MANAGEMENT INFORMATION SYSTEMS TITLES

MIS:

Jessup/Valacich, *Information Systems Today 2/e* © 2006
Laudon/Laudon, *Management Information Systems 9/e* © 2006
Laudon/Laudon, *Essentials of Business Information Systems 7/e* © 2007
Luftman et al., *Managing the IT Resource* © 2004
Malaga, *Information Systems Technology* © 2005
Martin et al., *Managing IT 5/e* © 2005
McLeod/Schell, *Management Information Systems 10/e* © 2007
McNurlin/Sprague, *Information Systems Management In Practice 7/e* © 2006
Miller, *MIS: Decision Making with Application Software (Cases) 3/e* © 2007
Senn, *Information Technology 3/e* © 2004

Database Management:

Bordoloi/Bock, *Oracle SQL* © 2004
Bordoloi/Bock, *SQL for SQL Server* © 2004
Frost/Day/VanSlyke, *Database Design and Development: A Visual Approach* © 2006
Hoffer/Prescott/McFadden, *Modern Database Management 8/e* © 2007
Kroenke, *Database Concepts 2/e* © 2005
Kroenke, *Database Processing 10/e* © 2006

Systems Analysis and Design:

Hoffer/George/Valacich, *Modern Systems Analysis and Design 4/e* © 2005
Kendall/Kendall, *Systems Analysis and Design 6/e* © 2005
Valacich/George/Hoffer, *Essentials of Systems Analysis and Design 3/e* © 2006

Object-Oriented Systems Analysis and Design:

Stumpf/Teague, *Object-Oriented Systems Analysis and Design with UML* © 2005
George/Batra/Valacich/Hoffer, *Object-Oriented Systems Analysis and Design* © 2004

Decision Support Systems:

Turban/Aronson/Liang, *Decision Support Systems 8/e* © 2007
Marakas, *Decision Support Systems 2/e* © 2003
Marakas, *Modern Data Warehousing, Mining, and Visualization* © 2003

Data Communications & Networking:

Dooley, *Business Data Communications* © 2005
Panko, *Business Data Networks and Telecommunications 6/e* © 2007

Electronic Commerce:

Turban/King/Lee/Viehland, *Electronic Commerce 4/e* © 2006
Awad, *Electronic Commerce 3/e* © 2007

Project Management:

Fuller/Valacich/George, *IT Project Management* © 2007

Enterprise Resource Planning:

Sumner, *Enterprise Resource Planning* © 2005

IS Communications:

Liebowitz/Agresti/Djavanshir, *Communicating as IT Professionals* © 2006

Knowledge Management:

Awad/Ghaziri, *Knowledge Management* © 2004
Becerra-Fernandez/Gonzalez/Sabherwal, *Knowledge Management* © 2004

Corporate Security:

Panko, *Corporate Computer and Network Security* © 2004
Volonino/Robinson, *Principles and Practice of Information Security* © 2004

For more information on these titles and the rest of Prentice Hall's best-selling Management Information Systems list, please visit www.prenhall.com/mis.

MODERN

DATABASE

MANAGEMENT

EIGHTH EDITION

JEFFREY A. HOFFER
University of Dayton

MARY B. PRESCOTT
University of Tampa

FRED R. McFADDEN
University of Colorado–Colorado Springs

PEARSON
Prentice
Hall

Upper Saddle River, New Jersey 07458

Library of Congress Cataloging-in-Publication Data

Hoffer, Jeffrey A.
    Modern database management / Jeffrey A. Hoffer, Mary B. Prescott, Fred R.
McFadden.—8th ed.
        p. cm.
    Includes bibliographical references and index.
    ISBN 0-13-2212110
        1. Database management. I. Prescott, Mary B. II. McFadden, Fred R.,
        III. Title.

QA76.9.D3M395 2007
005.74—dc22   2006068969

AVP/Executive Editor: Bob Horan
VP/Editorial Director: Jeff Shelstad
Manager, Product Development: Pamela Hersberger
Editorial Assistant/Project Manager: Ana Cordero
Media Project Manager: Peter Snell
AVP/Executive Marketing Manager: Debbie Clare
Marketing Assistant: Joanna Sabella
Senior Managing Editor (Production): Cynthia Regan
Senior Production Editor: Anne Graydon
Associate Director of Manufacturing: Vincent Scelta
Production Manager: Arnold Vila
Manufacturing Buyer: Diane Peirano
Design/Composition Manager: Christy Mahon
Composition Liaison: Suzanne Duda
Art Director/Cover Designer: Jayne Conte
Cover Photo: Getty Images, Inc.
Manager, Multimedia Production: Richard Bretan
Composition: TechBooks
Full-Service Project Management: Penny Walker/TechBooks
Printer/Binder: Quebecor
Typeface: 10/12 New Baskerville

Credits and acknowledgments borrowed from other sources and reproduced, with
permission, in this textbook appear on the appropriate page within the text.

Microsoft® and Windows® and Microsoft Access® are registered trademarks of the
Microsoft Corporation in the U.S.A. and other countries. Screen shots and icons
reprinted with permission from the Microsoft Corporation. This book is not
sponsored or endorsed by or affiliated with the Microsoft Corporation.

Pearson Education LTD.   Pearson Education Australia PTY, Limited
Pearson Education Singapore, Pte. Ltd   Pearson Education North Asia Ltd
Pearson Education, Canada, Ltd   Pearson Educación de Mexico, S.A. de C.V.
Pearson Education–Japan   Pearson Education Malaysia, Pte. Ltd

10 9 8 7 6 5 4 3 2
ISBN 0-13-221211-0

To Patty, for her sacrifices, encouragement, and support.
To my students and colleagues for being receptive and critical and for
challenging me to be a better teacher.

—J.A.H.

To Larry, for his constant support throughout this revision.
To Jeff, for his management of the process and his unfailing enthusiasm for
responding to our colleagues' suggestions for improvement.

—M.B.P.

To Evelyn, for her patience, love, and support. And to my colleagues and
students, from whom I continue to learn so much.

—F.R.M.

Brief Contents

Contents

2   The Database Development Process   36

Part II Database Analysis

Part III   Database Design

Part IV   Implementation

Part V　Advanced Database Topics

Part V　Overview　482

Preface

This text is designed for an introductory course in database management. Such a course is usually required as part of an information systems curriculum in business schools, computer technology programs, and applied computer science departments. The Association of Information Technology Professionals (AITP), Association for Computing Machinery (ACM), and the International Federation of Information Processing Societies (IFIPS) curriculum guidelines (e.g., IS 2002) all outline this type of database management course. Previous editions of our text have been used successfully for more than 20 years at both the undergraduate and graduate levels, as well as in management and professional development programs.

This text represents a meaningful update of the seventh edition of *Modern Database Management*. These revisions are necessary to accommodate the practical, technical, managerial, and methodological changes occurring at an ever-increasing pace in this field. However, we have endeavored to retain the best features of our previous editions. We have made every effort to justify the title *Modern Database Management*, which was introduced in the fourth edition.

For Those New to *Modern Database Management*

Modern Database Management has been a leading text since its first edition. In spite of this market leadership position, some faculty have used other good database management texts. Why might you want to switch at this time? There are several good reasons to switch to *Modern Database Management*, including:

- This text has, in every edition, led other books in coverage of the latest principles, concepts, and technologies. See what we have added for the eighth edition below in "New to This Edition". In the past, we have led in coverage of object-oriented data modeling and UML, Internet databases, data warehousing, and the use of CASE tools in support of data modeling.

- While remaining current, this text focuses on what leading practitioners say is most important for database developers. We work with many practitioners, including the professionals of the Data Management Association (DAMA), leading consultants, technology leaders, and authors of articles in the most widely read professional publications. We draw on these experts to ensure that what the book includes is important and covers not only important entry-level knowledge and skills, but also those fundamentals and mindsets that lead to long-term career success.

- As a highly successful book in its eighth edition, material is presented in a way that has been viewed as very accessible to students. Our methods have been refined through continuous market feedback for over 20 years. Overall, the pedagogy of the book is sound. We use many illustrations that help to make important concepts and techniques clear. We use the most modern notations.

The organization of the book is flexible, so you can use chapters in whatever sequence makes sense for your students.

- You may have particular interest in introducing SQL early in your course. Our text can accommodate this. First, we cover SQL in depth, devoting two full chapters to this core technology of the database field. Second, we include many SQL examples in early chapters. Third, many faculty have successfully used the two SQL chapters early in their course. Although logically appearing in the life cycle of systems development as Chapters 7 and 8, part of the implementation section of the text, many faculty have used these chapters immediately after Chapter 2 or in parallel with other early chapters.

- We have the latest in supplements and Web site support for the text. See The Supplement Package for details on all the resources available to you and your students.

- This text is written to be part of a modern information systems curriculum, with a strong business systems development focus. Topics are included and addressed so as to reinforce principles from other typical courses, such as systems analysis and design, networking, Web site design and development, MIS principles, and computer programming. Emphasis is on the development of the database component of modern information systems and on the management of the data resource. Thus, the text is practical, supports projects and other hands-on class activities, and encourages linking database concepts to concepts being learned throughout the curriculum the student is taking.

New to This Edition

The eighth edition of *Modern Database Management* updates and expands materials in areas undergoing rapid change due to improved managerial practices, database design tools and methodologies, and database technology. The themes of the eighth edition reflect the major trends in the information systems field and the skills required of modern information systems graduates:

- Data quality and database processing accuracy, which are extremely important with the national and international regulations such as Sarbanes-Oxley, Basel II, COSI, and HIPAA that now require organizations to comply with standards for reporting accurate financial data and ensuring data privacy.

- Web-enabled systems design and programming within an overall client/server architecture for systems, including Web services.

- Large-scale online (e-commerce) databases and data warehouses, and the renewal of concerns about database processing performance.

- Clarifying system requirements through thorough systems modeling and design, and using industry and business function commercial data models to speed up the systems development process.

- SQL as a standard for database querying.

In all the chapters, new screen captures are included to reflect the latest database technologies and an extensively updated Web Resources section lists Web sites that can provide the student with information on the latest database trends and expanded background details on important topics covered in the text. Major changes to the text include:

- The length of the printed book has been significantly reduced without any loss of content. The reduced length is more consistent with what our reviewers say can be covered in a database course today, given the need for depth of coverage in the most important topics. Specifically, we have moved full, updated versions of Chapters 13–15 to the textbook's Web site, and included short overviews of these chapters in the printed text. Care has been given to the layout of figures and tables to also reduce the length of the book. The reduced length should encourage more students to purchase and read the text, without any loss of coverage and learning.

- The client/server section of the book has been extensively updated to describe the latest, evolving technologies and concepts for databases in multi-tier systems and on the Internet, including Web services and XML.

- Material on database security has been updated and now consolidated into one, consistent location in Chapter 12 as part of data and database administration.

- The entity-relationship diagramming notation has been changed to be consistent with the predominant data model drawing and CASE tools used in the field. We have moved away from the original Chen notation involving, for example, attribute ovals, to the contemporary notation used by ERWin, PowerDesigner, Visio, Oracle and others, with attributes within the entity rectangle. This will make it much easier for students to use such tools with this textbook. We still show a variety of modeling conventions so students can be flexible to work with different standards in different organizations.

- Slightly more coverage is given to the increasingly popular universal data models provided by industry experts for specific industries and business functions. The new material focuses on building the fundamental constructs of these data models rather than introducing these models, which was the focus in the seventh edition. Students are now better prepared to understand why these data models are important and how to read and work with (tailor) them.

- The Mountain View Community Hospital case study within each chapter has been thoroughly updated to reflect modern hospital and health care management practices, information processing issues, and regulations (HIPAA). This case now has more and greater variety of exercises that address a rich set of database development and management issues.

The following presents a chapter-by-chapter description of the major changes in this edition. Each chapter description presents a statement of the purpose of that chapter, followed by a description of the changes and revisions that have been made from the seventh edition. Each paragraph concludes with a description of the strengths that have been retained from the seventh edition.

Part I: The Context of Database Management

Chapter 1: The Database Environment This chapter discusses the role of databases in organizations and previews the major topics in the remainder of the text. The chapter introduces a revised classification scheme that now recognizes five types of databases—personal, workgroup, departmental/divisional, enterprise, and Web-enabled. The explanation of enterprise databases includes databases that are part of enterprise resource planning systems and data warehouses. The chapter updates the discussion of the evolution of database technologies from pre-database files to modern object-relational and Web-enabled systems, including mobile databases. The chapter continues to present a well-organized comparison of database technology and conventional file-processing systems.

Chapter 2: The Database Development Process This chapter presents a detailed discussion of the role of database development within the broader context of information systems development. The chapter explains the process of database development for both structured life cycle and prototyping methodologies. The presentation has been made more consistent with the companion systems analysis text by Hoffer,

George, and Valacich. The chapter discusses important issues in database development, including management of the diverse group of people involved in database development and frameworks for understanding database architectures and technologies (e.g., the three-schema architecture). The chapter also continues to emphasize the information engineering methodology in database development, including the role of the enterprise data model. An introduction to the increasingly popular and standard-setting packaged data models (so-called "universal data models") for industries and business functional areas is also included. Reviewers frequently note the compatibility of this chapter with what students learn in systems analysis and design classes.

Part II: Database Analysis

Chapter 3: Modeling Data in the Organization   This chapter presents a thorough introduction to conceptual data modeling with the entity-relationship (E-R) model. The chapter title emphasizes the reason for the entity-relationship model: to unambiguously document the rules of the business that influence database design. Specific subsections explain in detail how to name and define elements of a data model, which are essential in developing an unambiguous E-R diagram. New to the chapter is the diagramming notation—we have changed from the original Chen notation to the contemporary notation more consistent with the widely used E-R diagramming tools. The chapter continues to proceed from simple to more complex examples, and it concludes with a comprehensive E-R diagram for the Pine Valley Furniture Company.

Chapter 4: The Enhanced E-R Model and Business Rules   This chapter presents a discussion of several advanced E-R data model constructs, primarily supertype/subtype relationships. As with Chapter 3, the notation for showing supertype/subtype relationships is consistent with modern E-R diagramming tools. New to the chapter is coverage of the fundamental components, such as the "party-role" constructs, used in universal (packaged) data models. The chapter continues to present a thorough coverage of supertype/subtype relationships and includes a comprehensive example of an extended E-R data model for the Pine Valley Furniture Company.

Part III: Database Design

Chapter 5: Logical Database Design and the Relational Model   This chapter describes the process of converting a conceptual data model to the relational data model as well as how to merge new relations into an existing normalized database. It features a discussion of the characteristics of foreign keys and introduces the important concept of a nonintelligent enterprise key. Enterprise keys (also called surrogate keys for data warehouses) are being emphasized as some concepts of object-orientation migrate into the relational technology world. The chapter now places more importance on the use of functional dependencies and determinants as the basis for normalization. The chapter continues to emphasize the basic concepts of the relational data model and the role of the database designer in the logical design process.

Chapter 6: Physical Database Design and Performance   This chapter describes the steps that are essential in achieving an efficient database design. The chapter contains a new emphasis on ways to improve database performance, with references to specific techniques available in Oracle and other DBMSs to improve database processing performance. The discussion of indexes includes descriptions of the types of indexes (primary and secondary indexes, join index, hash index table) that are widely available in database technologies as techniques to improve query processing speed. The discussion of denormalization has been improved to better motivate its importance for achieving database processing goals for very large databases. The chapter continues to emphasize the physical design process and the goals of that process.

Part IV: Implementation

Chapter 7: Introduction to SQL   This chapter presents a thorough introduction to the SQL used by most DBMSs (SQL:99) and introduces the changes that are included in the latest standard (SQL:2003). The coverage of SQL is extensive and divided into this and the next chapter. This chapter includes examples of SQL code, using mostly SQL:99 and SQL:2003 syntax and some Oracle 10g syntax. Views, both dynamic and materialized, are also covered. Chapter 7 explains the SQL commands needed to create and maintain a database and to program single-table queries. The chapter continues to use the Pine Valley Furniture Company case to illustrate a wide variety of practical queries and query results.

Chapter 8: Advanced SQL   This chapter continues the description of SQL with a careful explanation of multiple-table queries, transaction integrity, data dictionaries, triggers and stored procedures, and embedded SQL in other programming language programs. All forms of the OUTER JOIN command are covered. Standard SQL is also used in Chapter 8. This chapter illustrates how to store the results of a query in a derived table, the CAST command to convert data between different data types, and the CASE command for doing conditional processing in SQL. The chapter also outlines the new online analytical processing (OLAP) features of SQL:2003, which are necessary for SQL to be useful as a data access tool for data warehouses. New data types, extensions, and other features accessible to the novice database student are introduced. Emphasis continues on the set-processing style of SQL compared with the record-processing of programming languages with which the student may be familiar. The chapter continues to contain a clear explanation of subqueries and cor-related subqueries, two of the most complex and powerful constructs in SQL. Security issues have been consolidated in Chapter 12. Additional examples of more complex and realistic queries have been added.

Chapter 9: The Client/Server Database Environment   This chapter provides a thor-oughly modern discussion of the client/server architecture, applications, middleware, and client database access in contemporary database environments. This chapter lays the technology groundwork for the Internet topics in the remainder of the text. Many figures are included to show the options in multitiered networks, including application and database servers, database processing distribution alternatives among network tiers, and browser (thin) clients. Security topics have been consoli-dated in Chapter 12. The chapter continues with coverage of the three-tier client/ server architecture, application partitioning, and the role of the mainframe. Symmetric multiprocessing (SMP) and massively parallel processing (MPP) architec-tures have been moved to a piece on database performance optimization on the Web site. Microsoft Access QBE coverage has been removed due to the increasing sophis-tication of today's database students.

Chapter 10: The Internet Database Environment   The purpose of this chapter is to describe how databases are connected with Web-based applications. This chapter includes a discussion of scripting languages and embedded SQL in scripts. The Web site shopping cart has been updated using ASP.NET. The chapter also includes a review of the Internet-related terminology and concepts (such as firewall, proxy server, static and dynamic Web pages, HTML/SGML/XML/XHTML languages, Cascading Style Sheets, Common Gateway Interface, and servlets) necessary to understand how to connect a database to a Web page. The role of Web servers and server-side extensions for database connectivity is addressed. Web security issues have been consolidated into Chapter 12. Introduced in the seventh edition, coverage of Web services, associated standards and technologies and its role in seamless, secure movement of data in Web-based applications has been increased. A brief introduction to service-oriented architecture, SOA, has been added. XML has been given more prominence in the chapter, including more illustrations of XML and an expanded discussion of its future in database management. This chapter continues to present the networking concepts that are important for connecting databases to Web-based applications.

Chapter 11: Data Warehousing   This chapter describes the basic concepts of data warehousing, the reasons data warehousing is regarded as critical to competitive advantage in many organizations, and the database design activities and structures unique to data warehousing. Topics include alternative data warehouse architectures, techniques for data transformation and reconciliation, and the dimensional data model (or star schema) for data warehouses. Operational data store; independent, dependent, and logical data marts; and various forms of online analytical processing (OLAP) are defined. User interfaces, including OLAP and data mining, are also described. New to this edition is a summary of award-winning, best practices of data warehousing that illustrate how leading organizations have drastically reduced the chance of data warehousing project failure. We have also updated the explanations of active (or real-time) data warehousing, which is becoming increasingly common as organizations attempt to decrease the delays among business intelligence, decision making, and actions.

Part V: Advanced Database Topics

Chapter 12: Data and Database Administration   This extensively revised chapter presents a thorough discussion of the importance and roles of data and database administration and describes a number of the key issues that arise when these functions are being performed. This chapter emphasizes the changing roles and approaches of data and database administration, with emphasis on data quality and high performance. It contains a thorough discussion of database backup procedures, an extensively expanded and consolidated coverage of data security threats and responses, and an updated description of managing data quality and availability. The data security topics now include considerable new material on database security policies, procedures, and technologies (including encryption and smart cards). By moving all the data security coverage to this chapter, we have made it easier for the student to find and integrate the wide variety of techniques for data security. This one section can be referenced when students read other chapters, such as those on SQL, physical database design, and Internet databases. Also new is an expanded discussion of open-source DBMS to cover more on the benefits and hazards of this technology and how to choose an open-source DBMS. In addition, the topic of heartbeat queries is included in the coverage of database performance improvements. The chapter continues to emphasize the critical importance of data and database management in managing data as a corporate asset.

Chapter 13: Distributed Databases   This chapter reviews the role, technologies, and unique database design opportunities of distributed databases. The objectives and trade-offs for distributed databases, data replication alternatives, factors in selecting a data distribution strategy, and distributed database vendors and products are covered. This chapter, along with Chapter 12, provides thorough coverage of database concurrency access controls. New for this chapter is that the full version of this chapter has been moved to the textbook's Web site. Many reviewers indicated that they seldom are able to cover this chapter in an introductory course, but having the material available is critical for advanced students or special topics. Having an overview in the printed text with the full chapter available to students provides the greatest flexibility and economy.

Chapter 14: Object-Oriented Data Modeling   This chapter presents an introduction to object-oriented modeling using the Unified Modeling Language (UML) of Booch, Jacobson, and Rumbaugh. This chapter has been updated to illustrate the latest UML notations, including the notation for stereotypes. UML provides an industry-standard notation for representing classes and objects. The chapter continues to emphasize basic object-oriented concepts, such as inheritance and aggregation. As with Chapter 13, the full version of this chapter has been moved to the textbook's Web site, with a suitable overview included in the printed text.

Chapter 15: Object-Oriented Database Development   The purpose of this chapter is to show how to translate object-oriented models (explained in Chapter 14) into class, object, relationship, and operation definitions for an object-oriented DBMS. The chapter also introduces the latest format for object definition language (ODL) and object query language (OQL), the standard language for ODBMSs. The chapter includes an object-oriented database definition using ODL for the Pine Valley Furniture database design of the previous chapter. The chapter concludes with an updated survey of ODBMSs—both vendors and products. As with Chapters 13 and 14, the full version of this chapter has been moved to the textbook's Web site, with a suitable overview included in the printed text.

Appendices

The eighth edition contains four appendices intended for persons who wish to explore certain topics in greater depth.

Appendix A: E-R Modeling Tools and Notation   This extensively updated appendix addresses a need raised by many readers—how to translate the E-R notation in the text into the form used by the CASE tool or DBMS used in class. Specifically, this appendix compares the notations of Microsoft Visio Pro 2003, Computer Associates' AllFusion ERwin Data Modeler 4.1 SP1, Sybase PowerDesigner, and Oracle Designer. Tables and illustrations show the notations used for the same constructs in each of these popular software packages.

Appendix B: Advanced Normal Forms   This appendix presents a description (with examples) of Boyce-Codd and fourth normal forms, including an example of BCNF to show how to handle overlapping candidate keys. Other normal forms are briefly introduced. The Web Resources section has been expanded to include information on many advanced normal form topics.

Appendix C: Data Structures   This appendix describes several data structures that often underlie database implementations. Topics include the use of pointers, stacks, queues, sorted lists, inverted lists, and trees.

Appendix D: Object-Relational Databases   This appendix presents a description of object-relational database management systems (ORDBMSs). Topics include features of an ORDBMS, enhanced SQL, advantages of the object-relational approach, and a summary of ORDBMS vendors and products. Examples are included to show how relational DBMSs such as Oracle include object-oriented data specifications.

Pedagogy

A number of additions and improvements have been made to chapter-end materials to provide a wider and richer range of choices for the user. The most important of these improvements are the following:

1. *Review Questions*   Questions have been updated to support new and enhanced chapter material.
2. *Problems and Exercises*   This section has been updated in every chapter and contains new problems and exercises to support updated chapter material. Of special interest are questions in many chapters that give students opportunities to use the datasets provided for the text.
3. *Field Exercises*   This section provides a set of "hands-on" minicases that can be assigned to individual students or to small teams of students. Field exercises range from directed field trips to Internet searches and other types of research exercises.

4. *Case*   The Mountain View Community Hospital (MVCH) case has been thoroughly updated to present a more challenging and rich student project experience. In each chapter, the case begins with a description of a realistic, modern hospital situation as it relates to that chapter. The case then presents a series of case questions and exercises that focus on specific aspects of the case. The final section includes project assignments, which tie together some issues and activities across chapters. These project assignments can be completed by individual students or by small project teams. This case provides an excellent means for students to gain hands-on experience with the concepts and tools they have studied. Some cases include questions for students to use the MVCH dataset provided for the text.
5. *Web Resources*   Each chapter contains a list of updated and validated URLs for Web sites that contain information that supplements the chapter. These Web sites cover online publication archives, vendors, electronic publications, industry standards organizations, and many other sources. These sites allow students and faculty to find updated product information, innovations that have appeared since the printing of the book, background information to explore topics in greater depth, and resources for writing research papers.

We have also updated the pedagogical features that helped make the seventh edition widely accessible to instructors and students. These features include the following:

1. *Learning objectives* appear at the beginning of each chapter to preview the major concepts and skills students will learn from that chapter. The learning objectives also provide a great study review aid for students as they prepare for assignments and examinations.
2. *Chapter introductions and summaries* both encapsulate the main concepts of each chapter and link material to related chapters, providing students with a comprehensive conceptual framework for the course.
3. The *chapter review,* which includes the Review Questions, Problems and Exercises, and Field Exercises discussed earlier, also contains *key terms* to test the student's grasp of important concepts, basic facts, and significant issues.
4. A *running glossary* defines key terms in the page margins as they are discussed in the text. These terms are also defined at the end of the text in the *Glossary of Terms.* Also included is an end-of-book *Glossary of Acronyms* for abbreviations commonly used in database management.

Organization

We encourage instructors to customize their use of this book to meet the needs of both their curriculum and student career paths. The modular nature of the text, its broad coverage, extensive illustrations, and inclusion of advanced topics and emerging issues make customization easy. The many references to current publications and Web sites can help instructors develop supplemental reading lists or expand classroom discussion beyond material presented in the text. The use of appendices for several advanced topics allows instructors to easily include or omit these topics.

The modular nature of the text allows the instructor to omit certain chapters or to cover chapters in a different sequence. For example, an instructor who wishes to emphasize data modeling may cover Chapter 14 on object-oriented data modeling along with or instead of Chapters 3 and 4. An instructor who wishes to cover only basic entity-relationship concepts (but not the enhanced E-R model or business rules) may skip Chapter 4 or cover it after Chapter 5 on the relational model.

We have contacted many adopters of *Modern Database Management* and asked them to share with us their syllabi. Most adopters cover the chapters in sequence, but several alternative sequences have also been successful. These alternatives include:

- Covering Chapter 12 on data and database administration immediately after Chapter 6 on physical database design and the relational model.

- To cover SQL as early as possible, instructors have effectively covered Chapters 7 and 8 immediately after Chapter 5; some have even covered Chapter 7 immediately after Chapter 2.

- Many faculty have students read appendices along with chapters, such as reading Appendix A on data modeling notations with Chapters 3 or 4 on E-R modeling, Appendix B on advanced normal forms can be read with Chapter 5 on the relational model, and Appendix C on data structures can be read with Chapter 6.

Case Tools

Modern Database Management, eighth edition, offers adopters the option of acquiring outstanding CASE tools, software packages from Microsoft, Oracle, and Visible Systems. Students can purchase this book packaged with the full editions of Microsoft Visio Pro, Oracle Designer, Oracle Forms and Reports (Developer), Personal Oracle, or Visible Analyst at a greatly reduced fee. We are proud to offer such highly valued, powerful software packages to students at such a low cost. These packages can be used to draw data models, generate normalized relations from conceptual data models, and generate database definition code, among other tasks. These tools also are useful in other courses on information systems development.

The Supplement Package: www.prenhall.com/hoffer

A comprehensive and flexible technology support package is available to enhance the teaching and learning experience. All instructor and student supplements are available on the text Web site: **www.prenhall.com/hoffer.**

For Students   The following online resources are available to students:

- The *Web Resources* module includes the Web links referenced at the end of each chapter in the text to help students further explore database management topics on the Web.
- *PowerPoint Presentation Slides* feature lecture notes that highlight key terms and concepts.
- A full *glossary* is available both alphabetically and by chapter, along with a glossary of acronyms.

- *Links to sites where students can use our datasets* are provided. Although our datasets are provided to you in formats that are easily loaded on computers at your university or on student PCs, some faculty will not want the responsibility of supporting local datasets. The application service providers with whom we have developed arrangements provide thin-client interfaces to SQL coding environments. See the text's Web site for more details.

- *Complete chapters on distributed databases, object-oriented data modeling, and object-oriented DBMSs* allow you to learn in depth about topics that are overviewed in Chapters 13–15 of the textbook. A new resource, *Achieving Optimal Database Performance*, provides an introduction to current practices in database performance tuning.

For Instructors   The following online resources are available to instructors:

- The *Instructor's Resource Manual* by John P. Russo, Wentworth Institute of Technology, provides chapter-by-chapter instructor objectives, classroom ideas, and answers to Review Questions, Problems and Exercises, Field Exercises, and Project Case Questions. The Instructor's Resource Manual is also available in print and from the faculty area of the text's Web site.

- The *Test Item File and TestGen* by John P. Russo, Wentworth Institute of Technology, includes a comprehensive set of test questions in multiple-choice, true-false, and short-answer format, ranked according to level of difficulty and referenced with page numbers and topic headings from the text. The Test Item File is available in Microsoft Word and as the computerized Prentice Hall TestGen. TestGen is a comprehensive suite of tools for testing and assessment. It allows instructors to easily create and distribute tests for their courses, either by printing and distributing through traditional methods or by online delivery via a Local Area Network (LAN) server. Test Manager features Screen Wizards to assist you as you move through the program, and the software is backed with full technical support.

- *PowerPoint Presentation Slides* by Michel Mitri, James Madison University, feature lecture notes that highlight key terms and concepts. Professors can customize the presentation by adding their own slides or editing existing ones.

- The *Image Library* is a collection of the text art organized by chapter. It includes all figures, tables, and screenshots (as permission allows) and can be used to enhance class lectures and PowerPoint slides.

PINE VALLEY FURNITURE

- *Accompanying databases* are also provided. Three versions of the Pine Valley Furniture case have been created and populated for the seventh edition. One version is scoped to match the textbook examples. A second version is fleshed out with sample forms, reports, and modules coded in Visual Basic. This version is not complete, however, so that students may create missing tables and additional forms, reports, and modules. The third version is a data warehousing environment, and special exercises for using this dataset are located on the text's Web site. A version of the Mountain View Community Hospital case is also included. Oracle scripts are included to create the tables and insert sample data for both Pine Valley Furniture and Mountain View Community Hospital. Robert Lewis of the University of South Florida has created these datasets and applications for us.

- The *shopping cart application* mentioned in Chapter 10 provides the starting point for some interesting student exercises. The code and documentation for a "bare bones" shopping cart, with an ASP.NET connection, are included on the book's Web site. The shopping carts can be run on the student's personal PC without having to establish a live Web site. Most students should be able to read the code and then build enhancements to their shopping cart as they desire. This experiential learning opportunity, aided by simple code that gives the student the ability to examine the connection of a database to the Web and to enhance that application, is a significant strength of the book that addresses the learning styles of many current students.

Materials for Your Online Course

Prentice Hall supports our adopters using online courses by providing files ready for upload into both WebCT and Blackboard course management systems for our testing, quizzing, and other supplements. Please contact your local Prentice Hall representative or mis_service@prenhall.com for further information on your particular course.

Acknowledgments

We are grateful to numerous individuals who contributed to the preparation of *Modern Database Management*, eighth edition. First, we wish to thank our reviewers for their detailed suggestions and insights, characteristic of their thoughtful teaching style. As always, analysis of topics and depth of coverage provided by the reviewers was crucial. Our reviewers include Bijoy Bordoloi, Southern Illinois University, Edwardsville; Traci Carte, University of Oklahoma; Jon Gant, Syracuse University; Monica Garfield, Bentley University; Brian Mennecke, Iowa State University; Dat-Dao Nguyen, California State University, Northridge; John Russo, Wentworth Institute of Technology; Richard Segall, Arkansas State University; and Chelley Vician, Michigan Technology Institute.

We received excellent input from people in industry, including Todd Walter, Carrie Ballinger, Rob Armstrong, and Dave Schoeff (all of Teradata Division of NCR); Derek Strauss (Gavroshe International); Richard Hackatorn (University of Colorado, Bolder); and Michael Alexander (Open Access Technology, Int'l.).

We also thank Klara Nelson at the University of Tampa, who authored the Mountain View Community Hospital case study. This extensive update is a notable addition to the text. We also value her great insights on the textbook, bringing the perspective of an impertinent adopter of our book. Linda Jayne, formerly operations manager of Suncoast Hospital, Largo, Florida provided many relevant stories and validation of the situations faced by Mountain View Community Hospital in the eighth edition. We appreciate her taking the time to meet with us and to review the existing case.

This edition of the textbook will be accompanied by more sample database applications that faculty and students can explore than any previous edition. Our thanks for creating these supplements go to Robert Lewis, University of South Florida, for the Pine Valley Furniture Company and Mountain View Community Hospital cases. We also want to thank a former student who is always ready to help out, Harrison Hamilton, for updating Michael Alexander's ASP shopping cart to ASP.NET.

Thanks are also due Willard Baird, Progress Telecom, a highly experienced Oracle database administrator, who has co-authored the new website piece, *Achieving Optimal Database Performance* with us. Willard is able to convey trends in database administration to us very clearly and in a timely fashion, and his experience with the trend toward more holistic approaches to database optimization that have occurred over the last few years have led to our decision to put up a piece on the Web site for students and instructors who desire a deeper understanding of this area.

We are also very grateful to the staff and associates of Prentice Hall for their support and guidance throughout this project. In particular, we wish to thank Executive Editor Bob Horan, who coordinated the planning for the text, Editorial assistant and Project Manager Ana Cordero, who kept us on track and made sure everything was complete, Production Editor Anne Graydon, Executive Marketing Manager Debbie Clare, and Marketing Assistant Joanna Sabella. We extend special thanks to Penny Walker at TechBooks, whose supervision of the production process was excellent.

Finally, we give immeasurable thanks to our spouses, who endured many evenings and weekends of solitude for the thrill of seeing a book cover hang on a den wall. In particular, we marvel at the commitment of Patty Hoffer, who has lived the lonely life of a textbook author's spouse through eight editions over more than twenty years. Now, Larry Prescott has shown his support through four editions, including leading several "contemplation excursions" to Tampa Bay and treks across country in an RV. Much of the value of this text is due to their patience, encouragement, and love, but we alone bear the responsibility for any errors or omissions between the covers.

Jeffrey A. Hoffer
Mary B. Prescott

Part ONE

The Context of
Database Management

● **Chapter 1**
The Database Environment

● **Chapter 2**
The Database Development Process

An Overview of Part ONE

Part I consists of two chapters that set the context and provide basic database concepts and definitions used throughout the text. In this part, we portray database management as an exciting, challenging, and growing field that provides numerous career opportunities for information systems students. Databases continue to become a more common part of everyday living and a more central component of business operations. From the database that stores contact information in your personal digital assistant (PDA) to the very large databases that support enterprisewide information systems, databases have become the central points of data storage that were envisioned decades ago. Customer relationship management and Internet shopping are examples of two database-dependent activities that have developed in recent years. The development of data warehouses that provide managers the opportunity for deeper and broader historical analysis of data also continues to take on more importance.

Chapter 1 (The Database Environment) provides basic definitions of data, databases, metadata, database management systems, data warehouses, intranets, extranets, and other terms associated with this environment. We compare databases with the older file management systems they replaced and describe several important advantages that are enabled by the carefully planned use of databases. We describe typical database applications and their characteristics for personal, workgroup, departmental/divisional, enterprise, and Web-enabled databases. Enterprise databases include enterprise resource planning systems and data warehouses. We describe the major components of the database environment in detail later in the text. Finally, we provide a brief history of the evolution of database systems, including object-relational and Web-enabled systems, and the forces that have driven and continue to drive their development. The Pine Valley Furniture Company case is introduced and used to illustrate many of the principles and concepts of database management. This case is used throughout the text as a continuing example of the use of database management systems.

Chapter 2 (The Database Development Process) describes the general steps followed in the analysis, design, implementation, and administration of databases. This chapter also describes how the database development process fits into the overall information systems development process. Database development for both structured life cycle and prototyping methodologies is explained. We introduce enterprise data modeling, which sets the range and general contents of organizational databases. This is often the first step in database development. We also present the concept of an information systems architecture that may be used as a blueprint for information systems in organizations. We describe and illustrate information engineering, which is a data-oriented methodology used to create and maintain information systems. We present issues in database development, including management of the diverse group of people involved in database development and frameworks for understanding database architectures and technologies.

We describe and illustrate the systems development life cycle in this chapter, and the alternative use of prototyping, which is an iterative development process. We describe the importance and use of computer-aided software engineering (CASE) tools and discuss the role of a repository in the information systems development process. We introduce the concept of schemas and a three-schema architecture, which is the dominant approach in modern database systems. Finally, we describe the roles of the various people who are typically involved in a database development project.

It is essential that you gain a clear understanding of the various concepts and definitions presented in Part I. These concepts and definitions are used throughout the remainder of the text. To ensure that an adequate understanding has been gained, answer a number of the review questions and exercises at the end of each chapter and ask your instructor to clarify any concepts that remain unclear.

Chapter 1

The Database Environment

LEARNING OBJECTIVES

After studying this chapter, you should be able to:

- Concisely define each of the following key terms: **data, database, database management system, information, metadata, enterprise data model, entity, relational database, enterprise resource planning (ERP) system, database application, data warehouse, data independence, repository, user view,** and **constraint.**
- Explain why databases will continue to grow in number and importance into the next century.
- Name several limitations of conventional file processing systems.
- Identify five categories of databases and several key decisions that must be made for each category.
- Explain at least ten advantages of the database approach, compared to traditional file processing.
- Identify several costs and risks of the database approach.
- List and briefly describe nine components of a typical database environment.
- Briefly describe the evolution of database systems.

DATA MATTERS!

The world has become a very complex place. The advantage goes to people and organizations that collect, manage, and interpret information effectively. To make our point, let's visit Continental Airlines. A little over a decade ago, Continental was in real trouble, ranking at the bottom of U.S. airlines in on-time performance, mishandled baggage, customer complaints, and overbooking. Speculation was that Continental would have to file

bankruptcy for the third time. In the last 10 years, Continental had had ten CEOs. Could more effective collection, management, and interpretation of Continental's data and information help Continental's situation? The answer is, yes. Today Continental is one of the most respected global airlines and has been named the Most Admired Global Airline by *Fortune Magazine* on its 2004 and 2005 lists of Most Admired Global Companies. It was recognized as Airline of the Year, Best Airline Based in North America, and Best Executive/Business Class by the 2004 OAG Airline of the Year awards.

Continental's president and COO, Larry Kellner, points to the use of real-time business intelligence as a significant factor in Continental's turnaround. How? Implementation of a real-time or "active" data warehouse has supported the company's business strategy, dramatically improving customer service and operations, creating cost savings, and generating revenue. Eleven years ago, Continental could not even track a customer's travel itinerary if more than one stop was involved. Now, employees who deal with travelers know if a high-value customer is currently experiencing a delay in a trip, where and when the customer will arrive at the airport, and the gate where the customer must go to make the next airline connection. High-value customers receive letters of apology if they experience travel delays on Continental and sometimes a trial membership in the President's Club.

Incorporation of Continental's data into a data warehouse began by integrating the data necessary for revenue management. The integration of flight schedule, customer, and inventory data supported management's ability to set prices and manage revenue. Customer information, finance, flight information, and security followed. Following is a list of some of the wins that came from the data warehousing project:

1. Optimization of airfares using mathematical programming models, adjusting number of seats sold at a particular fare on the fly as real-time sales data is analyzed after a fare is announced

2. Improvement of customer relationship management focused on Continental's most profitable customers

3. Immediate availability of customer profiles to sales personnel, marketing managers, and flight personnel, such as ticket agents and flight attendants

4. Support for union negotiations, including analysis of pilot staffing that allows management and union negotiators to evaluate the appropriateness of work assignment decisions

5. Development of fraud profiles that can be run against the data to identify transactions that appear to fit one of over 100 fraud profiles

To emphasize this last win, Continental's ability to meet Homeland Security requirements has been greatly aided by the real-time data warehouse. During the period immediately following the terrorist attacks of September 11, 2001, Continental was able to work with the FBI to determine whether any terrorists on the FBI watch list were attempting to board a Continental flight. The data warehouse's ability to identify fraudulent activity and monitor passengers contributes significantly to Continental's goal of keeping all its passengers and crew members safe. (Anderson-Lehman et al., 2004).

Continental's turnaround has been based on its corporate culture, which places a high value on customer service, and the effective use of information through the integration of data in the data warehouse. Data does, indeed, matter. The topics covered in this textbook will equip you with a deeper understanding of data and how to collect, organize, and manage it. This understanding will give you the power to support any business strategy, and the deep satisfaction that comes from knowing how to organize data so that financial, marketing, or customer service questions can be answered almost as soon as they are asked. Enjoy!

INTRODUCTION

Over the past two decades there has been enormous growth in the number and importance of database applications. Databases are used to store, manipulate, and retrieve data in nearly every type of organization, including business, health care, education, government, and libraries. Database technology is routinely used by individuals on personal computers, by workgroups accessing databases on network servers, and by employees using enterprisewide distributed applications. Databases are also accessed by customers and other remote users through diverse technologies, such as automated teller machines, Web browsers, digital phones, PDAs, and scanning devices.

Following this period of rapid growth, will the demand for databases and database technology level off? Certainly not. In the highly competitive environment of the early 2000s, there is every indication that database technology will assume even greater importance. Managers seek to use knowledge derived from databases for competitive advantage. For example, detailed sales databases can be mined to determine customer buying patterns as a basis for advertising and marketing campaigns. Organizations embed procedures called "alerts" in databases to warn of unusual conditions, such as impending stockouts or opportunities to sell additional products, and to trigger appropriate actions. Many organizations build separate databases called data warehouses for this type of decision support application (Anderson-Lehman et al., 2004).

Use of databases to support customer relationship management, online shopping, and employee relationship management is increasingly important. For example, Blockbuster Video uses its customer relationship management system to understand diverse customer needs across some eight thousand retail stores. This system, which is based on a five-terabyte data warehouse and a global operational data store, enables Blockbuster to ensure that the right movies are available in each store, at the right time, and in the right quantity. You will study this type of database technology in Chapter 11.

Although the future of databases is assured, much work remains to be done. Many organizations have a proliferation of incompatible databases that were developed to meet immediate needs, rather than based on a planned strategy or a well-managed evolution. Much of the data are trapped in older, "legacy" systems, and the data are often of poor quality. New skills are required to design and manage data warehouses and to integrate databases with Internet applications. There is a shortage of skills in areas such as database analysis, database design, data administration, and database administration. We address these and other important issues in this textbook.

A course in database management has emerged as one of the most important courses in the information systems curriculum today. Many schools have added an additional elective course in data warehousing or database administration to provide in-depth coverage of these important topics. As an information systems professional, you must be prepared to analyze database requirements and design and implement databases within the context of information systems development. You also must be prepared to consult with end users and show them how they can use databases (or data warehouses) to build decision support systems and executive information systems for competitive advantage. And, the widespread use of databases attached to Web sites that return dynamic information to users of the Web site requires that you understand not only how to attach databases to the Web, but also how to secure those databases so that their contents may be viewed but not compromised by outside users.

In this chapter, we introduce the basic concepts of databases and database management systems (DBMSs). We describe traditional file management systems and some of their shortcomings that led to the database approach. Next we consider the benefits, costs, and risks of using the database approach. We describe the range of database applications, from personal computers and digital assistants to workgroup, departmental or divisional, and enterprise databases. We conclude the chapter with a summary of the evolution of database systems and a review of the range of technologies used to build, use, and manage databases. This chapter is intended to serve as a preview of the topics in the remainder of the text.

BASIC CONCEPTS AND DEFINITIONS

Database: An organized collection of logically related data.

We define a database as an organized collection of logically related data. A **database** may be of any size and complexity. For example, a salesperson may maintain a small database of customer contacts on her laptop computer consisting of a few megabytes of data. A large corporation may build a large database consisting of several terabytes of data (a *terabyte* is a trillion bytes) on a large mainframe computer that is used for decision support applications (Winter, 1997). Very large data warehouses contain more than a petabyte of data. (A petabyte is a quadrillion bytes.) (We assume throughout the text that all databases are computer based.)

Data

Historically, the term data referred to facts concerning objects and events that could be recorded and stored on computer media. For example, in a salesperson's database, the data would include facts such as customer name, address, and telephone number. This type of data is called *structured* data. The most important structured data types are numeric, character, and dates. Structured data are stored in tabular form (in tables, relations, arrays, spreadsheets, etc.) and are most commonly found in traditional databases and data warehouses.

The traditional definition of data now needs to be expanded to reflect a new reality: Databases today are used to store objects such as documents, maps, photographic images, sound, and video segments in addition to structured data. For example, the salesperson's database might include a photo image of the customer contact. It might also include a sound recording or video clip about the most recent product. This type of data is referred to as unstructured data, or as multimedia data. Multimedia data are most often found on Web servers and on Web-enabled databases. Multimedia data require much more storage space than typical structured data do; this increase in data item size requires an understanding of data retrieval methods and storage methods if the fast response time expected by users is to be met.

Data: Stored representations of objects and events that have meaning and importance in the user's environment.

We now define **data** as stored representations of objects and events that have meaning and importance in the user's environment. This definition includes structured and unstructured data types. Today structured and unstructured data are often combined in the same database to create a true multimedia environment. For example, an automobile repair shop can combine structured data (describing customers and automobiles) with multimedia data (photo images of the damaged autos and scanned images of insurance claim forms).

Data Versus Information

Information: Data that have been processed in such a way as to increase the knowledge of the person who uses the data.

The terms *data* and *information* are closely related, and in fact are often used interchangeably. However, it is useful to distinguish between data and information. We define **information** as data that have been processed in such a way that the knowledge of the person who uses the data is increased. For example, consider the following list of facts:

Baker, Kenneth D.	324917628
Doyle, Joan E.	476193248
Finkle, Clive R.	548429344
Lewis, John C.	551742186
McFerran, Debra R.	409723145
Sisneros, Michael	392416582

These facts satisfy our definition of data, but most people would agree that the data are useless in their present form. Even if we guess that this is a list of people's names

Figure 1-1
Converting data to information
(a) Data in context

Class Roster

| Course: | MGT 500 Business Policy | Semester: Spring 200X |

Section: 2

Name	ID	Major	GPA
Baker, Kenneth D.	324917628	MGT	2.9
Doyle, Joan E.	476193248	MKT	3.4
Finkle, Clive R.	548429344	PRM	2.8
Lewis, John C.	551742186	MGT	3.7
McFerran, Debra R.	409723145	IS	2.9
Sisneros, Michael	392416582	ACCT	3.3

(b) Summarized data

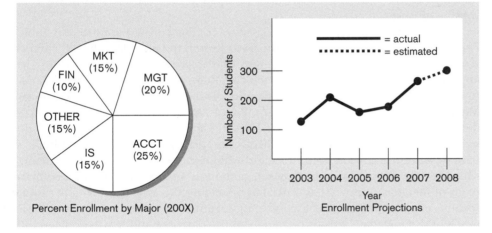

Percent Enrollment by Major (200X)

Enrollment Projections

paired with their Social Security numbers, the data remain useless because we have no idea what the entries mean. Notice what happens when we place the same data in a context, as shown in Figure 1-1a. By adding a few additional data items and providing some structure, we recognize a class roster for a particular course. This is useful information to some users, such as the course instructor and the registrar's office.

Another way to convert data into information is to summarize them or otherwise process and present them for human interpretation. For example, Figure 1-1b shows summarized student enrollment data presented as graphical information. This information could be used as a basis for deciding whether to add new courses or to hire new faculty members.

In practice, according to our definitions, databases today may contain either data or information (or both). For example, a database may contain an image of the class roster document shown in Figure 1-1a. Also, data are often preprocessed and stored in summarized form in databases that are used for decision support. Throughout this text we use the term database without distinguishing its contents as data or information.

Metadata

As we have indicated, data only become useful when placed in some context. The primary mechanism for providing context for data is metadata. **Metadata** are data that describe the properties or characteristics of end-user data and the context of that data. Some of the properties that are typically described include data names,

Metadata: Data that describe the properties or characteristics of end-user data, and the context of that data.

Table 1-1 Example Metadata for Class Roster

Data Item					Value	
Name	**Type**	**Length**	**Min**	**Max**	**Description**	**Source**
Course	Alphanumeric	30			Course ID and name	Academic Unit
Section	Integer	1	1	9	Section number	Registrar
Semester	Alphanumeric	10			Semester and year	Registrar
Name	Alphanumeric	30			Student name	Student IS
ID	Integer	9			Student ID (SSN)	Student IS
Major	Alphanumeric	4			Student major	Student IS
GPA	Decimal	3	0.0	4.0	Student grade point average	Academic Unit

definitions, length (or size), and allowable values. Metadata describing data context include the source of the data, where the data are stored, ownership (or steward-ship), and usage.

Some sample metadata for the Class Roster (Figure 1-1a) are listed in Table 1-1. For each data item that appears in the Class Roster, the metadata show the data item name, the data type, length, minimum and maximum allowable values (where appropriate), a brief description of each data item, and the source of the data (some-times called the *system of record*). Notice the distinction between data and metadata. Metadata are once removed from data. That is, metadata describe the properties of data but are separate from that data. Thus, the metadata shown in Table 1-1 do not include any sample data from the Class Roster of Figure 1-1a. Metadata enable data-base designers and users to understand what data exist, what the data mean, and what the fine distinctions are between seemingly similar data items. The manage-ment of metadata is at least as crucial as managing the associated data because data without clear meaning can be confusing, misinterpreted, or erroneous. Typically, much of the metadata are stored as part of the database and may be retrieved using the same approaches that are used to retrieve data or information.

Database Management Systems

Database Management System (DBMS): A software system that is used to create, maintain, and provide controlled access to user databases.

A **database management system (DBMS)** is a software system that is used to cre-ate, maintain, and provide controlled access to user databases. A DBMS provides a systematic method of creating, updating, storing, and retrieving data in a database. It enables end users and application programmers to share data, and it enables data to be shared among multiple applications rather than propagated and stored in new files for every new application (Mullins, 2002). A DBMS also provides facilities for controlling data access, enforcing data integrity, managing concurrency control, and restoring a database. We describe these DBMS features in detail in Chapter 12.

Data Models

Data model: Graphical systems used to capture the nature and relation-ships among data.

Designing a database properly is fundamental to establishing a database that meets the needs of the users. **Data models** capture the nature of and relationships among data and are used at different levels of abstraction as a database is conceptu-alized and designed. Chapters 3 and 4 are devoted to developing your understanding of data modeling, as is Chapter 14, which addresses a different approach using object-oriented data modeling. The effectiveness and efficiency of a database is directly associated with the structure of the database. Various graphical systems exist that convey this structure and are used to produce data models that can be under-stood by end users, systems analysts, and database designers.

Enterprise data model: A graphical model that shows the high-level enti-ties for the organization and the rela-tionships among those entities.

Data models are created at both the enterprise and project levels. **Enterprise data models** are the less detailed of the two and capture the major categories of data

Figure 1-2
Comparison of enterprise and project level data models

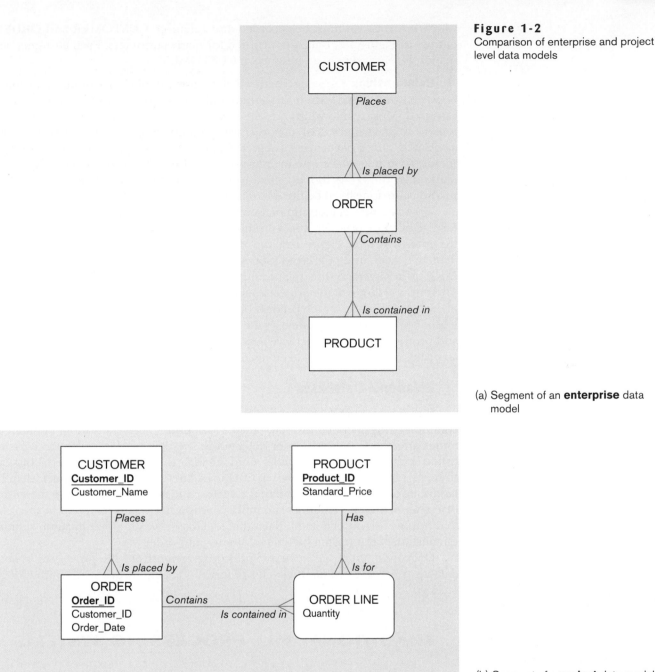

(a) Segment of an **enterprise** data model

(b) Segment of a **project** data model

and the relationships between data, such as between a customer and his order. Enterprise data models are comprehensive to the whole (or large portion of the) organization. They are used to explain the scope of data covered in the database. Project-level data models are more detailed and more closely match the way the data must be included in the database, and hence, are used in the process of developing a database and applications against it. The details of a customer order may be included in a project-level data model, but not in an enterprise-level data model. See Figure 1-2 for a simple comparison of the difference between an enterprise-level and a project-level data model.

Entities   Customers and orders are objects about which a business maintains information. They are referred to as "entities." An **entity** is like a noun in that it describes a person, place, object, event, or concept in the business environment for

Entity: A person, place, object, event, or concept in the user environment about which the organization wishes to maintain data.

which information must be recorded and retained. CUSTOMER and ORDER are entities in Figure 1-2. Data are recorded for many customers. Each customer's information is referred to as an instance of CUSTOMER.

Relationships   A well-structured database establishes the many *relationships* between entities that exist in organizational data so that desired information can be retrieved. Most relationships are one-to-many (*1:M*) or many-to-many (*M:N*). A customer can place more than one order with a company. However, each order is usually associated with a particular customer. Figure 1-2 shows the *1:M* relationship of customers who may place one or more orders; the *1:M* nature of the relationship is marked by the crows foot attached to the rectangle (entity) labeled ORDER. This relationship appears to be the same in Figures 1-2a and 1-2b.

However, the relationship between orders and products is *M:N*. An order may be for one or more products and a product may be included on more than one order. At the enterprise level, Figure 1-2a, the *M:N* relationship between orders and products is depicted, again using the crows foot. At the project level, an additional entity, ORDER LINE, is depicted, and its relationships with ORDER and PRODUCT are each *1:M*. This entity is shown at the project level because it allows for the inclusion of the details of each order. That is, each product ordered can be recorded. At the enterprise level, it is only necessary to include only the higher level relationships of customers, orders, and products. At the project level, additional detail, such as the exact composition of an order, needs to be included to meet the functional needs of the organization.

Relational Databases

Relational database: A database that represents data as a collection of tables in which all data relationships are represented by common values in related tables.

Relational databases establish the relationships between entities by means of common fields included in a file, called a "relation." The relationship between a customer and the customer's order depicted in the data models in Figure 1-2 is established by including the customer number with the customer's order. Thus, a customer's identification number is included in the file (or relation) that holds customer information such as name, address, and so forth. Every time the customer places an order, the customer identification number is also included in the relation that holds order information. Relational databases use the identification number to establish the relationship between customer and order.

Over time, there has been a logical progression from file processing systems to databases and data warehouses. This progression is briefly described in the following section.

TRADITIONAL FILE PROCESSING SYSTEMS

When computer-based data processing was first available, there were no databases. Computers that were considerably less powerful than today's personal computers filled large rooms and were used almost exclusively for scientific and engineering calculations. Gradually computers were introduced into the business world. To be useful for business applications, computers had to store, manipulate, and retrieve large files of data. Computer file processing systems were developed for this purpose. Although these systems have evolved over time, their basic structure and purpose have changed little over several decades.

As business applications became more complex, it became evident that traditional file processing systems had a number of shortcomings and limitations (described next). As a result, these systems have been replaced by database processing systems in most critical business applications today. Nevertheless, you should have at least some familiarity with file processing systems for the following reasons:

1. File processing systems are still widely used today, especially for backing up database systems.

2. Understanding the problems and limitations inherent in file processing systems can help us avoid these same problems when designing database systems.

In the remainder of this section, we describe file processing systems and discuss their limitations by means of a realistic case example. In the next section, we use the same case example to introduce and compare database processing systems.

File Processing Systems at Pine Valley Furniture Company

Early computer applications at Pine Valley Furniture (during the 1980s) used the traditional file processing approach. This approach to information systems design met the data processing needs of individual departments rather than the overall information needs of the organization. The information systems group typically responded to users' requests for new systems by developing (or acquiring) new computer programs for individual applications such as inventory control, accounts receivable, or human resource management. Each application program or system that was developed was designed to meet the needs of the requesting department or user group and no overall map, plan, or model guided application growth.

Three of the computer applications based on the file processing approach are shown in Figure 1-3. The systems illustrated are Order Filling, Invoicing, and Payroll. The figure also shows the major data files associated with each application. A file is a collection of related records. For example, the Order Filling System has three files: Customer Master, Inventory Master, and Back Order. Notice that there is duplication of some of the files used by the three applications, which is typical of file processing systems.

Disadvantages of File Processing Systems

Several disadvantages are associated with conventional file processing systems. These disadvantages are listed in Table 1-2 and described briefly here.

Table 1-2 Disadvantages of File Processing Systems

Program-data dependence
Duplication of data
Limited data sharing
Lengthy development times
Excessive program maintenance

Figure 1-3
Old file processing systems at
Pine Valley Furniture Company

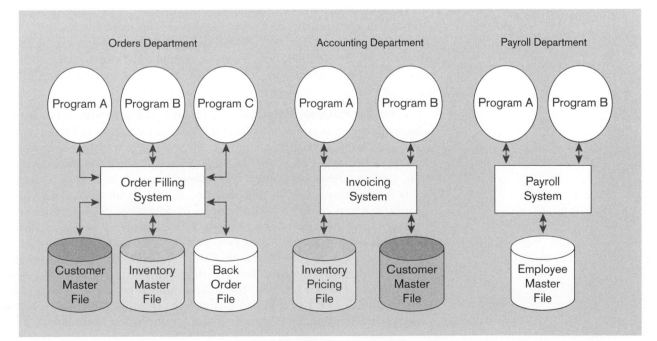

Database application: An application program (or set of related programs) that is used to perform a series of database activities (create, read, update, and delete) on behalf of database users.

Program-Data Dependence   File descriptions are stored within each **database application** program that accesses a given file. For example, in the Invoicing System in Figure 1-3, Program A accesses the Inventory Pricing File and the Customer Master File. Because the program contains a detailed file description for these files, any change to a file structure requires changes to the file descriptions for all programs that access the file.

Notice in Figure 1-3 that the Customer Master File is used in the Order Filling System and the Invoicing System. Suppose it is decided to change the customer address field length in the records in this file from 30 to 40 characters. The file descriptions in each program that is affected (up to five programs) would have to be modified. It is often difficult even to locate all programs affected by such changes. What is worse, errors are often introduced when making such changes.

Duplication of Data   Because applications are often developed independently in file processing systems, unplanned duplicate data files are the rule rather than the exception. For example, in Figure 1-3 the Order Filling System contains an Inventory Master File, whereas the Invoicing System contains an Inventory Pricing File. These files contain data describing Pine Valley Furniture Company's products, such as product description, unit price, and quantity on hand. This duplication is wasteful because it requires additional storage space and increased effort to keep all files up to date. Data formats may be inconsistent or data values may not agree (or both). Reliable metadata are very difficult to establish in file processing systems. For example, the same data item may have different names in different files, or conversely, the same name may be used for different data items in different files.

Limited Data Sharing   With the traditional file processing approach, each application has its own private files and users have little opportunity to share data outside their own applications. Notice in Figure 1-3, for example, that users in the Accounting Department have access to the Invoicing System and its files, but they probably do not have access to the Order Filling System or to the Payroll System and their files. Managers often find that a requested report requires a major programming effort because data must be drawn from several incompatible files in separate systems. When different organizational units own these different files, additional management barriers must be overcome.

Lengthy Development Times   With traditional file processing systems, each new application requires that the developer essentially start from scratch by designing new file formats and descriptions and then writing the file access logic for each new program. The lengthy development times required are inconsistent with today's fast-paced business environment, in which time to market (or time to production for an information system) is a key business success factor.

Excessive Program Maintenance   The preceding factors all combined to create a heavy program maintenance load in organizations that relied on traditional file processing systems. In fact, as much as 80 percent of the total information system's development budget might be devoted to program maintenance in such organizations, leaving little opportunity for developing new applications.

It is important to note that many of the disadvantages of file processing we have mentioned can also be limitations of databases if an organization does not properly apply the database approach. For example, if an organization develops many separately managed databases (say, one for each division or business function) with little or no coordination of the metadata, then uncontrolled data duplication, limited data sharing, lengthy development time, and excessive program maintenance can occur. Thus, the database approach, which is explained in the next section, is as much a way to manage organizational data as it is a set of technologies for defining, creating, maintaining, and using these data.

THE DATABASE APPROACH

The database approach emphasizes the integration and sharing of data throughout the organization (or at least across major segments of the organization). This approach requires a fundamental reorientation or shift in thought processes, starting with top management. Such a reorientation is difficult for most organizations, but most mid-size and larger organizations have made this shift today and appreciate the use of information as a competitive weapon. These organizations expect to gain certain advantages through the use of databases, primarily based on a relational model, and data warehouses, based on an integrated historical perspective. The primary advantages are summarized in Table 1-3 and described below.

It may also help you begin to understand the differences by comparing Figures 1-3 and 1-4. Figure 1-4 depicts the data model for the data files shown in Figure 1-3. Now, there is only one entity, CUSTOMER, rather than two Customer Master Files. Both the Order Filling System and the Invoicing System will access the data contained in the CUSTOMER entity, enabling them to achieve the advantages listed below. No relationships are depicted for the EMPLOYEE entity, but it would have relationships with other entities, such as EMPLOYEE HISTORY, DEPARTMENT, and so forth. Remember that the data models shown here and elsewhere in this text are very simple compared to those used in real businesses. Data models for mid-sized and larger organizations may include thousands of entities and relationships. This may seem overwhelming to a novice database designer, administrator, or user. However, the number of entities used regularly by any one employee will depend on the scope and nature of their position. Database developers learn that there are basic relationships that are common to organizations and database administrators learn database management procedures and principles applicable to the entire database. Users typically access only those entities that are necessary to meet their job requirements, resulting in a database scope that is easier to grasp. Such constraints on access are achieved by granting users permissions to access only certain data, and the data they can see constitutes their view of the database.

Table 1-3 Advantages of the Database Approach

Program-data independence

Planned data redundancy

Improved data consistency

Improved data sharing

Increased productivity of application development

Enforcement of standards

Improved data quality

Improved data accessibility and responsiveness

Reduced program maintenance

Improved decision support

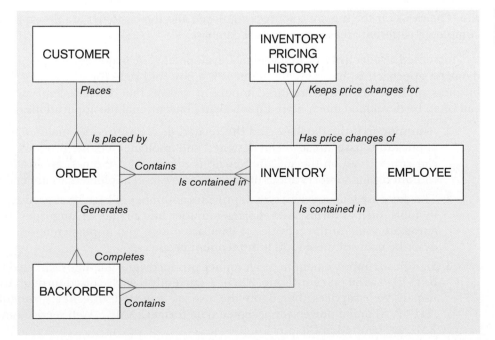

Figure 1-4
Enterprise data model for Figure 1-3 segments

Advantages of The Database Approach

Program-Data Independence   The separation of data descriptions (metadata) from the application programs that use the data is called **data independence.** With the database approach, data descriptions are stored in a central location called the *repository*. This property of database systems allows an organization's data to change and evolve (within limits) without changing the application programs that process the data.

Data independence: The separation of data descriptions from the application programs that use the data.

Planned Data Redundancy   Good database design attempts to integrate previously separate (and redundant) data files into a single, logical structure. Ideally, each primary fact is recorded in only one place in the database. For example, facts about a product, such as Pine Valley's oak computer desk, its finish, price, and so forth are recorded together in one place in the Product table, which contains data about each of Pine Valley's products. The database approach does not eliminate redundancy entirely, but it enables the designer to control the type and amount of redundancy. For example, each order in the Order table will contain a Customer_ID to establish the relationship between orders and customers. At other times it may be desirable to include some limited redundancy to improve database performance, as we will see in later chapters.

Improved Data Consistency   By eliminating or controlling data redundancy, we greatly reduce the opportunities for inconsistency. For example, if a customer address is stored only once, we cannot disagree about the customer's address. When the customer's address changes, recording the new address is greatly simplified because the address is stored in one place only. Finally, we avoid the wasted storage space that results from redundant data storage.

Improved Data Sharing   A database is designed as a shared corporate resource. Authorized internal and external users are granted permission to use the database, and each user (or group of users) is provided one or more user views into the database to facilitate this use. A **user view** is a logical description of some portion of the database that is required by a user to perform some task. A user view is often developed by identifying a form or report that the user needs on a regular basis. For example, an employee working in Human Resources will need access to confidential employee data; a customer needs access to the product catalog available on Pine Valley's Web site. The views for the human resources employee and the customer are drawn from completely different areas of one unified database.

User view: A logical description of some portion of the database that is required by a user to perform some task.

Increased Productivity of Application Development   A major advantage of the database approach is that it greatly reduces the cost and time for developing new business applications. There are three important reasons that database applications can often be developed much more rapidly than conventional file applications:

1. Assuming that the database and the related data capture and maintenance applications have already been designed and implemented, the programmer can concentrate on the specific functions required for the new application, without having to worry about file design or low-level implementation details.

2. The database management system provides a number of high-level productivity tools, such as forms and report generators, and high-level languages that automate some of the activities of database design and implementation. We describe many of these tools in subsequent chapters.

3. Significant improvement in programmer productivity, sometime estimated to be as high as 60 percent (Long, 2005), is currently being realized through the use of Web services, based on the use of standard Internet protocols (HTTP/S) and a universally accepted data format (XML). Web services and XML are covered in Chapter 10.

Enforcement of Standards   When the database approach is implemented with full management support, the database administration function should be granted single-point authority and responsibility for establishing and enforcing data standards. These standards will include naming conventions, data quality standards, and uniform procedures for accessing, updating, and protecting data. The data repository provides database administrators with a powerful set of tools for developing and enforcing these standards. Unfortunately, the failure to implement a strong database administration function is perhaps the most common source of database failures in organizations. We describe the database administration (and related data administration) functions in Chapter 12.

Improved Data Quality   Concern with poor quality data is a common theme in strategic planning and database administration today. In fact, a recent report by The Data Warehousing Institute (TDWI) estimated that data quality problems currently cost U.S. businesses some $600 billion each year (Hudica, 2003). The database approach provides a number of tools and processes to improve data quality. Two of the more important are the following:

1. Database designers can specify integrity constraints that are enforced by the DBMS. A **constraint** is a rule that cannot be violated by database users. We describe numerous types of constraints (also called "business rules") in Chapters 3 and 4. If a customer places an order, the constraint that ensures that the customer and the order remain associated is called a "relational integrity constraint," and it prevents an order from being entered without specifying who placed the order.

   Constraint: A rule that cannot be violated by database users.

2. One of the objectives of a data warehouse environment is to clean up (or "scrub") operational data before they are placed in the data warehouse (Jordan, 1996). Do you ever receive multiple copies of a catalog? The company that sends you three copies of each of its mailing pieces could recognize significant postage and printing savings if its data were scrubbed, and its understanding of its customers would also be enhanced if it could determine a more accurate count of existing customers. We describe data warehouses and the potential for improving data quality in Chapter 11.

Improved Data Accessibility and Responsiveness   With a relational database, end users without programming experience can often retrieve and display data, even when it crosses traditional departmental boundaries. For example, an employee can display information about computer desks at Pine Valley Furniture Company with the following query:

```
SELECT *
FROM PRODUCT
WHERE Product_Name = "Computer Desk";
```

The language used in this query is called Structured Query Language, or SQL. (You study this language in detail in Chapters 7 and 8.) Although the queries constructed can be *much* more complex, the basic structure of the query is easy for novice, non-programmers to grasp. If they understand the structure and names of the data that fit within their view of the database, they soon gain the ability to retrieve answers to new questions without having to rely on a professional programmer. This can be dangerous; queries should be thoroughly tested to be sure they are returning accurate data before relying on their results, and novices may not understand that challenge.

Reduced Program Maintenance   Stored data must be changed frequently for a variety of reasons: new data item types are added, data formats are changed, and so on. A celebrated example of this problem was the well-known "year 2000" problem, in which common two-digit year fields were extended to four digits to accommodate the rollover from the year 1999 to the year 2000.

In a file processing environment, the data descriptions and the logic for accessing data are built into individual application programs (this is the program-data dependence issue described earlier). As a result, changes to data formats and access methods inevitably result in the need to modify application programs. In a database environment, data are more independent of the application programs that use them. Within limits, we can change either the data or the application programs that use the data without necessitating a change in the other factor. As a result, program maintenance can be significantly reduced in a modern database environment.

Improved Decision Support Some databases are designed expressly for decision support applications. For example, some databases are designed to support customer relationship management, whereas others are designed to support financial analysis or supply chain management. You will study how databases are tailored for different decision support applications and analytical styles in Chapter 11.

Cautions About Database Benefits

This section has identified ten major potential benefits of the database approach. However, we must caution you that many organizations have been frustrated in attempting to realize some of these benefits. For example, the goal of data independence (and, therefore, reduced program maintenance) has proven elusive due to the limitations of older data models and database management software. Fortunately, the relational model (as well as the newer object-oriented model) provide a significantly better environment for achieving these benefits. Another reason for failure to achieve the intended benefits is poor organizational planning and database implementation—even the best data management software cannot overcome such deficiencies. For this reason, we stress database planning and design throughout this text.

Costs and Risks of The Database Approach

As with any business decision, the database approach entails some additional costs and risks that must be recognized and managed when it is implemented. (see Table 1-4).

New, Specialized Personnel Frequently, organizations that adopt the database approach need to hire or train individuals to design and implement databases, provide database administration services, and manage a staff of new people. Further, because of the rapid changes in technology, these new people will have to be retrained or upgraded on a regular basis. This personnel increase may be more than offset by other productivity gains, but an organization should not minimize the need for these specialized skills, which are required to obtain the most from the potential benefits. We discuss the staff requirements for database management in Chapter 12.

Installation and Management Cost and Complexity A multiuser database management system is a large and complex suite of software that has a high initial cost, requires a staff of trained personnel to install and operate, and has substantial annual maintenance and support costs. Installing such a system may also require upgrades to the hardware and data communications systems in the organization. Substantial training is normally required on an ongoing basis to keep up with new releases and upgrades. Additional or more sophisticated and costly database software may be needed to provide security and to ensure proper concurrent updating of shared data.

Conversion Costs The term *legacy system* is widely used to refer to older applications in an organization that are based on file processing and/or older database technology. The cost of converting these older systems to modern database technology—measured in terms of dollars, time, and organizational commitment—may often seem prohibitive to an organization. The use of data warehouses is one strategy for

Table 1-4 Costs and Risks of the Database Approach

New, specialized personnel

Installation and management cost and complexity

Conversion costs

Need for explicit backup and recovery

Organizational conflict

COMPONENTS OF THE DATABASE ENVIRONMENT

continuing to use older systems while at the same time exploiting modern database technology and techniques (Ritter, 1999).

Need for Explicit Backup and Recovery   A shared corporate database must be accurate and available at all times. This requires that comprehensive procedures be developed and used for providing backup copies of data and for restoring a database when damage occurs. These considerations have acquired increased urgency in today's security-conscious environment. A modern database management system normally automates many more of the backup and recovery tasks than a file system. We describe procedures for security, backup, and recovery in Chapter 12.

Organizational Conflict   A shared database requires a consensus on data definitions and ownership, as well as responsibilities for accurate data maintenance. Experience has shown that conflicts on data definitions, data formats and coding, rights to update shared data, and associated issues are frequent and often difficult to resolve. Handling these issues requires organizational commitment to the database approach, organizationally astute database administrators, and a sound evolutionary approach to database development.

If strong top management support of and commitment to the database approach is lacking, end-user development of stand-alone databases is likely to proliferate. These databases do not follow the general database approach that we have described, and they are unlikely to provide the benefits described earlier. In the extreme, they may lead to a pattern of inferior decision making that threatens the well-being or existence of an organization.s

COMPONENTS OF THE DATABASE ENVIRONMENT

The major components of a typical database environment and their relationships are shown in Figure 1-5. You have already been introduced to some (but not all) of these components in previous sections. Following is a brief description of the nine components shown in Figure 1-5.

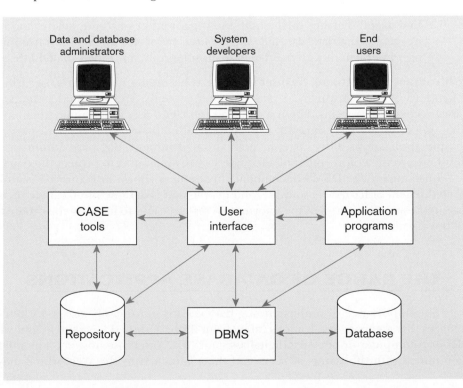

Figure 1-5
Components of the database environment

1. **Computer-aided software engineering (CASE) tools**   Automated tools used to design databases and application programs. We describe the use of CASE tools for database design and development throughout the text.

2. **Repository**   Centralized knowledge base for all data definitions, data relationships, screen and report formats, and other system components. A **repository** contains an extended set of metadata important for managing databases as well as other components of an information system. We describe the repository in Chapter 12.

3. **DBMS**   A software system that is used to create, maintain, and provide controlled access to user databases. We describe the functions of a DBMS in Chapters 12 and 13.

4. **Database**   An organized collection of logically related data, usually designed to meet the information needs of multiple users in an organization. It is important to distinguish between the database and the repository. The repository contains definitions of data, whereas the database contains occurrences of data. We describe the activities of database design in Chapters 5 and 6 and of implementation in Chapters 7 through 11.

5. **Application programs**   Computer programs that are used to create and maintain the database and provide information to users. Key database programming skills are described in Chapters 7 through 11.

6. **User interface**   Languages, menus, and other facilities by which users interact with various system components, such as CASE tools, application programs, the DBMS, and the repository. User interfaces are illustrated throughout this text.

7. **Data and database administrators**   Data administrators are persons who are responsible for the overall management of data resources in an organization. Database administrators are responsible for physical database design and for managing technical issues in the database environment. We describe these functions in detail in Chapter 12.

8. **System developers**   Persons such as systems analysts and programmers who design new application programs. System developers often use CASE tools for system requirements analysis and program design.

9. **End users**   Persons throughout the organization who add, delete, and modify data in the database and who request or receive information from it. All user interactions with the database must be routed through the DBMS.

Repository: A centralized knowledge base of all data definitions, data relationships, screen and report formats, and other system components.

With advances in software, the user interface is becoming increasingly user friendly. Examples of such advances are menu-driven systems, Web-enabled systems, and voice-recognition systems. These systems promote end-user computing, which means that users who are not computer experts can define their own reports, displays, and simple applications. Of course, in such an environment, database administration must ensure the enforcement of adequate security measures to protect the database.

In summary, the DBMS operational environment shown in Figure 1-5 is an integrated system of hardware, software, and people that is designed to facilitate the storage, retrieval, and control of the information resource and to improve the productivity of the organization.

THE RANGE OF DATABASE APPLICATIONS

The importance of understanding databases is more easily grasped when one realizes that database applications range from those designed for a single user with a desktop computer or personal digital assistant (PDA) to those hosted on mainframe computers with thousands of users and those attached to the Web, which may be accessed almost without limit. Although there is some overlap, we divide database applications into five categories: personal databases, workgroup databases, departmental/divisional databases, enterprise databases, and Web-enabled databases. We introduce each category with a typical example, followed by some issues that generally arise within that category of use.

Personal Databases

Personal databases are designed to support one user. Personal databases have long resided on personal computers (PCs), including laptops. Recently the introduction of PDAs has incorporated personal databases into handheld devices that function not only as computing devices, but also as cellular phones, fax senders, cameras, and Web browsers. Simple database applications that store customer information and the details of contacts with each customer can be used from a PC or a PDA and easily transferred from one device to the other for backup and work purposes. For example, consider a company that has a number of salespersons who call on actual or prospective customers. If each salesperson also has other applications, such as a graphics-intensive sales presentation and a pricing program that helps the salesperson determine the best combination of quantity and type of items for the customer to order, a laptop computer may be appropriate because of storage and performance requirements. If the salespersons need to keep only their contact list, a PDA with a contacts management application that uses a small database may be best. Typical data from a customer contact list are shown in Figure 1-6.

Figure 1-6
Typical data from a personal database

Some of the key decisions that must be made in developing personal databases are the following:

1. Should the application be purchased from an outside vendor or developed within the organization?

2. If the database application is developed internally, should it be developed by the end user or by a professional within the information systems (IS) department?

3. What data are required by the user and how should the database be designed?

4. What commercial DBMS product should be used for the application?

5. How should data in the personal database be synchronized with data in other databases?

6. Who is responsible for the accuracy of the data in the personal database?

Personal databases are widely used because they can often improve personal productivity. However, they entail a risk: The data cannot easily be shared with other users. For example, suppose the sales manager wants a consolidated view of customer contacts. This cannot be quickly or easily provided from an individual salesperson's databases. This illustrates a very common problem: If data are of interest to one person, they probably are or will soon become of interest to others as well. For this reason, personal databases should be limited to those rather special situations (such as in a very small organization) where the need to share the data among users of the personal database is unlikely to arise.

Workgroup Databases

A workgroup is a relatively small team of people who collaborate on the same project or application or on a group of similar projects or applications. A workgroup typically comprises fewer than twenty-five persons. These persons might be engaged (for example) with a construction project or with developing a new computer application. A workgroup database is designed to support the collaborative efforts of such a team.

Consider a workgroup that develops both standard and custom objects (or software components) that are sold to software vendors as well as to end users. Table 1-5 is a list of some of the software objects that have been developed recently. Typically, one or more persons work on a given object or component at a given time. The group needs a database that will track each item as it is developed and allow the data to be easily shared by the team members.

The method of sharing the data in this database is shown in Figure 1-7. Each member of the workgroup has a notebook computer, and the computers are linked by means of a docking station and a wireless LAN. The database is stored on a central

Table 1-5 List of Software Objects in an Example Workgroup Database

Object Place, Inc.
400 Magnolia St.
Atlanta, GA 02103

Name	Language	Description	Price
123Xtender	Visual Basic	Spreadsheet wrapper	595
DSSObjects	C++	Decision support generator	595
ObjectSuite	Smalltalk	Set of 6 generic objects	5000
OrderObject	Smalltalk	Generic order object	1000
PatientObject	Visual Basic	Generic patient object	1000

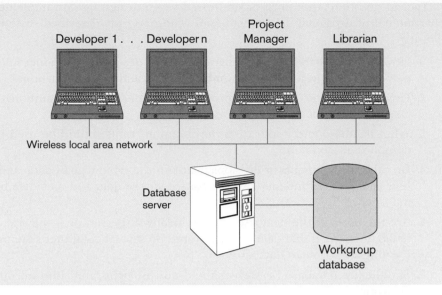

Figure 1-7
Workgroup database with wireless
local area network

device called the "database server," which is also connected to the network. Thus, each member of the workgroup has access to the shared data. Different types of group members (e.g., developer or project manager) may have different user views of this shared database. This arrangement overcomes the principal objection to PC databases, which is that the data are not easily shared (at least data are easily shared within the workgroup). This arrangement, however, introduces many data management issues not present with personal (single-user) databases, such as data security and data integrity with concurrent user data updating. Also, because an organization is composed of many workgroups, and an individual may be part of many different workgroups at the same or different times, it is possible to generate many databases, just as with the use of personal databases.

In establishing a workgroup database, the organization must answer the same questions that applied to personal databases. In addition, the following database management questions arise:

1. How can the design of the database be optimized for a variety of group members' information requirements?

2. How can the various members use the database concurrently without compromising the integrity of the database?

3. Which database processing operations should be performed at a workstation and which should occur on the server?

Departmental/Divisional Databases

A department is a functional unit within an organization. Typical examples of departments are personnel, marketing, manufacturing, and accounting. A department is generally larger than a workgroup (typically between 25 and 100 persons) and is responsible for a more diverse range of functions. Divisions are even larger administrative units, generally focused on a line of business within the organization.

Departmental and divisional databases are designed to support the various functions and activities of a department or division. They are the most common of the five types of databases described in this section. For example, consider a personnel database that is designed to track data concerning employees, jobs, skills, and job assignments. After the relevant data are stored in the database, users can query the database to obtain answers to most personnel-related questions.

Typical questions that must be addressed when designing and implementing departmental or divisional databases (besides those already described) include the following:

1. How can the database and its environment be designed to produce adequate performance, given the large number of users and user transactions?
2. How can adequate security be provided to protect against unauthorized disclosure or distribution of sensitive data?
3. What database and application development tools should be used in this complex environment?
4. Do other departments or divisions maintain the same type of data, and if so, how can data redundancy and the consistency of data and metadata best be managed?
5. Are the users of the database geographically dispersed or is the size of the database so great that data must be stored on several computer systems, thus creating a distributed database?
6. Should the database be Web-enabled and incorporated into an intranet environment?

Enterprise Databases

An enterprise database is one whose scope is the entire organization or enterprise (or, at least, many different departments). Such databases are intended to support organizationwide operations and decision making. Note that an organization may have several enterprise databases, so such a database is not inclusive of all organizational data. A single, operational, enterprise database is impractical for many medium to large organizations due to difficulties in performance for very large databases, diverse needs of different users, and the complexity of achieving a single definition of data (metadata) for all database users. An enterprise database does, however, support information needs from many departments. Over the last decade, the evolution of enterprise databases has resulted in two major developments:

1. Enterprise resource planning (ERP) systems
2. Data warehousing implementations

Enterprise resource planning (ERP): A business management system that integrates all functions of the enterprise, such as manufacturing, sales, finance, marketing, inventory, accounting, and human resources. ERP systems are software applications that provide the data necessary for the enterprise to examine and manage its activities.

Data warehouse: An integrated decision support database whose content is derived from the various opertional databases.

Enterprise resource planning (ERP) systems have evolved from the materials requirements planning (MRP) and manufacturing resources planning (MRP-II) systems of the 1970s and 1980s. Whereas MRP systems scheduled the raw materials, components, and subassembly requirements for manufacturing processes, MRP-II systems also scheduled shop floors and product distribution. Next, extension to the remaining business functions resulted in enterprisewide management systems, or ERP systems. All ERP systems are heavily dependent on databases to store the data required by the ERP applications.

Whereas ERP systems work with the current operational data of the enterprise, **data warehouses** collect their content from the various operational databases, including personal, workgroup, department, and ERP databases. Data warehouses provide users with the opportunity to work with historical data to identify patterns and trends and answers to strategic business questions. We describe data warehouses in detail in Chapter 11.

Consider a large health-care organization that operates a group of medical centers that includes hospitals, clinics, and nursing homes. As shown in Figure 1-8, each of these medical centers has a separate database (or databases) to support the various operations at that facility. These databases contain data concerning patients, physicians, medical services, business operations, and other related entities.

Figure 1-8
An enterprise data warehouse

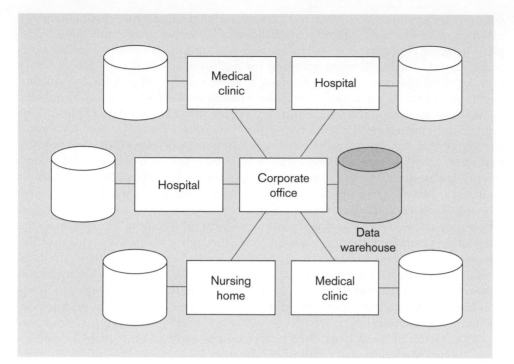

The databases provide adequate support for most functions at each individual medical center. However, the organization also needs a single, consolidated view of the entire organization, for example, to see the total activities with a single patient or supplier. Operating efficiencies can be achieved, for example, by the central ordering of supplies for all medical units and by scheduling staff and services across all units. An ERP system makes these approaches possible. Corporate decision making, dealing with external suppliers (such as insurance companies), and reporting to various agencies requires compiled historical data and information. To satisfy these requirements, the organization has created a data warehouse that is maintained at the corporate office. Data in the data warehouse are derived by extracting and summarizing data from the individual databases on a periodic basis and transmitting those data by means of a telecommunications network to the corporate data warehouse.

Several questions that often arise in the context of an enterprise database are the following:

1. How should the data be distributed among the various locations in the corporate structure?

2. How can the organization develop and maintain standards concerning data names, definitions, formats, and related issues?

3. What actions must be taken to integrate numerous systems successfully, including legacy data from earlier systems that are desired for analysis?

Web-Enabled Databases

The most recent change, and one that has dramatically affected the database environment is the ascendance of the Internet, a worldwide network that easily connects users of multiple platforms through an interface known as a Web browser. Acceptance of the Internet by businesses has resulted in important changes in long-established business models. Very successful companies have been shaken by competition from new businesses that have employed the Internet to provide improved customer information and service, to eliminate traditional marketing channels and distribution channels, and to implement employee relationship management. For example, customers configure and order their personal computers directly from the computer manufacturers. Bids are accepted for airline tickets and collectables within minutes of submission, sometimes resulting in savings of over 40 percent. Information about open positions and company activities is readily available within many companies.

Each of these applications requires database support, and many applications require universal access. The easy connection of multiple platforms enables companies to reorganize their operations and develop new applications faster and at lower cost. A standard interface allows users to be productive with less training and to require less support. Central to the development of useful applications is the ability to attach a database from which current information may be retrieved. When a database is Web-enabled, the Web browser interface enables users to ask unique and specific questions and receive answers based on current information. The answer to the question is automated; there is no need to go through a series of options over the telephone and wait for a human to offer assistance. Web-enabled databases are indispensable to the development of online shopping sites. Companies are scrambling to collect information about their customers (purchase patterns, site navigation, duration of stay at each screen, and so forth) to improve their customer relationship management (CRM) efforts.

Most of the examples just cited reflect business-to-customer (BtoC) relationships, though some businesses' customers are other businesses. Such interactions are commonly referred to as BtoB relationships. The Internet is used to facilitate BtoC relationships because customers are necessarily external to the business, and the capability of the customer to access business data or information is critical to the success of the relationship. Allowing such external access to a business database raises data security and integrity issues that are new to the management of information systems, where data have traditionally been closely guarded and secured within each company. These issues are covered in more detail in Chapters 10 and 12.

Companies have traded information by means of electronic data interchange (EDI) for years. Many companies continue to use their EDI systems to conduct their BtoB business. Some companies, particularly those who are new or did not previously use EDI for intercompany information exchange, have set up extranets to conduct their BtoB exchanges. An extranet uses Internet technology, but access to the extranet is not universal as is the case with an Internet application. Rather, access is restricted to business suppliers and customers with whom an agreement has been reached about legitimate access and use of each other's data and information. Typically, these suppliers and customers have access to a part of the company's intranet, discussed next. This access facilitates the business relationship by providing faster and more efficient processing or access to information.

As previously mentioned, many companies have used Internet technology to create private networks intended for information management within an organization. In appearance, an intranet page is not distinguishable from an Internet page, but access to the page is limited to those within the organization. Thus, access to company databases is restricted. Intranets may also be able to establish an Internet connection, but that connection will be protected by a firewall, which prevents external users from connecting to the intranet.

One of the most interesting changes in the database environment since the early 2000s has been the utilization of XML-defined Web services. Discussed in more detail in Chapter 10, the development of a new integration methodology that works with any language, operating system, or network and transforms sites into reusable components is exciting (Long, 2005). While it is still a challenge to find reliable Web services for a particular business application, XML Web services are now available for almost every business purpose, such as calculating taxes (state, national, or international), or determining shipping rates or shipping dates.

Table 1-6 Summary of Database Applications (adapted from White, 1995)

Type of Database	Typical Number of Users	Typical Architecture	Typical Size of Database
Personal	1	Desktop/laptop computer, PDA	Megabytes
Workgroup	5–25	Client/server (two-tier)	Megabytes–gigabytes
Department/Division	25–100	Client/server (three-tier)	Gigabytes
Enterprise	>100	Client/server (distributed or parallel server)	Gigabytes–terabytes
Web-enabled	>1000	Web server and application servers	Megabytes–gigabytes

Several questions that often arise in the context of Web-enabled databases are the following:

1. What technology (Web services, middleware, protocols, etc.) should be used to link Web applications to client databases?
2. What special measures are required to protect the security and privacy of data in this environment?
3. How should an organization manage the mountains of data that are generated through Internet transactions?
4. How can an organization maintain data quality when so much data are generated outside the organization?

Summary of Database Applications

A summary of the various types of database applications that we have described in this section is shown in Table 1-6. For each type of database, the table shows the typical number of users, the typical database architecture (client/server architectures are explained in Chapter 9), and the typical range of database size.

EVOLUTION OF DATABASE SYSTEMS

Many new database students today have only experienced a Windows or Mac operating system and assume that a database system is an easy solution to the automation of most business processes. Interfaces have improved to the point that many are able to create small working systems with little understanding of the programming and architectural structures that lie behind the interface. Database professionals and those who must work with database professionals to obtain the system they require do need a deeper understanding, including a sense of the flow from file processing systems to the present. We attempt to provide you with a sense that "data are data" and we are involved in meeting the continuous challenge of processing business requirements as safely, accurately, and efficiently as possible. We hope you can share our excitement about achieving a more seamless and efficient database environment and spending a lot less time doing it.

Database management systems were first introduced during the 1960s and have continued to evolve during subsequent decades. Figure 1-9 sketches this evolution by highlighting the database technology (or technologies) that were dominant during each decade. In most cases, the period of introduction was quite long, and the technology was first introduced during the decade preceding the one shown in the figure. For example, the relational model was first defined by E. F. Codd, an

Figure 1-9
Evolution of database technologies

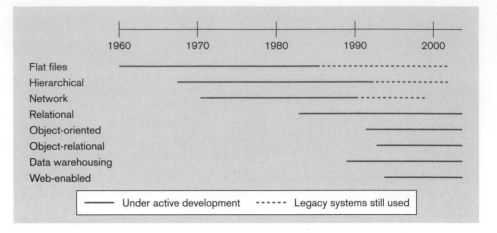

IBM research fellow, in a paper published in 1970 (Codd, 1970). However, the relational model did not realize widespread commercial success until the 1980s.

Database management systems were developed to overcome the limitations of file processing systems, described in a previous section. To summarize, some of the following four objectives generally drove the development and evolution of database technology:

1. The need to provide greater independence between programs and data, thereby reducing maintenance costs

2. The desire to manage increasingly complex data types and structures

3. The desire to provide easier and faster access to data for users who have neither a background in programming languages nor a detailed understanding of how data are stored in databases

4. The need to provide ever more powerful platforms for decision support applications

1960s

File processing systems were still dominant during this period. However, the first database management systems were introduced during this decade and were used primarily for large and complex ventures such as the Apollo moon-landing project. We can regard this as an experimental "proof-of-concept" period in which the feasibility of managing vast amounts of data with a DBMS was demonstrated. Also, the first efforts at standardization were taken with the formation of the Data Base Task Group in the late 1960s.

1970s

During this decade the use of database management systems became a commercial reality. The hierarchical and network database management systems were developed, largely to cope with increasingly complex data structures such as manufacturing bills of materials that were extremely difficult to manage with conventional file processing methods. The hierarchical and network models are generally regarded as first-generation DBMS. Both approaches were widely used, and in fact many of these systems continue to be used today. However, they have some major disadvantages:

1. Difficult access to data, based on navigational record-at-a-time procedures. As a result, complex programs have to be written to answer even simple queries.

2. Very limited data independence, so that programs are not insulated from changes to data formats.

3. No widely accepted theoretical foundation for either model, unlike the relational data model.

1980s

To overcome these limitations, E. F. Codd and others developed the relational data model during the 1970s. This model, considered second-generation DBMS, received widespread commercial acceptance and diffused throughout the business world during the 1980s. With the relational model, all data are represented in the form of tables. A relatively simple fourth-generation language called SQL is used for data retrieval. Thus, the relational model provides ease of access for nonprogrammers, overcoming one of the major objections to first-generation systems. The relational model has also proven well-suited to client/server computing, parallel processing, and graphical user interfaces (Gray, 1996).

1990s

The 1990s ushered in a new era of computing, first with client/server computing, and then with data warehousing and Internet applications becoming increasingly important. Whereas the data managed by a DBMS during the 1980s were largely structured (such as accounting data), multimedia data (including graphics, sound, images, and video) became increasingly common during the 1990s. To cope with these increasingly complex data, object-oriented databases (considered third generation) were introduced during the late 1980s (Grimes, 1998). We describe object-oriented databases in detail in Chapters 14 and 15.

Because organizations must manage a vast amount of structured and unstructured data, both relational and object-oriented databases are of great importance today. In fact, some vendors are developing combined object-relational DBMSs that can manage both types of data. We describe object-relational databases in Appendix D.

2000 and Beyond

We are naturally led to speculate on what directions database technology will take during the next decade. While there will undoubtedly be some surprises, we can expect several well-established trends to continue:

1. The ability to manage increasingly complex data types. These types include multidimensional data, which have already assumed considerable importance in data warehouse applications. We discuss multidimensional data in Chapter 11.

2. The continued development of "universal servers." Based on object-relational DBMS, these are database servers that can manage a wide range of data types transparently to users. They will become especially important to Internet applications.

3. While fully distributed databases have become a reality, the current trend toward centralization of databases will continue. With communications costs coming down as the volume of data increases, the cost to locate and access centralized data is going down. The lower cost of high-performance computing also encourages centralization.

4. Content-addressable storage will become more popular. With this approach, users can retrieve data by specifying the data they desire, rather than how to retrieve them. For example, a user can scan a photograph and have the computer search for the closest match to that photo.

5. Database and other technologies, such as artificial intelligence and television-like information services, will make database access much easier for untrained

users. For example, users will be able to request data in a more natural language, and database technology will anticipate users' data needs based on past queries and relevant database changes.

6. Work on developing data mining algorithms that scale to handle very large data sets will result in organizations being able to efficiently analyze their huge data stores. Improving abilities to discern patterns, trends, and correlations about customers, employees, products, and suppliers will influence strategic decision making by organizations. This capability will also be applied to the large volume of data being collected from Web site activity, for example, clickstream analysis (Riggs, 2000).

7. On the other end of the scale, the proliferation of PDAs will lead to improved synchronization of small databases and improvement of wireless transmission rates. Several wireless standards, including Bluetooth and Wi-Fi, will greatly accelerate development of wireless PDAs that connect to the Internet. This development will accentuate the importance of protecting data security in an increasingly wireless world.

8. The use of Web services will become more widespread as reliable XML Web services become more available. Increases in developer productivity and greatly improved ease of integration across platforms will drive this trend.

9. Improved ability to reconstruct historical positions will be developed, pushed by recent legislation such as Sarbanes-Oxley, HIPPA, and the Basel Convention.

10. The development of computer forensics will continue to increase emphasis and expectations that electronic discovery and electronic evidence will be available to help enforce accounting procedures and the above legislative requirements.

Summary

Over the past two decades there has been enormous growth in the number and importance of database applications. Databases are used to store, manipulate, and retrieve data in every type of organization. In the highly competitive environment of the 2000s, there is every indication that database technology will assume even greater importance. A course in modern database management is one of the most important courses in the information systems curriculum.

A database is an organized collection of logically related data. We define data as stored representations of objects and events that have meaning and importance in the user's environment. Information is data that have been processed in such a way that the knowledge of the person who uses the data increases. Both data and information may be stored in a database.

Metadata are data that describe the properties or characteristics of end-user data and the context of that data. A database management system (or DBMS) is a software system that is used to create, maintain, and provide controlled access to user databases. A DBMS stores metadata in a repository, which is a central storehouse for all data definitions, data relationships, screen and report formats, and other system components.

Computer file processing systems were developed early in the computer era so that computers could store, manipulate, and retrieve large files of data. These systems (still in use today) have a number of important limitations such as dependence between programs and data, data duplication, limited data sharing, and lengthy development times. The database approach was developed to overcome these limitations. This approach emphasizes the integration and sharing of data across the organization. Advantages of this approach include program-data independence, improved data sharing, minimal data redundancy, and improved productivity of application development.

Database applications can be arranged into the following categories: personal databases, workgroup databases, departmental databases, enterprise databases, and Web-enabled databases. Enterprise databases include data warehouses and integrated decision support databases whose content is derived from the various operational databases. Enterprise resource planning (ERP) systems rely heavily on enterprise databases.

Database technology has evolved steadily since it was first introduced during the 1960s. The major objectives driving this evolution have included the desire to provide greater program-data independence, the need to manage increasingly complex data structures, and the desire to provide faster and easier access to all users. Today, both object-oriented and object-relational databases are increasingly being used to satisfy these objectives.

CHAPTER REVIEW

Key Terms

Constraint
Data
Data independence
Data warehouse
Database
Database application

Database management
  system (DBMS)
Enterprise data model
Enterprise resource planning
  (ERP) systems
Entity

Information
Metadata
Relational database
Repository
User view

Review Questions

1. Define each of the following key terms:
   a. data
   b. information
   c. metadata
   d. database application
   e. data warehouse
   f. constraint
   g. database
   h. entity
   i. database management system

2. Match the following terms and definitions:
   _____ data
   _____ database application
   _____ constraint
   _____ repository
   _____ metadata
   _____ data warehouse
   _____ information
   _____ user view
   _____ database management system
   _____ data independence
   _____ database

   a. data placed in context or summarized
   b. application program(s)
   c. facts, text, graphics, images, etc.
   d. a graphical model that shows the high-level entities for the organization and the relationships among those entities
   e. organized collection of related data
   f. includes data definitions and constraints
   g. centralized storehouse for all data definitions
   h. separation of data description from programs

   _____ enterprise resource systems planning (ERP)
   _____ enterprise data model

   i. a business management system that integrates all functions of the enterprise
   j. logical description of portion of database
   k. a software application that is used to create, maintain and provide controlled access to user databases
   l. a rule that cannot be violated by database users
   m. integrated decision support database

3. Contrast the following terms:
   a. data dependence; data independence
   b. structured data; unstructured data
   c. data; information
   d. repository; database
   e. entity; enterprise data model
   f. data warehouse; ERP system

4. List five disadvantages of file processing systems.

5. Describe two ways to convert data into information.

6. List and briefly describe five categories of databases and give an example of each type.

7. Why has the definition of data been expanded in today's business environment?

8. List the nine major components in a database system environment.

9. How are relationships between tables expressed in a relational database?

10. List some key questions that must typically be answered for each of the following types of databases: personal, workgroup, departmental, enterprise, Internet.

11. What does the term data independence mean and why is it an important goal?

12. List 10 potential benefits of the database approach over conventional file systems.

13. List five costs or risks associated with the database approach.

14. For each decade from the 1960s to the 1990s, list the dominant database technology (or technologies). Indicate the generation generally associated with each technology.

15. Pine Valley Furniture Company has introduced Internet technology to their application. Discuss why this would be beneficial to the company. What potential problems could arise from implementing such a system?

16. Why might Pine Valley Furniture Company need a data warehouse?

17. Compare and contrast intranets, the Internet, and extranets.

18. Discuss the database technology trends that will continue in the 2000s.

19. As the ability to handle large amounts of data improves, describe three business areas where these very large databases are being used effectively.

20. Perform a search on the Internet of relational DBMS vendors. Pick two competing products and discuss whether each is scalable and if it can be used for a personal, workgroup, departmental, enterprise, or Internet database.

Problems and Exercises

1. For each of the following entities in a university, indicate whether (under typical circumstances) there is a one-to-many or a many-to-many relationship. Then, using the shorthand notation introduced in the text, draw a diagram for each of the relationships.
   a. STUDENT and COURSE (students register for courses)
   b. BOOK and BOOK COPY (books have copies)
   c. COURSE and SECTION (courses have sections)
   d. SECTION and ROOM (sections are scheduled in rooms)
   e. INSTRUCTOR and COURSE

2. Examine the personal database for customer contacts. (Figure 1-6). Is the relationship between CUSTOMER and CONTACT HISTORY one-to-many or many-to-many? Using the shorthand notation introduced in the text, draw a diagram showing this relationship.

3. Reread the definitions for data and database in this chapter. Database management systems only recently included the capability to store and retrieve more than numeric and textual data. What special data storage, retrieval, and maintenance capabilities do images, sound, video, and other advanced data types require that are not required or are simpler with numeric and textual data?

4. Table 1-1 shows example metadata for a set of data items. Identify three other columns for these data (i.e., three other metadata characteristics for the listed attributes) and complete the entries of the table in Table 1-1 for these three additional columns.

5. In the section Disadvantages of File Processing Systems, the statement is made that the disadvantages of file processing systems can also be limitations of databases, depending on how an organization manages its databases. First, why do organizations create multiple databases, not just one all-inclusive database supporting all data processing needs? Second, what organizational and personal factors are at work that might lead an organization to have multiple, independently managed databases (and, hence, not completely follow the database approach)?

6. Consider a student club or organization in which you are a member. What are the data entities of this enterprise? List and define each entity. Then, develop an enterprise data model (such as Figure 1-2a) showing these entities and important relationships between them.

7. In the section of this chapter titled The Range of Database Applications, five different categories of databases are introduced. For each category, a series of key decisions are outlined. Later in the text you will learn how to deal with these and other decisions; however, you should be able to anticipate partial responses for these decisions from your reading of this chapter and your overall familiarity with computer technologies. For the following categories and key decisions, explain what choice you think should be made or what factors should be considered in making a choice within any organization.
   a. Personal database: Who is responsible for the accuracy of the data in a personal database?
   b. Workgroup database: Which database processing operations should be performed at a workstation and which should occur on the server?
   c. Departmental/divisional database: How can adequate security be provided to protect against unauthorized disclosure or distribution of sensitive data?
   d. Enterprise database: How can the organization develop and maintain standards concerning data names, definitions, formats, and related issues?
   e. Web-enabled database: With applets and code modules on different servers and browsers, how can all components have a shared understanding of the meaning of data?

8. One of the biggest challenges of building e-commerce sites has been the ability to quickly deliver merchandise ordered by customers over the Web. From what you have learned about databases in this first chapter and your own experience with ordering over the Web, why do you think companies are turning to database solutions to help them improve

their supply chain management and expedite the filling and delivery of orders?

9. A driver's license bureau maintains a database of licensed drivers. State whether each of the following represents data or metadata. If it represents data, state whether it is structured or unstructured data. If it represents metadata, state whether it is a fact describing a property of data or a fact describing the context of data.

   a. Driver's name, address, and birthdate

   b. The fact that the driver's name is a 30-character field

   c. A photo image of the driver

   d. An image of the driver's fingerprint.

   e. The make and serial number of the scanning device that was used to scan the fingerprint

   f. The resolution (in megapixels) of the camera that was used to photograph the driver

   g. The fact that the driver's birthdate must precede today's date by at least 16 years

10. Consider an online catalog business in which customers can place orders for merchandise. All orders consist of one or more items.

   a. Is the relationship between customer and order one-to-one, one-to-many, or many-to-many?

   b. Is the relationship between order and item one-to-one, one-to-many, or many-to-many?

11. Develop an enterprise data model (such as Figure 1-2a) for the online catalog business described in Problem and Exercise 10. Show all entities and the relationships between them.

12. Using a table similar to Table 1-1, define metadata for the customer entity in Problem and Exercise 10.

13. Great Lakes Insurance would like to implement a relational database for both its in-house as well as outside agents. The outside agents will use notebook computers to keep track of customers and policy information. Based on what you have learned in this chapter, what type (or types) of database(s) would you recommend for this application?

14. Figure 1-8 shows a data warehouse for a large organization. Suggest any data elements that would be common among all of the separate databases for the enterprise.

15. Research the Internet for a Business-to-Business success story. Discuss how the application was implemented using databases.

16. The following figure shows an enterprise data model for a pet store.

   a. What is the relationship between Pet and Store (one-to-one, many-to-many, or one-to-many)?

   b. What is the relationship between Customer and Pet?

   c. Do you think there should be a relationship between Customer and Store?

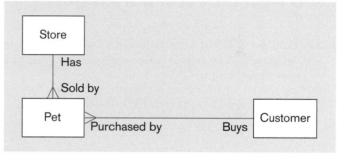

Figure 1–10
Data model for Problem and Exercise 16

Field Exercises

For Questions 1 through 4, choose an organization with a fairly extensive information systems department and set of information system applications. Use the same organization for each question.

1. Investigate whether the organization follows more of a traditional file processing approach or the database approach to organizing data. How many different databases does the organization have? Try to draw a figure, similar to Figure 1-3, to depict some or all of the files and databases in this organization.

2. Talk with a database administrator or designer from the organization. What type of metadata does this organization maintain about its databases? Why did the organization choose to keep track of these and not other metadata? What tools are used to maintain these metadata?

3. Identify, if possible, one database of each of the five types of databases listed in this chapter (personal, workgroup, departmental/divisional, enterprise, and Web-enabled) used by the organization. Does this organization have a data warehouse? If so, how is the data warehouse formed from data in all the other databases? Does this organization use an ERP system?

4. Determine the company's use of intranet, extranet, or other Web-enabled business processes. For each type of process, determine its purpose and the database management system that is being used in conjunction with the networks. Ask what the company's plans are for the next year with regard to using intranets, extranets, or the Web in their business activities. Ask what new skills they are looking for in order to implement these plans.

5. You may want to keep a personal journal of ideas and observations about database management while you are studying this book. Use this journal to record comments you hear, summaries of news stories or professional articles you read, original ideas or hypotheses you create, Uniform Resource Locators (URLs) for and comments about Web sites related to databases, and questions that require further analysis. Keep your eyes and ears open for anything related to database management. Your instructor may ask you to turn in a copy of your journal from time to time in order to provide feedback and reactions. The journal is an unstructured set of personal notes that will supplement your class notes and can stimulate you to think beyond the topics covered within the time limitations of most courses.

References

Anderson-Lehman, R., H. J. Watson, B. Wixom, and J. A. Hoffer 2004. "Continental Airlines Flies High with Real-Time Business Intelligence." *MIS Quarterly Executive* 3.4 (December).

Codd, E. F. 1970. "A Relational Model of Data for Large Shared Data Banks." *Communications of the ACM* 13,6 (June): 377–87.

Gray, J. 1996. "Data Management: Past, Present, and Future." *IEEE Computer* 29,10: 38–46.

Grimes, S. 1998. "Object/Relational Reality Check." *Database Programming & Design* 11,7 (July): 26–33.

Hudica, J. 2003. "Develop a Data Quality Strategy." *DM Review* 13,3 (March): 58–60.

Jordan, A. 1996. "Data Warehouse Integrity: How Long and Bumpy the Road?" *Data Management Review* 6,3 (March): 35–37.

Long, D. 2005. Presentation. ".Net Overview", Tampa Bay Technology Leadership Association, May 19, 2005.

Mullins, C. S. 2002. *Database Administration: The Complete Guide to Practices and Procedures.* New York: Addison-Wesley.

Riggs, S. 2000. "Collecting Webdata." *Teradata Review* 3,1 (Spring): 12–19.

Ritter, D. 1999. "Don't Neglect Your Legacy." *Intelligent Enterprise* 2,5 (March 30): 70,72.

Winter, R. 1997. "What, After All, Is a Very Large Database?" *Database Programming & Design* 10,1 (January): 23–26.

Further Reading

Ballou, D. P., and G. K. Tayi. 1999. "Enhancing Data Quality in Data Warehouse Environments." *Communications of the ACM* 42,1 (January): 73–78.

Date, C. J. 1998. "The Birth of the Relational Model, Part 3." *Intelligent Enterprise* 1,4 (December 10): 45–48.

Hoffer, J. A., J. F. George, and J. S. Valacich. 2005. *Modern Systems Analysis and Design*, 4th ed. Upper Saddle River, NJ: Prentice Hall.

Ritter, D. 1999. "The Long View." *Intelligent Enterprise* 2,12 (August 24): 58, 63, 67.

Web Resources

www.dbazine.com An online portal for database issues and solutions.

www.webopedia.com An online dictionary and search engine for computer terms and Internet technology.

www.techrepublic.com A portal site for information technology professionals that users can customize to their own particular interests.

www.zdnet.com A portal site where users can review recent articles on information technology subjects.

www.dmreview.com *DM Review* magazine Web site. Tagline is "Covering Business Intelligence, Integration and Analytics." Provides a comprehensive list of links to relevant resource portals in addition to providing many of the magazine articles online.

www.dbta.com *Data Base Trends & Applications* magazine Web site. Addresses enterprise-level information issues.

Databases.about.com A comprehensive site with many feature articles, links, interactive forum, chat rooms, and so forth.

http://www.pwcglobal.com/Extweb/NewCoAtWork.nsf/docid/ D0D7F79003C6D64485256CF30074D66C PriceWaterhouse-Coopers' summary site regarding Sarbanes-Oxley legislation.

http://dchealth.dc.gov/hipaa/hipaaoverview.shtm Web site offering an overview of the healthcare legislation contained in HIPPA.

http://www.basel.int/ United Nations page offering an overview of the Basel Convention, which addresses global waste issues.

MOUNTAIN VIEW COMMUNITY HOSPITAL

Case

INTRODUCTION

This case is included to provide you an opportunity to apply the concepts and techniques you will learn in each chapter. The case can also be used to support a semester-long database project built throughout the term that results in a complete application. We have selected a hospital for this case because it is a type of organization that is at least somewhat familiar to most persons and because health care institutions are of such importance in our society today. A segment of the case is included at the end of each chapter in this text. Each segment includes a brief description of the case as it relates to the material in the chapter followed by questions and exercises related to the material. Additional requirements, assignments, and project deliverables are provided in support of a semester project.

CASE DESCRIPTION

Mountain View Community Hospital (MVCH) is a not-for-profit, short-term, acute care general hospital. It is a relatively small hospital, with some 150 beds. The basic goal is to provide high-quality, cost-effective health care services for the surrounding community in a compassionate, caring, and personalized manner.

Mountain View Community Hospital has computer applications that support the following areas (among others): patient care administration, clinical services, financial management, and administrative services. Many of these applications have been purchased from outside vendors, but a few have been developed internally. Most of the computer applications are implemented using relational database and client/server technology. In the client/server environment, the client runs the database applications that request the data. The server runs the DBMS software, which fulfills the requests and handles the functions required for concurrent, shared data access to the database. Most of the databases (as well as the applications) are departmental, using the classification introduced in this chapter.

The relational databases at Mountain View Community Hospital contain a number of tables. Two of these tables, with some sample data, are shown in MVCH Figure 1-1. The

PATIENT table contains data concerning current or recent patients at the hospital, whereas the PATIENT CHARGES table contains data describing charges that have been incurred by those patients. These tables have been simplified for this chapter, but will be expanded in later chapters.

CASE QUESTIONS

1. The goal of Mountain View Community Hospital is to provide high-quality, cost-effective health care services for the surrounding community in a compassionate, caring, and personalized manner. Give some examples of how the use of databases in the hospital might improve health-care quality or contain costs. How else could a well-managed database help the hospital achieve its mission?

2. How can database technology be used to help Mountain View Community Hospital comply with the security standards of the Health Insurance Portability and Accountability Act of 1996 (HIPAA)? HIPAA requires health care providers to maintain reasonable and appropriate administrative, technical, and physical safeguards to ensure that the integrity, confidentiality, and availability of electronic health information they collect, maintain, use, or transmit is protected. (For more details on HIPAA, visit http://www.cms.hhs.gov/hipaa/hipaa2/regulations/security/03-3877.pdf.)

3. What are some of the costs and risks of using databases that the hospital must manage carefully?

4. How critical are data quality requirements in the hospital environment? For which applications might quality requirements be more restrictive?

5. At present, Mountain View Community Hospital is using relational database technology. Although this technology is appropriate for structured data, such as patient or accounting data, it is less well-suited to unstructured data, such as graphical data and images. Can you think of some types of data maintained by a hospital that fit this latter category? What types of database technology rather than relational might be better suited to these data types?

PATIENT

Patient Number	Patient Last Name	Patient First Name	Patient Address
8379	Dimas	Selena	617 Valley Vista
4238	Dolan	Mark	818 River Run
3047	Larreau	Annette	127 Sandhill
5838	Wiggins	Brian	431 Walnut
6143	Thomas	Wendell	928 Logan

PATIENT CHARGES

Item Description	Item Code	Patient Number	Amount
Room Semi-Priv	200	4238	1600
Speech Therapy	350	3047	750
Radiology	275	4238	150
Physical Therapy	409	5838	600
EKG Test	500	8379	200
Room Semi-Priv	200	3047	800
Standard IV	470	8379	150
EEG Test	700	4238	200

MVCH Figure 1-1
Two database tables from Mountain View Community Hospital

6. How are data in the PATIENT and PATIENT CHARGES tables related? That is, how can a user find the relevant charges for a particular patient?

7. Give an example of how the hospital could use each of the types of databases described in this chapter: personal, workgroup, departmental/divisional, enterprise, and Web-enabled.

8. How could the hospital use Web-based applications? What are some of the benefits and risks associated with Web-based applications for the hospital?

CASE EXERCISES

1. Using the notation introduced in this chapter, draw a diagram showing the relationship between the entities PATIENT and PATIENT CHARGES.

2. Develop a metadata chart for the data attributes in the PATIENT and PATIENT CHARGES tables using (at minimum) the columns shown in Table 1-1. You may include other metadata characteristics that you think are appropriate for the management of data at Mountain View Community Hospital.

3. One of the important database views for the hospital is the Patient Bill (MVCH Figure 1-2). Following is a highly simplified version of this view. Fill in the missing data in this view, using the data from MVCH Figure 1-1.

4. Using the notation introduced in this chapter, draw a single diagram that represents the following relationships in the hospital environment.

   • A HOSPITAL has on its staff one or more PHYSICIANs. A PHYSICIAN is on the staff of only one HOSPITAL.

   • A PHYSICIAN may admit one or more PATIENTs. A PATIENT is admitted by only one PHYSICIAN.

Patient Name:	Dolan, Mark
Patient Number:	
Patient Address:	

Item Code	Item Description	Amount

MVCH Figure 1-2
Partial Patient Bill

- Each PATIENT may incur any number of CHARGEs. A particular CHARGE may be incurred by any number of PATIENTs.

- A HOSPITAL has one or more WARDs. Each WARD is located in exactly one HOSPITAL.

- A WARD has any number of EMPLOYEEs. An EMPLOYEE may work in one or more WARDs.

5. Use the MVCH database files for the following exercises:

a. Develop a metadata chart for the EMPLOYEE_t table similar to Table 1-1 in Chapter 1.

b. What types of relationships (*1:1, 1:M,* or *M:N*) exist between the PATIENT_t table and other tables in the database:? How did you determine that?

c. MVCH hospital administrators regularly need information about their patient population. Based on the distinction between *data* and *information* discussed in Chapter 1, explain why a print-out of the PATIENT_t table will not satisfy these information needs, and

d. Create a report that organizes the data from the PATIENT_t table to provide hospital administrators with useful information about the patient population at MVCH.

6. Chapter 1 shows an SQL query that displays information about computer desks at Pine Valley Furniture company:

SELECT *

FROM PRODUCT

WHERE Product_Name="Computer Desk";

Following this example, create a SQL query for the PATIENT_t table that displays information about the outpatients.

PROJECT ASSIGNMENTS

P1. Identify and list entities other than the ones listed in the case description that are of interest in a hospital environment.

P2. Identify and list other user views that occur in a hospital environment.

P3. Using the notation introduced in this chapter, create a preliminary enterprise data model for Mountain View Community Hospital similar to the one shown in Figure 1-2a.

chapter 2

The Database Development Process

After studying this chapter, you should be able to:

● Concisely define each of the following key terms: **enterprise data modeling, information systems architecture (ISA), information engineering, top-down planning, business functions, functional decomposition, systems development lifecycle (SDLC), prototyping, computer-aided software engineering (CASE), project, incremental commitment, conceptual schema, logical schema, physical schema,** and **client/server architecture.**

● Describe the life cycle of a systems development project, with emphasis on the purpose of database analysis, design, and implementation activities.

● Explain the prototyping approach to database and application development.

● Explain the roles of individuals who design, implement, use, and administer databases.

● Explain the differences between external, conceptual, and internal schemas and the reasons for a three-schema architecture for databases.

● Explain the role of packaged (or generic) data models in database development.

● Explain the three-tiered location architecture for databases and database processing.

● Explain the scope of a database design and development class project.

● Draw simple data models that show the scope of a database.

INTRODUCTION

Chapter 1 introduced the database approach to information systems and the database application environment found in many organizations. An example organization, Pine Valley Furniture Company, was used to illustrate many of the principles and concepts of the database approach to information systems. You will again see Pine Valley Furniture Company in this, as well as subsequent chapters, as a continuing example of the application of database management.

Chapter 2 presents an overview of the general steps followed in the analysis, design, implementation, and administration of databases. Because a database is one part of an information system, this chapter will examine how the database development process fits into the overall information systems development process. The chapter emphasizes the need to coordinate database development with all the other activities in the development of a complete information system. The chapter includes highlights from a hypothetical database development process at Pine Valley Furniture Company. In this example, the chapter introduces tools for developing databases on personal computers and the process of extracting data from enterprise databases for use in stand-alone applications.

There are several reasons for discussing database development at this point. First, although you may have used the basic capabilities of a database management system, such as Microsoft Access, you may not yet have developed an understanding of how the database was developed. As you start to work with database developers and administrators, you will hear tales of successful database development projects that are exciting because of the benefits and strategic advantage provided to an organization. You will also hear tales of database development disasters that were completed behind schedule, incurred costs higher than those budgeted, and/or did not meet system requirements. The primary goal of this text is to introduce you to the concepts and many of the skills you will use to design and build database applications so that your projects will have a better chance of being successful. Using simple examples, this chapter briefly illustrates what you will be able to do after you complete a database course using this text. Thus, this chapter helps you to develop a vision and context for each topic developed in detail in subsequent chapters.

Second, many students learn best from a text full of concrete examples. Although all of the chapters in this text contain numerous examples, illustrations, and actual database designs and code, each chapter concentrates on a specific aspect of database management. We have designed this chapter to help you understand how all of these individual aspects of database management are related. Although we keep the technical details to a minimum, we hope you will develop a thirst to learn more about the data modeling and development skills presented in subsequent chapters.

Finally, many instructors want you to begin the initial steps of a database development group or individual course project early in your database course. Because of the logical progression of topics in this book, you will study many pages before you see your target for the project. This chapter gives you an idea of how to structure a database development project sufficient to begin a course exercise. Obviously, because this is only Chapter 2, many of the examples and notations we will use will be much simpler than those required for your project, for other course assignments, or in a real organization.

One note of caution: You will not learn how to design or develop databases just from this chapter. We have purposely kept the content of this chapter introductory and simplified. Many of the notations used in this chapter are not exactly like the ones you will learn in subsequent chapters. Our purpose in Chapter 2 is to give you a general understanding of the key steps and types of skills, not to teach you specific techniques. You will, however, develop an intuition and motivation for the skills and knowledge presented in later chapters.

DATABASE DEVELOPMENT WITHIN INFORMATION SYSTEMS DEVELOPMENT

In many organizations, database development begins with **enterprise data modeling**, which establishes the range and general contents of organizational databases. This step typically occurs during information systems planning for an organization. Its purpose is to create an overall picture or explanation of organizational data, not the design for a particular database. A particular database provides the data for one or more information systems, whereas an enterprise data model, which may

Enterprise data modeling: The first step in database development, in which the scope and general contents of organizational databases are specified.

encompass many databases, describes the scope of data maintained by the organization. In enterprise data modeling, you review current systems, analyze the nature of the business areas to be supported, describe the data needed at a very high level of abstraction, and plan one or more database development projects. Figure 2-1, a duplicate of Figure 1-2a, shows a segment of an enterprise data model for Pine Valley Furniture Company using a simplified version of the notation you will learn in Chapters 3 and 4.

Information Systems Architecture

An enterprise data model, such as Figure 2-1, is only one part of an overall **information systems architecture (ISA),** or blueprint, for information systems in an organization. You would develop an enterprise data model as part of a total information systems architecture or an organizational plan for data resources. According to Zachman (1987) and Sowa and Zachman (1992), an information systems architecture consists of six key components:

Information systems architecture (ISA): A conceptual blueprint or plan that expresses the desired future structure for the information systems in an organization.

1. *Data* (can be represented at a general level, as in Figure 2-1, but there are other representations, some of which are depicted in the next section on information systems planning)
2. *Processes* that manipulate data (these can be represented by data flow diagrams, object-models with methods, or other notations)
3. *Networks* that transport data around the organization and between the organization and its key business partners (which can be shown by a schematic of the network links and topology)
4. *People* who perform processes and are the sources and receivers of data and information (people can be shown on process models as senders and receivers of data)
5. *Events and points in time* when processes are performed (these can be shown by state-transition diagrams and other means)
6. *Reasons* for events and rules that govern the processing of data (often shown in textual form; but some diagramming tools, such as decision tables, exist for rules)

So, why is such a high-level approach important to data management? First, you cannot create a database without a plan, just as a house cannot be built without a blueprint and a site plan for the community in which it exists. Second, it is difficult to manage the inevitable changes in the database without a plan that anticipates change. Finally, with an enterprise data model, it is much easier to build applications because you know exactly what data exist and what needs to be added. On a practical level, organizations with whom we have talked about enterprise data modeling say that the most important reason for a data architecture is reusability. One organization has reported to us that with their enterprise data model, they have been able to reuse 60 to 90 percent of the data as each new application is developed. Without the enterprise data model, they most likely would have developed multiple databases, creating many problems.

A detailed description of the information systems architecture is beyond the scope of this text. However, you can view an online description of the architecture and its relationship to the systems development life cycle at **members.ozemail.com. au/~visible/papers/zachman3.htm.**

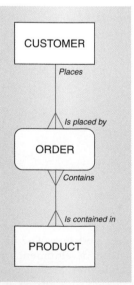

Figure 2-1
Segment from an enterprise data model (Pine Valley Furniture Company)

Information Engineering

An information systems architecture is developed by information systems planners following a particular methodology for IS planning. One such formal and popular methodology is information engineering. **Information engineering** emphasizes the importance of understanding relevant data when creating and maintaining information systems. With information engineering, data are modeled in the context of the enterprise, not by detailed consideration of data usage or technology. Because the business context changes more slowly than specific data or technology, this makes for more stable databases. A brief explanation of information engineering can be helpful as you begin to understand how databases are identified and defined. Information engineering follows a **top-down planning** approach. That is, specific information systems are deduced from a broad understanding of information needs (e.g., we need data about our customers, products, suppliers, salespersons, work centers, etc.) rather than from consolidating many specific information requests (such as requests for an order entry screen or sales summary by territory report). Top-down planning offers the advantages of a broad perspective, a way to look at integration of individual system components, an understanding of the relationship of information systems to business objectives, and an understanding of the impact of information systems across the whole organization.

Information engineering includes four steps: planning, analysis, design, and implementation. The planning phase of information engineering results in the high-level components of an information systems architecture, including an enterprise data model. We review the planning phase of information engineering in the next section. Although this book does not follow the information engineering methodology per se, the remaining chapters address activities that fall under the other three phases of information engineering.

Information engineering: A formal, top-down methodology that uses a data orientation to create and maintain information systems.

Top-down planning: A generic information systems planning methodology that attempts to gain a broad understanding of the information system needs of the entire organization.

Information Systems Planning

The goal of information systems planning is to align information technology with the business strategies of the organization. Such an alignment is important in order to achieve the maximum benefits from investments in information systems and technologies. As depicted in Table 2-1, the planning phase of the information engineering methodology includes three steps, which are discussed in the following three sections.

Identifying Strategic Planning Factors The strategic planning factors are organization goals, critical success factors, and problem areas. The purpose of identifying these factors is to develop the planning context and to link information systems plans to the strategic business plans. Table 2-2 shows some strategic planning factors for Pine Valley Furniture Company. These factors help information systems managers to set priorities to address requests for new information systems and, hence, the development of databases. For example, the problem area of inaccurate sales forecasts might cause information systems managers to place additional historical

Table 2-1 Information Engineering Planning Phase

Step	Explanation
1.	Identify strategic planning factors
	a. Goals
	b. Critical success factors
	c. Problem areas
2.	Identify corporate planning objects
	a. Organizational units
	b. Locations
	c. Business functions
	d. Entity types
3.	Develop an enterprise model
	a. Functional decomposition
	b. Entity-relationship diagram
	c. Planning matrixes

Table 2-2 Example Results of Information Engineering Planning Phase (Pine Valley Furniture Company)

Planning Factor	Examples
Goals	Maintain 10% per year growth rate
	Maintain 15% before-tax return on investment
	Avoid employee layoffs
	Be a responsible corporate citizen
Critical success factors	High-quality products
	On-time deliveries of finished products
	High productivity of employees
Problem areas	Inaccurate sales forecasts
	Increasing competition
	Stockouts of finished products

PINE VALLEY FURNITURE

sales data, new market research data, or data concerning results from test trials of new products in organizational databases.

Identifying Corporate Planning Objects The corporate planning objects define the business scope. The scope limits subsequent systems analysis and where information system changes can occur. Five key planning objects are as follows. (See Table 2-3 for examples of these for Pine Valley Furniture Company.)

1. *Organizational units* The various departments of the organization.

2. *Organizational locations* The places where business operations occur.

3. *Business functions* Related groups of business processes that support the mission of the organization. Note that business functions are different from organizational units; in fact, a function may be assigned to more than one organizational unit (e.g., product development, which is a function, may be the joint responsibility of the Sales and Manufacturing departments).

4. *Entity types* Major categories of data about the people, places, and things managed by the organization.

Business function: A related group of business processes that support some aspects of the mission of an enterprise.

Table 2-3 Example Corporate Planning Objects (Pine Valley Furniture Company)

Planning Object	Examples

Organizational units	Sales Department
	Orders Department
	Accounting Department
	Manufacturing
	   Fabrication Department
	   Assembly Department
	   Finishing Department
	   Purchasing Department

Organizational locations	Corporate Headquarters Durango Plant Western Regional Sales Office Lumber Mill

Business functions	Business planning
	Product development
	Materials management
	Marketing and sales
	   Order fulfillment
	   Order shipment
	   Sales summarization
	Production operations
	Finance and accounting

Entity types	CUSTOMER PRODUCT RAW MATERIAL ORDER WORK CENTER INVOICE EQUIPMENT EMPLOYEE

Information systems	Transaction processing systems
	   Order tracking
	   Order processing
	   Plant scheduling
	   Payroll
	Management information systems
	   Sales management
	   Inventory control
	   Production scheduling

5. *Information systems*   The application software and supporting procedures for handling sets of data.

Developing an Enterprise Model   A comprehensive enterprise model consists of three major components: a functional breakdown (or decomposition) model of each business function, an enterprise data model, and various planning matrixes. **Functional decomposition** is the process of breaking down the functions of an organization into progressively greater levels of detail. Functional decomposition is a classical process employed in systems analysis to simplify problems, isolate attention, and identify components. An example of decomposition of an order fulfillment function for Pine Valley Furniture Company appears in Figure 2-2. Often, many databases are necessary to handle the full set of business functions and supporting functions (e.g., all of the functions and subfunctions listed in Table 2-3), whereas a particular database may support only a subset of the supporting functions (e.g., those in Figure 2-2). It is helpful, however, to have a total, high-level enterprise view to minimize redundancy of data and make the data purposeful.

Functional decomposition: An iterative process of breaking down the description of a system into finer and finer detail in which one function is described in greater detail by a set of other, supporting functions.

An enterprise data model is often described using entity-relationship diagramming, which is explained in Chapters 3 and 4. Besides such a graphical depiction of the entity types, a thorough enterprise data model would also include business-oriented descriptions of each entity type and a compendium of various statements about how the business operates, called business rules, which govern the validity of data. Business rules are also defined and illustrated in Chapters 3 and 4.

An enterprise data model shows not only the entity types, but also the relationships between entities. Other relationships, between various planning objects, are also depicted during enterprise modeling. A common format for showing the interrelationships between planning objects is matrixes. The planning matrixes serve an important function because they provide an explicit approach for describing business requirements without requiring that the database be explicitly modeled. Often elicited from the business rules, planning matrixes aid in setting development priorities, sequencing development activities, and scheduling those activities from the top-down view sought by taking an enterprisewide approach. A wide variety of planning matrixes can be used. Several common ones are:

- *Location-to-function*   Indicates which business functions are being performed at which business locations
- *Unit-to-function*   Identifies which business functions are performed by or are the responsibility of which business units

Figure 2-2
Example process decomposition of an order fulfillment function (Pine Valley Furniture Company)

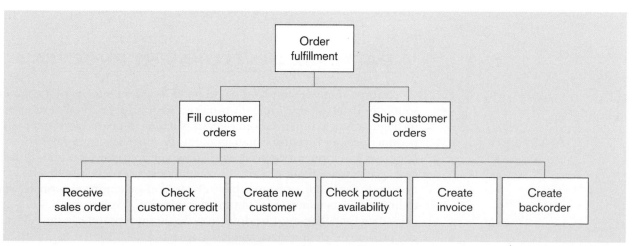

Figure 2-3
Example business function-to-data
entity matrix

Business Functions \ Data Entity Types	Customer	Product	Raw Material	Order	Work Center	Work Order	Invoice	Equipment	Employee
Business Planning	X	X						X	X
Product Development		X	X		X			X	
Materials Management		X	X	X	X	X		X	
Order Fulfillment	X	X	X	X	X	X	X	X	X
Order Shipment	X	X		X	X			X	X
Sales Summarization	X	X		X				X	X
Production Operations		X	X	X	X	X		X	X
Finance and Accounting	X	X	X	X	X			X	X	X

X = data entity (column) is used within business function (row)

- *Information system-to-data entity*   Explains how each information system interacts with each data entity (e.g., whether each system creates, retrieves, updates, or deletes data in each entity)
- *Supporting function-to-data entity*   Identifies which data are captured, used, updated, or deleted within each function
- *Information system-to-objective*   Shows which information systems support each business objective

Figure 2-3 illustrates a possible function-to-data entity matrix. Such a matrix could be used for various purposes, including the following three:

1. *Identify orphans*   Indicate which data entities are not used by any function or which functions do not use any entities
2. *Spot missing entities*   Employees involved with each function who examine the matrix can identify any entities that may have been missed.
3. *Prioritize development*   If a given function has a high priority for systems development (maybe because it is related to important organizational objectives), then the entities used by that area also have a high priority in database development

See Hoffer et al. (2005) for a more thorough description of how to use planning matrixes for information engineering and systems planning.

DATABASE DEVELOPMENT PROCESS

Information systems planning, which is based on information engineering, is one source of database development projects. Such projects often develop new databases to meet strategic organizational needs, such as improved customer support, better production and inventory management, or more accurate sales forecasting. Many database development projects arise, however, in a more bottom-up fashion. In this case, projects are requested by information systems users, who need certain information to do their jobs, or from other information systems professionals, who see a need to improve data management in the organization. Even in the bottom-up case, enterprise data modeling must be done in order to understand whether existing databases can provide the desired data, and if not, what new databases, data entities, and attributes need to be added to the current organizational data resource.

Whether identified from strategic or operational information needs, each database development project usually focuses on one database. Some database projects concentrate only on defining, designing, and implementing a database as a foundation for subsequent information systems development. In most cases, however, a database and the associated information processing functions are developed together as part of a comprehensive information systems development project.

Systems Development Life Cycle

A traditional process for conducting an information systems development project is called the **systems development life cycle (SDLC)**. The SDLC is a complete set of steps that a team of information systems professionals, including database designers and programmers, follow in an organization to specify, develop, maintain, and replace information systems. Textbooks and organizations use many variations on the life cycle, and may identify anywhere from three to twenty different phases. This process is depicted in Figure 2-4 (Hoffer et al., 2005). The process appears to be circular and is intended to convey the iterative nature of systems development projects. The steps may overlap in time, they may be conducted in parallel, and it is possible to backtrack to previous steps when prior decisions need to be reconsidered.

Systems development life cycle (SDLC): The traditional methodology used to develop, maintain, and replace information systems.

Figure 2-4
Systems development life cycle (SDLC)

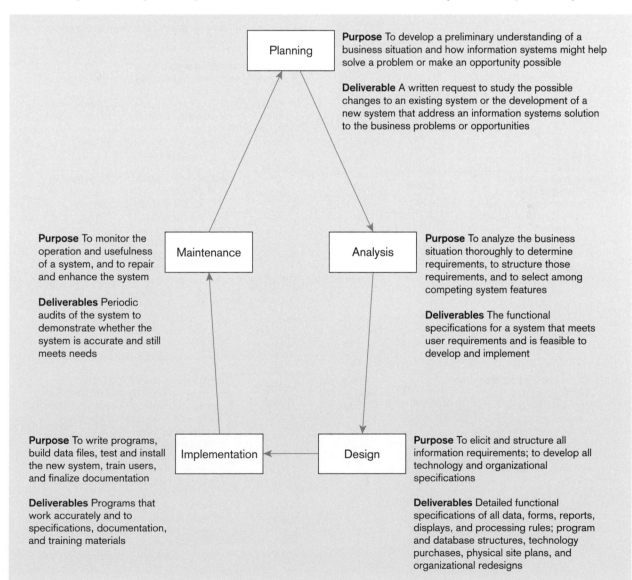

Some feel that the most common path through the development process is to cycle through the steps depicted in Figure 2-4, but at more detailed levels on each pass, as the requirements of the system become more concrete. However the organization conceives of its particular systems development life cycle, that cycle provides a structure that guides each successful system development project.

Figure 2-5 is annotated with an outline of the database development activities typically included in each phase. Note that there is not always a one-to-one correspondence between SDLC phases and database development steps: Conceptual data modeling occurs in both the Planning and the Analysis phases. We will briefly illustrate each of these database development steps for Pine Valley Furniture Company later in this chapter.

Planning–Enterprise Modeling   The database development process begins with a review of the enterprise modeling components that were developed during the information systems planning process. During this step, analysts review current

Figure 2-5
Database development activities during the systems development life cycle (SDLC)

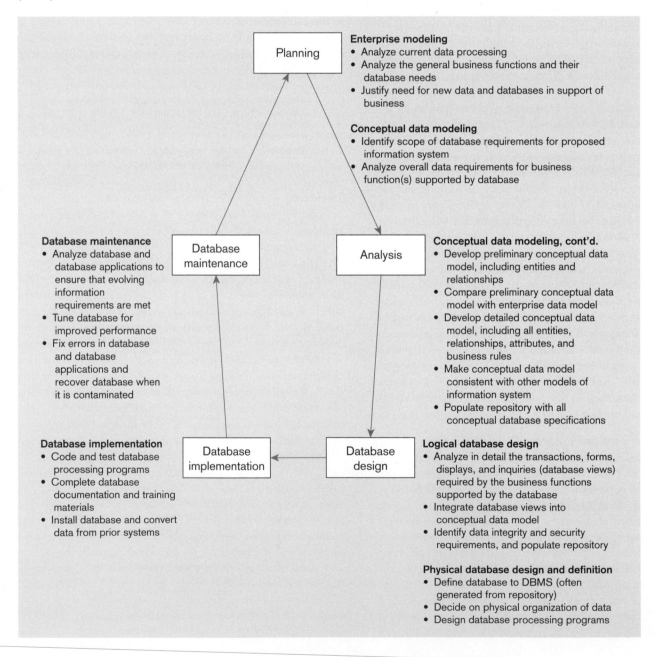

databases and information systems, analyze the nature of the business area that is the subject of the development project, and describe, in very general terms, the data needed for each information system under consideration for development. They determine which of that data are already available in existing databases and what new data will need to be added to support the proposed new project. Only selected projects move into the next phase based on the projected value of each project to the organization.

Planning–Conceptual Data Modeling   For an information systems project that is initiated, the overall data requirements of the proposed information system must be analyzed. This is done in two stages. First, during the Planning phase, the analyst develops a diagram similar to Figure 2-1 as well as other documentation, to outline the scope of data involved in this particular development project without consideration of what databases already exist. Only high-level categories of data (entities) and major relationships are included at this point. This step in the SDLC is critical for improving the chances of a successful development process. The better the definition of the specific needs of the organization, the closer the conceptual model should come to meeting the needs of the organization, and the less recycling back through the SDLC should be needed.

Analysis–Conceptual Data Modeling   Then, during the Analysis phase of the SDLC, the analyst produces a detailed data model that identifies all the organizational data that must be managed for this information system. Every data attribute is defined, all categories of data are listed, every business relationship between data entities is represented, and every rule that dictates the integrity of the data is specified. It is also during the analysis phase that the conceptual data model (also called a conceptual schema later in this chapter) is checked for consistency with other types of models developed to explain other dimensions of the target information system, such as processing steps, rules for handling data, and the timing of events. However, even this detailed conceptual data model is preliminary, because subsequent SDLC activities may find missing elements or errors when designing specific transactions, reports, displays, and inquiries. Thus, it is often said that conceptual data modeling is done in a top-down fashion, driven from a general understanding of the business area, not from specific information processing activities. Again, the detailed data modeling uncovers specific and sometimes unique practices of the organization. With experience, the database developer gains mental models of common business functions, such as sales or financial record keeping, but must always remain alert for the exceptions to common practices followed by an organization.

Design–Logical Database Design   Logical database design approaches database development from two perspectives. First, the conceptual data model must be transformed into a logical data model, which describes the data in terms of the data management technology that will be used to implement the database. For example, if relational technology will be used, the conceptual data model is transformed to constructs of the relational model (you will learn how to conduct this important process in Chapter 5). Then, as each computer program in the information system is designed, including the program's input and output formats, the analyst performs a detailed review of the transactions, reports, displays, and inquiries supported by the database. During this so-called bottom-up analysis, the analyst verifies exactly what data are to be maintained in the database and the nature of those data as needed for each transaction, report, and so forth.

The analysis of each individual report, transaction, and so on considers a detailed, limited view of the database. It may be necessary to refine the conceptual data model as each report, transaction, and other user view is analyzed. Especially on larger projects, different teams of analysts and systems developers may work independently on different programs or sets of programs. The details of all of their work may not be revealed until well into the logical design phase. In this case, one must combine, or integrate, the original conceptual data model along with these individual user views into a comprehensive design during logical database design. It is also possible that additional information processing requirements will be identified during logical information systems design, in which case these new requirements must be integrated into the previously identified logical database design.

The final step in logical database design is to transform the combined and reconciled data specifications into basic, or atomic, elements following well-established rules for well-structured data specifications. For most databases today, these rules come from relational database theory and a process called normalization, which we will describe in detail in Chapter 5. The result is a complete picture of the database without any reference to a particular database management system for managing these data. With a final logical database design in place, the analyst begins to specify the logic of the particular computer programs and queries needed to maintain and report the database contents.

Design–Physical Database Design and Definition   Physical database design requires a knowledge of the specific DBMS that will be used to implement the database. In physical database design and definition, an analyst decides on the organization of physical records, the choice of file organizations, the use of indexes, and so on. To do this, a database designer needs to outline the programs to process transactions and to generate anticipated management information and decision-support reports. The goal is to design a database that will efficiently and securely handle all data processing against it. Thus, physical database design is done in close coordination with the design of all other aspects of the physical information system: programs, computer hardware, operating systems, and data communications networks.

Implementation–Database Implementation   In database implementation, a designer writes, tests, and installs the programs that process the database. The designer might program with standard programming languages (such as COBOL, C, or Visual Basic), in special database processing languages (such as SQL), or use special-purpose nonprocedural languages to produce stylized reports and displays, possibly including graphs. Also, during implementation, the designer will finalize all database documentation, train users, and put procedures into place for the ongoing support of information system (and database) users. The last step is to load data from existing information sources (files and databases from legacy applications plus new data now needed). Loading is often done by first unloading data from existing files and databases into a neutral format (such as binary or text files) and then loading these data into the new database. Finally, the database and its associated applications are put into production for data maintenance and retrieval by the actual users. During production, the database should be periodically backed up and recovered in case of contamination or destruction.

Maintenance–Database Maintenance   The database evolves during database maintenance. In this step, the designer adds, deletes, or changes characteristics of the structure of a database in order to meet changing business conditions, to correct errors in database design, or to improve the processing speed of database applications. The designer might also need to rebuild a database if it becomes contaminated or destroyed due to a program or computer system malfunction. This is typically the longest step of database development, because it lasts throughout the life of the database and its associated applications. Each time the database evolves, view it as an abbreviated database development process in which conceptual data modeling, logical and physical database design, and database implementation occur to deal with proposed changes.

Alternative IS Development Approaches

The systems development life cycle or slight variations on it are often used to guide the development of information systems and databases. The SDLC is a methodical, highly structured approach, which includes many checks and balances to ensure that each step produces accurate results and the new or replacement information system is consistent with existing systems with which it must communicate or for which there needs to be consistent data definitions. Consequently, the SDLC is often criticized for the length of time needed until a working system is produced, which occurs only at the end of the process. Instead, organizations increasingly use rapid application development (RAD) methods, which follow an iterative process of rapidly repeating analysis, design, and implementation steps until they converge on the system the user wants. These RAD methods work best when most of the necessary database structures already exist, and hence for systems that primarily retrieve data, rather than for those that populate and revise databases.

One of the most popular RAD methods is **prototyping**, which is an iterative process of systems development in which requirements are converted to a working system that is continually revised through close work between analysts and users. Figure 2-6 shows the prototyping process. This figure includes annotations to indicate roughly which database development activities occur in each prototyping phase. Typically, you make only a very cursory attempt at conceptual data modeling when the information system problem is identified. During the development of the initial prototype, you simultaneously design the displays and reports the user wants while understanding any new database requirements and defining a database to be used by the prototype. This is typically a new database, which is a copy of portions of existing databases, possibly with new content. If new content is required, it will usually come from external data sources, such as market research data, general economic indicators, or industry standards.

Database implementation and maintenance activities are repeated as new versions of the prototype are produced. Often security and integrity controls are

Prototyping: An iterative process of systems development in which requirements are converted to a working system that is continually revised through close work between analysts and users.

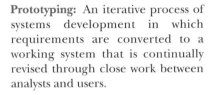

Figure 2-6
The prototyping methodology and database development process
Source: Adapted from Naumann and Jenkins (1982).

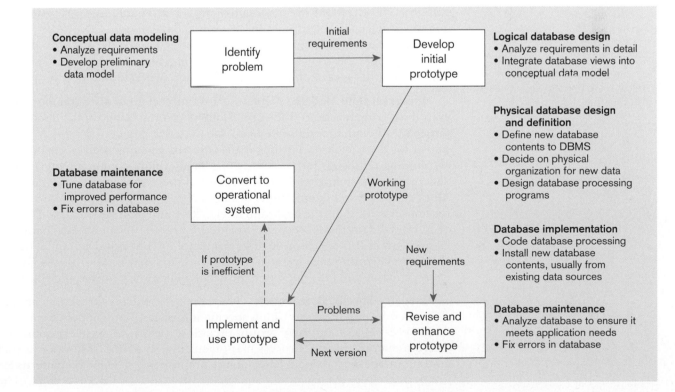

minimal because the emphasis is on getting working prototype versions ready as quickly as possible. Also, documentation tends to be delayed until the end of the project, and user training occurs from hands-on use. Finally, after an accepted prototype is created, the developer and the user decide whether the final prototype, and its database, can be put into production as is. If the system, including the database, is too inefficient, the system and database will be reprogrammed and reorganized to meet performance expectations.

With the increasing popularity of visual programming tools (such as Visual Basic, Java, Visual C++, and fourth-generation languages) that make it easy to modify the interface between user and system, prototyping is becoming the systems development methodology of choice to develop new applications internally. With prototyping, it is relatively easy to change the content and layout of user reports and displays. During this process, new database requirements may be identified, and hence existing databases used by the evolving application will need to change. It is even possible to use prototyping for a system that requires a new database. In this case, sample data are acquired to build and rebuild the database prototype as the system requirements evolve through the iterative development process.

Role of Packaged Data Models

Fortunately, the art and science of data modeling have progressed to the point where it is seldom necessary for an organization to develop its data models internally in their entirety. Instead, packaged data models (or model components) can be purchased at comparatively low cost and, after suitable customization, assembled into full-scale data models. These generic data models are developed by industry specialists, consultants, and database technology vendors based on their expertise and experience in dozens of organizations across multiple industry types. The models are displayed in graphical form either in books or on the Internet. An optional CD-ROM (or Internet download) is also generally available that contains electronic versions that enable users to manipulate and customize their models easily using standard data modeling tools, such as ERWin (see Appendix A for an illustration of ERWin). The CD-ROM often contains scripts that enable users to generate logical and physical data models from the conceptual data model.

There are two principal types of packaged data models: universal data models, which are applicable to nearly any business or organization, and industry-specific data models. We discuss each of these types briefly and provide references for each type.

Universal Data Models   Numerous core subject areas are common to many (or even most) organizations, such as customers, products, accounts, documents, and projects. Although they differ in detail, the underlying data structures are often quite similar for these subjects. Further, many core business functions, such as purchasing, accounting, receiving, and project management, follow common patterns. Universal data models are templates for one or more of these subject areas and/or functions. All of the expected components of data models are generally included: entities, relationships, attributes, primary and foreign keys, and even sample data. Two examples of universal data model sets are provided by Hay (1996) and Silverston (2001a). Figure 4-15 in this text provides an example of a Universal data model designed to support relationship management applications. You may want to glance ahead at the figure, knowing you will understand the details better when you are studying Chapter 4.

Industry-Specific Data Models   These are generic data models that are designed to be used by organizations within specific industries. Data models are available for nearly every major industry group, including health care, telecommunications, discrete manufacturing, process manufacturing, banking, insurance, and higher education. These models are based on the premise that data model patterns for organizations are very similar within a particular industry. (A bank is a bank.) However, the data models for one industry (e.g., banking) are quite different than those for another (e.g., hospitals). Prominent examples of industry-specific data models are provided by Silverston (2001b), Kimball and Ross (2002), and Inmon (look at the Data Model section of **www.BillInmon.com** at what Inmon calls a generic data model for many examples for various industries and business functions).

You may wonder about the value of universal and industry-specific data models. The answer is that for many support functions, such as purchasing, accounting, and document management, the data model patterns across industries are often quite similar. Universal data models are often appropriate for these types of applications. However, for most mainstream functions, such as manufacturing and operations, the data model patterns are quite different (e.g., from a university to an insurance company). For these applications, industry-specific data models are probably most appropriate. We conclude that most organizations can probably benefit from both types of packaged data models by saving considerable time in data modeling.

Summary   The use of packaged data models can provide two major benefits to an organization:

1. *Dramatically reduced implementation times and costs*   The time required to design and implement a large data model can be reduced by weeks or months by using this approach.

2. *Higher quality models*   Packaged data models are constructed and tested by knowledgeable developers based on their experience with many industries and organizations. They tend to represent "best practice" data modeling techniques whose quality often exceeds that which can be achieved by internal development teams, given typical organizational pressures.

Of course, packaged data models are no substitute for sound database analysis and design. Skilled analysts and designers are still required to determine database requirements and to select, modify, install, and integrate any packaged systems that are used.

The Role of CASE and a Repository

At several points in the preceding section we mentioned the role of CASE tools in information systems development. **Computer-aided software engineering (CASE)** tools are software that provide automated support for some portion of the systems development process. For our purposes in the study of database development, CASE tools have three relevant features. First is the ability to help us draw data models using entity-relationship (E-R) and other notations (see Figure 2-1 for an example of a form of E-R notation) A CASE tool's drawing capabilities are "database intelligent" in that each symbol represents specific data modeling constructs, and these symbols can be used only in ways consistent with the properties of the associated constructs. Database drawing tools are used in enterprise modeling, conceptual data modeling, logical database design, and physical data modeling. CASE tools can help us ensure consistency across diagrams. For example, a CASE tool will make sure that each use of the PRODUCT entity on any diagram has exactly the same meaning. CASE drawing tools enforce unique names for each data object and may be able to automatically redraw a data model when characteristics of data objects change.

Often, different drawing tools and associated methods are used for different stages of the database development process. For example, one tool is used for enterprise modeling to draw high-level diagrams and matrixes. Still another tool may be used in conceptual data modeling, and yet another in logical database design.

The second important feature of CASE tools is the ability to generate code. Most often, this code contains the database definition commands to be given to a database management system. During database implementation, the CASE tool will refer to all

Computer-aided software engineering (CASE): Software tools that provide automated support for some portion of the systems development process.

the conceptual, logical, and physical data specifications and compose SQL commands to create relational tables, define each attribute of each table, and define key indexes. Although less common, some CASE tools can generate C or other language code for the rudiments of database retrieval and updating programs.

As with drawing tools, many organizations use separate tools ("best of breed") for code generation as well as for drawing. If these tools and methods are to be effective, they must be integrated. In particular, the tools must be able to share the metadata that are developed during each stage of the process. Unfortunately, the ability to share such information among CASE tools has not been common, especially among tools from different vendors. A so-called integrated-CASE (or I-CASE) tool provides support across the whole life cycle, but such tools are rarely used because they tend to be strong in supporting certain phases and weak in supporting other phases of the systems development process. Tools that support the SDLC from the Project Identification and Selection phase through Physical Design are called "upper-CASE tools;" tools that support the Implementation and Maintenance phases are called "lower-CASE tools."

Tool integration depends on a formal, detailed architecture for building and maintaining information systems. This architecture includes formal definitions of interfaces between tools, data model standards among tools, and common controls across the life cycle. This leads to the third feature of CASE tools important to our discussion of the database development process: an information repository (or repository for short). A repository (which was defined in Chapter 1) is a knowledge base of information about the facts that an enterprise must be able to access and the processes it must perform to be successful (Moriarty, 1991). Thus, for example, all of the information that is collected during the six stages of database development is maintained in a repository. In a sense, a repository is a database itself, which contains information needed to generate all the diagrams, form and report definitions, and other system documentation. A repository helps systems and database analysts achieve a seamless integration of data from several CASE tools.

MANAGING THE PEOPLE INVOLVED IN DATABASE DEVELOPMENT

Project: A planned undertaking of related activities to reach an objective that has a beginning and an end.

As implied in Figure 2-5, a database is developed as part of a project. A **project** is a planned undertaking of related activities to reach an objective that has a beginning and an end. A project begins with the first steps of the Project Initiation and Planning phase and ends with the last steps of the Implementation phase. A senior systems or database analyst will be assigned to be project leader. This person is responsible for creating detailed project plans as well as staffing and supervising the project team. A good project leader will possess skills in leadership, management, customer relations and communications, technical problem solving, conflict management, team building, and risk and change management.

A project is initiated and planned in the Planning phase, executed during Analysis, Logical Design, Physical Design, and Implementation phases, and closed down at the end of implementation. During initiation the project team is formed. A systems or database development team can include one or more of each the following:

- *Business analysts*   Work with both management and users to analyze the business situation and develop detailed system and program specifications for projects
- *Systems analysts*   May perform business analyst activities but also specify computer systems requirements and typically have a stronger programming background than business analysts do

- *Database analysts and data modelers* Concentrate on determining the requirements and design for the database component of the information system
- *Users* Provide assessment of their information needs and monitor that the developed system meets their needs
- *Programmers* Design and write computer programs that have commands to maintain and access data in the database embedded in them
- *Database architects* Establish standards for data in business units, striving to attain optimum data location, currency, and quality
- *Data administrators* Have responsibility for existing and future databases and ensure consistency and integrity across databases, and as experts on database technology, provide consulting and training to other project team members
- *Project managers* Oversee assigned projects, including team composition, analysis, design, implementation and support of projects
- *Other technical experts* For example, networking, operating systems, testing, data warehousing and documentation

It is the responsibility of the project leader to select and manage all of these people as an effective team. See Hoffer et al. (2005) for details on how to manage a systems development project team. See Henderson et al. (2005) for a more detailed description of career paths and roles in data management.

Project closedown occurs when the project is naturally or unnaturally terminated. An unnatural termination occurs when the system no longer appears to have business value, when the performance of the system or the development team is unacceptable, or when the project runs out of time, funding, or support. To determine whether a project is progressing on time and within budget, the project leader develops detailed schedules of project activities. Often these schedules are depicted in graphical form that show when project activities begin and end, who is responsible for doing each activity, how much effort is required to do each activity, and the precedence relationships between activities (i.e., which activities depend on the output of other activities).

A characteristic of successful systems development projects is frequent review points, when project team members report the results of the project to date. Often these results are reported to people outside the project team, including other users, those who are providing the funding for the project, and senior information systems and possibly general management. The reasons for these review points are to:

- Validate that the project is progressing in a satisfactory way
- Step back from the details of daily activities and verify that all the parts of the project are coming together
- Gain renewed commitment from all parties to the project (especially important for projects that last more than a few months)

Central to the third reason is the concept of incremental commitment. **Incremental commitment** is a strategy in systems development projects in which the project is reviewed after each phase and continuation of the project is rejustified in each of these reviews. Incremental commitment allows those interested in the project to commit only to the next phase (with limited time and cost) and then to reassess whether further commitment of resources (people and money) is warranted after some results are shown. Thus, significant resources are not wasted when the original concept for the system does not prove valuable. Incremental commitment also allows a project to be easily redirected or killed.

Incremental commitment: A strategy in systems development projects in which the project is reviewed after each phase and continuation of the project is rejustified in each of these reviews.

THREE-SCHEMA ARCHITECTURE FOR DATABASE DEVELOPMENT

The explanation earlier in this chapter of the database development process referred to several different, but related, views or models of databases developed on a systems development project. These data models and the primary phase of the SDLC in which they are developed are as follows:

- Enterprise data model (during the Information Systems Planning phase)—defined in Chapter 1
- External schema, or user view (during the Analysis and Logical Design phases)—defined as user view in Chapter 1
- Conceptual schema (during the Analysis phase)—defined below
- Logical schema (during the Logical Design phase)—defined below
- Physical schema (during the Physical Design phase)—defined below

In this section, we summarize the properties of these schemas. We also relate them to the classical three-schema architecture that has guided database thinking for several decades. Remarkably, the three-schema architecture is still valid and plays an important role in the multitier computer environments of today (as discussed later in this chapter).

Three-Schema Components

In 1978, an industry committee commonly known as ANSI/SPARC published an important document that described a three-schema architecture for describing the structure of data. The three schemas (depicted down the center of Figure 2-7) are the following:

1. *External schema*   This is the view (or views) of managers and other employees who are the database users. As shown in Figure 2-7, the external schema can be represented as a combination of the enterprise data model (a top-down view) and a collection of detailed (or bottom-up) user views.

2. *Conceptual schema*   This schema combines the different external views into a single, coherent definition of the enterprise's data. The conceptual schema represents the view of the data architect or data administrator.

3. *Internal schema*   As shown in Figure 2-7, internal schema today really consists of two separate schemas: a logical schema and a physical schema. The logical schema is the representation of data for a type of data management technology (e.g., relational). The physical schema describes how data are to be represented and stored in secondary storage using a particular DBMS (e.g., Oracle).

Database development and database technologies are based on encouraging the distinction among these three schemas, or views, of databases. However, it is important to keep in mind that the different views are all models of the same organizational data.

Summary of Schemas

In this section, we summarize the desired properties of each component of the three-schema architecture and indicate where each component is discussed in greater detail in this text.

Enterprise Data Model   This is a high-level model that identifies, defines, and relates the major entities of interest in an organization. The modeling process begins by listing the high-level entities. (Most small- to medium-sized organizations can be described by between one and two dozen such entities.) A clear business-oriented

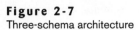
Figure 2-7
Three-schema architecture

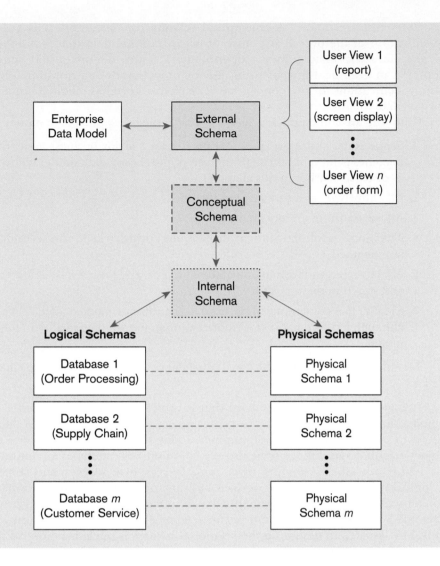

definition of each entity is recorded. The relationships between entities are named and described, as are important business rules or constraints. An entity-relationship model is then usually created (see MVCH Figure 2-3 at the end of this chapter for an example). Because enterprise data models are high level, they are quite abstract, and more detailed information, such as attributes or primary keys are not usually identified at this level. Many-to-many relationships between entities are allowed, but subtype relationships are normally not included. E-R diagramming techniques appropriate to creating an enterprise data model are described in Chapters 3 and 4.

User Views   Each user view is a logical description of some portion of an enterprise database that is required by a user to perform some task. For example, an online order form used by customers of Pine Valley Furniture Company is a view that enables customers (external users) to order Pine Valley Furniture products. A logical version of a user view can be represented as an E-R or object diagram or as a set of relations. The process of translating an E-R diagram into relations and then merging relations (view integration) into one complete relational description of a database is described in Chapter 5. Remember that these user views will be integrated with the enterprise level data model to define the conceptual schema.

Conceptual schema: A detailed, technology-independent specification of the overall structure of organizational data.

Conceptual Schema A **conceptual schema** (or data model) is a detailed specification of the overall structure of organizational data that is independent of any database management technology. Usually, a conceptual schema is depicted in graphical format using E-R or object-modeling notations. In addition, specifications for the conceptual schema are stored as metadata in a repository or data dictionary.

Following are contemporary design goals for the conceptual data model:

1. Scope is the entire organization, or at least a major business area (this goal becomes achievable through the use of purchased data model components, as discussed earlier in this chapter)

2. All entity types and subtypes are included

3. All relationships are documented

4. The model is fully attributed; all attributes, primary keys, and secondary keys are included

5. All data types and formats, attribute domains, and business rules are specified and stored in the repository

6. Ideally, the conceptual data model is fully normalized (see Chapter 5), although it is acceptable (and more common today) to normalize in the logical model

Techniques for designing the conceptual data model are described in Chapters 3 and 4.

Logical schema: The representation of a database for a particular data management technology.

Logical Schema Each database that is implemented has a separate logical schema. Each **logical schema** is the representation of data for a type of data management technology. (The most common today is relational, but others such as object-oriented and dimensional also are common.) Elements of a relational data model include tables, columns, rows, primary keys, foreign keys, and constraints. A logical relational schema is derived by transforming relevant portions of the conceptual schema to these elements. We describe this transformation process in Chapter 5. Some CASE tools can perform some (or even most) of these steps as well. The last step in designing the relational schema is normalization, which also is described in Chapter 5.

Physical schema: Specifications for how data from a logical schema are stored in a computer's secondary memory by a database management system.

Physical Schema A **physical schema** is a set of specifications that describe how data from a logical schema are stored in a computer's secondary memory by a specific database management system. There is one physical schema for each logical schema. The physical schema describes the organization of physical records, the choice of file organizations, the uses of indexes, and so on.

Ideally, there will be one logical and associated physical schema for a conceptual schema, but this is not usually the case in most organizations, especially larger ones. Most organizations have many logical and physical databases, possibly using different database technologies. There will be several operational databases, often supporting different organizational units or business processes. In Chapter 11, we discuss the increasingly popular approach of consolidating these databases into one operational data store and data warehouse, which are, however, usually additional, separate databases.

Strategies for Development

As shown in Figure 2-8, the conceptual and external schemas are typically developed iteratively. To read Figure 2-8, start at the upper-left corner where the Enterprise data model and general understanding of the project's database requirements are portrayed. First you will develop a first-cut conceptual schema based on the organization's enterprise data model and a general understanding of the organization's

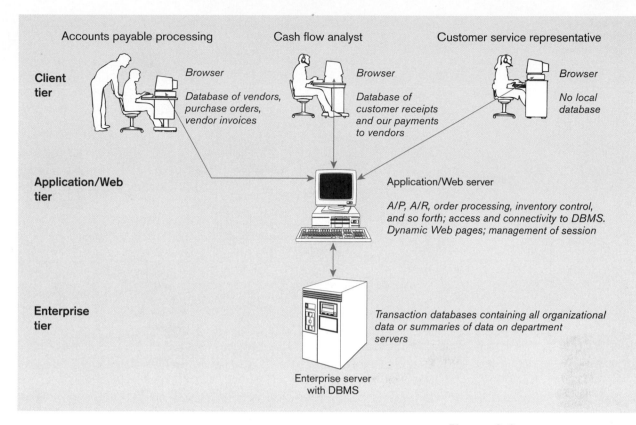

Figure 2-9
Three-tiered client/server database architecture

The most significant implication for database development from the use of a multiple-tiered client/server architecture is the ease of separating the development of the database and the modules that maintain the database from the information system modules that present the contents of the database to end users. Presentation routines can use languages such as PowerBuilder, Java, and Visual Basic to provide easy-to-use, graphic user interfaces. Through middleware (see Chapter 9), the presentation routines can interact through the tiers to access the routines that access the required data and analyze these data to form the needed information. As a database developer and programmer, you might work at any of these tiers, developing the requisite software. We will consider the client/server architecture in more detail in Chapter 9, which outlines how to decide where to distribute data across the multiple tiers of the computer network.

DEVELOPING A DATABASE APPLICATION FOR PINE VALLEY FURNITURE COMPANY

Pine Valley Furniture Company was introduced in Chapter 1. By the early 1990s, competition in furniture manufacturing had intensified, and competitors seemed to respond more rapidly than Pine Valley Furniture to new business opportunities. While there were many reasons for this trend, managers felt that the computer information systems they had been using (based on traditional file processing) had become outdated. The company started a development effort that eventually led to adopting a database approach for the company. Figure 2-10 displays a general schematic of the computer network within Pine Valley Furniture Company.

Figure 2-10
Computer system for Pine Valley
Furniture Company

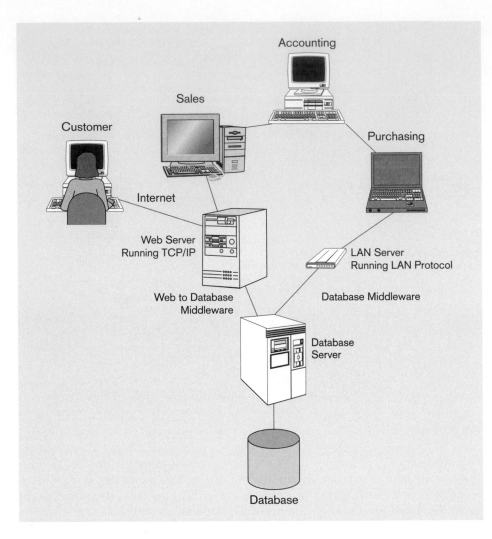

Data previously stored in separate files have been integrated into a single database structure. Also, the metadata that describe these data reside in the same structure. The DBMS provides the interface between the various database applications for organizational users and the database (or databases). The DBMS allows users to share the data and to query, access, and update the stored data.

Before addressing a request that has been received for direct access to sales data from Helen Jarvis, product manager for home office furniture, let's review the process that Pine Valley Furniture Company followed as they originally moved into a database environment. Pine Valley Furniture Company's first step in converting to a database approach was to develop a list of the high-level entities that support the business activities of the organization. From Chapter 1, remember that an entity is an object or concept that is important to the business. Some of the high-level entities identified at Pine Valley Furniture are the following: CUSTOMER, PRODUCT, EMPLOYEE, CUSTOMER ORDER, and DEPARTMENT. After these entities were identified and defined, the company proceeded to develop an enterprise data model. Remember that an enterprise data model is a graphical model that shows the high-level entities for the organization and associations among those entities.

The results of preliminary studies convinced management of the potential advantages of the database approach. After additional data modeling steps had been completed, the company decided to implement a modern relational database management system that views all data in the form of tables. (We cover relational databases in more detail in Chapter 5.) A simplified segment of the project data model used is discussed next.

Simplified Project Data Model Example

A segment of the project data model containing four entities and three pertinent associations is shown in Figure 2-11. The entities shown in this model segment are the following:

- CUSTOMER   People and organizations that buy or may potentially buy products from Pine Valley Furniture
- ORDER   The purchase of one or more products by a customer
- PRODUCT   The items Pine Valley Furniture makes and sells
- ORDER LINE   Details about each product sold on a particular customer order (such as quantity and price)

The three associations (called relationships in database terminology) shown in the figure (represented by the three lines connecting entities) capture three fundamental business rules, as follows:

1. Each CUSTOMER Places any number of ORDERs. Conversely, each ORDER Is placed by exactly one CUSTOMER.
2. Each ORDER Contains any number of ORDER LINEs. Conversely, each ORDER LINE Is contained in exactly one ORDER.
3. Each PRODUCT Has any number of ORDER LINEs. Conversely, each ORDER LINE Is for exactly one PRODUCT.

Places, Contains, and Has are called one-to-many relationships because, for example, one customer places potentially many orders and one order is placed by exactly one customer.

The type of diagram shown in Figure 2-11 is referred to as an entity-relationship diagram. Entity-relationship (or E-R) diagrams are of such importance in database applications that we devote two chapters (3 and 4) to this type of model. Chapter 3 describes basic data modeling using E-R diagrams and related notations, whereas Chapter 4 describes advanced data modeling. Both of these chapters also describe the various types of business rules and how they are captured and modeled.

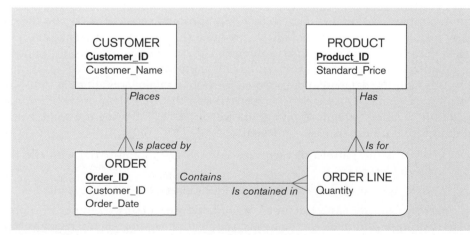

Figure 2-11
Segment of a project data model

Notice the following characteristics of the project data model:

1. It is a model of the organization that provides valuable information about how the organization functions, as well as important constraints.

2. The project data model focuses on entities, relationships, and business rules. It also includes attribute labels for each piece of data that will be stored in each entity. Many entities would include more attributes than we list in Figure 2-11, but there are enough demonstrated to help you begin to understand how the data will be stored in a database.

Figure 2-12 shows the following four tables with sample data: Customer, Product, Order, and Order_Line. Notice that these tables represent the four entities shown in the project data model (Figure 2-11). Each column of a table represents an attribute (or characteristic) of an entity. For example, the attributes shown for Customer are Customer_ID and Customer_Name. Each row of a table represents an instance (or occurrence) of the entity. An important property of the relational model is that it represents relationships between entities by values stored in the columns of the corresponding tables. For example, notice that Customer_ID is an attribute of both the Customer table and the Order table. As a result, we can easily link an order to its associated customer. For example, we can determine that Order_ID 1003 is associated with Customer_ID 15. Can you determine which Product_IDs are associated with Order_ID 1004? In subsequent chapters, you will learn how to retrieve data from these tables by using a powerful query language, SQL, that exploits these linkages.

To facilitate the sharing of data and information, Pine Valley Furniture Company uses a local area network (LAN) that links employee workstations in the various departments to a database server, as shown in Figure 2-10. During the early 2000s, the company mounted a two-phase effort to introduce Internet technology. First, to improve intracompany communication and decision making, an intranet was installed that uses Web-based technology and is accessible only from within the company. Each employee's workstation may be used as a Web browser, gaining fast access to company information, including phone directories, furniture design specifications, e-mail, and so forth. Or, the workstation may be used as a personal computer and connected directly to the database server as needed through the LAN. Pine Valley Furniture Company also added a Web interface to some of its business applications, such as order entry, so that more internal business activities can be conducted by employees through its intranet.

In the second phase, Pine Valley Furniture Company opened its intranet to their customers by linking it to the Internet. This enables the furniture retail outlets that sell their lines of furniture to browse the product catalogs (including pictures and product specifications) and determine the availability of furniture pieces in Pine Valley's inventory. Then the retailers can provide this information to their customers and order items online from Pine Valley Furniture Company. The Internet connection is configured as an extranet, so that only approved retailers can access the company intranet. Opening Pine Valley's product and inventory information to the retailers raises information security questions that will be addressed in Chapter 12 and platform issues that will be discussed in Chapter 10.

Although the database quite adequately supports daily operations at Pine Valley Furniture Company, managers soon learned that the same database is often inadequate for decision support applications. For example, following are some types of questions that cannot be easily answered:

1. What is the pattern of furniture sales this year, compared with the same period last year?

2. Who are our ten largest customers, and what are their buying patterns?

3. Why can't we easily obtain a consolidated view of any customer who orders through different sales channels, rather than viewing each contact as representing a separate customer?

Figure 2-12
Four relations (Pine Valley Furniture Company)

(a) Order and Order Line tables

		Order_ID	Order_Date	Customer_ID
▶	+	1001	10/21/2006	4
	+	1002	10/21/2006	3
	+	1003	10/22/2006	1
	+	1004	10/22/2006	6
	+	1005	10/24/2006	4
	+	1006	10/24/2006	2
	+	1007	10/27/2006	11
	+	1008	10/30/2006	12
	+	1009	11/5/2006	4
	+	1010	11/5/2006	1
✳		0		0

Record: I◀ ◀ 　1　 ▶ ▶I ▶✳ of 10

Order : Table

	Order_ID	Product_ID	Quantity
	1001	1	2
	1001	2	2
	1001	4	1
	1002	3	5
	1003	3	3
	1004	5	2
	1004	8	2
	1005	4	4
	1006	4	1
	1006	7	2
	1007	1	3
	1007	2	2
	1008	3	3
	1008	8	3
	1009	4	1
	1009	7	3
	1010	8	10
▶	0	0	0

Record: I◀ ◀ 　18　 ▶ ▶I ▶✳ of 18

Order Line : Table

(b) Customer table

Customer : Table

		Customer_ID	Customer_Name
	+	1	Contemporary Casuals
	+	2	Value Furniture
	+	3	Home Furnishings
	+	4	Eastern Furniture
	+	5	Impressions
	+	6	Furniture Gallery
	+	7	Period Furniture
	+	8	California Classics
	+	9	M and H Casual Furniture
	+	10	Seminole Interiors
	+	11	American Euro Lifestyles
	+	12	Battle Creek Furniture
	+	13	Heritage Furnishings
	+	14	Kaneohe Homes
	+	15	Mountain Scenes
▶			

Record: I◀ ◀ 　16　 ▶ ▶I ▶✳ of 16

(c) Product table

Product : Table

	Product_ID	Standard_Price
+	1	$175.00
+	2	$200.00
+	3	$375.00
+	4	$650.00
+	5	$325.00
+	6	$750.00
+	7	$150.00
+	8	$250.00
▶		$0.00

Record: I◀ ◀ 　9　 ▶ ▶I ▶✳

To answer these and other questions, an organization often needs to build a separate database that contains historical and summarized information. Such a database is usually called a "data warehouse," or in some cases, a "data mart." Also, analysts need specialized decision support tools to query and analyze the database. One class of tools used for this purpose is called "online analytical processing (or OLAP) tools." We describe data warehouses, data marts, and related decision support tools in Chapter 11. There you will learn of the interest in building a data warehouse that is now growing within Pine Valley Furniture Company.

A Current Pine Valley Furniture Company Project Request

Helen Jarvis, product manager for home office furniture at Pine Valley Furniture Company, knows that competition has become fierce in this growing product line. Thus, it is increasingly important to Pine Valley Furniture that Helen be able to analyze sales of her products more thoroughly. Often these analyses are ad hoc, driven by rapidly changing and unanticipated business conditions, comments from furniture store managers, trade industry gossip, or personal experience. Helen has requested that she be given direct access to sales data with an easy-to-use interface so that she can search for answers to the various marketing questions she will generate.

Chris Martin is a systems analyst in Pine Valley Furniture's information systems development area. Chris has worked at Pine Valley Furniture for five years, and has experience with information systems from several business areas within Pine Valley. From the various systems development projects Chris has worked on, his information systems education at Western Florida University, and the extensive training Pine Valley has given him, he has become one of Pine Valley's best systems developers. Chris is skilled in data modeling and is familiar with several relational database management systems used within the firm. Because of his experience, expertise, and availability, the head of information systems has assigned Chris to work with Helen on her request for a marketing support system.

Because Pine Valley Furniture has been careful in the development of its systems, especially since adopting the database approach, the company already has a fairly complete information systems architecture, including databases for all operational business functions. Thus, it is likely that Chris will be able to extract the data Helen needs from existing databases. Pine Valley's information systems architecture calls for such systems as Helen is requesting to be built on stand-alone databases so that the unstructured and unpredictable use of data will not interfere with the access to the operational databases needed to support efficient transaction processing systems.

Further, because Helen's needs are for data analysis, not creation and maintenance, and are personal, not institutional, Chris decides to follow a combination of prototyping and life cycle approaches in developing the system Helen has requested. This means that Chris will follow all the life cycle steps, but he will conduct very quickly and in a cursory way those steps not integral to prototyping. Thus, he will very quickly address project planning (including placing this project within the company's information system architecture), then use an iterative cycle of analysis, design, and implementation to work closely with Helen to develop a working prototype of the system she needs. Because the system will be personal and likely will require a database with limited scope, Chris hopes the prototype will end up being the actual system Helen will use. Chris has chosen to develop the system using Microsoft Access, Pine Valley's preferred technology for personal databases. However, in most cases, the SQL necessary to define the database structure will also be illustrated, because these commands can be used to define a database using any relational database management system.

Matching User Needs to the Information Systems Architecture

Chris begins the project to develop the database and associated marketing support system for the home office furniture area by interviewing Helen. Chris asks

Helen about her business area, taking notes about business area objectives, business functions, data entity types, and other business objects with which she deals. At this point, Chris listens more than he talks so that he can concentrate on understanding Helen's business area; he interjects questions and makes sure that Helen does not try to jump ahead to talk about what she thinks she needs with regards to computer screens and reports from the information system. Chris asks very general questions, using business and marketing terminology as much as possible. For example, Chris asks Helen what issues she faces managing the home office products; what people, places, and things are of interest to her in her job; how far back in time she needs data to go to do her analyses; and what events occur in the business that are of interest to her.

Table 2-4 summarizes what Chris learns from this initial interview. The table lists the various business objects Helen mentioned and indicates which of these are already in Pine Valley Furniture's information systems architecture. There are a few

Table 2-4   Business Objects for Product Line Marketing Support System (Pine Valley Furniture Company)

Planning Object	Objects for Home Office Product Line Tracking	Does Object Exist in Pine Valley Information Systems Architecture?
Objectives	Increase annual sales ($) of home office products by at least 16%	No
	Increase annual profit margin of home office product line by at least 10%	No
	Increase same customer repeat sales ($) of home office products by at least 5%	No
	Exceed sales goals for each product finish category of home office products	No
	Have home office products perform above average for all Pine Valley products	No
	Reduce time to fill office product orders by 5%	No
	Reduce time to receive final payment on office product invoices by 5%	No
Organizational units	Marketing Department	Yes
	Office Furniture Product Line Management	No
	Accounting Department	Yes
	Orders Department	Yes
Organizational locations	Regional Sales Offices	Yes
	Corporate Headquarters	Yes
Business functions	Payment receipt	Yes
	Product development	–
	Demographics analysis	No
	Target market analysis	Yes
	Marketing and sales	–
	Order fulfillment	Yes
	Sales summarization	Yes
	Order taking	Yes
Entity types	CUSTOMER	Yes
	PRODUCT	Yes
	PRODUCT LINE	Yes
	ORDER	Yes
	INVOICE	Yes
	PAYMENT	Yes
Information systems	Order processing	Yes
	Sales management	Yes

entries in the figure that are not in the information systems architecture. However, all of the major categories of data Helen mentioned are covered in the architecture and are managed in existing information systems. Thus, Chris is confident that most, if not all, of the data Helen might want already exist within company databases.

Chris does two quick analyses before talking with Helen again. First, he identifies all of the databases that contain data associated with the data entities Helen mentioned. From these databases, Chris makes a list of all of the data attributes from these data entities that he thinks might be of interest to Helen in her analyses of the home office furniture market. Chris's previous involvement in projects that developed Pine Valley's standard sales tracking and forecasting system and cost accounting system helps him to extrapolate from the information in Table 2-4 the kinds of data Helen might want. For example, the objective to exceed sales goals for each product finish category of office furniture suggests that Helen wants product annual sales goals in her system; also, the objective of achieving at least a 16 percent annual sales growth means that the prior year's orders for each product need to be included. He also concludes that Helen's database must include all products, not just those in the office furniture line, because she wants to compare her line to others. However, he is able to eliminate many of the data attributes kept on each data entity. For example, Helen does not appear to need various customer data such as address, phone number, contact person, store size, and salesperson. Chris does, though, include a few attributes, customer type and zip code, which are not obvious from Table 2-4. He includes these because they were important attributes in the sales forecasting system.

Second, from this list, Chris draws a graphic data model that represents the data entities with the associated data attributes, as well as the major relationships between these data entities. Chris's hope is that he can reduce the time for the analysis phase of the systems development process (and hence the time to do conceptual data modeling) by presenting this data model to Helen. A graphic of the data model for the preliminary database that Chris produces appears in Figure 2-13. The data attributes of each entity Chris thinks Helen wants for the system are listed in Table 2-5. Chris lists in Table 2-5 only basic data attributes from existing databases, because Helen will likely want to combine these data in various ways for the analyses she will want to do.

Figure 2-13
Preliminary data model for Home Office product line marketing support system

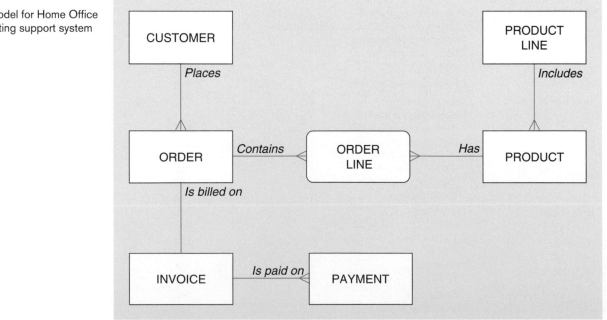

Table 2-5 Data Attributes for Entities in Preliminary Data Model

Entity Type	Attribute
CUSTOMER	Customer_Identifier
	Customer_Name
	Customer_Type
	Customer_ZIPCODE
PRODUCT	Product_Identifier
	Product_Description
	Product_Finish
	Product_Price
	Product_Cost
	Product_Annual_Sales_Goal
	Product_Line_Name
PRODUCT LINE	Product_Line_Name
	Product_Line_Annual_Sales_Goal
ORDER	Order_Number
	Order_Placement_Date
	Order_Fulfillment_Date
	Customer_Identifier
ORDERED PRODUCT	Order_Number
	Product_Identifier
	Order_Quantity
INVOICE	Invoice_Number
	Order_Number
	Invoice_Date
PAYMENT	Invoice_Number
	Payment_Date
	Payment_Amount

Analyzing Database Requirements

Chris's initial meeting with Helen lasted only 45 minutes, but he feels that it served to generate a lot of ideas to share with Helen from the data he collected at the meeting and his subsequent work. He schedules a longer session (two hours) with Helen to go over these findings. Prior to the meeting, he sends Helen a rough project schedule outlining the steps he plans to follow and the estimated length of time each step will take. Because prototyping is a user-driven process, in which the user says when to stop iterating on the new prototype versions, Chris can provide only rough estimates of the duration of certain project steps. For this reason, Chris's boss has decided that this project should be billed to Helen on a consulting time basis, not at a fixed cost.

Chris does more of the talking at this second meeting. He methodically walks through each data entity in Figure 2-13, explaining what it means, what each data attribute associated with it (in Table 2-5) means, and what business policies and procedures are represented by each line between entities. For example, Chris explains that each order is billed on one invoice and each invoice is a bill for exactly one order. An Order_Number uniquely identifies each order, and an order is placed by one customer. Other data about an order Chris thinks Helen might want to know include the date when the order was placed and the date when the order was filled. (This would be the latest shipment date for the products on the order.) Chris also explains that the Payment_Date attribute represents the most recent date when the customer made any payments, in full or partial, for the order.

During this discussion, Helen tells Chris about some additional data she wants (the number of years a customer has purchased products from Pine Valley Furniture Company and the number of shipments necessary to fill each order). Helen also notes that Chris has only one year of sales goals indicated for a product line. She

Table 2-6　Data Attributes for Entities in Final Data Model

Entity Type	Attribute*
CUSTOMER	Customer_Identifier
	Customer_Name
	Customer_Type
	Customer_ZIPCODE
	Customer_Years
PRODUCT	Product_Identifier
	Product_Description
	Product_Finish
	Product_Price
	Product_Cost
	Product_Prior_Year_Sales_Goal
	Product_Current_Year_Sales_Goal
	Product_Line_Name
PRODUCT LINE	Product_Line_Name
	Product_Line_Prior_Year_Sales_Goal
	Product_Line_Current_Year_Sales_Goal
ORDER	Order_Number
	Order_Placement_Date
	Order_Fulfillment_Date
	Order_Number_of_Shipments
	Customer_Identifier
ORDERED PRODUCT	Order_Number
	Product_Identifier
	Order_Quantity
INVOICE	Invoice_Number
	Order_Number
	Invoice_Date
PAYMENT	Invoice_Number
	Payment_Date
	Payment_Amount

*Changes from preliminary list of attributes appear in italics.

reminds him that she wants these data for both the past and current years. As she reacts to the data model, Chris asks her how she intends to use the data she wants. Chris does not try to be thorough at this point, because he knows that Helen has not worked with an information set like the one being developed; thus, she may not yet be positive what data she wants or what she wants to do with the data. Rather, Chris's objective is to understand a few ways in which Helen intends to use the data so he can develop an initial prototype, including the database and several computer displays or reports. The final list of attributes that Helen agrees she needs appears in Table 2-6.

Designing the Database

Because Chris is following a prototyping methodology, and because the first two sessions with Helen quickly identified the data Helen might need, Chris is able to immediately begin to build the prototype. First, Chris creates extracts from the corporate databases the data entities and attributes that Helen suggested. Chris is able to create all of these files using the SQL query language. Some of the data Helen wants are computed from raw, operational data (e.g., Customer_Years), but SQL makes it easy for Chris to specify these calculations. This extracting results in a single ASCII file for each data entity; each row in a file contains all of the data attributes associated with that data entity in the data model, and the rows are different instances of the entity. For example, each row of the ASCII file for the PRODUCT LINE data entity contains data for product line names and the annual sales goals for the past and current years.

```
CREATE TABLE PRODUCT_LINE
    (PRODUCT_LINE_NAME          VARCHAR (40)   NOT NULL PRIMARY KEY,
    PL_PRIOR_YEAR_GOAL          DECIMAL,
    PL_CURRENT_YEAR_GOAL        DECIMAL);
```

Figure 2-14
SQL definition of PRODUCT_LINE
table

Second, Chris translates the final data model from his discussion with Helen into a set of tables for which the columns are data attributes and the rows are different sets of values for those attributes. Tables are the basic building blocks of a relational database, which is the database style for Microsoft Access. The definitions of the PRODUCT LINE and PRODUCT tables Chris created, including associated data attributes, are shown in Figures 2-14 and 2-15. The tables are defined using SQL, a language commonly used for relational databases. Chris did this translation so that each table had an attribute, called the table's "primary key," which will be distinct for each row in the table. The other major properties of each table are that there is only one value for each attribute in each row, and if we know the value of the identifier, there can be only one value for each of the other attributes. For example, for any product line, there can be only one value for the current year's sales goal.

The design of the database includes specifying the format, or properties, for each attribute (Access calls attributes *fields*). These design decisions were easy in this case because most of the attributes were already specified in the corporate data dictionary A few attributes, such as Order_Number_of_Shipments on the ORDER table, were computed from raw data in Pine Valley Furniture Company databases, so Chris had to create the specifications for such attributes.

The other major decision Chris has to make about database design is how to physically organize the database to respond fastest to the queries Helen will write. Because the database will be used for decision support, neither Chris nor Helen can anticipate all of the queries that will arise; thus, Chris must make the physical design choices from experience rather than precise knowledge of the way the database will be used. The key physical database design decision that SQL allows a database designer to make is on which attributes to create indexes. (An index is like a card catalog in the library, through which rows with common characteristics can be quickly located.) All primary key attributes (like Order_Number for the ORDER table), those with unique values across the rows of the table, are indexed. In addition to this, Chris uses a general rule of thumb: Create an index for any attribute that has more than 10 different values and that Helen might use to segment the database. For example, Helen indicated that one of the ways she wants to use the database is to look at sales by product finish. Thus, it might make sense to create an index on the PRODUCT table using the Product_Finish attribute.

```
CREATE TABLE PRODUCT
    (PRODUCT_ID                 INTEGER NOT NULL PRIMARY KEY,
    PRODUCT_DESCRIPTION         VARCHAR (20),
    PRODUCT_FINISH              VARCHAR (50),
    PRODUCT_PRICE               DECIMAL,
    PRODUCT_COST                DECIMAL,
    PR_PRIOR_YEAR_GOAL          DECIMAL,
    PR_CURRENT_YEAR_GOAL        DECIMAL,
    PRODUCT_LINE_NAME           VARCHAR (40),
FOREIGN KEY (PRODUCT_LINE_NAME) REFERENCES
    PRODUCT_LINE (PRODUCT_LINE_NAME));
```

Figure 2-15
SQL definition of PRODUCT table

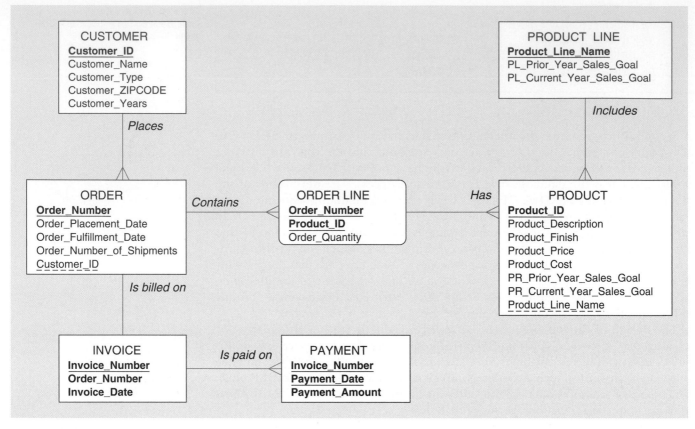

Figure 2-16
Project data model for Home Office
product line marketing support system

However, Pine Valley uses only six product finishes, or types of wood, so this is not a useful index candidate. On the other hand, Order_Placement_Date (called a secondary key because there may be more than one row in the ORDER table with the same value of this attribute), which Helen also wants to use to analyze sales in different time periods, is a good index candidate.

Figure 2-16 shows the prototype project data model developed by Chris for the home office marketing database. Each box represents one table in the database; the attributes of a table are listed inside the associated box. The project data model shows how the relations will be linked by including foreign keys, which will be covered in detail in Chapter 5. The foreign keys have a dashed underline in the model. For example, the attribute Product_Line is the primary identifier in the PRODUCT-LINE relation, and is also included in the PRODUCT table, This linkage makes it possible to compare current sales to sales goals by product line.

Using the Database

Helen will use the database Chris has built mainly for ad hoc questions, so Chris will train her so that she can access the database and build queries to answer her ad hoc questions. Helen has indicated a few standard questions she expects to ask periodically. Chris will develop several types of prewritten routines that can make it easier for Helen to answer these standard questions (so she does not have to program these questions from scratch). Chris develops the following prewritten routines:

- *Form*   A set of attributes, in a predetermined format, all based on a single database record. Thus, a form might contain the data about a given customer or it might contain the data about a specific order and the customer attributes for the customer associated with the order.

```
SELECT PRODUCT.PRODUCT_ID, PRODUCT.PRODUCT_DESCRIPTION,
       PRODUCT.PR_CURRENT_YEAR_SALES_GOAL,
       (ORDER_QUANTITY*PRODUCT_PRICE) AS Sales to Date
FROM ORDER, ORDER_LINE, PRODUCT, PRODUCT_LINE
WHERE ORDER.ORDER_NUMBER = ORDER_LINE.ORDER_NUMBER
AND PRODUCT.PRODUCT_ID = ORDERED_PRODUCT.PRODUCT_ID
AND PRODUCT.PRODUCT_ID = PRODUCT_LINE.PRODUCT_ID
AND PRODUCT.PRODUCT_LINE_NAME = "Home Office";
```

Figure 2-17
SQL query for Home Office sales-to-goal comparison

- *Report* A set of attributes, in a predetermined format, based on many unrelated records. A report usually contains the same attributes about each record. For example, a report might list the product identifier, current year sales, and current year sales goal for all the products for which sales are below goal. A report usually includes page numbers, titles on each page, the date the report was printed, and other descriptive information.

- *Query* A question to be answered from the database as posed in a particular querying language, Query-by-Example. The result of a query is a table in which the columns are the attributes the user wants to see and the rows are different instances of those attributes that satisfy the qualification entered by the user.

During the prototyping development process Chris may develop many examples of each of these routines as Helen communicates more clearly what she wants the system to be able to do. At this early stage of development, however, Chris wants to develop one routine to create the first prototype. One of the standard sets of information Helen says she wants is a list of each of the products in the Home Office line showing each product's total sales to date compared with its current year sales goal. Helen may want the results of this query to be displayed in a more stylized fashion—an opportunity to use a report—but for now Chris will present this feature to Helen only as a query.

The query to produce this list of products appears in Figure 2-17, with sample output in Figure 2-18. The query in Figure 2-17 uses SQL. You can see three of the six standard SQL clauses in this query: SELECT, FROM, and WHERE. SELECT indicates which attributes will be shown in the result. One calculation is also included and given the label "Sales to Date". FROM indicates which tables must be accessed to retrieve data. WHERE defines the links between the tables and indicates that only results from the Home Office product line are to be included. Only limited data are included for this example, so the Total Sales results in Figure 2-18 are fairly small, but the format is the result of the query in Figure 2-17.

Figure 2-18
Home Office product line sales comparison

Product_ID	Product_Description	PR_Current_Year_Sales_ Goal	Sales to Date
3	Computer Desk	$23,500.00	5625
10	96" Bookcase	$22,500.00	4400
5	Writer's Desk	$26,500.00	650
3	Computer Desk	$23,500.00	3750
7	48" Bookcase	$17,000.00	2250
5	Writer's Desk	$26,500.00	3900

Chris is now ready to meet with Helen again to see if the prototype is beginning to meet her needs. Chris shows Helen the system. As Helen makes suggestions, Chris is able to make a few changes online, but many of Helen's observations will have to wait for more careful work at his desk.

Space does not permit us to review the whole project to develop the Home Office marketing support system. Chris and Helen ended up meeting about a dozen times before Helen was satisfied that all the attributes she needed were in the database; that the standard queries, forms, and reports Chris wrote were of use to her; and that she knew how to write queries for unanticipated questions. Chris will be available to Helen at any time to provide consulting support when she has trouble with the system, including writing more complex queries, forms, or reports. One final decision that Chris and Helen made was that the performance of the final prototype was efficient enough that the prototype did not have to be rewritten or redesigned. Helen was now ready to use the system.

Administering the Database

The administration of the Home Office marketing support system is fairly simple. Helen decided that she could live with weekly downloads of new data from Pine Valley's operational databases into her Access database. Chris wrote a C program with SQL commands embedded in it to perform the necessary extracts and wrote an MS Access program in Visual Basic to rebuild the Access tables from these extracts; he scheduled these jobs to run every Sunday evening. Chris also updated the corporate information systems architecture model to include the Home Office marketing support system. This step was important so that when changes occurred to formats for data included in Helen's system, the corporate CASE tool could alert Chris that changes might have to be made also in her system.

Summary

This chapter discussed the process of developing databases and the applications that used them. Database development begins with enterprise data modeling, during which the range and general contents of organizational databases are established. Enterprise data modeling is part of an overall process that develops an information systems architecture (including data, processes, network, people, events, and reasons) for an organization. One popular methodology for developing an information systems architecture is information engineering, a top-down information systems planning approach.

Information systems planning must consider organization goals, critical success factors, and problem areas of the organization. During information systems planning, data entities need to be related to other organizational planning objects: organizational units, locations, business functions, and information systems. Business functions can be represented at various levels of detail by breaking them down through a process called functional decomposition. Relationships between data entities and the other

organizational planning objects can be represented at a high level by planning matrixes, which can be manipulated to understand patterns of relationships.

Once the need for a database is identified either from information systems planning or from a specific request (such as the one from Helen Jarvis for a Home Office products marketing support system), a project team is formed to develop all elements. The project team follows a systems development process, such as the systems development life cycle or prototyping. The systems development life cycle can be represented by five methodical steps: (1) planning, (2) analysis, (3) design, (4) implementation, and (5) maintenance. Database development activities occur in each of these overlapping phases, and feedback may occur that causes a project to return to a prior phase. In prototyping, a database and its applications are iteratively refined through a close interaction of systems developers and users. Prototyping works best when the database application is small and stand-alone, and a small number of users exist. Packaged (or generic) data models can often be used to shorten the development process and improve the quality of resulting data models. However, competent database analysis and design techniques are required to exploit the potential benefits of these models.

Throughout the systems development process, CASE tools are used to develop data models and to maintain the metadata for the database and applications. A repository maintains all the documentation. Various people might use the CASE tools and associated repository during a database development project: systems analysts, database analysts, users, programmers, database and data administrators, and other technical specialists. As a significant new portion of a project is completed and entries are made in the repository, a review point occurs so that those working on the project and funding the human and capital resources of the project can assess progress and renew commitment based on incremental achievements.

Those working on a database development project deal with three views, or schemas, for a database: (1) conceptual schema, which provides a complete, technology-independent picture of the database; (2) internal schema, which specifies the complete database as it will be stored in computer secondary memory in terms of a logical schema and a physical schema; and (3) an external schema or user view, which describes the database relevant to a specific set of users in terms of a set of user views combined with the enterprise data model.

A modern database and the applications that use it may be located on multiple computers. Although any number of tiers may exist (from one to many), three tiers of computers relate to the client/server architecture for database processing: (1) the client tier, where database contents are presented to the user; (2) the application/Web server tier, where analyses on database contents are made and user sessions are managed; and (3) the enterprise server tier, where the data from across the organization are merged into an organizational asset.

We closed the chapter with the review of a hypothetical database development project at Pine Valley Furniture Company. This system to support marketing a Home Office furniture product line illustrated the use of a personal database management system and SQL coding for developing a retrieval-only database. The database in this application contained data extracted from the enterprise databases and then stored in a separate database on the client tier. Prototyping was used to develop this database application because the user, Helen Jarvis, had rather unstructured needs that could best be discovered through an iterative process of developing and refining the system.

CHAPTER REVIEW

Key Terms

Business function
Client/server architecture
Computer-aided software
    engineering (CASE)
Conceptual schema
Enterprise data modeling

Functional decomposition
Incremental commitment
Information engineering
Information systems
    life cycle (SDLC)
Logical schema

Physical schema
Project
Prototyping
Systems development
    architecture (ISA)
Top-down planning

Review Questions

1. Define each of the following key terms:
   a. information systems architecture (ISA)
   b. systems development life cycle (SDLC)
   c. client/server architecture
   d. incremental commitment
   e. enterprise data model
   f. conceptual data model
   g. logical data model
   h. physical data model

2. Match the following terms and definitions:
   _____ conceptual schema
   _____ business function
   _____ prototyping
   _____ systems development life cycle
   _____ functional decomposition
   _____ top-down planning

   a. consist of the enterprise data model and multiple user views
   b. repeatedly breaking a function into finer and finer detail
   c. periodic review points in a systems development project

_____ incremental commitment

_____ internal schema

_____ external schema

d. a rapid approach to systems development

e. consists of two data models: a logical model and a physical model

f. a comprehensive description of business data

g. gains a broad understanding of information system needs

h. a related group of business processes

i. a structured, step-by-step approach to systems development

3. Contrast the following terms:
   a. internal schema; conceptual schema
   b. systems development life cycle; prototyping
   c. top-down planning; functional decomposition
   d. enterprise data modeling; information engineering
   e. repository; computer-aided software engineering
   f. enterprise data model; conceptual data model

4. List and explain the four steps of information engineering.

5. Describe the three steps in the information engineering planning phase.

6. List and explain the three information engineering strategic planning factors.

7. List and define the five key corporate planning objects.

8. Explain the significance of functional decomposition in information systems and database development.

9. Explain the use of information system planning matrixes in information systems development.

10. Name the five phases of the traditional systems development life cycle, and explain the purpose and deliverables of each phase.

11. In which of the five phases of the SDLC do database development activities occur?

12. Define the steps in the prototyping systems development process. Which database development activities occur in each prototyping step?

13. Explain the differences between user views, a conceptual schema, and an internal schema as different views of the same database.

14. Are the design of external schemas and a conceptual schema done in a particular sequence? Why or why not?

15. Define a three-tiered database architecture.

16. In the three-tiered database architecture, is it possible for there to be no database on a particular tier? If not, why? If yes, give an example.

17. List the six key components of an information systems architecture (ISA). Which of these components relate to database design? Why?

18. When during the database development process might an entity-relationship diagram be drawn? How do these different diagrams of the same database differ from one another?

19. In the three-schema architecture:
   a. The view of a manager or other type of user is called the _____ schema.
   b. The view of the data architect or data administrator is called the _____ schema.
   c. The view of the database administrator is called the _____ schema.

20. Explain the similarities and differences between an enterprise-level data model and a project-level data model. What are the differences in how the different types of data models are used?

Problems and Exercises

1. What is your reaction to the representation of the systems development life cycle included in Chapter 2? Explain any problems you have with it.

2. Rearrange the rows and columns of Figure 2-3 into a more useful sequence. Why did you choose this new sequence of rows and columns? For what purpose can you now use the rearranged matrix?

3. List three additional entities that might appear in an enterprise data model for Pine Valley Furniture Company (Figure 2-1).

4. Consider your business school or other academic unit as a business enterprise.
   a. Define several functions and do a functional decomposition to at least three levels.
   b. Define several major data entity types, and draw a preliminary enterprise data model (similar in notation to Figure 2-1).

   c. Develop a planning matrix with the lowest level functions from part a of the exercise as rows and data entity types from part b as columns. Fill in the cells of this matrix similar to Figure 2-3.
   d. Define four critical success factors for the academic unit.
   e. Would your business school or academic unit benefit from a multiple-tiered architecture for data? Why or why not?

5. Consider a student club in which you are involved.
   a. Define several information systems (manual or automated) used by this club.
   b. Define several major data entity types, and draw a preliminary enterprise data model (similar in notation to Figure 2-1).

c. Develop an Information System-to-Data Entity planning matrix. Fill in the cells to show how each information system interacts with each data entity. (Code the cell with a C for create new instances of that entity, R for retrieves data about that entity, U for updates values of data for that entity, and D for deletes instances of that entity.)

d. Reorganize the rows and columns of your answer to part c of this exercise to create, as best you can, a matrix with cells with entries along the main diagonal and empty cells off the main diagonal. What does this reorganized matrix tell you?

6. Imagine a planning matrix of Business Functions-to-Data Entities. Suppose that by studying this matrix you determine that three of the business functions provide the bulk of the use of five of the data entities. What implications might this have for identifying databases for development?

7. Consider Table 2-3. Develop a hypothetical Information System-to-Entity Type matrix from the information in this table. Make assumptions about which information systems create, retrieve, update, and delete data from each data entity. Code the cells to indicate create (C), retrieve (R), update (U), and delete (D). Because the information systems listed include both transaction processing and management information systems, what patterns of entity usage do you observe?

8. Consider Table 2-3. Develop a hypothetical functional decomposition of the Product development business function, similar to that shown for the Order fulfillment function in Figure 2-2. Do any of the same subfunctions appear in both Figure 2-2 and your diagram? Why?

9. Explain the differences between an enterprise data model and a conceptual data model. How many databases does each represent? What scope of the organization does each address? What are other salient differences?

10. Is it possible that during the physical database design and creation step of database development you might want to return to the logical database design activity? Why or why not? If it is possible, give an example of what might arise during physical database design and creation that would cause you to want to reconsider the conceptual and external database designs from prior steps.

11. Contrast the top-down nature of database development during conceptual data modeling with the bottom-up nature of database development during logical database design. What major differences exist in the type of information considered in each of these two database development steps?

12. The objective of the prototyping systems development methodology is to rapidly build and rebuild an information system as the user and systems analyst learn from use of the prototype what features should be included in the evolving information system. Because the final prototype does not have to become the working system, where do you think would be an ideal location to develop a prototype: on a personal computer, workgroup computer, department computer, or enterprise server? Does your answer depend on any assumptions?

13. Consider an organization with which you frequently interact, such as a bank, credit card company, university, or insurance company, from which you receive several computer-generated messages, such as monthly statements, transaction slips, and so forth. Depict the data included in each message you receive from the organization as its own user view; use the notation of Figure 2-1 to represent these views. Now, combine all of these user views together into one conceptual data model, also using the notation of Figure 2-1. What did you observe about the process of combining the different user views? Were there inconsistencies across the user views? Once you have created the conceptual data model, would you like to change anything about any of the user views?

14. Consider Figure 2-9, which depicts a hypothetical three-tiered database architecture. Identify potential duplications of data across all the databases listed on this figure. What problems might arise because of this duplication? Does this duplication violate the principles of the database approach outlined in Chapter 1? Why or why not?

15. Consider Figure 2-13. Explain the meaning of the line that connects ORDER to INVOICE and the line that connects INVOICE to PAYMENT. What does this say about how Pine Valley Furniture Company does business with its customers?

16. Answer the following questions concerning Figures 2-14 and 2-15:

a. What will be the field size for the Product_Line_Name field in the PRODUCT table? Why?

b. In Figure 2-15, how is the Product_ID field in the PRODUCT table specified to be required? Why is it a required attribute?

c. In Figure 2-15, explain the function of the FOREIGN KEY definition?

17. Consider the SQL query in Figure 2-17.

a. How is Sales to Date calculated?

b. How would the query have to change if Helen Jarvis wanted to see the results for all of the product lines, not just the Home Office product line?

18. Helen Jarvis wants to determine the most important customers for Home Office products. She requests a listing of total dollar sales year-to-date for each customer who bought these products, as revealed by invoiced payments. The list is to be sorted in descending order, so that the largest customer heads the list.

a. Look at Figure 2-16 and determine what entities are required to produce this list.

b. Which entities will be involved in the SQL query that will give Helen the information she needs?

19. If you look ahead to Figure 3-22 in Chapter 3, you will see an E-R diagram for part of the Pine Valley organization database.

a. How is the entity PRODUCT LINE diagrammed?

b. How has Chris diagrammed the PRODUCT_LINE entity in the draft prepared for Helen?

c. Explain the differences you note between the two definitions of PRODUCT LINE.

20. In this chapter, we described four important data models and their properties: enterprise, conceptual, logical, and physical. In the following table, summarize the important properties of these data models by entering a "Y" (for Yes) or an "N" (for No) in each cell of the table.

	All Entities?	All Attributes?	Technology Independent?	DBMS Independent?	Record Layouts?
Enterprise					
Conceptual					
Logical					
Physical					

Field Exercises

1. Interview systems and database analysts at several organizations. Ask them to describe their systems development process. Does it resemble more the systems development life cycle or prototyping? Do they use methodologies similar to both? When do they use their different methodologies? Explore the methodology used for developing applications to be used through the Web. How have they adapted their methodology to fit this new systems development process?

2. Choose an organization with which you are familiar, possibly where you work, your university, or an organization where a friend works. For this organization, describe its information systems architecture (ISA). Does it have a formally prepared architecture or did you have to create one? Interview information system managers in this organization to find out why they do or do not have a formally recognized information systems architecture.

3. Choose an organization with which you are familiar, possibly your employer, your university, or an organization where a friend works. Consider a major database in this organization, such as one supporting customer interactions, accounting, or manufacturing. What is the architecture for this database? Is the organization using some form of client/server architecture? Interview information systems

managers in this organization to find out why they chose the architecture for this database.

4. Choose an organization with which you are familiar, possibly your employer, your university, or an organization where a friend works. Interview a systems analyst or database analyst and ask questions about the typical composition of an information systems development team. Specifically, what role does a database analyst play in project teams? Is a database analyst used throughout the systems development process or is the database analyst used only at selected points?

5. Choose an organization with which you are familiar, possibly your employer, your university, or an organization where a friend works. Interview a systems analyst or database analyst and ask questions about how that organization uses CASE tools in the systems development process. Concentrate your questions on how CASE tools are used to support data modeling and database design and how the CASE tool's repository maintains the information collected about data, data characteristics, and data usage. If multiple CASE tools are used on one or many projects, ask how the organization attempts to integrate data models and data definitions. Finally, inquire how satisfied the systems and database analysts are with CASE tool support for data modeling and database design.

References

Hay, D. 1996. *Data Model Patterns: Conventions of Thought.* New York: Dorset House Publishing.

Henderson, D., B. Champlin, D. Coleman, P. Cupoli, J. Hoffer, L. Howarth et al. "Model Curriculum Framework for Post Secondary Education Programs in Data Resource Management." The Data Management Association International Foundation Committee on the Advancement of Data Management in Post Secondary Institutions Sub Committee on Curriculum Framework Development. DAMA International Foundation.

Hoffer, J. A., J. F. George, and J. S. Valacich. 2005. *Modern Systems Analysis and Design,* 4th ed. Upper Saddle River, NJ: Prentice Hall.

Inmon, W. 2003. "A Data Warehouse Development Methodology" available at www.billinmon.com/library/methods/dwmeth_frame.asp (access verified October 28, 2003).

Kimball, R., and M. Ross. 2002. The *Data Warehouse Toolkit: The Complete Guide to Dimensional Data Modeling,* 2d ed. New York: Wiley.

Moriarty, T. 1991. "Framing Your System." *Database Programming & Design* 4,6 (June): 38–43.

Naumann, J. D. and A. M. Jenkins. 1982. "Prototyping: The New Paradigm for Systems Development." *MIS Quarterly* 6(3): 29-44.

Silverston, L. 2001a. *The Data Model Resource Book, Vol. 1: A Library of Universal Data Models for all Enterprises.* New York: Wiley.

Silverston, L. 2001b. *The Data Model Resource Book, Vol 2: A Library of Data Models for Specific Industries.* New York: Wiley.

Silverston, L. 2002. "A Universal Data Model for Relationship Development." *DM Review* 12,3 (March): 44–47, 65.

Sowa, J. F., and J. A. Zachman. 1992. "Extending and Formalizing the Framework for Information Systems Architecture." *IBM Systems Journal* 31,3 (September): 590–616.

Thompson, C. 1997. "Committing to Three-Tier Architecture." *Database Programming & Design* 10,8 (August): 26–30, 32, 33.

Zachman, J. A. 1987. "A Framework for Information Systems Architecture." *IBM Systems Journal* 26,1 (March): 276–92.

Further Reading

Finkelstein, C. 1989. *An Introduction to Information Engineering.* Reading, MA: Addison-Wesley.

Shank, M. E., A. C. Boynton, and R. W. Zmud. 1985. "Critical Success Factor Analysis as a Methodology for IS Planning." *MIS Quarterly* 9,2 (June): 121–29.

Web Resources

www.usdoj.gov/jmd/irm/lifecycle/table.htm The Department of Justice Systems Development Life Cycle Guidance Document. This is an example of a systems methodology that you may want to look over.

www.qucis.queensu.ca/Software-Engineering/ The software engineering archives for USENET newsgroup comp.software-eng. This site contains many links that you may want to explore.

www.acinet.org/acinet/ This site, America's Career InfoNet, provides information about careers, outlook, requirements, and so forth.

www.collegegrad.com/salaries/index.shtml Find recent salary information for a wide range of careers, including database-related careers.

www.essentialstrategies.com/publications/methodology/zachman.htm David Hay's Web site, which has considerable information on universal data models as well as how database development fits into the Zachman information systems architecture.

www.billinmon.com Web site for one of the pioneers of data warehousing.

Case

CASE DESCRIPTION

You were introduced to Mountain View Community Hospital in Chapter 1. Here are a few more facts about the hospital. Within the last fiscal year, the hospital performed more than one million laboratory procedures and over 110,000 radiology procedures. During that time, the hospital had 9,192 admissions and 112,230 outpatient visits, brought 1,127 babies into the world, and performed 2,314 inpatient and 1,490 outpatient surgeries. Patients who receive outpatient surgeries do not remain in the hospital overnight. With an average of 2,340 patients a month, the emergency department experienced approximately 28,200 visits throughout the year. Approximately 30 percent of the patients admitted to the hospital were first treated in the emergency room, and about 13 percent of emergency room visits resulted in hospital admission. The hospital employs 740 full-time and 439 part-time personnel, among them 264 full-time and 176 part-time registered nurses, and 10 full-time and 6 part-time licensed practical nurses. The hospital's active medical staff includes over 250 primary physicians, specialists, and sub-specialists. Volunteers are an integral part of MVCH's culture and contribute greatly to the well-being of patients and their families. Approximately 300 volunteers from different backgrounds and of all ages devote their time, energy, and talents to many areas of the hospital. They greet visitors and patients and help them find their way through the hospital, deliver mail and flowers to patient rooms, escort patients, aid staff with clerical duties, work in the gift shop, assist at community and fund-raising events, and help out in a host of other areas.

Mountain View Hospital provides a number of key services, including general medical and surgical care, general intensive care, a cardiology department, open-heart surgery, a neurology department, pediatric medical and surgical care, obstetrics, an orthopedics department, oncology, and a 24-hour emergency department. The hospital also offers a wide range of diagnostic services. A specialty service within the neurology department is the recently opened Multiple Sclerosis (MS) Center which provides comprehensive and expert care for patients with multiple sclerosis in order to improve their quality of life. Using an interdisciplinary team approach, the center emphasizes all aspects of MS care from diagnosis and treatment of MS symptoms and secondary complications, to individual and family counseling, rehabilitation therapy, and social services. Headed by Dr. Zequida, called Dr. "Z" by staff and patients, the MS Center is a member of a consortium of MS centers.

The current organizational chart for Mountain View Community Hospital is shown in MVCH Figure 2-1. Like most general hospitals, Mountain View Community is divided into two primary organizational groups. The physicians, headed by Dr. Browne (chief of staff), are responsible for the quality of medical care provided to their patients. The group headed by Ms. Baker (CEO and President) provides the nursing, clinical, and administrative support the physicians need to serve their patients. According to Ms. Baker, the most pressing issues affecting the hospital within the last year have been financial challenges such as bad debt, personnel shortages, particularly registered nurses and imaging technicians, and malpractice insurance. Other critical issues are the quality of care, patient safety, compliance with HIPAA, and technological innovation, which is seen as a major enabler for decreasing costs and improving quality. The trend toward managed care and the need to maintain costs while maintaining/ improving clinical outcomes requires the hospital to track and analyze both clinical and financial data related to patient care services.

Goals and Critical Success Factors As stated in Chapter 1, Mountain View Community Hospital's basic goal is to provide high-quality, cost-effective health care services for the surrounding community in a compassionate, caring, and personalized manner. Mountain View Community Hospital strives to meet the needs of a community of about 60,000 with an annual growth rate of 10 percent, a trend that is expected to continue since the surrounding area is attracting many retirees. To serve the health care needs of this growing community, Mountain View Community Hospital plans to expand its capacity by adding another 50 beds over the next five years, and opening a managed care retirement center with independent

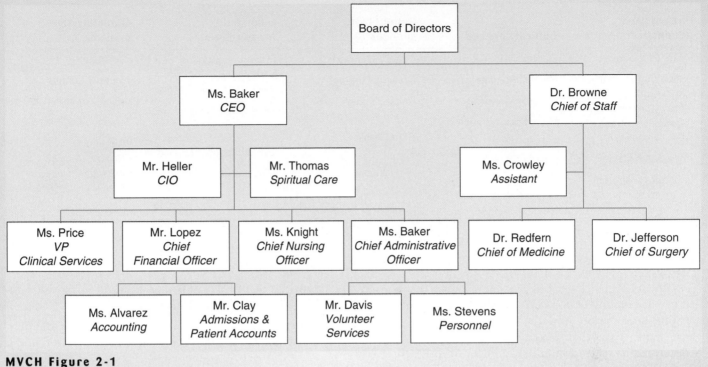

MVCH Figure 2-1
Organizational chart

apartments and assisted living facilities. Adequate land exists for expansion adjacent to the current hospital facilities. Because of the expansion, Mountain View Community Hospital expects to increase the size of its administrative and medical staff, create a new department of Retirement Living under Ms. Baker, and create a new department of Geriatric Medicine under Dr. Browne.

In response to the steady growth and expansion plans at Mountain View Community Hospital, a special study team including Mr. Heller, Mr. Lopez, Dr. Jefferson, and a consultant has been developing a long-term strategic plan, including an information systems plan for the Hospital. Their work is not complete, but they have begun to identify many of the elements necessary to build the plan. To meet the goals of high-quality health care, cost containment, and expansion into new services, the team concluded that the Hospital has four critical success factors (CSFs): quality of medical care, control of operating costs, control of capital costs, and recruitment and retention of skilled personnel. The development of improved information systems is viewed as an enabler in dealing with each of these CSFs.

The team is currently at work to generate two to four short- or long-term objectives for each CSF. So far they have developed the following four objectives related to the control of the operating costs CSF:

1. Reduce costs for purchased items
2. More efficiently schedule staff
3. Lower cost of liability insurance
4. Expand volunteer services

The study team described each of these CSFs and objectives in more detail and stored these descriptions in a repository managed by the CASE tool used by the information systems department.

Enterprise Modeling The study team also has developed a preliminary list of business functions that describe the administrative and medical activities within the Hospital. These functions consider the organizational goals and CSFs explained in the prior section. At this point, the study team has identified five major business functions that cut across all of the organizational units:

1. *Patient care administration* Manage the logistical and record-keeping aspects of patient care
2. *Clinical services* Provide laboratory testing and procedures, and patient monitoring and screening
3. *Patient care services* Provide patients with medical care and support services
4. *Financial management* Manage the financial resources and operations of the hospital
5. *Administrative services* Provide general management and support services not directly related to patient care

The study team has been able to break each of these high-level functions into lists of more detailed functions

Patient care administration	Clinical services	Patient care services	Financial management	Administrative services
Patient scheduling	Electrodiagnosis	Dietary/Nutrition	Patient accounting	Purchasing
Patient registration	Psychiatric testing	Nursing Surgery	• *Bill patient*	Inventory control
• *Admit patient*	Patient monitoring	Rehabilitation	• *Account for receivables*	Housekeeping
• *Assign patient to bed*	Multiphasic screening	• *Perform physical therapy*	Cost accounting	Personnel
• *Transfer patient*	Radiology	Blood banking	Payroll	Volunteering
• *Discharge patient*	• *Perform x-rays*		General accounting	• *Recruit volunteers*
Physician orders	Laboratory		Risk management	• *Schedule volunteers*
Laboratory reporting	• *Perform blood tests*			• *Evaluate volunteers*

MVCH Figure 2-2
Business functions

(see MVCH Figure 2-2), but the team knows that these lists are not complete nor well defined at this point.

The study team initially has a preliminary set of eleven entity types that describe the data required by the hospital for its operation and administration: FACILITY, PHYSICIAN, PATIENT, DIAGNOSTIC UNIT, WARD, STAFF, ORDER, SERVICE/DRUG, MEDICAL/SURGICAL ITEM, SUPPLY ITEM, and VENDOR. From discussions with hospital staff, reviewing hospital documents, and studying existing information systems, the study team developed a list of business rules describing the policies of the hospital and nature of the hospital's operation that govern the relationships between these entities. Some of these rules are:

1. A FACILITY maintains one or more DIAGNOSTIC UNITS (radiology, clinical laboratory, cardiac diagnostic unit, etc.).

2. A FACILITY contains a number of WARDs (obstetrics, oncology, geriatrics, etc.).

3. Each WARD is assigned a certain number of STAFF members (nurses, secretaries, etc.); a STAFF member may be assigned to multiple WARDs.

4. A FACILITY staffs its medical team with a number of PHYSICIANs. A PHYSICIAN may be on the staff of more than one FACILITY.

5. A PHYSICIAN treats PATIENTs, and a PATIENT is treated by any number of PHYSICIANs.

6. A PHYSICIAN diagnoses PATIENTs, and a PATIENT is diagnosed by any number of PHYSICIANs.

7. A PATIENT may be assigned to a WARD (outpatients are not assigned to a WARD). The hospital cares only about the current WARD a patient is assigned to (if assigned at all).

8. A PATIENT uses MEDICAL/SURGICAL ITEMS, which are supplied by VENDORs. A VENDOR also provides SUPPLY ITEMs that are used for housekeeping and maintenance purposes.

9. A PHYSICIAN writes one or more ORDERS for a PATIENT. Each ORDER is for a given PATIENT, and a PATIENT may have many ORDERs.

10. An ORDER can be for a diagnostic test (lab tests such as lipid profile, CBC, liver function tests; diagnostic imaging such as MRIs and X-rays) or a drug.

They recognized that certain business functions, such as risk management and volunteering, were not adequately represented in the set of data entities and business rules, but they decided to deal with these and other areas later. The study team stored descriptions of these data entities and the business rules in the CASE repository for later analysis. Using the identified entities and business rules, the study team developed a preliminary enterprise data model (see MVCH Figure 2-3). Again, this conceptual model is preliminary and does not follow all the conventions used in the information systems department for drawing data models, but the purpose of this enterprise model is to give only a general overview of organizational data.

Developing Planning Matrixes   The study team used the CASE tool to produce a first version of a function-to-entity type matrix (see MVCH Figure 2-4). This matrix maps the business function from MVCH Figure 2-2 to the 11 data entities. The cells of the matrix are coded as follows:

M = Function maintains instances of entity (creates, updates, and deletes)

R = Function reads or uses data about entity

Because this was an initial pass of the matrix, the study team decided not to separately code data creation, update, and deletion activities.

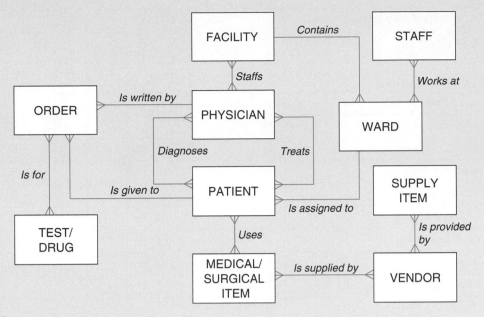

MVCH Figure 2-3
Preliminary enterprise data model

The study team created another planning matrix shown in MVCH Figure 2-5 to relate business functions to the four critical success factors. The codes in this table are:

E = Doing the function well is <u>e</u>ssential in achieving the CSF

D = Doing the function well is <u>d</u>esirable for/helps in achieving the CSF

The study team is looking for ways to combine the results shown in MVCH Figures 2-4 and 2-5 to help them set some priorities for information systems development.

CASE QUESTIONS

1. Which information system planning matrixes (among those shown in this case study or others not shown) might assist the study team at Mountain View Community Hospital to determine a tiered location plan for databases? Why?

2. In the case description, objectives are listed for one of the four critical success factors, operating cost control. Write plausible objectives, given the structure and plans of the hospital, for the other three CSFs.

3. What additional activities might occur within the "volunteering" business function?

4. What activities might occur within the "risk management" business function?

5. Do you think that the study team will be able to identify all the data entities by doing the kind of analysis they have been doing? If not, what other database development steps will need to be done and when?

6. Why do you think the people on the business planning study team were selected for this assignment? Would you have chosen different people? Should additional people be included? If so, who?

7. The case description lists ten business rules. The study team used these rules to develop MVCH Figure 2-3. Are there any other business rules implied by or depicted in that figure? What are they?

8. Even though capital cost control is a critical success factor, only two business functions in MVCH Figure 2-5 mention this CSF. Why? What would need to be done to enhance this figure so that more entries indicated a relationship between business functions and this CSF?

CASE EXERCISES

1. Rearrange the rows and columns of MVCH Figure 2-4 so that the entries form a block diagonal pattern. What conclusions do you reach from analyzing this pattern?

2. Redraw MVCH Figure 2-1 to reflect the structure of the hospital after its planned future expansion and growth. Given this expansion and growth, what else would need to change about MVCH Figures 2-2, 2-3, and 2-4?

3. Carefully compare the enterprise data model in MVCH Figure 2-3 to the business rules listed in the case segment. Are all entities and relationships represented? If not, redraw MVCH Figure 2-3 to account for any entities and relationships that were overlooked by MVCH's study team.

Data Entity Types → / Business Functions ↓	Facility	Physician	Patient	Ward	Staff	Diagnostic Unit	Test/Drug	Medical/ Surgical	Supply Item	Vendor	Other
Patient Scheduling		R	R	R		R	R				R
Patient Registration			M	R							R
Physician Orders		R	R				R	R			M
Laboratory Reporting			R			R	R				R
Electrodiagnosis			R				M				R
Psychiatric Testing			R				M				R
Patient Monitoring			R	R			R				R
Multiphasic Screening			R			R	M				R
Radiology			R			R	M				R
Dietary			R	R							R
Nursing			R	R			R	R			R
Surgery		R	R	R			R	R			R
Rehabilitation			R	R			R				R
Blood Banking			R	R		R					R
Patient Accounting			R	R		R	R				R
Cost Accounting	R		R	R		R					
Payroll		R		R	R						
General Accounting	M			M		M					
Risk Management	R	R	R		R			R		R	R
Purchasing								M	M	M	
Inventory Control					R			R	R		
Housekeeping					R				R		
Personnel		M			M				R		
Volunteering	R		R	R	R	R					

M = data entity (column) is maintained by business function (row)

R = data entity (column) is used by business function (row)

MVCH Figure 2-4
Business function-to-data entity matrix

Business Functions \ Critical success factors	Quality Care	Operating Cost Control	Capital Cost Control	Staff. Recruitment and Retention
Patient Scheduling	D			
Patient Registration				
Physician Orders	D			
Laboratory Reporting	D			
Electrodiagnosis			D	
Psychiatric Testing	D			
Patient Monitoring	E			
Multiphasic Screening	E			
Radiology	D			
Dietary	E			
Nursing	E	E		E
Surgery	D	D	E	
Rehabilitation	E			
Blood Banking	D			
Patient Accounting	D	E		
Cost Accounting		E		
Payroll				D
General Accounting				
Risk Management		E		D
Purchasing		E		
Inventory Control		E		
Housekeeping		D		
Personnel				E
Volunteering		E		E

E = business function (row) is essential in achieving CSF (column)

D = business function (row) is desirable in achieving CSF (column)

MVCH Figure 2-5
Business function-to-CSF matrix

4. Based on MVCH Figures 2-4 and 2-5, determine which data entities are essential for operating cost control. What implications does this result have for information systems development?

5. One of the important outputs from the "bill patient" business function is the Patient Bill. Case Exercise 2 in Chapter 1 introduced a reduced version of this bill, which is repeated here. That exercise asked you to add missing data that would typically appear on a patient bill. Using your result from that exercise, verify that the enterprise data model in MVCH Figure 2-3 contains the data necessary to generate a patient bill. Explain what you have to do to perform this verification. What did you discover from your analysis?

Patient Name: Dolan, Mark

Patient Number: _____

Patient Address: _____

Item Code	Item Description	Amount
_____	_____	_____
_____	_____	_____
_____	_____	_____

6. The manager of the risk management area, Ms. Jamieson, is anxious to receive computerized support for her activities. The hospital is increasingly facing malpractice claims and litigation, and she does not believe she can wait for improved information services until the information systems and database plans are set. Specifically, Ms. Jamieson wants a system that will track claims, legal suits, lawyers, judges, medical staff, disbursements against claims, and judgments. How would you proceed to deal with this request for improved information services? What methodology would you apply to design or acquire the systems and databases she needs? Why?

7. Consider again the request of the manager of risk management from Project Exercise 5. On what tier or tiers would you recommend the system and database he needs be developed? Why?

PROJECT ASSIGNMENTS

P1. The study team's activities described in this case study are still in the very early stages of information system and database development. Outline the next steps that should be followed within the Information Systems unit to align current systems and databases to the future information systems needs of the hospital.

P2. Carefully read through the case description, exercises, and questions again and:

a. Modify the enterprise data model shown in MVCH Figure 2-3 to include any additional entities and relationships that you identify.

b. Modify the list of business rules from the case description to include the additional entities and relationships you identified.

c. Draw a context diagram of MVCH's improved information system similar to the one for a burger restaurant shown in MVCH Figure 2-6. A context diagram provides the highest-level view of a system and shows the system boundaries, external entities that interact with the system, and major information flows between the entities and the system.

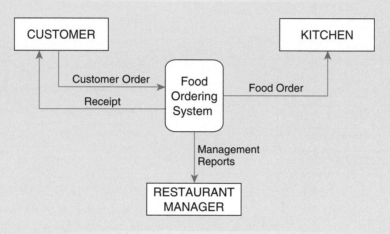

MVCH Figure 2-6
Context diagram example
Adapted from Hoffer et al. (2005), p. 203.

Part TWO

Database Analysis

● **Chapter 3**
Modeling Data in the Organization

● **Chapter 4**
The Enhanced E-R Model and Business Rules

An Overview of Part TWO

The first step in database development is database analysis, in which we determine user requirements for data and develop data models to represent those requirements. The two chapters in Part II describe in depth the de facto standard for conceptual data modeling—entity-relationship diagramming. A conceptual data model represents data from the viewpoint of the organization, independent of any technology that will be used to implement the model.

Chapter 3 (Modeling Data in the Organization) begins with an orientation toward data modeling by describing business rules, which are the policies and rules about the operation of a business that a data model represents. Characteristics of good business rules are described and the process of gathering business rules is discussed. General guidelines for naming and defining elements of a data model are presented within the context of business rules. This chapter introduces the notations and main constructs of this modeling technique, including entities, relationships, and attributes; for each construct, we provide specific guidelines for naming and defining these elements of a data model. We distinguish between strong and weak entity types and the use of identifying relationships. We describe different types of attributes including required versus optional, simple versus composite attributes, single-valued versus multivalued attributes, derived attributes, and identifiers. We contrast relationship types and instances and introduce associative entities. We describe and illustrate relationships of various degrees, including unary, binary, and ternary relationships. We also describe the various relationship cardinalities that arise in modeling situations. We discuss the common problem of how to model time-dependent data. Finally, we describe the situation where multiple relationships are defined between a given set of entities. The E-R modeling concepts are illustrated with an extended example for Pine Valley Furniture Company. This final example, as well as a few other examples throughout the chapter, is presented also using Microsoft Visio, which shows how many data modeling tools represent data models.

Chapter 4 (The Enhanced E-R Model and Business Rules) presents advanced concepts in entity-relationship modeling and introduces recently developed notation for capturing more complex business rules on E-R diagrams. These additional modeling features are often required to cope with the increasingly complex business environment encountered in organizations today.

The most important modeling construct incorporated in the enhanced entity-relationship (or EER) diagram is supertype/subtype relationships. This facility allows us to model a general entity type (called a supertype) and then subdivide it into several specialized entity types called subtypes. For example, sports cars and sedans are subtypes of automobiles. We introduce a simple notation for representing supertype/subtype relationships and several refinements. We also introduce generalization and specialization as two contrasting techniques for identifying supertype/subtype relationships. Supertype/subtype notation is necessary for the increasingly popular universal data model, which is discussed in Chapter 4. The comprehensiveness of a well-documented relationship can be overwhelming, so we introduce a technique called entity clustering for simplifying the presentation of an E-R diagram to meet the needs of a given audience.

Business rules are statements that define or constrain some aspect of the business. We develop a classification for the different types of business rules that are commonly encountered. We then describe and illustrate a declarative approach for expressing business rules, together with a notation for the rules that is superimposed on the EER diagram.

There is another, alternative notation for data modeling—the UML class diagrams for systems developed using object-oriented technologies. This technique is presented later, in Chapter 14, in Part IV. It is possible to read Chapter 14 immediately after Chapter 4 if you want to compare these alternative, but conceptually similar, approaches.

The conceptual data modeling concepts presented in the two chapters in Part II provide the foundation for your career in database analysis and design. As a database analyst you will be expected to apply the E-R notation in modeling user requirements for data and information.

Chapter 3

Modeling Data in the Organization

LEARNING OBJECTIVES

After studying this chapter, you should be able to:

- Concisely define each of the following key terms: **business rule, term, fact, entity-relationship model (E-R model), entity-relationship diagram (E-R diagram), entity, entity type, entity instance, strong entity type, weak entity type, identifying owner, identifying relationship, attribute, required attribute, optional attribute, composite attribute, simple attribute, multivalued attribute, derived attribute, identifier, composite identifier, relationship type, relationship instance, associative entity, degree, unary relationship, binary relationship, ternary relationship, cardinality constraint, minimum cardinality, maximum cardinality,** and **time stamp.**

- State reasons why many system developers believe that data modeling is the most important part of the system development process.

- Write good names and definitions for entities, relationships, and attributes.

- Distinguish unary, binary, and ternary relationships and give a common example of each.

- Model each of the following constructs in an E-R diagram: composite attribute, multivalued attribute, derived attribute, associative entity, identifying relationship, and minimum and maximum cardinality constraints.

- Draw an E-R diagram to represent common business situations.

- Convert a many-to-many relationship to an associative entity type.

- Model simple time-dependent data using time stamps and relationships in an E-R diagram.

INTRODUCTION

You have already been introduced to modeling data and the entity-relationship model through simplified examples in the first two chapters of this text. In this chapter, we formalize data modeling based on the powerful concept of business rules and describe the entity-relationship (E-R) data model in detail.

Business rules are derived from policies, procedures, events, functions, and other business objects, and state constraints on the organization. Business rules represent the language and fundamental structure of an organization (Hay, 2003). Business rules formalize the understanding of the organization by organization owners, managers, and leaders with that of the information systems architects.

Business rules are important in data modeling because they govern how data are handled and stored.

Basic business rules are data names and definitions. This chapter explains guidelines for the clear naming and definition of data objects in a business. In terms of conceptual data modeling, names and definitions must be provided for entity types, attributes, and relationships. Other business rules may state constraints on these data objects. These constraints can be captured in a data model, such as an entity-relationship diagram, and associated documentation. Additional business rules govern the people, places, events, processes, networks, and objectives of the organization, which are all linked to the data requirements through other system documentation.

After some years of use, the E-R model remains the mainstream approach for conceptual data modeling. Its popularity stems from factors such as relative ease of use, widespread CASE tool support, and the belief that entities and relationships are natural modeling concepts in the real world.

The E-R model is most often used as a tool for communications between database designers and end users during the analysis phase of database development (described in Chapter 2). The E-R model is used to construct a conceptual data model, which is a representation of the structure and constraints of a database that is independent of the software (such as a database management system) and its associated data model that will be used to implement the database.

Some authors introduce terms and concepts peculiar to the relational data model when discussing E-R modeling. In particular, they recommend that the E-R model be completely normalized, with full resolution of primary and foreign keys. However, we believe that this forces a premature commitment to the relational data model. In today's database environment, the database may be implemented with object-oriented technology or with a mixture of object-oriented and relational technology. Therefore, we defer discussion of normalization concepts to Chapter 5.

The entity-relationship model was introduced in a key article by Chen (1976), in which he described the main constructs of the E-R model—entities and relationships—and their associated attributes. The model has subsequently been extended to include additional constructs by Chen and others; for example, see Teorey et al. (1986) and Storey (1991). The E-R model continues to evolve, but unfortunately there is not yet a standard notation for E-R modeling. Song et al. (1995) present a side-by-side comparison of ten different E-R modeling notations, explaining the major advantages and disadvantages of each approach. You may be asked to use notations other than the Chen notation, possibly because of the computer-based data diagramming tool you will use. Because such tools are now commonly used by professional data modelers, we adopt for use in this text a variation of the notation used in professional modeling tools. Appendix A will help you translate between our notation and other popular E-R diagramming notations.

Many systems developers believe that data modeling is the most important part of the systems development process. This belief is based on three important reasons (Hoffer et al., 2005):

1. The characteristics of data captured during data modeling are crucial in the design of databases, programs, and other system components. The facts and rules captured during the process of data modeling are essential in assuring data integrity in an information system.

2. Data rather than processes are the most complex aspect of many modern information systems and hence require a central role in structuring system requirements. Often the goal is to provide a rich data resource that might support any type of information inquiry, analysis, and summary.

3. Data tend to be more stable than the business processes that use that data. Thus, an information system design that is based on a data orientation should have a longer useful life than one based on a process orientation.

In this chapter, we present the main features of E-R modeling, using common notation and conventions. We begin by defining the basic constructs of the E-R model: entities, attributes, and relationships. We define three types of entities that are common in E-R modeling: strong entities, weak entities, and associative entities; a few more entity types are defined in Chapter 4. We also define several important types of attributes, including required and optional attributes, single- and multivalued attributes, derived attributes, and composite attributes. We then introduce three important concepts associated with relationships: the degree of a relationship, the cardinality of a relationship, and participation constraints in a relationship. We conclude with an extended example of an E-R diagram for Pine Valley Furniture Company. We begin, however, with the core topic of data modeling—modeling the rules of the organization—which is the reason for entity-relationship diagramming.

MODELING THE RULES OF THE ORGANIZATION

We will see in this and the next chapter how to use data models, in particular the entity-relationship notation, to document rules and policies of an organization. *In fact, documenting rules and policies of an organization that govern data is exactly what data modeling is all about.* Business rules and policies govern creating, updating, and removing data in an information processing and storage system, thus they must be described along with the data to which they are related. For example, a policy that "every student in the university must have a faculty adviser" forces data (in a database) about each student to be associated with data about some student adviser. Also, the statement that "a student is any person who has applied for admission or taken a course or training program from any credit or noncredit unit of the university" not only defines the concept of "student," but also states a policy of the university (e.g., implicitly, alumni are students, and a high school student who attended a college fair but has not applied is not a student, assuming the college fair is not a noncredit training program).

Business rules and policies are not universal; different universities may have different policies for student advising and may include different types of people as students. Also, the rules and policies of an organization may change (usually slowly) over time; a university may decide that a student does not have to be assigned a faculty adviser until the student chooses a major.

Your job as a database analyst is to

- Identify and understand those rules *that govern data*
- Represent those rules so that they can be unambiguously understood by information systems developers and users
- Implement those rules in database technology

Data modeling is an important tool in this process. Because the purpose of data modeling is to document business rules about data, we introduce the discussion of data modeling and the entity-relationship notation with an overview of business rules. Data models cannot represent all business rules (and do not need to, because not all business rules govern data); data models along with associated documentation and other types of information system models (e.g., models that document the processing of data) represent all business rules that must be enforced through information systems.

Overview of Business Rules

A **business rule** is "a statement that defines or constrains some aspect of the business. It is intended to assert business structure or to control or influence the behavior of the business … rules prevent, cause, or suggest things to happen" (Guide Business

Business rule: A statement that defines or constrains some aspect of the business. It is intended to assert business structure or to control or influence the behavior of the business.

Rules Project, 1997). For example, the following two statements are common expressions of business rules that affect data processing and storage:

- "A student may register for a section of a course only if he or she has successfully completed the prerequisites for that course."
- "A preferred customer qualifies for a 10 percent discount, unless he has an overdue account balance."

Most organizations (and their employees) today are guided by thousands of combinations of such rules. In the aggregate, these rules influence behavior and determine how the organization responds to its environment (Gottesdiener, 1997). Capturing and documenting business rules is an important, complex task. Thoroughly capturing and structuring business rules, then enforcing them through database technologies, helps to ensure that information systems work right and that users of the information understand what they enter and see.

The Business Rules Paradigm   The concept of business rules has been used in information systems for some time. However, it has been more common (especially in the database world) to use the related term "integrity constraint" when referring to such rules. The intent of this term is somewhat more limited in scope, usually referring to maintaining valid data values and relationships in the database.

Today the term "business rules" has a much broader scope, so that it includes all rules (such as the two examples presented earlier) that have an impact on the databases in an organization (some refer to this broader scope as "standards and procedures"). In fact, a business rules approach has been advocated by a number of authors as a new paradigm for specifying information systems requirements (von Halle, 1997). This approach is based on the following premises:

- Business rules are a core concept in an enterprise because they are an expression of business policy and guide individual and aggregate behavior. Well-structured business rules can be stated in natural language for end users and in a data model for systems developers.
- Business rules can be expressed in terms that are familiar to end users. Thus, users can define and then maintain their own rules.
- Business rules are highly maintainable. They are stored in a central repository, and each rule is expressed only once, then shared throughout the organization. Each rule is discovered and documented only once, to be applied in all systems development projects.
- Enforcement of business rules can be automated through the use of software that can interpret the rules and enforce them using the integrity mechanisms of the database management system (Moriarty, 2000).

Although much progress has been made, the industry has not realized all of these objectives to date. Research and tools development is continuing, especially on automating business rules (Owen, 2004), and the business rules approach holds considerable promise for the future. Possibly the premise with greatest potential benefit is "Business rules are highly maintainable." The ability to specify and maintain the requirements for information systems as a set of rules has considerable power when coupled with an ability to generate automatically information systems from a repository of rules. Automatic generation and maintenance of systems will not only simplify the systems development process but also will improve the quality of systems.

Scope of Business Rules

In this and the next chapter, we are concerned with business rules that impact only an organization's databases. Most organizations have a host of rules and/or

Table 3-1 Characteristics of a Good Business Rule

Characteristic	Explanation
Declarative	A business rule is a statement of policy, not how policy is enforced or conducted; the rule does not describe a process or implementation, but rather describes what a process validates
Precise	With the related organization, the rule must have only one interpretation among all interested people, and its meaning must be clear
Atomic	A business rule marks one statement, not several; no part of the rule can stand on its own as a rule (that is, the rule is indivisible, yet sufficient)
Consistent	A business rule must be internally consistent (that is, not contain conflicting statements) and must be consistent with (and not contradict) other rules
Expressible	A business rule must be able to be stated in natural language, but it will be stated in a structured natural language so that there is no misinterpretation
Distinct	Business rules are not redundant, but a business rule may refer to other rules (especially refer to definitions)
Business-oriented	A business rule is stated in terms business people can understand, and since it is a statement of business policy, only business people can modify or invalidate a rule; thus, a business rule is owned by the business

Adapted from Gottesdiener (1999) and Plotkin (1999).

policies that fall outside this definition. For example, the rule "Friday is business casual dress day" may be an important policy statement, but it has no immediate impact on databases. In contrast, the rule "A student may register for a section of a course only if he or she has successfully completed the prerequisites for that course" is within our scope because it constrains the transactions that may be processed against the database. In particular, it causes any transaction to be rejected that attempts to register a student who does not have the necessary prerequisites. Some business rules cannot be represented in common data modeling notation; those rules that cannot be represented in a variation of an entity-relationship diagram are stated in natural language, and some can be represented in the relational data model, which we describe in Chapter 5.

Good Business Rules Whether stated in natural language, a structured data model, or other information systems documentation, a business rule will have certain characteristics if it is to be consistent with the premises outlined above. These characteristics are summarized in Table 3-1. These characteristics will have a better chance of being satisfied if a business rule is defined, approved, and owned by business, not technical, people. Business people become stewards of the business rules. You, as the database analyst, facilitate the surfacing of the rules and the transformation of ill-stated rules into ones that satisfy the desired characteristics.

Gathering Business Rules Business rules appear (possibly implicitly) in descriptions of business functions, events, policies, units, stakeholders, and other objects. These descriptions can be found in interview notes from individual and group information systems requirements collection sessions, organizational documents (e.g., personnel manuals, policies, contracts, marketing brochures, and technical instructions), and other sources. Rules are identified by asking questions about the who, what, when, where, why, and how of the organization. Usually, the data analyst has to be persistent in clarifying initial statements of rules because initial statements may be vague or imprecise (what some people have called "business ramblings"). Thus, precise rules are formulated from an iterative inquiry process. You should be prepared to ask such questions as "Is this always true," "Are there special circumstances when an alternative occurs," "Are there distinct kinds of that person,"

"Is there only one of those or are there many," and "Is there a need to keep a history of those, or is the current data all that is useful?" Such questions can be useful for surfacing rules for each type of data modeling construct we introduce in this and the subsequent chapter.

Data Names and Definitions

Fundamental to understanding and modeling data are naming and defining data objects. Data objects must be named and defined before they can be used unambiguously in a model of organizational data. In the entity-relationship notation you will learn in this chapter, you have to give entities, relationships, and attributes clear and distinct names and definitions.

Data Names   We will provide specific guidelines for naming entities, relationships, and attributes as we develop the entity-relationship data model, but there are some general guidelines about naming any data object. Data names should (Salin, 1990)

- *Relate to Business, not Technical (Hardware or Software) Characteristics;* so, Customer is a good name, but File10, Bit7, and PayrollReportSortKey are not good names.
- *Be Meaningful,* almost to the point of being self-documenting (i.e., the definition will refine and explain the name without having to state the essence of the object's meaning); you should avoid using generic words such as "has," "is," "person," or "it."
- *Be Unique* from the name used for every other distinct data object; words should be included in a data name if they distinguish the data object from other similar data objects (e.g., HomeAddress versus CampusAddress).
- *Be Readable,* so that the name is structured as the concept would most naturally be said (e.g., GradePointAverage is a good name, whereas AverageGradeRelativeToA, although possibly accurate, is an awkward name).
- *Be Composed of Words Taken from an Approved List;* each organization often chooses a vocabulary from which significant words in data names must be chosen (e.g., maximum is preferred, never upper limit, ceiling, or highest); alternative, or alias names, also can be used as can approved abbreviations (e.g., CUST for Customer), and you may be encouraged to use the abbreviations so that data names are short enough to meet maximum length limits of database technology.
- *Be Repeatable,* meaning that different people or the same person at different times should develop exactly or almost the same name; this often means that there is a standard hierarchy or pattern for names (e.g., the birth date of a student would be StudentBirthDate and the birth date of an employee would be EmployeeBirthDate).

Salin (1990) suggests that you develop data names by

1. Preparing a definition of the data (we talk about definitions next).
2. Removing insignificant or illegal words (words not on the approved list for names); note that the presence of AND and OR in the definition may imply that two or more data objects are combined, and you may want to separate the objects and assign different names.
3. Arranging the words in a meaningful, repeatable way.
4. Assigning a standard abbreviation for each word.
5. Determining whether the name already exists, and if so, adding other qualifiers that make the name unique.

We will see examples of good data names as we develop a data modeling notation in this chapter.

Data Definitions   A definition (sometimes called a structural assertion) is considered a type of business rule (GUIDE Business Rules Project, 1997). A definition is an explanation of a term or a fact. A **term** is a word or phrase that has a specific meaning for the business. Examples of terms are "course," "section," "rental car," "flight," "reservation," and "passenger." Terms are often the key words used to form data names. Terms must be defined carefully and concisely. However, there is no need to define common terms such as "day," "month," "person," or "television," because these terms are understood without ambiguity by most persons.

> **Term:** A word or phrase that has a specific meaning for the business.

A **fact** is an association between two or more terms. A fact is documented as a simple declarative statement that relates terms. Examples of facts that are definitions are the following (the defined terms are underlined):

> **Fact:** An association between two or more terms.

- "A <u>course</u> is a module of instruction in a particular subject area." This definition associates two terms: *module of instruction* and *subject area*. We assume that these are common terms that do not need to be further defined.

- "A <u>customer</u> may request a <u>model of car</u> from a <u>rental branch</u> on a particular <u>date</u>." This fact, which is a definition of *model rental request,* associates the four underlined terms (GUIDE Business Rules Project, 1997). Three of these terms are business-specific terms that would need to be defined individually (date is a common term).

A fact statement places no constraints on instances of the fact. For example, it is inappropriate in the second fact statement to add that a customer may not request two different car models on the same date. Such constraints are separate business rules.

Good Data Definitions   We will illustrate good definitions for entities, relationships, and attributes as we develop the entity-relationship notation in this and the next chapters. There are, however, some general guidelines to follow (Aranow, 1989).

- Definitions (and all types of business rules) are gathered from the same sources as all requirements for information systems. Thus, systems and data analysts should be looking for data objects and their definitions as these sources of information systems requirements are studied.

- Definitions will usually be accompanied by diagrams, such as entity-relationship diagrams. The definition does not need to repeat what is shown on the diagram, but rather supplement the diagram. A definition will state such characteristics of a data object as

  - Subtleties

  - Special or exceptional conditions

  - Examples

  - Where, when, and how the data are created or calculated in the organization

  - Whether the data are static or changes over time

  - Whether the data are singular or plural in its atomic form

  - Who determines the value for the data

  - Who owns the data (i.e., who controls the definition and usage)

  - Whether the data are optional or if empty (what we will call null) values are allowed

  - Whether the data can be broken down into more atomic parts or is often combined with other data into some more composite or aggregate form

If not included in a data definition, then these characteristics need to be documented elsewhere, where other metadata are stored.

- A data object should not be added to a data model, such as an entity-relationship diagram, until after it has been carefully defined (and named) and there is agreement on this definition. But, expect the definition of the data to change once you place the object on the diagram because the process of developing a data model tests your understanding of the meaning of data (in other words, *modeling data is an iterative process*).

There is an unattributed phrase in data modeling that highlights the importance of good data definitions. This phrase is "He who controls the meaning of data controls the data." It might seem that obtaining concurrence in an organization on the definitions to be used for the various terms and facts should be relatively easy. However, this is usually far from the case. In fact, it is likely to be one of the most difficult challenges you will face in data modeling or, for that matter, in any other endeavor. It is not unusual for an organization to have multiple definitions (perhaps a dozen or more) for common terms such as "customer" or "order."

To illustrate the problems inherent in developing definitions, consider a data object of Student found in a typical university. A sample definition for Student is "a person who has been admitted to the school and who has registered for at least one course during the past year." This definition is certain to be challenged, because it is probably too narrow. A person who is a student typically proceeds through several stages in relationship with the school, such as the following:

1. Prospect—some formal contact, indicating an interest in the school
2. Applicant—applies for admission
3. Admitted applicant—admitted to the school and perhaps to a degree program
4. Matriculated student—registers for at least one course
5. Continuing student—registers for courses on an ongoing basis (no substantial gaps)
6. Former student—fails to register for courses during some stipulated period (now may reapply)
7. Graduate—satisfactorily completes some degree program (now may apply for another program)

Imagine the difficulty of obtaining consensus on a single definition in this situation! It would seem you might consider three alternatives:

1. *Use Multiple Definitions to Cover the Various Situations.*   This is likely to be highly confusing if there is only one entity type, and is not recommended (multiple definitions are not good definitions). It might be possible to create multiple entity types, one for each student situation. However, because there is likely considerable similarity across the entity types, the fine distinctions between the entity types may be confusing, and the data model will show many constructs.

2. *Use a Very General Definition That Will Cover Most Situations.*   This approach may necessitate adding additional data about students to record a given student's actual status. For example, data for a student's status, with values of prospect, applicant, and so forth might be sufficient. On the other hand, if the same student could hold multiple statuses (e.g., prospect for one degree and matriculated for another degree), this may not work.

3. *Consider Using Multiple, But Related, Data Objects for Student.*   For example, we could create a general entity type for Student, and then other specific entity

types for kinds of students with unique characteristics. We describe the conditions that suggest this approach in Chapter 4.

THE E-R MODEL: AN OVERVIEW

An **entity-relationship model** (or E-R model) is a detailed, logical representation of the data for an organization or for a business area. The E-R model is expressed in terms of entities in the business environment, the relationships (or associations) among those entities, and the attributes (or properties) of both the entities and their relationships. An E-R model is normally expressed as an **entity-relationship diagram** (or E-R diagram, or simply ERD), which is a graphical representation of an E-R model.

Entity-relationship model (E-R model): A logical representation of the data for an organization or for a business area.

Entity-relationship diagram (E-R diagram or ERD): A graphical representation of an entity-relationship model.

Sample E-R Diagram

To jump-start your understanding of E-R diagrams, Figure 3-1 presents a simplified E-R diagram for a small furniture manufacturing company, Pine Valley Furniture (this figure, which does not include attributes, is often called an *enterprise data model*, which we introduced in prior chapters). This company can purchase items from a number of different suppliers, who then ship the items to the manufacturer. The items are assembled into products that are sold to customers who order the products. Each customer order may include one or more lines corresponding to the products appearing on that order.

The diagram in Figure 3-1 shows the entities and relationships for this company (attributes are omitted to simplify the diagram for now). Entities are represented by the rectangle symbol, whereas relationships between entities are represented by lines connecting the related entities. The entities in Figure 3-1 are:

- CUSTOMER A person or organization who has ordered or might order products. *Example:* L. L. Fish Furniture.

Figure 3-1
Sample E-R diagram

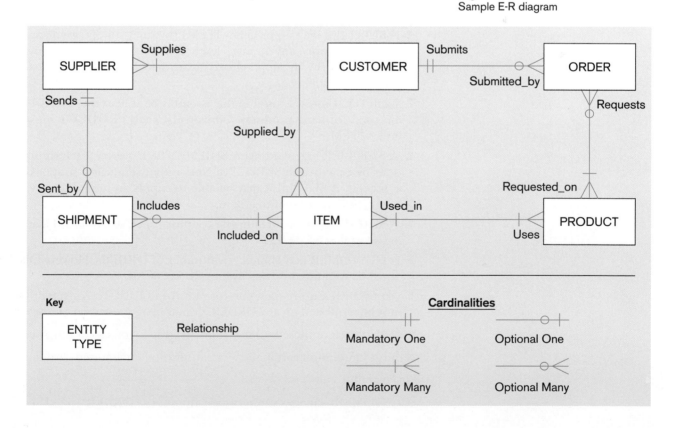

- PRODUCT A type of furniture made by Pine Valley Furniture that may be ordered by customers. Note that a product is not a specific bookcase, because individual bookcases do not need to be tracked. *Example*: A 6-foot, 5-shelf, oak bookcase called O600.

- ORDER The transaction associated with the sale of one or more products to a customer and identified by a transaction number from sales or accounting. *Example*: The event of L. L. Fish buying one product O600 and four products O623 on September 10, 2006.

- ITEM A type of component that goes into making one or more products and can be supplied by one or more suppliers. *Example*: A 4-inch, ball-bearing caster called I-27–4375.

- SUPPLIER Another company that may provide items to Pine Valley Furniture. *Example*: Sure Fasteners, Inc.

- SHIPMENT The transaction associated with items received in the same package by Pine Valley Furniture from a supplier. All items in a shipment appear on one bill-of-lading document. *Example*: The receipt of 300 I-27-4375 and 200 I-27-4380 items from Sure Fasteners, Inc. on September 9, 2006.

Note that it is important to clearly define, as metadata, each entity. For example, it is important to know that the CUSTOMER entity includes persons or organizations that have not yet purchased products from Pine Valley Furniture. It is common for different departments in an organization to have different meanings for the same term (homonyms). For example, Accounting may designate as customers only those persons or organizations who have ever made a purchase, thus excluding potential customers, whereas Marketing designates as customers anyone they have contacted or who has purchased from Pine Valley Furniture or any known competitor. An accurate and thorough ERD without clear metadata may be interpreted in different ways by different people.

The symbols at the end of each line on an ERD represent relationship cardinalities. On examining Figure 3-1, we can see that these cardinality symbols express the following business rules:

1. A SUPPLIER may supply many ITEMs (by "may supply" we mean the supplier may not supply any items). Each ITEM is supplied by any number of SUPPLIERs (by "is supplied" we mean that the item must be supplied by at least one supplier).

2. Each ITEM must be used in the assembly of at least one PRODUCT and may be used in many products. Conversely, each PRODUCT must use one or more ITEMs.

3. A SUPPLIER may send many SHIPMENTs. However, each shipment must be sent by exactly one SUPPLIER. Notice that sends and supplies are separate concepts. A SUPPLIER may be able to supply an item, but may not yet have sent any shipments of that item.

4. A SHIPMENT must include one (or more) ITEMs. An ITEM may be included on several SHIPMENTs.

5. A CUSTOMER may submit any number of ORDERs. However, each ORDER must be submitted by exactly one CUSTOMER.

6. An ORDER must request one (or more) PRODUCTs. A given PRODUCT may not be requested on any ORDER, or may be requested on one or more orders.

Note that each of these business rules roughly follows a certain grammar:

<entity> <minimum cardinality> <relationship> <maximum cardinality> <entity>

For example, rule 5 is:

<CUSTOMER> <may> <submit> <any number> <ORDER>

This grammar gives you a standard way to put each relationship into a natural English business rule statement.

E-R Model Notation

The notation we use for E-R diagrams is shown in Figure 3-2. As indicated in the previous section, there is no industry standard notation (in fact, you saw a slightly simpler notation in Chapters 1 and 2). The notation in Figure 3-2 combines most of the desirable features of the different notations that are commonly used in E-R drawing tools today and also allows us to model accurately most situations that are encountered in practice. We introduce additional notation for enhanced entity-relationship models (including class-subclass relationships) in Chapter 4.

In many situations, however, a simpler E-R notation is sufficient. Most drawing tools, either stand-alone ones such as Microsoft Visio or those in CASE tools such as Oracle Designer, All Fusion ERWin, or PowerDesigner, do not show all the entity and attribute types we use. It is important to note that any notation requires special annotations, not always present in a diagramming tool, to show all the business rules of the organizational situation you are modeling. We will use the Visio notation for a few examples throughout the chapter and at the end of the chapter so that you can see the differences. Appendix A illustrates the E-R notation from several commonly used guidelines and diagramming tools. This appendix may help you translate between the notations in the text and the notation you use in classes.

Figure 3-2
Basic E-R notation

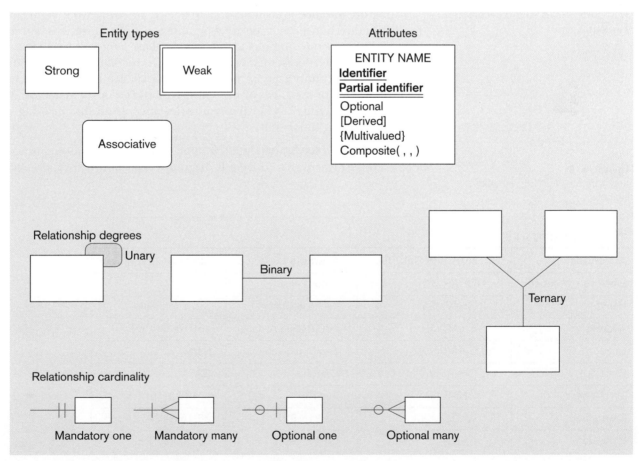

MODELING ENTITIES AND ATTRIBUTES

The basic constructs of the entity-relationship model are entities, relationships, and attributes. As shown in Figure 3-2, the model allows numerous variations for each of these constructs. The richness of the E-R model allows designers to model real-world situations accurately and expressively, which helps account for the popularity of the model.

Entities

Entity: A person, place, object, event, or concept in the user environment about which the organization wishes to maintain data.

An **entity** is a person, place, object, event, or concept in the user environment about which the organization wishes to maintain data. Thus, an entity has a noun name. Some examples of each of these *kinds* of entities follow:

Person:	EMPLOYEE, STUDENT, PATIENT
Place:	STORE, WAREHOUSE, STATE
Object:	MACHINE, BUILDING, AUTOMOBILE
Event:	SALE, REGISTRATION, RENEWAL
Concept:	ACCOUNT, COURSE, WORK CENTER

Entity type: A collection of entities that share common properties or characteristics.

Entity Type Versus Entity Instance   There is an important distinction between entity types and entity instances. An **entity type** is a collection of entities that share common properties or characteristics. Each entity type in an E-R model is given a name. Because the name represents a collection (or set) of items, it is always singular. We use capital letters for names of entity type(s). In an E-R diagram, the entity name is placed inside the box representing the entity type (see Figure 3-1).

Entity instance: A single occurrence of an entity type.

An **entity instance** is a single occurrence of an entity type. Figure 3-3 illustrates the distinction between an entity type and two of its instances. An entity type is described just once (using metadata) in a database, whereas many instances of that entity type may be represented by data stored in the database. For example, there is one EMPLOYEE entity type in most organizations, but there may be hundreds (or even thousands) of instances of this entity type stored in the database. We often use the single term "entity" rather than entity instance when the meaning is clear from the context of our discussion.

Entity Type Versus System Input, Output, or User   A common mistake made when people are just learning to draw E-R diagrams, especially if they already are familiar

Figure 3-3
Entity type EMPLOYEE with two instances

Entity type: EMPLOYEE			
Attributes	**Attribute Data Type**	**Example Instance**	**Example Instance**
Employee_Number	CHAR (10)	642-17-8360	534-10-1971
Name	CHAR (25)	Michelle Brady	David Johnson
Address	CHAR (30)	100 Pacific Avenue	450 Redwood Drive
City	CHAR (20)	San Francisco	Redwood City
State	CHAR (2)	CA	CA
Zip_Code	CHAR (9)	98173	97142
Date_Hired	DATE	03-21-1992	08-16-1994
Birth_Date	DATE	06-19-1968	09-04-1975

with data process modeling (such as data flow diagramming), is to confuse data entities with other elements of an overall information systems model. A simple rule to avoid such confusion is that a true data entity will have many possible instances, each with a distinguishing characteristic, as well as one or more other descriptive pieces of data.

Consider Figure 3-4a, which might be drawn to represent a database needed for a college sorority's expense system. (For simplicity in this and some figures, we show only one name for a relationship.) In this situation, the sorority treasurer manages accounts, receives expense reports, and records expense transactions against each account. However, do we need to keep track of data about the Treasurer (the TREASURER entity type) and her supervision of accounts (the Manages relationship) and receipt of reports (the Receives relationship)? The Treasurer is the person entering data about accounts and expenses and receiving expense reports. That is, she is a user of the database. Because there is only one Treasurer, TREASURER data do not need to be kept. Further, is the EXPENSE REPORT entity necessary? Because an expense report is computed from expense transactions and account balances, it is the result of extracting data from the database and received by the Treasurer. Even though there will be multiple instances of expense reports given to the Treasurer over time, data needed to compute the report contents each time are already represented by the ACCOUNT and EXPENSE entity types.

Another key to understanding why the ERD in Figure 3-4a might be in error is the nature of the *relationship names,* Receives and Summarizes. These relationship names refer to business activities that transfer or translate data, not to simply the association of one kind of data with another kind of data. The simple E-R diagram in Figure 3-4b shows entities and a relationship that would be sufficient to handle the sorority expense system as described here. See Problem and Exercise 23 for a variation on this situation.

Strong Versus Weak Entity Types   Most of the basic entity types to identify in an organization are classified as strong entity types. A **strong entity type** is one that exists independently of other entity types. Examples include STUDENT, EMPLOYEE, AUTOMOBILE, and COURSE. Instances of a strong entity type always have a unique

Strong entity type: An entity that exists independently of other entity types.

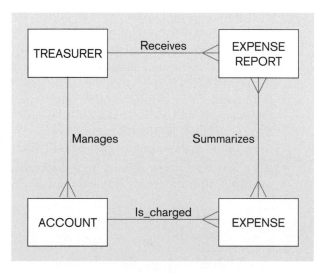

Figure 3-4
Example of inappropriate entities
(a) System user (Treasurer) and output (Expense Report) shown as entities

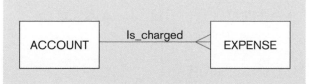

(b) E-R diagram with only the necessary entities

characteristic (called an *identifier*)—that is, an attribute or combination of attributes that uniquely distinguish each occurrence of that entity.

Weak entity type: An entity type whose existence depends on some other entity type.

Identifying owner (owner): The entity type on which the weak entity type depends.

In contrast, a **weak entity type** is an entity type whose existence depends on some other entity type. A weak entity type has no business meaning in an E-R diagram without the entity on which it depends. The entity type on which the weak entity type depends is called the **identifying owner** (or simply owner for short). A weak entity type does not have its own identifier. Generally, on an E-R diagram, a weak entity type has an attribute that serves as a *partial* identifier. During a later design stage (described in Chapter 5), a full identifier will be formed for the weak entity by combining the partial identifier with the identifier of its owner.

An example of a weak entity type with an identifying relationship is shown in Figure 3-5a. EMPLOYEE is a strong entity type with identifier Employee_ID (we note the identifier attribute by underlining it). DEPENDENT is a weak entity type, as indicated by the double-lined rectangle. The relationship between a weak entity type and its owner is called an **identifying relationship**. In Figure 3-5, "Carries" is the identifying relationship (indicated by the double-line). The attribute Dependent_Name serves as a *partial* identifier (Dependent_Name is a composite attribute that can be broken into component parts, as we describe later). We use a double underline to indicate a partial identifier. During a later design stage, Dependent_Name will be combined with Employee_ID (the identifier of the owner) to form a full identifier for DEPENDENT.

Identifying relationship: The relationship between a weak entity type and its owner.

Naming and Defining Entity Types   In addition to the general guidelines for naming and defining data objects, there are a few special guidelines for *naming* entity types, which follow:

- An entity type name is a *singular noun* (such as CUSTOMER, STUDENT, or AUTOMOBILE); an entity is a person, place, object, event, or concept and the name is for the entity type, which represents a set of entity instances (i.e., STUDENT represents students Hank Finley, Jean Krebs, and so forth). It is common to also specify the plural form (possibly in a CASE tool repository accompanying the E-R diagram), because sometimes the E-R diagram is read best by using plurals. For example, in Figure 3-1, we would say that a SUPPLIER may supply ITEMs. Because plurals are not always formed by adding an "s" to the singular noun, it is best to document the exact plural form.

- An entity type name should be *specific to the organization*. Thus, one organization may use the entity type name CUSTOMER and another organization may use the term CLIENT. The name should be descriptive for everyone in the organization and distinct from all other entity type names within that organization. For example, a PURCHASE ORDER for orders placed with suppliers is distinct from CUSTOMER ORDER for orders placed with us by our customers. Both of these entity types cannot be named ORDER.

- An entity type name should be *concise*, using as few words as possible. For example, in a university database, an entity type REGISTRATION for the

Figure 3-5
Example of a weak entity and its identifying relationship

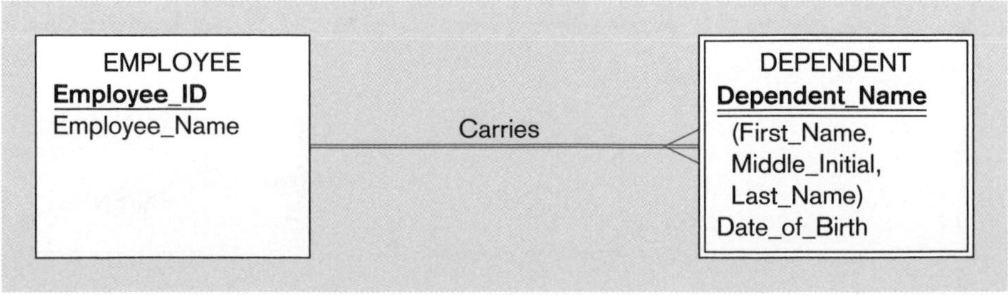

event of a student registering for a class is probably a sufficient name for this entity type; STUDENT REGISTRATION FOR CLASS, although precise, is probably too wordy because the reader will understand REGISTRATION from its use with other entity types.

- An *abbreviation or short name* should be specified for each entity type name, and the abbreviation may be sufficient to use in the E-R diagram; abbreviations must follow all of the same rules as do the full entity names.

- *Event entity types* should be named for the result of the event, not the activity or process of the event. For example, the event of a project manager assigning an employee to work on a project results in an ASSIGNMENT, and the event of a student contacting his or her faculty adviser seeking some information is a CONTACT.

- The *name* used for the same entity type *should be the same* on all E-R diagrams on which the entity type appears. Thus, as well as being specific to the organization, the name used for an entity type should be a standard, adopted by the organization for all references to the same kind of data. However, some entity types will have aliases, or alternative names, which are synonyms used in different parts of the organization. For example, the entity type ITEM may have aliases of MATERIAL (for production) and DRAWING (for engineering). Aliases are specified in documentation about the database, such as the repository of a CASE tool.

There are also some specific guidelines for *defining* entity types, which follow:

- An entity type definition usually *starts with* "An X is …". This is the most direct and clear way to state the meaning of an entity type.

- An entity type definition should include a statement of *what the unique characteristic is for each instance* of the entity type. In many cases, stating the identifier for an entity type helps to convey the meaning of the entity. For example, for Figure 3-4b, "An expense is a payment of the purchase of some good or service. An expense is identified by a journal entry number."

- An entity type definition should make it clear what *entity instances are included and not included* in the entity type; often, it is necessary to list the kinds of entities that are excluded. For example, "A customer is a person or organization that has placed an order for a product from us or one that we have contacted to advertise or promote our products. A customer does not include persons or organizations that buy our products only through our customers, distributors, or agents."

- An entity type definition often includes a description of *when an instance of the entity type is created and deleted*. For example, in the previous bullet point, a customer instance is implicitly created when the person or organization places its first order; because this definition does not specify otherwise, implicitly a customer instance is never deleted, or it is deleted based on general rules that are specified about the purging of data from the database. A statement about when to delete an entity instance is sometimes referred to as the retention of the entity type. A possible deletion statement for a customer entity type definition might be "A customer ceases to be a customer if it has not placed an order for more than 3 years."

- For some entity types, the definition must specify *when an instance might change into an instance of another entity type*. For example, consider the situation of a construction company for which bids accepted by potential customers become contracts. In this case, a bid might be defined by "A bid is a legal offer by our organization to do work for a customer. A bid is created when an officer of our company signs the bid document; a bid becomes an instance of contract when we receive a copy of the bid signed by an officer of the customer." This definition is also a good example to note how one definition can use other entity type names (in this case, the definition of bid uses the entity type name Customer).

- For some entity types, the definition must specify *what history is to be kept about instances of the entity type.* For example, the characteristics of an ITEM in Figure 3-1 may change over time, and we may need to keep a complete history of the individual values and when they were in effect. As we will see in some examples later, such statements about keeping history may have ramifications about how we represent the entity type on an E-R diagram and eventually how we store data for the entity instances.

Attributes

Attribute: A property or characteristic of an entity or relationship type that is of interest to the organization.

Each entity type has a set of attributes associated with it. An **attribute** is a property or characteristic of an entity type that is of interest to the organization (later we will see that some types of relationships may also have attributes). Thus, an attribute has a noun name. Following are some typical entity types and their associated attributes:

STUDENT	Student_ID, Student_Name, Home_Address, Phone_Number, Major
AUTOMOBILE	Vehicle_ID, Color, Weight, Horsepower
EMPLOYEE	Employee_ID, Employee_Name, Payroll_Address, Skill

In naming attributes, we use an initial capital letter followed by lowercase letters. If an attribute name consists of two words, we use an underscore character to connect the words and we start each word with a capital letter; for example: Employee_Name. In E-R diagrams, we represent an attribute by placing its name in the entity it describes. Attributes may also be associated with relationships, as described later. Note that an attribute is associated with exactly one entity or relationship.

Notice in Figure 3-5 that all of the attributes of DEPENDENT are characteristics only of an employee's dependent, not characteristics of an employee. In traditional E-R notation, an entity type (not just weak entities but any entity) does not include attributes of entities to which it is related (what might be called foreign attributes). For example, DEPENDENT does not include any attribute that indicates to which employee this dependent is associated. This nonredundant feature of the E-R data model is consistent with the shared data property of databases. Because of relationships, which we discuss shortly, someone accessing data from a database will be able to associate attributes from related entities (e.g., show on a display screen a Dependent_Name and the associated Employee_Name).

Required attribute: An attribute that must have a value for every entity (or relationship) instance.

Optional attribute: An attribute that may not have a value for every entity (or relationship) instance.

Required Versus Optional Attributes   Each entity (or instance of an entity type) potentially has a value associated with each of the attributes of that entity type. An attribute that must be present for each entity instance is called a **required attribute**, whereas an attribute that may not have a value is called an **optional attribute**. For example, Figure 3-6 shows two STUDENT entities (instances) with their respective attribute values. The only optional attribute for STUDENT is Major. (Some students, specifically Melissa Kraft in this example, have not chosen a major yet.) However, every student must, by the rules of the organization, have values for all the other attributes. In various E-R diagramming notations, a symbol might appear in front of each attribute to indicate if it is required (e.g., "*") or optional ("o") or required attributes will be in boldface, whereas optional attributes will be in normal font (the format we use in this text); in many cases, required or optional is indicated within supplemental documentation. Later in Chapter 4 when we consider entity

Entity type: STUDENT				
Attributes	**Attribute Data Type**	**Required or Optional**	**Example Instance**	**Example Instance**
Student_ID	CHAR (10)	Required	876-24-8217	822-24-4456
Student_Name	CHAR (40)	Required	Michael Grant	Melissa Kraft
Home_Address	CHAR (30)	Required	314 Baker St.	1422 Heft Ave
Home_City	CHAR (20)	Required	Centerville	Miami
Home_State	CHAR (2)	Required	OH	FL
Home_Zip_Code	CHAR (9)	Required	45459	33321
Major	CHAR (3)	Optional	MIS	

Figure 3-6
Entity type STUDENT with required and optional attributes

supertypes and subtypes, we will see how sometimes optional attributes imply that there are different types of entities. (For example, we may want to consider students who have not declared a major as a subtype of the student entity type.) A database is, in essence, the collection of all of these attribute values for all of the entities; an attribute without a value is said to be null. Thus, each entity has an identifying attribute, which we discuss in a subsequent section, plus one or more other attributes. If you try to create an entity that has only an identifier, that entity is likely not legitimate. Such a data structure may simply hold a list of legal values for some attribute, which is better kept outside the database.

Simple Versus Composite Attributes   Some attributes can be broken down into meaningful component, detailed parts. A common example is Name, which we saw in Figure 3-5 ; another is an employee's Address, which can usually be broken down into the following components: Street_Address, City, State, and Postal_Code. A **composite attribute** is an attribute, such as Address, that has meaningful component parts. Figure 3-7 shows the notation that we use for composite attributes applied to this example. Most drawing tools do not have a notation for composite attributes, so you simply list all the component parts.

Composite attribute: An attribute that has meaningful component parts.

Composite attributes provide considerable flexibility to users, who can either refer to the composite attribute as a single unit or else refer to individual components of that attribute. Thus, for example, a user can either refer to Address or refer to one of its components, such as Street_Address. The decision whether to subdivide an attribute into its component parts depends on whether users will need to refer to those individual components, and hence, they have organizational meaning. Of course, the designer must always attempt to anticipate possible future usage patterns for the database.

A **simple (or atomic) attribute** is an attribute that cannot be broken down into smaller components that are meaningful for the organization. For example, all of the attributes associated with AUTOMOBILE are simple: Vehicle_ID, Color, Weight, and Horsepower.

Simple (or atomic) attribute: An attribute that cannot be broken down into smaller components that are meaningful to the organization.

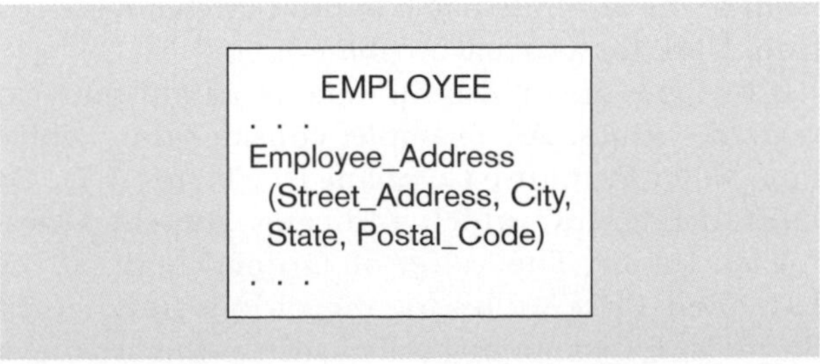

Figure 3-7
A composite attribute

```
          EMPLOYEE
         . . .
       Employee_Address
        (Street_Address, City,
         State, Postal_Code)
         . . .
```

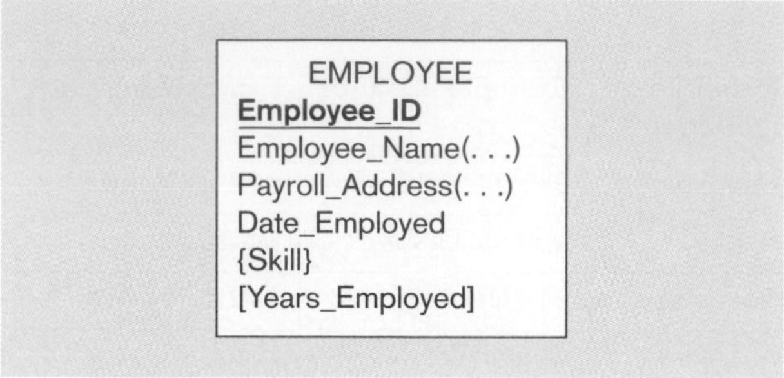

Figure 3-8
Entity with multivalued attribute (Skill)
and derived attribute (Years_Employed)

```
        ┌─────────────────────────────┐
        │        EMPLOYEE             │
        │   **Employee_ID**          │
        │   Employee_Name(. . .)     │
        │   Payroll_Address(. . .)   │
        │   Date_Employed            │
        │   {Skill}                  │
        │   [Years_Employed]         │
        └─────────────────────────────┘
```

Multivalued attribute: An attribute that may take on more than one value for a given entity (or relationship) instance.

Single-Valued Versus Multivalued Attributes   Figure 3-6 shows two entity instances with their respective attribute values. For each entity instance, each of the attributes in the figure has one value. It frequently happens that there is an attribute that may have more than one value for a given instance. For example, the EMPLOYEE entity type in Figure 3-8 has an attribute named Skill, whose values record the skill (or skills) for that employee. Of course, some employees may have more than one skill, such as PHP Programmer and C++ Programmer. A **multivalued attribute** is an attribute that may take on more than one value for a given entity (or relationship) instance. In this text we indicate a multivalued attribute with curly brackets around the attribute name, as shown for the Skill attribute in the EMPLOYEE example in Figure 3-8. In Microsoft Visio, once an attribute is placed in an entity, you can edit that attribute (column), select the Collection tab, and choose one of the options (typically, MultiSet will be your choice, but one of the other options may be more appropriate for a given situation). Other E-R diagramming tools may use an '*' after the attribute name, or you may have to use supplemental documentation to specify a multivalued attribute.

Multivalued and composite are different concepts, although beginner data modelers often confuse these terms. Skill, a multivalued attribute, may occur multiple times for each employee; Employee_Name and Payroll_Address are both likely composite attributes, each of which occurs once for each employee, but which have component, more atomic attributes, which are not shown in Figure 3-8 for simplicity. See Problem and Exercise 22 to review the concepts of composite and multivalued attributes.

Derived attribute: An attribute whose values can be calculated from related attribute values.

Stored Versus Derived Attributes   Some attribute values that are of interest to users can be calculated or derived from other related attribute values that are stored in the database. For example, suppose that for an organization, the EMPLOYEE entity type has a Date_Employed attribute. If users need to know how many years a person has been employed, that value can be calculated using Date_Employed and today's date. A **derived attribute** is an attribute whose values can be calculated from related attribute values (plus possibly data not in the database, such as today's date, the current time, or a security code provided by a system user). We indicate a derived attribute in an E-R diagram by using square brackets around the attribute name, as shown in Figure 3-8 for the Years_Employed attribute. Some E-R diagramming tools use a notation of a forward slash ('/') in front of the attribute name to indicate that it is derived. (This notation is borrowed from UML for a virtual attribute.)

In some situations, the value of an attribute can be derived from attributes in related entities. For example, consider the invoice created for each customer at Pine Valley Furniture Company (see Figure 1-7). Order_Total is an attribute of the INVOICE entity, which indicates the total dollar amount that is billed to the customer. The value of Order_Total can be computed by summing the Extended_Price values for the various line items that are billed on the invoice. Formulas for computing values such as this are one type of business rule.

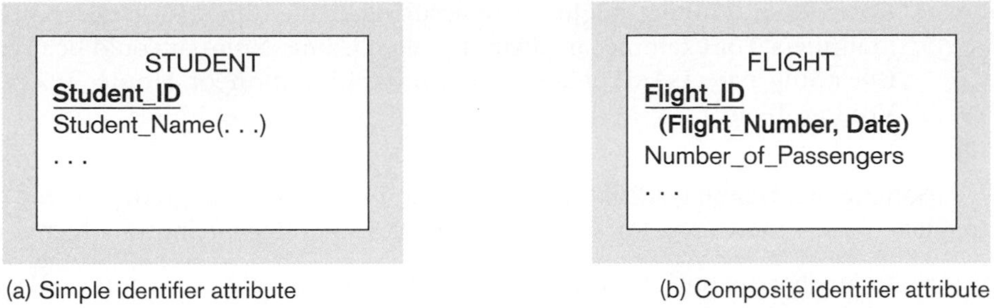

```
┌─────────────────────────────┐          ┌─────────────────────────────┐
│          STUDENT            │          │           FLIGHT            │
│  Student_ID                 │          │  Flight_ID                  │
│  Student_Name(. . .)        │          │  (Flight_Number, Date)      │
│  . . .                      │          │  Number_of_Passengers       │
│                             │          │  . . .                      │
└─────────────────────────────┘          └─────────────────────────────┘
```

(a) Simple identifier attribute   (b) Composite identifier attribute

Figure 3-9
Simple and composite identifier attributes

Identifier Attribute   An **identifier** is an attribute (or combination of attributes) that distinguishes individual instances of an entity type. That is, no two instances of the entity type may have the same value for the identifier attribute. The identifier for the STUDENT entity type introduced earlier is Student_ID, whereas the identifier for AUTOMOBILE is Vehicle_ID. Notice that an attribute such as Student_Name is not a candidate identifier, because many students may potentially have the same name, and students, like all people, can change their names. To be a candidate identifier, each entity instance must have a single value for the attribute and the attribute must be associated with the entity. We underline identifier names on the E-R diagram, as shown in the STUDENT entity type example in Figure 3-9a. To be an identifier, the attributed is also required (so the distinguishing value must exist), so an identifier is also in bold.

For some entity types, there is no single (or atomic) attribute that can serve as the identifier (i.e., that will ensure uniqueness). However, two (or more) attributes used in combination may serve as the identifier. A **composite identifier** is an identifier that consists of a composite attribute. Figure 3-9b shows the entity FLIGHT with the composite identifier Flight_ID. Flight_ID in turn has component attributes Flight_Number and Date. This combination is required to identify uniquely individual occurrences of FLIGHT. We use the convention that the composite attribute (Flight_ID) is underlined to indicate it is the identifier, while the component attributes are not underlined. Some data modelers think of a composite identifier as "breaking a tie" created by a simple identifier. Even with Flight_ID, a data modeler would ask a question, such as "Can two flights with the same number occur on the same date?" If so, yet another attribute is needed to form the composite identifier and to break the tie.

Some entities may have more than one candidate identifier. If there is more than one candidate identifier, the designer must choose one of them as the identifier. Bruce (1992) suggests the following criteria for selecting identifiers:

1. Choose an identifier that will not change its value over the life of each instance of the entity type. For example, the combination of Employee_Name and Payroll_ Address (even if unique) would be a poor choice as an identifier for EMPLOYEE because the values of Employee_Name and Payroll_Address could easily change during an employee's term of employment.

2. Choose an identifier such that for each instance of the entity, the attribute is guaranteed to have valid values and not be null (or unknown). If the identifier is a composite attribute, such as Flight_ID in Figure 3-9b, make sure that all parts of the identifier will have valid values.

3. Avoid the use of so-called intelligent identifiers (or keys), whose structure indicates classifications, locations, and so on. For example, the first two digits of an identifier may indicate the warehouse location. Such codes are often changed as conditions change, which renders the identifier values invalid.

Identifier: An attribute (or combination of attributes) that uniquely distinguishes individual instances of an entity type.

Composite identifier: An identifier that consists of a composite attribute.

4. Consider substituting single-attribute surrogate identifiers for large composite identifiers. For example, an attribute called Game_Number could be used for the entity type GAME instead of the combination of Home_Team and Visiting_Team.

Naming and Defining Attributes In addition to the general guidelines for naming data objects, there are a few special guidelines for naming attributes, which follow:

- An attribute name is a *singular noun or noun phrase* (such as Customer_ID, Age, Product_Minimum_Price, or Major). Attributes, which materialize as data values, are concepts or physical characteristics of entities. Concepts and physical characteristics are described by nouns.

- An attribute name should be *unique*. No two attributes of the same entity type may have the same name, and it is desirable, for clarity purposes, that no two attributes across all entity types have the same name.

- To make an attribute name unique and for clarity purposes, *each attribute name should follow a standard format*. For example, your university may establish Student_GPA, as opposed to GPA_of_Student, as an example of the standard format for attribute naming. The format to be used will be established by each organization. A common format is: [Entity type name{[_Qualifier]}_]Class, where [...] is an optional clause, and {...} indicates that the clause may repeat. *Entity type name* is the name of the entity with which the attribute is associated. The entity type name may be used to make the attribute name explicit. It is almost always used for the identifier attribute (e.g., Customer_ID) of each entity type. *Class* is a phrase from a list of phrases defined by the organization that are the permissible characteristics of entities (or abbreviations of these characteristics). For example, permissible values (and associated approved abbreviations) for Class might be Name (Nm), Identifier (ID), Date (Dt), or Amount (Amt). Class is, obviously, required. *Qualifier* is a phrase from a list of phrases defined by the organization that are used to place constraints on classes. One or more qualifiers may be needed to make each attribute of an entity type unique. For example, a qualifier might be Maximum (Max), Hourly (Hrly), or State (St). A qualifier may not be necessary: Employee_Age and Student_Major are both fully explicit attribute names. Sometimes a qualifier is necessary. For example, Employee_Birth_Date and Employee_Hire_Date are two attributes of Employee that require one qualifier. More than one qualifier may be necessary. For example, Employee_Residence_City_Name (or Emp_Res_Cty_Nm) is the name of an employee's city of residence, and Employee_Tax_City_Name (or Emp_Tax_Cty_Nm) is the name of the city in which an employee pays city taxes.

- *Similar attributes* of different entity types *should use the same qualifiers and classes*, as long as those are the names used in the organization. For example, the city of residence for faculty and students should be, respectively, Faculty_Residence_City_Name and Student_Residence_City_Name. Using similar names makes it easier for users to understand that values for these attributes come from the same possible set of values, what we will call *domains*. Users may want to take advantage of common domains in queries (e.g., find students who live in the same city as their adviser), and it will be easier for users to recognize that such a matching may be possible if the same qualifier and class phrases are used.

There are also some specific guidelines for defining attributes, which follow:

- An attribute definition states *what the attribute is and possibly why it is important*. The definition will often parallel the attribute's name; for example,

Student_Residence_City_Name could be defined as "The name of the city in which a student maintains his or her permanent residence."

- An attribute definition should make it clear *what is included and not included* in the attribute's value; for example, "Employee_Monthly_Salary_Amount is the amount of money paid each month in the currency of the country of residence of the employee exclusive of any benefits, bonuses, reimbursements, or special payments."

- Any *aliases*, or alternative names, for the attribute can be specified in the definition, or may be included elsewhere in documentation about the attribute, possibly stored in the repository of a CASE tool used to maintain data definitions.

- It may also be desirable to state in the definition *the source of values for the attribute*. Stating the source may make the meaning of the data clearer. For example, "Customer_Standard_Industrial_Code is an indication of the type of business for the customer. Values for this code come from a standard set of values provided by the Federal Trade Commission and are found on a CD we purchase named SIC provided annually by the FTC."

- An attribute definition (or other specification in a CASE tool repository) also should indicate *if a value for the attribute is required or optional*. This business rule about an attribute is important for maintaining data integrity. The identifier attribute of an entity type is, by definition, required. If an attribute value is required, then to create an instance of the entity type, a value of this attribute must be provided. Required means that an entity instance must always have a value for this attribute, not just when an instance is created. Optional means that a value may not exist for an instance of an entity instance to be stored. Optional can be further qualified by stating whether once a value is entered, a value must always exist. For example, "Employee_Department_ID is the identifier of the department to which the employee is assigned. An employee may not be assigned to a department when hired (so this attribute is initially optional), but once an employee is assigned to a department, the employee must always be assigned to some department."

- An attribute definition (or other specification in a CASE tool repository) may also indicate *whether a value for the attribute may change* once a value is provided and before the entity instance is deleted. This business rule also controls data integrity. Nonintelligent identifiers may not change values over time. To assign a new nonintelligent identifier to an entity instance, that instance must first be deleted and then recreated.

- For a multivalued attribute, the attribute definition should indicate *the maximum and minimum number of occurrences of an attribute value for an entity instance*. For example, "Employee_Skill_Name is the name of a skill an employee possesses. Each employee must possess at least one skill, and an employee can choose to list at most ten skills." The reason for a multivalued attribute may be that a history of the attribute needs to be kept. For example, "Employee_Yearly_Absent_Days_Number is the number of days in a calendar year the employee has been absent from work. An employee is considered absent if he or she works less than 50 percent of the scheduled hours in the day. A value for this attribute should be kept for each year in which the employee works for our company."

- An attribute definition may also indicate *any relationships that attribute has with other attributes*. For example, "Employee_Vacation_Days_Number is the number of days of paid vacation for the employee. If the employee has a value of 'Exempt' for Employee_Type, then the maximum value for

Employee_Vacation_Days_Number is determined by a formula involving the number of years of service for the employee."

MODELING RELATIONSHIPS

Relationships are the glue that holds together the various components of an E-R model. Intuitively, a *relationship* is an association representing an interaction among the instances of one or more entity types that is of interest to the organization. Thus, a relationship has a verb phrase name. But to understand this definition more clearly, we must distinguish between relationship types and relationship instances. To illustrate, consider the entity types EMPLOYEE and COURSE, where COURSE represents training courses that may be taken by employees. To track courses that have been completed by particular employees, we define a relationship called Completes between the two entity types (see Figure 3-10a). This is a many-to-many relationship, because each employee may complete any number of courses, whereas a given course may be completed by any number of employees. For example, in Figure 3-10b, the employee Melton has completed three courses (C++, COBOL, and Perl). The SQL course has been completed by two employees (Celko and Gosling).

In this example, there are two entity types (EMPLOYEE and COURSE) that participate in the relationship named Completes. In general, any number of entity types (from one to many) may participate in a relationship.

We frequently use in this and subsequent chapters the convention of a single verb phrase label to represent a relationship. Because relationships often occur due to an organizational event, entity instances are related because an action was taken;

Figure 3-10
Relationship type and instances
(a) Relationship type (Completes)

(b) Relationship instances

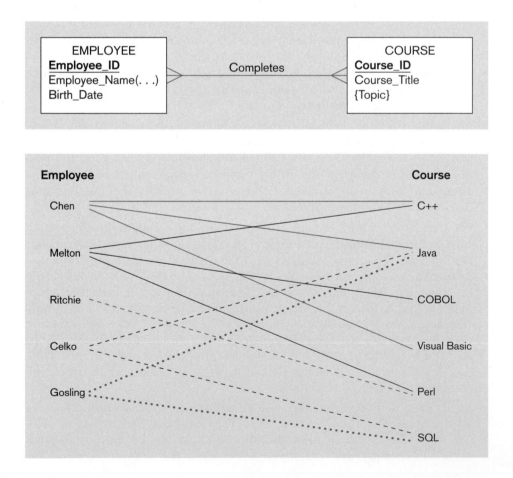

thus a verb phrase is appropriate for the label. This verb phrase should be in the present tense and descriptive. There are, however, many ways to represent a relationship. Some data modelers prefer the format with two relationship names. One or two verb phrases have the same structural meaning, so you may use either format as long as the meaning of the relationship in each direction is clear.

Basic Concepts and Definitions in Relationships

A **relationship type** is a meaningful association between (or among) entity types. The phrase "meaningful association" implies that the relationship allows us to answer questions that could not be answered given only the entity types. A relationship type is denoted by a line labeled with the name of the relationship, as in the example shown in Figure 3-10a, or with two names, as in Figure 3-1. We suggest you use a short, descriptive verb phrase that is meaningful to the user in naming the relationship. (We say more about naming and defining relationships later in this section.)

> **Relationship type:** A meaningful association between (or among) entity types.

A **relationship instance** is an association between (or among) entity instances, where each relationship instance includes exactly one entity from each participating entity type (Elmasri and Navathe, 1994). For example, in Figure 3-10b, each line in the figure represents a relationship instance between one employee and one course, indicating that the employee has completed that course.

> **Relationship instance:** An association between (or among) entity instances where each relationship instance includes exactly one entity from each participating entity type.

Attributes on Relationships Attributes may be associated with a many-to-many (or one-to-one) relationship, as well as with an entity. For example, suppose the organization wishes to record the date (month and year) when an employee completes each course. This attribute is named Date_Completed. For some sample data, see Table 3-2.

Where should the attribute Date_Completed be placed on the E-R diagram? Referring to Figure 3-10a, you will notice that Date_Completed has not been associated with either the EMPLOYEE or COURSE entity. That is because Date_Completed is a property of the relationship Completes, rather than a property of either entity. In other words, for each instance of the relationship Completes, there is a value for Date_Completed. One such instance (for example) shows that the employee named Melton completed the course titled C++ on 06/2005.

A revised version of the ERD for this example is shown in Figure 3-11a. In this diagram, the attribute Date_Completed is in a rectangle connected to the Completes relationship line. Other attributes might be added to this relationship if appropriate, such as Course_Grade, Instructor, and Room_Location.

Associative Entities The presence of one or more attributes on a relationship suggests to the designer that the relationship should perhaps instead be represented as an entity type. To emphasize this point, most E-R drawing tools require that such

Table 3-2   Instances Showing Date_Completed

Employee_Name	Course_Title	Date_Completed
Chen	C++	06/2005
Chen	Java	09/2005
Chen	Visual Basic	10/2005
Melton	C++	06/2005
Melton	COBOL	02/2006
Melton	SQL	03/2005
Ritchie	Perl	11/2005
Celko	Java	03/2005
Celko	SQL	03/2006
Gosling	Java	09/2005
Gosling	Perl	06/2005

Figure 3-11
An associative entity
(a) Attribute on a relationship

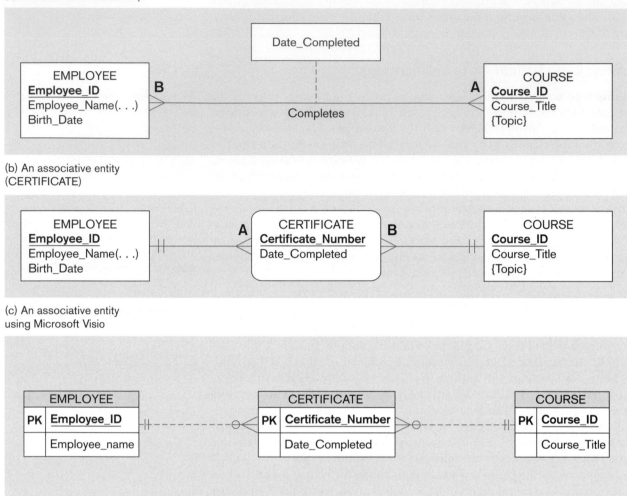

(b) An associative entity
(CERTIFICATE)

(c) An associative entity
using Microsoft Visio

Associative entity: An entity type that associates the instances of one or more entity types and contains attributes that are peculiar to the relationship between those entity instances.

attributes be placed in an entity type. An **associative entity** is an entity type that associates the instances of one or more entity types and contains attributes that are peculiar to the relationship between those entity instances. The associative entity CERTIFICATE is represented with the rectangle with rounded corners, as shown in Figure 3-11b. Most E-R drawing tools do not have a special symbol for an associative entity. Associative entities are sometimes referred to as gerunds, because the relationship name (a verb) is usually converted to an entity name that is a noun. Note in Figure 3-11b that there are no relationship names on the lines between an associative entity and a strong entity. This is because the associative entity represents the relationship. Figure 3-11c shows how associative entities are drawn using Microsoft Visio, which is representative of tools that do not use diamonds for relationships and do not allow attributes on relationships. The relationship lines are dashed because CERTIFICATE does not include the identifiers of the related entities in its identifier. (Certificate_Number is sufficient.)

How do you know whether or not to convert a relationship to an associative entity type? Following are four conditions that should exist:

1. All of the relationships for the participating entity types are "many" relationships.
2. The resulting associative entity type has independent meaning to end users and, preferably, can be identified with a single-attribute identifier.

3. The associative entity has one or more attributes in addition to the identifier.

4. The associative entity participates in one or more relationships independent of the entities related in the associated relationship.

Figure 3-11b shows the relationship Completes converted to an associative entity type. In this case, the training department for the company has decided to award a certificate to each employee who completes a course. Thus, the entity is named CERTIFICATE, which certainly has independent meaning to end users. Also, each certificate has a number (Certificate_Number) that serves as the identifier. The attribute Date_Completed is also included. Note also in Figure 3-11b and the Visio version of Figure 3-11c that both EMPLOYEE and COURSE are mandatory participants in the two relationships with CERTIFICATE. This is exactly what occurs when you have to represent a many-to-many relationship (Completes in Figure 3-11a) as two one-to-many relationships (the ones associated with CERTIFICATE in Figures 3-11b and 3-11c).

Notice that converting a relationship to an associative entity has caused the relationship notation to move. That is, the "many" cardinality now terminates at the associative entity, rather than at each participating entity type. In Figure 3-11, this shows that an employee, who may complete one or more courses (notation A in Figure 3-11a), may be awarded more than one certificate (notation A in Figure 3-11b); and that a course, which may have one or more employees complete it (notation B in Figure 3-11a), may have many certificates awarded (notation B in Figure 3-11b). See Problem and Exercise 21 for an interesting variation on Figure 3-11a, which emphasizes the rules for when to convert a many-to-many relationship, such as Completes, into an associative entity.

Degree of a Relationship

The **degree** of a relationship is the number of entity types that participate in that relationship. Thus, the relationship Completes in Figure 3-11 is of degree 2, because there are two entity types: EMPLOYEE and COURSE. The three most common relationship degrees in E-R models are unary (degree 1), binary (degree 2), and ternary (degree 3). Higher-degree relationships are possible, but they are rarely encountered in practice, so we restrict our discussion to these three cases. Examples of unary, binary, and ternary relationships appear in Figure 3-12. (Attributes are not shown in some figures for simplicity.)

Degree: The number of entity types that participate in a relationship.

As you look at Figure 3-12, understand that any particular data model represents a specific situation, not a generalization. For example, consider the Manages relationship in Figure 3-12a. In some organizations, it may be possible for one employee to be managed by many other employees (e.g., in a matrix organization). It is important when you develop an E-R model that you understand the business rules of the particular organization you are modeling.

Unary Relationship A **unary relationship** is a relationship between the instances of a *single* entity type. (Unary relationships are also called *recursive* relationships.) Two examples are shown in Figure 3-12a. In the first example, "Is_married_to" is shown as a one-to-one relationship between instances of the PERSON entity type. Because this is a one-to-one relationship, this notation indicates that only the current marriage, if one exists, needs to be kept about a person. In the second example, "Manages" is shown as a one-to-many relationship between instances of the EMPLOYEE entity type. Using this relationship, we could identify (for example) the employees who report to a particular manager. The third example is one case of using a unary relationship to represent a sequence, cycle, or priority list. In this example, sports teams are related by their standing in their league (the Stands_after relationship). (Note: In these examples, we ignore whether these are mandatory- or optional-cardinality relationships or whether the same entity instance can repeat in the same relationship instance; we will introduce mandatory and optional cardinality in a later section of this chapter.)

Unary relationship: A relationship between the instances of a single entity type.

Figure 3-12
Examples of relationships of different degrees
(a) Unary relationships

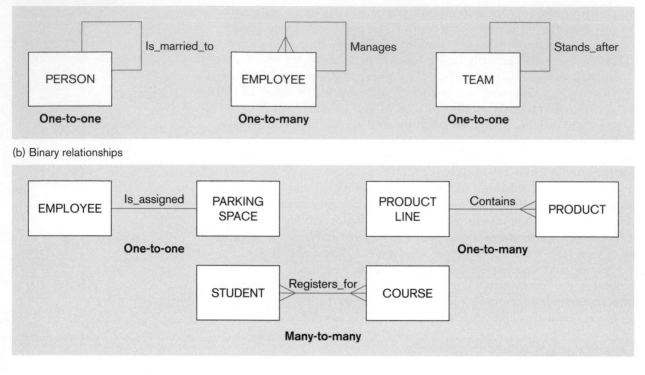

(b) Binary relationships

(c) Ternary relationship

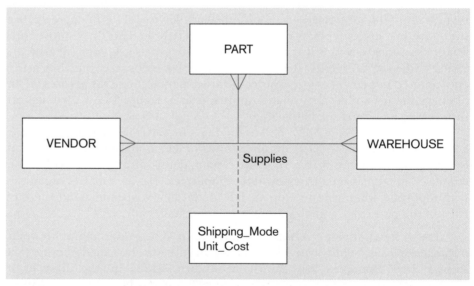

Figure 3-13 shows an example of another unary relationship, called a *bill-of-materials structure*. Many manufactured products are made of assemblies, which in turn are composed of subassemblies and parts, and so on. As shown in Figure 3-13a, we can represent this structure as a many-to-many unary relationship. In this figure, the entity type ITEM is used to represent all types of components, and we use "Has_components" for the name of the relationship type that associates lower-level items with higher-level items.

Two occurrences of this bill-of-materials structure are shown in Figure 3-13b. Each of these diagrams shows the immediate components of each item as well as the quantities of that component. For example, item TX100 consists of item BR450

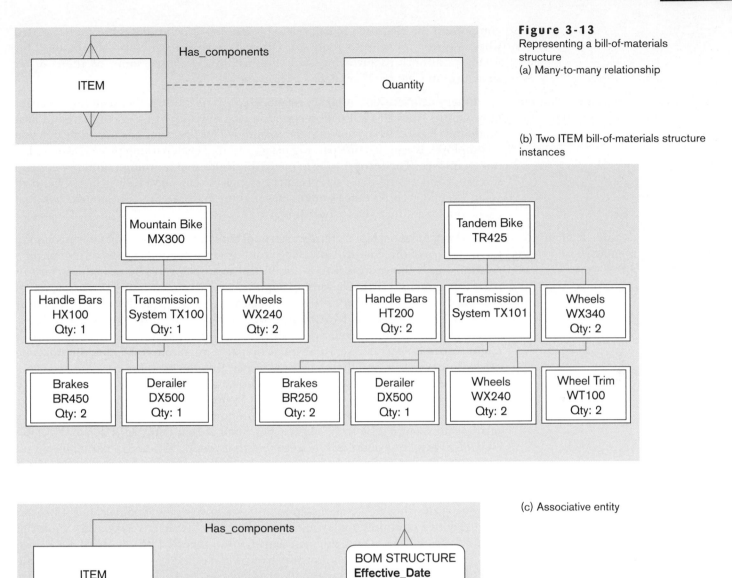

Figure 3-13
Representing a bill-of-materials
structure
(a) Many-to-many relationship

(b) Two ITEM bill-of-materials structure
instances

(c) Associative entity

(quantity 2) and item DX500 (quantity 1). You can easily verify that the associations are in fact many-to-many. Several of the items have more than one component type (e.g., item MX300 has three immediate component types: HX100, TX100, and WX240). Also, some of the components are used in several higher-level assemblies. For example, item WX240 is used in both item MX300 and item WX340, even at different levels of the bill-of-materials. The many-to-many relationship guarantees that, for example, the same subassembly structure of WX240 (not shown) is used each time item WX240 goes into making some other item.

The presence of the attribute Quantity on the relationship suggests that the analyst consider converting the relationship "Has_components" to an associative entity. Figure 3-13c shows the entity type BOM_STRUCTURE, which forms an association between instances of the ITEM entity type. A second attribute (named Effective_Date) has been added to BOM_STRUCTURE to record the date when this component was first used in the related assembly. Effective dates are often needed when a history of valves is required. Other data model structures can be used for unary relationships involving such hierarchies; we show some of these other structures in Chapter 11 on data warehousing.

Binary relationship: A relationship between the instances of two entity types.

Binary Relationship   A **binary relationship** is a relationship between the instances of two entity types and is the most common type of relationship encountered in data modeling. Figure 3-12b shows three examples. The first (one-to-one) indicates that an employee is assigned one parking place, and that each parking place is assigned to one employee. The second (one-to-many) indicates that a product line may contain several products, and that each product belongs to only one product line. The third (many-to-many) shows that a student may register for more than one course, and that each course may have many student registrants.

Ternary relationship: A simultaneous relationship among the instances of three entity types.

Ternary Relationship   A **ternary relationship** is a *simultaneous* relationship among the instances of three entity types. A typical business situation that leads to a ternary relationship is shown in Figure 3-12c. In this example, vendors can supply various parts to warehouses. The relationship Supplies is used to record the specific parts that are supplied by a given vendor to a particular warehouse. Thus there are three entity types: VENDOR, PART, and WAREHOUSE. There are two attributes on the relationship Supplies: Shipping_Mode and Unit_Cost. For example, one instance of Supplies might record the fact that vendor X can ship part C to warehouse Y, that the shipping mode is next-day air, and that the cost is $5 per unit.

Note that a ternary relationship is not the same as three binary relationships. For example, Unit_Cost is an attribute of the Supplies relationship in Figure 3-12c. Unit_Cost cannot be properly associated with any one of the three possible binary relationships among the three entity types, such as that between PART and WARE-HOUSE. Thus, for example, if we were told that vendor X can ship part C for a unit cost of $8, those data would be incomplete because they would not indicate to which warehouse the parts would be shipped.

As usual, the presence of an attribute on the relationship Supplies in Figure 3-12c suggests converting the relationship to an associative entity type. Figure 3-14 shows an alternative (and preferable) representation of the ternary relationship shown in Figure 3-12c. In Figure 3-14, the (associative) entity type SUPPLY SCHEDULE is used to replace the Supplies relationship from Figure 3-12c. Clearly the entity type SUPPLY SCHEDULE is of independent interest to users. However, notice that an identifier has not yet been assigned to SUPPLY SCHEDULE. This is acceptable. If no identifier is assigned to an associative entity during E-R modeling, an identifier (or key) will be assigned during logical modeling (discussed in Chapter 5). This will be a composite identifier whose components will consist of the identifier for each of the

Figure 3-14
Ternary relationship as an associative entity

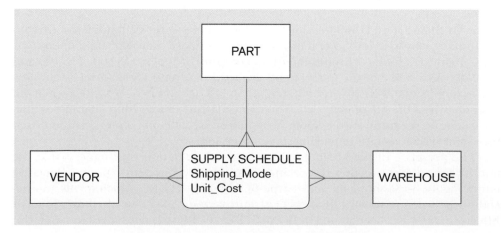

participating entity types (in this example, PART, VENDOR, and WAREHOUSE). Can you think of other attributes that might be associated with SUPPLY SCHEDULE?

As noted earlier, we do not label the lines from SUPPLY SCHEDULE to the three entities. This is because these lines do not represent binary relationships. To keep the same meaning as the ternary relationship of Figure 3-12c, we cannot break the Supplies relationship into three binary relationships, as we have already mentioned.

We strongly recommend that you convert all ternary (or higher) relationships to associative entities, as in this example. Song et al. (1995) show that participation constraints (described in the next section) cannot be accurately represented for a ternary relationship, given the notation with attributes on the relationship line. However, by converting to an associative entity, the constraints can be accurately represented. Also, many E-R diagram drawing tools, including most CASE tools, cannot represent ternary relationships. So, although not semantically accurate, you must use these tools to represent the ternary relationship with an associative entity and three binary relationships, which have a mandatory association with each of the three related entity types.

Attributes or Entity?

Figure 3-15 includes three examples of situations when an attribute could be represented via an entity type. We use this textbook's E-R notation in the left column and the notation from Microsoft Visio in the right column. In Figure 3-15a, the potentially multiple prerequisites of a course (shown as a multivalued attribute in the Attribute cell) are also courses (and a course may be a prerequisite for many other courses). Thus, prerequisite could be viewed as a bill-of-materials structure (shown in the Relationship & Entity cell) between courses, not a multivalued attribute of COURSE. Representing prerequisites via a bill-of-materials structure also means that finding the prerequisites of a course and finding the courses for which a course is prerequisite both deal with relationships between entity types. When a prerequisite is a multivalued attribute of COURSE, finding the courses for which a course is a prerequisite means looking for a specific value for a prerequisite across all COURSE instances. As was shown in Figure 3-13a, such a situation could also be modeled as a unary relationship among instances of the COURSE entity type. In Visio, this specific situation requires creating the equivalent of an associative entity (see the Relationship & Entity cell in Figure 3-15a; Visio does not use the rectangle with rounded corners symbol). By creating the associative entity, it is now easy to add characteristics to the relationship, such as a minimum grade required. In Figure 3-15b, employees potentially have multiple skills (shown in the Attribute cell), but skill could be viewed instead as an entity type (shown in the Relationship & Entity cell as the equivalent of an associative entity) about which the organization wants to maintain data (the unique code to identify each skill, a descriptive title, and the type of skill, or example technical or managerial). An employee has skills, which are not viewed as attributes, but rather as instances of a related entity type. In the cases of Figures 3-15a and 3-15b, representing the data as a multivalued attribute rather than via a relationship with another entity type may, in the view of some people, simplify the diagram. On the other hand, the right-hand drawings in these figures are closer to the way the database would be represented in a standard relational database management system, the most popular type of DBMS in use today. Although we are not concerned with implementation during conceptual data modeling, there is some logic for keeping the conceptual and logical data models similar. Further, as we will see in the next example, there are times when an attribute, whether simple, composite, or multivalued, should be in a separate entity.

So, when *should* an attribute be linked to an entity type via a relationship? The answer is: when the attribute is the identifier or some other characteristic of an entity type in the data model and multiple entity instances need to share these same attributes.

Figure 3-15

Using relationships and entities to link related attributes

(a) Multivalued attribute versus relationships via bill-of-materials structure

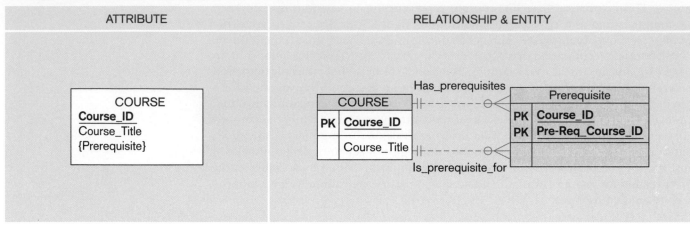

(b) Composite, multivalued attribute versus relationship

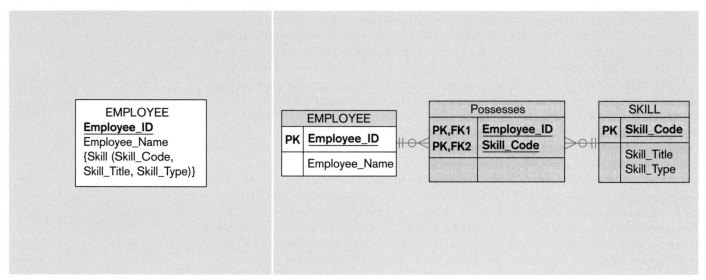

(c) Composite attribute of data shared with other entity types

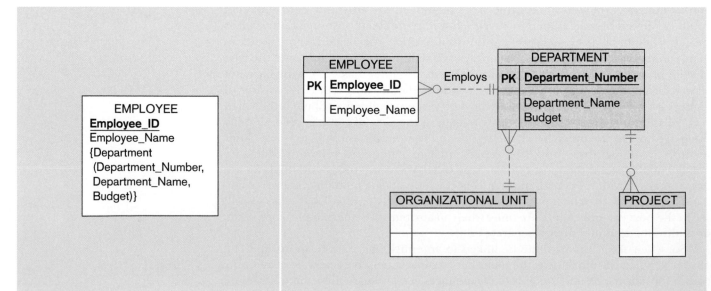

Figure 3-15c represents an example of this rule. In this example, EMPLOYEE has a composite attribute of Department. Because Department is a concept of the business, and multiple employees will share the same department data, department data could be represented (nonredundantly) in a DEPARTMENT entity type, with attributes for the data about departments that all other related entity instances need to know. With this approach, not only can different employees share the storage of the same department data, but projects (which are assigned to a department) and organizational units (which are composed of departments) also can share the storage of this same department data.

Cardinality Constraints

Suppose there are two entity types, A and B, that are connected by a relationship. A **cardinality constraint** specifies the number of instances of entity B that can (or must) be associated with each instance of entity A. For example, consider a video store that rents videotapes of movies. Because the store may stock more than one videotape for each movie, this is intuitively a "one-to-many" relationship, as shown in Figure 3-16a. Yet it is also true that the store may not have any tapes of a given movie in stock at a particular time (e.g., all copies may be checked out). We need a more precise notation to indicate the range of cardinalities for a relationship. This notation was introduced in Figure 3-2, which you may want to review at this time.

Cardinality constraint: Specifies the number of instances of one entity that can (or must) be associated with each instance of another entity.

Minimum Cardinality   The **minimum cardinality** of a relationship is the minimum number of instances of entity B that may be associated with each instance of entity A. In our videotape example, the minimum number of videotapes for a movie is zero. When the minimum number of participants is zero, we say that entity type B is an optional participant in the relationship. In this example, VIDEOTAPE (a weak entity type) is an optional participant in the "Is_stocked_as" relationship. This fact is indicated by the symbol zero through the line near the VIDEOTAPE entity in Figure 3-16b.

Minimum cardinality: The minimum number of instances of one entity that may be associated with each instance of another entity.

Maximum Cardinality   The **maximum cardinality** of a relationship is the maximum number of instances of entity B that may be associated with each instance of entity A. In the video example, the maximum cardinality for the VIDEOTAPE entity type is "many"—that is, an unspecified number greater than one. This is indicated by the "crow's foot" symbol on the line next to the VIDEOTAPE entity symbol in Figure 3-16b.

Maximum cardinality: The maximum number of instances of one entity that may be associated with each instance of another entity.

A relationship is, of course, bidirectional, so there is also cardinality notation next to the MOVIE entity. Notice that the minimum and maximum are both one (see Figure 3-16b). This is called a *mandatory one* cardinality. In other words, each videotape of a movie must be a copy of exactly one movie. In general, participation in a relationship

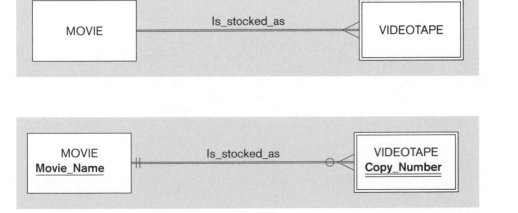

Figure 3-16
Introducing cardinality constraints
(a) Basic relationship

(b) Relationship with cardinality constraints

may be optional or mandatory for the entities involved. If the minimum cardinality is zero, participation is optional; if the minimum cardinality is one, participation is mandatory.

In Figure 3-16b, some attributes have been added to each of the entity types. Notice that VIDEOTAPE is represented as a weak entity. This is because a videotape cannot exist unless the owner movie also exists. The identifier of MOVIE is Movie_Name. VIDEOTAPE does not have a unique identifier. However, Copy_Number is a *partial* identifier, which, together with Movie_Name, would uniquely identify an instance of VIDEOTAPE.

Some Examples Examples of three relationships that show all possible combinations of minimum and maximum cardinalities appear in Figure 3-17. Each example states the business rule for each cardinality constraint and shows the associated E-R notation. Each example also shows some relationship instances to clarify the nature of the relationship. You should study each of these examples carefully. Following are the business rules for each of the examples in Figure 3-17:

1. PATIENT Has_recorded PATIENT HISTORY (Figure 3-17a). Each patient has one or more patient histories. (The initial patient visit is always recorded as an instance of PATIENT HISTORY.) Each instance of PATIENT HISTORY "belongs to" exactly one PATIENT.

Figure 3-17
Examples of cardinality constraints
(a) Mandatory cardinalities

(b) One optional, one mandatory cardinality

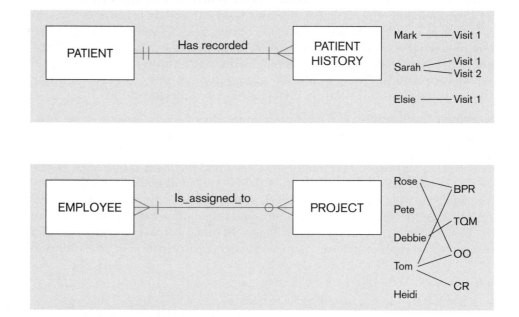

(c) Optional cardinalities

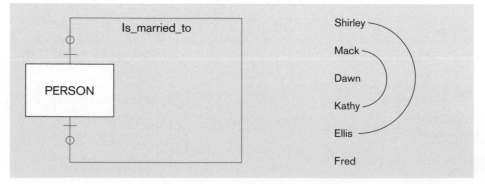

2. EMPLOYEE Is_assigned_to PROJECT (Figure 3-17b). Each PROJECT has at least one EMPLOYEE assigned to it. (Some projects have more than one.) Each EMPLOYEE may or (optionally) may not be assigned to any existing PROJECT (e.g., employee "Pete"), or may be assigned to one or more PROJECTs.

3. PERSON Is_married_to PERSON (Figure 3-17c). This is an optional zero or one cardinality in both directions, because a person may or may not be married.

It is possible for the maximum cardinality to be a fixed number, not an arbitrary "many" value. For example, suppose corporate policy states that an employee may work on at most five projects at the same time. We could show this business rule by placing a 5 above or below the crow's foot next to the PROJECT entity in Figure 3-17b.

A Ternary Relationship We showed the ternary relationship with the associative entity type SUPPLY SCHEDULE in Figure 3-14. Now let's add cardinality constraints to this diagram, based on the business rules for this situation. The E-R diagram, with the relevant business rules, is shown in Figure 3-18. Notice that PART and WAREHOUSE must relate to some SUPPLY SCHEDULE instance, whereas a VENDOR optionally may not participate. The cardinality at each of the participating entities is a mandatory one, because each SUPPLY SCHEDULE instance must be related to exactly one instance of each of these participating entity types. (Remember, SUPPLY SCHEDULE is an associative entity.)

As noted earlier, a ternary relationship is not equivalent to three binary relationships. Unfortunately, you are not able to draw ternary relationships with many CASE tools; instead, you are forced to represent ternary relationships as three binaries (i.e., an associative entity with three binary relationships). If you are forced to draw three binary relationships, then do not draw the binary relationships with names, and be sure that the cardinality next to the three strong entities is a mandatory one.

Modeling Time-Dependent Data

Database contents vary over time. With renewed interest today in traceability and reconstruction of a historical picture of the organization for various regulatory requirements, such as HIPPA and Sarbanes-Oxley, the need to include a time series of data has become essential. For example, in a database that contains product

Figure 3-18
Cardinality constraints in a ternary relationship

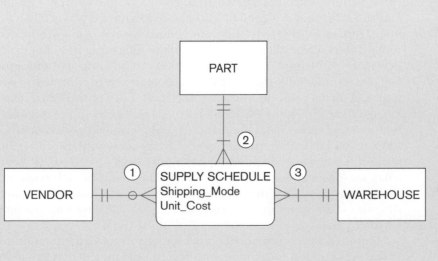

Figure 3-19
Simple example of time stamping

```
                    PRODUCT
                    Product_ID
                    {Price_History
                       (Effective_Date, Price)}
```

information, the unit price for each product may be changed as material and labor costs and market conditions change. If only the current price is required, Price can be modeled as a single-valued attribute. However for accounting, billing, financial reporting, and other purposes, we are likely to need to preserve a history of the prices and the time period during which each was in effect. As Figure 3-19 shows, we can conceptualize this requirement as a series of prices and the effective date for each price. This results in the (composite) multivalued attribute named Price_History. The components of Price_History are Price and Effective_Date. An important characteristic of such a composite, multivalued attribute is that the component attributes go together. Thus, in Figure 3-19, each Price is paired with the corresponding Effective_Date.

In Figure 3-19, each value of the attribute Price is time stamped with its effective date. A time stamp is simply a time value, such as date and time, that is associated with a data value. A **time stamp** may be associated with any data value that changes over time when we need to maintain a history of those data values. Time stamps may be recorded to indicate the time the value was entered (transaction time), the time the value becomes valid or stops being valid, or the time when critical actions were performed, such as updates, corrections, or audits. This situation is similar to the employee skill diagrams in Figure 3-15b; thus, an alternative, not shown in Figure 3-19, is to make Price History a separate entity type, as was done with Skill using Microsoft Visio.

Time stamp: A time value that is associated with a data value.

PINE VALLEY FURNITURE

The use of simple time stamping (as in the preceding example) is often adequate for modeling time-dependent data. However, time often introduces subtler complexities to data modeling. For example, Figure 3-20a represents a portion of an ERD for Pine Valley Furniture Company. Each product is assigned (i.e., current assignment) to a product line (or related group of products). Customer orders are processed throughout the year, and monthly summaries are reported by product line and by product within product line.

Suppose that in the middle of the year, due to a reorganization of the sales function, some products are reassigned to different product lines. The model shown in Figure 3-20a is not designed to track the reassignment of a product to a new product line. Thus, all sales reports will show cumulative sales for a product based on its current product line, rather than the one at the time of the sale. For example, a product may have total year-to-date sales of $50,000 and be associated with product line B, yet $40,000 of those sales may have occurred while the product was assigned to product line A. This fact will be lost using the model in Figure 3-20a. The simple design change shown in Figure 3-20b will correctly recognize product reassignments. A new relationship, called Sales_for_product_line, has been added between ORDER and PRODUCT LINE. As customer orders are processed, they are credited to both the correct product (via Sales_for_product) and the correct product line (via Sales_for_product_line) as of the time of the sale. The approach of Figure 3-20b is similar to what is done in a data warehouse to retain historical records of the precise situation at any point in time. (We will return to dealing with the time dimension in Chapter 11.)

Another aspect of modeling time is recognizing that although the requirements of the organization today may be to record only the current situation, the design of the database may need to change if the organization ever decides to keep history. In

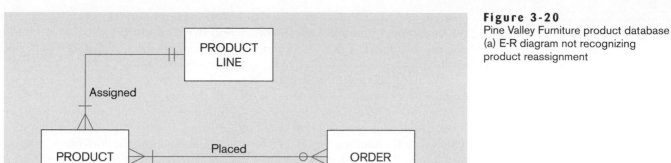

Figure 3-20
Pine Valley Furniture product database

(a) E-R diagram not recognizing
product reassignment

(b) E-R diagram recognizing product
reassignment

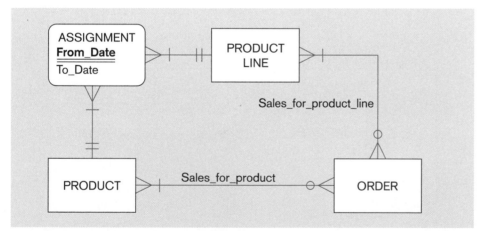

(c) E-R diagram with associative entity
for product assignment to product line
over time

Figure 3-20b, we know the current product line for a product and the product line for the product each time it is ordered. But, what if the product were ever reassigned to a product line during a period of zero sales for the product? Based on this data model in Figure 3-20b, we would not know of these other product line assignments. A common solution to this need for greater flexibility in the data model is to consider whether a one-to-many relationship, such as Assigned, should become a many-to-many relationship. Further, to allow for attributes on this new relationship, this relationship should actually be an associative entity. Figure 3-20c shows this alternative data model with the ASSIGNMENT associative entity for the Assigned relationship. The advantage of the alternative is that we now will not miss recording any product line assignment, and we can record information about the assignment (such as the from and to effective dates of the assignment); the disadvantage is that the data model no longer has the restriction that a product may be assigned to only one product line at a time. We will need additional notation, introduced in Chapter 4 on the topic of business rules, to represent this constraint.

We have discussed the problem of time-dependent data with managers in several organizations who are considered leaders in the use of data modeling and database management. Before the recent wave of financial reporting disclosure regulations, these discussions revealed that data models for operational databases were generally inadequate for handing time-dependent data, and that organizations often ignored this problem and hoped that the resulting inaccuracies balanced out. However, with these new regulations, you need to be alert to the complexities posed by time-dependent data as you develop data models in your organization.

Multiple Relationships

In some situations, an organization may wish to model more than one relationship between the same entity types. Two examples are shown in Figure 3-21. Figure 3-21a shows two relationships between the entity types EMPLOYEE and DEPARTMENT. In this figure we use the notation with names for the relationship in each direction; this notation makes explicit what the cardinality is for each direction of the relationship (which becomes important for clarifying the meaning of the unary relationship on EMPLOYEE). One relationship associates employees with the department in which they work. This relationship is one-to-many in the Has_workers direction and is mandatory in both directions. That is, a department must have at least one employee who works there (perhaps the department manager), and each employee must be assigned to exactly one department. (Note: These are specific business rules we assume for this illustration. It is crucial when you develop an E-R diagram for a particular situation that you understand the business rules that apply for that setting.

Figure 3-21
Examples of multiple relationships
(a) Employees and departments

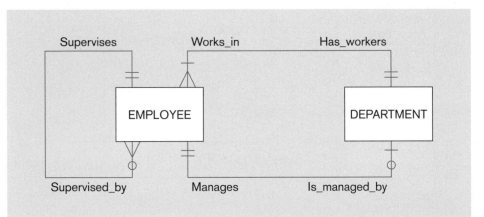

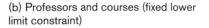

(b) Professors and courses (fixed lower limit constraint)

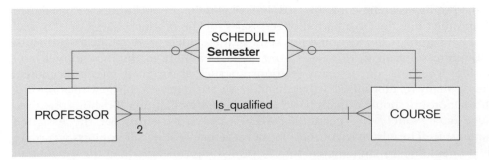

For example, if EMPLOYEE were to include retirees, then each employee may not be currently assigned to exactly one department; further, the E-R model in Figure 3-21a assumes that the organization needs to remember in which DEPARTMENT each EMPLOYEE currently works, rather than remembering the history of department assignments. Again, the structure of the data model reflects the information the organization needs to remember.)

The second relationship between EMPLOYEE and DEPARTMENT associates each department with the employee who manages that department. The relationship from DEPARTMENT to EMPLOYEE (called Is_managed_by in that direction) is mandatory one, indicating that a department must have exactly one manager. From EMPLOYEE to DEPARTMENT, the relationship (Manages) is optional because a given employee either is or is not a department manager.

Figure 3-21a also shows the unary relationship that associates each employee with his or her supervisor, and vice versa. This relationship records the business rule that each employee must have exactly one supervisor (Supervised_by). Conversely, each employee may supervise any number of employees, or may not be a supervisor.

The example in Figure 3-21b shows two relationships between the entity types PROFESSOR and COURSE. The relationship Is_qualified associates professors with the courses they are qualified to teach. A given course must have at a minimum two qualified instructors (an example of how to used a fixed value for a minimum or maximum cardinality). This might happen, for example, so that a course is never the "property" of one instructor. Conversely, each instructor must be qualified to teach at least one course (a reasonable expectation).

The second relationship in this figure associates professors with the courses they are actually scheduled to teach during a given semester. Because Semester is a characteristic of the relationship, we place an associative entity, SCHEDULE, between PROFESSOR and COURSE.

The ERD in Figure 3-21b captures the basic cardinality constraints. Often, however, there are other business rules that cannot easily be captured on a basic E-R diagram. What if a professor could not be scheduled to teach more than four courses in a semester? Or, consider the following rule: An instructor who is scheduled to teach a course must be qualified to teach that course (another reasonable rule). In Chapter 4, we discuss techniques for capturing such rules as part of the overall modeling process.

Naming and Defining Relationships

In addition to the general guidelines for naming data objects, there are a few special guidelines for naming relationships, which follow:

- A relationship name is a *verb phrase* (such as Assigned_to, Supplies, or Teaches). Relationships represent actions being taken, usually in the present tense, so transitive verbs (an action on something) are the most appropriate. A relationship name states the action taken, not the result of the action (e.g., use Assigned_to, not Assignment). The name states the essence of the interaction between the participating entity types, not the process involved (e.g., use an Employee is *Assigned_to* a project, not an Employee is *Assigning* a project).

- You should *avoid vague names*, such as Has or Is_related_to. Use descriptive, powerful verb phrases, often taken from the action verbs found in the definition of the relationship.

There are also some specific guidelines for defining relationships, which follow:

- A relationship definition *explains what action is being taken and possibly why it is important.* It may be important to state who or what does the action, but it is not important to explain how the action is taken. Stating the business objects involved in the relationship is natural, but because the E-R diagram shows what entity types are involved in the relationship and other definitions explain the entity types, you do not have to describe the business objects.

- It may also be important to *give examples to clarify the action*. For example, for a relationship of Registered_for between student and course, it may be useful to explain that this covers both on-site and online registration and includes registrations made during the drop/add period.

- The definition should explain any *optional participation*. You should explain what conditions lead to zero associated instances, whether this can happen only when an entity instance is first created, or whether this can happen at any time. For example, "Registered_for links a course with the students who have signed up to take the course, and the courses a student has signed up to take. A course will have no students registered for it before the registration period begins and may never have any registered students. A student will not be registered for any courses before the registration period begins and may not register for any classes (or may register for classes and then drop any or all classes)."

- A relationship definition should also *explain the reason for any explicit maximum cardinality* other than many. For example, "Assigned_to links an employee with the projects to which that employee is assigned and the employees assigned to a project. Due to our labor union agreement, an employee may not be assigned to more than four projects at a given time." This example, typical of many upper-bound business rules, suggests that maximum cardinalities tend not to be permanent. In this example, the next labor union agreement could increase or decrease this limit. Thus, the implementation of maximum cardinalities must be done to allow changes.

- A relationship definition should *explain any mutually exclusive relationships*. Mutually exclusive relationships are ones for which an entity instance can participate in only one of several alternative relationships. We will show examples of this situation in Chapter 4. For now, consider the following example: "Plays_on links an intercollegiate sports team with its student players and indicates on which teams a student plays. Students who play on intercollegiate sports teams cannot also work in a campus job (i.e., a student cannot be linked to both an intercollegiate sports team via Plays_on and a campus job via the Works_on relationship)." Another example of a mutually exclusive restriction is when an employee cannot both be Supervised_by and be Married_to the same employee.

- A relationship definition should *explain any restrictions on participation in the relationship*. Mutual exclusivity is one restriction, but there can be others. For example, "Supervised_by links an employee with the other employees he or she supervises and links an employee with the other employee who supervises him or her. An employee cannot supervise him- or herself, and an employee cannot supervise other employees if his or her job classification level is below 4."

- A relationship definition should *explain the extent of history that is kept in the relationship*. For example, "Assigned_to links a hospital bed with a patient. Only the current bed assignment is stored. When a patient is not admitted, that patient is not assigned to a bed, and a bed may be vacant at any given point in time." Another example of describing history for a relationship is "Places links a customer with the orders they have placed with our company and links an order with the associated customer. Only 2 years of orders are maintained in the database, so not all orders can participate in this relationship."

- A relationship definition should explain whether an entity instance involved in a relationship instance can transfer participation to another relationship instance. For example, "Places links a customer with the orders they have placed with our company and links an order with the associated customer. An order is not transferable to another customer." Another example is "Categorized_as links a product line with the products sold under that heading and links a product to its associated product line. Due to changes in organization structure and product design features, products may be recate-gorized to a different product line. Categorized_as keeps track of only the current product line to which a product is linked."

E-R MODELING EXAMPLE: PINE VALLEY FURNITURE COMPANY

PINE VALLEY FURNITURE

Developing an E-R diagram can proceed from one (or both) of two perspectives. With a top-down perspective, the designer proceeds from basic descriptions of the business, including its policies, processes, and environment. This approach is most appropriate for developing a high-level E-R diagram with only the major entities and relationships and with a limited set of attributes (such as just the entity identifiers). With a bottom-up approach, the designer proceeds from detailed discussions with users, and from a detailed study of documents, screens, and other data sources. This approach is necessary for developing a detailed, "fully attributed" E-R diagram.

In this section, we develop a high-level ERD for Pine Valley Furniture Company, based largely on the first of these approaches (see Figure 3-22 for a Microsoft Visio version). For simplicity, we do not show any composite or multivalued attributes (e.g., skill is shown as a separate entity type associated with EMPLOYEE via an asso-ciative entity, which allows and employee to have many skills and a skill to be held by many employees).

From a study of the business processes at Pine Valley Furniture Company, we have identified the following entity types. An identifier is also suggested for each entity, together with selected important attributes.

- The company sells a number of different furniture products. These products are grouped into several product lines. The identifier for a product is Product_ID, whereas the identifier for a product line is Product_Line_ID. We identify the following additional attributes for product: Product_Description, Product_Finish, and Standard_Price.[1] Another attribute for product line is Product_Line_Name. A product line may group any number of products but must group at least one product. Each product must belong to exactly one product line.

- Customers submit orders for products. The identifier for an order is Order_ID, and another attribute is Order_Date. A customer may submit any number of orders, but need not submit any orders. Each order is submitted by exactly one customer. The identifier for a customer is Customer_ID. Other attributes include Customer_Name, Customer_Address, and Postal_Code.

- A given customer order must request at least one product and only one product per order line item. Any product sold by Pine Valley Furniture may not appear on any order line item or may appear on one or more order line items. An attribute associated with each order line item is Ordered_Quantity.

- Pine Valley Furniture has established sales territories for its customers. Each cus-tomer may do business in any number of these sales territories or may not do business in any territory. A sales territory has one-to-many customers. The iden-tifier for a sales territory is Territory_ID and an attribute of a Territory_Name.

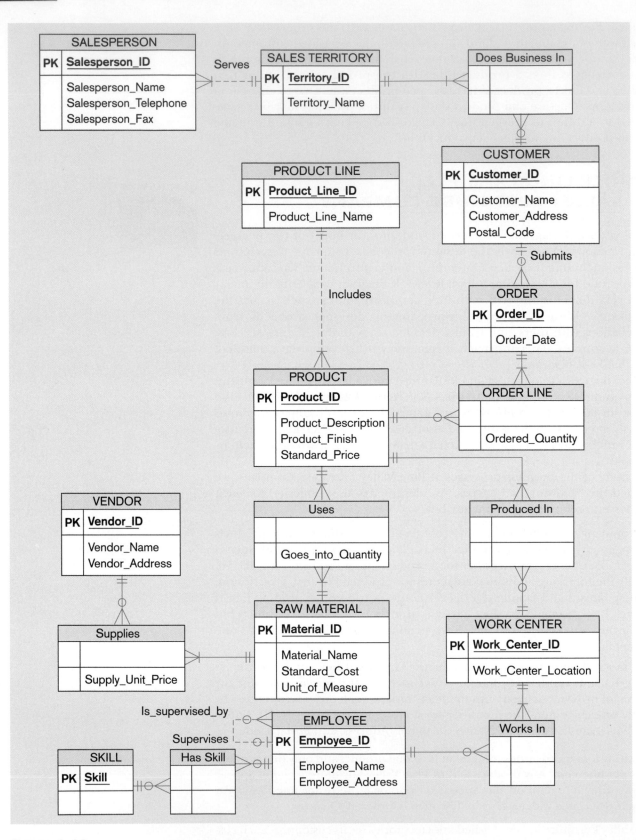

Figure 3-22
Data model for Pine Valley Furniture Company in Microsoft Visio notation

- Pine Valley Furniture Company has several salespersons. The identifier for a salesperson is Salesperson_ID. Other attributes include Salesperson_Name, Salesperson_Telephone, and Salesperson_Fax. A salesperson serves exactly one sales territory. Each sales territory is served by one or more salespersons.

- Each product is assembled from a specified quantity of one or more raw materials. The identifier for the raw material entity is Material_ID. Other attributes include Unit_of_Measure, Material_Name, and Standard_Cost. Each raw material is assembled into one or more products, using a specified quantity of the raw material for each product.

- Raw materials are supplied by vendors. The identifier for a vendor is Vendor_ID. Other attributes include Vendor_Name and Vendor_Address. Each raw material can be supplied by one or more vendors. A vendor may supply any number of raw materials or may not supply any raw materials to Pine Valley Furniture. An attribute of the relationship between vendor and raw material is Supply_Unit_Price.

- Pine Valley Furniture has established a number of work centers. The identifier for a work center is Work_Center_ID. Another attribute is Work_Center_Location. Each product is produced in one or more work centers. A work center may be used to produce any number of products or may not be used to produce any products.

- The company has over 100 employees. The identifier for employee is Employee_ID. Other attributes include Employee_Name, Employee_Address, and Skill. An employee may have more than one skill. Each employee may work in one or more work centers. A work center must have at least one employee working in that center, but may have any number of employees.

- Each employee has exactly one supervisor except managers, who have no supervisor. An employee who is a supervisor may supervise any number of employees, but not all employees are supervisors.

DATABASE PROCESSING AT PINE VALLEY FURNITURE

The purpose of the data model diagram in Figure 3-22 is to provide a conceptual design for the Pine Valley Furniture Company database. It is important to check the quality of such a design through frequent interaction with the persons who will use the database after it is implemented. An important and often performed type of quality check is to determine whether the E-R model can easily satisfy user requests for data and/or information. Employees at Pine Valley Furniture have many data retrieval and reporting requirements. In this section, we show how a few of these information requirements can be satisfied by database processing against the database shown in Figure 3-22.

We use the SQL database processing language (explained in Chapters 7 and 8) to state these queries. To fully understand these queries, you will need to understand concepts introduced in Chapter 5. However, a few simple queries in this chapter should help you to understand the capabilities of a database to answer important organizational questions and give you a jump-start toward understanding SQL queries in Chapter 7 as well as in later chapters.

Showing Product Information

Many different users have a need to see data about the products Pine Valley Furniture produces; for example, salespersons, inventory managers, and product managers. One specific need is for a salesperson who wants to respond to a request from a customer for a list of products of a certain type. An example of this query is:

List all details for the various computer desks that are stocked by the company.

The data for this query is maintained in the PRODUCT entity (see Figure 3-22). The query scans this entity and displays all the attributes for products that contain the description "Computer Desk."

The SQL code for this query is:

```
SELECT *
FROM PRODUCT
WHERE Product_Description LIKE "Computer Desk%";
```

Typical output for this query is:

Product_ID	Product_Description	Product_Finish	Standard_Price
3	Computer Desk 48"	Oak	375.00
8	Computer Desk 64"	Pine	450.00

SELECT * FROM PRODUCT says display all attributes of PRODUCT entities. The WHERE clause says to limit the display to only products whose description begins with the phrase "Computer Desk."

Showing Customer Information

Another common information need is to show data about Pine Valley Furniture customers. One specific type of person who needs this information is a territory sales manager. The following is a typical query from a territory sales manager:

List the details of customers in the Northwest sales territory.

The data for this query are maintained in the CUSTOMER entity. As we explain in Chapter 5, the attribute Territory_ID will be added to the CUSTOMER entity when a data model in Figure 3-22 is translated into a database that can be accessed via SQL. The query scans that entity and displays all attributes for customers who are in the selected territory.

The SQL code for this query is:

```
SELECT *
FROM CUSTOMER
WHERE Territory_ID = "Northwest";
```

Typical output for this query is:

Customer_ID	Customer_Name	Customer_Address	Territory_ID
5	Value Furniture	394 Rainbow Dr., Seattle, WA 97954	Northwest
9	Furniture Gallery	816 Peach Rd., Santa Clara, CA 96915	Northwest

The explanation of this SQL query is similar to the previous one.

Showing Customer Order Status

The previous two queries were relatively simple, involving data from only one table in each case. Often, data from multiple tables are needed in one information request. Although the query was simple, we did have to look through the whole database to find the entity and attributes needed to satisfy the request.

To simplify query writing and for other reasons, many database management systems support creating restricted views of a database suitable for the information needs of a particular user. For queries related to customer order status, Pine Valley utilizes such a user view called "Orders for customers" shown in Figure 3-23a. This user view allows users to see only CUSTOMER and ORDER entities in the database, and only the attributes of these entities shown in the figure. As we explain in Chapter 5, the attribute Customer_ID will be added to the ORDER entity (as shown in Figure 3-23a). A typical order status query is:

How many orders have we received from "Value Furniture"?

Assuming all the data we need are pulled together into this one user view, or virtual entity, called ORDERS_FOR_CUSTOMER, we can simply write the query as follows:

```
SELECT COUNT(Order_ID)
FROM ORDERS_FOR_CUSTOMERS
WHERE Customer_Name = "Value Furniture";
```

Without the user view, we can write the SQL code for this query in several ways. The way we have chosen is to compose a query within a query, called a subquery. The query is performed in two steps. First, the subquery (or inner query) scans the CUSTOMER entity to determine the Customer_ID for the customer named "Value Furniture." (The ID for this customer is 5, as shown in the output for the previous query.) Then the query (or outer query) scans the ORDER entity and counts the order instances for this customer.

The SQL code for this query without the "Orders for customer" user view is as follows:

```
SELECT COUNT (Order_ID)
FROM ORDER
WHERE Customer_ID =
 (SELECT Customer_ID
 FROM CUSTOMER
 WHERE Customer_Name = "Value Furniture");
```

Typical output for this query using either of the query approaches above is:

```
COUNT(Order_ID)
    4
```

Showing Product Sales

Salespersons, territory managers, product managers, production managers, and others have a need to know the status of product sales. One kind of sales question is what products are having an exceptionally strong sales month. Typical of this question is the following query:

What products have had total sales exceeding $25,000 during the past month (June, 2006)?

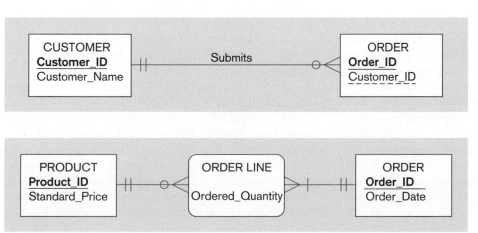

Figure 3-23
Two user views for Pine Valley Furniture
(a) User View 1: Orders for customers

(b) User View 2: Orders for products

This query can be written using the user view "Orders for products" shown in Figure 3-23b. Data to respond to the query are obtained from the following sources:

- Order_Date from the ORDER entity (to find only orders in the desired month)
- Ordered_Quantity for each product on each order from the associative entity ORDER LINE for an ORDER entity in the desired month
- Standard_Price for the product ordered from the PRODUCT entity associated with the ORDER LINE entity

For each item that has been ordered during the month of June 2006, the query needs to multiply Ordered_Quantity times Standard_Price to get the dollar value of a sale. The total amount is then obtained for that item by summing all orders. Data are displayed only if the total exceeds $25,000.

The SQL code for this query is beyond the scope of this chapter, because it requires techniques introduced in Chapter 8. We show this SQL query in that chapter. We introduce this query now only to suggest the power that a database such as the one shown in Figure 3-22 has to find information for management from detailed data. In many organizations today, users can use a Web browser to obtain the information described here. The programming code associated with a Web page then invokes the required SQL commands to obtain the requested information.

Summary

This chapter has described the fundamentals of modeling data in the organization. Business rules, derived from policies, procedures, events, functions, and other business objects, state constraints that govern the organization and, hence, how data are handled and stored. It was argued that business rules are a powerful way to describe the requirements for an information system, especially a database. The power of business rules results from business rules being core concepts of the business, being able to be expressed in terms familiar to end users, being highly maintainable, and being able to be enforced through automated means, mainly through a database. Good business rules are ones that are declarative, precise, atomic, consistent, expressible, distinct, and business oriented.

Basic business rules are data names and definitions. This chapter explained guidelines for the clear naming and definition of data objects in a business. In terms of conceptual data modeling, names and definitions must be provided for entity types, attributes, and relationships. Other business rules may state constraints on these data objects. These constraints can be captured in a data model and associated documentation.

The data modeling notation most frequently used today is the entity-relationship data model. An E-R model is a detailed, logical representation of the data for an organization. An E-R model is usually expressed in the form of an E-R diagram, which is a graphical rep-

resentation of an E-R model. The E-R model was introduced by Chen in 1976. However, at the present time there is no standard notation for E-R modeling. Notations, such as those found in Microsoft Visio, are used in many CASE tools.

The basic constructs of an E-R model are entity types, relationships, and related attributes. An entity is a person, place, object, event, or concept in the user environment about which the organization wishes to maintain data. An entity type is a collection of entities that share common properties, whereas an entity instance is a single occurrence of an entity type. A strong entity type is an entity that has its own identifier and can exist without other entities. A weak entity type is an entity whose existence depends on the existence of a strong entity type. Weak entities do not have their own identifier, although they normally have a partial identifier. Weak entities are identified through an identifying relationship with their owner entity type.

An attribute is a property or characteristic of an entity or relationship that is of interest to the organization. There are several types of attributes. A required attribute must have a value for an entity instance, whereas an optional attribute value may be null. A simple attribute is one that has no component parts. A composite attribute is an attribute that can be broken down into component parts. For example, Person_Name can be broken down into the parts First_Name, Middle_Initial, and Last_Name.

A multivalued attribute is one that can have multiple values for a single instance of an entity. For example, the attribute College_Degree might have multiple values for an individual. A derived attribute is one whose values can be calculated from other attribute values. For example, Average_Salary can be calculated from values of Salary for all employees.

An identifier is an attribute that uniquely identifies individual instances of an entity type. Identifiers should be chosen carefully to ensure stability and ease of use. Identifiers may be simple attributes, or they may be composite attributes with component parts.

A relationship type is a meaningful association between (or among) entity types. A relationship instance is an association between (or among) entity instances. The degree of a relationship is the number of entity types that participate in the relationship. The most common relationship types are unary (degree 1), binary (degree 2), and ternary (degree 3).

In developing E-R diagrams, we sometimes encounter many-to-many (and one-to-one) relationships that have one or more attributes associated with the relationship, rather than with one of the participating entity types. This suggests that we consider converting the relationship to an associative entity. This type of entity associates the instances of one or more entity types and contains attributes that are peculiar to the relationship. Associative entity types may have their own simple identifier, or they may be assigned a composite identifier during logical design.

A cardinality constraint is a constraint that specifies the number of instances of entity B that may (or must) be associated with each instance of entity A. Cardinality constraints normally specify the minimum and maximum number of instances. The possible constraints are mandatory one, mandatory many, optional one, optional many, and a specific number. The minimum cardinality constraint is also referred to as the participation constraint. A minimum cardinality of zero specifies optional participation, whereas a minimum cardinality of one specifies mandatory participation.

CHAPTER REVIEW

Key Terms

Associative entity	Entity-relationship diagram (E-R diagram)	Multivalued attribute
Attribute		Optional attribute
Binary relationship	Entity-relationship model (E-R model)	Relationship instance
Business rule		Relationship type
Cardinality constraint	Entity type	Required attribute
	Fact	Simple attribute
Composite attribute	Identifier	Strong entity type
Composite identifier	Term	Ternary relationship
Degree	Identifying owner	Time stamp
Derived attribute	Identifying relationship	Unary relationship
Entity	Minimum cardinality	Weak entity type
Entity instance	Maximum cardinality	

Review Questions

1. Define each of the following terms:
   a. entity type
   b. entity-relationship model
   c. entity instance
   d. attribute

e. relationship type

f. identifier

g. multivalued attribute

h. associative entity

i. cardinality constraint

j. weak entity

k. identifying relationship

l. derived attribute

m. multivalued attribute

n. business rule

2. Match the following terms and definitions.

_____ composite attribute

_____ associative entity

_____ unary relationship

_____ weak entity

_____ attribute

_____ entity

_____ relationship type

_____ cardinality constraint

_____ degree

_____ identifier

_____ entity type

_____ ternary

_____ bill-of-materials

a. uniquely identifies entity instances

b. relates instances of a single entity type

c. specifies maximum and minimum number of instances

d. relationship modeled as an entity type

e. association between entity types

f. collection of similar entities

g. number of participating entity types in relationship

h. property of an entity

i. can be broken into component parts

j. depends on the existence of another entity type

k. relationship of degree 3

l. many-to-many unary relationship

m. person, place, object, concept, event

3. Contrast the following terms:

a. Stored attribute; derived attribute

b. Simple attribute; composite attribute

c. Entity type; relationship type

d. Strong entity type; weak entity type

e. Degree; cardinality

f. Required attribute; optional attribute

g. Composite attribute; multivalued attribute

4. Give three reasons why many system designers believe that data modeling is the most important part of the systems development process.

5. Give four reasons why a business rules approach is advocated as a new paradigm for specifying information systems requirements.

6. Explain where you can find business rules in an organization.

7. State six general guidelines for naming data objects in a data model.

8. State four criteria for selecting identifiers for entities.

9. State three conditions that suggest the designer should model a relationship as an associative entity type.

10. List the four types of cardinality constraints, and draw an example of each.

11. Give an example, other than those described in this chapter, of a weak entity type. Why is it necessary to indicate an identifying relationship?

12. What is the degree of a relationship? List the three types of relationship degrees described in the chapter, and give an example of each.

13. Give an example (other than those described in this chapter) for each of the following:

a. Derived attribute

b. Multivalued attribute

c. Composite attribute

14. Give an example of each of the following, other than those described in this chapter.

a. Ternary relationship

b. Unary relationship

15. Give an example of the use of effective (or effectivity) dates as attributes of an entity.

16. State a rule that says when to extract an attribute from one entity type and place it in a linked entity type.

17. What are the special guidelines for naming relationships?

18. In addition to explaining what action is being taken, what else should a relationship definition explain?

19. For the Manages relationship in Figure 3-12a, describe one or more situations that would result in different cardinalities on the two ends of this unary relationship. Based on your description to this example, do you think it is always clear simply from an E-R diagram what the business rule is that results in certain cardinalities? Justify your answer.

20. Explain the distinction between entity type and entity instance.

Problems and Exercises

1. You may have been assigned a CASE or a drawing tool to develop conceptual data models. Using this tool, attempt to redraw all of the E-R diagrams in this chapter. What difficulties did you encounter? What E-R notations did not translate well to your tool? How did you incorporate the E-R notation that did not directly translate into the tool's notation?

2. Contrast the terms "term" and "fact" as they apply to business rules. Give an example of a business rule and indicate the terms and facts in that rule.

3. There is a bulleted list associated with Figure 3-22 that describes the entities and their relationships in Pine Valley Furniture. For each of the ten points in the list, identify the subset of Figure 3-22 described by that point.

4. Draw an ERD for each of the following situations. (If you believe that you need to make additional assumptions, clearly state them for each situation.) Draw the same situation using the tool you have been told to use in the course.

   a. A company has a number of employees. The attributes of EMPLOYEE include Employee_ID (identifier), Name, Address, and Birthdate. The company also has several projects. Attributes of PROJECT include Project_ID (identifier), Project_Name, and Start_Date. Each employee may be assigned to one or more projects, or may not be assigned to a project. A project must have at least one employee assigned and may have any number of employees assigned. An employee's billing rate may vary by project, and the company wishes to record the applicable billing rate (Billing_Rate) for each employee when assigned to a particular project. Do the attribute names in this description follow the guidelines for naming attributes? If not, suggest better names.

   b. A university has a large number of courses in its catalog. Attributes of COURSE include Course_Number (identifier), Course_Name, and Units. Each course may have one or more different courses as prerequisites or may have no prerequisites. Similarly, a particular course may be a prerequisite for any number of courses or may not be prerequisite for any other course. Provide a good definition of COURSE. Why is your definition a good one?

   c. A laboratory has several chemists who work on one or more projects. Chemists also may use certain kinds of equipment on each project. Attributes of CHEMIST include Employee_ID (identifier), Name, and Phone_No. Attributes of PROJECT include Project_ID (identifier) and Start_Date. Attributes of EQUIPMENT include Serial_No and Cost. The organization wishes to record Assign_Date—that is, the date when a given equipment item was assigned to a particular chemist working on a specified project. A chemist must be assigned to at least one project and one equipment item. A given equipment item need not be assigned, and a given project need not be assigned either a chemist or an equipment item. Provide good definitions for all of the relationships in this situation.

   d. A college course may have one or more scheduled sections, or may not have a scheduled section. Attributes of COURSE include Course_ID, Course_Name, and Units. Attributes of SECTION include Section_Number and Semester_ID. Semester_ID is composed of two parts: Semester and Year. Section_Number is an integer (such as "1" or "2") that distinguishes one section from another for the same course but does not uniquely identify a section. How did you model SECTION? Why did you choose this way versus alternative ways to model SECTION?

   e. A hospital has a large number of registered physicians. Attributes of PHYSICIAN include Physician_ID (the identifier) and Specialty. Patients are admitted to the hospital by physicians. Attributes of PATIENT include Patient_ID (the identifier) and Patient_Name. Any patient who is admitted must have exactly one admitting physician. A physician may optionally admit any number of patients. Once admitted, a given patient must be treated by at least one physician. A particular physician may treat any number of patients, or may not treat any patients. Whenever a patient is treated by a physician, the hospital wishes to record the details of the treatment (Treatment_Detail). Components of Treatment_Detail include Date, Time, and Results. Did you draw more than one relationship between physician and patient? Why or why not?

   f. The loan office in a bank receives from various parties requests to investigate the credit status of a customer. Each credit request is identified by a Request_ID and is described by a Request_Date and Requesting_Party_Name. The loan office also received results of credit checks. A credit check is identified by a Credit_Check_ID and is described by the Credit_Check_Date and the Credit_Rating. The loan office matches credit requests with credit check results. A credit request may be recorded before its result arrives; a particular credit result may be used in support of several credit requests. Draw an ERD for this situation. Now, assume that credit results may not be reused for multiple credit requests. Redraw the ERD for this new situation using two entity types, and then redraw it again using one entity type. Which of these two versions do you prefer and why?

   g. Companies, identified by Company_ID and described by Company_Name and Industry_Type, hire consultants, identified by Consultant_ID and described by Consultant_Name, Consultant_Specialty, which is multivalued. Assume that a consultant can work for only one company at a time, and we need to track only current consulting engagements. Draw an ERD for this situation. Now, consider a new attribute, which is the Hourly_Rate a consultant charges a company for her services. Redraw the ERD to include this new attribute. Now, consider that each time a consultant works for a company a contract is written describing the terms for this consulting engagement. Contract is identified by a composite identifier of Company_ID, Consultant_ID, and Contract_Date.

Assuming that a consultant can still work for only one company at a time, redraw the ERD for this new situation. Did you move any attributes to different entity types in this latest situation? As a final situation, now consider that although a consultant can work for only one company at a time, we now need to keep the complete history of all consulting engagements for each consultant and company. Draw an ERD for this final situation. Explain why these different changes to the situation led to different data models, if they did.

5. Figure 3-24 shows a Grade Report that is mailed to students at the end of each semester. Prepare an ERD reflecting the data contained in Grade Report. Assume that each course is taught by one instructor. Also draw this data model using the tool you have been told to use in the course.

6. The entity type STUDENT has the following attributes: Student_Name, Address, Phone, Age, Activity, and No_of_Years. Activity represents some campus-based student activity, whereas No_of_Years represents the number of years the student has engaged in this activity. A given student may engage in more than one activity. Draw an ERD for this situation.

7. Prepare an ERD for a real estate firm that lists property for sale. Also prepare a definition for each entity type, attribute, and relationship on your diagram. In addition, draw a data model for this situation using the tool you have been told to use in your course. The following describes this organization:

   - The firm has a number of sales offices in several states. Attributes of sales office include Office_Number (identifier) and Location.
   - Each sales office is assigned one or more employees. Attributes of employee include Employee_ID (identifier) and Employee_Name. An employee must be assigned to only one sales office.
   - For each sales office, there is always one employee assigned to manage that office. An employee may manage only the sales office to which he or she is assigned.
   - The firm lists property for sale. Attributes of property include Property_ID (identifier) and Location.

Components of Location include Address, City, State, and Zip_Code.
   - Each unit of property must be listed with one (and only one) of the sales offices. A sales office may have any number of properties listed or may have no properties listed.
   - Each unit of property has one or more owners. Attributes of owners are Owner_ID (identifier) and Owner_Name. An owner may own one or more units of property. An attribute of the relationship between property and owner is Percent_Owned.

8. Add minimum and maximum cardinality notation to each of the following figures, as appropriate:

   a. Figure 3-5
   b. Figure 3-10a
   c. Figure 3-11b
   d. Figure 3-12 (all parts)
   e. Figure 3-13c
   f. Figure 3-14

9. After completing a course in database management, you have been asked to develop a preliminary ERD for a symphony orchestra. You discover the following entity types that should be included:

   - CONCERT SEASON The season during which a series of concerts will be performed. Identifier is Opening_Date, which includes Month, Day, and Year.
   - CONCERT A given performance of one or more compositions. Identifier is Concert_Number. Another important attribute is Concert_Date, which consists of the following: Month, Day, Year, and Time. Each concert typically has more than one concert date.
   - COMPOSITION Compositions to be performed at each concert. Identifier is Composition_ID, which consists of the following: Composer_Name and Composition_Name. Another attribute is Movement_ID, which consists of two parts: Movement_Number and Movement_Name. Many, but not all, compositions have multiple movements.
   - CONDUCTOR Person who will conduct the concert. Identifier is Conductor_ID. Another attribute is Conductor_Name.

Figure 3-24
Grade report

MILLENNIUM COLLEGE
GRADE REPORT
FALL SEMESTER 200X

NAME: Emily Williams   ID: 268300458
CAMPUS ADDRESS: 208 Brooks Hall
MAJOR: Information Systems

COURSE ID	TITLE	INSTRUCTOR NAME	INSTRUCTOR LOCATION	GRADE
IS 350	Database Mgt.	Codd	B104	A
IS 465	System Analysis	Parsons	B317	B

- SOLOIST Solo artist who performs a given composition on a particular concert. Identifier is Soloist_ID. Another attribute is Soloist_Name.

During further discussions you discover the following:

- A concert season schedules one or more concerts. A particular concert is scheduled for only one concert season.
- A concert includes the performance of one or more compositions. A composition may be performed at one or more concerts or may not be performed.
- For each concert there is one conductor. A conductor may conduct any number of concerts or may not conduct any concerts.
- Each composition may require one or more soloists or may not require a soloist. A soloist may perform one or more compositions at a given concert or may not perform any composition. The symphony orchestra wishes to record the date when a soloist last performed a given composition (Date_Last_Performed).

Draw an ERD to represent what you have discovered. Identify a business rule in this description and explain how this business rule is modeled on the E-R diagram. Also draw a data model for this situation using the tool you have been told to use in your course.

10. Obtain several common user views such as a credit card receipt, credit card statement, and annual summary, or some other common document from one organization with which you interact.

    a. Prepare an ERD for one of these documents. Also prepare a data model for this document using the tool you have been told to use in your course.

    b. Prepare an ERD for another of these documents. Also prepare a data model for this document using the tool you have been told to use in your course.

    c. Do you find the same entities, attributes, and relationships in the two ERDs you developed for parts a and b? What differences do you find in modeling the same data entities, attributes, and relationships between the two ERDs? Can you combine the two ERDs into one ERD for which the original two are subsets? Do you encounter any issues in trying to combine the ERDs? Suggest some issues that might arise if two different data modelers had independently developed the two data models.

    d. How might you use data naming and definition standards to overcome the issues you identified in part c?

11. Draw an ERD for some organization that you are familiar with—Boy Scouts/Girl Scouts, sports team, etc. Also draw a data model for this organization using the tool you have been told to use in your course.

12. Draw an ERD for the following situation (Batra et al., 1988). Also, develop the list of words for qualifiers and classes that you use to form attribute names. Explain why you chose the words on your list. Also, draw a data model for this situation using the tool you have been told to use in your course.

    Projects, Inc., is an engineering firm with approximately 500 employees. A database is required to keep track of all employees, their skills, projects assigned, and departments worked in. Every employee has a unique number assigned by the firm, required to store his or her name and date of birth. If an employee is currently married to another employee of Projects, Inc., the date of marriage and who is married to whom must be stored; however, no record of marriage is required if an employee's spouse is not also an employee. Each employee is given a job title (for example, engineer, secretary, and so on). An employee does only one type of job at any given time, and we only need to retain information for an employee's current job.

    There are eleven different departments, each with a unique name. An employee can report to only one department. Each department has a phone number.

    To procure various kinds of equipment, each department deals with many vendors. A vendor typically supplies equipment to many departments. We are required to store the name and address of each vendor and the date of the last meeting between a department and a vendor.

    Many employees can work on a project. An employee can work on many projects (e.g., Southwest Refinery, California Petrochemicals, and so on) but can only be assigned to at most one project in a given city. For each city, we are interested in its state and population. An employee can have many skills (preparing material requisitions, checking drawings, and so on), but she or he may use only a given set of skills on a particular project. (For example, an employee MURPHY may prepare requisitions for the Southwest Refinery project and prepare requisitions as well as check drawings for California Petrochemicals.) Employees use each skill that they possess in at least one project. Each skill is assigned a number, and we must store a short description of each skill. Projects are distinguished by project numbers, and we must store the estimated cost of each project.

13. Draw an ERD for the following situation. (State any assumptions you believe you have to make in order to develop a complete diagram.) Also, draw a data model for this situation using the tool you have been told to use in your course: Stillwater Antiques buys and sells one-of-a-kind antiques of all kinds (e.g., furniture, jewelry, china, and clothing). Each item is uniquely identified by an item number and is also characterized by a description, asking price, condition, and open-ended comments. Stillwater works with many different individuals, called clients, who sell items to and buy items from the store. Some clients only sell items to Stillwater, some only buy items, and some others both sell and buy. A client is identified by a client number and is also described by a client name and client address. When Stillwater sells an item in stock to a client, the owners want to record the commission paid, the actual selling price, sales tax (tax of zero indicates a tax exempt sale), and date sold. When Stillwater buys an item from a client, the owners want to record the purchase cost, date purchased, and condition at time of purchase.

14. Draw an ERD for the following situation. (State any assumptions you believe you have to make in order to develop a complete diagram.) Also, draw a data model for this situation using the tool you have been told to use in your course: The H. I. Topi School of Business operates international business programs in ten locations throughout Europe. The

School had its first class of 9,000 graduates in 1965. The School keeps track of each graduate's student number, name when a student, country of birth, current country of citizenship, current name, current address, and the name of each major the student completed. (Each student has one or two majors.) To maintain strong ties to its alumni, the School holds various events around the world. Events have a title, date, location, and type (e.g., reception, dinner, or seminar). The School needs to keep track of which graduates have attended which events. For an attendance by a graduate at an event, a comment is recorded about information School officials learned from that graduate at that event. The School also keeps in contact with graduates by mail, e-mail, telephone, and fax interactions. As with events, the School records information learned from the graduate from each of these contacts. When a School official knows that he or she will be meeting or talking to a graduate, a report is produced showing the latest information about that graduate and the information learned during the past two years from that graduate from all contacts and events the graduate attended.

15. Assume that at Pine Valley Furniture each product (described by product number, description, and cost) comprises at least three components (described by component number, description, and unit of measure), and components are used to make one or many products. In addition, assume that components are used to make other components and that raw materials are also considered to be components. In both cases of components, we need to keep track of how many components go into making something else. Draw an ERD for this situation, and place minimum and maximum cardinalities on the diagram. Also, draw a data model for this situation using the tool you have been told to use in your course.

16. Emerging Electric wishes to create a database with the following entities and attributes:
    • Customer, with attributes Customer_ID, Name, Address (Street, City, State, Zip code), Telephone
    • Location, with attributes Location_ID, Address (Street, City, State, Zip code), Type (values of Business or Residential)
    • Rate, with attributes RateClass, Rateperkwh

    After interviews with the owners, you have come up with the following business rules:
    • Customers can have one or more locations.
    • Each location can have one or more rates, depending on the time of day.

    Draw an ERD for this situation, and place minimum and maximum cardinalities on the diagram. Also, draw a data model for this situation using the tool you have been told to use in your course. State any assumptions that you have made.

17. Each semester, each student must be assigned an adviser who counsels students about degree requirements and helps students register for classes. Each student must register for classes with the help of an adviser, but if the student's assigned adviser is not available, the student may register with any adviser. We must keep track of students, the

assigned adviser for each, and the name of the adviser with whom the student registered for the current term. Represent this situation of students and advisers with an E-R diagram. Also, draw a data model for this situation using the tool you have been told to use in your course.

18. Because Visio does not explicitly show associative entities, it is not clear in Figure 3-22 which entity types are associative. List the associative entities in this figure. Why are there so many associative entities in Figure 3-22 ?

19. Wally Los Gatos, owner of Wally's Wonderful World of Wallcoverings, has hired you as a consultant to design a database management system for his chain of three stores that sell wallpaper and accessories. He would like to track sales, customers, and employees. After an initial meeting with Wally, you have developed a list of business rules and specifications to begin the design of an E-R Model:
    • Customers place orders through a branch.
    • Wally would like to track the following about customers: Name, Address, City, State, Zip code, Telephone, Date of Birth, Primary Language.
    • A customer may place many orders.
    • A customer does not always have to order through the same branch all the time.
    • Customers may have one or more accounts, although they may also have no accounts.
    • The following information needs to be recorded about accounts: Balance, Last payment date, Last payment amount, Type.
    • A branch may have many customers.
    • The following information about each branch needs to be recorded: Branch Number, Location (Address, City, State, Zip code), Square Footage.
    • A branch may sell all items or may only sell certain items.
    • Orders are composed of one or more items.
    • The following information about each order needs to be recorded: Order date, Credit authorization status.
    • Items may be sold by one or more branches.
    • We wish to record the following about each item: Description, Color, Size, Pattern, Type.
    • An item can be composed of multiple items; for example, a dining room wallcovering set (item 20) may consist of wallpaper (item 22) and borders (item 23).
    • Wally employs fifty-six employees.
    • He would like to track the following information about employees: Name, Address (Street, City, State, Zip code), Telephone, Date of Hire, Title, Salary, Skill, Age.
    • Each employee works in one and only one branch.
    • Each employee may have one or more dependents. We wish to record the name of the dependent as well as the age and relationship.
    • Employees can have one or more skills.

    Based upon this information, draw an E-R model. Please indicate any assumptions that you have made. Also, draw a data model for this situation using the tool you have been told to use in your course.

20. Our friend Wally Los Gatos (see Problem and Exercise 19), realizing that his wallcovering business had a few wrinkles in it, decided to pursue a law degree at night. After graduating, he has teamed up with Lyla El Pàjaro to form Peck and Paw, Attorneys at Law. Wally and Lyla have hired you to design a database system based upon the following set of business rules. It is in your best interest to perform a thorough analysis, to avoid needless litigation. Please create an ERD based upon the following set of rules:

- An ATTORNEY is retained by one or more CLIENTS for each CASE.
- Attributes of ATTORNEY are: Attorney_ID, Name, Address, City, State, Zip_Code, Specialty (may be more than one), Bar (may be more than one).
- A CLIENT may have more than one ATTORNEY for each CASE.
- Attributes of CLIENT are Client_ID, Name, Address, City, State, Zip_Code, Telephone, Date of Birth.
- A CLIENT may have more than one CASE.
- Attributes of CASE are Case_ID, Case_Description, Case_Type.
- An ATTORNEY may have more than one CASE.
- Each CASE is assigned to one and only one COURT.
- Attributes of COURT are Court_ID, Court_Name, City, State, Zip_Code.
- Each COURT has one or more JUDGES assigned to it.
- Attributes of JUDGE are Judge_ID, Name, Years in Practice.
- EACH JUDGE is assigned to exactly one court.

Please state any assumptions that you have made. Also, draw a data model for this situation using the tool you have been told to use in your course.

21. Modify Figure 3-11a to model the following additional information requirements: The training director decides, for each employee who completes each class, who (what employees) should be notified of the course completion. The training director needs to keep track of which employees are notified about each course completion by a student. The date of notification is the only attribute recorded about this notification.

22. Review Figure 3-8 and Figure 3-22.

a. Identify any attributes in Figure 3-22 that might be composite attributes but are not shown that way. Justify your suggestions. Redraw the ERD to reflect any changes you suggest.

b. Identify any attributes in Figure 3-22 that might be multivalued attributes but are not shown that way. Justify your suggestions. Redraw the ERD to reflect any changes you suggest.

c. Is it possible for the same attribute to be both composite and multivalued? If no, justify your answer; if yes, give an example (Hint: Consider the CUSTOMER attributes in Figure 3-22).

23. In the chapter, when describing Figure 3-4a, it was argued that the Received and Summarizes relationships and TREASURER entity were not necessary. Within the context of this explanation, this is true. Now, consider a slightly different situation. Suppose it is necessary, for compliance purposes (e.g., Sarbanes-Oxley compliance), to know when each expense report was produced and which officers (not just the treasurer) received each expense report and when they each signed off on that report. Redraw Figure 3-4a, now including any attributes and relationships required for this revised situation.

Field Exercises

1. Interview a database or systems analyst and document how he or she decides on names for data objects in data models. Does the organization in which this person works have naming guidelines? If so, describe the pattern used. If there are no guidelines, ask whether your contact has ever had any problems because guidelines did not exist.

2. Visit two local small businesses, one in the service sector (such as a dry cleaner, auto repair shop, veterinarian, or bookstore) and one that manufactures tangible goods. Interview employees from these organizations to elicit from them the entities, attributes, and relationships that are commonly encountered in these organizations. Use this information to construct E-R diagrams. What differences and similarities are there between the diagrams for the service- and the product-oriented companies? Does the E-R diagramming technique handle both situations equally well? Why or why not?

3. Ask a database or systems analyst to give you examples of unary, binary, and ternary relationships that the analyst has dealt with personally at his or her company. Ask which is most common and why.

4. Ask a database or systems analyst in a local company to show you an E-R diagram for one of the organization's primary databases. Ask questions to be sure you understand what each entity, attribute, and relationship means. Does this organization use the same E-R notation used in this text? If not, what other or alternative symbols are used and what do these symbols mean? Does this organization model associative entities on the E-R diagram? If not, how are associative entities modeled? What metadata are kept about the objects on the E-R diagram?

5. For the same E-R diagram used in Field Exercise 4 or for a different database in the same or a different organization, identify any uses of time stamping or other means to model time-dependent data. Why are time-dependent data necessary for those who use this database? Would the E-R diagram be much simpler if it were not necessary to represent the history of attribute values?

6. Search on the Internet for products that help document and manage business rules, standards, and procedures. One such site is **www.axisboulder.com.** Choose a couple of tools and summarize their capabilities and discuss how they would be useful in managing business rules.

References

Aranow, E. B. 1989. "Developing Good Data Definitions." *Database Programming & Design* 2,8 (August): 36–39.

Batra, D., J. A. Hoffer, and R. B. Bostrom. 1988. "A Comparison of User Performance Between the Relational and Extended Entity Relationship Model in the Discovery Phase of Database Design." *Proceedings of the Ninth International Conference on Information Systems.* Minneapolis, Nov. 30–Dec. 3: 295–306.

Bruce, T. A. 1992. *Designing Quality Databases with IDEF1X Information Models.* New York: Dorset House.

Chen, P. P.-S. 1976. "The Entity-Relationship Model—Toward a Unified View of Data." *ACM Transactions on Database Systems* 1,1(March): 9–36.

Elmasri, R., and S. B. Navathe. 1994. *Fundamentals of Database Systems.* 2d ed. Menlo Park, CA: Benjamin/Cummings.

Gottesdiener, E. 1997. "Business Rules Show Power, Promise." *Application Development Trends* 4,3 (March): 36–54.

Gottesdiener, E. 1999. "Turning Rules into Requirements." *Application Development Trends* 6,7 (July): 37–50.

Hay, D. C. 2003. "What Exactly IS a Data Model?" Parts 1, 2, and 3 *DM Review* Vol 13, Issues 2 (February: 24–26), 3 (March: 48–50), and 4 (April: 20–22, 46).

GUIDE. "GUIDE Business Rules Project." Final Report, revision 1.2. October 1997.

Hoffer, J. A., J. F. George, and J. S. Valacich. 2005. *Modern Systems Analysis and Design.* 4th ed. Upper Saddle River, NJ: Prentice Hall.

Moriarty, T. 2000. "The Right Tool for the Job." *Intelligent Enterprise* 3,9 (June 5): 68, 70–71.

Owen, J. 2004. "Putting Rules Engines to Work." *InfoWorld* (June 28): 35–41.

Plotkin, D. 1999. "Business Rules Everywhere." *Intelligent Enterprise* 2,4 (March 30): 37–44.

Salin, T. 1990. "What's in a Name?" *Database Programming & Design* 3,3 (March): 55–58.

Song, I.-Y., M. Evans, and E. K. Park. 1995. "A Comparative Analysis of Entity-Relationship Diagrams." *Journal of Computer & Software Engineering* 3,4: 427–59.

Storey, V. C. 1991. "Relational Database Design Based on the Entity-Relationship Model." *Data and Knowledge Engineering* 7: 47–83.

Teorey, T. J., D. Yang, and J. P. Fry. 1986. "A Logical Design Methodology for Relational Databases Using the Extended Entity-Relationship Model." *Computing Surveys* 18,2 (June): 197–221.

von Halle, B. 1997. "Digging for Business Rules." *Database Programming & Design* 8,11: 11–13.

Further Reading

Batini, C., S. Ceri, and S. B. Navathe. 1992. *Conceptual Database Design: An Entity-Relationship Approach.* Menlo Park, CA: Benjamin/Cummings.

Bodart, F, A. Patel, M. Sim, and R. Weber. 2001. "Should Optional Properties Be Used in Conceptual Modelling? A Theory and Three Empirical Tests." *Information Systems Research* 12,4 (December): 384–405.

Carlis, J., and J. Maguire. 2001. *Mastering Data Modeling: A User-Driven Approach.* Upper Saddle River, NJ: Addison-Wesley.

Keuffel, W. 1996. "Battle of the Modeling Techniques." *DBMS* 9,8 (August): 83, 84, 86, 97.

Moody, D. 1996. "The Seven Habits of Highly Effective Data Modelers." *Database Programming & Design* 9,10 (October): 57, 58, 60–62, 64.

Teorey, T. 1999. *Database Modeling & Design.* 3d ed. San Francisco, CA: Morgan Kaufman.

Tillman, G. 1994. "Should You Model Derived Data?" *DBMS* 7,11 (November): 88, 90.

Tillman, G. 1995. "Data Modeling Rules of Thumb." *DBMS* 8,8 (August): 70, 72, 74, 76, 80–82, 87.

Web Resources

www.adtmag.com *Application Development Trends* is a leading publication on the practice of information systems development.

www.axisboulder.com Web site for one vendor of business rules software.

www.businessrulesgroup.org The Business Rules Group, formerly part of GUIDE International, formulates and supports standards about business rules.

datadmn.disa.mil This site contains many E-R diagrams and other documentation as examples of data and systems modeling.

www.intelligententerprise.com *Intelligent Enterprise* is a leading publication on database management and related areas. This magazine is the result of combining two previous publications, *Database Programming & Design* and *DBMS.*

www.tdan.com *The Data Administration Newsletter* is an on-line journal that includes articles on a wide variety of data management topics. This Web site is considered a "must follow" Web site for data management professionals.

MOUNTAIN VIEW COMMUNITY HOSPITAL

Case

CASE DESCRIPTION

After completing a course in database management, you have been hired as a summer intern by Mountain View Community Hospital. Your first assignment is to work as part of a team of three people to develop a high-level E-R diagram for the hospital. You conduct interviews with a number of hospital administrators and staff to identify the key entity types for the hospital. You have also seen the preliminary enterprise-level diagram shown in MVCH Figure 2-3 and subsequent revisions. As a result, your team has identified the following entity types:

- *Care Center*—a treatment center within the hospital. Examples of care centers are maternity, emergency care, or multiple sclerosis center. Each care center has a care center ID (identifier) and a care center name.

- *Patient*—a person who is either admitted to the hospital or is registered as an outpatient. Each patient has an identifier, the medical record number (MRN), and a name.

- *Physician*—a member of the hospital medical staff who may admit patients to the hospital and who may administer medical treatments. Each physician has a physician ID (identifier) and name.

- *Bed*—a hospital bed that may be assigned to a patient who is admitted to the hospital. Each bed has a bed number (identifier), a room number, and a care center ID.

- *Item*—any medical or surgical item that may be used in treating a patient. Each item has an item number (identifier), description, and unit cost.

- *Employee*—any person employed as part of the hospital staff. Each employee has an employee number (identifier) and name.

- *Diagnosis*—a patient's medical condition diagnosed by a physician. Each diagnosis has a diagnosis ID/code and diagnosis name. Mountain View Community Hospital

is using the HIPAA-mandated ICD-9-CM Volume 1 diagnosis codes[1] for patient conditions (e.g., 00.50, STAPH FOOD POISONING, 173.3, BASAL CELL CARCINOMA, 200.2, MALIGNANT MELANOMA, BURKITT'S TYPE, or 776.5. CONGENITAL ANEMIA).

- *Treatment*—any test or procedure ordered by and/or performed by a physician for a patient. Each treatment has a treatment ID/treatment code and treatment name using standard codes. HIPAA-mandated ICD-9-CM Volume 3 Procedure Codes are used for diagnostic and therapeutic procedures, e.g., 03.31, SPINAL TAP, 14.3, REPAIR OF RETINAL TEAR, 87.44, ROUTINE CHEST X-RAY, or 90.5, MICROSCOPIC EXAMINATION OF BLOOD).

- *Order*—any order issued by a physician for treatment and/or services such as diagnostic tests (radiology, laboratory) and therapeutic procedures (physical therapy, diet orders), or drugs and devices (prescriptions). Each order has an order_ID, and order date, and order time.

The team next recorded the following information concerning relationships:

- Each hospital employee is assigned to work in one or more care centers. Each care center has at least one employee and may have any number of employees. The hospital records the number of hours per week that a given employee works in a particular care center.

- Each care center has exactly one employee who is designated nurse-in-charge for that care center.

- A given patient may or may not be assigned to a bed (since some patients are outpatients). Occupancy rates are seldom at 100 percent, so a bed may or may not be assigned to a patient.

- A patient may be referred to the hospital by exactly one physician. A physician may refer any number of patients or may not refer any patients.

---

[1]Note: ICD refers to the International Classification of Diseases which, in the United States, is the HIPAA-mandated coding system used in medical billing. More information can be found at http://www.cms.hhs.gov/medlearn/icd9code.asp.

- A patient must be admitted to the hospital by exactly one physician. A physician may admit any number of patients or may not admit any patients.

- Prior to being seen by a physician, a nurse typically obtains and records relevant information about the patient. This includes the patient's weight, blood pressure, pulse, and temperature. The nurse who assesses the vital signs also records the date and time. Finally, the reasons for the visit and any symptoms the patient describes are recorded.

- Physicians diagnose any number of conditions affecting a patient, and a diagnosis may apply to many patients. The hospital records the following information: date and time of diagnosis, diagnosis code, and description.

- Physicians may order and perform any number of services/treatments for a patient or may not perform any treatment. A treatment or service may be performed on any number of patients, and a patient may have treatments performed or ordered by any number of physicians. For each treatment or service rendered, the hospital records the following information: physician ordering the treatment, treatment date, treatment time, and results.

- A patient may also consume any number of items. A given item may be consumed by one or more patients, or may not be consumed. For each item consumed by a patient, the hospital records the following: date, time, quantity, and total cost (which can be computed by multiplying quantity times unit cost).

CASE QUESTIONS

1. Why would Mountain View Community Hospital want to use E-R modeling to understand its data requirements? What other ways might the hospital want to model its information requirements?

2. Is Mountain View Community Hospital itself an entity type in the data model? Why or why not?

3. Do there appear to be any of the following in the description of the Mountain View Community Hospital data requirements? If so, what are they?
   a. weak entities
   b. multivalued attributes
   c. multiple relationships

4. When developing an E-R diagram for Mountain View Community Hospital, what is the significance of the business rule that states that some patients are assigned to a bed, but outpatients are not assigned to a bed?

5. Do you think that *Items* should be split into two separate entities, one for nonreusable and one for reusable items? Why or why not?

6. What quality check(s) would you perform to determine whether the E-R model you developed can easily satisfy user requests for data and/or information?

CASE EXERCISES

1. Study the case description very closely. What other questions would you like to ask to understand the data requirements at Mountain View Community Hospital?

2. Develop an E-R diagram for Mountain View Community Hospital. State any assumptions you made in developing the diagram. If you have been assigned a particular data modeling tool, redraw your E-R diagram using this tool.

3. The case describes an entity type called *Item*. Given your answer to Case Exercise 2, will this entity type also be able to represent in-room TVs as a billable item to patients? Why or why not?

4. Suppose the attribute bed number were a composite attribute, composed of care center ID, room number, and individual bed number. Redraw any parts of your answer to Case Exercise 2 that would have to change to handle this composite attribute.

5. Consider your new E-R diagram for Case Exercise 4. Now, additionally assume that a care center contains many rooms, and each room may contain items that are billed to patients assigned to that room. Redraw your E-R diagram to accommodate this new assumption.

6. Does your answer to Case Exercise 2 allow more than one physician to perform a treatment on a patient at the same time? If not, redraw your answer to Case Exercise 2 to accommodate this situation. Make any additional assumptions you consider necessary to represent this situation.

7. Does your answer to Case Exercise 2 allow the same treatment to be performed more than once on the same patient by the same physician? If not, redraw your answer to Case Exercise 2 to accommodate this situation. Make any additional assumptions you consider necessary in order to represent this situation.

PROJECT ASSIGNMENTS

P1. Develop an E-R diagram for Mountain View Hospital based on the enterprise data model you developed in Chapter 2, and the case description, questions, and exercises presented above. Using the notation described in Chapter 3, clearly indicate the different types of entities, attributes (identifiers, multivalued attributes, composite attributes, derived attributes) and relationships that apply in this case.

P2. Develop a list of well-stated business rules for your E-R diagram.

P3. Prepare a list of questions that have arisen as a result of your E-R modeling efforts, and that need to be answered to clarify your understanding of Mountain View Community Hospital's business rules and data requirements.

4

The Enhanced E-R Model
and Business Rules

LEARNING OBJECTIVES

After studying this chapter, you should be able to:

- Concisely define each of the following key terms: **enhanced entity-relationship (EER) model, subtype, supertype, attribute inheritance, generalization, specialization, completeness constraint, total specialization rule, partial specialization rule, disjointness constraint, disjoint rule, overlap rule, subtype discriminator, supertype/subtype hierarchy, entity cluster, universal data model, derivation, structural assertion, action assertion, derived fact, anchor object, action,** and **corresponding object.**

- Recognize when to use subtype/supertype relationships in data modeling.

- Use both specialization and generalization as techniques for defining supertype/subtype relationships.

- Specify both completeness constraints and disjointness constraints in modeling supertype/subtype relationships.

- Develop a supertype/subtype hierarchy for a realistic business situation.

- Develop an entity cluster to simplify presentation of an E-R diagram.

- Explain the major features and data modeling structures of a universal data model.

- Name the various categories of business rules.

- Define a simple operational constraint using a graphical model or structured English statement.

INTRODUCTION

The basic E-R model described in Chapter 3 was first introduced during the mid-1970s. It has been suitable for modeling most common business problems and has enjoyed widespread use. However, the business environment has changed dramatically since that time. Business relationships are more complex, and as a result, business data are much more complex as well. For example, organizations must be prepared to segment their markets and to customize their products, which places much greater demands on organizational databases.

To cope better with these changes, researchers and consultants have continued to enhance the E-R model so that it can more accurately represent the complex

Enhanced entity-relationship (EER) model: The model that has resulted from extending the original E-R model with new modeling constructs.

data encountered in today's business environment. The term **enhanced entity-relationship (EER) model** is used to identify the model that has resulted from extending the original E-R model with these new modeling constructs. These extensions make the EER model semantically similar to the object-oriented data modeling, which we cover in Chapter 14.

The most important modeling construct incorporated in the EER model is supertype/subtype relationships. This facility enables us to model a general entity type (called the *supertype*) and then subdivide it into several specialized entity types (called *subtypes*). Thus, for example, the entity type CAR can be modeled as a supertype, with subtypes SEDAN, SPORTS CAR, COUPE, and so on. Each subtype inherits attributes from its supertype and in addition may have special attributes and be involved in relationships of its own. Adding new notation for modeling supertype/subtype relationships has greatly improved the flexibility of the basic E-R model.

E-R, and especially EER, diagrams can become large and complex, requiring multiple pages (or very small font) for display. Some commercial databases include hundreds of entities. Many users and managers specifying requirements for a database do not need to see all the entities, relationships, and attributes to understand the part of the database with which they are most interested. Entity clustering is a way to turn a part of an entity-relationship data model into a more macro-level view of the same data. Entity clustering is a hierarchical decomposition technique, which can make E-R diagrams easier to read. By grouping entities and relationships, you can lay out an E-R diagram to allow you to give attention to the details of the model that matter most in a given data modeling task.

Universal and industry-specific generalizable data models, which extensively utilized EER capabilities, have become very important for contemporary data modelers. These packaged data models and data model patterns have made data modelers more efficient and produce data models of higher quality. The EER features of supertypes/subtypes are essential to create generalizable data models; additional generalizing constructs, such as typing entities and relationships, are also employed.

Enhanced E-R diagrams are used to capture important business rules such as constraints in supertype/subtype relationships. However, most organizations use a multitude of business rules to guide behavior. Many of these rules cannot be expressed with basic E-R diagrams, or even with enhanced E-R diagrams. Promising research at present is directed at developing new ways of expressing business rules that would allow end users with some training to define their own rules to the system. These rules then automatically become constraints that are enforced by the database management system and are used to maintain the database in a consistent or valid state. This business-rules approach enables organizations to respond much more quickly to changing business conditions than previous approaches to systems development.

REPRESENTING SUPERTYPES AND SUBTYPES

Recall from Chapter 3 that an entity type is a collection of entities that share common properties or characteristics. Although the entity instances that compose an entity type are similar, we do not expect them to be identical. For example, recall required and optional attributes from Chapter 3. One way to view these types of attributes is that different entity instances have some of the same attributes, but not exactly the same ones, and hence, maybe there are different types of similar entities. One of the major challenges in data modeling is to recognize and clearly represent entities that are almost the same; that is, entity types that share common properties but also have one or more distinct properties that are of interest to the organization.

Subtype: A subgrouping of the entities in an entity type that is meaningful to the organization and that shares common attributes or relationships distinct from other subgroupings.

For this reason, the E-R model has been extended to include supertype/subtype relationships. A **subtype** is a subgrouping of the entities in an entity type that is meaningful to the organization. For example, STUDENT is an entity type in a university. Two subtypes of STUDENT are GRADUATE STUDENT and UNDERGRADUATE

STUDENT. In this example, we refer to STUDENT as the supertype. A **supertype** is a generic entity type that has a relationship with one or more subtypes.

In the E-R diagramming we have done so far, supertypes and subtypes have been hidden. For example, consider again Figure 3-22, which is the E-R diagram (in Microsoft Visio) for Pine Valley Furniture Company. Notice that it is possible for a customer to not do business in any territory (i.e., no associated instances of Does_Business_In relationships). Why is this? One possible reason is that there are two types of customers—national account customers and regular customers—and only regular customers are assigned to a sales territory. Thus, in Figure 3-22, the reason for the optional cardinality next to the Does_Business_In relationship coming from CUSTOMER is obscured. Explicitly drawing a customer entity supertype and several entity subtypes will help us to make the E-R diagram more meaningful. Later in this chapter, we show a revised E-R diagram for Pine Valley Furniture, which demonstrates several EER notations to make vague aspects of Figure 3-22 more explicit.

Basic Concepts and Notation

The notation that is used for supertype/subtype relationships in this text is shown in Figure 4-1a. The supertype is connected with a line to a circle, which in turn is connected by a line to each subtype that has been defined. The U-shaped symbol on each line connecting a subtype to the circle emphasizes that the subtype is a subset of the supertype. It also indicates the direction of the subtype/supertype relationship. (This U is optional because the meaning and direction of the supertype/subtype relationship is usually obvious; in most examples, we will not include this symbol). Figure 4-1b shows the type of EER notation used by Microsoft Visio (which is very similar to that used in this text), and Figure 4-1c shows the type of EER notation used by some CASE tools (e.g., Oracle Designer); the notation in Figure 4-1c is also the form often used for universal and industry-specific data models. These

Supertype: A generic entity type that has a relationship with one or more subtypes.

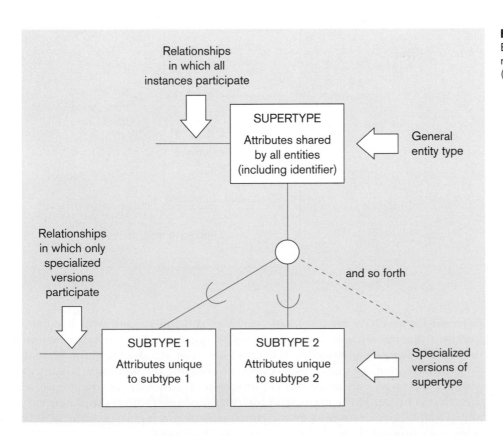

Figure 4-1 (Continues)
Basic notation for supertype/subtype relationships
(a) EER notation

Figure 4-1 (Continued)
(b) Microsoft Visio notation

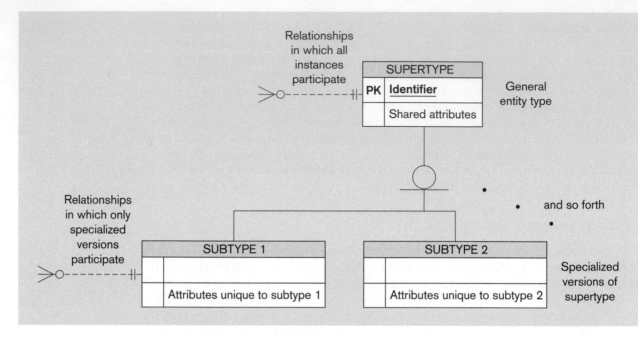

(c) Subtypes inside supertypes notation

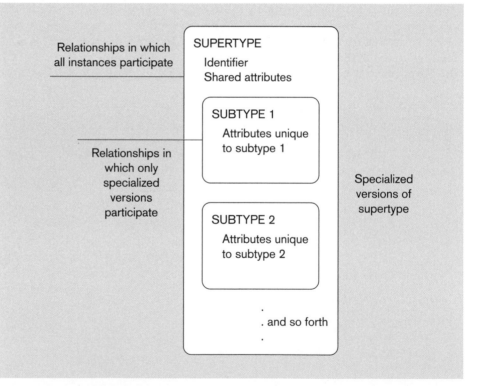

different formats have identical basic features, and you should easily become comfortable using any of these forms. We primarily use the text notation for examples in this chapter because advanced EER features are more standard with this format.

Attributes that are shared by all entities (including the identifier) are associated with the supertype. Attributes that are unique to a particular subtype are associated with that subtype. The same is true for relationships. Other components will be added to this notation to provide additional meaning in supertype/subtype relationships as we proceed through the remainder of this chapter.

An Example Let us illustrate supertype/subtype relationships with a simple yet common example. Suppose that an organization has three basic types of employees: hourly employees, salaried employees, and contract consultants. Some of the important attributes for each of these types of employees are the following:

- *Hourly employees* Employee_Number, Employee_Name, Address, Date_Hired, Hourly_Rate
- *Salaried employees* Employee_Number, Employee_Name, Address, Date_Hired, Annual_Salary, Stock_Option
- *Contract consultants* Employee_Number, Employee_Name, Address, Date_Hired, Contract_Number, Billing_Rate

Notice that all of the employee types have several attributes in common: Employee_Number, Employee_Name, Address, and Date_Hired. In addition, each type has one or more attributes distinct from the attributes of other types (e.g., Hourly_Rate is unique to hourly employees). If you were developing a conceptual data model in this situation, you might consider three choices:

1. Define a single entity type called EMPLOYEE. Although conceptually simple, this approach has the disadvantage that EMPLOYEE would have to contain all of the attributes for the three types of employees. For an instance of an hourly employee (for example), attributes such as Annual_Salary and Contract_Number would not apply (optional attributes) and would be null or not used. When taken to a development environment, programs that use this entity type would necessarily need to be quite complex to deal with the many variations.

2. Define a separate entity type for each of the three entities. This approach would fail to exploit the common properties of employees, and users would have to be careful to select the correct entity type when using the system.

3. Define a supertype called EMPLOYEE with subtypes for HOURLY EMPLOYEE, SALARIED EMPLOYEE, and CONSULTANT. This approach exploits the common properties of all employees, yet recognizes the distinct properties of each type.

Figure 4-2 shows a representation of the EMPLOYEE supertype with its three subtypes, using enhanced ER notation. Attributes shared by all employees are associated

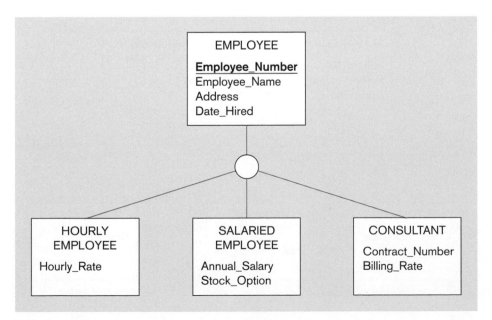

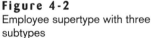

Figure 4-2
Employee supertype with three subtypes

with the EMPLOYEE entity type. Attributes that are peculiar to each subtype are included with that subtype only.

Attribute Inheritance   A subtype is an entity type in its own right. An entity instance of a subtype represents the same entity instance of the supertype. For example, if "Therese Jones" is an occurrence of the CONSULTANT subtype, then this same person is necessarily an occurrence of the EMPLOYEE supertype. As a consequence, an entity in a subtype must possess not only values for its own attributes, but also values for its attributes as a member of the supertype, including the identifier.

Attribute inheritance is the property by which subtype entities inherit values of all attributes of the supertype. This important property makes it unnecessary to include supertype attributes redundantly with the subtypes. For example, Employee_Name is an attribute of EMPLOYEE (Figure 4-2), but not of the subtypes of EMPLOYEE. Thus, the fact that the employee's name is "Therese Jones" is inherited from the EMPLOYEE supertype. However, the Billing_Rate for this same employee is an attribute of the subtype CONSULTANT.

We have established that a member of a subtype must be a member of the supertype. Is the converse also true—that is, is a member of the supertype also a member of one (or more) of the subtypes? This may or may not be true, depending on the business situation. We discuss the various possibilities later in this chapter.

When to Use Supertype/Subtype Relationships   Whether to use supertype/subtype relationships is a decision that the data modeler must make in each situation. You should consider using subtypes when either (or both) of the following conditions are present:

1. There are attributes that apply to some (but not all) instances of an entity type. For example, see the EMPLOYEE entity type in Figure 4-2.

2. The instances of a subtype participate in a relationship unique to that subtype.

Figure 4-3 is an example of the use of subtype relationships that illustrates both of these situations. The hospital entity type PATIENT has two subtypes: OUTPATIENT and RESIDENT PATIENT. (The identifier is Patient_ID.) All patients have an Admit_Date attribute, as well as a Patient_Name. Also, every patient is cared for by a RESPONSIBLE PHYSICIAN who develops a treatment plan for the patient.

Each subtype has an attribute that is unique to that subtype. Outpatients have a Checkback_Date, whereas resident patients have a Date_Discharged. Also, resident

Attribute inheritance: A property by which subtype entities inherit values of all attributes of the supertype.

Figure 4-3
Supertype/subtype relationships in a hospital

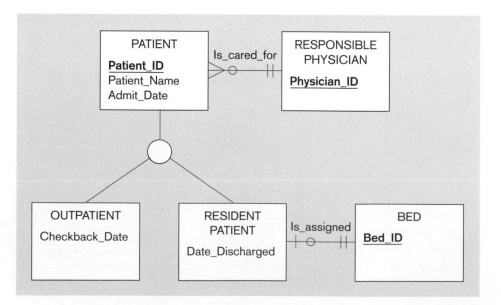

patients have a unique relationship that assigns each patient to a bed. (Notice that this is a mandatory relationship; it would be optional if it were attached to PATIENT.) Each bed may or may not be assigned to a patient.

Earlier we discussed the property of attribute inheritance. Thus, each outpatient and each resident patient inherits the attributes of the parent supertype PATIENT: Patient_ID, Patient_Name, and Admit_Date. Figure 4-3 also illustrates the principle of relationship inheritance. OUTPATIENT and RESIDENT PATIENT are also instances of PATIENT; therefore, each Is_cared_for by a RESPONSIBLE PHYSICIAN.

Representing Specialization and Generalization

We have described and illustrated the basic principles of supertype/subtype relationships, including the characteristics of "good" subtypes. But in developing real-world data models, how can you recognize opportunities to exploit these relationships? There are two processes—specialization and generalization—that serve as mental models in developing supertype/subtype relationships.

Generalization   A unique aspect of human intelligence is the ability and propensity to classify objects and experiences and to generalize their properties. In data modeling, **generalization** is the process of defining a more general entity type from a set of more specialized entity types. Thus generalization is a bottom-up process.

An example of generalization is shown in Figure 4-4. In Figure 4-4a, three entity types have been defined: CAR, TRUCK, and MOTORCYCLE. At this stage, the data

Generalization: The process of defining a more general entity type from a set of more specialized entity types.

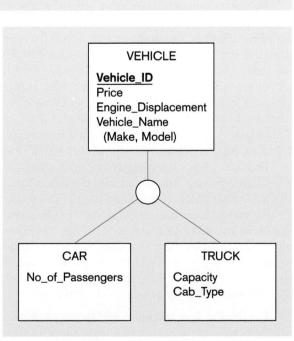

Figure 4-4
Example of generalization
(a) Three entity types: CAR, TRUCK, and MOTORCYCLE

(b) Generalization to VEHICLE supertype

modeler intends to represent these separately on an E-R diagram. However, on closer examination we see that the three entity types have a number of attributes in common: Vehicle_ID (identifier), Vehicle_Name (with components Make and Model), Price, and Engine_Displacement. This fact (reinforced by the presence of a common identifier) suggests that each of the three entity types is really a version of a more general entity type.

This more general entity type (named VEHICLE) together with the resulting supertype/subtype relationships is shown in Figure 4-4b. The entity CAR has the specific attribute No_of_Passengers, whereas TRUCK has two specific attributes: Capacity and Cab_Type. Thus, generalization has allowed us to group entity types along with their common attributes and at the same time preserve specific attributes that are peculiar to each subtype.

Notice that the entity type MOTORCYCLE is not included in the relationship. Is this simply an omission? No. Instead, it is deliberately not included because it does not satisfy the conditions for a subtype discussed earlier. Comparing Figure 4-4 parts a and b, you will notice that the only attributes of MOTORCYCLE are those that are common to all vehicles; there are no attributes specific to motorcycles. Furthermore, MOTORCYCLE does not have a relationship to another entity type. Thus there is no need to create a MOTORCYCLE subtype.

The fact that there is no MOTORCYCLE subtype suggests that it must be possible to have an instance of VEHICLE that is not a member of any of its subtypes. We discuss this type of constraint in the section on specifying constraints.

Specialization: The process of defining one or more subtypes of the supertype and forming supertype/subtype relationships.

Specialization As we have seen, generalization is a bottom-up process. **Specialization** is a top-down process, the direct reverse of generalization. Suppose that we have defined an entity type with its attributes. Specialization is the process of defining one or more subtypes of the supertype and forming supertype/subtype relationships. Each subtype is formed based on some distinguishing characteristic, such as attributes or relationships specific to the subtype.

An example of specialization is shown in Figure 4-5. Figure 4-5a shows an entity type named PART, together with several of its attributes. The identifier is Part_No, and other attributes include Description, Unit_Price, Location, Qty_on_Hand, Routing_Number, and Supplier. (The last attribute is multivalued and composite because there may be more than one supplier with an associated unit price for a part.)

In discussions with users, we discover that there are two possible sources for parts: Some are manufactured internally, whereas others are purchased from outside suppliers. Further, we discover that some parts are obtained from both sources. In this case, the choice depends on factors such as manufacturing capacity, unit price of the parts, and so on.

Some of the attributes in Figure 4-5a apply to all parts regardless of source. However, others depend on the source. Thus Routing_Number applies only to manufactured parts, whereas Supplier_ID and Unit_Price apply only to purchased parts. These factors suggest that PART should be specialized by defining the subtypes MANUFACTURED PART and PURCHASED PART (Figure 4-5b).

In Figure 4-5b, Routing_Number is associated with MANUFACTURED PART. The data modeler initially planned to associate Supplier_ID and Unit_Price with PURCHASED PART. However, in further discussions with users, the data modeler suggested instead that they create a SUPPLIER entity type and an associative entity linking PURCHASED PART with SUPPLIER. This associative entity (named SUPPLIES in Figure 4-5b) allows users to more easily associate purchased parts with their suppliers. Notice that the attribute Unit_Price is now associated with the associative entity, so that the unit price for a part may vary from one supplier to another. In this example, specialization has permitted a preferred representation of the problem domain.

Combining Specialization and Generalization Specialization and generalization are both valuable techniques for developing supertype/subtype relationships. The

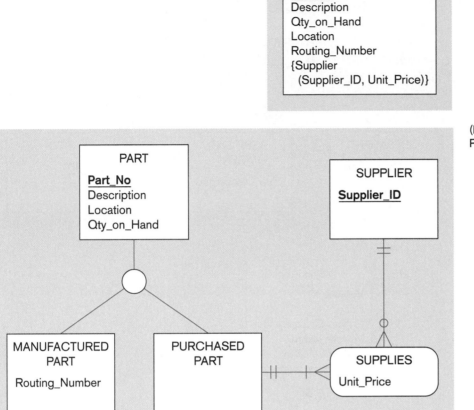

Figure 4-5
Example of specialization
(a) Entity type PART

(b) Specialization to MANUFACTURED
PART and PURCHASED PART

technique you use at a particular time depends on several factors, such as the nature of the problem domain, previous modeling efforts, and personal preference. You should be prepared to use both approaches and to alternate back and forth as dictated by the preceding factors.

SPECIFYING CONSTRAINTS IN SUPERTYPE/SUBTYPE RELATIONSHIPS

So far we have discussed the basic concepts of supertype/subtype relationships and introduced some basic notation to represent these concepts. We have also described the processes of generalization and specialization, which help a data modeler recognize opportunities for exploiting these relationships. In this section, we introduce additional notation to represent constraints on supertype/subtype relationships. These constraints allow us to capture some of the important business rules that apply to these relationships. The two most important types of constraints that are described in this section are completeness and disjointness constraints (Elmasri and Navathe, 1994).

Specifying Completeness Constraints

A **completeness constraint** addresses the question of whether an instance of a supertype must also be a member of at least one subtype. The completeness constraint

Completeness constraint: A type of constraint that addresses the question whether an instance of a supertype must also be a member of at least one subtype.

Figure 4-6
Examples of completeness constraints
(a) Total specialization rule

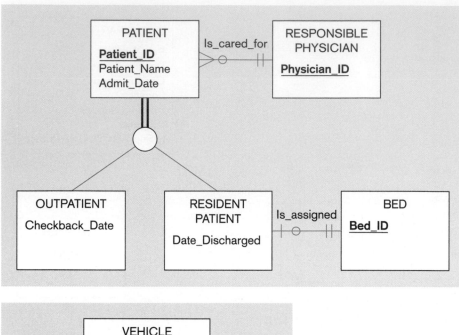

(b) Partial specialization rule

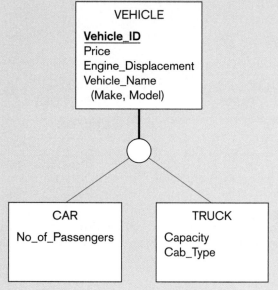

Total specialization rule: Specifies that each entity instance of the supertype must be a member of some subtype in the relationship.

Partial specialization rule: Specifies that an entity instance of the supertype is allowed not to belong to any subtype.

has two possible rules: total specialization and partial specialization. The **total specialization rule** specifies that each entity instance of the supertype must be a member of some subtype in the relationship. The **partial specialization rule** specifies that an entity instance of the supertype is allowed not to belong to any subtype. We illustrate each of these rules with earlier examples from this chapter (see Figure 4-6).

Total Specialization Rule   Figure 4-6a repeats the example of PATIENT (Figure 4-3) and introduces the notation for total specialization. In this example, the business rule is the following: A patient must be either an outpatient or a resident patient. (There are no other types of patient in this hospital.) Total specialization is indicated by the *double* line extending from the PATIENT entity type to the circle. (In the Microsoft Visio notation, total specialization is called "Category is complete" and is shown also by a *double* line under the category circle between the supertype and associated subtypes.)

In this example, every time a new instance of PATIENT is inserted into the supertype, a corresponding instance is inserted into either OUTPATIENT or RESIDENT PATIENT. If the instance is inserted into RESIDENT PATIENT, an instance of the relationship Is_assigned is created to assign the patient to a hospital bed.

Partial Specialization Rule   Figure 4-6b repeats the example of VEHICLE and its subtypes CAR and TRUCK from Figure 4-4. Recall that in this example, motorcycle is a type of vehicle, but it is not represented as a subtype in the data model. Thus, if a vehicle is a car, it must appear as an instance of CAR, and if it is a truck, it must appear as an instance of TRUCK. However, if the vehicle is a motorcycle, it cannot appear as an instance of any subtype. This is an example of partial specialization, and it is specified by the single line from the VEHICLE supertype to the circle.

Specifying Disjointness Constraints

A **disjointness constraint** addresses the question of whether an instance of a supertype may simultaneously be a member of two (or more) subtypes. The disjointness constraint has two possible rules: the disjoint rule and the overlap rule. The disjoint rule specifies that if an entity instance (of the supertype) is a member of one subtype, it cannot simultaneously be a member of any other subtype. The overlap rule specifies that an entity instance can simultaneously be a member of two (or more) subtypes. An example of each of these rules is shown in Figure 4-7.

Disjointness constraint: A constraint that addresses the question whether an instance of a supertype may simultaneously be a member of two (or more) subtypes.

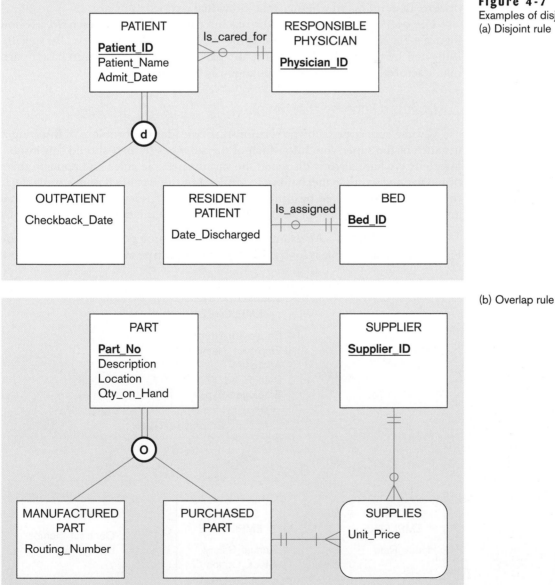

Figure 4-7
Examples of disjointness constraint
(a) Disjoint rule

(b) Overlap rule

Disjoint Rule   Figure 4-7a shows the PATIENT example from Figure 4-6a. The business rule in this case is the following: *At any given time*, a patient must be either an outpatient or a resident patient, but cannot be both. This is the disjoint rule, as specified by the letter "d" in the circle joining the supertype and its subtypes. Note in this figure, the subclass of a PATIENT may change over time, but at a given time, a PATIENT is of only one type. (The Microsoft Visio notation does not have a way to designate disjointness or overlap; however, you can place a "d" or an "o" inside the category circle using the Text Tool.)

Overlap Rule   Figure 4-7b shows the entity type PART with its two subtypes, MANUFACTURED PART and PURCHASED PART (from Figure 4-5b). Recall from our discussion of this example that some parts are both manufactured and purchased. Some clarification of this statement is required. In this example, an instance of PART is a particular part number (i.e., a *type of part*), not an individual part (indicated by the identifier, which is Part_No). For example, consider part number 4000. At a given time, the quantity on hand for this part might be 250, of which 100 are manufactured and the remaining 150 are purchased parts. In this case, it is not important to keep track of individual parts. When tracking individual parts is important, each part is assigned a serial number identifier, and the quantity on hand is one or zero, depending on whether that individual part exists or not.

The overlap rule is specified by placing the letter "o" in the circle, as shown in Figure 4-7b. Notice in this figure that the total specialization rule is also specified, as indicated by the double line. Thus, any part must be either a purchased part or a manufactured part, or it may simultaneously be both of these.

Defining Subtype Discriminators

Given a supertype/subtype relationship, consider the problem of inserting a new instance of the supertype. Into which of the subtypes (if any) should this instance be inserted? We have already discussed the various possible rules that apply to this situation. We need a simple mechanism to implement these rules, if one is available. Often this can be accomplished by using a subtype discriminator. A **subtype discriminator** is an attribute of the supertype whose values determine the target subtype or subtypes.

> **Subtype discriminator:** An attribute of the supertype whose values determine the target subtype or subtypes.

Disjoint Subtypes   An example of the use of a subtype discriminator is shown in Figure 4-8. This example is for the EMPLOYEE supertype and its subtypes, introduced

Figure 4-8
Introducing a subtype discriminator
(disjoint rule)

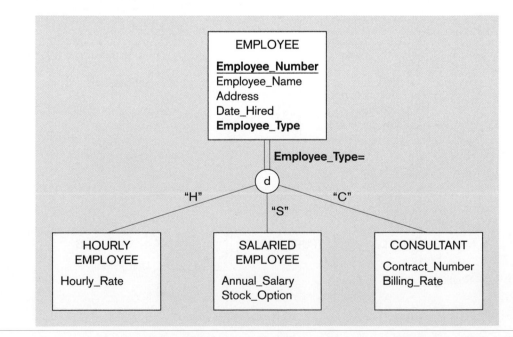

in Figure 4-2. Notice that the following constraints have been added to this figure: total specialization and disjoint subtypes. Thus, each employee must be either hourly, salaried, or a consultant.

A new attribute (Employee_Type) has been added to the supertype, to serve as a subtype discriminator. When a new employee is added to the supertype, this attribute is coded with one of three values, as follows: "H" (for Hourly), "S" (for Salaried), or "C" (for Consultant). Depending on this code, the instance is then assigned to the appropriate subtype. (An attribute of the supertype may be selected in the Microsoft Visio notation as a Discriminator, which is shown similarly next to the category symbol.)

The notation we use to specify the subtype discriminator is also shown in Figure 4-8. The expression "Employee_Type=" (which is the left side of a condition statement) is placed next to the line leading from the supertype to the circle. The value of the attribute that selects the appropriate subtype (in this example, either "H," "S," or "C") is placed adjacent to the line leading to that subtype. Thus, for example, the condition "Employee_Type = S" causes an entity instance to be inserted into the SALARIED EMPLOYEE subtype.

Overlapping Subtypes   When subtypes overlap, a slightly modified approach must be applied for the subtype discriminator. The reason is that a given instance of the supertype may require that we create an instance in more than one subtype.

An example of this situation is shown in Figure 4-9 for PART and its overlapping subtypes. A new attribute named Part_Type has been added to PART. Part_Type is a composite attribute with components Manufactured? and Purchased? Each of these attributes is a Boolean variable (i.e., it takes on only the values yes, "Y," and no, "N"). When a new instance is added to PART, these components are coded as follows:

Type of Part	Manufactured?	Purchased?
Manufactured only	"Y"	"N"
Purchased only	"N"	"Y"
Purchased and manufactured	"Y"	"Y"

The method for specifying the subtype discriminator for this example is shown in Figure 4-9. Notice that this approach can be used for any number of overlapping subtypes.

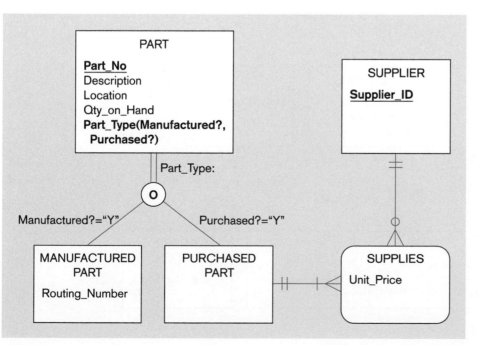

Figure 4-9
Subtype discriminator (overlap rule)

Defining Supertype/Subtype Hierarchies

We have considered a number of examples of supertype/subtype relationships in this chapter. It is possible for any of the subtypes in these examples to have other subtypes defined on it (in which case, the subtype becomes a supertype for the newly defined subtypes). A **supertype/subtype hierarchy** is a hierarchical arrangement of supertypes and subtypes, where each subtype has only one supertype (Elmasri and Navathe, 1994).

We present an example of a supertype/subtype hierarchy in this section in Figure 4-10. (For simplicity, we do not show subtype discriminators in this and most subsequent examples. See Problem and Exercise 21). This example includes most of the concepts and notation we have used in this chapter to this point. It also presents a methodology (based on specialization) that you can use in many data modeling situations.

An Example   Suppose that you are asked to model the human resources in a university. Using specialization (a top-down approach), you might proceed as follows. Starting at the top of a hierarchy, model the most general entity type first. In this case, the most general entity type is PERSON. List and associate all attributes of PERSON. The attributes shown in Figure 4-10 are SSN (identifier), Name, Address, Gender, and Date_of_Birth. The entity type at the top of a hierarchy is sometimes called the root.

Supertype/subtype hierarchy: A hierarchical arrangement of supertypes and subtypes, where each subtype has only one supertype.

Figure 4-10
Example of supertype/subtype hierarchy

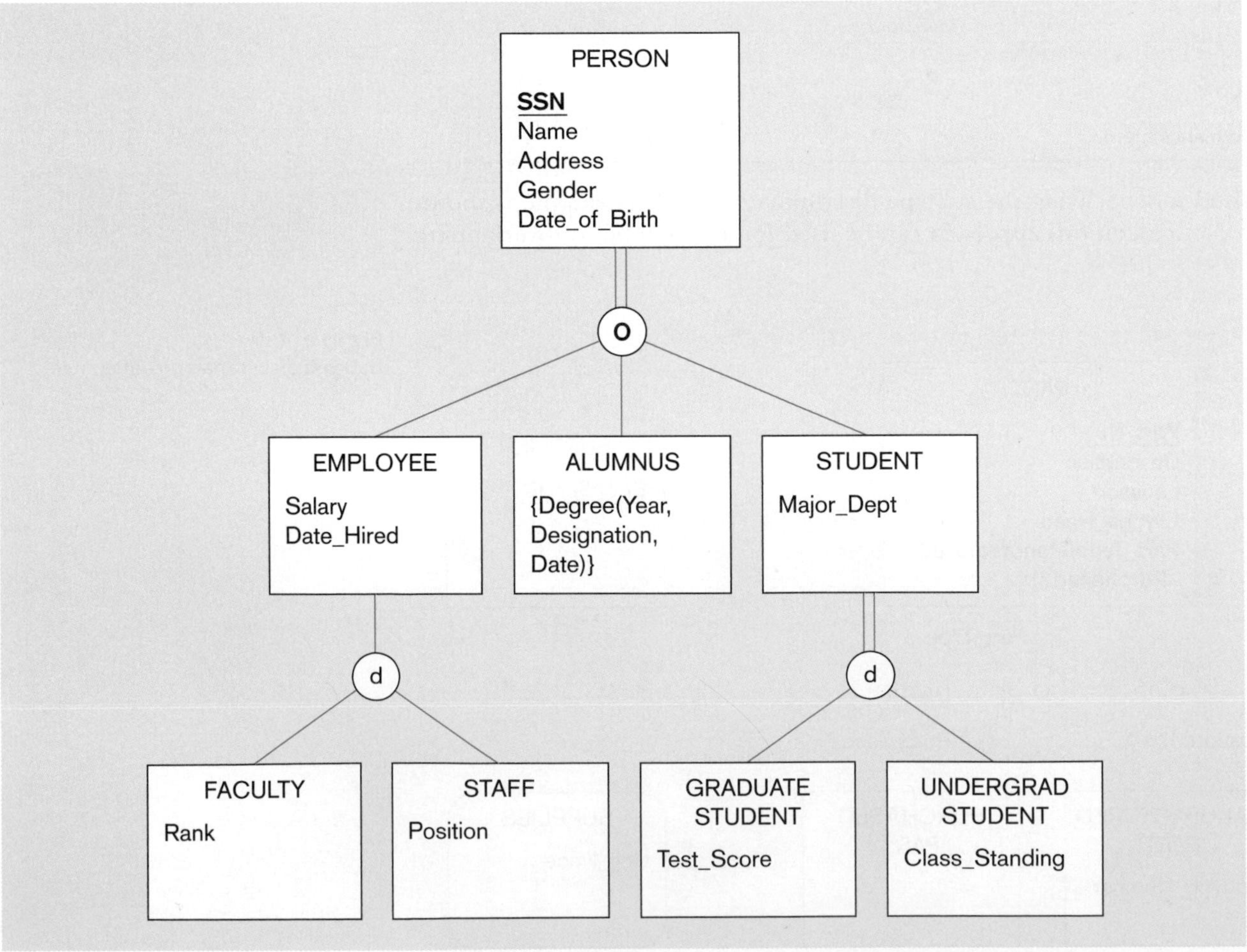

Next, define all major subtypes of the root. In this example, there are three subtypes of PERSON: EMPLOYEE (persons who work for the university), STUDENT (persons who attend classes), and ALUMNUS (persons who have graduated). Assuming there are no other types of persons of interest to the university, the total specialization rule applies, as shown in the figure. A person might belong to more than one subtype (e.g., ALUMNUS and EMPLOYEE), so the overlap rule is used. Note that overlap allows for any overlap. (A PERSON may be simultaneously in any pair or in all three subtypes.) If certain combinations are not allowed, a more refined supertype/subtype hierarchy would have to be developed to eliminate the prohibited combinations.

Attributes that apply specifically to each of these subtypes are shown in the figure. Thus, each instance of EMPLOYEE has a value for Date_Hired and Salary. Major_Dept is an attribute of STUDENT, and Degree (with components Year, Designation, and Date) is a multivalued, composite attribute of ALUMNUS.

The next step is to evaluate whether any of the subtypes already defined qualify for further specialization. In this example, EMPLOYEE is partitioned into two subtypes: FACULTY and STAFF. FACULTY has the specific attribute Rank, whereas STAFF has the specific attribute Position. Notice that in this example the subtype EMPLOYEE becomes a supertype to FACULTY and STAFF. Because there may be types of employees other than faculty and staff (such as student assistants), the partial specialization rule is indicated. However, an employee cannot be both faculty and staff at the same time. Therefore, the disjoint rule is indicated in the circle.

Two subtypes are also defined for STUDENT: GRADUATE STUDENT and UNDERGRAD STUDENT. UNDERGRAD STUDENT has the attribute Class_Standing, whereas GRADUATE STUDENT has the attribute Test_Score. Notice that total specialization and the disjoint rule are specified; you should be able to state the business rules for these constraints.

Summary of Supertype/Subtype Hierarchies   We note two features concerning the attributes contained in the hierarchy shown in Figure 4-10.

1. Attributes are assigned at the highest logical level that is possible in the hierarchy. For example, because SSN (i.e., Social Security Number) applies to all persons, it is assigned to the root. In contrast, Date_Hired applies only to employees, so it is assigned to EMPLOYEE. This approach ensures that attributes can be shared by as many subtypes as possible.

2. Subtypes that are lower in the hierarchy inherit attributes not only from their immediate supertype, but from all supertypes higher in the hierarchy, up to the root. Thus, for example, an instance of faculty has values for all of the following attributes: SSN, Name, Address, Gender, and Date_of_Birth (from PERSON); Date_Hired and Salary (from EMPLOYEE); and Rank (from FACULTY).

In the student case at the end of this chapter, we ask you to develop an enhanced E-R diagram for Mountain View Community Hospital using the same procedure we outlined in this section.

EER MODELING EXAMPLE: PINE VALLEY FURNITURE

In Chapter 3, we presented an example E-R diagram for Pine Valley Furniture. (This diagram, developed using Microsoft Visio, is repeated in Figure 4-11.) After studying this diagram, you might use some questions to help you clarify the meaning of entities and relationships. Three such areas of questions are:

PINE VALLEY FURNITURE

1. Why do some customers not do business in one or more sales territories?

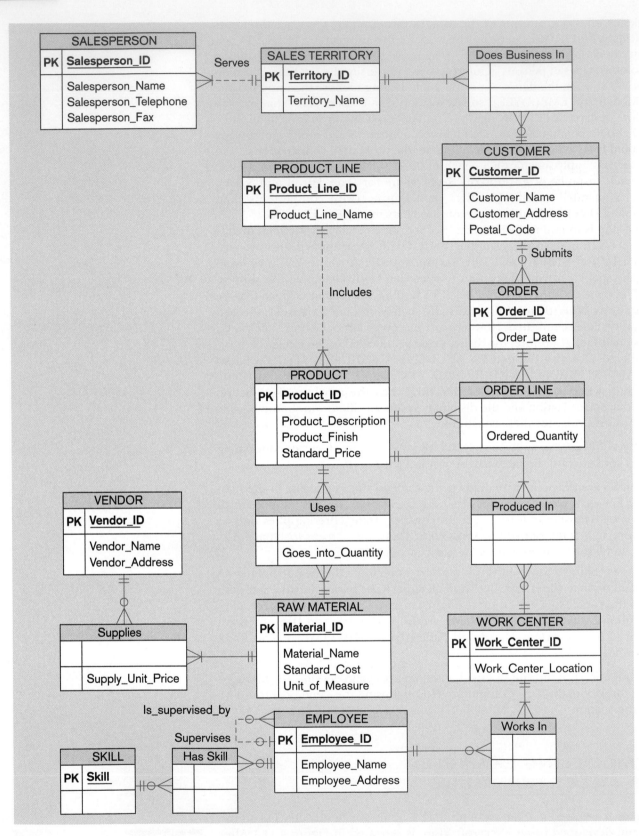

Figure 4-11
E-R diagram for Pine Valley Furniture Company

2. Why do some employees not supervise other employees, and why are they not all supervised by another employee? And, why do some employees not work in a work center?

3. Why do some vendors not supply raw materials to Pine Valley Furniture?

You may have other questions, but we will concentrate on these three to illustrate how supertype/subtype relationships can be used to convey a more specific (semantically rich) data model.

After some investigation into these three questions, we discover the following business rules that apply to how Pine Valley Furniture does business:

1. There are two types of customers: regular and national account. Only regular customers do business in sales territories. A sales territory exists only if it has at least one regular customer associated with it. A national account customer is associated with an account manager. It is possible for a customer to be both a regular and a national account customer.

2. Two special types of employees exist: management and union. Only union employees work in work centers, and a management employee supervises union employees. There are other kinds of employees besides management and union. A union employee may be promoted into management, at which time that employee stops being a union employee.

3. Pine Valley Furniture keeps track of many different vendors, not all of which have ever supplied raw materials to the company. A vendor is associated with a contract number once that vendor becomes an official supplier of raw materials.

These business rules have been used to modify the E-R diagram in Figure 4-11 into the EER diagram in Figure 4-12. (We have left most attributes off of this diagram except for those that are essential to see the changes that have occurred.) Rule 1 means that there is a total, overlapping specialization of CUSTOMER into REGULAR CUSTOMER and NATIONAL ACCOUNT CUSTOMER. A composite attribute of CUSTOMER, Customer_Type (with components National and Regular), is used to designate whether a customer instance is a regular customer, a national account, or both. Because only regular customers do business in sales territories, only regular customers are involved in the Does Business In relationship (associative entity).

Rule 2 means that there is a partial, disjoint specialization of EMPLOYEE into MANAGEMENT EMPLOYEE and UNION EMPLOYEE. An attribute of EMPLOYEE, Employee_Type, discriminates between the two special types of employees. Specialization is partial because there are other kinds of employees besides these two types. Only union employees are involved in the Works In relationship, but all union employees work in some work center, so the minimum cardinality of next to Works In from UNION EMPLOYEE is now mandatory. Because an employee cannot be both management and union at the same time (although they can change status over time), the specialization is disjoint.

Rule 3 means that there is a partial specialization of VENDOR into SUPPLIER because only some vendors become suppliers. A supplier, not a vendor, has a contract number. Because there is only one subtype of VENDOR, there is no reason to specify a disjoint or overlap rule. Because all suppliers supply some raw material, the minimum cardinality next to RAW MATERIAL in the Supplies relationship (associative entity in Visio) now is one.

This example shows how an E-R diagram can be transformed into an EER diagram once generalization/specialization of entities is understood. Not only are supertype and subtype entities now in the data model, but additional attributes, including discriminating attributes, also are added, minimum cardinalities change (from optional to mandatory), and relationships move from the supertype to a subtype.

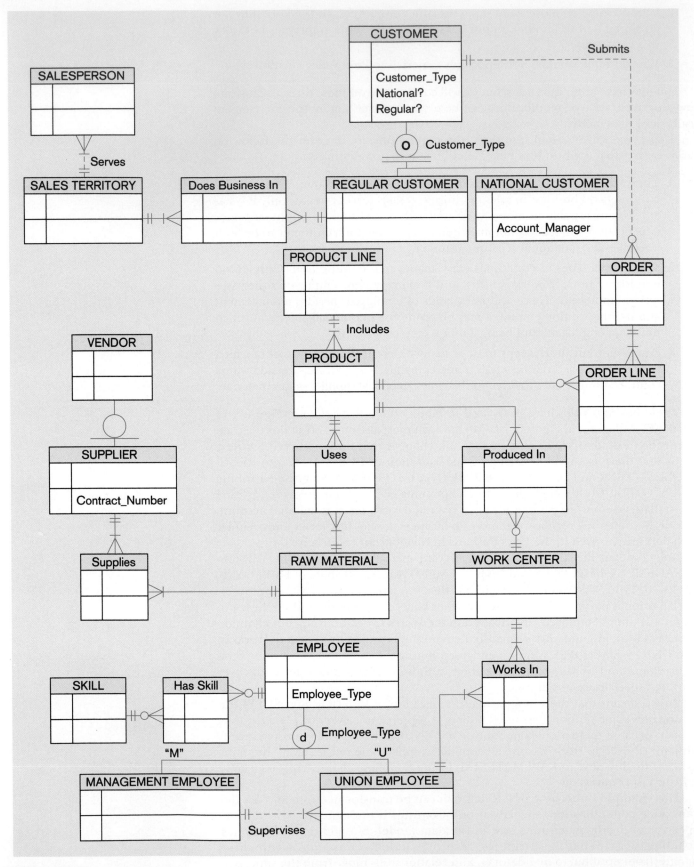

Figure 4-12
EER diagram for Pine Valley Furniture
Company using Microsoft Visio

This is a good time to emphasize a point made earlier about data modeling. A data model is a conceptual picture of the data required by an organization. A data model does not map one-for-one to elements of an implemented database. For example, a database designer may choose to put all customer instances into one database table, not separate ones for each type of customer. Such details are not important now. The purpose now is to explain all the rules that govern data, not how data will be stored and accessed to achieve efficient, required information processing. We will address technology and efficiency issues in subsequent chapters when we cover database design and implementation.

Although the EER diagram in Figure 4-12 clarifies some questions and makes the data model in Figure 4-11 more explicit, it still can be difficult for some people to comprehend. Some people will not be interested in all types of data, and some may not need to see all the details in the EER diagram to understand what the database will cover. The next section addresses how we can simplify a complete and explicit data model for presentation to specific user groups and management.

ENTITY CLUSTERING

Some enterprisewide information systems have over 1,000 entity types and relationships. How do we present such an unwieldy picture of organizational data to developers and users? One approach is to create multiple, E-R diagrams, each showing the details of different (possibly overlapping) segments or subsets of the data model (e.g., different segments that apply to different departments, information system applications, business processes, or corporate divisions). This works, but is really insufficient by itself because a total picture would not exist.

Entity clustering (Teorey, 1999) is a useful way to present a data model for a large and complex organization. An **entity cluster** is a set of one or more entity types and associated relationships grouped into a single abstract entity type. Because an entity cluster behaves like an entity type, entity clusters and entity types can be further grouped to form a higher-level entity cluster. Entity clustering is a hierarchical decomposition of a macro-level view of the data model into finer and finer views, eventually resulting in the full, detailed data model.

Entity cluster: A set of one or more entity types and associated relationships grouped into a single abstract entity type.

Figure 4-13 illustrates one possible result of entity clustering for the Pine Valley Furniture Company data model of Figure 4-12. Figure 4-13a shows the complete data model with shaded areas around possible entity clusters; Figure 4-13b shows the final result of transforming the detailed EER diagram into an EER diagram of only entity clusters and relationships. (An EER diagram may include both entity clusters and entity types, but this diagram includes only entity clusters.) In this figure, the entity cluster

- *SELLING UNIT*   represents the SALESPERSON and SALES TERRITORY entity types and the Serves relationship
- *CUSTOMER*   represents the CUSTOMER entity supertype, its subtypes, and the relationship between supertype and subtypes
- *ITEM SALE*   represents the ORDER entity type and ORDER LINE associative entity as well as the relationship between them
- *ITEM*   represents the PRODUCT LINE and PRODUCT entity types and the Includes relationship
- *MANUFACTURING*   represents the WORK CENTER and EMPLOYEE supertype entity and its subtypes as well as the Works In associative entity and Supervises relationships and the relationship between the supertype and its subtypes. (Figure 4-14 shows an explosion of the MANUFACTURING entity cluster into its components.)

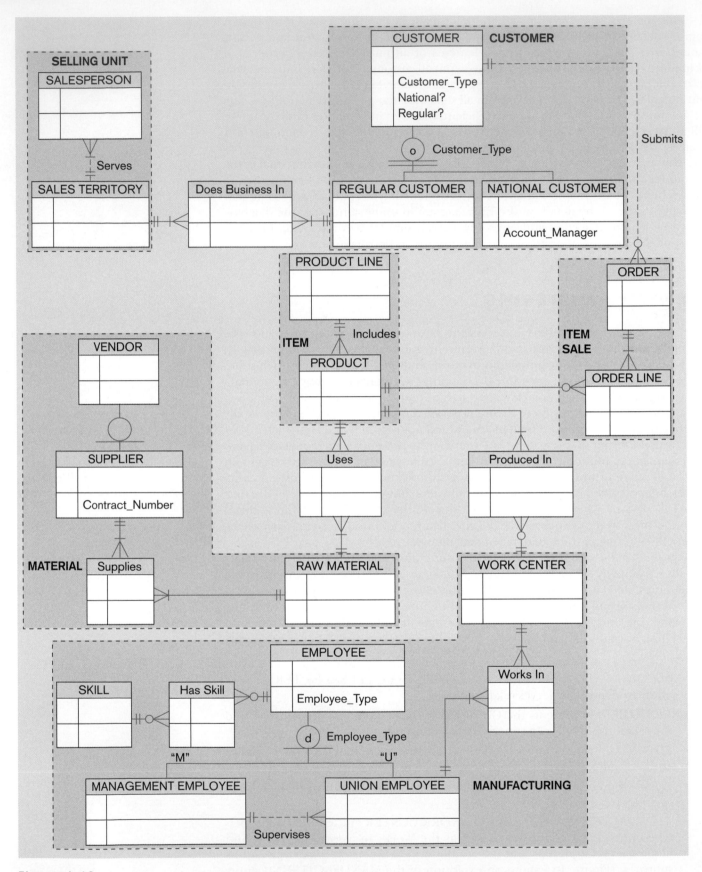

Figure 4-13
Entity clustering for Pine Valley Furniture Company
(a) Possible entity clusters (using Microsoft Visio)

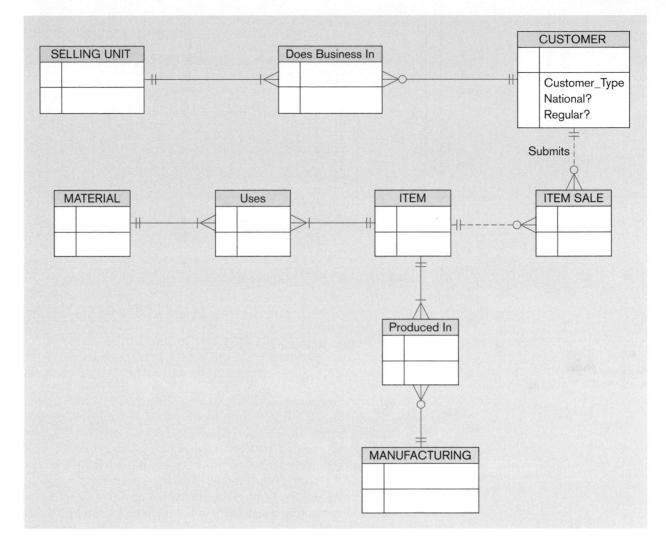

Figure 4-13 (Continued)
(b) EER diagram of entity clusters
(using Microsoft Visio)

- *MATERIAL* represents the RAW MATERIAL and VENDOR entity types, the SUPPLIER subtype, the Supplies associative entity, and the supertype/subtype relationship between VENDOR and SUPPLIER.

The E-R diagrams in Figures 4-13 and 4-14 can be used to explain details to people most concerned with assembly processes and the information needed to support this part of the business. For example, an inventory control manager can see in Figure 4-13b that the data about manufacturing can be related to item data (the Produced_in relationship). Furthermore, Figure 4-14 shows what detail is kept about the production process involving work centers and employees. This person probably does not need to see the details about, for example, the selling structure, which is embedded in the SELLING UNIT entity cluster.

Entity clusters in Figure 4-13 were formed (1) by abstracting a supertype and its subtype (see the CUSTOMER entity cluster) and (2) by combining directly related entity types and their relationships (see the SELLING UNIT, ITEM, MATERIAL, and MANUFACTURING entity clusters). An entity cluster can also be formed by combining a strong entity and its associated weak entity types (not illustrated here). Because entity clustering is hierarchical, if it were desirable, we could draw another EER diagram in which we combine the SELLING UNIT and CUSTOMER entity clusters with the Does_business_in relationship into one entity cluster, because these are directly related entity clusters.

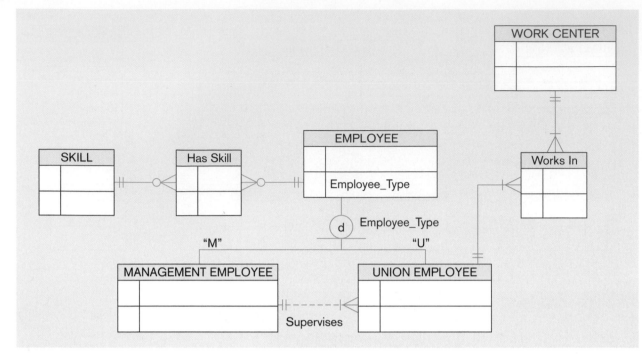

Figure 4-14
MANUFACTURING entity cluster

An entity cluster should focus on an area of interest to some community of users, developers, or managers. Which entity types and relationships are grouped to form an entity cluster depends on your purpose. For example, the ORDER entity type could be grouped in with the CUSTOMER entity cluster and the ORDER LINE entity type could be grouped in with the ITEM entity cluster in the example of entity clustering for the Pine Valley Furniture data model. This regrouping would eliminate the ITEM SALE cluster, which might not be of interest to any group of people. Also, you can do several different entity clusterings of the full data model, each with a different focus.

PACKAGED DATA MODELS

According to Len Silverston (Silverston, 1998) "The age of the data modeler as artisan is passing. Organizations can no longer afford the labor or time required for handcrafting data models from scratch. In response to these constraints, the age of the data modeler as engineer is dawning."

An increasingly popular approach of beginning a data modeling project is by acquiring a packaged or predefined data model, either a so-called universal model or an industry specific model. Then the data modeler customizes the predefined model to fit the business rules of the organization. The key assumption of this data modeling approach is that underlying structures or patterns of enterprises in the same industry or functional area are similar. Packaged data models are available from various consultants and database technology vendors. Although not inexpensive, many believe the total cost is lower and the quality of data modeling is better by using such resources. Some generic data models can be found in publications (e.g., see articles and books by Hay and by Silverston listed at the end of this chapter).

A **universal data model** is a generic or template data model that can be reused as a starting point for a data modeling project. Some people call these data model patterns, similar to the notion of patterns of reusable code for programming. A universal data model is not the "right" data model, but it is a successful starting point for developing an excellent data model for an organization.

Universal data model: A generic or template data model that can be reused as a starting point for a data modeling project.

Why has this approach of beginning from a universal data model for conducting a data modeling project become so popular? The following are some of the most compelling reasons professional data modelers are adopting this approach:

- Data models can be developed using proven components developed from cumulative experiences.

- Projects take less time and effort because the essential components and structures are already defined and only need to be customized to the particular situation.

- Data models are less likely to miss important components or make modeling errors due to not recognizing common possibilities.

- Because of a holistic view and development from best practices found in a universal data model, the resulting data model for a particular enterprise tends to be easier to evolve as additional data requirements are identified for the given situation.

- The generic model provides a starting point for asking requirements questions so that most likely all areas of the model are addressed during requirements determination.

- Data models of an existing database are easier to read by data modelers and other data management professionals the first time because they are based on common components seen in similar situations.

- Extensive use of supertype/subtype hierarchies and other structures in universal data models promotes reusing data and taking a holistic, rather than narrow, view of data in an organization.

- Extensive use of many-to-many relationships and associative entities even where a data modeler might place a one-to-many relationship gives the data model greater flexibility to fit any situation, and naturally handles time stamping and retention of important history of relationships, which can be important to comply with regulations and financial record keeping rules.

Central to the universal data model approach are supertype/subtype hierarchies. For example, a core structure of any universal data model is the entity type PARTY, which generalizes persons or organizations as actors for the enterprise, and an associated entity type PARTY ROLE, which generalizes various roles parties can play at different times. A PARTY ROLE instance is a situation in which a PARTY acts in a particular ROLE TYPE. These notions of PARTY, PARTY ROLE, and ROLE TYPE supertypes and their relationship are shown in Figure 4-15a. We use the supertype/subtype notation from Figure 4-1c because this is the notation most frequently used by the leading proponents of universal data models. This is a very generic data model (albeit simple to begin our discussion). This type of structure allows a specific party to serve in different roles during different time periods. It allows attribute values of a party to be "overridden" (if necessary in the organization) by values pertinent to the role being played during the given time period (e.g., although a PERSON of the PARTY supertype has a Current_Last_Name as of now, when in the party role of BILL_TO_CUSTOMER a different Current_Last_Name could apply during the particular time period (From_Date to Thru_Date) of that role). Note that even for this simple situation, the data model is trying to capture the most general circumstances. For example, an instance of the EMPLOYEE subtype of the PERSON ROLE subtype of PARTY ROLE would be associated with an instance of the ROLE TYPE that describes the employee-person role-party role. Thus, one description of a role type explains all the instances of the associated party roles of that role type.

An interesting aspect of Figure 4-15a is that PARTY ROLE actually simplifies what could be a more extensive set of subtypes of PARTY. Figure 4-15b shows one PARTY supertype with many subtypes covering many party roles. With partial specialization

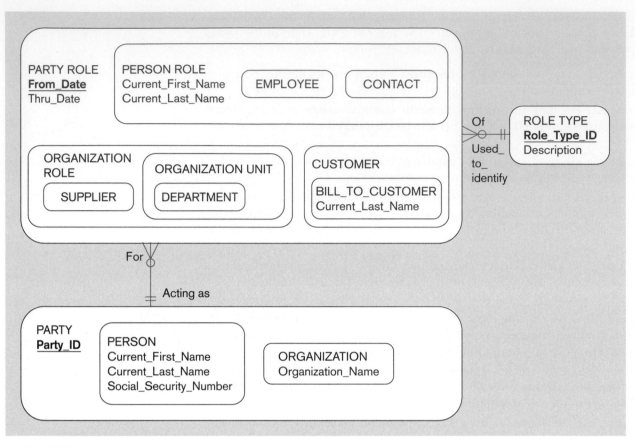

(a) Basic PARTY universal data model

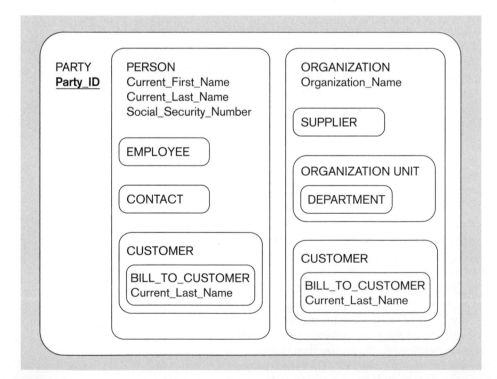

Figure 4-15
PARTY, PARTY ROLE, and ROLE TYPE in a universal data model
(b) PARTY supertype/subtype hierarchy

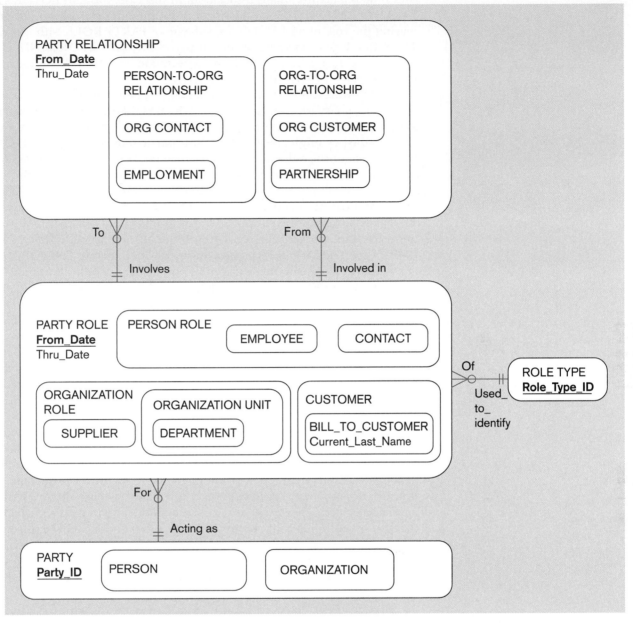

Figure 4-16
Extension of a universal data model to
include PARTY RELATIONSHIPs

and overlap of subtypes, this alternative would appear to accomplish the same data modeling semantics as Figure 4-15a. However, Figure 4-15a recognizes the important distinction between enterprise actors (PARTYs) and the roles each plays from time to time (PARTY ROLEs). Thus, the PARTY ROLE concept actually adds to the generalization of the data model and the universal applicability of the predefined data model.

The next basic construct of most universal data models is the representation of relationships between parties in the roles they play. Figure 4-16 shows this next extension of the basic universal data model. PARTY RELATIONSHIP is an associative entity, which hence allows any number of parties to be related as they play particular roles. Each instance of a relationship between PARTYs in PARTY ROLEs would be a separate instance of a PARTY RELATIONSHIP subtype. For example, consider the employment of a person by some organization unit during some time span, which over time is a many-to-many association. In this case, the EMPLOYMENT subtype of PARTY RELATIONSHIP would (for a given time period) likely link one PERSON playing the role of an EMPLOYEE subtype of PARTY ROLE with one ORGANIZA-TION ROLE playing some pertinent party role, such as ORGANIZATION UNIT. (That is, a person is employed in an organization unit during a period of From_Date to Thru_Date in PARTY RELATIONSHIP.)

PARTY RELATIONSHIP is represented very generally, so it really is an associative entity for a unary relationship among PARTY ROLE instances. This makes for a very general, flexible pattern of relationships. What might be obscured, however, are which subtypes might be involved in a particular PARTY RELATIONSHIP, and stricter relationships that are not many-to-many, probably because we don't need to keep track of the relationship over time. For example, because the Involves and Involved in relationships link the PARTY ROLE and PARTY RELATIONSHIP super-types, this does not restrict EMPLOYMENT to an EMPLOYEE with an ORGANIZA-TION UNIT. Also, if the enterprise needs to track only current employment associa-tions, the data model in Figure 4-16 will not enforce that a PERSON PARTY in an EMPLOYEE PARTY ROLE can be associated with only one ORGANIZATION UNIT at a time. We will see in the next section how we can include additional business rule notation on an EER diagram to make this specific. Alternatively, we could draw spe-cific relationships from just the EMPLOYEE PARTY ROLE and the ORGANIZATION UNIT PARTY ROLE to the EMPLOYMENT PARTY RELATIONSHIP to represent this particular one-to-many association. As you can imagine, to handle very many spe-cial cases like this would create a diagram with a large number of relationships between PARTY ROLE and PARTY RELATIONSHIP, and, hence, a very busy dia-gram. Thus, more restrictive cardinality rules (at least most of them) would likely be implemented outside the data model (e.g., in database stored procedures or applica-tion programs) when using a prepackaged data model.

We could continue introducing various common, reusable building blocks of universal data models. However, Silverston in a two volume set (2001) and Hay (1996) provide extensive coverage. To bring our discussion of packaged, universal data models to a conclusion, we show in Figure 4-18 a universal data model for a rela-tionship development organization. In this figure, we use the original notation of Silverston, which is pertinent to Oracle data modeling tools (see Appendix A). Now that you have studied EER concepts and notations and have been introduced to uni-versal data models, you can understand more about the power of this data model.

To help you better understand the EER diagram in Figure 4-17, consider the definitions of the highest level entity type in each supertype/subtype hierarchy, as follows:

- *PARTY*   Persons and organizations independent of the roles they play
- *PARTY ROLE*   Information about a party for an associated role, thus allowing a party to act in multiple roles
- *PARTY RELATIONSHIP*   Information about two parties (those in the "to" and "from" roles) within the context of a relationship
- *EVENT*   Activities that may occur within the context of relationships (e.g., a CORRESPONDENCE can occur within the context of a PERSON-CUSTOMER relationship in which the to party is a CUSTOMER role for an ORGANIZA-TION and the from party is an EMPLOYEE role for a PERSON)
- *PRIORITY TYPE*   Information about a priority that may set the priority for a given PARTY RELATIONSHIP
- *STATUS TYPE*   Information about the status (e.g., active, inactive, pending) of events or party relationships
- *EVENT ROLE*   Information about all of the PARTYs involved in an EVENT
- *ROLE TYPE*   Information about the various PARTY ROLEs and EVENT ROLEs

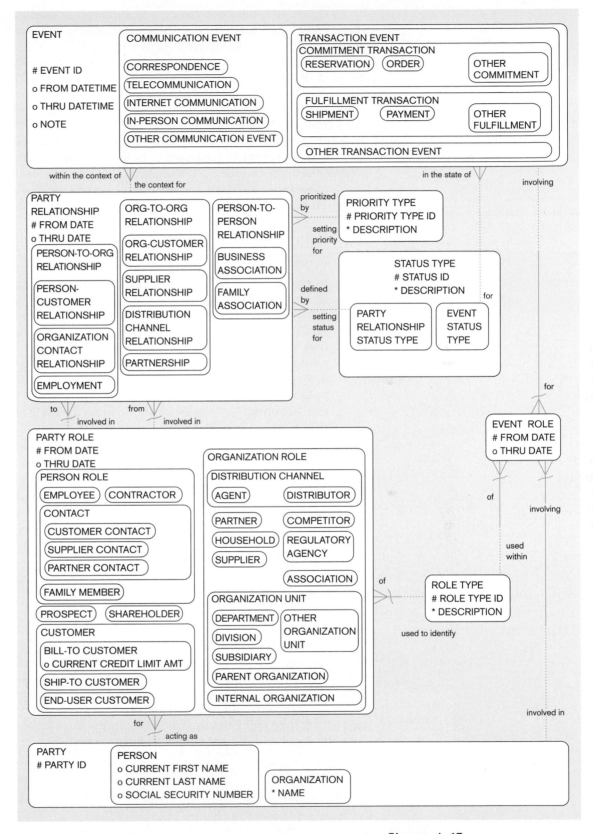

Figure 4-17
A universal data model for Relationship Development
Source: Silverston (2002)

In Figure 4-17, supertype/subtype hierarchies are used extensively. For example, in the PARTY ROLE entity type, the hierarchy is as many as four levels deep (e.g., PARTY ROLE to PERSON ROLE to CONTACT to CUSTOMER CONTACT). Attributes can be located with any entity type in the hierarchy [e.g., PARTY has the identifier of PARTY ID ("#" means identifier), PERSON has three optional attributes ("o" means optional), and ORGANIZATION has a required attribute ("*" means required)]. Relationships can be between entity types anywhere in the hierarchy. For example, any EVENT is "in the state of" an EVENT STATUS TYPE, a subtype, whereas any EVENT is "within the context of" a PARTY RELATIONSHIP, a supertype.

As stated previously, packaged data models are not meant to be exactly right straight out of the box for a given organization; they are meant to be customized. To be the most generalized, such models have certain properties before they are customized for a given situation:

1. Relationships are connected to the highest level entity type in a hierarchy that makes sense. Relationships can be renamed, eliminated, added, and moved as need be for the organization.

2. Strong entities almost always have *M:N* relationships between them (e.g., EVENT and PARTY), so at least one, and sometimes many, associative entities are used. Consequently, all relationships are *1:M*, and there is an entity type in which to store intersection data. Intersection data are often dates, showing over what span of time the relationship was valid. Thus, the packaged data model is designed to allow tracking of relationships over time. (Recall, this is a common issue that was discussed with Figure 3-20.) *1:M* relationships are optional, at least on the many side (e.g., the dotted line next to EVENT for the "involving" relationship signifies an EVENT may involve an EVENT ROLE, as is done with Oracle Designer).

3. Although not clear on this diagram, all supertype/subtype relationships follow the total specialization and overlap rules, which makes the diagram as thorough and flexible as possible.

4. Most entities on the many side of a relationship are weak, thus inheriting the identifier of the entity on the one side (e.g., the "~" on the "acting as" relationship from PARTY to PARTY ROLE signifies that PARTY ROLE implicitly includes PARTY ID).

BUSINESS RULES REVISITED

We have seen that E-R diagrams (and enhanced E-R diagrams) are a useful means for expressing certain types of business rules. Thus, for example, the participation and disjointness constraints associated with supertypes and subtypes discussed in this chapter are an expression of the business rules associated with those relationships. However, there are many other types of business rules in an organization that cannot be expressed with this notation. In this section, we develop a general framework for business rules and show how to express some important types of rules that elude the standard E-R (and enhanced E-R) notation.

Classification of Business Rules

There are many different types of business rules. You have already seen examples in Chapter 3 and in this chapter of some of these, such as rules about relationships between entity types (e.g., cardinality values), supertype/subtype relationships, and facts about attributes and entity types (e.g., definitions). Figure 4-18, adapted from the GUIDE Business Rules Project, shows an E-R diagram that classifies business rules and the potential relationships between different types of rules.

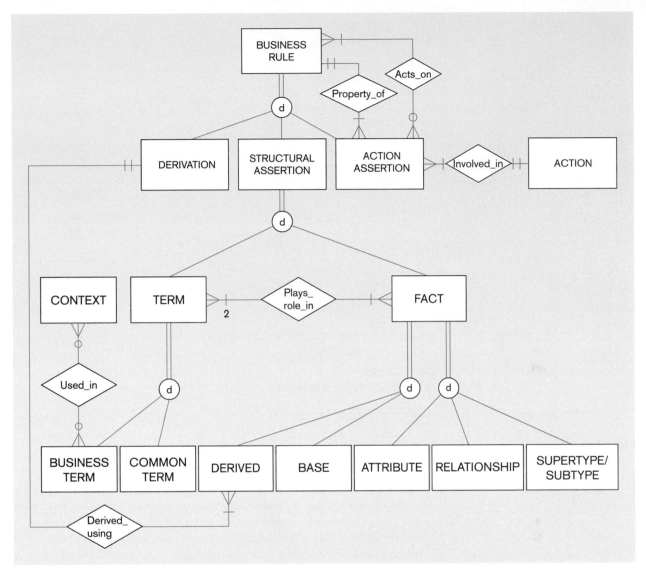

Figure 4-18
EER diagram to describe business rules (Adapted from GUIDE Business Rules Project, 1997)

There are three main types of business rules: derivation, structural assertion, and action assertion. A **derivation** is a statement derived from other knowledge in the business. Most commonly, a derivation is a mathematical or logical inference involving literals and facts. Since in data modeling we are concerned more with derived facts, which are derived by using derivations, we will address derivations only indirectly when we discuss derived facts in a subsequent section. A **structural assertion** is a statement that expresses some aspect of the static structure of the organization. E-R diagrams are a common way to show structural assertions. As shown in Figure 4-18, a structural assertion is stated either as a term or a fact. (Term and fact were defined in Chapter 3.) Terms play a role in the statement of a fact. A term is either a common term, one that is generally understood, or a business term, one that can be understood only within the context of a given setting. An **action assertion** is a statement of a constraint or control on the actions of the organization. An action assertion is the property of some business rule and states under what conditions a particular action can be performed on which business rules. (Remember, a business rule can be as simple as the definition of an entity type, relationship, or attribute.) For example, an action assertion can state under what conditions a new customer can be created or a new purchase order written.

Derivation: A statement derived from other knowledge in the business.

Structural assertion: A statement that expresses some aspect of the static structure of the organization.

Action assertion: A statement of a constraint or control on the actions of the organization.

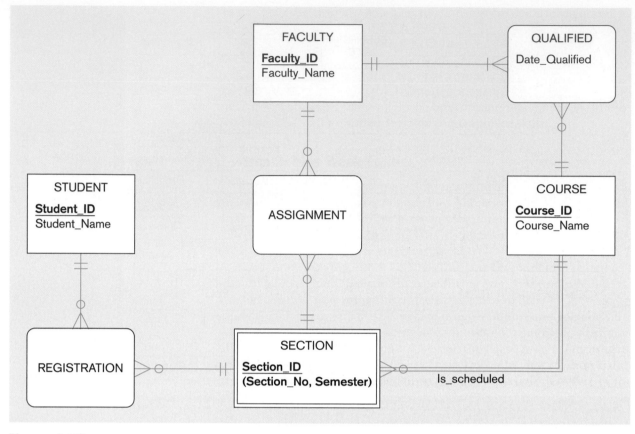

Figure 4-19
Data model segment for class scheduling

Another common type of an action assertion states what values a particular attribute may hold (sometimes called a domain constraint).

In the following sections, we describe various forms of structural assertions, which are commonly shown in E-R and EER diagrams and in associated database documentation. Then, in the following section, we explain action assertions, which can be implemented in a database as triggers and stored procedures, which we discuss later in the text. We use a simple data model for class scheduling to illustrate these assertions. The E-R model for this example is shown in Figure 4-19.

The E-R model in Figure 4-19 contains four entity types: FACULTY, COURSE, SECTION, and STUDENT. It also shows the relationships and associative entities between these entity types. Notice that SECTION is a weak entity type, because it cannot exist without the COURSE entity type. The identifying relationship for SECTION is Is_scheduled, and the partial identifier is Section_ID (a composite attribute). Only sample attributes are shown for the various entity types to simplify the diagram.

Stating a Structural Assertion

A structural assertion says that something of importance to the organization either exists or exists in relationship with other things of interest. A structural assertion can be as simple as the definition of a term, or a fact, which is a statement of a relationship between terms. Four examples of facts are:

1. A course is a module of instruction in a particular subject area. This *definition of the term* course associates two terms: module of instruction and subject area. We assume these are common terms that do not need to be further defined or placed in a business context.

2. Student name is an *attribute* of student. This fact is shown in Figure 4-19 by the Student_Name attribute in the STUDENT entity type.

3. A student may register for many sections, and a section may be registered for by many students. This fact states the participation of entity types in a *relationship*. Both student and section are business terms that require definitions. This fact is shown in Figure 4-19 by the Is_registered associative entity.

4. A faculty is an employee of the university. Although not shown in Figure 4-19, this fact designates a *supertype/subtype* relationship between the subtype of faculty and its supertype of employee.

Derived Facts   The type of facts described above are called base facts; that is, they are fundamental facts that cannot be derived from other terms or facts. Another type of fact (shown in Figure 4-18) is called a derived fact. A **derived fact** is a fact that is derived from business rules using an algorithm or inference. A derived fact may be treated just like a base fact (e.g., because a derived fact is a type of business rule, an action assertion may be a property of a derived fact). A derived attribute, defined in Chapter 3, is an example of a derived fact. Following are two examples of derived facts:

> **Derived fact:** A fact that is derived from business rules using an algorithm or inference.

- Student_GPA = Quality_Points/Total_Hours_Taken
     where Quality_Points =
     sum [for all courses attempted]
     (Credit_Hours*Numerical_Grade)

    In this example, Student_GPA is derived from other base and derived facts. Quality_Points and Total_Hours are also derived facts. Student_GPA could be shown in Figure 4-19 as an attribute of STUDENT within square brackets, Numerical_Grade as an attribute of REGISTRATION, and Credit_Hours as an attribute of COURSE.

- A student is taught by the faculty assigned to the sections for which the student is registered. You can see how this fact can be derived by traversing from STUDENT or SECTION via the REGISTRATION associative entity and then the ASSIGNMENT associative entity from SECTION to FACULTY in the E-R diagram in Figure 4-19.

Stating an Action Assertion

Whereas a structural assertion deals with the static structure of an organization, an action assertion deals with the dynamic aspects of the organization. Action assertions impose "must (must not)" and "should (should not)" constraints on handling data. An action assertion is the property of some business rule (called the **anchor object**); for a data handling **action** (e.g., create, update, delete, or read), it states how other business rules (called the **corresponding objects**) act on the anchor object. Some examples of action assertions are:

> **Anchor object:** A business rule (a fact) on which actions are limited.
>
> **Action:** An operation, such as create, delete, update, or read, which may be performed on data objects.
>
> **Corresponding object:** A business rule (a fact) that influences the ability to perform an action on another business rule.

- A course (anchor object) must have a course name (corresponding object). In this example, the action is updating the course name property of a course.

- A student (anchor object) must have a value of 2.0 or greater for Student_GPA (corresponding object) to graduate (action). In this example, the anchor object is a structural assertion, but it is possible for the anchor object to be another action assertion.

- A student cannot register for (the anchor object is the REGISTRATION associative entity) a section of a course for which there is no qualified faculty (the corresponding object is the QUALIFIED associative entity).

Types of Action Assertions   For simplicity, we do not show in Figure 4-18 the various types of action assertions that exist. There are three ways to classify action assertions:

1. Action assertions can be classified based on the type of result from the assertion. Looking at action assertions in this way yields three types of assertions:

   a. *Condition,* which states that if something is true, then another business rule will apply. The third example of an action assertion above could be stated as a condition in the form of "If a course has a qualified faculty, then students can register for a section of that course."

   b. *Integrity constraint,* which states something that must always be true. The first example of an action assertion above illustrates an integrity constraint. Another example would be "The date a faculty becomes qualified to teach a course cannot be after the semester in which the faculty is assigned to teach a section of that course."

   c. *Authorization,* which states a privilege; for example, only department chairs (a type of user) can qualify a faculty to teach a course.

2. Action assertions can be classified based on the form of the assertion. Looking at action assertions in this way yields three types of assertions:

   a. *Enabler,* which, if true, permits or leads to the existence of the corresponding object. An example of an enabler is "A faculty can be created once the faculty is qualified to teach at least one course."

   b. *Timer,* which enables (disables) or creates (deletes) an action. An example of a timer assertion is "When a student has a GPA above 2.0 and a total credit hours above 125, then student may graduate." Note, the action of graduating does not occur because of this timer assertion, but rather the timer enables the action to occur.

   c. *Executive,* which causes the execution of one or more actions. An executive action assertion can be thought of as a trigger for some action. An example of an executive assertion is "When a student has a GPA below 2.0, then the student goes on academic probation." This executive action might result in a status attribute of the student to be updated to the value of "probation."

3. Action assertions can be classified based on the rigor of the assertion. Looking at action assertions in this way yields two types of assertions:

   a. *Controlling,* which state that something must or must not be or happen. The examples we have used so far all fall in this category.

   b. *Influencing,* which are guidelines or items of interest for which a notification must occur. An example of an influencing action assertion is "When the number of students registered for a section exceeds 90 percent of the capacity of that section, notify the responsible department chair." In this situation, nothing is controlled (students may continue to register for the near-capacity section and no additional sections are created), but management wants to know that a particular condition has occurred.

Representing and Enforcing Business Rules

Most organizations have hundreds (or thousands) of such rules. Action assertions have traditionally been implemented in procedural logic buried deep within individual application programs in a form that is virtually unrecognizable, unmanageable, and inconsistent. This approach places a heavy burden on the programmer, who must know all the constraints that an action may violate and must include checks for each of these constraints. An omission, misunderstanding, or error by the programmer will likely leave the database in an invalid state.

The more modern approach is to declare action assertions at a conceptual level without specifying how the rule will be implemented. Thus, there needs to be a specification language for business rules. We have seen that the EER notation works well for specifying many types of business rules. In fact, the EER notation was invented to allow more business rules to be shown in graphical form than the simpler E-R notation. An alternative to a graphical notation would be a structured grammar (such as a limited form of English). Whether graphical or grammatical, two desirable features for a business rule specification language would be:

1. It should be relatively simple so that end users not only can understand the rule statements, but also can define the rules themselves.

2. The language should be sufficiently structured to be automatically convertible to the computer code that enforces the specifications.

In the following section, we illustrate both graphical and structured grammar approaches to specifying business rules. The graphical approach we used is adapted from Ross (1997), a leader in the development of business rule specifications.

Sample Business Rules   In this section, we augment the data model for class scheduling, Figure 4-19, with two new business rules. You will be asked to add additional rules in the problems and exercises at the end of the chapter.

> **Business Rule 1** For a faculty member to be assigned to teach a section of a course, the faculty member must be qualified to teach the course for which that section is scheduled.

This rule refers to three entity types in Figure 4-19: FACULTY, SECTION, and COURSE. The question is whether a faculty member can be assigned to teach a section (of a course). Thus, the anchor object is the ASSIGNMENT associative entity. We are not constraining the faculty member, nor are we constraining the section. Rather, we are constraining the assignment of the faculty member to the section. Figure 4-20 shows the dashed line from ASSIGNMENT to the action assertion symbol.

What are the corresponding objects in this rule? For a faculty member to be assigned to teach a section of a course, two conditions are necessary:

1. The faculty member must be qualified to teach the course. (This information is recorded by the QUALIFIED associative entity.)

2. The section must be scheduled for the course. (This information is recorded by the Is_scheduled relationship.)

Thus, in this case, there are two corresponding objects. This fact is represented by the dashed lines from the action assertion symbol to each of the two objects.

> **Business Rule 2** For a faculty member to be assigned to teach a section of a course, the faculty member must not be assigned to teach a total of more than three course sections.

This rule imposes a limitation on the total number of sections a faculty member may teach at a given time. Because the rule involves a total, it requires a modification of the previous notation.

As shown in Figure 4-21, the anchor object is again the relationship Is_assigned. However, in this case, the corresponding object is also the relationship Is_assigned! In particular, it is a count of the total sections assigned to the faculty member. The letters "LIM" in the action assertion symbol stand for "limit." The arrow leaving this symbol then points to a circle with the letter "U," which stands for "upper." The second circle then contains the number 3, which is the upper limit. Thus, the constraint

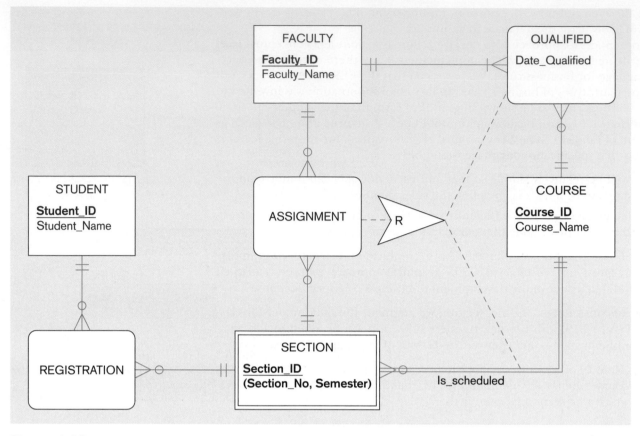

Figure 4-20
Business Rule 1: For a faculty member to be assigned to teach a section of a course, the faculty member must be qualified to teach the course for which the section is Scheduled. (The letter "R" inside the symbol represents "Restricted," which is one of the many options for constraints.)

is read as follows: "The corresponding object is a count of the number of sections assigned to the faculty member, which has an upper limit of three." If a faculty member is already assigned three sections, any transaction that attempts to add another section will be rejected.

You can implement business rules such as those presented here using the SQL language, and then store the rules as part of the database definitions. One way to implement a rule with SQL is to use the CREATE ASSERTION statement, which is included in the most recent version of this language (SQL2). For example, consider Business Rule 2. The following statement creates an assertion named "Overload_Protect:"

```
CREATE ASSERTION Overload_Protect
CHECK (SELECT COUNT(*)
FROM ASSIGNED
WHERE Faculty_ID = '12345') <= 3;
```

This statement checks whether the total number of course sections assigned to a particular faculty member is less than or equal to the limit (three). The database management system is responsible for ensuring that this constraint is not violated.

Many other business rules, besides the few examples of this section, are possible. See Ross (1997) for a comprehensive list and associated notation.

Identifying and Testing Business Rules

You have seen in this chapter a wide variety of business rules and how they can be represented in structured grammar and EER diagrams and extensions. It is

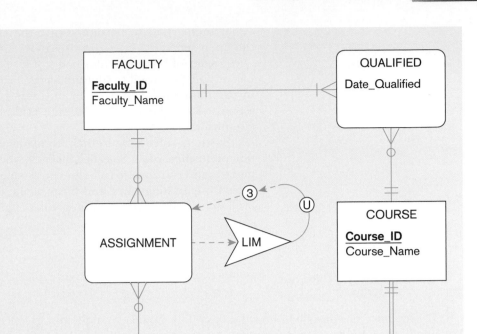

Figure 4-21
Business Rule 2: For a faculty member to be assigned to teach a section of a course, the faculty member must not be assigned to teach a total of more than three course sections.

your job as a data analyst to document the specifications of business rules and then ensure that the business rules are enforced as much as possible through database technologies. But, before business rules can be specified, they must be identified. Then, once specified, they should be tested before being implemented in technology.

An approach to identifying and testing business rules is scenarios (Moriarty, 1993). A scenario is a story or script that describes how a business reacts to a given situation. A scenario is similar to the concept of a use case, which is an important tool in object modeling (see Chapters 14 and 15). For example, a scenario related to the E-R diagram of Figure 4-19 would focus on the events related to a student. Events include being admitted, registering for (and dropping) classes, obtaining grades for a class, and graduating. A scenario would trace through these events for a given individual. The scenario is used to identify elements (business rules) for the data model or to test that the data model handles all possible circumstances for these events (e.g., a student trying to register for a nonexistent class, a student on probation trying to register, or a graduated student trying to register).

A student scenario might read as follows:

Missi Davies logs on to the class registration system to sign up for classes next semester. Missi enters her student ID and password to gain authorization to sign up for classes. Missi is an MIS major in good academic standing. Missi wants to make sure she gets into the courses required in her major, so she searches among the list of MIS courses for the required database course. Missi discovers that there are two sections of this course offered in the next semester, but one is already closed. Thus, for the online registration system, Missi must register for the open section. Depending on her overall schedule, Missi may see the department chair to be signed into the closed section and drop registration in the open section.

If a set of business rules had not already been identified, this and other scenarios could be used to identify terms, facts, and action assertions to be included in the data model. If a set of business rules already exist, then statements in scenarios can be used to validate that the business rules handle all possible circumstances.

Business rules software help to manage the construction, testing, and application of business rules. So-called business rules engines consolidate rules into one dictionary, and can analyze rules for consistency. Business rules engines can also deduce rules from existing rules, and break a rule down into components. See Frye (2002) for a status report on the business rules engine market.

Summary

This chapter has described how the basic E-R model has been extended to include supertype/subtype relationships. A *supertype* is a generic entity type that has a relationship with one or more subtypes. A *subtype* is a grouping of the entities in an entity type that is meaningful to the organization. For example, the entity type PERSON is frequently modeled as a supertype. Subtypes of PERSON may include EMPLOYEE, VOLUNTEER, and CLIENT. Subtypes inherit the attributes and relationships associated with their supertype.

Supertype/subtype relationships should normally be considered in data modeling with either (or both) of the following conditions present: First, there are attributes that apply to some (but not all) of the instances of an entity type. Second, the instances of a subtype participate in a relationship unique to that subtype.

The techniques of generalization and specialization are important guides in developing supertype/subtype relationships. Generalization is the bottom-up process of defining a generalized entity type from a set of more specialized entity types. Specialization is the top-down process of defining one or more subtypes of a supertype that has already been defined.

The EER notation allows us to capture the important business rules that apply to supertype/subtype relationships. The completeness constraint allows us to specify whether an instance of a supertype must also be a member of at least one subtype. There are two cases: With total specialization, an instance of the supertype must be a member of at least one subtype. With partial specialization, an instance of a supertype may or may not be a member of any subtype. The disjointness constraint allows us to specify whether an instance of a supertype may simultaneously be a member of two or more subtypes. Again, there are two cases. With the disjoint rule, an instance can be a member of only one subtype at a given time. With the overlap rule, an entity instance can simultaneously be a member of two (or more) subtypes.

A subtype discriminator is an attribute of a supertype whose values determine to which subtype (or subtypes) a supertype instance belongs. A supertype/subtype hierarchy is a hierarchical arrangement of supertypes and subtypes, where each subtype has only one supertype.

There are extensions to the E-R notation other than supertype/subtype relationships. One of the other more useful extensions is aggregation, which represents how some entities are part of other entities (e.g., a PC is composed of a disk drive, RAM, motherboard, etc.). For space limitations we have not discussed these extensions here. Most of these extensions, like aggregation, are also a part of object-oriented data modeling, which is explained in Chapters 14 and 15.

E-R diagrams can become large and complex, including hundreds of entities. Many users and managers do not need to see all the entities, relationships, and attributes to understand the part of the database with which they are most interested. Entity clustering is a way to turn a part of an entity-relationship data model into a more macro-level view of the same data. An entity cluster is a set of one or more entity types and associated relationships grouped into a single abstract entity type. Several entity clusters and associated relationships can be further grouped into even a higher entity cluster, so entity clustering is a hierarchical decomposition technique. By grouping entities and relationships, you can lay out an E-R diagram to allow you to give attention to the details of the model that matter most in a given data modeling task.

Packaged data models, so called universal and industry-specific data models, extensively utilize EER features. These generalizable data models often use multiple level supertype/subtype hierarchies and associative entities. Subjects and the roles subjects play are separated, creating many entity types; this complexity can be simplified when customized for a given organization, and entity clusters can be used to present simpler views of the data model to different audiences.

A business rule is a statement that defines or constrains some aspect of the business. It is intended to assert business structure or control or to influence the behavior of the business. Rules can be divided into three major categories: derivations, structural assertions, and action assertions. Structural assertions define the static structure of the organization, while action assertions are rules that constrain the dynamic operations of the organization. A structural assertion is a term or a fact. A term is a definition of a concept about the business, and a fact is a statement involving the association of two or more terms. Facts can be base, or fundamental, facts or derivations from mathematical or logical manipulations of other facts; they can deal with an attribute, relationship, or supertype/subtype association between facts.

Action assertions state that the actions (such as create, delete, update, and read) on some business rule, called the anchor object, are constrained by other corresponding objects. Constraints can be if … then … else conditions, integrity rules, or authorization privileges. An action assertion can permit the existence of the corresponding object, enable or disable an action, or cause an action to be taken. Other types of action assertions are simply guidelines that trigger notification of special conditions.

CHAPTER REVIEW

Key Terms

Action
Action assertion
Anchor object
Attribute inheritance
Completeness constraint
Corresponding object
Derivation
Derived fact
Disjoint rule
Disjointness constraint
Enhanced entity-relationship (EER) model
Entity cluster
Generalization
Overlap rule
Partial specialization rule
Specialization
Structural assertion
Subtype
Subtype discriminator
Supertype
Supertype/subtype hierarchy
Total specialization rule
Universal data model

Review Questions

1. Define each of the following terms:
   a. supertype
   b. subtype
   c. specialization
   d. entity cluster
   e. structural assertion
   f. anchor object
   g. subtype discriminator
   h. total specialization rule
   i. generalization
   j. disjoint rule
   k. overlap rule
   l. action assertion
   m. universal data model

2. Match the following terms and definitions.
   ____ supertype
   ____ entity cluster
   ____ structural assertion
   ____ subtype
   ____ specialization
   ____ anchor object
   ____ action
   ____ subtype discriminator
   ____ attribute inheritance

   a. subset of supertype
   b. entity belongs to two subtypes
   c. subtype gets supertype attributes
   d. rule on which actions are limited
   e. business rule that influences an action
   f. create, delete, update, or read
   g. calculated using an algorithm
   h. generalized entity type
   i. static structure of organization
   j. creating subtypes for an entity type

____ overlap rule

____ corresponding object

____ derived fact

k. a group of associated entity types and relationships

l. locates target subtype for an entity

3. Contrast the following terms:

   a. Supertype; subtype

   b. Generalization; specialization

   c. Anchor object; corresponding object

   d. Disjoint rule; overlap rule

   e. Structural assertion; action assertion

   f. Total specialization rule; partial specialization rule

   g. PARTY; PARTY ROLE

4. State two conditions that indicate when a designer should consider using supertype/subtype relationships.

5. State the reason for entity clustering.

6. Give an example (other than those discussed in the chapter) of a supertype/subtype relationship.

7. Give an example (other than those discussed in the chapter) of each of the following:

   a. Structural assertion

   b. Action assertion

8. Discuss the types of action assertions.

9. Give an example of how one might use an enabler action assertion.

10. State one executive action assertion for the Pine Valley Furniture example in this chapter.

11. What is attribute inheritance? Why is it important?

12. Give an example of each of the following:

    a. A supertype/subtype relationship where the disjoint rule applies

    b. A supertype/subtype relationship where the overlap rule applies

13. What types of business rules are normally captured in an EER diagram?

14. What is the purpose of a subtype discriminator?

15. When would a packaged data model be useful?

16. Search the Web for industry-specific packaged data models. One Web site to look at is **www.inmoncif.com.** Did you find a packaged data model that could possibly be used for Pine Valley Furniture Company? How do you think that it would need to be modified?

17. When might a supertype/subtype hierarchy be useful?

18. When is a member of a supertype always a member of at least one subtype?

19. Based on your understanding of the Pine Valley Furniture Company system, state five structural assertions.

20. Can you think of any derived facts for the Pine Valley Furniture Company system?

Problems and Exercises

1. Examine the hierarchy for the university EER diagram (Figure 4-10). As a student, you are an instance of one of the subtypes: either UNDERGRAD STUDENT or GRADUATE STUDENT. List the names of all the attributes that apply to you. For each attribute, record the data value that applies to you.

2. Add a subtype discriminator for each of the supertypes shown in Figure 4-10. Show the discriminator values that assign instances to each subtype. Use the following subtype discriminator names and values:

   a. PERSON: Person_Type (Employee?, Alumnus?, Student?)

   b. EMPLOYEE: Employee_Type (Faculty, Staff)

   c. STUDENT: Student_Type (Grad, Undergrad)

3. Draw an EER diagram for the following problem using this textbook's EER notation, the Visio notation, or the subtypes inside supertypes notation, as specified by your instructor. A nonprofit organization depends on a number of different types of persons for its successful operation. The organization is interested in the following attributes for all of these persons: SSN, Name, Address, City/State/Zip, and Telephone. Three types of persons are of greatest interest: employees, volunteers, and donors. Employees have only a Date_Hired attribute, and volunteers have only a Skill attribute. Donors have only a relationship (named Donates) with an Item entity type. A donor must have donated one or more items, and an item may have no donors, or one or more donors.

   There are persons other than employees, volunteers, and donors who are of interest to the organization, so that a person need not belong to any of these three groups. On the other hand, at a given time a person may belong to two or more of these groups (e.g., employee and donor).

4. Add a subtype discriminator (named Person_Type) to the diagram you created in Problem and Exercise 3.

5. A rental car agency classifies the vehicles it rents into four categories: compact, mid-size, full-size, and sport utility. The agency wants to record the following data for all vehicles: Vehicle_ID, Make, Model, Year, and Color. There are no unique attributes for any of the four classes of vehicle. The entity type vehicle has a relationship (named Rents) with a customer entity type. None of the four vehicle classes has a unique relationship with an entity type. Would you consider creating a supertype/subtype relationship for this problem? Why or why not?

6. At a weekend retreat, the entity type PERSON has three subtypes: CAMPER, BIKER, and RUNNER. Draw a separate EER diagram segment for each of the following situations:

a. At a given time, a person must be exactly one of these subtypes.

b. A person may or may not be one of these subtypes. However, a person who is one of these subtypes cannot at the same time be one of the other subtypes.

c. A person may or may not be one of these subtypes. On the other hand, a person may be any two (or even three) of these subtypes at the same time.

d. At a given time, a person must be at least one of these subtypes.

7. A bank has three types of accounts: checking, savings, and loan. Following are the attributes for each type of account:

CHECKING: Acct_No, Date_Opened, Balance, _Service_ Charge

SAVINGS: Acct_No, Date_Opened, Balance, _Interest_Rate

LOAN: Acct_No, Date_Opened, Balance, Interest_Rate, Payment

Assume that each bank account must be a member of exactly one of these subtypes. Using generalization, develop an EER model segment to represent this situation using the traditional EER notation, the Visio notation, or the subtypes inside supertypes notation, as specified by your instructor. Remember to include a subtype discriminator.

8. Refer to the employee EER diagram (Figure 4-2) to perform the following exercises. Make any assumptions that you believe are necessary.

a. Develop a sample definition for each entity type, attribute, and relationship in the diagram.

b. Develop sample integrity constraint action assertions for all of the attributes in the figure.

9. Refer to the data model for class scheduling (Figure 4-19). Add graphical notation to the figure to express each of the following business rules:

a. For a section of a course to be scheduled, there must be a faculty member who is qualified to teach that course (Hint: See Figure 4-20.)

b. For a student to register in a section of a course, that student may not be registered in a total of more than six course sections at a given time (Hint: See Figure 4-21.)

10. Refer to the EER diagram for hospital relationships (Figure 4-3). Add notation to express the following business rule: A resident patient can be assigned a bed only if that patient has been assigned a responsible physician. In this example, what is (are):

a. the anchor object?

b. the corresponding object(s)?

11. Consider the following "business" rule: "A student may attend a concert only if that student has completed his (her) homework."

a. Draw an EER diagram segment to portray the entities and relationships implied in this rule.

b. Add a suitable notation to express the business rule.

c. Identify each of the following: (i) anchor object; (ii) corresponding object(s).

12. Refer to the EER diagram for patients (Figure 4-3) and perform the following exercises. Make any assumptions you believe are necessary.

a. Develop sample definitions for each entity type, attribute, and relationship in the diagram.

b. Develop sample integrity constraint action insertions for each attribute in the diagram.

13. Figure 4-13 shows the development of entity clusters for the Pine Valley Furniture E-R diagram. In Figure 4-13b, explain the following:

a. Why the minimum cardinality next to the Does_business_in relationship coming from CUSTOMER is zero.

b. What the attributes of ITEM would be (refer to Figure 3-22).

c. What the attributes of MATERIAL would be (refer to Figure 3-22).

14. Refer to your answer to Problem and Exercise 7 in Chapter 3. Develop entity clusters for this E-R diagram and redraw the diagram using the entity clusters. Explain why you chose the entity clusters you used.

15. Refer to your answer to Problem and Exercise 12 in Chapter 3. Develop entity clusters for this E-R diagram and redraw the diagram using the entity clusters. Explain why you chose the entity clusters you used.

16. Develop an EER model for the following situation using the traditional EER notation, the Visio notation, or the subtypes inside supertypes notation, as specified by your instructor:

A person may be employed by one or more organizations, and each organization may be the employer of one or more persons. An organization can be an internal organizational unit or an external organization. For persons and organizations, we want to know their ID, name, address, and phone number. For persons, we want to know their birthdate, and for organizations, we want to know their budget number. For each employment, we want to know the employment date, termination date, and bonus.

Employment of a person by an organization may result in the person holding many positions over time. For each position, we want to know its title, and each time someone holds that position, we need to know the start date and termination date and salary. An organization is responsible for each position. It is possible for a person to be employed by one organization and hold a position for which another organization is responsible.

17. You have seen in Chapter 4 many examples of this textbook's EER notation, Visio notation, and subtypes within supertypes notation. Create a table or figure that summarizes how each notation shows the same EER concept (e.g., disjoint rule, subtype discriminator).

18. Develop an EER model for the following situation using the traditional EER notation, the Visio notation, or the subtypes inside supertypes notation, as specified by your instructor:

An international school of technology has hired you to create a database management system to assist in scheduling classes. After several interviews with the president, you have come up with the following list of entities, attributes, and initial business rules:

• Room is identified by Building_ID and Room_NO and also has a Capacity. A room can be either a lab or a classroom. If it is a classroom, it has an additional attribute called Board_type.

- Media is identified by Mtypeid and has attributes of MediaType and Type Description. Note: Here we are tracking type of media (such as a VCR, projector, etc.), not the individual piece of equipment. Tracking of equipment is outside of the scope of this project.

- Computer is identified by Ctypeid and has attributes ComputerType, TypeDescription, DiskCapacity, and ProcessorSpeed. Please note: As with MediaType, we are tracking only the type of computer, not an individual computer. You can think of this as a class of computers (e.g., PIII 900MHZ).

- Instructor has identified by Emp_ID and has attributes Name, Rank, and Office_Phone.

- Timeslot has identifier TSIS and has attributes DayofWeek, StartTime, and EndTime.

- Course has identifier CourseID and has attributes CourseDescription and Credits. Courses can have one, none, or many prerequisites. Courses also have one or more sections.

- Section has identifier SectionID and attribute EnrollmentLimit.

After some further discussions, you have come up with some additional business rules to help you create the initial design:

- An instructor teaches one, none, or many sections of a course in a given semester.

- An instructor specifies preferred timeslots.

- Scheduling data are kept for each semester, uniquely identified by semester and year.

- A room can be scheduled for one section or no section during one timeslot in a given semester of a given year. However, one room can participate in many schedules, one schedule, or no schedules; one timeslot can participate in many schedules, one schedule, or no schedules; one section can participate in many schedules, one schedule, or no schedules. Hint: Can you associate this to anything that you have seen before?

- A room can have one type of media, several types of media, or no media.

- Instructors are trained to use one, none, or many types of media.

- A lab has one or more computer types. However, a classroom does not have any computers.

- A room cannot be both a classroom and a lab. There also are no other room types to be incorporated into the system.

19. Develop an EER model for the following situation using the traditional EER notation, the Visio notation, or the subtypes inside supertypes notation, as specified by your instructor:

Wally Los Gatos and his partner Henry Chordate have formed a new limited partnership, Fin and Finicky Security Consultants. Fin and Finicky consults with corporations to determine their security needs. You have been hired by Wally and Henry to design a database management system to help them manage their business.

Due to a recent increase in business, Fin and Finicky has decided to automate their client tracking system. You and your team have done a preliminary analysis and come up with the following set of entities, attributes, and business rules:

Consultant

There are two types of consultants: business consultants and technical consultants. Business consultants are contacted by a business in order to first determine security needs and provide an estimate for the actual services to be performed. Technical consultants perform services according to the specifications developed by the business consultants.

Attributes of business consultant are the following: EmployeeID (identifier), Name, Address (which is composed of Street, City, State, and Zip Code), Telephone, DateofBirth, Age, Business Experience (which is composed of Number of Years, Type of Business [or businesses], and Degrees Received).

Attributes of technical consultant are the following: EmployeeID (identifier), Name, Address (which is composed of Street, City, State, and ZipCode), Telephone, DateofBirth, Age, Technical Skills, and Degrees Received.

Customer

Customers are businesses that have asked for consulting services. Attributes of customer are CustomerID (identifier), Company Name, Address (which is composed of Street, City, State, and ZipCode), ContactName, ContactTitle, ContactTelephone, BusinessType, and NumberOfEmployees.

Location

Customers can have multiple locations. Attributes of location are CustomerID (identifier), LocationID (which is unique only for each CustomerID), Address (which is composed of Street, City, State, and ZipCode), Telephone, and BuildingSize.

Service

A security service is performed for a customer at one or more locations. Before services are performed, an estimate is prepared. Attributes of service are ServiceID (identifier), Description, Cost, Coverage, and ClearanceRequired.

Additional Business Rules

In addition to the entities outlined above, the following information will need to be stored to tables and should be shown in the model. These may be entities, but they also reflect a relationship between more than one entity.

- Estimates, which have characteristics of Date, Amount, Business Consultant, Services, Customer

- Services Performed, which have characteristics of Date, Amount, Technical Consultant, Services, Customer

In order to construct the EER Diagram, you may assume the following:

A customer can have many consultants providing many services. We wish to track both actual services performed as well as services offered. Therefore, there should be two relationships between customer, service, and consultant, one to show services performed and one to show services offered as part of the estimate.

20. Based on the EER diagram constructed for Problem and Exercise 19, complete the following:

a. Develop sample definitions for each entity type, attribute, and relationship in the diagram.

b. Develop sample integrity constraint action insertions for each attribute in the diagram.

21. For simplicity, subtype discriminators were left off many figures in this chapter. Add subtype discriminator notation in each figure listed below. If necessary, create a new attribute for the discriminator.

    a. Figure 4-2.
    b. Figure 4-3.
    c. Figure 4-4b.
    d. Figure 4-7a.
    e. Figure 4-7b.

22. Add the following to Figure 4-16: an EMPLOYMENT party relationship is further explained by the positions and assignments to positions during the time a person is employed. A position is defined by an organization unit, and a unit may define many positions over time. Over time, positions are assigned to various employment relationships (i.e., somebody employed by some organization unit is assigned a particular position. For example, a position of Business Analyst is defined by the Systems Development organization unit. Carl Gerber, while employed by the Data Warehousing organization unit is assigned the position of Systems Analyst. In the spirit of universal data modeling, enhance Figure 4-16 for the most general case consistent with this description.

Field Exercises

1. Interview a friend or family member to elicit common examples of the following things they may come into contact with at work.

    a. *Supertype/subtype relationships.* You will have to explain the meaning of this term to the person you are interviewing and provide a common example, such as PROPERTY: RESIDENTIAL, COMMERCIAL or BONDS: CORPORATE, MUNICIPAL. Use the information the person provides to construct an EER diagram segment and present it to the person. Revise, if necessary, until it seems appropriate to you and your friend or family member.

    b. *Business rules.* Give the person you are interviewing examples of business rules, using the ones provided in this chapter (Figures 4-20 and 4-21). When your informant gives you a rule from his or her environment, restructure it, if necessary, to conform to the syntax of this chapter.

2. Visit two local small businesses, one in the service sector and one in manufacturing. Interview employees from these organizations to obtain examples of both supertype/subtype relationships and business rules (such as "A customer can return merchandise only with a valid sales slip"). In which of these environments is it easier to find examples of these constructs? Why?

3. Ask a database administrator or database or systems analyst in a local company to show you an EER (or E-R) diagram for one of the organization's primary databases. Does this organization model supertype/subtype relationships? If so, what notation is used and does the CASE tool the company uses support these relationships? Also, what types of business rules are included during the EER modeling phase? How are business rules represented, and how and where are they stored?

4. Read the summary of business rules published by the GUIDE Business Rules Project (1997) and the article by Gottesdiener (1997). Search the Web for additional information on business rules. Then write a three-page executive summary of current directions in business rules and their potential impact on systems development and maintenance.

5. Research business rules engine software. Include in your summary at least four softwares. Explain the features, price, and stated values or benefits of each.

6. Research universal data models. Find articles on universal (or prepackaged, industry, or functional area) data models, or find information on some commercial offerings. Identify common features across these models as well as different ways to model the same concepts. Discuss what you think are the advantages and disadvantages of the different ways used to model the same concepts.

References

Elmasri, R., and S. B. Navathe. 1994. *Fundamentals of Database Systems.* Menlo Park, CA: Benjamin/Cummings.

Frye, C. 2002. "Business Rules Are Back." *Application Development Trends* 9,7 (July): 29–35.

Gottesdiener, E. 1997. "Business Rules Show Power, Promise." *Application Development Trends* 4,3 (March): 36–54.

GUIDE. "GUIDE Business Rules Project." Final Report, revision 1.2. October 1997.

Hay, D. C. 1996. *Data Model Patterns: Conventions of Thought.* New York, NY: Dorset House Publishing.

Moriarty, T. "Using Scenarios in Information Modeling: Bringing Business Rules to Life." *Database Programming & Design* 6,8 (August): 65–67.

Ross, R. G. 1997. *The Business Rule Book.* Version 4. Boston: Business Rule Solutions, Inc.

Silverston, L. 1998. "Is Your Organization Too Unique to Use Universal Data Models?" *DM Review* 8,8 (September) accessed at http://www.dmreview.com/article_sub.cfm?articleId=425.

Silverston, L. 2001. *The Data Model Resource Book, Volume 1.* Revised Edition. New York, NY: Wiley.

Silverston, L. 2001. *The Data Model Resource Book, Volume 2.* Revised Edition. New York, NY: Wiley.

Silverston, L. 2002. "A Universal Data Model for Relationship Development." *DM Review* 12,3 (March): 44–47, 65.

Teorey, T. 1999. *Database Modeling & Design.* San Francisco, CA: Morgan Kaufman Publishers.

Further Reading

Ross, R. G. 1998. Business Rule Concepts: The New Mechanics of Business Information Systems. Boston: Business Rule Solutions, Inc.

Ross, R. G. 2003. *Principles of the Business Rule Approach*. Boston: Addison-Wesley.

Schmidt, B. 1997. "A Taxonomy of Domains." *Database Programming & Design* 10,9 (September): 95, 96, 98, 99.

Silverston, L. 2002. Silverston has a series of articles in *DM Review* that discuss universal data models in different settings. See in particular Vol. 12 issues 1 (January) on clickstream analysis, 5 (May) on health care, 7 (July) on financial services, and 12 (December) on manufacturing.

von Halle, B. 1996. "Object-Oriented Lessons." *Database Programming & Design* 9,1 (January): 13–16.

von Halle, B. 2001. von Halle has a series of articles in *DM Review* on building a business rules system. These articles are in Vol. 11, issues 1–5 (January–May).

von Halle, B., and R. Kaplan. 1997. "Is IT Falling Short?" *Database Programming & Design* 10,6 (June): 15–17.

Web Resources

www.adtmag.com *Application Development Trends* is a leading publication on the practice of information systems development.

www.brsolutions.com Business Rules Solutions is the consulting company of Ronald Ross, a leader in the development of a business rule methodology. Or you can check out **www.BRCommunity.com,** which is a virtual community site for people interested in business rules (sponsored by Business Rules Solutions).

www.businessrulesgroup.org The Business Rules Group, formerly part of GUIDE International, formulates and supports standards about business rules.

datadmn.disa.mil This site contains many E-R diagrams and other documentation as examples of data and system modeling.

www.intelligententerprise.com *Intelligent Enterprise* is a leading publication on database management and related areas. This magazine is the result of combining two previous publications, *Database Programming & Design* and *DBMS*.

www.kpiusa.com The homepage for Knowledge Partners, Inc., founded by Barbara von Halle. This site has some interesting case studies and white papers about business rules.

www.tdan.com The Data Administration Newsletter regularly publishes new articles, special reports, and news on a variety of data modeling and administration topics.

MOUNTAIN VIEW COMMUNITY HOSPITAL

Case

CASE DESCRIPTION

After developing a preliminary ER model and discussing it with the rest of your team, you realize that you need to delve deeper into the interview notes and documentation you obtained to add more detail to the model and possibly add entities and relationships you had overlooked. Several issues need to be addressed.

As a large service organization, Mountain View Community Hospital depends on four major groups of persons for its continued success: employees, physicians, patients, and volunteers. A small number of persons in the hospital community do not belong to any of these four groups. A particular person may belong to two (or more) of these groups at a given time. For example, a volunteer or employee may also be a patient at the hospital at some point in time.

The four groups of people listed above share many common characteristics such as a unique identifier, Name, Address, City/State/Zip, Birth_Date, Phone, and e-mail. Then there are characteristics that apply to only one of these groups. For example, a hire date (Date_Hired) is recorded for employees only. Volunteer Services records skills and interests of their volunteers in order to place them appropriately. Physicians have pager number (pager#) and a DEA number (a physician needs a DEA registration number from the Drug Enforcement Administration to be able to prescribe controlled substances). For patients, the hospital records the date of first contact with the hospital (Contact_Date). There are also characteristics that apply to some, but not all of the groups. For example, both physicians and nurses have a specialty (e.g., pediatrics, oncology, etc.).

In addition to the characteristics already mentioned, the hospital records a number of other characteristics about its patients: emergency contact information (last and first name, relationship to patient, address, and phone), insurance information (insurance company name, policy number, group number, and insurance phone number), information about the insurance subscriber in case the patient is not the insurance subscriber (last and first name, relationship to patient, address, and phone), and contact information for the patient's primary care physician or other physician who referred the patient to the hospital.

At Mountain View Community Hospital, each patient has one (and only one) physician responsible for that patient. A given physician may not be responsible for a patient at a given time or may be responsible for one or more patients. The primary patient segments are resident patients and outpatients. Outpatients may come in for many reasons, including routine examinations at an outpatient care center (e.g., the MS Center), ambulatory/outpatient surgery, diagnostic services, or emergency room care. Each outpatient is scheduled for zero or more visits. A visit has several attributes: a unique identifier (Visit#), date, and time. Notice that an instance of visit cannot exist without an outpatient owner entity. Some patients that are seen as outpatients, for example, in the emergency room, are subsequently admitted to the hospital and become resident patients. Each resident patient has a Date_Admitted attribute as well as a Discharge_Date.

The volunteer application form in MVCH Figure 4-1 shows all the information that Volunteer Services under Mr. Davis requires from persons interested in volunteering. Volunteers work in many areas of the hospital based on their interests and skills. Volunteer Services keeps track of a person's time of service (begin and end date), work unit where a person works as a volunteer, and the volunteer's supervisor. Each volunteer is supervised by an employee or physician, but not all employees and physicians supervise volunteers. Volunteer Services also keep track of a volunteer's number of hours worked and recognizes outstanding volunteers at an annual awards ceremony.

Employees fall into three categories: nurses, technicians, and staff. Nurses have a certificate/degree, which indicates their qualification as RNs or LPNs. (LPNs work under the direction of RNs at MVCH.) They must also have a current Colorado nursing license, and may hold certifications in special fields such as dialysis, pediatrics, anesthesia, critical care, pain management, and so on. Most nurses are assigned to one (and only one) care

Mountain View Community Hospital
VOLUNTEER APPLICATION

Last Name _____ First Name _____ Date of Birth _____

Street Address _____ City _____ State _____ Zip _____

Home Phone: (___) _____ Work Phone: (___) _____ E-Mail _____

Have you been *convicted of a felony* within the past seven years?

    ○ NO ○ YES If YES, please explain _____

Emergency Contact Last Name _____ First Name _____

Relationship _____ Phone: (___) _____

References (Not Relatives)

Last Name _____	Last Name _____
First Name _____	First Name _____
Relationship _____ Phone (___)	Relationship _____ Phone (___)
Address: _____	Address _____
City _____ State _____ Zip _____	City _____ State _____ Zip _____

Current or Last Employment

Name of Employer _____

Employer Address _____

Position (Type of work) _____ Dates of Employment _____

Prior Volunteer Service

Have you volunteered at Mountain Valley Community Hospital before?

    ○ NO ○ YES If YES, please list _____

Do you have previous volunteer experience elsewhere?

    ○ NO ○ YES If YES, please list _____

Interests & Preferences

Why do you want to become a volunteer? _____

What are your hobbies, skills, other interests? _____

Which languages do you speak? _____

What do you envision yourself doing as a volunteer? _____

	Mon	Tues	Wed	Thur	Fri	Sat	Sun
Morning							
Afternoon							
Evening							

Please indicate days and times when you are available to volunteer.

Applicant's Signature _____ Date _____

MVCH Figure 4-1
Volunteer Application Form

center at a time, although over time, they may be working in more than one care center. Some nurses are floaters who are not assigned to a specific care center but instead work wherever they are needed. As described earlier, one of the nurses assigned to a care center is appointed nurse-in-charge (nurse_in_charge). Only nurses with a RN certificate can be appointed nurse-in-charge.

Specific job-related competency skills are recorded for the hospital's technicians. A cardiovascular technician for example may be skilled in specific equipment, such as setting up and getting readings from a Holter monitor, a portable device that monitors a patient's EKG for a period of 24 to 48 hours during routine activities. Medical laboratory technicians need to be able to set up, operate, and control equipment, perform a variety of tests, analyze the test data, and summarize test results for physicians who use them to diagnose and treat patients Emergency room technicians skills include the ability to perform CPR, or set up an IV. Dialysis technicians, who may be skilled in different types of dialysis, (e.g., pediatric dialysis, outpatient dialysis) need a variety of skills related to setting up treatment, assessing the patient during dialysis, and assessing and troubleshooting equipment problems during dialysis. Each technician is assigned to a Work Unit in the hospital (a care center, the central medical laboratory, radiology, etc.).

Staff members have a job classification (Job_Class), such as, secretary, administrative assistant, admitting specialist, collection specialist, and so on. Like the technicians, each staff member is assigned to a Work Unit in the hospital (a care center, the central medical laboratory, radiology, etc.).

Work units such as a care center have a Name (identifier) and Location. The location denotes the facility (e.g., main building) and floor (e.g., 3 West, 2 South). A care center often has one or more beds (up to any number) assigned to it, but there are also care centers without assigned beds. The only attribute of bed is the identifier Bed_ID, which consists of two components: Bed# and Room#. Each resident patient must be assigned to a bed. Because Mountain Valley Community Hospital doesn't always fill all its beds, a bed may or may not have a resident patient assigned to it at a given time.

CASE QUESTIONS

1. Is the ability to model supertype/subtype relationships important in a hospital environment such as Mountain View Community Hospital? Why or why not?

2. Can the business rules paradigm and the ability to define, implement, and maintain business rules be used as a competitive advantage in a hospital environment such as Mountain View Community Hospital? Why or why not?

3. Do there appear to be any weak entities, multivalued attributes, or multiple relationships in the description of the data requirements in this case segment? If so, what are they?

4. Can you think of any other business rules (other than the one explicitly described in the case) that are likely to be used in a hospital environment?

5. Are there any universal data models that can be reused as a starting point for modeling Mountain View Community Hospital's data requirements? Would you recommend using such as model for the Mountain View Community Hospital project? Why or why not?

CASE EXERCISES

1. Draw an EER diagram to represent the requirements described in this case segment carefully following the notation from this chapter.

2. Suppose each care center had two nurses-in-charge, one for the day shift, and another one for the evening shift. How would that change the diagram you developed in Case Exercise 1?

3. Develop definitions for each of the following types of objects in your EER diagram from Case Exercise 1. Consult with some member of the hospital or health care community (if one is available); do some research on the Internet, or otherwise make reasonable assumptions based on your own knowledge and experience.

   a. Entity types

   b. Attributes

   c. Relationships

4. Figure 4-17 in Chapter 4 shows the following entity types in a universal data model: PARTY, PARTY ROLE, PARTY RELATIONSHIP, EVENT, PRIORITY TYPE, STATUS TYPE, EVENT ROLE, and ROLE TYPE. How would these apply to the Mountain View Community Hospital case? Give examples of each entity type based on the information provided in the case descriptions up to this point.

5. Derive and clearly state the business rules that are implicit in the Volunteer Application Form shown in MVCH Figure 4-1.

6. You should recognize the statement "Only nurses with a RN certificate can be appointed nurse-in-charge" as a statement of a business rule.

   a. What is the anchor object? Is it an entity, an attribute, a relationship, or some other object?

   b. What is the corresponding object (or objects, if more than one)? Is it an entity, an attribute, a relationship, or some other object?

7. Compare the EER diagram that you developed in this chapter with the E-R diagram you developed in Chapter 3. What are the differences between these two diagrams? Why are there differences?

PROJECT ASSIGNMENTS

P1. Revise the list of business rules you developed in Chapter 3 in light of the information provided in this case segment and your insights from Case Exercises 1, 2, 5, and 7.

P2. Following the notation from this chapter, merge your Chapter 3 E-R diagram with the EER diagram you developed for Case Exercises 1 and 2 to represent the data requirements for Mountain View Community Hospital's new system.

P3. Document and explain the decisions you made during merging.

Part **THREE**

Database Design

An Overview of Part THREE

By the end of the database analysis phase of database development, systems and database analysts have a fairly clear understanding of data storage and access requirements. However, the data model developed during analysis explicitly avoided any ties to database technologies. Before we can implement a database, the conceptual data model must be mapped into a data model that is compatible with the database management system to be used.

The activities of database design transform the requirements for data storage developed during database analysis into specifications to guide database implementation. There are two forms of specifications:

1. Logical, which maps the conceptual requirements into the data model associated with a specific database management system

2. Physical, which indicates all the parameters for data storage that are then input to database implementation, during which a database is actually defined using a data definition language

In Chapter 5 (Logical Database Design and the Relational Model), we describe logical database design, with special emphasis on the relational data model. Logical database design is the process of transforming the conceptual data model (described in Chapters 3 and 4) into a logical data model. Most database management systems in use today use the relational data model, so this data model is the basis for our discussion of logical database design.

In Chapter 5, we first define the important terms and concepts for this model, including relation, primary key, foreign key, anomaly, normal form, normalization, functional dependency, partial functional dependency, and transitive dependency. We next describe and illustrate the process of transforming an E-R model to the relational model. Many CASE tools support this transformation; however, it is important that you understand the underlying principles and procedures. We then describe and illustrate in detail the important concepts of normalization (the process of designing well-structured relations). Finally, we describe how to merge relations from separate logical design activities (e.g., different groups within a large project team) while avoiding common pitfalls that may occur in this process.

The purpose of physical database design, the topic of Chapter 6 (Physical Database Design and Performance), is to translate the logical description of data into the technical specifications for storing and retrieving data. The goal is to create a design for storing data that will provide adequate performance and ensure database integrity, security, and recoverability. Physical database design produces the technical specifications that programmers and others involved in information systems construction will use during the implementation phase, which we discuss in Chapters 7 through 11.

In Chapter 6, you will learn key terms and concepts for physical database design, including data type, page, pointer, denormalization, partitioning, indexed file organization, and hashed file organization. You will study the basic steps to develop an efficient physical database design. You will learn about choices for storing attribute values and how to select among these choices. You will also learn why normalized tables do not always form the best physical data files and how you can, if necessary, denormalize the data to achieve data retrieval speed improvements. You will learn about different file organizations and different types of indexes, which are important in speeding the retrieval of data. Chapter 6 also addresses how to use redundant data storage schemes (RAID) to provide improved performance and reliability to databases. In addition, you will learn physical database design choices that improve data quality, essential today with new regulations for validating the accuracy of financial reporting. Finally, you will address some techniques of database design and query handling that improve the speed of data access.

You must carefully perform physical database design because decisions made during this stage have a major impact on data accessibility, response times, security, user friendliness, information quality, and similarly important information system design factors. Database administration (described in Chapter 12) plays a major role in physical database design, so we will return to some advanced design issues in that chapter, and Chapter 13 addresses distributed database design issues.

Logical Database Design
and the Relational Model

LEARNING OBJECTIVES

After studying this chapter, you should be able to:

- Concisely define each of the following key terms: **relation, primary key, composite key, foreign key, null, entity integrity rule, referential integrity constraint, well-structured relation, anomaly, recursive foreign key, normalization, normal form, functional dependency, determinant, candidate key, first normal form, second normal form, partial functional dependency, third normal form, transitive dependency, synonyms, alias, homonym** and **enterprise key.**

- List five properties of relations.

- State two properties that are essential for a candidate key.

- Give a concise definition of each of the following: first normal form, second normal form, and third normal form.

- Briefly describe four problems that may arise when merging relations.

- Transform an E-R (or EER) diagram to a logically equivalent set of relations.

- Create relational tables that incorporate entity integrity and referential integrity constraints.

- Use normalization to decompose a relation with anomalies into well-structured relations.

INTRODUCTION

In this chapter, we describe logical database design, with special emphasis on the relational data model. Logical database design is the process of transforming the conceptual data model (described in Chapters 3 and 4) into a logical data model—one which is consistent and compatible with a type of database technology. An experienced database designer often will do logical database design in parallel with conceptual data modeling if he or she knows the type of database technology that will be used. As a beginner, it is important to treat these as separate steps so that you concentrate on each important part of database development. Conceptual data modeling is about understanding the organization—getting the right requirements. Logical database design is about creating stable database structures—getting the requirements right. Both are important steps that must be performed carefully.

Although there are other data models, we have two reasons for emphasizing the relational data model in this chapter. First, the relational data model is most commonly used in contemporary database applications. Second, some of the principles of logical database design for the relational model apply to the other logical models as well.

We have introduced the relational data model informally through simple examples in earlier chapters. It is important, however, to note that the relational data model is only one form of logical data model. Thus, an E-R data model is not a relational data model, and an E-R model may not obey the rules for a well-structured relational data model, called normalization, which we explain in this chapter. That is okay, because the E-R model was developed for other purposes—understanding data requirements and business rules about the data—not structuring the data for sound database processing, which is the goal of logical database design.

In this chapter, we first define the important terms and concepts for the relational data model. (We often use the abbreviated term *relational model* when referring to the relational data model.) We next describe and illustrate the process of transforming an E-R model into the relational model. Many CASE tools support this transformation today; however, it is important that you understand the underlying principles and procedures. We then describe the concepts of normalization in detail. Normalization, which is the process of designing well-structured relations, is an important component of logical design for the relational model. Finally, we describe how to merge relations while avoiding common pitfalls that may occur in this process.

The objective of logical database design is to translate the conceptual design (which represents an organization's requirements for data) into a logical database design that can be implemented via a chosen database management system. The resulting databases must meet user needs for data sharing, flexibility, and ease of access. The concepts presented in this chapter are essential to your understanding of the database development process.

THE RELATIONAL DATA MODEL

The relational data model was first introduced in 1970 by E. F. Codd, then of IBM (Codd, 1970). Two early research projects were launched to prove the feasibility of the relational model and to develop prototype systems. The first of these, at IBM's San Jose Research Laboratory, led to the development of System R (a prototype relational DBMS–RDBMS) during the late 1970s. The second, at the University of California at Berkeley, led to the development of Ingres, an academically oriented RDBMS. Commercial RDBMS products from numerous vendors started to appear about 1980. (See the Web site for this book for links to RDBMS and other DBMS vendors.) Today RDBMSs have become the dominant technology for database management, and there are literally hundreds of RDBMS products for computers ranging from PDAs and personal computers to mainframes.

Basic Definitions

The relational data model represents data in the form of tables. The relational model is based on mathematical theory and therefore has a solid theoretical foundation. However, we need only a few simple concepts to describe the relational model, and it is therefore easily understood and used by those unfamiliar with the underlying theory. The relational data model consists of the following three components (Fleming and von Halle, 1989):

1. *Data structure* Data are organized in the form of tables with rows and columns.

2. *Data manipulation* Powerful operations (using the SQL language) are used to manipulate data stored in the relations.

EMPLOYEE1			
<u>Emp_ID</u>	Name	Dept_Name	Salary
100	Margaret Simpson	Marketing	48,000
140	Allen Beeton	Accounting	52,000
110	Chris Lucero	Info Systems	43,000
190	Lorenzo Davis	Finance	55,000
150	Susan Martin	Marketing	42,000

Figure 5-1
EMPLOYEE1 relation with sample data

3. *Data integrity* Facilities are included to specify business rules that maintain the integrity of data when they are manipulated.

We discuss data structure and data integrity in this section. Data manipulation is discussed in Chapters 7, 8, and 10.

Relational Data Structure A **relation** is a named, two-dimensional table of data. Each relation (or table) consists of a set of named columns and an arbitrary number of unnamed rows. An attribute, consistent with its definition in Chapter 3, is a named column of a relation. Each row of a relation corresponds to a record that contains data (attribute) values for a single entity. Figure 5-1 shows an example of a relation named EMPLOYEE1. This relation contains the following attributes describing employees: Emp_ID, Name, Dept_Name, and Salary. The five rows of the table correspond to five employees. It is important to understand that the sample data in Figure 5-1 are intended to illustrate the structure of the EMPLOYEE1 relation; they are not part of the relation itself. Even if we add another row of data to the figure, it is still the same EMPLOYEE1 relation. Nor does deleting a row change the relation. In fact, we could delete all of the rows shown in Figure 5-1, and the EMPLOYEE1 relation would still exist. Stated differently, Figure 5-1 is an instance of the EMPLOYEE1 relation.

Relation: A named two-dimensional table of data.

We can express the structure of a relation by a shorthand notation in which the name of the relation is followed (in parentheses) by the names of the attributes in that relation. For EMPLOYEE1 we would have:

EMPLOYEE1(Emp_ID,Name,Dept_Name,Salary)

Relational Keys We must be able to store and retrieve a row of data in a relation, based on the data values stored in that row. To achieve this goal, every relation must have a primary key. A **primary key** is an attribute (or combination of attributes) that uniquely identifies each row in a relation. We designate a primary key by underlining the attribute name. For example, the primary key for the relation EMPLOYEE1 is Emp_ID. Notice that this attribute is underlined in Figure 5-1. In shorthand notation, we express this relation as follows:

Primary key: An attribute (or combination of attributes) that uniquely identifies each row in a relation.

EMPLOYEE1(<u>Emp_ID</u>,Name,Dept_Name,Salary)

The concept of a primary key is related to the term *identifier* defined in Chapter 3. The same attribute (or attributes) indicated as an entity's identifier in an E-R diagram may be the same attributes that compose the primary key for the relation representing that entity. There are exceptions; for example, associative entities do not have to have an identifier, and the identifier of a weak entity forms only part of a weak entity's primary key. In addition, there may be several attributes of an entity that may serve as the associated relation's primary key. All of these situations will be illustrated later in this chapter.

A **composite key** is a primary key that consists of more than one attribute. For example, the primary key for a relation DEPENDENT would likely consist of the combination Emp_ID and Dependent_Name. We show several examples of composite keys later in this chapter.

Composite key: A primary key that consists of more than one attribute.

Often we must represent the relationship between two tables or relations. This is accomplished through the use of foreign keys. A **foreign key** is an attribute (possibly composite)

Foreign key: An attribute in a relation of a database that serves as the primary key of another relation in the same database.

in a relation of a database that serves as the primary key of another relation in the same database. For example, consider the relations EMPLOYEE1 and DEPARTMENT:

EMPLOYEE1(Emp_ID,Name,Dept_Name,Salary)
DEPARTMENT(Dept_Name,Location,Fax)

The attribute Dept_Name is a foreign key in EMPLOYEE1. It allows a user to associate any employee with the department to which he or she is assigned. Some authors emphasize the fact that an attribute is a foreign key by using a dashed underline, such as

EMPLOYEE1(Emp_ID,Name,Dept_Name,Salary)

We provide numerous examples of foreign keys in the remainder of this chapter and discuss the properties of foreign keys under the heading, "Referential Integrity."

Properties of Relations We have defined relations as two-dimensional tables of data. However, not all tables are relations. Relations have several properties that distinguish them from nonrelational tables. We summarize these properties below.

1. Each relation (or table) in a database has a unique name.
2. An entry at the intersection of each row and column is atomic (or single valued). There can be no multivalued attributes in a relation.
3. Each row is unique; no two rows in a relation are identical.
4. Each attribute (or column) within a table has a unique name.
5. The sequence of columns (left to right) is insignificant. The columns of a relation can be interchanged without changing the meaning or use of the relation.
6. The sequence of rows (top to bottom) is insignificant. As with columns, the rows of a relation may be interchanged or stored in any sequence.

Removing Multivalued Attributes from Tables The second property of relations in the list states that there can be no multivalued attributes in a relation. Thus, a table that contains one or more multivalued attributes is not a relation. As an example, Figure 5-2a shows the employee data from the EMPLOYEE1 relation extended to include courses

Figure 5-2
Eliminating multivalued attributes
(a) Table with repeating groups

Emp_ID	Name	Dept_Name	Salary	Course_Title	Date_Completed
100	Margaret Simpson	Marketing	48,000	SPSS	6/19/200X
				Surveys	10/7/200X
140	Alan Beeton	Accounting	52,000	Tax Acc	12/8/200X
110	Chris Lucero	Info Systems	43,000	Visual Basic	1/12/200X
				C++	4/22/200X
190	Lorenzo Davis	Finance	55,000		
150	Susan Martin	Marketing	42,000	SPSS	6/16/200X
				Java	8/12/200X

(b) EMPLOYEE2 relation

EMPLOYEE2

Emp_ID	Name	Dept_Name	Salary	Course_Title	Date_Completed
100	Margaret Simpson	Marketing	48,000	SPSS	6/19/200X
100	Margaret Simpson	Marketing	48,000	Surveys	10/7/200X
140	Alan Beeton	Accounting	52,000	Tax Acc	12/8/200X
110	Chris Lucero	Info Systems	43,000	Visual Basic	1/12/200X
110	Chris Lucero	Info Systems	43,000	C++	4/22/200X
190	Lorenzo Davis	Finance	55,000		
150	Susan Martin	Marketing	42,000	SPSS	6/19/200X
150	Susan Martin	Marketing	42,000	Java	8/12/200X

that may have been taken by those employees. Because a given employee may have taken more than one course, the attributes Course_Title and Date_Completed are multivalued attributes. For example, the employee with Emp_ID 100 has taken two courses. If an employee has not taken any courses, the Course_Title and Date_Completed attribute values are null. (See employee with Emp_ID 190 for an example.)

We show how to eliminate the multivalued attributes in Figure 5-2b by filling the relevant data values into the previously vacant cells of Figure 5-2a. As a result, the table in Figure 5-2b has only single-valued attributes and now satisfies the atomic property of relations. The name EMPLOYEE2 is given to this relation to distinguish it from EMPLOYEE1. However, as you will see, this new relation does have some undesirable properties.

Example Database

A relational database consists of any number of relations. The structure of the database is described through the use of a schema (defined in Chapter 2), which is a description of the overall logical structure of the database. There are two common methods for expressing a schema:

a. Short text statements, in which each relation is named and the names of its attributes follow in parentheses. (See EMPLOYEE1 and DEPARTMENT relations defined earlier in this chapter.)

b. A graphical representation, in which each relation is represented by a rectangle containing the attributes for the relation.

Text statements have the advantage of simplicity. However, a graphical representation provides a better means of expressing referential integrity constraints (as you will see shortly). In this section, we use both techniques for expressing a schema so that you can compare them.

A schema for four relations at Pine Valley Furniture Company is shown in Figure 5-3. The four relations shown in this figure are CUSTOMER, ORDER, ORDER LINE, and PRODUCT. The key attributes for these relations are underlined, and other important attributes are included in each relation. We show how to design these relations using the techniques of normalization later in this chapter.

PINE VALLEY FURNITURE

Figure 5-3
Schema for four relations (Pine Valley Furniture Company)

CUSTOMER

Customer_ID	Customer_Name	Customer_Address	City *	State *	Postal_Code *

ORDER

Order_ID	Order_Date	Customer_ID

ORDER LINE

Order_ID	Product_ID	Ordered_Quantity

PRODUCT

Product_ID	Product_Description	Product_Finish	Standard_Price	Product_Line_ID

* Not in Figure 3-22 for simplicity.

Figure 5-4
Instance of a relational scheme (Pine Valley Furniture Company)

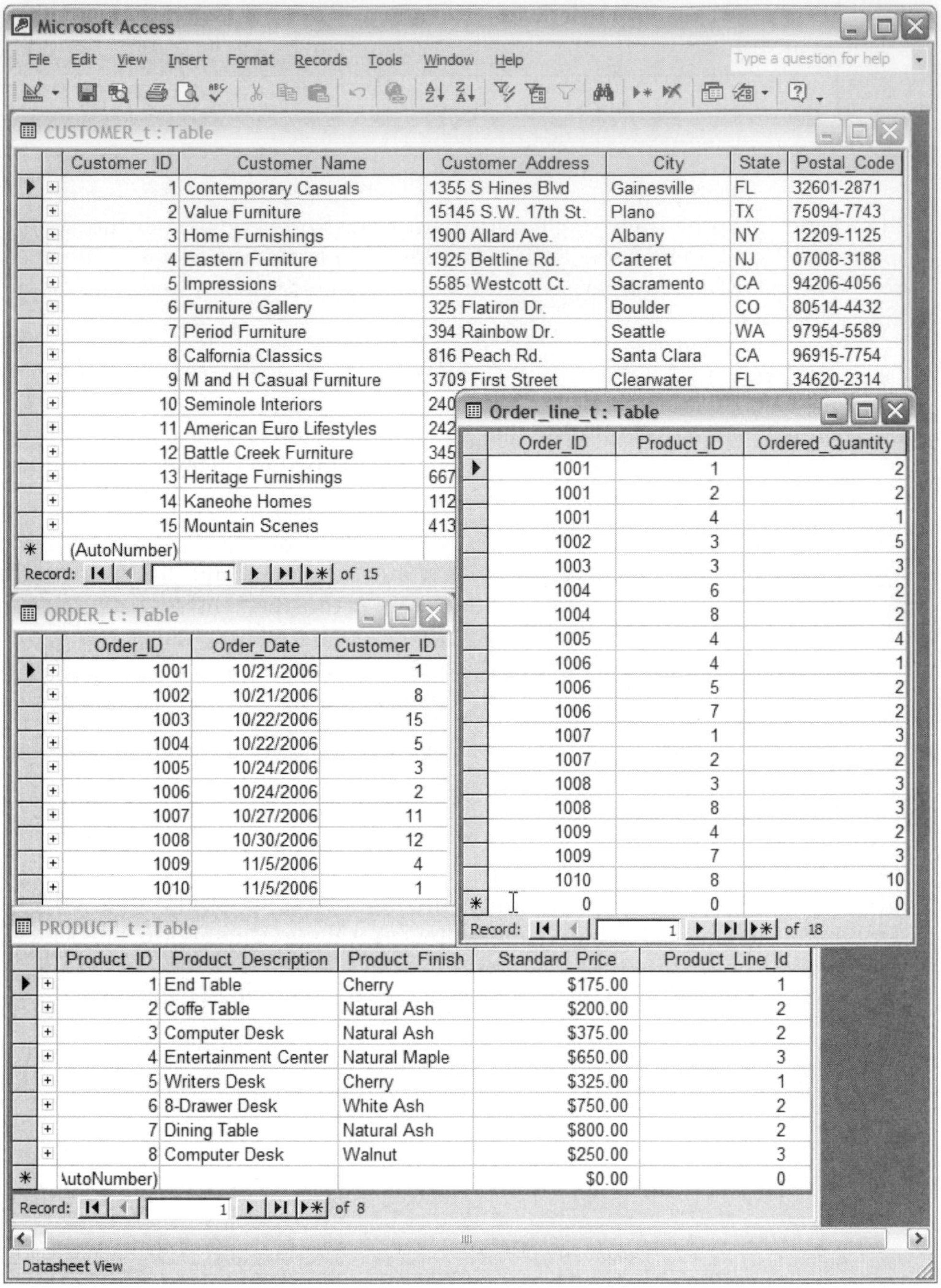

Microsoft Access

CUSTOMER_t : Table

Customer_ID	Customer_Name	Customer_Address	City	State	Postal_Code
1	Contemporary Casuals	1355 S Hines Blvd	Gainesville	FL	32601-2871
2	Value Furniture	15145 S.W. 17th St.	Plano	TX	75094-7743
3	Home Furnishings	1900 Allard Ave.	Albany	NY	12209-1125
4	Eastern Furniture	1925 Beltline Rd.	Carteret	NJ	07008-3188
5	Impressions	5585 Westcott Ct.	Sacramento	CA	94206-4056
6	Furniture Gallery	325 Flatiron Dr.	Boulder	CO	80514-4432
7	Period Furniture	394 Rainbow Dr.	Seattle	WA	97954-5589
8	Calfornia Classics	816 Peach Rd.	Santa Clara	CA	96915-7754
9	M and H Casual Furniture	3709 First Street	Clearwater	FL	34620-2314
10	Seminole Interiors	240			
11	American Euro Lifestyles	242			
12	Battle Creek Furniture	345			
13	Heritage Furnishings	667			
14	Kaneohe Homes	112			
15	Mountain Scenes	413			
(AutoNumber)					

Record: 1 of 15

ORDER_t : Table

Order_ID	Order_Date	Customer_ID
1001	10/21/2006	1
1002	10/21/2006	8
1003	10/22/2006	15
1004	10/22/2006	5
1005	10/24/2006	3
1006	10/24/2006	2
1007	10/27/2006	11
1008	10/30/2006	12
1009	11/5/2006	4
1010	11/5/2006	1

Order_line_t : Table

Order_ID	Product_ID	Ordered_Quantity
1001	1	2
1001	2	2
1001	4	1
1002	3	5
1003	3	3
1004	6	2
1004	8	2
1005	4	4
1006	4	1
1006	5	2
1006	7	2
1007	1	3
1007	2	2
1008	3	3
1008	8	3
1009	4	2
1009	7	3
1010	8	10
0	0	0

Record: 1 of 18

PRODUCT_t : Table

Product_ID	Product_Description	Product_Finish	Standard_Price	Product_Line_Id
1	End Table	Cherry	$175.00	1
2	Coffe Table	Natural Ash	$200.00	2
3	Computer Desk	Natural Ash	$375.00	2
4	Entertainment Center	Natural Maple	$650.00	3
5	Writers Desk	Cherry	$325.00	1
6	8-Drawer Desk	White Ash	$750.00	2
7	Dining Table	Natural Ash	$800.00	2
8	Computer Desk	Walnut	$250.00	3
(AutoNumber)			$0.00	0

Record: 1 of 8

Datasheet View

Following is a text description for the relations:

CUSTOMER(Customer_ID,Customer_Name,Customer_Address,City, State,Postal_Code)
ORDER(Order_ID,Order_Date,Customer_ID)
ORDER LINE((Order_ID,Product_ID,Ordered_Quantity)
PRODUCT(Product_ID,Product_Description,Product_Finish,Standard_Price, Product_Line_ID)

Notice that the primary key for ORDER LINE is a composite key consisting of the attributes Order_ID and Product_ID. Also, Customer_ID is a foreign key in the ORDER relation; this allows the user to associate an order with the customer who submitted the order. ORDER LINE has two foreign keys: Order_ID, and Product_ID. These keys allow the user to associate each line on an order with the relevant order and product.

An instance of this database is shown in Figure 5-4. This figure shows four tables with sample data. Notice how the foreign keys allow us to associate the various tables. It is a good idea to create an instance of your relational schema with sample data for three reasons:

1. The sample data provide a convenient way to check the accuracy of your design.

2. The sample data help improve communications with users in discussing your design.

3. You can use the sample data to develop prototype applications and to test queries.

INTEGRITY CONSTRAINTS

The relational data model includes several types of constraints, or business rules, whose purpose is to facilitate maintaining the accuracy and integrity of data in the database. The major types of integrity constraints are domain constraints, entity integrity, referential integrity, and action assertions.

Domain Constraints

All of the values that appear in a column of a relation must be taken from the same domain. A domain is the set of values that may be assigned to an attribute. A domain definition usually consists of the following components: domain name, meaning, data type, size (or length), and allowable values or allowable range (if applicable). Table 5-1 shows domain definitions for the domains associated with the attributes in Figures 5-3 and 5-4.

Entity Integrity

The entity integrity rule is designed to ensure that every relation has a primary key, and that the data values for that primary key are all valid. In particular, it guarantees that every primary key attribute is non-null.

In some cases, a particular attribute cannot be assigned a data value. There are two situations where this is likely to occur: Either there is no applicable data value, or the applicable data value is not known when values are assigned. Suppose, for example,

Table 5-1   Domain Definitions for INVOICE Attributes

Attribute	Domain Name	Description	Domain
Customer_ID	Customer_IDs	Set of all possible customer IDs	character: size 5
Customer_Name	Customer_Names	Set of all possible customer names	character: size 25
Customer_Address	Customer_Addresses	Set of all possible customer addresses	character: size 30
City	Cities	Set of all possible cities	character: size 20
State	States	Set of all possible states	character: size 2
Postal_Code	Postal_Codes	Set of all possible postal zip codes	character: size 10
Order_ID	Order_IDs	Set of all possible order IDs	character: size 5
Order_Date	Order_Dates	Set of all possible order dates	date format mm/dd/yy
Product_ID	Product_IDs	Set of all possible product IDs	character: size 5
Product_Description	Product_Descriptions	Set of all possible product descriptions	character size 25
Product_Finish	Product_Finishes	Set of all possible product finishes	character: size 15
Standard_Price	Unit_Prices	Set of all possible unit prices	monetary: 6 digits
Product_Line_ID	Product_Line_IDs	Set of all possible product line IDs	integer: 3 digits
Ordered_Quantity	Quantities	Set of all possible ordered quantities	integer: 3 digits

that you fill out an employment form that has a space reserved for a fax number. If you have no fax number, you leave this space empty because it does not apply to you. Or suppose that you are asked to fill in the telephone number of your previous employer. If you do not recall this number, you may leave it empty because that information is not known.

Null: A value that may be assigned to an attribute when no other value applies or when the applicable value is unknown.

The relational data model allows us to assign a null value to an attribute in the just described situations. A **null** is a value that may be assigned to an attribute when no other value applies or when the applicable value is unknown. In reality, a null is not a value but rather the absence of a value. For example, it is not the same as a numeric zero or a string of blanks. The inclusion of nulls in the relational model is somewhat controversial, because it sometimes leads to anomalous results (Date, 1995). However, Codd advocates the use of nulls for missing values (Codd, 1990).

Entity integrity rule: No primary key attribute (or component of a primary key attribute) can be null.

One thing on which everyone agrees is that primary key values must not be allowed to be null. Thus, the **entity integrity rule** states the following: No primary key attribute (or component of a primary key attribute) may be null.

Referential Integrity

In the relational data model, associations between tables are defined through the use of foreign keys. For example, in Figure 5-4, the association between the CUSTOMER and ORDER tables is defined by including the Customer_ID attribute as a foreign key in ORDER. This of course implies that before we insert a new row in the ORDER table, the customer for that order must already exist in the CUSTOMER table. If you examine the rows in the ORDER table in Figure 5-4, you will find that every customer number for an order already appears in the CUSTOMER table.

Referential integrity constraint: A rule that states that either each foreign key value must match a primary key value in another relation or the foreign key value must be null.

A **referential integrity constraint** is a rule that maintains consistency among the rows of two relations. The rule states that if there is a foreign key in one relation, either each foreign key value must match a primary key value in another relation, or the foreign key value must be null. You should examine the tables in Figure 5-4 to check whether the referential integrity rule has been enforced.

The graphical version of the relational schema provides a simple technique for identifying associations where referential integrity must be enforced. Figure 5-5

Figure 5-5
Referential integrity constraints (Pine Valley Furniture Company)

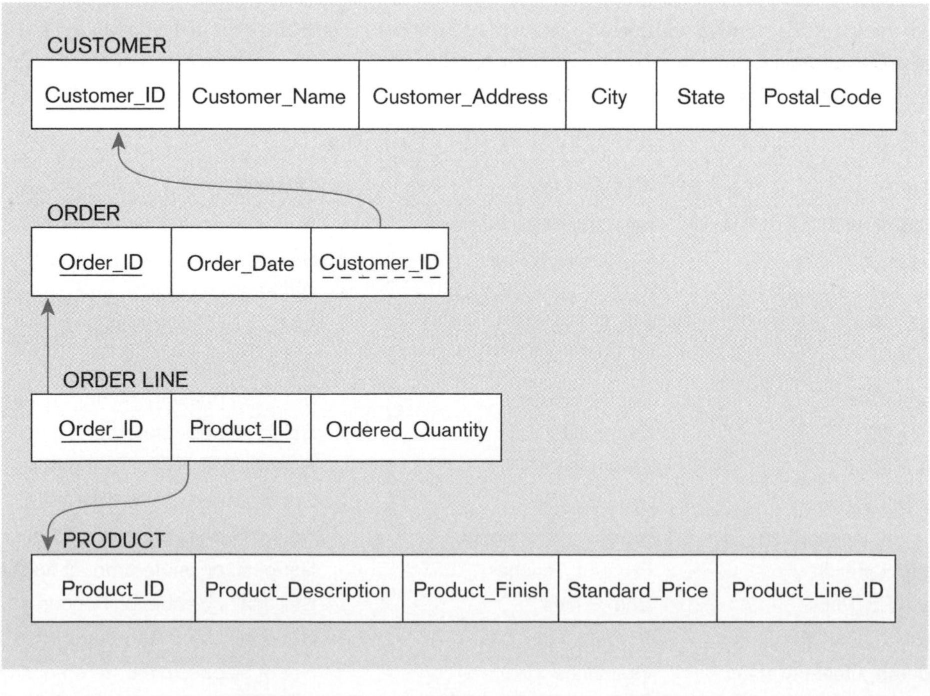

shows the schema for the relations introduced in Figure 5-3. An arrow has been drawn from each foreign key to the associated primary key. A referential integrity constraint must be defined for each of these arrows in the schema.

How do you know whether a foreign key is allowed to be null? If each order must have a customer (a mandatory relationship), then the foreign key of Customer_ID cannot be null in the ORDER relation. If the relationship is optional, then the foreign key could be null. Whether a foreign key can be null must be specified as a property of the foreign key attribute when the database is defined.

Actually, whether a foreign key can be null is more complex to model on an E-R diagram and to determine than we have shown so far. For example, what happens to order data if we choose to delete a customer who has submitted orders? We may want to see sales even if we do not care about the customer any more. Three choices are possible:

1. Delete the associated orders (called a cascading delete), in which case we lose not only the customer, but also all the sales history

2. Prohibit deletion of the customer until all associated orders are first deleted (a safety check)

3. Place a null value in the foreign key (an exception that says although an order must have a Customer_ID value when the order is created, Customer_ID can become null later if the associated customer is deleted)

We will see how each of these choices is implemented when we describe the SQL database query language in Chapter 7.

Action Assertions

In Chapter 4, we discussed business rules and introduced a new category of business rules we called action assertions. For example, a typical action assertion might state the following: "A person may purchase a ticket for the all-star game only if that person is a season-ticket holder." There are various techniques for defining and enforcing such rules. We discuss some of these techniques in later chapters.

Creating Relational Tables

In this section, we create table definitions for the four tables shown in Figure 5-5. These definitions are created using **CREATE TABLE** statements from the SQL data definition language. In practice, these table definitions are actually created during the implementation phase later in the database development process. However, we show these sample tables in this chapter for continuity and especially to illustrate the way the integrity constraints described above are implemented in SQL.

The SQL table definitions are shown in Figure 5-6. One table is created for each of the four tables shown in the relational schema (Figure 5-5). Each attribute for a table is then defined. Notice that the data type and length for each attribute is taken from the domain definitions (Table 5-1). For example, the attribute Customer_Name in the CUSTOMER relation is defined as VARCHAR (variable character) data type with length 25. By specifying **NOT NULL**, each attribute can be constrained from being assigned a null value.

The primary key for each table is specified for each table using the **PRIMARY KEY** clause at the end of each table definition. The ORDER_LINE table illustrates how to specify a primary key when that key is a composite attribute. In this example, the primary key of ORDER_LINE is the combination of Order_ID and Product_ID. Each primary key attribute in the four tables is constrained with **NOT NULL**. This enforces the entity integrity constraint described in the previous section. Notice that the **NOT NULL** constraint can also be used with non-primary-key attributes.

Figure 5-6
SQL table definitions

```
CREATE TABLE CUSTOMER
        (CUSTOMER_ID                    VARCHAR(5)          NOT NULL,
        CUSTOMER_NAME                   VARCHAR(25)         NOT NULL,
        CUSTOMER ADDRESS                VARCHAR(30)         NOT NULL,
        CITY                            VARCHAR(20)         NOT NULL,
        STATE                           CHAR(2)             NOT NULL,
        POSTAL_CODE                     CHAR(10)            NOT NULL,
PRIMARY KEY (CUSTOMER_ID);

CREATE TABLE ORDER
        (ORDER_ID                       CHAR(5)             NOT NULL,
        ORDER DATE                      DATE                NOT NULL,
        CUSTOMER_ID                     VARCHAR(5)          NOT NULL,
PRIMARY KEY (ORDER_ID),
FOREIGN KEY (CUSTOMER_ID) REFERENCES CUSTOMER (CUSTOMER_ID);

CREATE TABLE ORDER_LINE
        (ORDER_ID                       CHAR(5)             NOT NULL,
        PRODUCT_ID                      CHAR(5)             NOT NULL,
        ORDERED_QUANTITY                INT                 NOT NULL,
PRIMARY KEY (ORDER_ID, PRODUCT_ID),
FOREIGN KEY (ORDER_ID) REFERENCES ORDER (ORDER_ID),
FOREIGN KEY (PRODUCT_ID) REFERENCES PRODUCT (PRODUCT_ID);

CREATE TABLE PRODUCT
        (PRODUCT_ID                     CHAR(5)             NOT NULL,
        PRODUCT_DESCRIPTION             VARCHAR(25),
        PRODUCT_FINISH                  VARCHAR(12),
        STANDARD_PRICE                  DECIMAL(8,2)        NOT NULL,
        PRODUCT_LINE_ID                 INT                 NOT NULL,
PRIMARY KEY (PRODUCT_ID);
```

Referential integrity constraints are easily defined, using the graphical schema shown in Figure 5-5. An arrow originates from each foreign key and "points to" the related primary key in the associated relation. In the SQL table definition, a **FOREIGN KEY REFERENCES** statement corresponds to each of these arrows. Thus, for the table ORDER, the foreign key CUSTOMER_ID references the primary key of CUSTOMER, which is also CUSTOMER_ID. Although in this case the foreign key and primary keys have the same name, this need not be the case. For example, the foreign key attribute could be named CUST_NO instead of CUSTOMER_ID. However, the foreign and primary keys must be from the same domain.

The ORDER_LINE table provides an example of a table that has two foreign keys. Foreign keys in this table reference both the ORDER and PRODUCT tables.

Well-Structured Relations

Well-structured relation: A relation that contains minimal redundancy and allows users to insert, modify, and delete the rows in a table without errors or inconsistencies.

To prepare for our discussion of normalization, we need to address the following question: What constitutes a well-structured relation? Intuitively, a **well-structured relation** contains minimal redundancy and allows users to insert, modify, and delete the rows in a table without errors or inconsistencies. EMPLOYEE1 (Figure 5-1) is such a relation. Each row of the table contains data describing one employee, and any modification to an employee's data (such as a change in salary) is confined to one row of the table. In contrast, EMPLOYEE2 (Figure 5-2b) is not a well-structured relation. If you examine the sample data in the table, you will notice considerable redundancy. For example, values for Emp_ID, Name, Dept_Name, and Salary appear in two separate rows for employees 100, 110, and 150. Consequently, if the salary for employee 100 changes, we must record this fact in two rows (or more, for some employees).

Emp_ID	Course_Title	Date_Completed
100	SPSS	6/19/200X
100	Surveys	10/7/200X
140	Tax Acc	12/8/200X
110	Visual Basic	1/12/200X
110	C++	4/22/200X
150	SPSS	6/19/200X
150	Java	8/12/200X

Figure 5-7
EMP_COURSE

Redundancies in a table may result in errors or inconsistencies (called **anomalies**) when a user attempts to update the data in the table. Three types of anomalies are possible: insertion, deletion, and modification.

Anomaly: An error or inconsistency that may result when a user attempts to update a table that contains redundant data. The three types of anomalies are insertion, deletion, and modification.

1. *Insertion anomaly* Suppose that we need to add a new employee to EMPLOYEE2. The primary key for this relation is the combination of Emp_ID and Course_Title (as noted earlier). Therefore, to insert a new row, the user must supply values for both Emp_ID and Course_Title (because primary key values cannot be null or nonexistent). This is an anomaly, because the user should be able to enter employee data without supplying course data.

2. *Deletion anomaly* Suppose that the data for employee number 140 are deleted from the table. This will result in losing the information that this employee completed a course (Tax Acc) on 12/8/200X. In fact, it results in losing the information that this course had an offering that completed on that date.

3. *Modification anomaly* Suppose that employee number 100 gets a salary increase. We must record the increase in each of the rows for that employee (two occurrences in Figure 5-2); otherwise the data will be inconsistent.

These anomalies indicate that EMPLOYEE2 is not a well-structured relation. The problem with this relation is that it contains data about two entities: EMPLOYEE and COURSE. We will use normalization theory (described later in this chapter) to divide EMPLOYEE2 into two relations. One of the resulting relations is EMPLOYEE1 (Figure 5-1). The other we will call EMP_COURSE, which appears with sample data in Figure 5-7. The primary key of this relation is the combination of Emp_ID and Course_Title, and we underline these attribute names in Figure 5-7 to highlight this fact. Examine Figure 5-7 to verify that EMP_COURSE is free of the types of anomalies described above and is therefore well-structured.

TRANSFORMING EER DIAGRAMS INTO RELATIONS

During logical design you transform the E-R (and EER) diagrams that were developed during conceptual design into relational database schemas. The inputs to this process are the entity-relationship (and enhanced E-R) diagrams that you studied in Chapters 3 and 4. The outputs are the relational schemas described in the first two sections of this chapter.

Transforming (or mapping) E-R diagrams to relations is a relatively straightforward process with a well-defined set of rules. In fact, many CASE tools can automatically perform many of the conversion steps. However, it is important that you understand the steps in this process for three reasons:

1. CASE tools often cannot model more complex data relationships such as ternary relationships and supertype/subtype relationships. For these situations, you may have to perform the steps manually.

Figure 5-8
Mapping the regular entity CUSTOMER
(a) CUSTOMER entity type

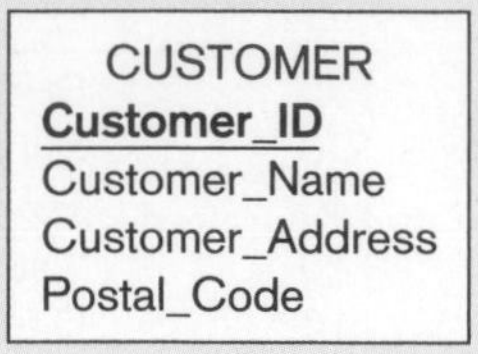

(b) CUSTOMER relation

CUSTOMER

Customer_ID	Customer_Name	Customer_Address	Postal_Code

2. There are sometimes legitimate alternatives where you will need to choose a particular solution.
3. You must be prepared to perform a quality check on the results obtained with a CASE tool.

In the following discussion, we illustrate the steps in the transformation with examples taken from Chapters 3 and 4. It will help for you to recall that we discussed three types of entities in those chapters:

1. *Regular entities* are entities that have an independent existence and generally represent real-world objects, such as persons and products. Regular entity types are represented by rectangles with a single line.
2. *Weak entities* are entities that cannot exist except with an identifying relationship with an owner (regular) entity type. Weak entities are identified by a rectangle with a double line.
3. *Associative entities* (also called gerunds) are formed from many-to-many relationships between other entity types. Associative entities are represented by a rectangle with a single line that encloses the diamond relationship symbol.

Step 1: Map Regular Entities

Each regular entity type in an ER diagram is transformed into a relation. The name given to the relation is generally the same as the entity type. Each simple attribute of the entity type becomes an attribute of the relation. The identifier of the entity type becomes the primary key of the corresponding relation. You should check to make sure that this primary key satisfies the desirable properties of identifiers outlined in Chapter 3.

Figure 5-8a shows a representation of the CUSTOMER entity type for Pine Valley Furniture Company from Chapter 3 (see Figure 3-22). The corresponding CUSTOMER relation is shown in graphical form in Figure 5-8b. In this figure and those that follow in this section, we show only a few key attributes for each relation to simplify the figures.

Composite Attributes When a regular entity type has a composite attribute, only the simple component attributes of the composite attribute are included in the new relation. Figure 5-9 shows a variation on the example of Figure 5-8, where Customer_Address is represented as a composite attribute with components Street, City, and State (see Figure 5-9a). This entity is mapped to the CUSTOMER relation, which contains the simple address attributes, as shown in Figure 5-9b. Although Customer_Name is modeled as a simple attribute in Figure 5-9a, you are aware that it

```
SELECT Component_No, Quantity
FROM COMPONENT
WHERE Item_No = 100;
```

Step 6: Map Ternary (and *n*-ary) Relationships

Recall from Chapter 3 that a ternary relationship is a relationship among three entity types. In that chapter, we recommended that you convert a ternary relationship to an associative entity to represent participation constraints more accurately.

To map an associative entity type that links three regular entity types, we create a new associative relation. The default primary key of this relation consists of the three primary key attributes for the participating entity types. (In some cases, additional attributes are required to form a unique primary key.) These attributes then act in the role of foreign keys that reference the individual primary keys of the participating entity types. Any attributes of the associative entity type become attributes of the new relation.

An example of mapping a ternary relationship (represented as an associative entity type) is shown in Figure 5-19. Figure 5-19a is an E-R segment (or view) that represents a *patient* receiving a *treatment* from a *physician*. The associative entity type PATIENT TREATMENT has the attributes Treatment_Date, Treatment_Time, and Results; values are recorded for these attributes for each instance of PATIENT TREATMENT.

The result of mapping this view is shown in Figure 5-19b. The primary key attributes Patient_ID, Physician_ID, and Treatment_Code become foreign keys in PATIENT TREATMENT. These attributes are components of the primary key of PATIENT TREATMENT. However, they do not uniquely identify a given treatment, because a patient may receive the same treatment from the same physician on more than one occasion. Does including the attribute Date as part of the primary key (along with the other three attributes) result in a primary key? This would be so if a given patient receives only one treatment from a particular physician on a given date. However, this is not likely to be the case. For example, a patient may receive a treatment

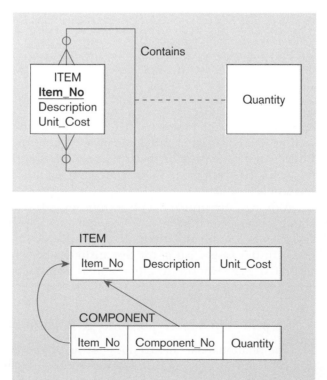

Figure 5-18
Mapping a unary *M:N* relationship
(a) Bill-of-materials relationships (*M:N*)

(b) ITEM and COMPONENT relations

Figure 5-19
Mapping a ternary relationship
(a) PATIENT TREATMENT ternary
relationship with associative entity

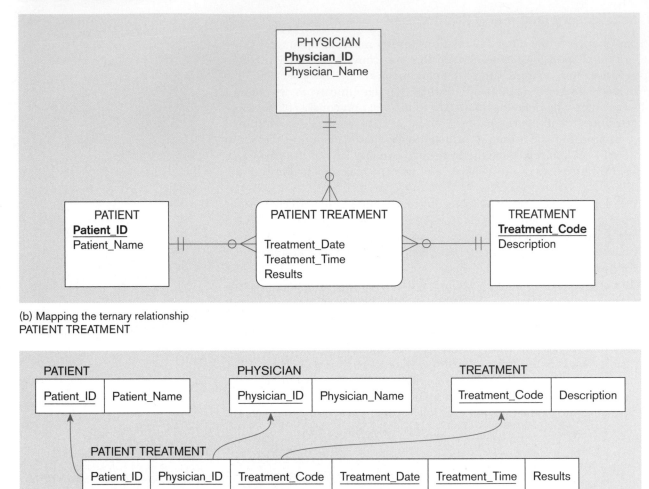

(b) Mapping the ternary relationship
PATIENT TREATMENT

in the morning, then the same treatment in the afternoon. To resolve this issue, we include Time as part of the primary key. Therefore, the primary key of PATIENT TREATMENT consists of the five attributes shown in Figure 5-19b: Patient_ID, Physician_ID, Treatment_Code, Date, and Time. The only nonkey attribute in the relation is Results.

Although this primary key is technically correct, it is complex and therefore difficult to manage and prone to errors. A better approach is to introduce a surrogate key, such as Treatment#, that is a serial number that uniquely identifies each treatment. In this case, each of the five attributes become foreign keys in the PATIENT TREATMENT relation. Another similar approach is to use an enterprise key, as described at the end of this chapter.

Step 7: Map Supertype/Subtype Relationships

The relational data model does not yet directly support supertype/subtype relationships. Fortunately, there are various strategies that database designers can use to represent these relationships with the relational data model (Chouinard, 1989). For

Figure 5-20
Supertype/subtype relationships

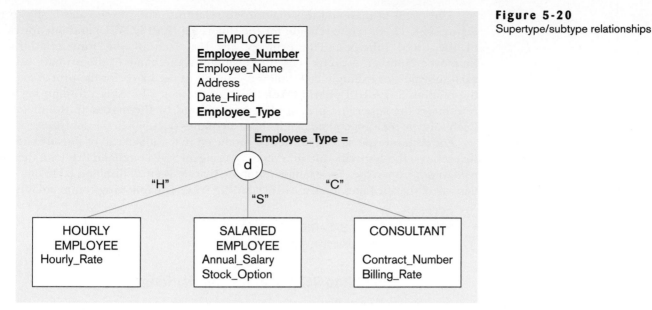

our purposes, we use the following strategy, which is the one most commonly employed:

1. Create a separate relation for the supertype and for each of its subtypes.

2. Assign to the relation created for the supertype the attributes that are common to all members of the supertype, including the primary key.

3. Assign to the relation for each subtype the primary key of the supertype and only those attributes that are unique to that subtype.

4. Assign one (or more) attributes of the supertype to function as the subtype discriminator. (The role of the subtype discriminator was discussed in Chapter 4.

An example of applying this procedure is shown in Figures 5-20 and 5-21. Figure 5-20 shows the supertype EMPLOYEE with subtypes HOURLY EMPLOYEE, SALARIED EMPLOYEE, and CONSULTANT. (This example is described in Chapter 4, and Figure 5-20 is a repeat of Figure 4-8). The primary key of EMPLOYEE is Employee_Number, and the attribute Employee_Type is the subtype discriminator.

Figure 5-21
Mapping supertype/subtype
relationships to relations

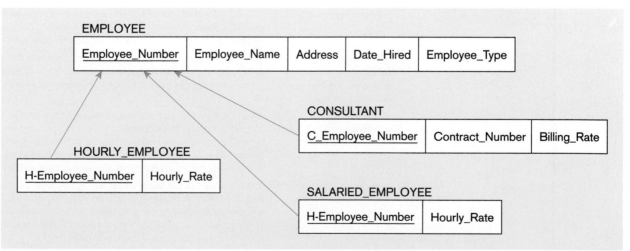

The result of mapping this diagram to relations using these rules is shown in Figure 5-21. There is one relation for the supertype (EMPLOYEE) and one for each of the three subtypes. The primary key for each of the four relations is Employee_Number. A prefix is used to distinguish the name of the primary key for each subtype. For example, S_Employee_Number is the name for the primary key of the relation SALARIED_EMPLOYEE. Each of these attributes is a foreign key that references the supertype primary key, as indicated by the arrows in the diagram. Each subtype relation contains only those attributes peculiar to the subtype.

For each subtype, a relation can be produced that contains all of the attributes of that subtype (both specific and inherited) by using an SQL command that joins the subtype with its supertype. For example, suppose that we want to display a table that contains all of the attributes for SALARIED_EMPLOYEE. The following command is used:

```
SELECT *
FROM EMPLOYEE, SALARIED_EMPLOYEE
WHERE Employee_Number = S_Employee_Number;
```

Summary of EER to Relational Transformations

The steps provide a comprehensive explanation of how each element of an EER diagram is transformed into parts of a relational data model. Table 5-2 is a quick reference to these steps and the associated figures that illustrate each type of transformation.

Table 5-2 Summary of E-R to Relational Transformations

E-R Structure	Relational Representation (example figure)
Regular entity	Create a relation with primary key and nonkey attributes (Figure 5-8)
Composite attribute	Each component of composite becomes separate attribute (Figure 5-9)
Multivalued attribute	Create separate relation for multivalued attribute with composite primary key, including primary key of entity (Figure 5-10)
Weak entity	Create a relation with a composite primary key (which includes the primary key of the entity on which this entity depends) and nonkey attributes (Figure 5-11)
Binary or unary 1:N relationship	Place the primary key of the entity on the one side of the relationship as a foreign key in the relation for the entity on the many side (Figure 5-12; Figure 5-17 for unary relationship)
Binary or unary M:N relationship or associative entity without its own key	Create a relation with a composite primary key using the primary keys of the related entities plus any nonkey attributes of the relationship or associative entity (Figure 5-13; Figure 5-15 for associative entity; Figure 5-18 for unary relationship)
Binary or unary 1:1 relationship	Place the primary key of either entity in the relation for the other entity or do this for both entities; if one side of the relationship is optional, place the foreign key of the entity on the mandatory side in the relation for the entity on the optional side (Figure 5-14)
Binary or unary M:N relationship or associative entity with its own key	Create a relation with the primary key associated with the associative entity plus any nonkey attributes of the associative entity and the primary keys of the related entities as foreign keys (Figure 5-16)
Ternary and n-ary relationships	Same as binary M:N relationships above; without its own key, include as part of primary key of relation for the relationship or associative entity the primary keys from all related entities; with its own key, the primary keys of the associated entities are included as foreign keys in the relation for the relationship or associative entity (Figure 5-19)
Supertype/subtype relationship	Create a relation for the superclass, which contains the primary key and all nonkey attributes in common with all subclasses, plus create a separate relation for each subclass with the same primary key (with the same or local name) but with only the nonkey attributes related to that subclass (Figure 5-20 and 5-21)

INTRODUCTION TO NORMALIZATION

Normalization is a formal process for deciding which attributes should be grouped together in a relation. For example, we used the principles of normalization to convert the EMPLOYEE2 table (with its redundancy) to EMPLOYEE1 (Figure 5-1) and EMP_COURSE (Figure 5-7). There are three major occasions during the overall database development process when you can usually benefit from using normalization:

1. During conceptual data modeling (described in Chapters 3 and 4). You should normalize the E-R diagrams that you develop during that phase.

2. During logical database design (described in this chapter). You should use normalization concepts as a quality check for the relations that are obtained from mapping the E-R diagrams.

3. Reverse-engineering older systems. Many of the tables and user views for older systems are redundant and subject to the anomalies we describe in this chapter.

We have presented an intuitive discussion of well-structured relations; however, we need formal definitions of such relations, together with a process for designing them. **Normalization** is the process of successively reducing relations with anomalies to produce smaller, well-structured relations. Following are some of the main goals of normalization:

Normalization: The process of decomposing relations with anomalies to produce smaller, well-structured relations.

1. Minimize data redundancy, thereby avoiding anomalies and conserving storage space

2. Simplify the enforcement of referential integrity constraints

3. Make it easier to maintain data (insert, update, and delete)

4. Provide a better design that is an improved representation of the real world and a stronger basis for future growth

Steps in Normalization

Normalization can be accomplished and understood in stages, each of which corresponds to a normal form (see Figure 5-22). A **normal form** is a state of a relation that results from applying simple rules regarding functional dependencies (or relationships between attributes) to that relation. We describe these rules briefly in this section and illustrate them in detail in the following sections.

Normal form: A state of a relation that results from applying simple rules regarding functional dependencies for relationships between attributes to that relation.

1. *First normal form* Any multivalued attributes (also called repeating groups) have been removed, so there is a single value (possibly null) at the intersection of each row and column of the table (as in Figure 5-2b).

2. *Second normal form* Any partial functional dependencies have been removed (i.e., nonkeys are identified by the whole primary key).

3. *Third normal form* Any transitive dependencies have been removed (i.e., nonkeys are identified by only the primary key).

4. *Boyce-Codd normal form* Any remaining anomalies that result from functional dependencies have been removed (because there was more than one primary key for the same nonkeys).

5. *Fourth normal form* Any multivalued dependencies have been removed.

6. *Fifth normal form* Any remaining anomalies have been removed.

We describe and illustrate first through third normal forms in this chapter. The remaining normal forms are described in Appendix B. These other normal forms are in an appendix only to save space in this chapter, not because they are less important.

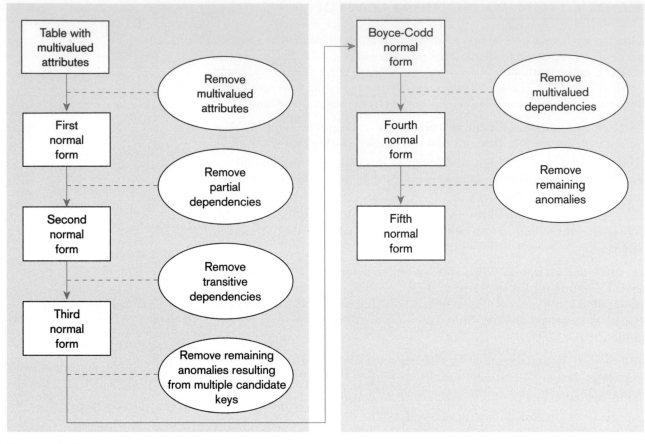

Figure 5-22
Steps in normalization

In fact, you can easily follow the subsequent section on third normal form with Appendix B.

Functional Dependencies and Keys

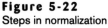

Functional dependency: A constraint between two attributes in which the value of one attribute is determined by the value on another attribute.

Normalization is based on the analysis of functional dependencies. A **functional dependency** is a constraint between two attributes or two sets of attributes. For any relation R, attribute B is functionally dependent on attribute A if, for every valid instance of A, that value of A uniquely determines the value of B (Dutka and Hanson, 1989). The functional dependency of B on A is represented by an arrow, as follows: A → B. A functional dependency is not a mathematical dependency—B cannot be computed from A. Rather, if you know the value of A there can be only one value for B. An attribute may be functionally dependent on a combination of two (or more) attributes, rather than on a single attribute. For example, consider the relation EMP_COURSE (Emp_ID,Course_Title,Date_Completed) shown in Figure 5-7. We represent the functional dependency in this relation as follows:

Emp_ID,Course_Title → Date_Completed

The comma between Emp_ID and Course_Title stands for the logical AND operator, because Date_Completed is functional dependent on Emp_ID and Course_Title in combination.

The functional dependency in this statement implies that the date a course is completely determined by the identity of the employee and the title of the course. Common examples of functional dependencies are the following:

1. SSN → Name, Address, Birthdate   A person's name, address, and birthdate are functionally dependent on that person's Social Security number.

2. VIN → Make, Model, Color   The make, model, and color of a vehicle are functionally dependent on the vehicle identification number.

3. ISBN → Title, First_Author_Name, Publisher   The title of a book, the name of the first author, and the publisher are functionally dependent on the book's International Standard Book Number (ISBN).

Determinants   The attribute on the left side of the arrow in a functional dependency is called a **determinant**. SSN, VIN, and ISBN are determinants (respectively) in the preceding three examples. In the EMP_COURSE relation (Figure 5-7) the combination of Emp_ID and Course_Title is a determinant.

> **Determinant:** The attribute on the left-hand side of the arrow in a functional dependency.

Candidate Keys   A **candidate key** is an attribute, or combination of attributes, that uniquely identifies a row in a relation. A candidate key must satisfy the following properties (Dutka and Hanson, 1989), which are a subset of the six properties of a primary key previously listed:

> **Candidate key:** An attribute, or combination of attributes, that uniquely identifies a row in a relation.

1. *Unique identification*   For every row, the value of the key must uniquely identify that row. This property implies that each nonkey attribute is functionally dependent on that key.

2. *Nonredundancy*   No attribute in the key can be deleted without destroying the property of unique identification.

Let's apply the preceding definition to identify candidate keys in two of the relations described in this chapter. The EMPLOYEE1 relation (Figure 5-1) has the following schema: EMPLOYEE1(Emp_ID,Name,Dept_Name,Salary). Emp_ID is the only determinant in this relation. All of the other attributes are functionally dependent on Emp_ID. Therefore, Emp_ID is a candidate key and (because there are no other candidate keys) also is the primary key.

We represent the functional dependencies for a relation using the notation shown in Figure 5-23. Figure 5-23a shows the representation for EMPLOYEE1. The horizontal line in the figure portrays the functional dependencies. A vertical line drops from the primary key (Emp_ID) and connects to this line. Vertical arrows then

Figure 5-23
Representing functional dependencies
(a) Functional dependencies in EMPLOYEE1

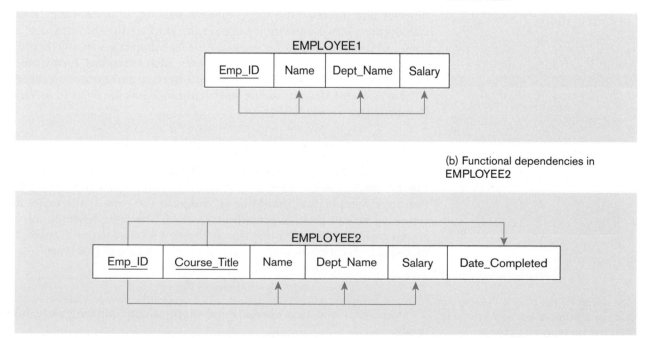

(b) Functional dependencies in EMPLOYEE2

point to each of the nonkey attributes that are functionally dependent on the primary key.

For the relation EMPLOYEE2 (Figure 5-2b), notice that (unlike EMPLOYEE1) Emp_ID does not uniquely identify a row in the relation. For example, there are two rows in the table for Emp_ID number 100. There are two functional dependencies in this relation:

1. Emp_ID → Name, Dept_Name, Salary
2. Emp_ID, Course_Title → Date_Completed

The functional dependencies indicate that the combination of Emp_ID and Course_Title is the only candidate key (and therefore the primary key) for EMPLOYEE2. In other words, the primary key of EMPLOYEE2 is a composite key. Neither Emp_ID nor Course_Title uniquely identifies a row in this relation and therefore (according to property 1) cannot by itself be a candidate key. Examine the data in Figure 5-2b to verify that the combination of Emp_ID and Course_Title does uniquely identify each row of EMPLOYEE2. We represent the functional dependencies in this relation in Figure 5-23b. Notice that Date_Completed is the only attribute that is functionally dependent on the full primary key consisting of the attributes Emp_ID and Course_Title.

We can summarize the relationship between determinants and candidate keys as follows. A candidate key is always a determinant, whereas a determinant may or may not be a candidate key. For example, in EMPLOYEE2, Emp_ID is a determinant but not a candidate key. A candidate key is a determinant that uniquely identifies the remaining (nonkey) attributes in a relation. A determinant may be a candidate key (such as Emp_ID in EMPLOYEE1), part of a composite candidate key (such as Emp_ID in EMPLOYEE2), or a nonkey attribute. We will describe examples of this shortly.

As a preview to the following illustration of what normalization accomplishes, normalized relations have as their primary key the determinant for each of the nonkeys, and within that relation there are no other functional dependencies.

NORMALIZATION EXAMPLE: PINE VALLEY FURNITURE COMPANY

Now that we have examined functional dependencies and keys, we are ready to describe and illustrate the steps of normalization. If an EER data model has been transformed into a comprehensive set of relations for the database, then each of these relations needs to be normalized. In other cases in which the logical data model is being derived from user interfaces, such as screens, forms, and reports, you will want to create relations for each user interface and normalize those relations.

For a simple illustration, we use a customer invoice from Pine Valley Furniture Company (see Figure 5-24.)

Step 0: Represent the View in Tabular Form

The first step (preliminary to normalization) is to represent the user view (in this case an invoice) as a single table, or relation, with the attributes recorded as column headings. Sample data should be recorded in the rows of the table, including any repeating groups that are present in the data. The table representing the invoice is shown in Figure 5-25. Notice that data for a second order (Order_ID 1007) are included in Figure 5-25 to clarify further the structure of this data.

Step 1: Convert to First Normal Form

First normal form (1NF): A relation that has a primary key and in which there are no repeating groups.

A relation is in **first normal form (1NF)** if the following two constraints both apply:

PVFC Customer Invoice

Customer ID	2			**Order ID**	1006	
Customer Name	Value Furniture			**Order Date**	10/24/2006	
Address	15145 S.W. 17th St.					
	Plano TX 750					

Product ID	Product Description	Finish	Quantity	Unit Price	Extended Price
7	Dining Table	Natural Ash	2	$800.00	$1,600.00
5	Writers Desk	Cherry	2	$325.00	$650.00
4	Entertainment Center	Natural Maple	1	$650.00	$650.00
				Total	$2,900.00

Figure 5-24
Invoice (Pine Valley Furniture Company)

1. There are no repeating groups in the relation (thus, there is a single fact at the intersection of each row and column of the table).

2. A primary key has been defined, which uniquely identifies each row in the relation.

Remove Repeating Groups As you can see, the invoice data in Figure 5-25 contains a repeating group for each product that appears on a particular order. Thus, Order_ID 1006 contains three repeating groups, corresponding to the three products on that order.

In a previous section, we showed how to remove repeating groups from a table by filling relevant data values into previously vacant cells of the table (see Figures 5-2a and 5-2b). Applying this procedure to the invoice table yields the new table (named INVOICE) shown in Figure 5-26.

Select the Primary Key There are four determinants in INVOICE, and their functional dependencies are the following:

Order_ID → Order_Date, Customer_ID, Customer_Name, Customer_Address
Customer_ID → Customer_Name, Customer_Address

Figure 5-25
INVOICE data (Pine Valley Furniture Company)

Order_ID	Order_Date	Customer_ID	Customer_Name	Customer_Address	Product_ID	Product_Description	Product_Finish	Unit_Price	Ordered_Quantity
1006	10/24/2006	2	Value Furniture	Plano, TX	7	Dining Table	Natural Ash	800.00	2
					5	Writer's Desk	Cherry	325.00	2
					4	Entertainment Center	Natural Maple	650.00	1
1007	10/25/2006	6	Furniture Gallery	Boulder, CO	11	4–Dr Dresser	Oak	500.00	4
					4	Entertainment Center	Natural Maple	650.00	3

Order_ID	Order_Date	Customer_ID	Customer_Name	Customer_Address	Product_ID	Product_Description	Product_Finish	Unit_Price	Ordered_Quantity
1006	10/24/2006	2	Value Furniture	Plano, TX	7	Dining Table	Natural Ash	800.00	2
1006	10/24/2006	2	Value Furniture	Plano, TX	5	Writer's Desk	Cherry	325.00	2
1006	10/24/2006	2	Value Furniture	Plano, TX	4	Entertainment Center	Natural Maple	650.00	1
1007	10/25/2006	6	Furniture Gallery	Boulder, CO	11	4–Dr Dresser	Oak	500.00	4
1007	10/25/2006	6	Furniture Gallery	Boulder, CO	4	Entertainment Center	Natural Maple	650.00	3

Figure 5-26
INVOICE relation (1NF) (Pine Valley Furniture Company)

Product_ID → Product_Description, Product_Finish, Unit_Price
Order_ID, Product_ID → Ordered_Quantity

Why do we know these are the functional dependencies? These business rules come from the organization. We know these from studying the nature of the Pine Valley Furniture Company business. We can also see that no data in Figure 5-26 violates any of these functional dependencies. But, because we don't see all possible roles of this table, we cannot be sure that there wouldn't be some invoice that would violate one of these functional dependencies. Thus, we must depend on our understanding of the rules of the organization.

As you can see, the only candidate key for INVOICE is the composite key consisting of the attributes Order_ID and Product_ID (because there is only one row in the table for any combination of values for these attributes). Therefore, Order_ID and Product_ID are underlined in Figure 5-26, indicating that they comprise the primary key.

When forming a primary key, you must be careful not to include redundant (therefore unnecessary) attributes. Thus, although Customer_ID is a determinant in INVOICE, it is not included as part of the primary key because all of the nonkey attributes are identified by the combination of Order_ID and Product_ID. We will see the role of Customer_ID in the normalization process that follows.

A diagram that shows these functional dependencies for the INVOICE relation is shown in Figure 5-27. This diagram is a horizontal list of all the attributes in INVOICE, with the primary key attributes (Order_ID and Product_ID) underlined. Notice that the only attribute that depends on the full key is Ordered_Quantity. All of the other functional dependencies are either partial dependencies or transitive dependencies (both are defined below).

Figure 5-27
Functional dependency diagram for INVOICE

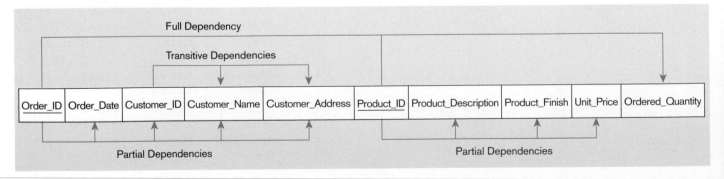

Anomalies in 1NF   Although repeating groups have been removed, the data in Figure 5-26 still contains considerable redundancy. For example, the Customer_ID, Customer_Name, and Customer_Address for Value Furniture are recorded in three rows (at least) in the table. As a result of these redundancies, manipulating the data in the table can lead to anomalies such as the following:

1. *Insertion anomaly*   If the customer calls and requests another product be added to his Order_ID 1007, a new row must be inserted in which the order date and all of the customer information must be repeated. This may lead to data entry errors (e.g., the customer name may be entered as "Valley Furniture").

2. *Deletion anomaly*   If the customer calls and requests that the Dining Table be deleted from her Order_ID 1006, this row must be deleted from the relation and we lose the information concerning this item's finish (Natural Ash) and price ($800.00).

3. *Update anomaly*   If Pine Valley Furniture (as part of a price adjustment) increases the price of the Entertainment Center (Product_ID 4) to $750.00, this change must be recorded in all rows containing that item. (There are two such rows in Figure 5-26.)

Step 2: Convert to Second Normal Form

We can remove many of the redundancies (and resulting anomalies) in the INVOICE relation by converting it to second normal form. A relation is in **second normal form (2NF)** if it is in first normal form and contains no partial dependencies. A **partial functional dependency** exists when a nonkey attribute is functionally dependent on part (but not all) of the primary key. As you can see, the following partial dependencies exist in Figure 5-27:

> **Second normal form (2NF):** A relation in first normal form in which every nonkey attribute is fully functionally dependent on the primary key.

> **Partial functional dependency:** A functional dependency in which one or more nonkey attributes are functionally dependent on part (but not all) of the primary key.

Order_ID → Order_Date, Customer_ID, Customer_Name, Customer_Address
Product_ID → Product_Description, Product_Finish, Unit_Price

The first of these partial dependencies (for example) states that the date on an order is uniquely determined by the order number and has nothing to do with the Product_ID.

To convert a relation with partial dependencies to second normal form, the following steps are required:

1. Create a new relation for each primary key attribute (or combination of attributes) that is a determinant in a partial dependency. That attribute is the primary key in the new relation.

2. Move the nonkey attributes that are dependent on this primary key attribute (or attributes) from the old relation to the new relation.

The results of performing these steps for the INVOICE relation are shown in Figure 5-28. Removal of the partial dependencies results in the formation of two new relations: PRODUCT and CUSTOMER_ORDER. The INVOICE relation is now left with just the primary key attributes (Order_ID and Product_ID) and Ordered_Quantity, which is functionally dependent on the whole key. We rename this relation ORDER_LINE, because each row in this table represents one line item on an order.

As indicated in Figure 5-28, the relations ORDER_LINE and PRODUCT are in third normal form. However, CUSTOMER_ORDER contains transitive dependencies and therefore (although in second normal form) is not yet in third normal form.

A relation that is in first normal form will be in second normal form if any one of the following conditions applies:

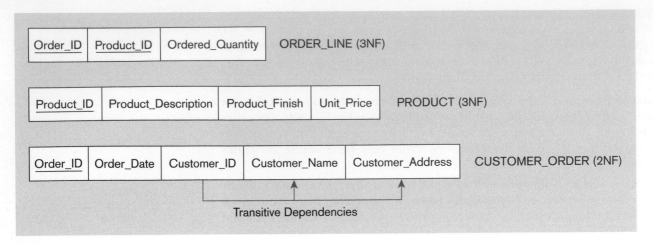

Figure 5-28
Removing partial dependencies

1. The primary key consists of only one attribute (such as the attribute Product_ID in the PRODUCT relation in Figure 5-28). By definition, there cannot be a partial dependency in such a relation.

2. No nonkey attributes exist in the relation (thus all of the attributes in the relation are components of the primary key). There are no functional dependencies in such a relation.

3. Every nonkey attribute is functionally dependent on the full set of primary key attributes (such as the attribute Ordered_Quantity in the ORDER_LINE relation in Figure 5-28).

Step 3: Convert to Third Normal Form

Third normal form (3NF): A relation that is in second normal form and has no transitive dependencies present.

Transitive dependency: A functional dependency between two (or more) nonkey attributes.

A relation is in **third normal form (3NF)** if it is in second normal form and no transitive dependencies exist. A **transitive dependency** in a relation is a functional dependency between two (or more) nonkey attributes. For example, there are two transitive dependencies in the CUST_ORDER relation shown in Figure 5-28:

Customer_ID → Customer_Name, and
Customer_ID → Customer_Address.

In other words, both customer name and address are uniquely identified by the Customer_ID, but Customer_ID is not part of the primary key (as we noted earlier). Transitive dependencies create unnecessary redundancy that may lead to the type of anomalies discussed earlier. For example, the transitive dependency in CUSTOMER_ORDER (Figure 5-28) requires that a customer's name and address be reentered every time a customer submits a new order, regardless of how many times they have been entered previously. You have no doubt experienced this type of annoying requirement when ordering merchandise online, visiting a doctor's office, or any number of similar activities.

Removing Transitive Dependencies You can easily remove transitive dependencies from a relation by means of a three-step procedure:

1. For each nonkey attribute (or set of attributes) that is a determinant in a relation, create a new relation. That attribute (or set of attributes) becomes the primary key of the new relation.

2. Move all of the attributes that are functionally dependent on the attribute from the old to the new relation.

3. Leave the attribute (which serves as a primary key in the new relation) in the old relation to serve as a foreign key that allows you to associate the two relations.

Figure 5-29
Removing transitive dependencies

Order_ID	Order_Date	Customer_ID	ORDER (3NF)

Customer_ID	Customer_Name	Customer_Address	CUSTOMER (3NF)

The results of applying these steps to the relation CUSTOMER_ORDER are shown in Figure 5-29. A new relation named CUSTOMER has been created to receive the components of the transitive dependency. The determinant Customer_ID becomes the primary key of this relation, and the attributes Customer_Name and Customer_Address are moved to the relation. CUST_ORDER is renamed ORDER, and the attribute Customer_ID remains as a foreign key in that relation. This allows us to associate an order with the customer who submitted the order. As indicated in Figure 5-29, these relations are now in third normal form.

Normalizing the data in the INVOICE view has resulted in the creation of four relations in third normal form: CUSTOMER, PRODUCT, ORDER, and ORDER_LINE. A relational schema showing these four relations and their associations (developed using Microsoft Visio) is shown in Figure 5-30. Note that Customer_ID is a foreign key in ORDER and Order_ID and Product_ID are foreign keys in ORDER_LINE. (Foreign keys are shown in Visio for logical, but not conceptual, data models.) Also note that minimum cardinalities are shown on the relationships even though the normalized relations provide no evidence of what the minimum cardinalities should be. Sample data for the relations might include, for example, a customer with no orders, thus providing evidence of the optional cardinality for the relationship Places. However, even if there were an order for every customer in a sample data set, this would not prove mandatory cardinality. Minimum cardinalities must be determined from business rules not illustrations of reports, screens, and transactions. The same statement is true for specific maximum cardinalities (for example, a business rule that no order may contain more than ten line items).

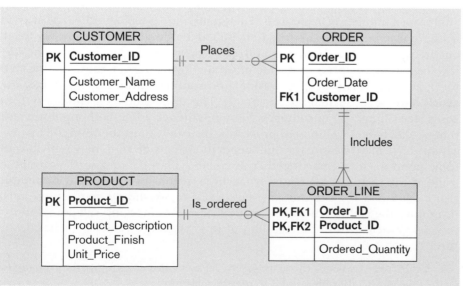

Figure 5-30
Relational scheme for INVOICE data
(Microsoft Visio)

Determinants and Normalization

We demonstrated normalization through 3NF in steps. There is an easy short cut, however. If you look back at the original set of four determinants and the associated functional dependencies for the invoice user view, each of these correspond to one of the relations in Figure 5-30, with each determinant being the primary key of a relation and the nonkeys of each relation are those attributes functionally dependent on each determinant. There is a subtle but important difference: Because Order_ID determines Customer_ID, Customer_Name, and Customer_Address and Customer_ID determines its dependent attributes, Customer_ID becomes a foreign key in the ORDER relation, which is where Customer_Name and Customer_Address are represented. The point is, if you can determine determinants that have no overlapping dependent attributes, then you have defined the relations. Thus, you can do normalization step by step as illustrated for the Pine Valley Furniture invoice, or you can create relations in 3NF straight from determinants functional dependencies.

Step 4: Further Normalization

After completing steps 0 through 3 all nonkeys will be dependent on the primary key, the whole primary key, and nothing but the primary key ("so help you Codd!"). Actually, normal forms are rules about functional dependencies and, hence, are the result of finding determinants and their associated nonkeys. The steps we outline are an aid in creating a relation for each determinant and its associated nonkeys.

You will recall from the beginning of our discussion of normalization that we identified additional normal forms beyond 3NF. The most commonly enforced of these additional normal forms are explained in Appendix B, which you might want to read on scan now.

MERGING RELATIONS

In a previous section, we described how to transform E-R diagrams to relations. This transformation occurs when we take the results of a top-down analysis of data requirements and begin to structure them for implementation in a database. We then described how to check the resulting relations to determine whether they are in third (or higher) normal form, and perform normalization steps if necessary.

As part of the logical design process, normalized relations may have been created from a number of separate E-R diagrams and (possibly) other user views (that is, there may be bottom-up or parallel database development activities for different areas of the organization as well as top-down ones). For example, besides the invoice used in the prior section to illustrate normalization, there may be an order form, account balance report, production routing, and other user views, each of which have been normalized separately. The three-schema architecture for databases (see Chapter 2) encourages the simultaneous use of both top-down and bottom-up database development processes. In reality, most medium to large organizations have many reasonably independent systems development activities that at some point need to come together to create a shared database. The result is that some of the relations generated from these various processes may be redundant; that is, they may refer to the same entities. If so, we should merge those relations to remove the redundancy. This section describes merging relations (also called *view integration*). An understanding of how to merge relations is important for three reasons:

1. On large projects, the work of several subteams comes together during logical design, so there is a need to merge relations.

2. Integrating existing databases with new information requirements often leads to the need to integrate different views.

3. New data requirements may arise during the life cycle, so there is a need to merge any new relations with what has already been developed.

An Example

Suppose that modeling a user view results in the following 3NF relation:

EMPLOYEE1(Employee_ID,Name,Address,Phone)

Modeling a second user view might result in the following relation:

EMPLOYEE2(Employee_ID,Name,Address,Jobcode,No_Years)

Because these two relations have the same primary key (Employee_ID), they likely describe the same entity and may be merged into one relation. The result of merging the relations is the following relation:

EMPLOYEE(Employee_ID,Name,Address,Phone,Jobcode,No_Years)

Notice that an attribute that appears in both relations (such as Name in this example) appears only once in the merged relation.

View Integration Problems

When integrating relations as in the preceding example, the database analyst must understand the meaning of the data and must be prepared to resolve any problems that may arise in that process. In this section, we describe and briefly illustrate four problems that arise in view integration: *synonyms, homonyms, transitive dependencies*, and *supertype/subtype relationships*.

Synonyms   In some situations, two (or more) attributes may have different names but the same meaning, as when they describe the same characteristic of an entity. Such attributes are called **synonyms**. For example, Employee_ID and Employee_No may be synonyms. When merging the relations that contain synonyms, you should obtain agreement (if possible) from users on a single, standardized name for the attribute and eliminate any other synonyms. (Another alternative is to choose a third name to replace the synonyms.) For example, consider the following relations:

> **Synonyms:** Two (or more) attributes having different names but the same meaning, as when they describe the same characteristic of an entity.

STUDENT1(Student_ID,Name)
STUDENT2(Matriculation_No,Name,Address)

In this case, the analyst recognizes that both the Student_ID and Matriculation_No are synonyms for a person's Social Security number and are identical attributes. (Another possibility is that these are both candidate keys, and only one of them should be selected as the primary keys.) One possible resolution would be to standardize on one of the two attribute names, such as Student_ID. Another option is to use a new attribute name, such as SSN, to replace both synonyms. Assuming the latter approach, merging the two relations would produce the following result:

STUDENT(SSN,Name,Address)

Often when there are synonyms, there is a need to allow some database users to refer to the same data by different names. Users may need to use familiar names that are consistent with terminology in their part of the organization. An **alias** is an alternative name used for an attribute. Many database management systems allow the definition of an alias that may be used interchangeably with the primary attribute label.

> **Alias:** An alternative name used for an attribute.

Homonym: An attribute that may have more than one meaning.

Homonyms   An attribute that may have more than one meaning is called a **homonym**. For example, the term "account" might refer to a bank's checking account, savings account, loan account, or other type of account (therefore, "account" refers to different data, depending on how it is used).

You should be on the lookout for homonyms when merging relations. Consider the following example:

STUDENT1(Student_ID,Name,Address)
STUDENT2(Student_ID,Name,Phone_No,Address)

In discussions with users, the analyst may discover that the attribute Address in STUDENT1 refers to a student's campus address, whereas in STUDENT2 the same attribute refers to a student's permanent (or home) address. To resolve this conflict, we would probably need to create new attribute names, so that the merged relation would become

STUDENT(Student_ID,Name,Phone_No,Campus_Address,Permanent_Address)

Transitive Dependencies   When two 3NF relations are merged to form a single relation, transitive dependencies (described earlier in this chapter) may result. For example, consider the following two relations:

STUDENT1(Student_ID,Major)
STUDENT2(Student_ID,Advisor)

Because STUDENT1 and STUDENT2 have the same primary key, the two relations may be merged:

STUDENT(Student_ID,Major,Advisor)

However, suppose that each major has exactly one advisor. In this case, Advisor is functionally dependent on Major:

Major → Advisor

If the preceding functional dependency exists, then STUDENT is in 2NF but not in 3NF, because it contains a transitive dependency. The analyst can create 3NF relations by removing the transitive dependency. Major becomes a foreign key in STUDENT:

STUDENT(Student_ID,Major)
MAJOR ADVISOR(Major,Advisor)

Supertype/Subtype Relationships   These relationships may be hidden in user views or relations. Suppose that we have the following two hospital relations:

PATIENT1(Patient_ID,Name,Address)
PATIENT2(Patient_ID,Room_No)

Initially, it appears that these two relations can be merged into a single PATIENT relation. However, the analyst correctly suspects that there are two different types of patients: resident patients and outpatients. PATIENT1 actually contains attributes common to all patients. PATIENT2 contains an attribute (Room_No) that is a characteristic only of resident patients. In this situation, the analyst should create supertype/subtype relationships for these entities:

PATIENT(Patient_ID,Name,Address)
RESIDENT PATIENT(Patient_ID,Room_No)
OUTPATIENT(Patient_ID,Date_Treated)

We have created the OUTPATIENT relation to show what it might look like if it were needed, but it is not necessary given only PATIENT1 and PATIENT2 user views. For an extended discussion of view integration in database design, see Navathe, Elmasri, and Larson (1986).

Figure 5-31 (Continued)
(d) Sample data after adding PERSON
relation

OBJECT

OID	Object_Type
1	EMPLOYEE
2	CUSTOMER
3	CUSTOMER
4	EMPLOYEE
5	EMPLOYEE
6	CUSTOMER
7	CUSTOMER
8	PERSON
9	PERSON
10	PERSON
11	PERSON
12	PERSON
13	PERSON
14	PERSON

PERSON

OID	Name
8	Jennings, Fred
9	Fred's Warehouse
10	Bargain Bonanza
11	Hopkins, Dan
12	Huber, Ike
13	Jasper's
14	Desks 'R Us

EMPLOYEE

OID	Emp_ID	Dept_Name	Salary	Person_ID
1	100	Marketing	50000	8
4	101	Purchasing	45000	11
5	102	Accounting	45000	12

CUSTOMER

OID	Cust_ID	Address	Person_ID
2	100	Greensboro, NC	9
3	101	Moscow, ID	10
6	102	Tallahassee, FL	13
7	103	Kettering, OH	14

Summary

Logical database design is the process of transforming the conceptual data model into a logical data model. The emphasis in this chapter has been on the relational data model, because of its importance in contemporary database systems. The relational data model represents data in the form of tables called relations. A relation is a named, two-dimensional table of data. A key property of relations is that they cannot contain multivalued attributes.

In this chapter, we described the major steps in the logical database design process. This process is based on transforming EER diagrams to normalized relations. The three steps in this process are the following: transform EER diagrams to relations, normalize the relations, and merge the relations. The result of this process is a set of relations in third normal form that can be implemented using any contemporary relational database management system.

Each entity type in the EER diagram is transformed to a relation that has the same primary key as the entity type. A one-to-many relationship is represented by adding a foreign key to the relation that represents the entity on the many side of the relationship. (This foreign key is the primary key of the entity on the one side of the relationship.) A many-to-many relationship is represented by creating a separate relation. The primary key of this relation is a composite key, consisting of the primary key of each of the entities that participate in the relationship.

The relational model does not directly support supertype/subtype relationships, but we can model these relationships by creating a separate table (or relation) for the supertype and for each subtype. The primary key of each subtype is the same (or at least from the same domain) as for the supertype. The supertype must have an attribute called the subtype discriminator that indicates to which subtype (or subtypes) each instance of the supertype belongs. The purpose of normalization is to derive well-structured relations that are free of anomalies (inconsistencies or errors) that would otherwise result when the relations are updated or modified. Normalization is based on the analysis of functional dependencies, which are constraints between two attributes (or two sets of attributes). It may be accomplished in several stages. Relations in first normal form (1NF) contain no multivalued attributes or repeating groups. Relations in second normal form (2NF) contain no partial dependencies, and relations in third normal form (3NF) contain no transitive dependencies. We can use diagrams that show the functional dependencies in a relation to help decompose that relation (if necessary) to obtain relations in third normal form. Higher normal forms (beyond 3NF) have also been defined; we discuss these normal forms in Appendix B.

We must be careful when combining relations to deal with problems such as synonyms, homonyms, transitive dependencies, and supertype/subtype relationships. In addition, before relations are defined to the database management system, all primary keys should be described as single attribute nonintelligent keys, and preferably, as enterprise keys.

CHAPTER REVIEW

Key Terms

Alias
Anomaly
Candidate key
Composite key
Determinant
Enterprise key
Entity integrity rule
First normal form

Foreign key
Functional dependency
Homonym
Normal form
Normalization
Null
Partial functional dependency
Primary key

Recursive foreign key
Referential integrity constraint
Relation
Second normal form
Synonyms
Third normal form
Transitive dependency
Well-structured relation

Review Questions

1. Define each of the following terms:
   a. determinant
   b. functional dependency
   c. transitive dependency
   d. recursive foreign key
   e. normalization
   f. composite key
   g. relation
   h. normal form
   i. partial functional dependency
   j. enterprise key

2. Match the following terms to the appropriate definitions:

   ____ well-structured relation
   ____ anomaly
   ____ functional dependency
   ____ determinant
   ____ composite key
   ____ 1NF
   ____ 2NF
   ____ 3NF
   ____ recursive foreign key

   a. constraint between two attributes
   b. functional dependency between nonkey attributes
   c. references primary key in same relation
   d. multivalued attributes removed
   e. inconsistency or error
   f. contains little redundancy
   g. contains two (or more) attributes
   h. contains no partial functional dependencies

_____ relation

_____ transitive dependency

i. transitive dependencies eliminated

j. attribute on left side of functional dependency

k. named two-dimensional table of data

3. Contrast the following terms:

a. normal form; normalization

b. candidate key; primary key

c. partial dependency; transitive dependency

d. composite key; recursive foreign key

e. determinant; candidate key

f. foreign key; primary key

4. Summarize six important properties of relations.

5. Describe two properties that must be satisfied by candidate keys.

6. Describe three types of anomalies that can arise in a table.

7. Fill in the blanks in each of the following statements.

a. A relation that has no partial functional dependencies is in _____ normal form.

b. A relation that has no multivalued attributes is in _____ normal form.

c. A relation that has no transitive dependencies is in _____ normal form.

8. What is a well-structured relation? Why are well-structured relations important in logical database design?

9. Describe how the following components of an E-R diagram are transformed into relations.

a. Regular entity type

b. Relationship (*1:M*)

c. Relationship (*M:N*)

d. Relationship (supertype/subtype)

e. Multivalued attribute

f. Weak entity

g. Composite attribute

10. Briefly describe four typical problems that often arise in merging relations and common techniques for addressing those problems.

11. List three conditions that you can apply to determine whether a relation that is in first normal form is also in second normal form.

12. Explain how each of the following types of integrity constraints are enforced in the **SQL CREATE TABLE** commands:

a. Entity integrity

b. Referential integrity

13. How are relationships between entities represented in the relational data model?

14. How do you represent a *1:M* unary relationship in a relational data model?

15. How do you represent an *M:N* ternary relationship in a relational data model?

16. How do you represent an associative entity in a relational data model?

17. What is the relationship between the primary key of a relation and the functional dependencies among all attributes within that relation?

18. Under what conditions must a foreign key not be null?

19. Explain what can be done with primary keys to eliminate key ripple effects as a database evolves.

20. Describe the difference between how a *1:M* unary relationship and a *M:N* unary relationship are implemented in a relational data model.

Problems and Exercises

1. For each of the following E-R diagrams from Chapter 3:

I. Transform the diagram to a relational schema that shows referential integrity constraints (see Figure 5-5 for an example of such a schema).

II. For each relation, diagram the functional dependencies (see Figure 5-23 for an example).

III. If any of the relations are not in 3NF, transform those relations to 3NF.

a. Figure 3-8   e. Figure 3-15a (relationship version)

b. Figure 3-9b   f. Figure 3-15b (attribute version)

c. Figure 3-11a   g. Figure 3-16b

d. Figure 3-11b   h. Figure 3-19

2. For each of the following EER diagrams from Chapter 4:

I. Transform the diagram into a relational schema that shows referential integrity constraints (see Figure 5-5 for an example of such a schema).

II. For each relation, diagram the functional dependencies (see Figure 5-23 for an example).

III. If any of the relations are not in 3NF, transform those relations to 3NF.

a. Figure 4-6b   c. Figure 4-9   e. Figure 4-12

b. Figure 4-7a   d. Figure 4-10   f. Figure 4-19

3. For each of the following relations, indicate the normal form for that relation. If the relation is not in third normal form, decompose it into 3NF relations. Functional dependencies (other than those implied by the primary key) are shown where appropriate.

a. CLASS(Course_No,Section_No)

b. CLASS(Course_No,Section_No,Room)

c. CLASS(Course_No,Section_No,Room,Capacity)
   Room→Capacity

d. CLASS(Course_No,Section_No,Course_Name, Room, Capacity)
   Course_No→ Course Name   Room→ Capacity

Figure 5-32
Class list (Millennium College)

MILLENNIUM COLLEGE
CLASS LIST
FALL SEMESTER 200X

COURSE NO.:   IS 460
COURSE TITLE: DATABASE
INSTRUCTOR NAME: NORMA L. FORM
INSTRUCTOR LOCATION: B 104

STUDENT NO.	STUDENT NAME	MAJOR	GRADE
38214	Bright	IS	A
40875	Cortez	CS	B
51893	Edwards	IS	A

Figure 5-33
EER diagram for bank cards

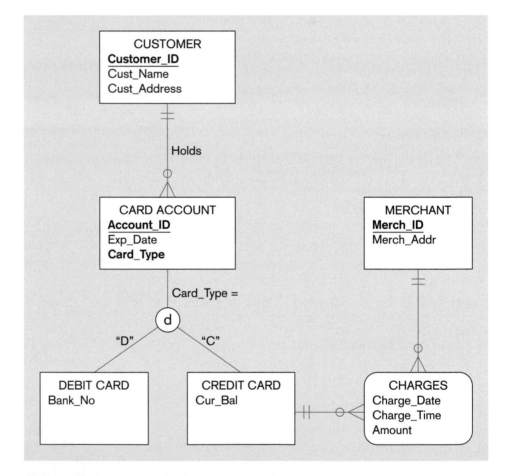

Table 5-3   Sample Data for Parts and Vendors

Part_No.	Description	Vendor_Name	Address	Unit_Cost
1234	Logic chip	Fast Chips	Cupertino	10.00
		Smart Chips	Phoenix	8.00
5678	Memory chip	Fast Chips	Cupertino	3.00
		Quality Chips	Austin	2.00
		Smart Chips	Phoenix	5.00

Table 5-4   GRADE REPORT Relation

GRADE REPORT

Student_ID	Student_ Name	Campus_ Address	Major	Course_ID	Course_ Title	Instructor_ Name	Instructor_ Location	Grade
168300458	Williams	208 Brooks	IS	IS 350	Database Mgt	Codd	B 104	A
268300458	Williams	208 Brooks	IS	IS 465	Systems Analysis	Parsons	B 317	B
543291073	Baker	104 Phillips	Acctg	IS 350	Database Mgt	Codd	B 104	C
543291073	Baker	104 Phillips	Acctg	Acct 201	Fund Acctg	Miller	H 310	B
543291073	Baker	104 Phillips	Acctg	Mktg 300	Intro Mktg	Bennett	B 212	A

4. Figure 5-32 shows a class list for Millennium College. Convert this user view to a set of 3NF relations using an enterprise key. Assume the following:

- An instructor has a unique location.
- A student has a unique major.
- A course has a unique title.

5. Figure 5-33 shows an EER diagram for a simplified credit card environment. There are two types of card accounts: debit cards and credit cards. Credit card accounts accumulate charges with merchants. Each charge is identified by the date and time of the charge as well as the primary keys of merchant and credit card.

   a. Develop a relational schema.

   b. Show the functional dependencies.

   c. Develop a set of 3NF relations using an enterprise key.

6. Table 5-3 contains sample data for parts and for vendors who supply those parts. In discussing these data with users, we find that part numbers (but not descriptions) uniquely identify parts, and that vendor names uniquely identify vendors.

   a. Convert this table to a relation (named PART SUPPLIER) in first normal form. Illustrate the relation with the sample data in the table.

   b. List the functional dependencies in PART SUPPLIER and identify a candidate key.

   c. For the relation PART SUPPLIER, identify each of the following: an insert anomaly, a delete anomaly, and a modification anomaly.

   d. Draw a relational schema for PART SUPPLIER and show the functional dependencies.

   e. In what normal form is this relation?

   f. Develop a set of 3NF relations from PART SUPPLIER.

   g. Show the 3NF relations using Microsoft Visio (or any other tool specified by your instructor).

7. Table 5-4 shows a relation called GRADE REPORT for a university. Your assignment is as follows:

   a. Draw a relational schema and diagram the functional dependencies in the relation.

   b. In what normal form is this relation?

   c. Decompose GRADE REPORT into a set of 3NF relations.

   d. Draw a relational schema for your 3NF relations and show the referential integrity constraints.

   e. Draw your answer to part d using Microsoft Visio (or any other tool specified by your instructor).

8. Table 5-5 shows a shipping manifest. Your assignment is as follows:

   a. Draw a relational schema and diagram the functional dependencies in the relation.

Table 5-5   Shipping Manifest

SHIPMENT ID:	00-0001	SHIPMENT DATE:	01/10/2006
ORIGIN:	BOSTON	EXPECTED ARRIVAL:	01/14/2006
DESTINATION:	BRAZIL		
SHIP NUMBER:	39	CAPTAIN:	002-15 Henry Moore

Item Number	Type Description	Weight	Quantity	Total	Weight
3223	BM	Concrete Form	500	100	50,000
3297	BM	Steel Beam	87	2,000	174,000
			Shipment Total:		224,000

Table 5-6   Parking Tickets at Millennium College

St_ID	L_Name	F_Name	Phone_No	St_Lic	Lic_No	Ticket#	Date	Code	Fine
38249	Brown	Thomas	111-7804	FL	BRY 123	15634	10/17/06	2	$25
						16017	11/13/06	1	$15
82453	Green	Sally	391-1689	AL	TRE 141	14987	10/05/06	3	$100
						16293	11/18/06	1	$15
						17892	12/13/06	2	$25

Table 5-7   Pine Valley Furniture Company Purchasing Data

Attribute Name	Sample Value
Material_ID	3792
Material_Name	Hinges 3" locking
Unit_of_Measure	each
Standard_Cost	$5.00
Vendor_ID	V300
Vendor_Name	Apex Hardware
Unit_Price	$4.75
Terms Code	1
Terms	COD

b. In what normal form is this relation?

c. Decompose MANIFEST into a set of 3NF relations.

d. Draw a relational schema for your 3NF relations and show the referential integrity constraints.

e. Draw your answer to part d using Microsoft Visio (or any other tool specified by your instructor).

9. Transform the relational schema developed in Problem and Exercise 8 into an EER diagram. State any assumptions that you have made.

10. Transform Figure 3-15b, attribute version, to 3NF relations. Transform Figure 3-15b, relationship version, to 3NF relations. Compare these two sets of 3NF relations with those in Figure 5-10. What observations and conclusions do you reach by comparing these different sets of 3NF relations?

11. The Public Safety office at Millennium College maintains a list of parking tickets issued to vehicles parked illegally on the campus. Table 5-6 shows a portion of this list for Fall semester. (Attribute names are abbreviated to conserve space.)

a. Convert this table to a relation in first normal form by entering appropriate data in the table. What are the determinants in this relation?

b. Draw a dependency diagram showing all functional dependencies in the relation, based on the sample data shown.

c. Give an example of one or more anomalies that can result in using this relation.

d. Develop a set of relations in third normal form. Include a new column with the heading Violation in the appropriate table to explain the reason for each ticket. Values in this column are: expired parking meter (ticket code 1), no parking permit (ticket code 2), and handicap violation (ticket code 3).

e. Develop an E-R diagram with the appropriate cardinality notations.

f. Draw your answer to art e using Microsoft Visio (or any other tool specified by your instructor).

12. The materials manager at Pine Valley Furniture Company maintains a list of suppliers for each of the material items purchased by the company from outside vendors. Table 5-7 shows the essential data required for this application.

a. Draw a dependency diagram for this data. You may assume the following:

- Each material item has one or more suppliers. Each supplier may supply one or more items or may not supply any items.

- The unit price for a material item may vary from one vendor to another.

- The terms code for a supplier uniquely identifies the terms of the sale (e.g., code 2 means 10% net 30 days, etc.). The terms for a supplier are the same for all material items ordered from that supplier.

b. Decompose this diagram into a set of diagrams in 3NF.

c. Draw an E-R diagram for this situation.

d. Draw a diagram in Microsoft Visio (or any other tool specified by your instructor) for this situation.

13. Table 5-8 shows a portion of a shipment table for a large manufacturing company. Each shipment (identified by Shipment#) uniquely identifies the shipment Origin, Destination, and Distance. The shipment Origin and Destination pair also uniquely identifies the Distance.

a. Develop a diagram that shows the functional dependencies in the SHIPMENT relation.

b. In what normal form is SHIPMENT? Why?

Table 5-8   SHIPMENT Relation

Shipment#	Origin	Destination	Distance
409	Seattle	Denver	1,537
618	Chicago	Dallas	1,058
723	Boston	Atlanta	1,214
824	Denver	Los Angeles	975
629	Seattle	Denver	1,537

c. Convert SHIPMENT to third normal form if necessary. Show the resulting table(s) with the sample data presented in SHIPMENT.

d. Draw your answer to part c using Microsoft Visio (or any other tool specified by your instructor).

14. Figure 5-34 shows an EER diagram for Vacation Property Rentals. This organization rents preferred properties in several states. As shown in the figure, there are two basic types of properties: beach properties and mountain properties.

a. Transform the EER diagram to a set of relations and develop a relational schema.

b. Diagram the functional dependencies and determine the normal form for each relation.

c. Convert all relations to third normal form if necessary and draw a revised relational schema.

d. Suggest an integrity constraint that would ensure that no property is rented twice during the same time interval.

15. Examine the set of relations in Figure 5-35. What normal form are these in? Why (that is, how do you know)? If they are in 3NF, convert the relations into an EER diagram.

16. A pet store currently uses a legacy, flat file system to store all of its information. The owner of the store, Peter Corona, wants to implement a Web-enabled database application. This would enable branch stores to enter data regarding inventory levels, ordering and so on. Presently, the data for inventory and sales tracking are stored in one file with the following format:

Store_Name, Pet_Name, Pet Description, Price, Cost, Supplier_Name, Shipping_Time, Quantity_on_Hand, Date_of_Last_Delivery, Date_of_Last_Purchase, Delivery_Date1, Delivery_Date2, Delivery_Date3, Delivery_Date4, Purchase_Date1, Purchase_Date2, Purchase_Date3, Purchase_

Figure 5-34
EER diagram for vacation property rentals

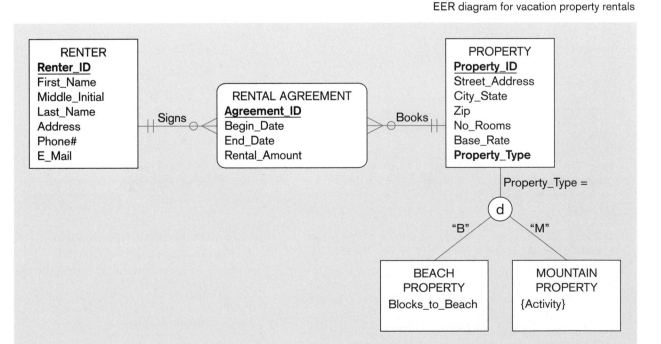

Figure 5-35
Relations for Problem
and Exercise 15

Attorney

Attorney_ID	Name	Address	City	State	ZipCode

Speciality_T

Attorney_ID	Speciality

Bar

Attorney_ID	Bar

Client

Client_ID	Name	Address	City	State	ZipCode	Telephone	DOB

Case

Case_ID	Description	CaseType	Court_ID

Retains

Attorney_ID	Case_ID	Client_ID	Date

Court

Court_ID	Court_Name	City	State	Zipcode

Judge

Judge_ID	Name	Years	Court_ID

Figure 5-36
EER diagram for university dining
services

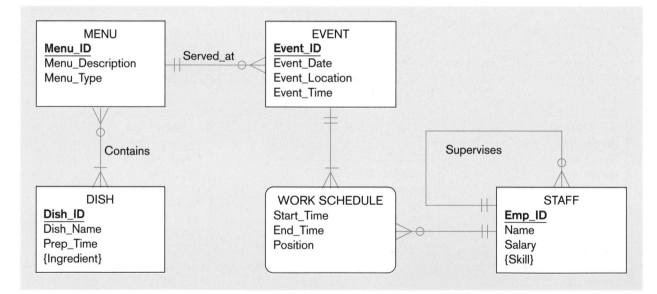

Date4, Last_Customer_Name, Customer_Name1, Customer_Name2, Customer_Name3, Customer_Name4

Assume that we want to track all purchase and inventory data, such as who bought the fish, the date that it was purchased, the date that it was delivered, and so on. The present file format allows only the tracking of the last purchase and delivery as well as four prior purchases and deliveries. We can assume that a type of fish is supplied by one supplier.

a. Show all functional dependencies.

b. What normal form is this table in?

c. Design a normalized data model for these data. Show that it is in 3NF.

17. For Problem and Exercise 16, draw the ER diagram based on the normalized relations.

Tempest Investment Services
12832 Parkside Drive
Boston, MA 02110
(800) 232-1322

Brokerage Account Summary Statement
Date: 9/2/2006
Period: 8/1/2006 – 8/31/2006

Client Name: Harold Smith, Jr.
Account Number: 392-21342
Agent: K. Weld

Symbol	Type	Description	Shares	Price	Total
T	Stock	ATT Common	1900	$20	$38,000
VZ	Stock	Verizon	2000	$40	$80,000
PG	Stock	Proctor and Gamble	10000	$90	$900,000
		Portfolio Total: $1,018,000			

Figure 5-37
Brokerage account summary

18. How would Problems and Exercises 16 and 17 change if a type of fish could be supplied by multiple suppliers?

19. Figure 5-36 shows an EER diagram for a university dining service. This organization provides dining services to a major university.

   a. Transform the EER diagram to a set of relations and develop a relational schema.

   b. Diagram the functional dependencies and determine the normal form for each relation.

   c. Convert all relations to third normal form, if necessary, and draw a revised relational schema.

20. Figure 5-37 contains a brokerage account summary with numerous investments.

   a. Draw a relational schema and diagram the functional dependencies in the relation.

   b. In what normal form is this relation?

   c. Decompose Brokerage_Account into a set of 3NF relations.

   d. Draw a relational schema for your 3NF relations and show the referential integrity constraints.

Field Exercises

1. Interview systems and database designers at several organizations. Ask them to describe the process they use for logical design. How do they transform their conceptual data models (e.g., E-R diagrams) to relational schema? What is the role of CASE tools in this process? Do they use normalization? If so, to what level?

2. Obtain a common document such as a sales slip, customer invoice from an auto repair shop, credit card statement, etc. Use the normalization steps (steps 0 through 4) described in this chapter to convert this user view to a set of relations in third normal form. You should also draw a relational schema. List several integrity rules that you would recommend to ensure the quality of the data in this application.

3. Obtain documentation for three popular PC-based CASE tools and compare the notation they use for representing relational schemas. You may use the following Internet addresses to obtain online information for the following four tools:

   a. Visible Analyst: **www.visible.com**

   b. Erwin: **www.cai.com/products/alm/erwin.htm**

   c. PowerDesigner: **www.sybase.com/products/developmentintegration/powerdesigner**

   d. DDS-Lite: **www.chillisource.com/**

4. Find a form or report from a business organization, possibly a statement, bill, or document you have received. Draw an EER diagram of the data in this form or report. Transform the diagram into a set of 3NF relations.

References

Chouinard, P. 1989. "Supertypes, Subtypes, and DB2." *Database Programming & Design* 2,10 (October): 50–57.

Codd, E. F. 1970. "A Relational Model of Data for Large Shared Data Banks." *Communications of the ACM* 13,6 (June): 77–87.

Codd, E. F. 1990. *The Relational Model for Database Management*, Version 2. Reading, MA: Addison-Wesley.

Date, C. J. 1995. *An Introduction to Database Systems*, 6th ed. Reading, MA: Addison-Wesley.

Dutka, A. F., and H. H. Hanson. 1989. *Fundamentals of Data Normalization*. Reading, MA: Addison-Wesley.

Fleming, C. C., and B. von Halle. 1989. *Handbook of Relational Database Design*. Reading, MA: Addison-Wesley.

Johnston, T. 2000. "Primary Key ReengineeringProjects: The Problem" and "Primary Key Reengineering Projects: The Solution." Available from **www.dmreview.com**.

Navathe, S., R. Elmasri, and J. Larson. 1986. "Integrating User Views in Database Design." *Computer* 19,1 (January): 50–62.

Further Reading

Elmasri, R., and S. Navathe. 1994. *Fundamentals of Database Systems*, 2nd ed. Menlo Park, CA: Benjamin Cummings.

Hoffer, J. A., J. F. George, and J. S. Valacich. 2005. *Modern Systems Analysis and Design*, 4th ed. Upper Saddle River, NJ: Prentice Hall.

Russell, T. and R. Armstrong. 2002 "13 Reasons why normalized tables help your business." *Database Administrator*, April 20.

Storey, V. C. 1991. "Relational Database Design Based on the Entity-Relationship Model." *Data and Knowledge Engineering* 7,1 (November): 47–83.

Web Resources

http://dev.mysql.com/tech-resources/articles/intro-to-normalization.html This article for mySQL developers, reviews first, second, and third normal forms.

http://en.wikipedia.org/wiki/Database_normalization This Wikipedia entry has a very thorough explanation of first, second, third, fourth, fifth, and Boyce-Codd normal forms.

www.bkent.net/Doc/simple5.htm Site presents a summary paper by William Kent entitled "A Simple Guide to Five Normal Forms in Relational Database Theory."

www.troubleshooters.com/codecorn/norm.htm This is a page on Steve Litt's site that contains various troubleshooting tips for avoiding programming and systems development problems.

MOUNTAIN VIEW COMMUNITY HOSPITAL

Case

You have been introduced to the Mountain View Community Hospital case in the preceding chapters. This chapter continues the case with special emphasis on logical design for the relational data model. Although the hospital will continue to evaluate newer technology (e.g., object-oriented databases, XML and XML databases), it is expected that relational technology will continue to dominate its systems development over the next few years.

CASE QUESTIONS

1. Should Mountain View Community Hospital continue to use relational technology for its systems development? Why or why not?

2. Should Mountain View Community Hospital use normalization in designing its relational databases? Why or why not?

3. Why are entity integrity constraints of importance to the hospital? Based on the case description from previous chapters, which attributes have you encountered that may be null?

4. Why are referential integrity constraints of importance to the hospital?

5. Physicians at Mountain View Community Hospital can be uniquely identified by their Social Security number, their license number, their DEA registration number, or a hospital assigned Physician_ID. Which attribute would you suggest using as the primary key for a PHYSICIAN relation? Why?

6. The chapter describes the importance of an *enterprise key*, which is a primary key that is unique across the whole database. Why might this be important in a hospital setting such as Mountain View Community Hospital? Explain.

7. Why might you need to revisit and potentially modify the EER Model you developed earlier during the logical design phase?

CASE EXERCISES

1. The assistant administrator at Mountain View Community Hospital has asked you to review the data used in the patient billing and accounting systems. Occasional errors have been discovered in patient statements and the patient records maintained by the hospital. As part of this effort, you have selected four user views for analysis. Simplified versions of these views are shown in MVCH Figures 5-1 through 5-4, and described briefly here.

- *Patient bill* (MVCH Figure 5-1). This statement is presented to the patient (or patient representative) when the patient is discharged. Assume that each item on the bill has a unique description, and that the charge for a particular item may vary from one patient to another.

- *Room Utilization Report* (MVCH Figure 5-2). This is a daily report that is distributed to qualified personnel. The information can also be retrieved online by a qualified staff member. It shows the status of each room and bed location in the hospital and is used primarily for scheduling and tracking the utilization of facilities. The Location column in this report records the room number and bed location in the room. The Accom column indicates the type of accommodation (PR = private, SP = semiprivate).

- *Patient display* (MVCH Figure 5-3). This display is presented on demand to any qualified doctor, nurse, or other staff member. Assume that for each location there is a unique telephone number.

- *Physician Report* (MVCH Figure 5-4). This report is prepared daily for each physician on the staff of MVCH. It shows the patients who have been treated on that day by the physician, and the name of the treatment (or procedure). To simplify the analysis, assume that each patient may receive only one treatment from a given physician on a given day. (We ask you to comment on this assumption later.)

MVCH Figure 5-1
Patient bill

INVOICE

MOUNTAIN VIEW COMMUNITY HOSPITAL
200 Forest Dr.
Mountain View, CO 80638

Mary Baker
200 Oak St.
Mountain View, CO 806338

INVOICE DATE:	10/24/2006
ACCOUNT NUMBER:	000976555
DUE DATE:	11/14/2006

PATIENT NAME	PATIENT #	DATE ADMITTED	DATE DISCHARGED
Mary Baker	3249	10/15/2006	10/18/2006

CODE	DESCRIPTION	TOTAL CHARGE
200	Room semi-pr	1,800.00
205	Television	75.00
307	X-ray	150.00
413	Lab tests	200.00

TOTAL CHARGES DUE	2,225.00

MVCH Figure 5-2
Room utilization report (excerpt)

ROOM UTILIZATION REPORT
Short Stay Surgical Ward
10/15/2006

LOCATION	ACCOM	PATIENT #	PATIENT NAME	EXP DISCHARGE DATE
100-1	PR	6213	Rose, David	10/17/2006
101-1	PR	1379	Cribbs, Ron	10/16/2006
102-1	SP			
102-2	SP	1239	Miller, Ruth	10/16/2006
103-1	PR	7040	Ortega, Juan	
104-1	PR			10/19/2006
105-1	SP	3249	Baker, Mary	10/18/2006

a. Using the normalization steps described in this chapter, develop a set of 3NF relations for each of the four user views.

b. For each user view, draw a relational schema for the 3NF relations you developed in Case Exercise 1a. Be sure to show the functional dependencies and referential integrity constraints for each schema.

c. Merge the relations for the four user views into a single set of 3NF relations, using the guidelines presented in this chapter. Draw a single relational schema for the four user views, and show the referential integrity constraints.

d. Suggest any refinements to the design in Case Exercise 1c that would promote data quality and integrity.

e. How would you change your approach to accommodate the rule that a patient may receive multiple treatments from a given physician on a given day?

MVCH Figure 5-3
Patient display

```
                    MVCH PATIENT DISPLAY
                                        09/16/2006  12:41 AM

PATIENT #:                  3249
PATIENT NAME:               Mary Baker
PATIENT ADDRESS:            300 Oak St.
CITY-STATE-ZIP:             Mountain View, CO 80638
DATE ADMITTED:              09-15-04
DATE DISCHARGED:
LOCATION:                   437-2
EXTENSION:                  529
INSURANCE:                  Blue Cross/Blue Shield
```

MVCH Figure 5-4
Physician report (excerpt)

```
            MOUNTAIN VIEW COMMUNITY HOSPITAL
                 DAILY PHYSICIAN REPORT
                      10/17/2006

   PHYSICIAN ID:  Gerald Wilcox     PHYSICIAN PHONE:   329-1848
```

PATIENT #	PATIENT NAME	LOCATION	PROCEDURE
6083	Brown, May	184-2	Tonsillectomy
1239	Miller, Ruth	102-2	Observation
4139	Major, Carl	107-3	Appendectomy
9877	Carlos, Juan	188-2	Herniorrhaphy
1277	Pace, Charles	187-8	Cholecystectomy

2. The Multiple Sclerosis Center headed by Dr. "Z." has been using a spreadsheet to keep track of information that patients provide upon signing in for a clinic visit. One of the staff members thought it would be better to use a relational database for recording this information and imported the spreadsheet as a table into a Microsoft Access database (MVCH Figure 5-5).

   a. What would you suggest as the primary key for this table?

   b. Is this table a relation? Why or why not?

   c. Can you identify any problems with this table structure? Are there any insertion, deletion, or update anomalies?

   d. Diagram the functional dependencies for this table.

   e. Using the normalization steps described in this chapter, develop a set of 3NF relations.

   f. Using a tool such as Microsoft Visio, draw the relational schema, clearly indicating referential integrity constraints.

   g. Write CREATE TABLE commands for all relations in your schema. Make reasonable assumptions concerning the data type for each attribute in each of the relations.

3. Dr. "Z." in the MS Center is using the MS Clinic Management System from an external vendor to keep track of clinical information regarding his patients. The application uses a relational database. Before seeing a patient, Dr. "Z." reviews a printout of the worksheet shown in MVCH Figure 5-6.

   a. Diagram the functional dependencies for this worksheet and develop a set of 3NF relations for the data on this worksheet.

   b. Draw the relational schema and clearly show the referential integrity constraints.

   c. Draw your answer to part b using Microsoft Visio (or any other tool specified by your instructor).

PROJECT ASSIGNMENTS

After developing conceptual data models for Mountain View Community Hospital's new system and

MVCH Figure 5-5
MS Center patient sign-in data

	Patient #	Name	First Seen	Social Worker	Visit Date	Visit Time	Reason for Visit	New symptoms	Level of Pain
	9844	John Miller	10/1/2004	Matt Baker	10/11/2005	2:30 pm	Severe leg pain	Severe leg pain for past 2 days	4
					10/18/2005	11:30 am	Follow-up, also need flu shot	None	2
					1/3/2006	10 am	Routine	None	0
					3/15/2006	10:30 am	Routine	None	0
	4211	Sheryl Franz	1/3/2005	Lynn Riley	1/3/2006	2PM	Referred by Primary care physician		0
					2/11/2006	9 am	Physical	None	0
					3/22/2006	4:00 pm	Routine and B12 Shot	Greater difficulties with writing & buttoning shirts	1
	8766	Juan Ortega	2/2/2005	Matt Baker	2/2/2006	9:30 am	Blurred vision in right eye		0
					2/14/2006	9:30 am	Follow-up		0
					3/18/2006	????	New symptoms	Pins/needles in both legs; trouble with balance	1

reviewing them with your team and key stakeholders at the hospital, you are ready to move on to the logical design for the relational data base. Your next deliverable is the relational schema. You may also have to modify the EER model you created earlier in Chapter 4.

P1. Map the EER diagram you developed in Chapter 4 to a relational schema, using the techniques described in this chapter. Be sure to underline all primary keys, include all necessary foreign keys, and clearly indicate referential integrity constraints.

P2. Analyze and diagram the functional dependencies in each relation. If any relation is not in 3NF, decompose that relation into 3NF relations using the steps described in this chapter. Revise the relational schema accordingly.

P3. Create enterprise keys for all relations and redefine all relations. Revise the relational schema accordingly.

P4. If necessary, revisit and modify the EER model you developed in Chapter 4, and explain the changes you made.

MVCH Figure 5-6
MS Center Patient Worksheet

Mountain View Community Hospital
MS CENTER PATIENT WORKSHEET

MRN# 7885	PATIENT NAME Michael J Olsen	Sex M	DOB June 16, 1949	STAGE Secondary Progressive MS	DATE PRINTED 07 July 2006

Presenting Symptoms
Tingling and numbness in both hands; spasticity in both legs, primarily the left one; significant loss of mobility, relies on wheelchair most days; episodes of severe muscular pain, primarily in left leg.

Active Medications

1. Aspirin, 325 mg, QD
2. Simvastatin, 40 mg, QHS
3. Baclofen, 10 mg, TID
4. Betaseron (interferon beta-1b), 250 mcg QOD, sc
5. Amantadine, 100 mg, BID
6. Plendil, 5 mg, QD

Clinical Laboratory Data

Lipid Profile	LDL(<100)	Trig(<200)	HDL(<35)	CHOL(<200)
06/23/2006	54	214	27	183
03/16/2006	54	325	24	217
12/13/2006	62	200	24	166

Radiology Data

Last Brain MRI: 05/23/2006   No new lesions; no expanding lesions

Clinic Data

Blood Pressure (<=120/80)		Weight		Last neurological assessment:
07/07/2006	135/80mmHg	07/07/2005	188	03/05 No change
06/07/2006	124/75 mmHg	06/07/2005	190	**Last Expanded Disability Status Scale (EDSS)**
05/20/2006	140/90 mmHg	05/20/2005	189	**Score:**
03/15/2006	135/86 mmHg	03/15/2005	188	03/05 5.5. (scale: 0-10)
01/17/2006	131/80 mmHg	01/17/2005	191	**Last Fatigue Severity Scale (FSS) Score:**
				03/052 (scale: 1-7)

Advisories

06/07/2006	Suggested follow-up lipid profile in 2 weeks
05/20/2006	Suggested follow-up for Triglycerides > 300, consider titrating Simvastatin up to 60 mg before initiating other therapies
03/15/2006	Discontinued Tizanidine; suggested follow-up for medication Baclofen

Chapter 6

Physical Database Design and Performance

LEARNING OBJECTIVES

After studying this chapter, you should be able to:

- Concisely define each of the following key terms: **field, data type, physical record, page, blocking factor, denormalization, horizontal partitioning, vertical partitioning, physical file, tablespace, extent, pointer, file organization, sequential file organization, indexed file organization, index, secondary key, bitmap index, join index, hashed file organization, hashing algorithm, hash index table, Redundant Array of Inexpensive Disks (RAID),** and **stripe.**
- Describe the physical database design process, its objectives, and deliverables.
- Choose storage formats for attributes from a logical data model.
- Select an appropriate file organization by balancing various important design factors.
- Describe three important types of file organization.
- Describe the purpose of indexes and the important considerations in selecting attributes to be indexed.
- Translate a relational data model into efficient database structures, including knowing when and how to denormalize the logical data model.

INTRODUCTION

In Chapters 3 through 5, you learned how to describe and model organizational data during the conceptual data modeling and logical database design phases of the database development process. You learned how to use EER notation, the relational data model, and normalization to develop abstractions of organizational data that capture the meaning of data; however, these notations do not explain how data will be processed or stored. The purpose of physical database design is to translate the logical description of data into the technical specifications for storing and retrieving data. The goal is to create a design for storing data that will provide adequate performance and ensure database integrity, security, and recoverability.

Physical database design does not include implementing files and databases (i.e., creating them and

240

loading data into them). Physical database design produces the technical specifications that programmers and others involved in information systems construction will use during the implementation phase, which we discuss in Chapters 7 through 11.

In this chapter, you study the basic steps required to develop an efficient and high integrity physical database design; security and recoverability are addressed in Chapter 12. We concentrate in this chapter on the design of a single, centralized database. Later, in Chapter 13, you learn about the design of databases that are stored at multiple, distributed sites. In Chapter 6, you learn how to estimate the amount of data that users will require in the database and determine how data are likely to be used. You learn about choices for storing attribute values and how to select from among these choices to achieve efficiency and data quality. Because of recent U.S. and international regulations (e.g., Sarbanes-Oxley) on financial reporting by organizations, proper controls specified in physical database design can be a sound foundation for compliance. Hence, we place special emphasis on data quality measures you can implement within the physical design. You will also learn why normalized tables do not always form the best physical data files and how you can denormalize the data to improve the speed of data retrieval. And, you will learn about different file organizations and about the use of indexes, which are important in speeding up the retrieval of data.

You must carefully perform physical database design, because the decisions made during this stage have a major impact on data accessibility, response times, data quality, security, user friendliness, and similarly important information system design factors. Database administration (described in Chapter 12) plays a major role in physical database design, so we return to some advanced design issues in that chapter.

PHYSICAL DATABASE DESIGN PROCESS

In most situations, many physical database design decisions are implicit or eliminated when you choose the database management technologies to use with the information system you are designing. Because many organizations have standards for operating systems, database management systems, and data access languages, you must deal only with those choices not implicit in the given technologies. Thus, we will cover only those decisions that you will make most frequently, as well as other selected decisions that may be critical for some types of applications, such an online data capture and retrieval.

The primary goal of physical database design is data processing efficiency. Today, with ever-decreasing costs for computer technology per unit of measure (both speed and space measures), it is typically very important for you to design the physical database to minimize the time required by users to interact with the information system. Thus, we concentrate on how to make processing of physical files and databases efficient, with less attention on efficient use of space.

Designing physical files and databases requires certain information that should have been collected and produced during prior system development phases. The information needed for physical file and database design includes these requirements:

- Normalized relations, including estimates for the number of rows in each table
- Definitions of each attribute, along with physical specifications such as maximum possible length
- Descriptions of where and when data are used: entered, retrieved, deleted, and updated (including frequencies)
- Expectations or requirements for response time and data security, backup, recovery, retention, and integrity
- Descriptions of the technologies (database management systems) used for implementing the database

Physical database design requires several critical decisions that will affect the integrity and performance of the application system. These key decisions include the following:

- Choosing the storage format (called *data type*) for each attribute from the logical data model. The format and associated parameters are chosen to minimize storage space and to maximize data integrity.

- Grouping attributes from the logical data model into *physical records*. You will discover that although the columns of a relational table are a natural definition for the contents of a physical record, this is not always the most desirable grouping of attributes.

- Arranging similarly structured records in secondary memory (primarily hard disks) so that individual and groups of records (called *file organizations*) can be stored, retrieved, and updated rapidly. Consideration must also be given to protecting data and recovering data after errors are found.

- Selecting structures (called *indexes* and *database architectures*) for storing and connecting files to make retrieving related data more efficient.

- Preparing strategies for handling queries against the database that will optimize performance and take advantage of the file organizations and indexes that you have specified. Efficient database structures will be of benefit only if queries and the database management systems that handle those queries are tuned to intelligently use those structures.

Data Volume and Usage Analysis

As mentioned above, data-volume and frequency-of-use statistics are critical inputs to the physical database design process. Thus, either the final step you need to take in logical database design or the first step you need to take in physical database design is to estimate the size and usage patterns of the database.

An easy way to show the statistics about data volumes and usage is by adding notation to the EER diagram that represents the final set of normalized relations from logical database design. Figure 6-1 shows the EER diagram (without attributes) for a simple inventory database in Pine Valley Furniture Company. This EER diagram represents the normalized relations constructed during logical database design for the original conceptual data model of this situation depicted in Figure 4-5b.

Both data volume and access frequencies are shown in Figure 6-1. For example, there are 1,000 PARTs in this database. The supertype PART has two subtypes, MANUFACTURED (40 percent of all PARTs are manufactured) and PURCHASED (70 percent are purchased; because some PARTs are of both subtypes, the percentages sum to more than 100 percent). The analysts at Pine Valley estimate that there are typically 50 SUPPLIERs, and Pine Valley receives on average 50 SUPPLIES instances from each SUPPLIER, yielding a total of 2,500 SUPPLIES. The dashed arrows represent access frequencies. So, for example, across all applications that use this database, there are on average 200 accesses per hour of PART data, and these yield, based on subtype percentages, 140 accesses per hour to PURCHASED PART data. There are an additional 60 direct accesses to PURCHASED PART data. Of this total of 200 accesses to PURCHASED PART, 80 accesses then also require SUPPLIES data and of these 80 accesses to SUPPLIES, there are 70 subsequent accesses to SUPPLIER data. For online and Web-based applications, usage maps should show the accesses per second. Several usage maps may be needed to show vastly different usage patterns for different times of day. Performance will also be affected by network specifications.

The volume and frequency statistics are generated during the systems analysis phase of the systems development process when systems analysts are studying current and proposed data processing and business activities. The data-volume

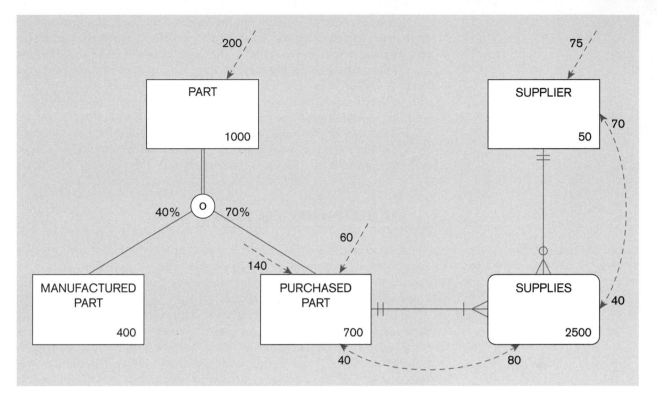

Figure 6-1
Composite usage map (Pine Valley Furniture Company)

statistics represent the size of the business, and should be calculated assuming business growth over at least a several-year period. The access frequencies are estimated from the timing of events, transaction volumes, the number of concurrent users, and reporting and querying activities. Because many databases support ad hoc accesses, and such accesses may change significantly over time, and known database access can peak and dip over a day, week, or month, the access frequencies tend to be less certain and even than the volume statistics are. Fortunately, precise numbers are not necessary. What is crucial is the relative size of the numbers, which will suggest where the greatest attention needs to be given during physical database design in order to achieve the best possible performance. For example, in Figure 6-1, notice that

- There are 1000 PART instances, so if PART has many attributes and some, like description, would be quite long, then the efficient storage of PART might be important.

- For each of the forty times per hour that SUPPLIES is accessed via SUPPLIER, PURCHASED PART is also accessed; thus, the diagram would suggest possibly combining these two co-accessed entities into a database table (or file). This act of combining normalized tables is an example of denormalization, which we discuss later in this chapter.

- There is only a 1 percent overlap between MANUFACTURED and PURCHASED parts, so it might make sense to have two separate tables for these entities and redundantly store data for those parts that are both manufactured and purchased; such planned redundancy is okay if purposeful. Further, there are a total of 200 accesses an hour of PURCHASED PART data (140 from access to PART and 60 independent access of PURCHASED PART) and only 80 accesses of MANUFACTURED PART per hour. Thus, it might make sense to organize tables for MANUFACTURED and PURCHASED PART data differently due to the significantly different access volumes.

It can be helpful for subsequent physical database design steps if you can also explain the nature of the access for the access paths shown by the dashed lines. For example, it can be helpful to know that of the 200 accesses to PART data, 150 ask for a part or a set of parts based on the primary key, Part_No (e.g., access a part with a particular number); the other 50 accesses qualify part data for access by the value of Qty_on_Hand. (These specifics are not shown in Figure 6-1.) This more precise description can help in selecting indexes, one of the major topics we discuss later in this chapter. It might also be helpful to know whether an access results in data creation, retrieval, update, or deletion. Such a refined description of access frequencies can be handled by additional notation on a diagram such as in Figure 6-1, or by text and tables kept in other documentation.

DESIGNING FIELDS

Field: The smallest unit of named application data recognized by system software.

A **field** is the smallest unit of application data recognized by system software, such as a programming language or database management system. A field corresponds to a simple attribute from the logical data model, so a field represents each component of a composite attribute.

The basic decisions you must make in specifying each field concern the type of data (or storage type) used to represent values of this field, data integrity controls built into the database, and how the DBMS should handle missing values for the field. Other field specifications, such as display format, also must be made as part of the total specification of the information system, but we will not be concerned here with those specifications typically handled by programs rather than the DBMS.

Choosing Data Types

Data type: A detailed coding scheme recognized by system software, such as a DBMS, for representing organizational data.

A **data type** is a detailed coding scheme recognized by system software, such as a DBMS, for representing organizational data. The bit pattern of the coding scheme is usually transparent to you, but the space to store data and the speed required to access data are of consequence in physical database design. The specific DBMS you will use will dictate which choices are available to you. For example, Table 6-1 lists some of the data types available in the Oracle 10i DBMS, a typical DBMS that uses the SQL data definition and manipulation language. Additional data types might be available for currency, voice, image, and user defined for some DBMSs.

Selecting a data type involves four objectives that will have different relative importances for different applications:

1. Minimize storage space
2. Represent all possible values
3. Improve data integrity
4. Support all data manipulations

The correct data type to choose for a field can, in minimal space, represent every possible value (but eliminate illegal values) for the associated attribute and can support the required data manipulation (e.g., numeric data types for arithmetic and character data types for string manipulation). Any attribute domain constraints from the conceptual data model are helpful in selecting a good data type for that attribute. Achieving these four objectives can be subtle. For example, consider a DBMS for which a data type has a maximum width of two bytes. Suppose this data type is sufficient to represent a quantity sold field. When quantity sold fields are summed, the sum may require a number larger than two bytes. If the DBMS uses the field's data type for results of any mathematics on that field, the two-byte length will not work. Some data types have special manipulation capabilities; for example, only the DATE data type allows true date arithmetic.

Table 6-1 *Commonly Used Data Types in Oracle 10i*

Data Type	Description
VARCHAR2	Variable-length character data with a maximum length of 4000 characters; you must enter a maximum field length (e.g., VARCHAR2(30) for a field with a maximum length of 30 characters). A value less than 30 characters will consume only the required space.
CHAR	Fixed-length character data with a maximum length of 2000 characters; default length is 1 character (e.g. CHAR(5) for a field with a fixed length of 5 characters, capable of holding a value from 0 to 5 characters long).
LONG	Capable of storing up to 2 gigabytes of one variable-length character data field (e.g., to hold a medical instruction or a customer comment).
NUMBER	Positive and negative numbers in the range 10^{-130} to 10^{126}; can specify the precision (total number of digits to the left and right of the decimal point) and the scale (the number of digits to the right of the decimal point) (e.g., NUMBER(5) specifies an integer field with a maximum of 5 digits and NUMBER(5,2) specifies a field with no more than 5 digits and exactly 2 digits to the right of the decimal point).
INTEGER	Positive and negative integers with up to 38 digits (same as SMALL INT).
DATE	Any date from January 1, 4712 B.C. to December 31, 4712 A.D.; date stores the century, year, month, day, hour, minute, and second.
BLOB	Binary large object, capable of storing up to 4 gigabytes of binary data (e.g., a photograph or sound clip).

Coding and Compression Techniques Some attributes have a sparse set of values or are so large that given data volumes, considerable storage space will be consumed. (Large data fields mean that data are farther apart, which yields slower data processing.) A field with a limited number of possible values can be translated into a code that requires less space. Consider the example of the product Finish field illustrated in Figure 6-2. Products at Pine Valley Furniture come in only a limited number of woods: Birch, Maple, and Oak. By creating a code or translation table, each Finish field value can be replaced by a code, a cross-reference to the look-up table, similar to a foreign key. This will decrease the amount of space for the Finish field, and hence for the PRODUCT file. There will be additional space for the FINISH look-up table, and when the Finish field value is needed, an extra access (called a join) to this look-up table will be required. If the Finish field is infrequently used or the number of distinct Finish values very large, the relative advantages of coding may outweigh the

Figure 6-2
Example code look-up table (Pine Valley Furniture Company)

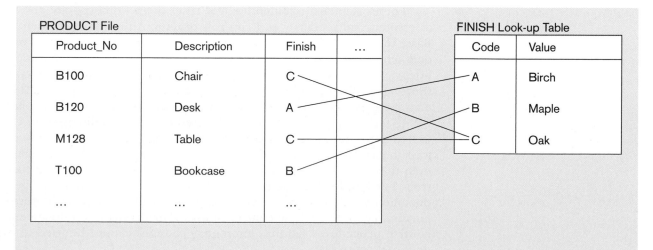

costs. Note that the code table would not appear in the conceptual or logical model. The code table is a physical construct to achieve data processing performance improvements, not a set of data with business value.

A form of a code table is used by data compression techniques, such as file zip routines. A data compression technique looks for patterns in data and then codes frequently appearing patterns with fewer bits. Although such routines are typically used to compress a whole file, such a routine could be used with some DBMSs to compress specific fields. Related to data compression techniques are encryption techniques, which translate a field into a secure format. In both cases, for a user to see the actual field value, software must know the reverse translation process.

Controlling Data Integrity–A Foundation for Sarbanes-Oxley Compliance

Accurate data are essential for compliance with new national and international regulations on financial reporting. These laws, such as Sarbanes-Oxley (SOX) in the United States and Basel II for international banking are reactions to recent cases of fraud and deception by executives in major corporations and partners in public accounting firms. The purpose of SOX is to protect investors by improving the accuracy and reliability of corporate disclosures made pursuant to the securities laws, and for other purposes. The Act requires all financial reports to include an internal control report. This is designed to show that not only are the company's financial data accurate, but the company has confidence in them because adequate controls (e.g., database integrity controls) are in place to safeguard financial data.

SOX is the most recent regulation in a stream of efforts to improve financial data reporting. COSO (the Committee of Sponsoring Organizations of the Treadway Commission) is a voluntary private sector organization dedicated to improving the quality of financial reporting through business ethics, effective internal controls, and corporate governance. COSO was originally formed in 1985 to sponsor the National Commission on Fraudulent Financial Reporting, an independent private sector initiative that studied the causal factors that can lead to fraudulent financial reporting and developed recommendations for public companies and their independent auditors, for the SEC and other regulators, and for educational institutions. COBIT (Control Objectives for Information and Related Technologies) is an open standard published by the IT Governance Institute and the Information Systems Audit and Control Association. It is an IT control framework built in part upon the COSO framework. ITIL stands for the IT Infrastructure Library, published by the Office of Government Commerce in Great Britain. It focuses on IT services and is often used to complement the COBIT framework.

Theses standards, guidelines, and rules focus on corporate governance, risk assessment, and security and controls of data. Although laws, such as SOX and Basel II, require comprehensive audits of all procedures that deal with financial data, compliance can be greatly enhanced by a strong foundation of basic data integrity controls. Because such preventive controls are applied consistently and thoroughly if designed into the database and enforced by the DBMS, field level data integrity controls can be viewed very positively in compliance audits. Other DBMS features, such as triggers and stored procedures, discussed in Chapter 8, as well as audit trails and activity logs, discussed in Chapter 12, provide even further ways to ensure that only legitimate data values are stored in the database. However, even these control mechanisms are only as good as the underlying field data controls. Further, for full compliance, all data integrity controls must be thoroughly documented; defining these controls for the DBMS is a form of documentation. Further, changes to these controls must occur through well documented change control procedures (so that temporary changes cannot be used to bypass well-designed controls).

For many DBMSs, data integrity controls (i.e., controls on the possible value a field can assume) can be built into the physical structure of the fields and controls enforced by the DBMS on those fields. The data type enforces one form of data integrity control because it may limit the type of data (numeric or character) and the length of a field value. Some other typical integrity controls that a DBMS may support are the following:

- *Default value* A default value is the value a field will assume unless a user enters an explicit value for an instance of that field. Assigning a default value to a field can reduce data entry time because entry of a value can be skipped and it can also help to reduce data entry errors for the most common value.

- *Range control* A range control limits the set of permissible values a field may assume. The range may be a numeric lower to upper bound or a set of specific values. Range controls must be used with caution because the limits of the range may change over time. A combination of range controls and coding led to the Year 2000 problem faced by many organizations, in which a field for year is represented by only the numbers 00 to 99. It is better to implement any range controls through a DBMS because range controls in programs may be inconsistently enforced, and it is more difficult to find and change them.

- *Null value control* A null value was defined in Chapter 5 as an empty value. Each primary key must have an integrity control that prohibits a null value. Any other required field may also have a null value control placed on it if that is the policy of the organization. For example, a university may prohibit adding a course to its database unless that course has a title as well as a value of the primary key, Course _ID. Many fields legitimately may have a null value, so this control should be used only when truly required by business rules.

- *Referential integrity* The term "referential integrity" was defined in Chapter 5. Referential integrity on a field is a form of range control in which the value of that field must exist as the value in some field in another row of the same or different table. That is, the range of legitimate values comes from the dynamic contents of a field in a database table, not from some prespecified set of values. Note that referential integrity guarantees that only some existing cross-referencing value is used, not that it is the correct one. A coded field will have referential integrity with the primary key of the associated look-up table.

Handling Missing Data When a field may be null, simply entering no value may be sufficient. For example, suppose a customer zip code field is null and a report summarizes total sales by month and zip code. How should sales to customers with unknown zip codes be handled? Two options for handling or preventing missing data have already been mentioned: using a default value and not permitting missing (null) values. Missing data are inevitable. According to Babad and Hoffer (1984), other possible methods for handling missing data are the following:

- Substitute an estimate of the missing value. For example, for a missing sales value when computing monthly product sales, use a formula involving the mean of the existing monthly sales values for that product indexed by total sales for that month across all products. Such estimates must be marked so that users know that these are not actual values.

- Track missing data so that special reports and other system elements cause people to resolve unknown values quickly. This can be done by setting up a trigger in the database definition. A trigger is a routine that will automatically execute when some event occurs or time period passes. One trigger could log the missing entry to a file when a null or other missing value is stored, and another trigger runs periodically to create a report of the contents of this log file.

- Perform sensitivity testing so that missing data are ignored unless knowing a value might significantly change results; if, for example, total monthly sales for a particular salesperson are almost over a threshold that would make a difference in that person's compensation. This is the most complex of the methods mentioned and hence requires the most sophisticated programming. Such routines for handling missing data may be written in application programs. Many modern DBMSs now have more sophisticated programming capabilities, such as case expressions, user-defined functions, and triggers, so that such logic can be available in the database for all users without application-specific programming.

DESIGNING PHYSICAL RECORDS AND DENORMALIZATION

Physical record: A group of fields stored in adjacent memory locations and retrieved and written together as a unit by a DBMS.

In a logical data model, you group into a relation those attributes that are determined by the same primary key. In contrast, a **physical record** is a group of fields stored in adjacent memory locations and retrieved and written together as a unit by a DBMS. The design of a physical record involves choosing the sequencing of fields into adjacent storage locations to achieve two goals: efficient use of secondary storage and data processing speed.

The efficient use of secondary storage is influenced by both the size of the physical record and the structure of secondary storage. Computer operating systems read data from hard disks in units called pages, not physical records. A **page** is the amount of data read or written by an operating system in one secondary memory input or output operation. The page size is fixed by system programmers and is selected to use most efficiently RAM across all applications. Depending on the computer system, a physical record may or may not be allowed to span two pages. Thus, if page length is not an integer multiple of the physical record length, wasted space may occur at the end of a page. The number of physical records per page is called the **blocking factor**. If storage space is scarce and physical records cannot span pages, creating multiple physical records from one logical relation will minimize wasted storage space. Some DBMSs will also block multiple physical records into a data block; in this case, the DBMS manages a data block, whereas the operating system manages a page.

Page: The amount of data read or written by an operating system in one secondary memory (disk) input or output (I/O) operation. For I/O with a magnetic tape, the equivalent term is record block.

Blocking factor: The number of physical records per page.

Denormalization

The preceding discussion of physical record design concentrated on efficient use of storage space (reducing redundancy). In most cases, the second goal of physical record design—efficient data processing—dominates the design process. Efficient processing of data, just like efficient accessing of books in a library, depends on how close together related data (books or indexes) are. Often all the attributes that appear within a relation are not used together, and data from different relations are needed together to answer a query or produce a report. Thus, although normalized relations solve data maintenance anomalies and minimize redundancies (and storage space), normalized relations, if implemented one for one as physical records, may not yield efficient data processing.

A fully normalized database usually creates many tables. For a frequently used query that requires data from multiple, related tables, the DBMS can spend considerable computer resources each time the query is submitted in matching up (called joining) related rows from each table required to build the query result. Because this joining work is so time-consuming, the processing performance difference between totally normalized and partially normalized databases can be dramatic. Inmon (1988) reports of a study to quantify fully and partially normalized databases. A fully normalized database contained eight tables with about 50,000 rows each, another partially normalized one had four tables with roughly 25,000 rows each, and yet another partially normalized database had two tables. The result showed that the less than fully normalized databases could be as much as an order of magnitude faster than the fully normalized one. Although such results depend greatly on the database and the type of processing against it, these results suggest that you should carefully consider whether the physical records should exactly match the normalized relations for a database.

Denormalization is the process of transforming normalized relations into unnormalized physical record specifications. We will review various forms of, reasons for, and cautions about denormalization in this section. In general, denormalization may partition a relation into several physical records, may combine attributes from several relations together into one physical record, or may do a combination of both.

Denormalize with Caution   Denormalization has it critics. As Finkelstein (1988) points out, denormalization can increase the chance of errors and inconsistencies (caused by reintroducing anomalies into the database) and can force the reprogramming of systems if business rules change. For example, redundant copies of the same data caused by a violation of second normal form are often not updated in a synchronized way. And, if they are, extra programming is required to ensure that all copies of exactly the same business data are updated together. Further, denormalization optimizes certain data processing at the expense of others, so if the frequencies of different processing activities change, the benefits of denormalization may no longer exist. Denormalization almost always also leads to more storage space for raw data and maybe more space for database overhead (e.g., indexes). Thus, denormalization should be an explicit act to gain significant processing speed when other physical design actions are not sufficient to achieve processing expectations.

Pascal (2002a and 2002b) passionately reports of the many dangers of denormalization. The motivation for denormalization is that a normalized database often creates many tables, and joining tables slows database processing. Pascal argues that this is not necessarily true, so the motivation for denormalization may be without merit in some cases. Overall, performance does not depend solely on the number of tables accessed, but rather also on how the tables are organized in the database (what we later call file organizations and clustering), the proper programming of queries, and the query optimization capabilities of the DBMS. Thus, to avoid the problems associated with the data anomalies in denormalized databases, Pascal recommends first attempting to use these other means to achieve the necessary performance. This often will be sufficient, but in those cases when further steps are needed, you must understand the opportunities for applying denormalization.

Hoberman (2002) has written a very useful two-part "denormalization survival guide," which summarizes the major factors (those outlined above and a few others) in deciding whether or not to denormalize.

Opportunities and Types of Denormalization   Rogers (1989) introduces several common denormalization opportunities (Figures 6-3 through Figure 6-5 show examples of normalized and denormalized relations for each of these three situations):

1. *Two entities with a one-to-one relationship*   Even if one of the entities is an optional participant, if the matching entity exists most of the time, then it may be wise to combine these two relations into one record definition (especially if the access frequency between these two entity types is high). Figure 6-3 shows student data with optional data from a standard scholarship application a student may complete. In this case, one record could be formed with four fields from the STUDENT and SCHOLARSHIP APPLICATION normalized relations (assuming Application_ID is no longer needed). (Note: In this case, fields from the optional entity must have null values allowed.)

Denormalization: The process of transforming normalized relations into unnormalized physical record specifications.

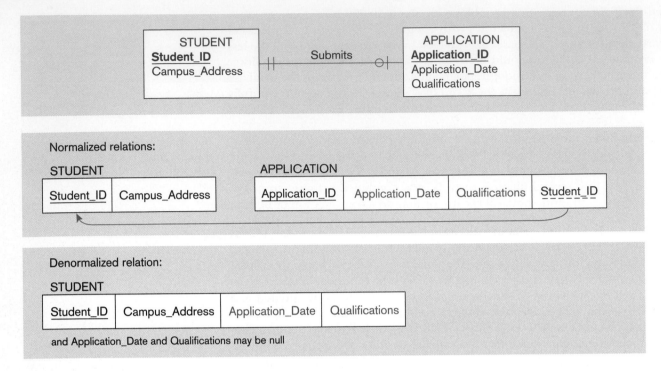

Figure 6-3
A possible denormalization situation: two entities with one-to-one relationship (*Note:* We assume Application_ID is not necessary when all fields are stored in one record, but this field can be included if it is required application data.)

2. *A many-to-many relationship (associative entity) with nonkey attributes*   Rather than joining three files to extract data from the two basic entities in the relationship, it may be advisable to combine attributes from one of the entities into the record representing the many-to-many relationship, thus avoiding one join operation in many data access modules. Again, this would be most advantageous if this joining occurs frequently. Figure 6-4 shows price quotes for different items from different vendors. In this case, fields from ITEM and PRICE QUOTE relations might be combined into one record to avoid having to join all three files together. (Note: This may create considerable duplication of data; in the example, the ITEM fields, such as Description, would repeat for each price quote. This would necessitate excessive updating if duplicated data change. Careful analysis of a composite usage map to study access frequencies and the number of occurrences of PRICE QUOTE per associated VENDOR or ITEM would be essential to understand the consequences of such possible denormalization.)

3. *Reference data*   Reference data exist in an entity on the one-side of a one-to-many relationship, and this entity participates in no other database relationships. You should seriously consider merging the two entities in this situation into one record definition when there are few instances of the entity on the many-side for each entity instance on the one-side. See Figure 6-5 in which several ITEMs have the same STORAGE INSTRUCTIONS and STORAGE INSTRUCTIONS only relate to ITEMs. In this case, the storage instruction data could be stored in the ITEM record creating, of course, redundancy and potential for extra data maintenance. (Instr_ID is no longer needed.)

The opportunities just listed all deal with combining tables to avoid doing joins. In contrast, denormalization can also be used to create more tables by partitioning a relation into multiple tables. Either horizontal or vertical partitioning, or a combination, is possible. **Horizontal partitioning** breaks a relation into multiple record specifications by placing different rows into different physical files based on common

Horizontal partitioning: Distributing the rows of a table into several separate files.

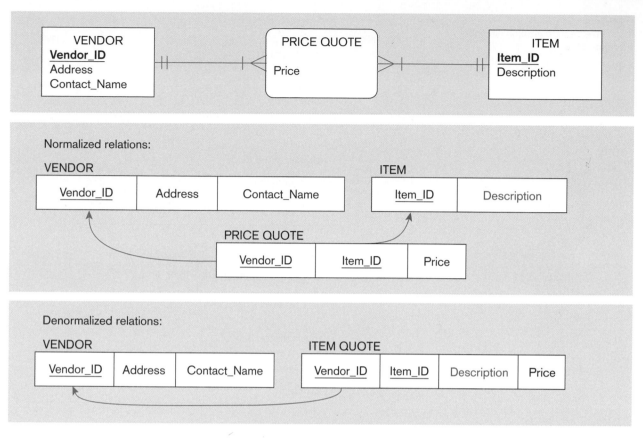

Figure 6-4
A possible denormalization situation: a many-to-many relationship with nonkey attributes

column values. In a library setting, horizontal partitioning is similar to placing the business journals in a business library, the science books in a science library, and so on. Each file created from the partitioning has the same record layout. For example, a customer relation could be broken into four regional customer files based on the value of a field Region.

Horizontal partitioning makes sense when different categories of rows of a table are processed separately; for example, for the customer table just mentioned, if a high percentage of the data processing needs to work with only one region at a time. Horizontal partitioning can also be more secure since file level security can be used to prohibit users from seeing certain rows of data. Also, each partitioned table can be organized differently, appropriate for the way it is individually used. It is likely also faster to recover one of the partitioned files than one file with all the rows. In addition, taking one of the partitioned files out of service because it was damaged or so it can be recovered still allows processing against the other partitioned files to continue. Finally, each of the partitioned files can be placed on a separate disk drive to reduce contention for the same drive and hence improve performance across the database. These advantages of horizontal partitioning (actually all forms of partitioning), along with the disadvantages, are summarized in Table 6-2.

Note that horizontal partitioning is very similar to creating a supertype/subtype relationship because different types of the entity (where the subtype discriminator is the field used for segregating rows) are involved in different relationships, hence different processing. In fact, when you have a supertype/subtype relationship, you need to decide if you will create separate tables for each subtype or combine them in various combinations. Combining makes sense when all subtypes are used about the same way, whereas partitioning the supertype entity into multiple files makes sense when the subtypes are handled differently in transactions, queries, and reports. When

Figure 6-5
A possible denormalization situation: reference data

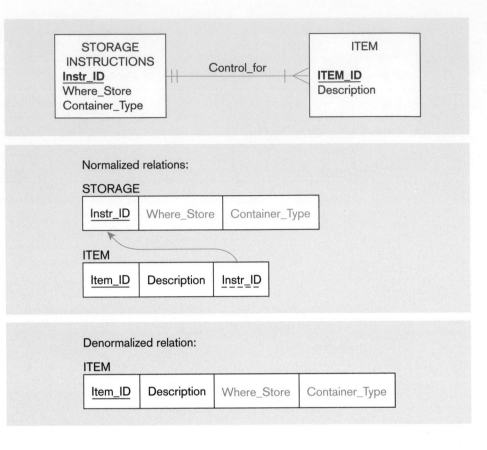

a relation is partitioned horizontally, the whole set of rows can be reconstructed by the SQL UNION operator (described in Chapter 7). Thus, for example, all customer data can be viewed together when desired.

The Oracle DBMS supports several forms of horizontal partitioning, designed in particular to deal with very large tables (Brobst et al., 1999). A table is partitioned

Table 6-2   Advantages and Disadvantages of Data Partitioning

Advantages of Partitioning

1. *Efficiency*:   Data used together are stored close to one another and separate from data not used together.

2. *Local optimization*:   Each partition of data can be stored to optimize performance for its own use.

3. *Security*:   Data not relevant to one group of users can be segregated from data they are allowed to use.

4. *Recovery and uptime*:   Smaller files will take less time to recover, and other files are still accessible if one file is damaged, so the effects of damage are isolated.

5. *Load balancing*:   Files can be allocated to different storage areas (disks or other media), which minimizes contention for access to the same storage area or even allows for parallel access to the different areas.

Disadvantages of Partitioning

1. *Inconsistent access speed*:   Different partitions may yield different access speeds, thus confusing users. Also, when data must be combined across partitions, users may have to deal with significantly slower response times than in a nonpartitioned approach.

2. *Complexity*:   Partitioning is usually not transparent to programmers, who will have to write more complex programs when combining data across partitions.

3. *Extra space and update time*:   Data may be duplicated across the partitions, taking extra storage space compared to storing all the data in normalized files. Updates which affect data in multiple partitions can take more time than if one file were used.

when it is defined to the DBMS using the SQL data definition language (you will learn about the CREATE TABLE command in Chapter 7); that is, in Oracle, there is one table with several partitions, not separate tables per se. Oracle 10i has three horizontal partitioning methods:

1. *Key range partitioning,* in which each partition is defined by a range of values (lower and upper key value limits) for one or more columns of the normalized table. A table row is inserted in the proper partition based on its initial values for the range fields. Because partition key values may follow patterns, each partition may hold quite a different number of rows. A partition key may be generated by the database designer to create a more balanced distribution of rows. A row may be restricted from moving between partitions when key values are updated.

2. *Hash partitioning,* in which data are evenly spread across partitions independent of any partition key value. Hash partitioning overcomes the uneven distribution of rows that is possible with key range partitioning.

3. *Composite partitioning,* which combines aspects of both key range and hash partitioning. Partitions can be transparent to the database user. (You need to refer to a partition only if you want to force the query processor to look at one or more partitions.) The part of the DBMS that optimizes the processing of a query will look at the definition of partitions for a table involved in a query and will automatically decide if certain partitions can be eliminated when retrieving the data needed to form the query results, which can drastically improve query processing performance.

For example, suppose a transaction date is used to define partitions in key range partitioning. A query asking for only recent transactions can be more quickly processed by looking at only the one or few partitions with the most recent transactions rather than scanning the database or even using indexes to find rows in the desired range from a nonpartitioned table. A partition on date also isolates insertions of new rows to one partition, which may reduce the overhead of database maintenance, and dropping "old" transactions will require simply dropping a partition. Indexes can still be used with a partitioned table and can improve performance even more than partitioning alone. See Brobst et al. (1999) for more details on the pros and cons of using dates for key range partitioning.

In hash partitioning, rows are more evenly spread across the partitions. If partitions are placed in different storage areas that can be processed in parallel, then query performance will improve noticeably compared to when all the data have to be accessed sequentially in one storage area for the whole table. As with key range partitioning, the existence of partitions can be transparent to a programmer of a query. With composite partitioning, partitions are defined by key ranges, and then subpartitions are defined by key hashing. Composite partitioning combines the advantages of range separation with the parallel processing of key hashing.

Vertical partitioning distributes the columns of a relation into separate physical records, repeating the primary key in each of the records. An example of vertical partitioning would be breaking apart a part relation by placing the part number along with accounting-related part data into one record specification, the part number along with engineering-related part data into another record specification, and the part number along with sales-related part data into yet another record specification. The advantages and disadvantages of vertical partitioning are similar to those for horizontal partitioning. When, for example, accounting-, engineering-, and sales-related part data need to be used together, these tables can be joined. Thus, neither horizontal nor vertical partitioning prohibits the ability to treat the original relation as a whole.

Combinations of horizontal and vertical partitioning are also possible. This form of denormalization—record partitioning—is especially common for a database

Vertical partitioning: Distributing the columns of a table into several separate physical records.

whose files are distributed across multiple computers. Thus, you study this topic again in Chapter 13.

A single physical table can be logically partitioned or several tables logically combined by using a concept of a user view, which will be defined in Chapter 7. With a user view, users can be given the impression that the database contains tables other than what are physically defined; you can create these logical tables by horizontal or vertical partitioning or other forms of denormalization. However, the purpose of any form of user view, including logical partitioning via views, is to simplify query writing and to create a more secure database, not to improve query performance. One form of a user view available in Oracle is called a Partition View. With a Partition View, physically separate tables with similar structures can be logically combined into one table using the SQL UNION operator. There are limitations to this form of partitioning. First, because there are actually multiple separate physical tables, there cannot be any global index on all the combined rows. Second, each physical table must be separately managed, so data maintenance is more complex (e.g., a new row must be inserted into a specific table). Third, the query optimizer has fewer options with a Partition View than with partitions of a single table for creating the most efficient query processing plan.

The final form of denormalization we introduce is data replication. With data replication, the same data are purposely stored in multiple places in the database. For example, consider again Figure 6-1. You learned earlier in this section that relations can be denormalized by combining data from an associative entity with data from one of the simple entities with which it is associated. So, in Figure 6-1, QUOTATION data might be stored with PURCHASED PART data in one expanded PURCHASED PART physical record specification. With data duplication, the same QUOTATION data might also be stored with its associated SUPPLIER data in another expanded SUPPLIER physical record specification. With this data duplication, once either a SUPPLIER or PURCHASED PART record is retrieved, the related QUOTATION data will also be available without any further access to secondary memory. This improved speed is worthwhile only if QUOTATION data are frequently accessed with SUPPLIER and with PURCHASED PART data and if the costs for extra secondary storage and data maintenance are not great.

DESIGNING PHYSICAL FILES

Physical file: A named portion of secondary memory (a magnetic tape or hard disk) allocated for the purpose of storing physical records.

A **physical file** is a named portion of secondary memory (such as a magnetic tape or hard disk) allocated for the purpose of storing physical records. Some computer operating systems allow a physical file to be split into separate pieces, sometimes called extents. In subsequent sections, we will assume that a physical file is not split and that each record in a file has the same structure. That is, subsequent sections address how to store and link relational table rows from a single database in physical storage space. In order to optimize the performance of the database processing, the person who administers a database, the database administrator, often needs to know extensive details about how the database management system manages physical storage space. This knowledge is very DBMS specific, but the principles described in subsequent sections are the foundation for the physical data structures used by most relational DBMSs.

Most database management systems store many different kinds of data in one operating system file. By an operating system file we mean a named file that would appear on a disk directory listing (such as a listing of the files in a folder on the C: drive of your personal computer). For example, an important structure for physical storage space in Oracle is a tablespace. A **tablespace** is a named set of disk storage elements in which data from one or more database tables may be stored. An instance of Oracle will include many tablespaces, for example, one for system data

Tablespace: A named set of disk storage elements in which physical files for database tables may be stored.

(data dictionary or data about data), one for temporary work space, one for database recovery, and several to hold user business data. One or more tablespaces are contained in a physical operating system file. Thus, Oracle has responsibility for managing the storage of data inside a tablespace, whereas the operating system has many responsibilities for managing a tablespace as a whole as it would any operating system file (e.g., handling file level security, allocating space, and responding to disk read and write errors).

Because an instance of Oracle usually supports many databases for many users, the database administrator usually will create many user tablespaces, which helps to achieve database security by giving each user selected rights to access each tablespace. As noted above, as an operating system file, a tablespace may be spread over several **extents,** where an extent is a contiguous section of disk storage space. When a tablespace needs to enlarge to hold more data, it is assigned another extent. Each database table is assigned to one or more tablespaces. (Each table row is in one and only one tablespace, but different rows from the same table may be in different tablespaces.) A tablespace may contain data from one or more tables. Managing tablespaces, or physical database files, is a significant job of a database administrator in an Oracle environment. For example, by locating different tablespaces on different devices or channels and spreading tables across tablespaces, a database administrator can minimize disk drive contention across concurrent database users. Because this is not a text on Oracle, we do not cover specific details on managing tablespaces; however, the general principles of physical database design apply to the design and management of Oracle tablespaces as they do to whatever the physical storage unit is for any database management system. Figure 6-6 is an EER model that shows the relationships between various physical and logical database terms related to physical database design in an Oracle environment.

Extent: A contiguous section of disk storage space.

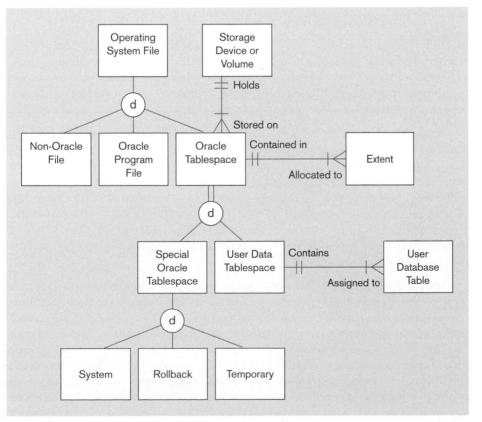

Figure 6-6
Physical file terminology in an Oracle environment

Pointer

Pointer: A field of data that can be used to locate a related field or record of data.

All files are organized by using two basic constructs to link one piece of data with another piece of data: sequential storage and pointers. With sequential storage, one field or record is stored right after another field or record. Although simple to implement and use, sometimes sequential storage is not the most efficient way to organize data. A **pointer** is a field of data that can be used to locate a related field or record of data. In most cases, a pointer contains the address, or location, of the associated data. Pointers are used in a wide variety of data storage structures; however, we will see only a few of their uses in this chapter. The interested reader can read Appendix C for a broader coverage of the use of pointers. We define pointer here only because knowing what a pointer is necessary for understanding file organizations. You will likely never work directly with pointers because the DBMS will handle all pointer use and maintenance automatically.

File Organizations

File organization: A technique for physically arranging the records of a file on secondary storage devices.

A **file organization** is a technique for physically arranging the records of a file on secondary storage devices. With modern relational DBMSs, you do not have to design file organizations, but you may be allowed to select an organization and its parameters for a table or physical file. In choosing a file organization for a particular file in a database, you should consider seven important factors:

1. Fast data retrieval
2. High throughput for processing data input and maintenance transactions
3. Efficient use of storage space
4. Protection from failures or data loss
5. Minimizing need for reorganization
6. Accommodating growth
7. Security from unauthorized use

Often these objectives conflict, and you must select a file organization that provides a reasonable balance among the criteria within resources available.

In this chapter, we consider the following families of basic file organizations: sequential, indexed, and hashed. Figure 6-7 illustrates each of these organizations with the nicknames of some university sports teams.

Sequential file organization: The storage of records in a file in sequence according to a primary key value.

Sequential File Organizations   In a **sequential file organization,** the records in the file are stored in sequence according to a primary key value (see Figure 6-7a). To locate a particular record, a program must normally scan the file from the beginning until the desired record is located. A common example of a sequential file is the alphabetical list of persons in the white pages of a telephone directory (ignoring any index that may be included with the directory). A comparison of the capabilities of sequential files with the other two types of files appears later in Table 6-3. Because of their inflexibility, sequential files are not used in a database, but may be used for files that back up data from a database.

Indexed file organization: The storage of records either sequentially or nonsequentially with an index that allows software to locate individual records.

Index: A table or other data structure used to determine the location of rows in a file that satisfy some condition.

Secondary key: One field or a combination of fields for which more than one record may have the same combination of values. Also called a nonunique key.

Indexed File Organizations   In an **indexed file organization,** the records are stored either sequentially or nonsequentially, and an index is created that allows the application software to locate individual records (see Figure 6-7b). Like a card catalog in a library, an **index** is a table that is used to determine the location of rows in a file that satisfy some condition. Each index entry matches a key value with one or more records. An index can point to unique records (a primary key index, such as on the Product_ID field of a product record) or to potentially more than one record. An index that allows each entry to point to more than one record is called a **secondary key** index. Secondary key indexes are important for supporting many reporting

Figure 6-7 (Continues)
Comparison of file organizations
(a) Sequential

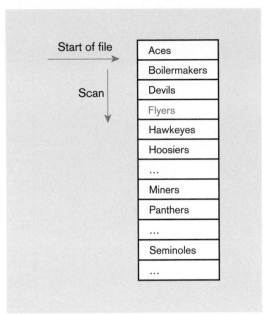

(b) Indexed

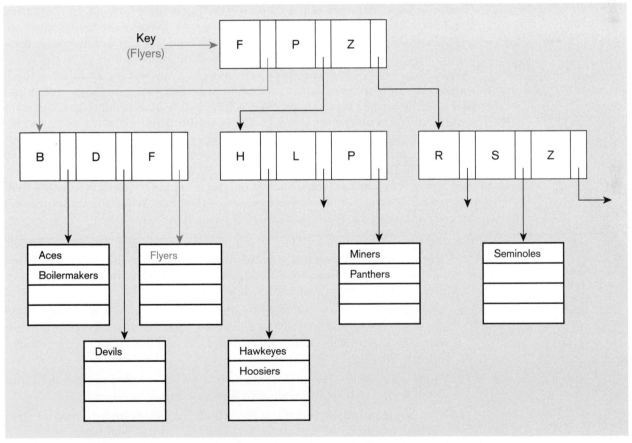

requirements and for providing rapid ad hoc data retrieval. An example would be an index on the Finish field of a product record. Because indexes are extensively used with relational DBMSs, and the choice of what index and how to store the index entries matters greatly in database processing performance, we review indexed file organizations in more detail than the other types of file organizations.

Figure 6-7 (Continued)
(c) Hashed

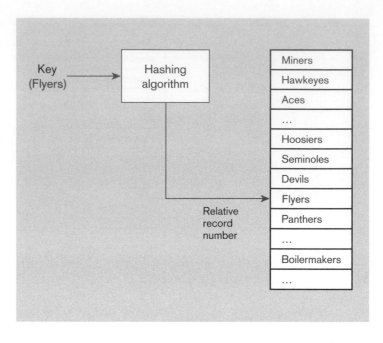

Some index structures influence where table rows are stored, and other index structures are independent of where rows are located. Because the actual structure of an index does not influence database design and is not important in writing database queries, we will not address the actual physical structure of indexes in this chapter. Thus, Figure 6-7b should be considered a logical view of how an index is used, not a physical view of how data are stored in an index structure. Some relational DBMSs use the term primary index (that is different from a primary key index) to designate an index that determines the physical location of data, whereas a secondary index (again, distinct from secondary key index) is an index that plays no role in determining the storage location of data. For these systems, a table will have one primary index and may have many secondary indexes. The primary index may use the primary key of the table or may not; and a secondary index may use a field that is unique or is not unique across the rows of the table. When the terms primary and secondary index are used, there are four types of indexes:

1. Unique primary index (UPI), which is an index on a unique field, possibly the primary key of the table, and that not only is used to find table rows based on this field value, but also is used by the DBMS to determine where to store a row based on the primary index field value.

2. Nonunique primary index (NUPI), which is an index on a nonunique field and which not only is used to find table rows based on this field value, but also is used by the DBMS to determine where to store a row based on the primary index field value.

3. Unique secondary index (USI), which is an index on a unique field and which is used only to find table rows based on this field value.

4. Nonunique secondary index (NUSI), which is an index on a nonunique field and which is used only to find table rows based on this field value.

The example in Figure 6-7b illustrates that indexes can be built on top of indexes, creating a hierarchical set of indexes. This may be desirable because an index itself is a file and, if it is very large, it too can be organized by indexing the index. Each index entry in Figure 6-7b has a key value and a pointer to another index or to a data record. For example, to find the record with key "Flyers," the file organization would start at the top index and take the pointer after the entry F, which points to another index for all keys that begin with the letters A through F in the alphabet. Then the software would follow the pointer after the F in this index, which represents all those records with keys that begin with the letters E through F. Eventually, the search through the indexes either locates the desired record or indicates that no such record exists.

One of the most powerful capabilities of indexed file organizations is the ability to create multiple indexes. Multiple indexes exist in a library, where there are indexes on title, author, and subject pointing to the same set of books and journals. Thus, we can virtually create another file by simply creating another index on the same set of data records, so the voluminous data are not replicated. Multiple indexes can be manipulated. For example, if we use the Finish index to find the addresses for the set of product records with the Birch finish and the Cost index to find the set of product records that cost under $500 to make, we can intersect these two intermediate result sets to find the addresses of those products, and only those products, that are Birch and cost under $500. This ability to use multiple indexes in one query is important in processing queries against a relational database. Logical AND, OR, and NOT operations can be handled by simply manipulating results from an index scan, thus avoiding the more costly access to data records that do not meet all the qualifications of the query.

The general structure of a hierarchical index like that in Figure 6-7b is called a tree (with the root node at the top and leaf nodes at the bottom—yes, the tree is upside down!). The performance of a tree of index entries is greatly influenced by the properties of the tree structure used. A common type of tree used by database management systems to store indexes is a balanced tree, or B-tree, and the most popular form of a B-tree is a B+-tree. In a B-tree, all the leaves (which typically contain the data records or pointers to each record) are stored at the same distance from the root, as in Figure 6-7b in which all the data records are stored two levels from the root. The operating system and DBMS transparently manage whatever index tree structure is used. As database designer, you may have no or only a few choices for the type or general parameters of an index you want to create (e.g., how much space to allocate for the index, where to store the index file relative to the associated data file). Appendix C includes a review of tree data structures and the parameters of a tree design over which you might have some control.

One choice you might have when defining an index is to create it as a **bitmap index**. A bitmap index (see Figure 6-8) assigns a bitmap for each key value. Suppose a Product table has 10 rows and the Price attribute has 4 different values (100, 200, 300, and 400) in these 10 rows. (This example is small for illustration purposes.) A bitmap index on the Price field would have four entries with ten bits per entry. Each bit in each bitmap entry matches a row in the Product table. If, for example, bit 8 is

Bitmap index: A table of bits in which each row represents the distinct values of a key and each column is a bit, which when on indicates that the record for that bit column position has the associated field value.

Figure 6-8
Bitmap index on Product Price attribute

Product Table Row Numbers										
Price	1	2	3	4	5	6	7	8	9	10
100	0	0	1	0	1	0	0	0	0	0
200	1	0	0	0	0	0	0	0	0	0
300	0	1	0	0	0	0	1	0	0	1
400	0	0	0	1	0	1	0	1	1	0

Products 3 and 5 have Price $100
Product 1 has Price $200
Products 2, 7, and 10 have Price $300
Products 4, 6, 8, and 9 have Price $400

on for the entry Price of $400, it indicates that row 8 of the Product table has Price $400. (Each bit column will have only one bit on.) A bitmap is ideal for attributes that have even a few possible values, which is not true for conventional tree indexes. A bitmap also often requires less storage space (possibly as little as 25 percent) than a conventional tree index does (Schumacher, 1997), but for an attribute with many distinct values, a bitmap index can exceed the storage space of a conventional tree index. In the proper situation, because bit manipulation and searching is so fast, the speed of query processing with a bitmap can be ten times faster than that of a conventional tree index.

An interesting feature of a bitmap index is that one bitmap can be used for multiple keys. For example, we could add another set of rows to the bottom of Figure 6-8 for all the values of the Room attribute. Then, each bit column would have two bits on, one for the associated Product row's price and one for room. A query looking for $100 products for the dining room can intersect the bit pattern for the $100 price row with the dining room row to find only those products that satisfy both conditions. Bit manipulation of this nature can be very efficient.

Transaction processing applications require rapid response to queries that involve one or a few related table rows. For example, to enter a new customer order, an order entry application needs to find the specific customer table row rapidly, a few product table rows for the items being purchased, possibly a few other product table rows based on the characteristics of the products the customer wants (e.g., product finish), and then one customer order and one customer shipment row need to be added by the application to the respective tables. The types of indexes discussed so far work very well in an application that is searching for a few, specific table rows.

Another increasingly popular type of index, especially in data warehousing and other decision support applications (see Chapter 11), is a join index. In decision support applications, the data accessing tends to want all rows from very large tables that are related to one another (e.g., all the customers who have bought items from the same store). A **join index** is an index on columns from two or more tables that come from the same domain of values. For example, consider Figure 6-9a, which shows two tables, Customer and Store. Each of these tables has a column, City. The join index of the City column indicates the row identifiers for rows in the two tables that have the

Join index: An index on columns from two or more tables that come from the same domain of values.

Figure 6-9
Join indexes
(a) Join index for common nonkey columns

Customer

RowID	Cust#	CustName	City	State
10001	C2027	Hadley	Dayton	Ohio
10002	C1026	Baines	Columbus	Ohio
10003	C0042	Ruskin	Columbus	Ohio
10004	C3861	Davies	Toledo	Ohio
. . .				

Store

RowID	Store#	City	Size	Manager
20001	S4266	Dayton	K2	E2166
20002	S2654	Columbus	K3	E0245
20003	S3789	Dayton	K4	E3330
20004	S1941	Toledo	K1	E0874
. . .				

Figure 6-9 (Continued)

Join Index

CustRowID	StoreRowID	Common Value*
10001	20001	Dayton
10001	20003	Dayton
10002	20002	Columbus
10003	20002	Columbus
10004	20004	Toledo
. . .		

*This column may or may not be included, as needed. Join index could be sorted on any of the three columns. Sometimes two join indexes are created, one as above and one with the two rowID columns reversed.

(b) Join index for matching a foreign key (FK) and a primary key (PK)

Order

RowID	Order#	Order Date	Cust#(FK)
30001	O5532	10/01/2001	C3861
30002	O3478	10/01/2001	C1062
30003	O8734	10/02/2001	C1062
30004	O9845	10/02/2001	C2027
. . .			

Customer

RowID	Cust#(PK)	CustName	City	State
10001	C2027	Hadley	Dayton	Ohio
10002	C1062	Baines	Columbus	Ohio
10003	C0042	Ruskin	Columbus	Ohio
10004	C3861	Davies	Toledo	Ohio
. . .				

Join Index

CustRowID	OrderRowID	Cust#
10001	30004	C2027
10002	30002	C1062
10002	30003	C1062
10004	30001	C3861
. . .		

same City value. Because of the way many data warehouses are designed, there is a high frequency for queries to find data (facts) in common to a store and a customer in the same city (or similar intersections of facts across multiple dimensions). Figure 6-9b shows another possible application for a join index. In this case, the join index precomputes the matching of a foreign key in the Order table with the associated customer in the Customer table. A join index precomputes the result of a relational join operator, which will be discussed in Chapter 7. Simply stated, a join says find rows in the same or different tables that have values that match some criterion.

A join index is created as rows are loaded into a database, so the index, like all other indexes previously discussed, is always up-to-date. Without a join index in the database of Figure 6-9a, any query that wants to find stores and customers in the same city would have to compute the equivalent of the join index each time the query is run. For very large tables, joining all the rows of one table with matching rows in another possibly large table can be very time consuming and can significantly delay responding to an online query. In Figure 6-9b, the join index provides one place for the DBMS to find information about related table rows. A join index, similar to any index, saves query processing time by finding data meeting a prespecified qualification at the expense of the extra storage space and maintenance of the index. Bontempo and Saracco (1996) discuss how to combine join indexing with bitmap indexing to speed up processing of certain types of join indexes.

Ballinger (1998) suggests an extension to a join index that may eliminate the need to access the actual data tables. For example, in Figure 6-9b, besides Cust#, other columns from either or both tables could be included as additional columns in the join index. Then, if the query using the join index requires only columns included in the join index, the base tables are not needed to process the query. When would it make sense to implement this extension? The answer is when the database is rather static, so that the join index, once created, has a fairly long life. This condition is true in many data warehousing environments, in which existing rows are not updated, and new rows are added and obsolete rows are deleted only periodically, for example, monthly. In this case when there are infrequent changes to the database but frequent and complex queries against very large data tables, an extended join index can be a very productive structure for improving query performance.

The use of databases for new applications, such as in data warehousing and online decision support, is generating the development of new types of indexes. We encourage you to investigate the indexing capabilities of the database management system you are using to understand fully when to apply each type of index and how to tune the performance of the index structures.

Hashed File Organizations

Hashed file organization: A storage system in which the address for each record is determined using a hashing algorithm.

Hashing algorithm: A routine that converts a primary key value into a relative record number (or relative file address).

In a **hashed file organization**, the address of each record is determined using a hashing algorithm (see Figure 6-7c). A **hashing algorithm** is a routine that converts a primary key value into a record address. Although there are several variations of hashed files, in most cases the records are located nonsequentially as dictated by the hashing algorithm. Thus, sequential data processing is impractical.

A typical hashing algorithm uses the technique of dividing each primary key value by a suitable prime number and then using the remainder of the division as the relative storage location. For example, suppose that an organization has a set of approximately 1,000 employee records to be stored on magnetic disk. A suitable prime number would be 997, because it is close to 1,000. Now consider the record for employee 12,396. When we divide this number by 997, the remainder is 432. Thus, this record is stored at location 432 in the file. Another technique (not discussed here) must be used to resolve duplicates (or overflow) that can occur with the division/remainder method when two or more keys hash to the same address (known as a "hash clash").

Hash index table: A file organization that uses hashing to map a key into a location in an index, where there is a pointer to the actual data record matching the hash key.

One of the severe limitations of hashing is that because data table row locations are dictated by the hashing algorithm, only one key can be used for hashing-based (storage and) retrieval. Hashing and indexing can be combined into what is called a hash index table to overcome this limitation. A **hash index table** uses hashing to map a key into a location in an index (sometimes called a scatter index table), where there is a pointer to the actual data record matching the hash key. The index is the target of the hashing algorithm, but the actual data are stored separately from the addresses generated by hashing. Because the hashing results in a position in an index, the table rows can be stored independently of the hash address, using whatever file organization for the data table makes sense (e.g., sequential or first available space). Thus, as with other indexing schemes but unlike most pure hashing schemes, there can be several primary and secondary keys, each with its own hashing algorithm and index table, sharing one data table. Also, because an index table is much smaller than a data table, the index can be more easily designed to reduce the likelihood of key collisions, or overflows, than can the more space-consuming data table. Again, the extra storage space for the index adds flexibility and speed for data retrieval, along with the added expense of storing and maintaining the index space. Another use of a hash index table is found in some data warehousing database technologies that use parallel processing. In this situation, the DBMS can evenly distribute data table rows across all storage devices to fairly distribute work across the parallel processors, yet use hashing and indexing to rapidly find on which processor desired data are stored.

One common caveat with all indexing techniques is the difficulty or cost for moving data once a table row is stored. If a row needs to move, then the pointer to it, in every index on the table, must be updated. This can be a significant overhead if the data must be frequently reorganized. (Sometimes this reorganization is caused by excessive deletion of rows and the creation of wasted space, or holes, in the middle of physical file reserved for data table rows.) On the other hand, pure hashing will not permit the moving of data except as part of handling hashing overflows. Thus, a hash index table scheme provides the advantages of very rapid retrieval of data based on multiple key values and the ability to move data, with the disadvantage of an overhead expense to update indexes, if reorganization of the data space becomes important.

As stated earlier, the DBMS will handle the management of any hashing file organization. You do not have to be concerned with handling overflows, accessing indexes, or the hashing algorithm. What is important for you, as a database designer, is to understand the properties of different file organizations so that you can choose the most appropriate one for the type of database processing required in the database and application you are designing. Also, understanding the properties of the file organizations used by the DBMS can help query programmers write a query in a way to take advantage of the file organization properties. As you will see in Chapters 7 and 8, many queries can be written in multiple ways in SQL; different query structures, however, can result in vastly different steps by the DBMS to answer the query. If you know how the DBMS thinks about using a file organization (e.g., what indexes it uses when and how and when it uses a hashing algorithm), you can design better databases and more efficient queries.

Summary of File Organizations

The three families of file organizations cover most of the file organizations you will have at your disposal as you design physical files and databases. Although more complex structures can be built using the data structures outlined in Appendix C, you are unlikely to be able to use these with a database management system.

Table 6-3 summarizes the comparative features of sequential, indexed, and hashed file organizations. You should review this table and study Figure 6-7 to see why each comparative feature is true.

Clustering Files

Some database management systems allow adjacent secondary memory space to contain rows from several tables. In this case, a physical file does not contain records with identical structures. For example, in Oracle, rows from one, two, or more related tables that are often joined together can be stored in the same disk area. A

Table 6-3 Comparative Features of Different File Organizations

Factor	File Organization		
	Sequential	**Indexed**	**Hashed**
Storage Space	No wasted space	No wasted space for data, but extra space for index	Extra space may be needed to allow for addition and deletion of records after initial set of records is loaded
Sequential Retrieval on Primary Key	Very fast	Moderately fast	Impractical, unless use hash index
Random Retrieval on Primary Key	Impractical	Moderately fast	Very fast
Multiple Key Retrieval	Possible, but requires scanning whole file	Very fast with multiple indexes	Not possible, unless use hash index
Deleting Records	Can create wasted space or require reorganizing	If space can be dynamically allocated, this is easy, but requires maintenance of indexes	Very easy
Adding New Records	Requires rewriting file	If space can be dynamically allocated, this is easy, but requires maintenance of indexes	Very easy, except multiple keys with same address require extra work
Updating Records	Usually requires rewriting file	Easy, but requires maintenance of indexes	Very easy

cluster is defined by the tables and the column or columns by which the tables are usually joined. For example, a Customer table and a Customer_Order table would be joined by the common value of Customer_ID, or the rows of a Price_Quote table (which contains prices on items purchased from vendors) might be clustered by common values of Item_ID. Clustering reduces the time to access related records compared to the normal allocation of different files to different areas of a disk. Time is reduced because related records will be closer to each other than if the records are stored in separate files in separate areas of the disk. Defining a table to be in only one cluster reduces retrieval performance for only those tables stored in the same cluster.

The following Oracle database definition commands show how a cluster is defined and tables are assigned to the cluster. First, the cluster (adjacent disk space) is specified, as in the following example:

```
CREATE CLUSTER ORDERING (CLUSTERKEY CHAR(25));
```

The term ORDERING names the cluster space; the term CLUSTERKEY is required but not used again.

Then tables are assigned to the cluster when the tables are created, such as:

```
CREATE TABLE CUSTOMER (
    CUSTOMER_ID          VARCHAR2(25) NOT NULL,
    CUSTOMER_ADDRESS     VARCHAR2(15)
    )
CLUSTER ORDERING (CUSTOMER_ID);

CREATE TABLE ORDER (
    ORDER_ID             VARCHAR2(20) NOT NULL,
    CUSTOMER_ID          VARCHAR2(25) NOT NULL,
    ORDER_DATE           DATE
    )
CLUSTER ORDERING (CUSTOMER_ID);
```

Access to records in a cluster can be specified in Oracle to be via an index on the cluster key or via a hashing function on the cluster key. Reasons for choosing an indexed versus a hashed cluster are similar to those for choosing between indexed and hashed files (see Table 6-3). Clustering records is best used when the records are fairly static. When records are frequently added, deleted, and changed, wasted space can arise, and it may be difficult to locate related records close to one another after the initial loading of records, which defines the clusters. Clustering is, however, one option a file designer has to improve the performance of tables that are frequently used together in the same queries and reports.

Designing Controls for Files

One additional aspect of a database file about which you may have design options is the types of controls you can use to protect the file from destruction or contamination or to reconstruct the file if it is damaged. Because a database file is stored in a proprietary format by the DBMS, there is a basic level of access control. You may require additional security controls on fields, files, or databases. We address these options in detail in Chapters 8 and 12. Briefly, files will be damaged, so the key is the ability to rapidly restore a damaged file. Backup procedures provide a copy of a file and of the transactions that have changed the file. When a file is damaged, the file copy or current file along with the log of transactions is used to recover the file to an uncontaminated state. In terms of security, the most effective method is to encrypt the contents of the file so that only programs with access to the decryption routine will be able to see the file contents. Again, these important topics will be covered later when you study the relational data manipulation language SQL in Chapter 8 and the activities of data and database administration in Chapter 12.

USING AND SELECTING INDEXES

Most database manipulations require locating a row (or collection of rows) that satisfies some condition. For example, we may want to retrieve all customers in a given zip code or all students with a particular major. Scanning every row in a table looking for the desired rows may be unacceptably slow, particularly when tables are large, as they often are in real-world applications. Using indexes, as described earlier, can greatly speed up this process, and defining indexes is an important part of physical database design.

As described in the section on indexes, indexes on a file can be created for either a primary or a secondary key or both. It is typical that an index would be created for the primary key of each table. The index is itself a table with two columns: the key and the address of the record or records that contain that key value. For a primary key, there will be only one entry in the index for each key value.

Creating a Unique Key Index

The Customer table defined in the section on clustering has a primary key of Customer_ID. A unique key index would be created on this field using the following SQL command:

```
CREATE UNIQUE INDEX CUSTINDEX ON CUSTOMER(CUSTOMER_ID);
```

In this command, CUSTINDEX is the name of the index file created to store the index entries. The ON clause specifies which table is being indexed and the column (or columns) that form the index key. When this command is executed, any existing records in the Customer table would be indexed. If there are duplicate values of Customer_ID, the CREATE INDEX command will fail. Once the index is created, the DBMS will reject any insertion or update of data in the CUSTOMER table that would violate the uniqueness constraint on Customer_IDs. Notice that every unique index creates overhead for the DBMS to validate uniqueness for each insertion or update of a table row on which there are unique indexes. We will return to this point later when reviewing when to create an index.

When a composite unique key exists, you simply list all the elements of the unique key in the ON clause. For example, a table of line items on a customer order might have a composite unique key of Order_ID and Product_ID. The SQL command to create this index for the Order_Line table would be as follows:

CREATE UNIQUE INDEX LINEINDEX ON ORDER_LINE(ORDER_ID, PRODUCT_ID);

Creating a Secondary (Nonunique) Key Index

Database users often want to retrieve rows of a relation based on values for various attributes other than the primary key. For example, in a Product table, users might want to retrieve records that satisfy any combination of the following conditions:

- All table products (Description = "Table")
- All oak furniture (Finish = "Oak")
- All dining room furniture (Room = "DR")
- All furniture priced below $500 (Price < 500)

To speed up such retrievals, we can define an index on each attribute that we use to qualify a retrieval. For example, we could create a nonunique index on the Description field of the Product table with the following SQL command:

CREATE INDEX DESCINDX ON PRODUCT(DESCRIPTION);

Notice that the term UNIQUE should not be used with secondary (nonunique) key attributes, because each value of the attribute may be repeated. As with unique keys, a secondary key index can be created on a combination of attributes.

To create a bitmap index, you follow a similar command structure. If we wanted a bitmap index for the Description field, the command would be:

CREATE BITMAP INDEX DESCBITINDX ON PRODUCT(DESCRIPTION);

When to Use Indexes

During physical database design, you must choose which attributes to use to create indexes. There is a trade-off between improved performance for retrievals through the use of indexes and degraded performance (because of the overhead for extensive index maintenance) for inserting, deleting, and updating the indexed records in a file. Thus, indexes should be used generously for databases intended primarily to support data retrievals, such as for decision support and data warehouse applications. Indexes should be used judiciously for databases that support transaction processing and other applications with heavy updating requirements, because the indexes impose additional overhead.

Following are some rules of thumb for choosing indexes for relational databases.

1. Indexes are most useful on larger tables.
2. Specify a unique index for the primary key of each table.
3. Indexes are most useful for columns that frequently appear in WHERE clauses of SQL commands either to qualify the rows to select (e.g., WHERE FINISH = "Oak," for which an index on Finish would speed retrieval) or for linking (joining) tables (e.g., WHERE PRODUCT.PRODUCT_ID = ORDER_LINE.PRODUCT_ID, for which a secondary key index on Product_ID in the Order_Line table and a primary key index on Product_ID in the Product

table would improve retrieval performance). In the latter case, the index is on a foreign key in the Order_Line table that is used in joining tables.

4. Use an index for attributes referenced in ORDER BY (sorting) and GROUP BY (categorizing) clauses. You do have to be careful, though, about these clauses. Be sure that the DBMS will, in fact, use indexes on attributes listed in these clauses (e.g., Oracle uses indexes on attributes in ORDER BY clauses but not GROUP BY clauses).

5. Use an index when there is significant variety in the values of an attribute. Oracle suggests that an index is not useful when there are fewer than 30 different values for an attribute, and an index is clearly useful when there are 100 or more different values for an attribute. Similarly, an index will be helpful only if the results of a query that uses that index do not exceed roughly 20 percent of the total number of records in the file (Schumacher, 1997).

6. Before creating an index on a field with long values, consider first creating a compressed version of the values (coding the field with a surrogate key) and then indexing on the coded version (Catterall, 2005). Large indexes, created from long index fields, can be slower to process than small indexes are.

7. If the key for the index is going to be used for determining the location where the record will be stored (what was called in a prior section a unique primary key or for clustering), then the key for this index should be a surrogate key so that the values cause records to be evenly spread across the storage space (Catterall, 2005). Many DBMSs have a say to create a sequence number so that each new row added to a table is assigned the next number in sequence; this is usually sufficient for creating a surrogate key.

8. Check your DBMS for the limit, if any, on the number of indexes allowable per table. Many systems permit no more than sixteen indexes and may limit the size of an index key value (e.g., no more than 2,000 bytes for each composite value). If there is such a limit in your system, you will have to choose those secondary keys that will most likely lead to improved performance.

9. Be careful indexing attributes that have null values. For many DBMSs, rows with a null value will not be referenced in the index (so they cannot be found from an *index search* of ATTRIBUTE = NULL). Such a search will have to be done by scanning the file.

Selecting indexes is arguably the most important physical database design decision, but it is not the only way you can improve the performance of a database. Other ways address such issues as reducing the costs to relocate records, optimizing the use of extra or so-called free space in files, and optimizing query processing algorithms [see Viehman (1994) for a discussion of these additional ways to enhance physical database design and efficiency]. We briefly discuss the topic of query optimization in a later section of this chapter because such optimization can be used to overrule how the DBMS would use certain database design options included because of their expected improvement in data processing performance in most instances.

RAID: IMPROVING FILE ACCESS PERFORMANCE BY PARALLEL PROCESSING

In previous sections of this chapter you learned about denormalization and clustering, two schemes for placing data used together close to one another in disk storage. Denormalization and clustering work well to minimize data access time if data used together in a program can be located within one physical data page. For small records, this is certainly possible. However, data used together or immediately after one another may have to be stored in separate pages; in this case, multiple, sequential disk input/output operations will be required for reading and writing these data. Thus, denormalization and clustering may not be sufficient schemes for significantly improving data read and write performance.

Two of the inevitable trends in computer technology are the constant reduction in cost and size of computer technologies. These two trends make redundancy of computer components, and thus fault tolerance, both economically and physically feasible. The feasibility of using multiple, small computer components also allows parallel processing of data. The result of parallel processing of data is that, for example, four input/output operations, when done in parallel, take as long as only one such operation. These features can be critical for the success of a very large database for an online application, such as e-commerce.

Parallel database processing and fault tolerance can be accomplished by a database designer using hardware or software technology called **Redundant Array of Inexpensive Disks (RAID)**. RAID storage uses a set, or array, of physical disk drives that appear to the database user (and programs) as if they form one large logical storage unit. Thus, RAID does not change the logical or physical structure of application programs or database queries.

To maximize input/output performance of RAID, all the disk drives must be kept busy. Striping accomplishes the balancing of the workload across the disk drives. Segments of data, called **stripes,** cut across all of the disk drives, as illustrated in Figure 6-10. Logically sequential pages of data (e.g., multiple pages for one record, a cluster of records, or several logically sequential records from one file) are stored in round-robin fashion across the physical disk drives. Thus, for the hypothetical RAID storage illustrated in Figure 6-10, it would be possible to read four logically sequen-

Redundant Array of Inexpensive Disks (RAID): A set, or array, of physical disk drives that appear to the database user (and programs) as if they form one large logical storage unit.

Stripe: The set of pages on all disks in a RAID that are the same relative distance from the beginning of the disk drive.

Figure 6-10
RAID with four disks and striping

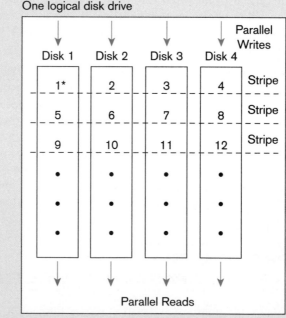

tial pages of data in parallel, in the elapsed time it takes to read just one page. A very long data record (containing possibly an audio or video field), which is stored in several physical pages, can be read in a fraction of the time it would take without RAID. Or multiple related records (a cluster) that span several pages can be read all at the same time.

Most multiuser operating systems today, including Microsoft NT, UNIX, and Novell NetWare, support some forms of RAID. Such operating systems initiate the parallel read operations and concatenate the results together into one logical record for the requesting program. These operating systems also permit multithreading, in which parallel input/output operations come from different user programs or tasks. RAID can also be implemented in hardware using special adapters, thus offloading from the host computer the work to break down input and output operations into parallel steps.

RAID has one important risk: the increased likelihood of a disk drive failure across the whole database. If the mean time between failures of an individual disk drive is, say, 1.2 million operations, then the mean time between failures of a RAID with, say, four disk drives will be 1.2 million divided by 4, or every 300,000 parallel disk operations. To cope with this risk and to make disk storage fault tolerant, many types of RAID technologies redundantly store data so that at least one copy of the data is accessible when demanded or store extra error correction codes so that damaged or lost data can be rebuilt.

A sufficient coverage of RAID is beyond the scope of this chapter. See Musciano (1999) for an excellent review of different forms of RAID. Briefly, these forms are:

- *RAID-0*   Very fast read/write times and efficient use of storage, primarily because there is no redundant storage of data (see Figure 6-10).

- *RAID-1*   A fully redundant, or disk mirror, image of data are stored. This improves fault tolerance, but each write operation has to be done redundantly in parallel. Falling disk storage prices have made RAID-1 arguably the most common form of RAID in use today.

- *RAID 0+1*   A very expensive combination of RAID-0 and RAID-1 (sometimes called RAID-10 or RAID-6) in which a second copy of a RAID-0 configuration is made. Used only in those environments that require extremely high uptime percentages with very rapid response, such as for real-time applications for military command and control, air traffic control, utility process control, and some electronic commerce situations (e.g., online investing).

- *RAID-2*   Involves dividing a table row across multiple disks (which then must be read in parallel to retrieve the whole row) and using error correction codes to detect errors and to reconstruct data when pages within the data stripes are damaged.

- *RAID-3*   Used for very long rows such that only one of the parallel drives is used to store error correction codes. This severely limits the ability to multithread requests from multiple programs; hence, RAID-3 works best in single-user environments with high volume of read and low volume of write activity.

- *RAID-4*   Similar to RAID-3 but for smaller rows so that multiple table rows can be stored in the same stripe. The bottleneck is the error correction code, or parity, drive, because it must be accessed to have an error correction page updated when any data record is rewritten. For databases with frequent record updates, such as for online transaction processing, this can create considerable contention (and hence delay) for the parity drive, reducing the advantages of parallel processing.

- *RAID-5*   Also called *Rotating Parity* Array, RAID-5 does not use a dedicated parity drive. Each drive contains both data and parity pages. Read operations can be done in parallel on all drives. A write operation will access its one or more drives to write the new record plus the parity drive *for that record*. Thus, write operations can also be done in parallel with less likelihood of delay compared to RAID-4 because random record updates will generate random error correction page updates randomly distributed across the drives.

So, which form of RAID is best? RAID-1 is best for fault-tolerant, database maintenance applications (those requiring a high percentage of uptime) or when only two disk drive controllers are affordable. RAID-1 can be costly, but is best for a variety of workloads. RAID-5 is best for read-intensive applications against very large data sets and at least three (and more typically five) disk drives are affordable. RAID-5 becomes less desirable as disk drives become larger.

Storage devices continue to be an area of rapid change. New technologies of storage area networks (SAN) and network-attached storage (NAS) are emerging for large enterprise storage environments (Shah, 1999).

DESIGNING DATABASES

Most modern information systems utilize database technologies, either database management systems or data warehouse systems, for data storage and retrieval. Recall that a database is a collection of logically related data, designed to meet the information needs of multiple users in an organization. The relationship between files in a database is due to relationships identified in the conceptual and logical data models. The relationships imply access paths between data. Each type of database technology allows different types of access paths. So, the process of choosing the appropriate type of DBMS or data warehousing technology is one of matching the needed access paths with the capabilities of the database technology.

As the designer of a database, the type of DBMS technologies available to you have likely been chosen by the organization for which you are designing a database. By far, the most popular database architectures in practice today are relational for transaction processing and multidimensional for data warehouses. However, other styles exist in legacy systems and are used for some specialized new databases. Figure 6-11 compares these five architectures:

1. *Hierarchical database model*   In this model, files are arranged in a top-down structure that resembles a tree or genealogy chart. Data are related in a nested, one-to-many set of relationships. The top file is called the root, the bottom files are called leaves, and intermediate files have one parent, or owner, file and one or several children files. Among the oldest of the database architectures, many hierarchical databases exist in larger organizations today. This technology is best applied when the conceptual data model also resembles a tree and when most data access begins with the same (root) file. Hierarchical database technology is used for high-volume transaction processing and MIS applications. Few new databases are developed with hierarchical DBMSs because newer applications tend to have broader needs than simply transaction processing or summarization of transaction data.

2. *Network database model*   In this model, each file may be associated with an arbitrary number of files. Although very flexible because any relationships can be implemented (a hierarchy is a special case of a network), the form of implementation, usually using pointers between related records in different files, creates significant overhead in storage space and maintenance time. Typically, network model systems support only one-to-many relationships along each arc in the network data model, but some support many-to-many relationships. Network model systems are still popular on powerful mainframes and for high-volume transaction processing applications. Because the database designer has such detailed control over data organizations, it is possible

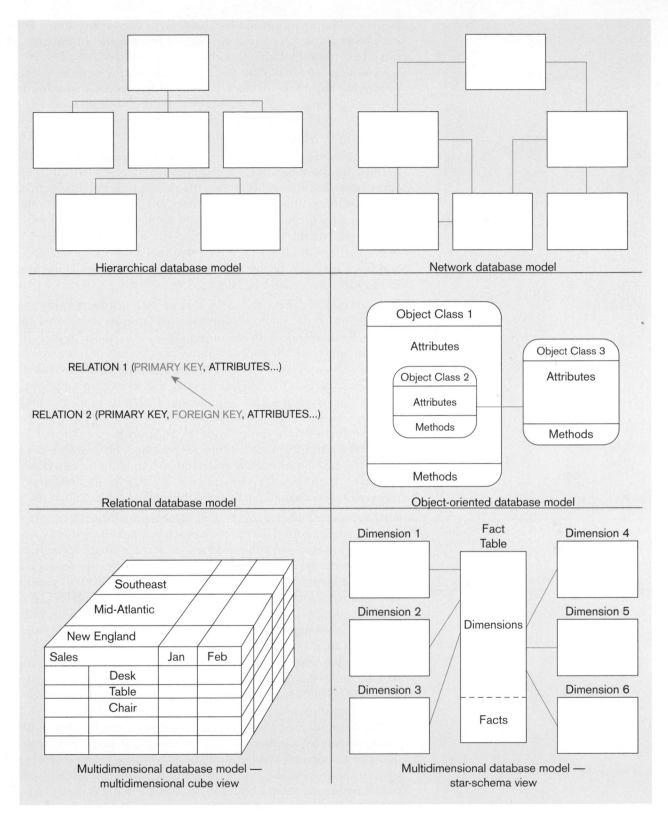

Hierarchical database model

Network database model

RELATION 1 (PRIMARY KEY, ATTRIBUTES...)

RELATION 2 (PRIMARY KEY, FOREIGN KEY, ATTRIBUTES...)

Relational database model

Object Class 1

Attributes

Object Class 2

Attributes

Methods

Methods

Object Class 3

Attributes

Methods

Object-oriented database model

Southeast
Mid-Atlantic
New England

Sales		Jan	Feb
	Desk		
	Table		
	Chair		

Multidimensional database model —
multidimensional cube view

Dimension 1
Dimension 2
Dimension 3

Fact
Table

Dimensions

Facts

Dimension 4
Dimension 5
Dimension 6

Multidimensional database model —
star-schema view

Figure 6-11
Database architectures

to design highly optimized databases with network systems. For example, each record type (a record type is shown by each box in the network) can be organized using hashing algorithms or located near another related record type—an early form of clustering. Network systems support a wider variety of processing requirements than do hierarchical database systems, but network systems still require significant programming and database design knowledge and time, and hence are used primarily in those organizations with significant expertise with such technologies.

3. *Relational database model*   The most common database model for new systems defines simple tables for each relation and many-to-many relationships. Cross-reference keys, representing the relationships between entities, link the tables together. Primary and secondary key indexes provide rapid access to data based on qualifications. Most new applications are built using relational DBMSs, and many relational DBMS products exist. See Chapter 5 for a thorough review of the features of the relational database model, and Chapters 7 and 8 for coverage of the SQL relational data manipulation language, the most widely used relational language.

4. *Object-oriented database model*   In this model, attributes and methods that operate on those attributes are encapsulated in structures called object classes. Relationships between object classes are shown, in part, by nesting or encapsulating one object class within another. New object classes are defined from more general object classes. A major advantage of this data model is that complex data types like graphics, video, and sound are supported as easily as simpler data types are. This is the newest DBMS technology, and larger organizations are gaining experience with it by selectively using it when complex data or event-driven programming is appropriate for the application. Chapters 14 and 15 provide extensive coverage of the use of the data model for conceptual data modeling and database implementation. Object-relational databases, highlighted in Appendix D, attempt to include some of the features of object-oriented databases within relational technologies.

5. *Multidimensional database model*   This database model is often used in data warehousing applications. Two ways of viewing this model exist. The first views data as a multidimensional cube in which each cell contains one or more simple attributes and the dimensions are ways to categorize the raw data. These categories, or dimensions, are the factors on which users want to summarize or segment the data, such as time periods, geography, lines of business, or people. A cell contains data relevant to the intersection of all of its dimension values. For example, a cell might hold the number-of-units-sold attribute for a given time period, location, line of business, and salesperson. The second (equivalent) view is called a star schema. At the center is a fact table, equivalent to the cell in the multidimensional view. This table contains all the raw attributes and a composite key made up of the primary keys of all the surrounding dimension tables. The surrounding dimension tables define each of the ways to categorize data, such as all the description data about each salesperson. The key design issue with the multidimensional database model is identifying in advance the lowest common denominator of data, and hence all the dimensions or categories by which users wish to summarize the raw facts. Although the multidimensional database model is a special case of both the relational and network data models, special DBMSs have been developed that optimize dimensional data processing. Chapter 11 deals with data warehousing and the multidimensional data model.

We have chosen to cover in greater detail in this textbook only the three newest of these database models: relational, object oriented, and multidimensional. If you want to know more about hierarchical and network database models, refer to some of the sources listed in Further Reading at the end of this chapter.

OPTIMIZING FOR QUERY PERFORMANCE

The primary purpose today for physical database design is to optimize the performance of database processing. Database processing includes adding, deleting, and modifying a database, as well as a variety of data retrieval activities. For databases that have greater retrieval traffic than maintenance traffic, optimizing the database for query performance (producing online or off-line anticipated and ad hoc screens and reports for end users) is the primary goal. This chapter has already covered most of the decisions you can make to tune the database design to meet the need of database queries (clustering, indexes, file organizations, etc.). In this final section of this chapter, we introduce a few additional advanced database design and processing options now available in many DBMSs.

The amount of work a database designer needs to put into optimizing query performance depends greatly on the DBMS. Because of the high cost of expert database developers, the less database and query design work developers have to do, the less costly will be the development and use of a database. Some DBMSs give very little control to the database designer or query writer over how a query is processed or the physical location of data for optimizing data reads and writes. Other systems give the application developers considerable control, and often demand extensive work to tune the database design and the structure of queries to obtain acceptable performance. Sometimes, the workload varies so much and the design options are so subtle that good performance is all that can be achieved. When the workload is fairly focused, say for data warehousing where there are a few batch updates and very complex queries requiring large segments of the database, performance can be well tuned either by smart query optimizers in the DBMS or by intelligent database and query design or a combination of both. For example, the NCR Teradata DBMS is highly tuned for parallel processing in a data warehousing environment. In this case, rarely can a database designer or query writer improve on the capabilities of the DBMS to store and process data. Because this situation is rare, as a database designer it is important to consider options for improving database processing performance.

Parallel Query Processing

One of the major computer architectural changes over the last few years is the increased use of multiple processors in database servers. Database servers frequently use symmetric multiprocessor (SMP) technology (Schumacher, 1997). To take advantage of this parallel processing capability, some of the more sophisticated DBMSs include strategies for breaking apart a query into modules that can be processed in parallel by each of the related processors. The most common approach is to replicate the query so that each copy works against a portion of the database, usually a horizontal partition (sets of rows). The partitions need to be defined in advance by the database designer. The same query is run against each portion in parallel on separate processors, and the intermediate results from each processor are combined to create the final query result as if the query were run against the whole database.

Suppose you have an Order table with several million rows for which query performance has been slow. To ensure that subsequent scans of this table are performed in parallel using at least three processors, you would alter the structure of the table with the SQL command:

ALTER TABLE ORDER PARALLEL 3

You need to tune each table to the best degree of parallelism, so it is not uncommon to alter a table several times until the right degree is found.

Parallel query processing speed can be impressive. Schumacher (1997) reports of a test in which the time to perform a query was cut in half with parallel processing compared to a normal table scan. Because an index is a table, indexes can also be given the parallel structure, so that scans of an index are also faster. Again, Schumacher (1997) shows an example where the cost, in time, to create an index by parallel processing was reduced from approximately seven minutes to five seconds!

Besides table scans, other elements of a query can be processed in parallel, such as certain types of joining of related tables, grouping query results into categories, combining several parts of a query result together (called union), sorting rows, and computing aggregate values. Row update, delete, and insert operations can also be processed in parallel. In addition, the performance of some database creation commands can be improved by parallel processing; these include creating and rebuilding an index and creating a table from data in the database. The Oracle environment must be preconfigured with a specification for the number of virtual parallel database servers to exist. Once this is done, the query processor will decide what it thinks is the best use of parallel processing for any command.

Sometimes the parallel processing is transparent to the database designer or query writer. With some DBMSs, the part of the DBMS that determines how to process a query, the query optimizer, uses physical database specifications and characteristics of the data (e.g., a count of the number of different values for a qualified attribute) to determine whether to take advantage of parallel processing capabilities.

Overriding Automatic Query Optimization

Sometimes, the query writer knows (or can learn) key information about the query that may be overlooked or unknown to the query optimizer module of the DBMS. With such key information in hand, a query writer may have an idea for a better way to process a query. But before you as the query writer can know you have a better way, you have to know how the query optimizer (which usually picks a query processing plan that will minimize expected query processing time, or cost) will process the query. This is especially true for a query you have not submitted before. Fortunately, with most relational DBMSs you can learn the optimizer's plan for processing the query before running the query. A command such as EXPLAIN or EXPLAIN PLAN (the exact command varies by DBMS) will display how the query optimizer intends to access indexes, use parallel servers, and join tables to prepare the query result. If you preface the actual relational command with the explain clause, the query processor displays the logical steps to process the query and stops processing before actually accessing the database. The query optimizer chooses the best plan based on statistics about each table, such as average row length and number of rows. It may be necessary to force the DBMS to calculate up-to-date statistics about the database (e.g., the Analyze command in Oracle) to get an accurate estimate of query costs. You may submit several explain commands with your query written in different ways to see if the optimizer predicts different performance. Then, you can submit the form of the query for actual processing that had the best predicted processing time, or you may decide not to submit the query because it will be too costly to run.

You may even see a way to improve query processing performance. With some DBMSs, you can force the DBMS to do the steps differently or to use the capabilities of the DBMS, such as parallel servers, differently than the optimizer thinks is the best plan.

For example, suppose we wanted to count the number of orders processed by a particular sales representative, Smith. In Oracle, parallel table processing works only when a table is scanned, not when it is accessed via an index. So, in Oracle, we may want to force both a full table scan as well as scanning in parallel. The SQL command for this query would be as follows:

```
SELECT /*+ FULL(ORDER) PARALLEL(ORDER,3) */ COUNT(*)
FROM ORDER
WHERE SALESPERSON = "SMITH";
```

The clause inside the /* */ delimiters is the hint to Oracle. This hint overrides whatever query plan Oracle would naturally create for this query. Thus, a hint is specific to each query, but the use of such hints must be anticipated by altering the structure of tables to be handled with parallel processing.

Picking Data Block Size

As mentioned earlier in the chapter, data are transferred between RAM and disk memory in blocks, or pages. The size of a data block can significantly affect the performance of queries. Too small a size may result in many physical I/O operations per table row being accessed or in accessing many rows. Too large a block size may result in extra data being transferred, with wasted time. Usually the minimum block size is 2K bytes; the upper limit is determined by the computer operating system, but a typical limit is 32K bytes or more. Once the block size is established for a database, it can be changed only by unloading the data, redefining the database, and reloading the data.

You make trade-offs among five performance factors as you switch from small to large block sizes. These factors are (Yuhanna, 2000):

1. *Block contention*   This is a measure of the need for concurrently accessing the same data block by several I/O commands. Smaller blocks create less contention. Contention matters the most in environments with many concurrent jobs running against the same database, such as when there are many online users.

2. *Random row access speed*   This is how fast one row from a table can be accessed. Again, smaller blocks are best. Random row accessing is common in online transaction processing applications.

3. *Sequential row access speed*   This is how fast a table is scanned. In this case, larger block sizes are better. Large block sizes allow many rows to be cached in RAM in one I/O operation so that fewer physical I/O operations are required to retrieve all the table rows needed for the query. A large block size fits well with clustering (discussed earlier in this chapter) because a whole cluster may be cached in one I/O operation. Sequential scans can occur in decision support and data warehousing applications and in applications that produce transaction summary reports.

4. *Row size*   This is the length of all the fields in a table row. It is usually best to try to match the block size with the physical table row size or a multiple of the row size.

5. *Overhead*   This is the cost, in time, for the DBMS to manage all the I/O operations needed to produce the result for a query or other database operation. Small block sizes produce more overhead than do large block sizes.

Rarely will all these factors point to one block size. In general, smaller block sizes are used for online transaction processing applications and larger block sizes are used for databases with a decision support or data warehousing system. Environments with a mixed workload can be very difficult to tune in terms of data block size.

Balancing I/O Across Disk Controllers

A disk controller manages the I/O operations for the disk drives attached to that controller. More controllers are better than a few (as before, more parallelism means better performance), but cost will limit the number of controllers you can have. The benefits of multiple controllers come when they can all be kept busy. Thus, you want to allocate database and DBMS system files to drives so that there is roughly the same workload on each controller, and better yet, each disk.

Tables can usually be easily moved from one disk to another after the tables contain data. So, the initial assignment of files to disks can be changed. To improve query processing performance:

- Understand what files are on which drives and which drives are attached to which controllers
- Understand the predefined programs and the nature of the ad hoc queries run against the database (you may need to concentrate on the most important programs or the most troublesome days or times)
- Collect statistics on disk and controller utilization and on table (or partition) accessing
- Rebalance the workload by moving tables between drives and controllers

In general, when it is not possible to have data required together in a query (or across concurrently running queries) stored in the same data block, then it is best to have those data on different disks on different controllers so that the data can be accessed in parallel. Again, it is difficult, if not impossible, to optimize this when there is a highly varied workload pattern. You may need to concentrate on a few of the most important applications (or the applications running with unacceptable performance today), do the analysis above for those applications, and balance file assignments to create the best possible performance for those applications without serious degradation for other applications.

Guidelines for Better Query Design

Prior sections of this chapter have provided many techniques and approaches for database and query design that result in fast query processing. Various database experts have developed additional guidelines that do not relate directly to the topics already covered. See DeLoach (1987) and Holmes (1996) for suggestions for improving query processing in a variety of settings. Also see the Web Resources at the end of the chapter for the link to **SearchDatabase.com**, where many query design suggestions are continually posted. We summarize below some of their suggestions that apply to many situations.

1. *Understand how indexes are used in query processing*   Many DBMSs will use only one index per table in a query, often the one that is the most discriminating (most key values). Some will never use an index with only a few values compared to the number of table rows. Others may balk at using an index for which the column has many null values across the table rows. Learn how the DBMS selects which index to use, and monitors accesses to indexes; then drop indexes that are infrequently used. This will improve the performance of database update operations. In general, queries that have equality criteria for selecting table rows (e.g., WHERE Finish = "Birch" OR "Walnut") will result in faster processing than queries involving more complex qualifications do (e.g., WHERE Finish NOT = "Walnut") because equality criteria can be evaluated via indexes. Again, learn how the DBMS treats different types of clauses in queries.

2. *Keep optimizer statistics up-to-date*   Some DBMSs do not automatically update the statistics needed by the query optimizer. If performance is degrading, force the running of an update-statistics-like command.

3. *Use compatible data types for fields and literals in Queries*   Compatible data types likely will mean that the DBMS can avoid having to convert data during query processing.

4. *Write simple queries*   Usually the simplest form of a query will be the easiest for the DBMS to process. For example, because relational DBMSs are based on set theory, write queries that manipulate sets of rows and literals.

5. *Break complex queries into multiple, simple parts*   Because the DBMS may use only one index per query, it is often good to break a complex query into multiple, simpler parts (which each use an index) and then combine the results of the smaller queries together. For example, because a relational DBMS works with sets, it is very easy for the DBMS to UNION two sets of rows that are the result of two simple, independent queries.

6. *Don't nest one query inside another query*   As you will see in Chapters 7 and 8, the SQL database language allows you to write one query inside another query (the query inside is called a subquery). Usually, such queries are less efficient than a query that avoids subqueries to produce the same result.

7. *Don't combine a table with itself*   Avoid, if possible, using the same table in two (or more) different roles in the same query. (This is called a self-join and is illustrated in Chapter 7.) It is usually better (more efficient for processing the query) to make a temporary copy of the table and then to relate the original table with the temporary one.

8. *Create temporary tables for groups of queries*   When possible, reuse data used in a sequence of queries. For example, if a series of queries all refer to the same subset of data from the database, it may be more efficient to first store this subset in one or more temporary tables and then refer to those temporary tables in the series of queries. This will avoid repeatedly combining the same data together or repeatedly scanning the database to find the same database segment for each query. The trade-off is that the temporary tables will not change if the original tables are updated when the queries are running.

9. *Combine update operations*   When possible, combine multiple update commands into one. This will reduce query processing overhead and allow the DBMS to seek ways to process the updates in parallel.

10. *Retrieve only the data you need*   This will reduce the data blocks accessed and transferred. This may seem obvious, but there are some shortcuts for query writing that violate this guideline. For example, in SQL the command SELECT * from EMP will retrieve all the fields from all the rows of the EMP table. But, if the user needs to see only some of the columns of the table, transferring the extra columns increases the query processing time.

11. *Don't have the DBMS sort without an index*   If data are to be displayed in sorted order and an index does not exist on the sort key field, then sort the data outside the DBMS after the unsorted results are retrieved. Usually a sort utility will be faster than a sort without the aid of an index by the DBMS.

12. *Learn!*   Track query processing times, review query plans with the EXPLAIN command, and improve your understanding of the way the DBMS determines how to process queries. Attend specialized training by your DBMS vendor on writing efficient queries, which will better inform you about the query optimizer.

13. *Finally, consider the total query processing time for ad hoc queries*   The total time includes the time it takes the programmer (or end user) to write the query as well as the time to process the query. Many times, for ad hoc queries, it is better to have the DBMS do extra work to allow the user to more quickly write a query. And isn't that what technology is supposed to accomplish—to allow people to be more productive? So, don't spend too much time, especially for ad hoc queries, trying to write the most efficient query. Write a query that is logically correct (produces the desired results), and let the DBMS do the work. (Of course, do an EXPLAIN first to be sure you haven't written "the query from hell" so that all other users will see a serious delay in query processing time.) This suggests a corollary: When possible, run your query when there is a light load on the database, because the total query

processing time includes delays induced by other load on the DBMS and database.

This concludes our discussion of advanced options for tuning the performance of a database. All options are not available with every DBMS, and each DBMS often has unique options due to its underlying design. You should refer to reference manuals for your DBMS to know which specific tuning options are available to you.

Summary

During physical database design, you, the designer, translate the logical description of data into the technical specifications for storing and retrieving data. The goal is to create a design for storing data that will provide adequate performance and ensure database integrity, security, and recoverability. In physical database design, you consider normalized relations and data volume estimates, data definitions, data processing requirements and their frequencies, user expectations, and database technology characteristics to establish field specifications, record designs, file organizations, and a database architecture.

A field is the smallest unit of application data, corresponding to an attribute in the logical data model. You must determine the data type, integrity controls, and how to handle missing values for each field, among other factors. A data type is a detailed coding scheme for representing organizational data. Data may be coded or compressed to reduce storage space. Field integrity control includes specifying a default value, range of permissible values, null value permission, and referential integrity.

A physical record is a group of fields stored in adjacent memory locations and retrieved together as a unit. Physical records are usually stored in a page (or data block), which is the amount of data read or written in one secondary memory I/O operation. The number of records in a page is called the blocking factor. For efficiency reasons, the attributes of one relation may not be stored in one physical record and attributes from several relations may be stored in one physical record. A process of denormalization transforms normalized relations into unnormalized physical record specifications. Denormalization is done to place in one physical record those attributes frequently needed together in an I/O operation. Denormalization includes horizontal partitioning, which breaks a relation into multiple record specifications by placing different rows into different records based on common column values. Denormalization also includes vertical partitioning, which distributes the columns of a relation into separate files, repeating the primary key in each of the files.

A physical file is a named portion of secondary memory allocated for the purpose of storing physical records. Data within a physical file are organized through a combination of sequential storage and pointers. A pointer is a field of data that can be used to locate a related field or record of data.

A file organization arranges the records of a file on a secondary storage device. The three major categories of file organizations are (1) sequential, which stores records in sequence according to a primary key value; (2) indexed, in which records are stored sequentially or nonsequentially and an index is used to keep track of where the records are stored; and (3) hashed, in which the address of each record is determined using an algorithm that converts a primary key value into a record address. Physical records of several types can be clustered together into one physical file in order to place records frequently used together close to one another in secondary memory.

The indexed file organization is one of the most popular in use today. An index may be based on a unique key or a secondary (nonunique) key, which allows more than one record to be associated with the same key value. The new form of an index, a bitmap index, creates a table of bits in which an on bit means that the related record has the related key value. A join index indicates rows from two or more tables that have common values for related fields. A hash index table makes the placement of data independent of the hashing algorithm and permits the same data to be accessed via several hashing functions on different fields. Indexes are important in speeding up data retrieval, especially when multiple conditions are used for selecting, sorting, or relating data. Indexes are useful in a wide variety of situations, including for large tables, for columns that are frequently used to qualify the data to be retrieved, when a field has a large number of distinct values, and when data processing is dominated by data retrieval rather than data maintenance.

File access efficiency and file reliability can be enhanced by the use of a Redundant Array of Inexpensive Disks (RAID), which allows blocks of data from one or several programs to be read and written in parallel to different disks, thus reducing the input/output delays with traditional sequential I/O operations on a single disk drive. Various levels of RAID allow a file and database designer to choose the combination of access efficiency, space utilization, and fault tolerance best suited for the database applications.

Database architectures in use today are hierarchical, network, relational, object oriented, and multidimensional. Hierarchical and network architectures primarily appear in legacy applications, whereas relational, object-oriented, and multidimensional architectures are used for new systems development.

The introduction of multiprocessor database servers has made possible new capabilities in database management systems. One major new feature is the ability to break a query apart and to process the query in parallel against segments of a table. Such parallel query processing can greatly improve the speed of query processing.

Also, database programmers can improve database processing performance by providing the DBMS with hints about the sequence in which to perform table operations. These hints override the cost-based optimizer of the DBMS. Both the DBMS and programmers can look at statistics about the database to determine how to process a query. A wide variety of guidelines for good query design were included in the chapter.

This chapter concludes the section of this book on database design. Having developed complete physical data specifications, you are now ready to begin implementing the database with database technology. Implementation means defining the database and programming client and server routines to handle the queries, reports, and transactions against the database. These are primary topics of the next five chapters, which cover relational database implementation on client platforms, server platforms, client/server environments, and data warehouse technologies.

CHAPTER REVIEW

Key Terms

Bitmap index	Hashed file organization	Physical record
Blocking factor	Hashing algorithm	Pointer
Data type	Horizontal partitioning	Redundant Array of Inexpensive Disks (RAID)
Denormalization	Index	Secondary key
Extent	Indexed file organization	Sequential file organization
Field	Join index	Stripe
File organization	Page	Tablespace
Hash index table	Physical file	Vertical partitioning

Review Questions

1. Define each of the following terms:
   a. file organization
   b. sequential file organization
   c. indexed file organization
   d. hashing file organization
   e. denormalization
   f. composite key
   g. secondary key
   h. data type
   i. bitmap index
   j. RAID
   k. join index
   l. stripe
   m. explain plan

2. Match the following terms to the appropriate definitions:

   ____ bitmap index
   ____ hashing algorithm
   ____ page
   ____ physical record
   ____ pointer
   ____ blocking factor
   ____ physical file

   a. data read in one I/O operation
   b. the number of records in a page
   c. named area of secondary memory
   d. a table of zeros and ones
   e. a field not containing business data
   f. converts a key value into an address
   g. adjacent fields

3. Contrast the following terms:
   a. horizontal partitioning; vertical partitioning
   b. physical file; tablespace
   c. physical record; physical file
   d. page; physical record
   e. secondary key; primary key

4. What are the major inputs into physical database design?

5. What are the key decisions in physical database design?

6. What information is shown on a composite usage map?

7. What decisions have to be made to develop a field specification?

8. What are the objectives of selecting a data type for a field?

9. Why are field values coded or compressed?

10. What options are available for controlling field integrity?

11. Describe three ways to handle missing field values.

12. Explain why normalized relations may not be efficient physical records.

13. List three common situations that suggest that relations be denormalized to form physical records.

14. What are the advantages and disadvantages of horizontal and vertical partitioning?

15. List seven important criteria in selecting a file organization.

16. Under what circumstances is a bitmap index desirable?

17. What are the benefits of a hash index table?

18. What is the purpose of clustering of data in a file?

19. State nine rules of thumb for choosing indexes.

20. Contrast the two ways of viewing multidimensional databases.

21. How can use of the EXPLAIN command help in writing a more efficient query?

22. Explain four options for optimizing query performance.

Problems and Exercises

1. Consider the following two relations for Millennium College:
   STUDENT (Student_ID, Student_Name, Campus_Address, GPA)
   REGISTRATION (Student_ID, Course_ID, Grade)

   Following is a typical query against these relations:
   SELECT STUDENT.STUDENT_ID, STUDENT_NAME, COURSE_ID, GRADE
   FROM STUDENT, REGISTRATION
       WHERE STUDENT.STUDENT_ID = REGISTRATION.STUDENT_ID
       AND   GPA > 3.0
   ORDER BY STUDENT_NAME;

   a. On what attributes should indexes be defined to speed up this query? Give the reasons for each attribute selected.
   b. Write SQL commands to create indexes for each attribute you identified in part a.

2. Choose Oracle data types for the attributes in the normalized relations in Figure 6-4.

3. Suppose you were designing a default value for the age field in a student record at your university. What possible values would you consider and why? How might the default vary by other characteristics about the student, such as school within the university or degree sought?

4. When a student has not chosen a major at a university, the university often enters a value of "Undecided" for the major field. Is "Undecided" a default value or a way to represent the null value?

5. Consider the following normalized relations from a database in a large retail chain:
   STORE (Store_ID, Region, Manager_ID, Square_Feet)

   EMPLOYEE (Employee_ID, Where_Work, Employee_Name, Employee_Address)
   DEPARTMENT (Department_ID, Manager_ID, Sales_Goal)
   SCHEDULE (Department_ID, Employee_ID, Date)

   What opportunities might exist for denormalizing these relations when defining the physical records for this database? Under what circumstances would you consider creating such denormalized records?

6. Assume that you have a hard disk file designated to accommodate a maximum of 1,000 records of 240 bytes each. Assume that a page is 4,000 bytes in length and that records may not span pages. How many bytes will be needed for this file?

7. What problems might arise from vertically partitioning a relation? Given these potential problems, what general conditions influence when to partition a relation vertically?

8. Is it possible with a sequential file organization to permit sequential scanning of the data based on several sorted orders? If not, why not? If it is possible, how?

9. Suppose each record in a file were connected to its prior and next record in key sequence using pointers. Thus, each record might have the following format:
   Primary key, other attributes, pointer to prior record, pointer to next record.
   a. What would be the advantages of this file organization compared with a sequential file organization?
   b. In contrast with a sequential file organization, would it be possible to keep the records in multiple sequences? Why or why not?

10. Assume that a student file in a university database had an index on Student_ID (the primary key) and indexes on Major, Age, Marital_Status, and Home_Zipcode (all secondary keys).

Further, assume that the university wanted a list of students majoring in MIS or Computer Science, over the age of 25, and married OR students majoring in Computer Engineering, single, and from the 45462 zip code. How could indexes be used so that only records that satisfy this qualification are accessed?

11. Consider again the student file described in Problem and Exercise 10. For which of the indexes would it make sense to use a bitmap index? What conditions have to hold for a bitmap index to make sense? Choose one of the keys that is a likely candidate for a bitmap index and draw a figure similar to Figure 6-8 showing the structure of that index.

12. Consider Figure 6-7c. Assuming that the empty rows in the leaves of this index show space where new records can be stored, explain where the record for "Sooners" would be stored. Where would the record for "Flashes" be stored? What might happen when one of the leaves is full and a new record needs to be added to that leaf?

13. Consider Figure 6-11, which compares the general characteristics of the most popular database architectures. For each of the two multidimensional database models, write equivalent relations.

14. Can clustering of files occur after the files are populated with records? Why or why not?

15. Parallel query processing, as described in this chapter, means that the same query is run on multiple processors and that each processor accesses in parallel a different subset of the database. Another form of parallel query processing, not discussed in this chapter, would partition the query so that each part of the query runs on a different processor, but that part accesses whatever part of the database it needs. Most queries involve a qualification clause that selects the records of interest in the query. In general, this qualification clause is of the form:

(condition OR condition OR_._._.) AND (condition OR condition OR...) AND...

Given this general form, how might a query be broken apart so that each parallel processor handles a subset of the query and then combines the subsets together after each part is processed?

Problems 16–19 refer to the large Pine Valley Furniture Company data set provided with the text.

16. Create a join index on the Customer_ID fields of the customer and order tables in Figure 5-4.

17. Consider the composite usage map in Figure 6-1. After a period of time, the assumptions for this usage map have changed as follows:

   a. There is an average of forty quotations (rather than fifty) for each supplier.

   b. Manufactured parts represent only 30 percent of all parts, and purchased parts represent 75 percent.

   c. The number of direct access to purchased parts increases to seventy-five per hour (rather than sixty).

   Draw a new composite usage map reflecting this new information to replace Figure 6-1.

18. Consider the EER diagram for Pine Valley Furniture shown in Figure 4-12. Let's look at the following portion of the EER diagram that is shown in Figure 6-12.

Figure 6-12
Figure for Problem and Exercise 18

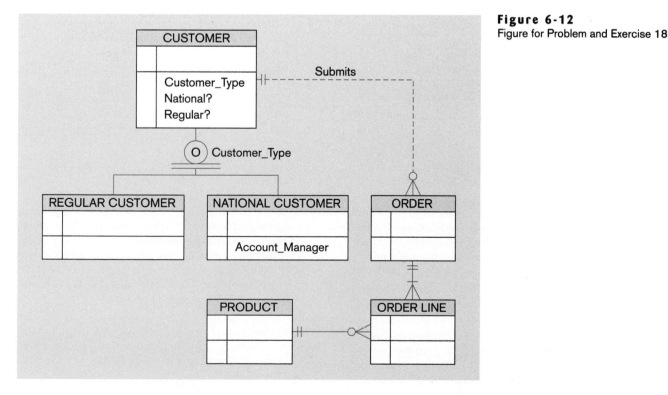

Let's make a few assumptions about the average usage of the system:

- There are 5,000 customers, of these, 80 percent represent regular accounts and 20 percent represent national accounts.
- Currently, the system stores 80,000 orders, although this number is constantly changing.
- Each order has an average of three products.
- There are 500 products.
- Approximately fifty orders are placed per hour.

  a. Based on these assumptions, draw a usage map for this portion of the EER diagram.
  b. Management would like employees only to use this database. Do you see any opportunities for denormalization?

19. Refer to Figure 5-5. For each of the following reports, indicate any indexes that you feel would help the report run faster as well as the type of index:

  a. State by products (user-specified period)

State By Products Report January 1, 2005 To March 31, 2005

State	Product Description	Total Quantity Ordered
CO	8-Drawer Dresser	1
CO	Entertainment Center	0
CO	Oak Computer Desk	1
CO	Writer's Desk	2
NY	Writer's Desk	1
VA	Writer's Desk	5

  b. Most frequently sold product finish in a user-specified month

Most Frequently Sold Product Finish Report March 1, 2005 to March 31, 2005

Product Finish	Units Sold
Cherry	13

  c. All orders placed last month

Monthly Order Report March 1, 2005 to March 31, 2005

Order_ID	Order Date	Customer ID	Customer Name
19	3/5/05	4	Eastern Furniture

Order Details:

Product Description	Quantity Ordered	Price	Extended Price
Cherry End Table	10	$75.00	$750.00
High Back Leather Chair	5	$362.00	$1,810.00

Order_ID	Order Date	Customer ID	Customer Name
24	3/10/05	1	Comtemporary Casuals

Order Details:

Product Description	Quantity Ordered	Price	Extended Price
Bookcase	4	$69.00	$276.00

  d. Total products sold by product line (user-specified period)

Products sold by Product Line March 1, 2005 to March 31, 2005

Product_Line	Quantity Sold
Basic	200
Antique	15
Modern	10
Classical	75

Field Exercises

1. Find out which database management systems are available at your university for student use. Investigate which data types these DBMSs support. Compare these DBMSs based on the data types supported and suggest which types of applications each DBMS is best suited for based on this comparison.

2. Using the Web site for this text and other Internet resources, investigate the parallel processing capabilities of several leading DBMSs. How do their capabilities differ?

3. Using the Web site for this text and other Internet resources, investigate the capabilities of object-oriented database products. How much do these DBMSs cost? For what types of applications do the vendors suggest using their products?

4. Contact a database designer or administrator in an organization with which you are familiar. Ask what file organizations are available in the various DBMSs used in that organization. Interview this person to learn what factors he or she considers when selecting an organization for database files. For indexed files, ask how he or she decides what indexes to create. Are indexes ever deleted? Why or why not?

5. Contact a database designer or administrator in an organization with which you are familiar. Ask if the person uses RAID technology with the organization's databases. Why or why not? If the person is using RAID, what level(s) are employed? Why?

References

Babad, Y. M., and J. A. Hoffer. 1984. "Even No Data Has a Value." *Communications of the ACM* 27,8 (August): 748–56.

Ballinger, C. 1998. "Introducing the Join Index." *Teradata Review* 1,3 (Fall): 18–23. [Note: *Teradata Review* is now *Teradata Magazine.*]

Bontempo, C. J., and C. M. Saracco. 1996. "Accelerating Indexed Searching." *Database Programming & Design* 9,7 (July): 37–43.

Brobst, S, S. Gant, and F. Thompson. 1999. "Partitioning Very Large Database Tables with Oracle8." *Oracle Magazine* 8,2 (March–April): 123–26.

Catterall, R. 2005. "The Keys to the Database." *DB2 Magazine* 10,2 (Quarter 2): 49–51.

DeLoach, A. 1987. "The Path to Writing Efficient Queries in SQL/DS." *Database Programming & Design* 1,1 (January): 26–32.

Finkelstein, R. 1988. "Breaking the Rules Has a Price." *Database Programming & Design* 1,6 (June): 11–14.

Hoberman, S. 2002. "The Denormalization Survival Guide–Parts I and II." Published in the online journal *The Data Administration Newsletter,* found in the April and July issues of Tdan.com; the two parts of this guide are at: **http://www.tdan.com/i020fe02.htm** and **http://www.tdan.com/i021ht03.htm,** respectively.

Holmes, J. "More Paths to Better Performance." *Database Programming & Design* 9 (February): 47–48.

Inmon, W. H. 1988. "What Price Normalization." *ComputerWorld* (October 17): 27, 31.

Musciano, C. 1999. "An Introduction to RAID." accessed via Web at **http://linux-sxs.org/hardware/raidintro.html**.

Pascal, F. 2002a. "The Dangerous Illusion: Denormalization, Performance and Integrity, Part 1." *DM Review* 12,6 (June): 52–53, 57.

Pascal, F. 2002b. "The Dangerous Illusion: Denormalization, Performance and Integrity, Part 2." *DM Review* 12,6 (June): 16, 18.

Rogers, U. 1989. "Denormalization: Why, What, and How?" *Database Programming & Design* 2,12 (December): 46–53.

Schumacher, R. 1997. "Oracle Performance Strategies." *DBMS* 10,5 (May): 89–93.

Shah, R. 1999. "Storage Beyond RAID." accessed via Web at **http://sunsite.uakom.sk/sunworldonline/swol-07-1999/swol-07-connectivity.html.**

Viehman, P. 1994. "Twenty-four Ways to Improve Database Performance." *Database Programming & Design* 7,2 (February): 32–41.

Yuhanna, N. 2000. *Oracle8i Database Administration.* Greenwich, CT: Manning Publications.

Further Reading

Elmasri, R. and S. Navathe. 1994. *Fundamentals of Database Systems,* 2nd ed. Menlo Park, CA: Benjamin/Cummings.

Loney, K., E. Aronoff, and N. Sonawalla. 1996. "Big Tips for Big Tables." *Database Programming & Design* 9,11 (November): 58–62.

Roti, S. 1996. "Indexing and Access Mechanisms." *DBMS* 9,5 (May): 65–70.

Web Resources

www.networkcomputing.com/605/605buyers.html "RAID Storage Solutions: Which is Right for You?" by J. Milne.

SearchDatabase.com This site contains a wide variety of information about database management and DBMSs. New "tips" are added daily, and you can subscribe to an alert service for new postings to the site. Many tips deal with improving the performance of queries through better database and query design.

www.teradatamagazine.com A journal for NCR Teradata data warehousing products that includes articles on database design. You can search the site for key terms from this chapter, such as join index, and find many articles on these topics.

www.win2000mag.com/Articles/Index.cfm?ArticleID=218 "RAID Levels" offers brief descriptions of common types of RAID.

MOUNTAIN VIEW COMMUNITY HOSPITAL

Case

Up to this point, you have developed the conceptual and logical models for Mountain View Community Hospital's database. After considering several options, the hospital has decided to use Microsoft SQL Server, a relational DBMS, for implementing the database. Before the functional database is actually created, it is necessary to specify its physical design to ensure that the database is effective and efficient. As you have learned, physical database design is specific to the target environment and must conform to the capabilities of the DBMS to be used. It requires a good understanding of the DBMS's features, such as available data types, indexing, support for referential integrity and other constraints, and many more. (You can alternatively assume that Mountain View Community Hospital chose another DBMS with which you are familiar, and then answer the following questions accordingly.)

CASE QUESTIONS

1. What additional kinds of information do you need for the physical database design of the MVCH database besides the 3NF relations you developed earlier for this case in Chapter 5?

2. What different types or forms of clinical data are collected at a hospital such as MVCH? Can you identify data that may not be easily accommodated by the standard data types provided by a DBMS? How would you handle that?

3. Are there opportunities for horizontal or vertical partitioning of this database? If you are not sure, what other information would you need to answer this question with greater certainty?

4. Do you see an opportunity for using a bitmap index or join index for this database? Why or why not?

5. Consider the following query against the Mountain View Community Hospital database:

   For each treatment ordered in the past 2 weeks, list by treatment ID and date (in reverse chronological order) the number of times a physician performed that treatment that day, sorted alphabetically by physician name.

   a. Which secondary key indexes would you suggest to optimize the performance of this query? Why? Make any assumptions you need to answer this question.

   b. Following the examples in Chapter 6, write the SQL statements that create these secondary key indexes.

6. Do you think that a hospital such as Mountain View should use RAID technology? Why or why not?

7. Chapter 6 describes the 2002 Sarbanes-Oxley Act, which is not focused on not-for-providers such as many community hospitals.

   a. Can you see how MVCH could benefit from voluntarily complying?

   b. How specifically can proper physical database design help with compliance and implement the following:

   • Improve accuracy and completeness of MVCH data;

   • Eliminate duplicates and data inconsistencies; and

   • Improve understandability of MVCH data?

CASE EXERCISES

1. In Case Exercise 2 from Chapter 5, you wrote CREATE TABLE commands for each relation of Dr. "Z's" small database which was to be created in MS Access. Since then, Dr. "Z" decided to use MS SQL Server consistent with other databases at MVCH. Reconsider your previous CREATE TABLE commands in answering the following questions:

   a. Would you choose different data types for any fields? Why?

   b. Are any fields candidates for coding? If so, what coding scheme would you use for each of these fields?

   c. Which fields require data values? Are there any fields that may take on a null value?

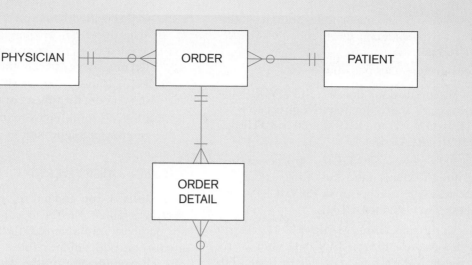

MVCH Figure 6-1
Partial data model

d. Suppose the *reason for a visit* or *the patient's social worker* are not entered. What procedures would you use for handling these missing data? Can you and should you use a default value for this field? Why or why not?

e. Using MS Visio (or other tool required by your instructor), draw the physical data model that shows the data types, primary keys, and foreign keys.

2. In Case Exercise 3 from Chapter 5, you developed the relational schema for Dr. "Z's" MS Clinic Management System.

a. Do you see any opportunities for user-defined data types? Which fields? Why?

b. Are any fields candidates for coding? If so, what coding scheme would you use for each of these fields?

c. Are there any fields that may take on a null value? If so, which ones?

d. Do you see any opportunities for denormalization of the relations you designed in Chapter 5? If not, why not? If yes, where and how might you denormalize?

e. Do you see an opportunity for using a bitmap index for this database? Why or why not?

f. Can you think of a situation with this set of tables where you might want to use a join index?

3. MVCH Figure 6-1 shows a portion of the data model for Mountain View Community Hospital's database that represents a set of normalized relations based on the enterprise model shown in MVCH Figure 2-1, and additional business rules provided in the Chapter 3 case segment. Recall that TREATMENT refers to any test or procedure ordered by a physician for a patient, and that ORDER refers to any order issued by a physician for treatment and/or services such as diagnostic tests (radiology, laboratory).

Using the information provided below regarding data volume and access frequencies, and following the example provided in Figure 6-1 in Chapter 6, modify the ER model shown in MVCH Figure 6-1 to create a preliminary composite usage map.

a. Data volume analysis

- Recall from an earlier case segment that the hospital performs more than a million laboratory procedures and over 110,000 radiology procedures annually. Add these two figures to arrive at the number of records for the ORDER DETAIL table.

- There are approximately 250 PHYSICIANS, 20,000 PATIENTS, and 200,000 physician ORDERS in this database.

- ICD-9 procedure codes for treatments (lab procedures, radiology procedures, etc.) fall into approximately 3,500 major categories. Use this number to approximate the number of TREAT-MENT records.

b. Data access frequencies per hour

- Across all applications that use the MVCH data-base, there are approximately 100 direct accesses to PHYSICIAN, 35 to ORDER, 200 to PATIENT, and 150 to TREATMENT.

- Of the 200 accesses to PATIENT, 30 accesses then also require ORDER data, and of these 30, there are 20 subsequent accesses to PHYSICIAN, and 30 accesses to ORDER DETAIL.

- Of the 35 direct accesses to ORDER, 10 accesses then also require PHYSICIAN data, and 20 re-quire access to PATIENT data, ORDER DETAIL data, and TREATMENT data.

- Of the 100 direct accesses to PHYSICIAN, 20 also access ORDER, ORDER DETAIL, and TREAT-MENT data.

- Of the 150 direct accesses to TREATMENT, 10 also access ORDER DETAIL data and associated ORDER and PHYSICIAN data.

4. In Case Exercise 3, you created a composite usage map for part of the Mountain View Community Hospital database based on MVCH Figure 6-1. Referring to this composite usage map, do you see any opportunities for clustering rows from two or more tables? Why or why not? Is the concept of clustering tables supported in SQL Server? Does it differ from Oracle's implemen-tation? If so, how?

5. This exercise is based on two different implementa-tions of the MVCH database that accompany this text-book and that are made available by your instructor: one using MS Access, the other one using the Teradata RDBMS (available at http://www.teradatastudentnet-work.com/). Your assignment consists of comparing data types that are used by both databases for the same table (e.g., Patient, Physician, Treatment, etc.). To dis-play the metadata for a table in Teradata, use the SHOW TABLE statement (e.g., SHOW TABLE Patient_t;). What are the differences? Are there data types in the Teradata RDBMS that are not available in MS Access? Which ones are they?

6. This exercise uses the MVCH MS Access database available from your instructor.

a. Review the data element properties for tables in this database. Do you think the data elements were

well specified based on a detailed physical design? Why or why not? Suggest changes that may be needed (e.g., different format, different data type, default values, specific range of values, etc).

b. Using a tools such as MS Visio, draw the physical data model for this set of tables.

c. Can you think of a situation with this set of tables where you might want to use a join index?

PROJECT ASSIGNMENTS

In Chapter 5, you created the relational schema for the MVCH database. Next, you will develop the specification for database implementation. Specifically, you need to identify and document choices regarding the properties of each data element in the database using the informa-tion provided in the case segments and options available in SQL Server (or other DBMS that you may be using for this assignment).

P1. Review the information provided in the case seg-ments and identify the data type for each field in the database.

- Do you see any opportunities for user-defined data types? Which fields? Why?

- Are any fields candidates for coding? If so, what cod-ing scheme would you use for each of these fields?

- Which fields may take on a null value? Why?

- Which fields should be indexed? What type of index?

P2. Create a data dictionary similar to the metadata table shown in Table 1-1 in Chapter 1 to document your choices. For each table in the relational schema you developed earlier, provide the following information for each field/data element: field name, defini-tion/description, data type, format, allowable values, if the field is required or optional, if the field is indexed and the type of index, if the field is a pri-mary key, if the field is a foreign key, and the table that is referenced by the foreign key field.

P3. Using Microsoft Visio (or similar tool designated by your instructor) create the physical data model for the MVCH relational schema you developed earlier in Chapter 5, clearly indicating data types, primary keys, and foreign keys.

P4. Identify five reports to be generated by the database, and create a composite usage map for each.

Part FOUR

Implementation

An Overview of Part FOUR

Part IV considers topics associated with implementing relational systems, including Web-enabled Internet applications and data warehouses. Database implementation, as indicated in Chapter 2, includes coding and testing database processing programs, completing database documentation and training materials, and installing databases and converting data, as necessary, from prior systems. Here, at last, is the point in the systems development life cycle for which we have been preparing. Our prior activities—enterprise modeling, conceptual data modeling, and logical and physical database design—are necessary previous stages. At the end of implementation, we expect a functioning system that meets users' information requirements. After that, the system will be put into production use, and database maintenance will be necessary for the life of the system. The chapters in Part IV help develop an initial understanding of the complexities and challenges of implementing a database system.

Chapter 7 describes Structured Query Language (SQL), which has become a standard language (especially on database servers) for creating and processing relational databases. In addition to a brief history of SQL that includes a thorough introduction to SQL:1999, currently used by most DBMSs, along with discussion of the SQL:2003 standard that is presently being implemented, the syntax of SQL is explored. Data definition language (DDL) commands used to create a database are included, as are single-table data manipulation language (DML) commands used to query the database. Dynamic and materialized views, which constrain a user's environment to relevant tables necessary to complete the user's work, are also covered.

Chapter 8 continues the explanation of more advanced SQL syntax and constructs. Multiple-table queries, along with subqueries and correlated subqueries, are demonstrated. These capabilities provide SQL with much of its power. Transaction integrity issues and an explanation of data dictionary construction place SQL within a wider context. Additional programming capabilities, including triggers and stored procedures, and embedding SQL in other programming language programs further demonstrate the capabilities of SQL. Online analytical processing (OLAP) features of SQL-1999 and SQL-2003, necessary for accessing data warehouses, are also covered.

Chapter 9 provides a discussion of the client/server architecture, applications, middleware, and client database access in contemporary database environments. It is important to understand this chapter because it lays the groundwork for understanding the Internet topics that are coming in Chapter 10. Multitiered architectures, including application and database servers, database processing alternatives for distribution among the tiers and browser (thin) clients are covered. Web-enabled database security and ODBC and JDBC connectivity material establish this chapter's connectivity to the Internet topics to come.

Chapter 10 describes the connectivity to databases from Web-based applications. Internet terminology is included for those who are less familiar with the Web. The use of scripting languages and embedding SQL in scripts are covered. Sample XML, SOAP, and PHP with MySQL coding are illustrated. A simple shopping cart application, implemented in ASP.NET and including code and documentation for installing and running the shopping carts, is included on the text's Web site. Try to explore the code in detail to see firsthand how to establish a Web-enabled database application. The role of Web servers and server-side extensions for database connectivity is addressed, as are Web services.

Chapter 11 describes the basic concepts of data warehousing, the reasons data warehousing is regarded as critical to competitive advantage in many organizations, and the database design activities and structures unique to data warehousing. Topics include alternative data warehouse architectures, techniques for data transformation and reconciliation, and the dimensional data model (star schema) for data marts. Database design for data marts, including surrogate keys, fact table grain, modeling dates and time, conformed dimensions, factless fact tables, and helper/hierarchy/reference tables, is explained and illustrated.

As indicated by the brief synopses of the chapters, Part IV provides both a conceptual understanding of the issues involved in implementing database applications and a practical initial understanding of the procedures necessary to construct a database prototype. The introduction of common strategies, such as client/server, Web enabled, Web services, and data warehousing, equip you to understand expected future developments in databases.

Chapter 7

Introduction to SQL

LEARNING OBJECTIVES

After studying this chapter, you should be able to:

- Concisely define each of the following key terms: **relational DBMS (RDBMS), catalog, schema, data definition language (DDL), data manipulation language (DML), data control language (DCL), base table, dynamic view, materialized view, referential integrity, scalar aggregate,** and **vector aggregate.**
- Interpret the history and role of SQL in database development.
- Define a database using the SQL data definition language.
- Write single table queries using SQL commands.
- Establish referential integrity using SQL.
- Discuss the SQL:1999 and SQL:2003 standards.

INTRODUCTION

Pronounced "S-Q-L" by some and "sequel" by others, SQL has become the de facto standard language for creating and querying relational databases. The primary purpose of this chapter is to introduce SQL, the most common language for relational systems. It has been accepted as an American standard by the American National Standards Institute (ANSI) and is a Federal Information Processing Standard (FIPS). It is also an international standard recognized by the International Organization for Standardization (ISO). ANSI has accredited the InterNational Committee for Information Technology Standards (INCITS) as a standards development organization. INCITS is working on the next version of the SQL standard to be released.

The ANSI SQL standards were first published in 1986 and updated in 1989, 1992 (SQL-92), 1999 (SQL:1999), and 2003 (SQL:2003). SQL-92 was a major revision and was structured into three levels: Entry, Intermediate, and Full. SQL:1999 established Core-level conformance, which must be met before any other level of conformance can be achieved and Core-level conformance requirements are unchanged in SQL:2003. In addition to fixes and enhancements of SQL:1999, SQL:2003 introduced a new set of SQL/XML standards, three new data types, various new built-in functions, and improved methods for generating values automatically. At the time of this writing, most database management systems claim SQL:1999 compliance and partial compliance with SQL:2003. Except where noted as a particular vendor's syntax, the examples in this chapter conform to the SQL standard. Concerns have been expressed about SQL:1999 and SQL:2003 being true standards because conformance with the standard is no longer certified by the U.S. Department of Commerce's National Institute of Standards and Technology (NIST) (Gorman, 2003). Vendor interpretations of the standards differ from each other and vendors extend their products' capabilities beyond the stated standards. This makes it difficult to port SQL from one vendor's product to another. One must become familiar with the particular version of SQL being used and not expect that it will transfer exactly as written to another vendor's version. Table 7-1 demonstrates differences in handling date and time values to illustrate discrepancies one encounters across vendors (IBM DB2, Microsoft SQL Server, MySQL [an open source DBMS], and Oracle).

SQL has been implemented in both mainframe and personal computer systems, so this chapter is relevant to both computing environments. Although many of the PC-database packages use a query-by-example (QBE) interface, they also include SQL coding as an option. QBE interfaces use graphic presentations and translate the QBE actions into SQL code before query execution occurs. In Microsoft Access, for example, it is possible to switch back and forth between the two interfaces; a query that has been built using a QBE interface can be viewed in SQL by clicking a button. This feature may aid the reader in learning SQL syntax. In client/server architectures, SQL commands are executed on the server, and the results are returned to the client workstation.

Table 7-1   Handling Date and Time Values (Adapted from Troels, 2005)

TIMESTAMP data type: A **core feature,** the standard required that this data type store year, month, day, hour, minute, second (with fractional seconds; default is six digits).

TIMESTAMP WITH TIME ZONE data type: **Extension to TIMESTAMP** also stores the time zone.

Implementation:

PRODUCT	FOLLOWS STANDARD?	COMMENTS
DB2	TIMESTAMP Only	Includes validity check and will not accept an entry such as '2006-02-29 00:05:00'.
MSSQL	NO	DATETIME stores date and time, with only 3 digits for fractional seconds. Validity check similar to DB2's is included.
MySQL	NO	TIMESTAMP updates to current date and time if certain criteria are met. DATETIME similar to MS-SQL, but validity checking is less accurate and may result in values of zero being stored.
Oracle	TIMESTAMP & TIMESTAMP WITH TIME ZONE	TIMESTAMP WITH TIME ZONE not allowed as part of a unique key. Includes validity check on dates.

The first commercial DBMS that supported SQL was Oracle in 1979. Oracle is now available in mainframe, client-server, and PC-based platforms for many operating systems, including various UNIX, Linux, and Microsoft Windows operating systems. IBM's DB2, Informix, and Microsoft SQL Server are available for this range of operating systems also. See Gulutzan (2002) for a detailed discussion of the move from SQL-92 to SQL:1999 compliance. See Eisenberg et al.(2004) for an overview of SQL:2003.

HISTORY OF THE SQL STANDARD

The concepts of relational database technology were first articulated in 1970 in a classic paper written by E. F. Codd entitled "A Relational Model of Data for Large Shared Data Banks." Workers at the IBM Research Laboratory in San Jose, California, undertook development of System R, a project whose purpose was to demonstrate the feasibility of implementing the relational model in a database management system. They used a language called Sequel, also developed at the San Jose IBM Research Laboratory. Sequel was renamed SQL during the project, which took place from 1974 to 1979. The knowledge gained was applied in the development of SQL/DS, the first relational database management system available commercially from IBM. SQL/DS was first available in 1981, running on the DOS/VSE operating system. A VM version followed in 1982, and the MVS version, DB2, was announced in 1983.

Because System R was well received at the user sites where it was installed, other vendors began developing relational products that used SQL. One product, Oracle, from Relational Software, was actually on the market before SQL/DS (1979). Other products included INGRES from Relational Technology (1981), IDM from Britton-Lee (1982), DG/SQL from Data General Corporation (1984), and Sybase from Sybase Inc. (1986). To provide some directions for the development of relational DBMSs, ANSI and the ISO approved a standard for the SQL relational query language (functions and syntax) that was originally proposed by the X3H2 Technical Committee on Database (Technical Committee X3H2—Database, 1986; ISO, 1987), often referred to as SQL/86. The 1986 standards have been extended to include an optional Integrity Enhancement Feature (IEF), often referred to as SQL/89. A related standard, Database Language Embedded SQL, was also adopted in the United States in 1989. The ISO and ANSI committees created SQL-92 (Technical Committee X3H2—Database, 1989; ISO, 1989, 1991), which was a more extensive expansion of SQL/86. This standard was ratified in late 1992 and is known as International Standard ISO/IEC 9075:1992, Database Language SQL. It was amended in 1994 and 1996. SQL:1999 was ratified in July, 1999 and SQL:2003 in 2003. The information included in this text about SQL:2003 has been taken from the Final Committee Draft (FCD) of ISO/IEC 9075-1:2003.

Many products are available that support SQL, and they run on all machine sizes, from small personal computers to large mainframes. The database market is maturing and the rate of significant changes in products may slow, but they will continue to be SQL-based. The number of relational database vendors with significant market share has continued to consolidate. According to International Data Corporation (IDC), Oracle, IBM, and Microsoft together garnered over 85 percent of the overall database market in 2003 (Tekrati, Inc, 2005), with Oracle controlling slightly over 41 percent of the market, IBM controlling about 31 percent, and Microsoft about 13 percent. MySQL, an open source version of SQL that runs on Linix, Unix, Windows, and Mac OS X operating systems has achieved considerable popularity. Download MySQL for free from http://www.mysql.com. Opportunities still exist for smaller vendors to prosper through industry-specific systems or niche applications. Upcoming product releases may change the relative strengths of the database management systems by the time you read this book. But all of them will continue to use SQL, and they will follow, to a certain extent, the standards described here.

THE ROLE OF SQL
IN A DATABASE ARCHITECTURE

With today's relational DBMSs and application generators, the importance of SQL within the database architecture is not usually apparent to the application users. Many users access database applications with no knowledge of SQL at all. For example, sites on the Web allow users to browse the catalog of the site being visited (e.g., see www.llbean.com). The information about an item that is presented, such as size, color, description, or availability, is stored in a database. The information has been retrieved using an SQL query, but the user has not issued an SQL command.

An SQL-based relational database application involves a user interface, a set of tables in the database, and a relational database management system (RDBMS) with an SQL capability. Within the RDBMS, SQL will be used to create the tables, translate user requests, maintain the data dictionary and system catalog, update and maintain the tables, establish security, and carry out backup and recovery procedures. A **relational DBMS (RDBMS)** is a data management system that implements a relational data model, one where data are stored in a collection of tables, and the data relationships are represented by common values, not links. This view of data was illustrated in Chapter 3 for the Pine Valley Furniture database system, and will be used throughout this chapter's SQL example queries.

Relational DBMS (RDBMS): A database management system that manages data as a collection of tables in which all data relationships are represented by common values in related tables.

The original purposes of the SQL standard follow:

1. To specify the syntax and semantics of SQL data definition and manipulation languages
2. To define the data structures and basic operations for designing, accessing, maintaining, controlling, and protecting an SQL database
3. To provide a vehicle for portability of database definition and application modules between conforming DBMSs
4. To specify both minimal (Level 1) and complete (Level 2) standards, which permit different degrees of adoption in products
5. To provide an initial standard, although incomplete, that will be enhanced later to include specifications for handling such topics as referential integrity, transaction management, user-defined functions, join operators beyond the equi-join, and national character sets (among others)

The Core SQL:1999 standard has been widely accepted, and most vendors indicate Core SQL:1999 compliance, which implies Core SQL:2003 compliance. However, each vendor's version of SQL also includes enhancements, features, and capabilities that extend their version beyond the baseline standards of SQL:1999. For example, Oracle includes a DESCRIBE command, which lists all attributes, their data types, and constraints for a table. This is a very useful feature, especially for students who are becoming familiar with a demonstration database, but it is a command that they will not find if they use another vendor's SQL, such as Microsoft Access. Thus, the SQL standards have always served as a minimum set of capabilities rather than as a completely specified set of capabilities. What are the advantages and disadvantages of having an SQL standard?

The benefits of such a standardized relational language include the following:

- *Reduced training costs*   Training in an organization can concentrate on one language. A large labor pool of IS professionals trained in a common language reduces retraining when hiring new employees.

- *Productivity*   IS professionals can learn SQL thoroughly and become proficient with it from continued use. The organization can afford to invest in tools to help IS professionals become more productive. And because they are familiar with the language in which programs are written, programmers can more quickly maintain existing programs.

- *Application portability*   Applications can be moved from machine to machine when each machine uses SQL. Further, it is economical for the computer software industry to develop off-the-shelf application software when there is a standard language.

- *Application longevity*   A standard language tends to remain so for a long time; hence there will be little pressure to rewrite old applications. Rather, applications will simply be updated as the standard language is enhanced or new versions of DBMSs are introduced.

- *Reduced dependence on a single vendor*   When a nonproprietary language is used, it is easier to use different vendors for the DBMS, training and educational services, application software, and consulting assistance; further, the market for such vendors will be more competitive, which may lower prices and improve service.

- *Cross-system communication*   Different DBMSs and application programs can more easily communicate and cooperate in managing data and processing user programs.

On the other hand, a standard can stifle creativity and innovation; one standard is never enough to meet all needs, and an industry standard can be far from ideal because it may be the offspring of compromises among many parties. A standard may be difficult to change (because so many vendors have a vested interest in it), so fixing deficiencies may take considerable effort. Another disadvantage of standards is that using special features added to SQL by a particular vendor may result in the loss of some advantages, such as application portability.

The original SQL standard has been widely criticized, especially for its lack of referential integrity rules and certain relational operators. Date and Darwen (1997) express concern that SQL seems to have been designed without adhering to established principles of language design and "As a result, the language is filled with numerous restrictions, ad hoc constructs, and annoying special rules" (p. 8). They feel that the standard is not explicit enough and that the problem of standard SQL implementations will continue to exist. Some of these limitations will be noticeable in this chapter.

THE SQL ENVIRONMENT

Figure 7-1 is a simplified schematic of an SQL environment, consistent with SQL:2003 standards. As depicted, an SQL environment includes an instance of an SQL database management system along with the databases accessible by that DBMS and the users and programs that may use that DBMS to access the databases. Each database is contained in a **catalog**, which describes any object that is a part of the database, regardless of which user created that object. Figure 7-1 shows two catalogs: DEV_C and PROD_C. Most companies keep at least two versions of any

Catalog: A set of schemas that, when put together, constitute a description of a database.

Figure 7-1
A simplified schematic of a typical SQL environment, as described by the SQL: 2003 standard

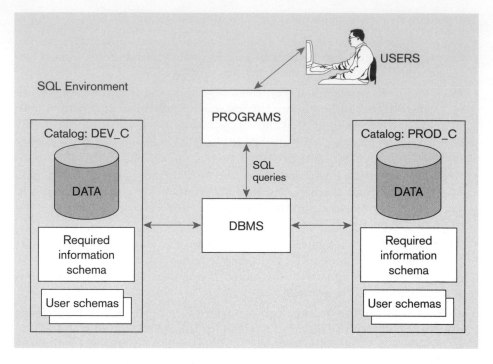

Figure 7-1
A simplified schematic of a typical SQL environment, as described by the SQL: 2003 standard

database they are using. The production version, PROD_C here, is the live version, which captures real business data and thus must be very tightly controlled and monitored. The development version, DEV_C here, is used when the database is being built and continues to serve as a development tool where enhancements and maintenance efforts can be thoroughly tested before being applied to the production database. Typically this database is not as tightly controlled or monitored, because it does not contain live business data. Each database will have named schema(s) associated with a catalog. The **schema** is a collection of related objects, including but not limited to, base tables and views, domains, constraints, character sets, triggers, roles, and so forth.

> **Schema:** That structure that contains descriptions of objects created by a user, such as base tables, views, and constraints, as part of a database.

If more than one user has created objects in the database, combining information about all users' schemas will yield information for the entire database. Each catalog must also contain an information schema, which contains descriptions of all schemas in the catalog, tables, views, attributes, privileges, constraints, and domains, along with other information relevant to the database. The information contained in the catalog is maintained by the DBMS as a result of the SQL commands issued by the users and does not require conscious action by the user to build it. It is part of the power of the SQL language that the issuance of syntactically simple SQL commands may result in complex data management activities being carried out by the DBMS software. Users can browse the catalog contents by using SQL select statements.

> **Data definition language (DDL):** Those commands used to define a database, including creating, altering, and dropping tables and establishing constraints.

SQL commands can be classified into three types. First, there are **data definition language (DDL)** commands. These commands are used to create, alter, and drop tables, and will be covered first in this chapter. In a production database, the ability to use DDL commands will generally be restricted to one or more database administrators in order to protect the database structure from unexpected changes. In development or student databases, DDL privileges will be granted to more users.

> **Data manipulation language (DML):** Those commands used to maintain and query a database, including updating, inserting, modifying, and querying data.

Next, there are **data manipulation language (DML)** commands. Many consider the DML commands to be the core commands of SQL. These commands are used for updating, inserting, modifying, and querying the data in the database. They may be issued interactively, so that a result is returned immediately following the execution of the statement, or they may be included within programs written in a procedural programming language, such as C, Java, or COBOL. Embedding SQL commands may provide the programmer with more control over timing of report generation, interface appearance, error handling, and database security (see Chapter 10 on embedding SQL in Web-based programs). Most of this chapter is devoted to covering basic DML commands, in interactive format. The general syntax of the SQL SELECT command used in DML is shown in Figure 7-2.

Last are **data control language (DCL)** commands. These commands help the DBA control the database; they include commands to grant or revoke privileges to access the database or particular objects within the database and to store or remove transactions that would affect the database.

Data control language (DCL): Commands used to control a database, including administering privileges and the committing (saving) of data.

Each DBMS has a defined list of data types that it can handle. All contain numeric, string, and date/time-type variables. Some also contain graphic data types, spatial data types, or image data types, which greatly increase the flexibility of data manipulation. When a table is created, the data type for each attribute must be specified. Selection of a particular data type is affected by the data values that need to be stored and the expected uses of the data. A unit price will need to be stored in a numeric format because mathematical manipulations such as multiplying unit price by the number of units ordered are expected. A phone number may be stored as string data, especially if foreign phone numbers are going to be included in the data set. Even though the phone number contains only digits, no mathematical operations, such as adding or multiplying phone numbers, make sense. Because character data will process more quickly, numeric data should be stored as character data if no arithmetic calculations are expected. Selecting a date field rather than a string field will allow the developer to take advantage of date/time interval calculation functions that cannot be applied to a character field. See Table 7-2 for a few examples of SQL data types. SQL:2003 includes three new data types BIGINT, MULTISET and XML. Watch for these new data types to be added to RDBMSs that had not previously introduced them as an enhancement of the existing standard.

```
SELECT [ALL/DISTINCT] column_list
FROM table_list
[WHERE conditional expression]
[GROUP BY group_by_column_list]
[HAVING conditional expression]
[ORDER BY order_by_column_list]
```

Figure 7-2
General syntax of the SELECT statement used in data manipulation language

Table 7-2   Sample SQL Data Types

String	CHARACTER (CHAR)	Stores string values containing any characters in a character set. CHAR is defined to be a fixed length.
	CHARACTER VARYING (VARCHAR)	Stores string values containing any characters in a character set, but of definable variable length.
	BINARY LARGE OBJECT (BLOB)	Stores binary string values in hexadecimal format. BLOB is defined to be a variable length.
Number	NUMERIC	Stores exact numbers with a defined precision and scale.
	INTEGER (INT)	Stores exact numbers with a predefined precision and scale of zero.
Temporal	TIMESTAMP	Stores a moment an event occurs, using a definable fraction of a second precision.
Boolean	BOOLEAN	Stores truth values, TRUE, FALSE, or UNKNOWN.

Figure 7-3
Sample Pine Valley Furniture Company data

CUSTOMER_t : Table

	Customer_ID	Customer_Name	Customer_Address	City	State	Postal_Code
+	1	Contemporary Casuals	1355 S Hines Blvd	Gainesville	FL	32601-2871
+	2	Value Furniture	15145 S.W. 17th St.	Plano	TX	75094-7743
+	3	Home Furnishings	1900 Allard Ave.	Albany	NY	12209-1125
+	4	Eastern Furniture	1925 Beltline Rd.	Carteret	NJ	07008-3188
+	5	Impressions	5585 Westcott Ct.	Sacramento	CA	94206-4056
+	6	Furniture Gallery	325 Flatiron Dr.	Boulder	CO	80514-4432
+	7	Period Furniture	394 Rainbow Dr.	Seattle	WA	97954-5589
+	8	California Classics	816 Peach Rd.	Santa Clara	CA	96915-7754
+	9	M and H Casual Furniture	3709 First Street	Clearwater	FL	34620-2314
+	10	Seminole Interiors	2400 Rocky Point Dr.	Seminole	FL	34646-4423
+	11	American Euro Lifestyles	2424 Missouri Ave N.	Prospect Park	NJ	07508-5621
+	12	Battle Creek Furniture	345 Capitol Ave. SW	Battle Creek	MI	49015-3401
+	13	Heritage Furnishings	66789 College Ave.	Carlisle	PA	17013-8834
+	14	Kaneohe Homes	112 Kiowai St.	Kaneohe	HI	96744-2537
+	15	Mountain Scenes	4132 Main Street	Ogden	UT	84403-4432
▶	(AutoNumber)					

Order_line_t : Table

Order_ID	Product_ID	Ordered_Quantity
1001	1	2
1001	2	2
1001	4	1
1002	3	5
1003	3	3
1004	6	2
1004	8	2
1005	4	4
1006	4	1
1006	5	2
1006	7	2
1007	1	3
1007	2	2
1008	3	3
1008	8	3
1009	4	2
1009	7	3
1010	8	10
▶ 0	0	0

ORDER_t : Table

	Order_ID	Order_Date	Customer_ID
+	1001	10/21/2006	1
+	1002	10/21/2006	8
+	1003	10/22/2006	15
+	1004	10/22/2006	5
+	1005	10/24/2006	3
+	1006	10/24/2006	2
+	1007	10/27/2006	11
+	1008	10/30/2006	12
+	1009	11/5/2006	4
+	1010	11/5/2006	1
▶	0		0

PRODUCT_t : Table

	Product_ID	Product_Description	Product_Finish	Standard_Price	Product_Line_ID
+	1	End Table	Cherry	$175.00	1
+	2	Coffee Table	Natural Ash	$200.00	2
+	3	Computer Desk	Natural Ash	$375.00	2
+	4	Entertainment Center	Natural Maple	$650.00	3
+	5	Writers Desk	Cherry	$325.00	1
+	6	8-Drawer Desk	White Ash	$750.00	2
+	7	Dining Table	Natural Ash	$800.00	2
+	8	Computer Desk	Walnut	$250.00	3
▶	(AutoNumber)			$0.00	0

With the advent of various graphic and image data types, it is necessary to consider business needs when deciding how to store data. For example, color may be stored as a descriptive character field, such as "sand drift" or "beige." But such descriptions will vary from vendor to vendor and do not contain the amount of information that could be contained in a spatial data type that includes exact red, green, and blue intensity values. Such data types are now available in universal servers, which handle data warehouses, and can be expected to appear in RDBMSs as well. In addition to the predefined data types included in Table 7-2, SQL:1999 and SQL:2003 support constructed data types and user-defined types. There are many more predefined data types than those shown in Table 7-2. It will be necessary to familiarize yourself with the available data types for each RDBMS with which you work to achieve maximum advantage from its capabilities.

We are almost ready to illustrate sample SQL commands. The sample data that we will be using are shown in Figure 7-3. Each table name follows a naming standard that places an underscore and the letter t at the end of each table name, such as Order_t or Product_t. When looking at these tables, please take notice of the following:

1. Each order must have a valid customer number included in the Order_t table.

2. Each item in an order must have both a valid product number and a valid order number associated with it in the Order_Line_t table.

3. These four tables represent a simplified version of one of the most common sets of relations in business database systems—that of the customer order for products. SQL commands necessary to create the Customer table and the Order table were included in Chapter 3, and are expanded here.

The remainder of the chapter will illustrate DDL, DML, and DCL commands. Figure 7-4 gives an overview of where the various types of commands are used

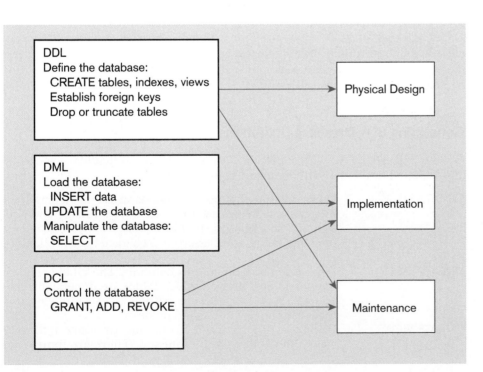

Figure 7-4
DDL, DML, DCL and the database development process

throughout the database development process. We will use the following notation in the illustrative SQL commands:

1. Capitalized words denote the command syntax. Type them exactly as shown, though capitalization may not be required by the RDBMSs.

2. Lowercase words denote values that must be supplied by the user.

3. Brackets enclose optional syntax.

4. Ellipses (. . .) indicate that the accompanying syntactic clause may be repeated as necessary.

5. Each SQL command ends with a semicolon (;). In interactive mode, when the user presses the RETURN key, the SQL command will execute. Be alert for alternative conventions, such as typing GO, or having to include a continuation symbol such as a hyphen at the end of each line used in the command. The spacing and indentations shown here are included for readability and are not a required part of standard SQL syntax.

DEFINING A DATABASE IN SQL

Most systems allocate storage space to contain base tables, views, constraints, indexes, and other database objects when a database is created. Because of this, the privilege of creating databases may be reserved for the database administrator, and you may need to ask to have a database created. Students at a university may be assigned an account that gives access to an existing database, or they may be allowed to create their own database. In any case, the basic syntax to create a database is CREATE SCHEMA database_name; AUTHORIZATION owner_user id. The database will be owned by the authorized user, although it is possible for other specified users to work with the database or even to transfer ownership of the database. Physical storage of the database is dependent on both the hardware and software environment and is usually the concern of the system administrator. The amount of control over physical storage that a database administrator is able to exert depends on the RDBMS being used. There is little control possible when using Microsoft Access 2002, but SQL Server 2000 allows for more control of the physical database. An Oracle 10g database administrator may exert considerable control over the placement of data, control files, index files, and so forth, thus improving the ability to tune the database to perform more efficiently.

Generating SQL Database Definitions

Several SQL DDL CREATE commands are included in SQL:2003 (each command is followed by the name of the object being created):

CREATE SCHEMA	Used to define that portion of a database that a particular user owns. Schemas are dependent on a catalog and contain schema objects, including base tables and views, domains, constraints, assertions, character sets, collations, and so forth.
CREATE TABLE	Defines a new table and its columns. The table may be a base table or a derived table. Tables are dependent on a schema. Derived tables are created by executing a query that uses one or more tables or views.
CREATE VIEW	Defines a logical table from one or more tables or views. Views may not be indexed. There are limitations

on updating data through a view. Where views can be updated, those changes can be transferred to the underlying base tables originally referenced to create the view.

Each of these CREATE commands may be reversed by using a DROP command. Thus, DROP TABLE *tablename* will destroy a table, including its definition, contents, and any constraints, views, or indexes associated with it. Usually only the table creator may delete the table. DROP SCHEMA or DROP VIEW will also destroy the named schema or view. ALTER TABLE may be used to change the definition of an existing base table by adding, dropping, or changing a column or by dropping a constraint.

There are also five other CREATE commands included:

CREATE CHARACTER SET	Allows the user to define a character set for text strings and aids in the globalization of SQL by enabling the use of languages other than English. Each character set contains a set of characters, a way to represent each character internally, a data format used for this representation, and a collation, or way of sorting the character set.
CREATE COLLATION	A named schema object that specifies the order that a character set will assume. Existing collations may be manipulated to create a new collation.
CREATE TRANSLATION	A named set of rules that maps characters from a source character set to a destination character set for translation or conversion purposes.
CREATE ASSERTION	A schema object that establishes a CHECK constraint that is violated if the constraint is false.
CREATE DOMAIN	A schema object that establishes a domain, or set of valid values, for an attribute. Data type will be specified, and a default value, collation, or other constraint may also be specified, if desired.

Creating Tables

Once the data model is designed and normalized, the columns needed for each table can be defined using the SQL CREATE TABLE command. The general syntax for CREATE TABLE is shown in Figure 7-5. Here is a series of steps to follow when preparing to create a table:

1. Identify the appropriate data type, including length, precision, and scale if required, for each attribute.

```
CREATE TABLE tablename
( {column definition   [table constraint] } . , . .
[ON COMMIT {DELETE | PRESERVE} ROWS] );

where column definition ::=
column_name
        {domain name | datatype [(size)] }
        [column_constraint_clause . . .]
        [default value]
        [collate clause]

and table constraint ::=
        [CONSTRAINT constraint_name]
        Constraint_type [constraint_attributes]
```

Figure 7-5
General syntax of the CREATE TABLE statement used in data definition language

```
CREATE TABLE CUSTOMER_T
            (CUSTOMER_ID              NUMBER(11, 0) NOT NULL,
            CUSTOMER_NAME             VARCHAR2(25)  NOT NULL,
            CUSTOMER_ADDRESS          VARCHAR2(30),
            CITY                      VARCHAR2(20),
            STATE                     VARCHAR2(2),
            POSTAL_CODE               VARCHAR2(9),
CONSTRAINT CUSTOMER_PK PRIMARY KEY (CUSTOMER_ID));

CREATE TABLE ORDER_T
            (ORDER_ID                 NUMBER(11, 0) NOT NULL,
            ORDER_DATE                DATE DEFAULT SYSDATE,
            CUSTOMER_ID               NUMBER(11, 0),
CONSTRAINT ORDER_PK PRIMARY KEY (ORDER_ID),
CONSTRAINT ORDER_FK FOREIGN KEY (CUSTOMER_ID) REFERENCES CUSTOMER_T(CUSTOMER_ID));

CREATE TABLE PRODUCT_T
            (PRODUCT_ID               INTEGER      NOT NULL,
            PRODUCT_DESCRIPTION       VARCHAR2(50),
            PRODUCT_FINISH            VARCHAR2(20)
                        CHECK (PRODUCT_FINISH IN ('Cherry', 'Natural Ash', 'White Ash',
                                    'Red Oak', 'Natural Oak', 'Walnut')),
            STANDARD_PRICE            DECIMAL(6,2),
            PRODUCT_LINE_ID           INTEGER,
CONSTRAINT PRODUCT_PK PRIMARY KEY (PRODUCT_ID));

CREATE TABLE ORDER_LINE_T
            (ORDER_ID                 NUMBER(11,0)  NOT NULL,
            PRODUCT_ID                NUMBER(11,0)  NOT NULL,
            ORDERED_QUANTITY          NUMBER(11,0),
CONSTRAINT ORDER_LINE_PK PRIMARY KEY (ORDER_ID, PRODUCT_ID),
CONSTRAINT ORDER_LINE_FK1 FOREIGN KEY(ORDER_ID) REFERENCES ORDER_T(ORDER_ID),
CONSTRAINT ORDER_LINE_FK2 FOREIGN KEY (PRODUCT_ID) REFERENCES PRODUCT_T(PRODUCT_ID));
```

Figure 7-6
SQL database definition commands for
Pine Valley Furniture Company (Oracle
10g)

2. Identify those columns that should accept null values, as discussed in Chapter 6. Column controls that indicate a column cannot be null are established when a table is created and are enforced for every update of the table when data are entered.

3. Identify those columns that need to be unique. When a column control of UNIQUE is established for a column, then the data in that column must have a different value (i.e., no duplicate values) for each row of data within that table. Where a column or set of columns is designated as UNIQUE, that column or set of columns is a candidate key, as discussed in Chapter 5. Although each base table may have multiple candidate keys, only one candidate key may be designated as a PRIMARY KEY. When a column(s) is specified as the PRIMARY KEY, that column(s) is also assumed to be NOT NULL, even if NOT NULL is not explicitly stated. UNIQUE and PRIMARY KEY are both column constraints. Note that a table with a composite primary key, Order_Line_t, is defined in Figure 7-6. The Order_Line_PK constraint includes both Order_ID and Product_ID in the primary key constraint, thus creating a composite key. Additional attributes may be included within the parentheses as needed to create the composite key.

4. Identify all primary key–foreign key mates, as presented in Chapter 5. Foreign keys can be established immediately, as a table is created, or later by

altering the table. The parent table in such a parent-child relationship should be created first so that the child table will reference an existing parent table when it is created. The column constraint REFERENCES can be used to enforce referential integrity.

5. Determine values to be inserted in any columns for which a default value is desired. DEFAULT can be used to define a value that is automatically inserted when no value is inserted during data entry. In Figure 7-6, the command that creates the ORDER_T table has defined a default value of SYSDATE (Oracle's name for the current date) for the ORDER_DATE attribute.

6. Identify any columns for which domain specifications may be stated that are more constrained than those established by data type. Using CHECK as a column constraint it may be possible to establish validation rules for values to be inserted into the database. In Figure 7-6, creation of the PRODUCT_T table includes a check constraint, which lists the possible values for PRODUCT_FINISH. Thus, even though an entry of 'White Maple' would meet the varchar data type constraints, it would be rejected because 'White Maple' is not in the checklist.

7. Create the table and any desired indexes using the CREATE TABLE and CREATE INDEX statements. (CREATE INDEX is not a part of the SQL:1999 standard because indexing is used to address performance issues, but is available in most RDBMSs.)

In Chapters 3 and 5, SQL database definition commands to create the Customer and Order tables for Pine Valley Furniture were shown that included establishing column constraints within the CREATE TABLE commands. In Figure 7-6, database definition commands using Oracle 10g are shown that include additional column constraints, and primary and foreign keys are given names. For example, the Customer table's primary key is CUSTOMER_ID. The primary key constraint is named CUSTOMER_PK. In Oracle, for example, once a constraint has been given a meaningful name by the user, a database administrator will find it easy to identify the primary key constraint on the customer table because its name, CUSTOMER_PK, will be the value of the constraint_name column in the DBA_CONSTRAINTS table. Without assigning a meaningful constraint name, a 16-byte system identifier would be assigned automatically. The identifiers are difficult to read and even more difficult to match up with user-defined constraints. Documentation about how system identifiers are generated is not available and it also can be changed without notification.

When a foreign key constraint is defined, referential integrity will be enforced. For example, if you try to add an order with an invalid CUSTOMER_ID value, you will receive an error message. Each DBMS vendor generates their own error messages, and they may be difficult to interpret. MS Access, being intended for both personal and professional use, provides simple error messages in dialogue windows. A referential integrity violation displays an error message: "You cannot add or change a record because a related record is required in table CUSTOMER_T." No record will be added to ORDER_T until that record references an existing customer in the CUSTOMER_T table.

Sometimes the user will want to create a table that is similar to one that already exists. SQL:1999 included the capability of adding a LIKE clause to the CREATE TABLE statement that allowed for the copying of the existing structure of one or more tables into a new table. For example, a table can be used to store data that are questionable until it can be reviewed by an administrator. This exception table has the same structure as the verified transaction table, and missing or conflicting data will be reviewed and resolved before those transactions are appended to the transaction table. SQL:2003 has expanded the CREATE...LIKE capability by allowing additional information, such as table constraints, from the original table to be easily ported to the new table when it is created. The new table exists independently of the original table. Inserting a new instance into the original table will have no effect on the new table. However, if the attempt to insert the new instance triggers an exception, the trigger can be written so that the data is stored in the new table to be reviewed later. The CREATE TABLE LIKE clause is covered in more detail in Chapter 8.

Creating Data Integrity Controls

Referential integrity: An integrity constraint specifying that the value (or existence) of an attribute in one relation depends on the value (or existence) of a primary key in the same or another relation.

We have seen the syntax that establishes foreign keys in Figure 7-6. To establish **referential integrity** between two tables with a *1:M* relationship in the relational data model, the primary key of the table on the one side will be referenced by a column in the table on the many side of the relationship. Referential integrity means that a value in the matching column on the many side must correspond to a value in the primary key for some row in the table on the one side or be NULL. The SQL REFERENCES clause prevents a foreign key value from being added if it is not already a valid value in the referenced primary key column, but there are other integrity issues.

If a CUSTOMER_ID value is changed, the connection between that customer and orders placed by that customer will be ruined. The REFERENCES clause prevents making such a change in the foreign key value, but not in the primary key value. This problem could be handled by asserting that primary key values cannot be changed once they are established. In this case, updates to the customer table will be handled in most systems by including an ON UPDATE RESTRICT clause. Then, any updates that would delete or change a primary key value will be rejected unless no foreign key references that value in any child table. See Figure 7-7 for the syntax associated with updates.

Another solution is to pass the change through to the child table(s) by using the ON UPDATE CASCADE option. Then, if a customer ID number is changed, that change will flow through (cascade) to the child table, ORDER_T, and the customer's ID will also be updated in the ORDER_T table.

A third solution is to allow the update on CUSTOMER_T but to change the involved CUSTOMER_ID value in the ORDER_T table to NULL by using the ON UPDATE SET NULL option. In this case, using the SET NULL option would result in losing the connection between the order and the customer, which is not a desired effect. The most flexible option to use would be the CASCADE option. Were a customer record to be deleted, ON DELETE RESTRICT, CASCADE, or SET NULL are also available. With DELETE RESTRICT, the customer record could not be deleted unless there were no orders from that customer in the ORDER_T table. With DELETE CASCADE, removing the customer would remove all associated order records from ORDER_T. With DELETE SET NULL, the order records for that customer would be set to null before the customer's record is deleted. With DELETE SET DEFAULT, the order records for that customer would be set to a default value before the customer's record is deleted. DELETE RESTRICT would probably make the most sense. Not all SQL RDBMSs provide for primary key referential integrity. In that case, update and delete permissions on the primary key column may be revoked.

Changing Table Definitions

Base table definitions may be changed by ALTERing column specifications. The ALTER TABLE command may be used to add new columns to an existing

Figure 7-7
Ensuring data integrity through updates

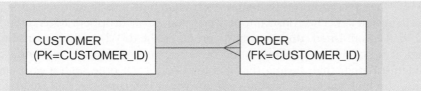

Restricted Update: A customer ID can only be deleted if it is not found in ORDER table.

CREATE TABLE CUSTOMER_T
    (CUSTOMER_ID   INTEGER DEFAULT 'C999' NOT NULL,
    CUSTOMER_NAME VARCHAR(40)   NOT NULL,
    . . .
CONSTRAINT CUSTOMER_PK PRIMARY KEY (CUSTOMER_ID),
ON UPDATE RESTRICT);

Cascaded Update: Changing a customer ID in the CUSTOMER table will result in that value changing in the ORDER table to match.

 . . . ON UPDATE CASCADE);

Set Null Update: When a customer ID is changed, any customer ID in the ORDER table that matches the old customer ID is set to NULL.

 . . . ON UPDATE SET NULL);

Set Default Update: When a customer ID is changed, any customer ID in the ORDER tables that matches the old customer ID is set to a predefined default value.

 . . . ON UPDATE SET DEFAULT);

---

table. Existing columns may also be altered. Table constraints may be added or dropped. The ALTER TABLE command may include keywords such as ADD, DROP, or ALTER and allow the column's names, data type, length, and constraints to be changed. Usually, when adding a new column, its null status will be NULL so that data that have already been entered in the table can be dealt with. When the new column is created, it is added to all of the instances in the table, and a value of NULL would be the most reasonable. The ALTER command cannot be used to change a view.

 Syntax:

 ALTER TABLE table_name alter_table_action;

Some of the alter_table_actions available are:

 ADD [COLUMN] column_definition
 ALTER [COLUMN] column_name **SET DEFAULT** default-value
 ALTER [COLUMN] column_name **DROP DEFAULT**
 DROP [COLUMN] column_name **[RESTRICT] [CASCADE]**
 ADD table_constraint

 Command: To add a customer type column named TYPE to the CUSTOMER
    table.

ALTER TABLE CUSTOMER_T
ADD COLUMN TYPE VARCHAR (2) DEFAULT "Commercial";

 The ALTER command is invaluable for adapting the database to inevitable modifications due to changing requirements, prototyping, evolutionary development, and mistakes. It is also useful when performing a bulk data load into a table that contains a foreign key. The constraint may be temporarily dropped. Later, after the bulk data load has finished, the constraint can be enabled. When the constraint is reenabled, it is possible to generate a log of any records that have referential integrity problems. Rather than having the data load balk each time such a problem occurs during the bulk load, the database administrator can simply review the log and reconcile the few (hopefully few) records that were problematic.

Removing Tables

To remove a table from a database, the owner of the table may use the DROP TABLE command. Views are dropped by using the similar DROP VIEW command.

Command: To drop a table from a database schema.

DROP TABLE CUSTOMER_T;

This command will drop the table and save any pending changes to the database. To drop a table, you must either own the table or have been granted the DROP ANY TABLE system privilege. Dropping a table will also cause associated indexes and privileges granted to be dropped. The DROP TABLE command can be qualified by the keywords RESTRICT or CASCADE. If RESTRICT is specified, the command will fail and the table will not be dropped if there are any dependent objects, such as views or constraints, that currently reference the table. If CASCADE is specified, all dependent objects will also be dropped as the table is dropped. Oracle allows users to retain the table's structure but remove all of the data that have been entered in the table with its TRUNCATE TABLE command. Commands for updating and deleting part of the data in a table are covered in the next section.

INSERTING, UPDATING, AND DELETING DATA

Once tables and views have been created, it is necessary to populate them with data and maintain those data before queries can be written. The SQL command that is used to populate tables is the INSERT command. When entering a value for every column in the table, you can use a command like the following, which was used to add the first row of data to the CUSTOMER_T table. Notice that the data values must be ordered in the same order as the columns in the table.

Command: To insert a row of data into a table where a value will be inserted for every attribute.

INSERT INTO CUSTOMER_T VALUES
(001, 'Contemporary Casuals', '1355 S. Himes Blvd.', 'Gainesville', 'FL', 32601);

When data will not be entered into every column in the table, either enter the value NULL for the empty fields or specify those columns to which data are to be added. Here, too, the data values must be in the same order as the columns have been specified in the INSERT command. For example, the following statement was used to insert one row of data into the PRODUCT_T table, because there was no product line ID for the end table.

Command: To insert a row of data into a table where some attributes will be left null.

INSERT INTO PRODUCT_T (PRODUCT_ID,
PRODUCT_DESCRIPTION,_PRODUCT_FINISH, STANDARD_PRICE)
    VALUES (1, 'End Table', 'Cherry', 175, 8);

In general, the INSERT command places a new row in a table based on values supplied in the statement, copies one or more rows derived from other database data into a table, or extracts data from one table and inserts them into another. If you want to populate a table, CA_CUSTOMER_T, that has the same structure as CUSTOMER_T, with only Pine Valley's California customers, you could use the following INSERT command.

Command: Populating a table by using a subset of another table with the same structure.

```
INSERT INTO CA_CUSTOMER_T
SELECT * FROM CUSTOMER_T
        WHERE CUSTOMER_STATE = 'CA';
```

The table identified in the INSERT command may be a view. However, the view must be updateable, so that data inserted through the view are also inserted into the base table on which the view is based. If the view definition included the WITH CHECK OPTION attempts to insert data through the view, it will be rejected when the data values do not meet the specifications of the WITH CHECK OPTION.

In many cases, we want to generate a unique primary identifier or primary key every time a row is added to a table. Customer identification numbers are a good example of a situation where this capability would be helpful. SQL:2003 had added a new feature, identity columns, that removes the previous need to create a procedure to generate a sequence and then apply it to the insertion of data. To take advantage of this, the CREATE TABLE CUSTOMER_T statement displayed in Figure 7-6 may be modified (emphasized by bold print) as follows:

```
CREATE TABLE CUSTOMER_T
(CUSTOMER_ID INTEGER GENERATED ALWAYS AS IDENTITY
        (START WITH 1
        INCREMENT BY 1
        MINVALUE 1
        MAXVALUE 10000
        NO CYCLE),
CUSTOMER_NAME           VARCHAR (25) NOT NULL,
CUSTOMER_ADDRESS        VARCHAR (30),
CITY                    VARCHAR (20),
STATE                   VARCHAR (2),
POSTAL_CODE             VARCHAR (9),
CONSTRAINT CUSTOMER_PK PRIMARY KEY (CUSTOMER_ID);
```

Only one column may be an identity column in a table. When a new customer is added, the CUSTOMER_ID value will be assigned implicitly if the vendor has implemented identity columns.

Thus, the command that adds a new customer to CUSTOMER_T will change from:

```
INSERT INTO CUSTOMER_T VALUES
(001, 'Contemporary Casuals', '1355 S. Himes Blvd.', 'Gainesville', 'FL', 32601);
```

to:

```
INSERT INTO CUSTOMER_T VALUES
('Contemporary Casuals', '1355 S. Himes Blvd.', 'Gainesville', 'FL', 32601);
```

The primary key value, 001, does not need to be entered, and the syntax to accomplish the automatic sequencing has been simplified in SQL:2003.

Batch Input

The INSERT command is used to enter one row of data at a time or to add multiple rows as the result of a query. Some versions of SQL have a special command or utility for entering multiple rows of data as a batch: the INPUT command. Oracle includes a program, SQL*Loader, which runs from the command line and can be used to load data from a file into the database. This popular program is tricky to use and is not within the scope of this text.

Deleting Database Contents

Rows can be deleted individually or in groups. Suppose Pine Valley Furniture decides that it will no longer deal with customers located in Hawaii. CUSTOMER_T rows for customers with addresses in Hawaii could all be eliminated by the next command.

Command: Deleting rows that meet a certain criterion from the CUSTOMER table.

```
DELETE FROM CUSTOMER_T
   WHERE CUSTOMER_STATE = 'HI';
```

The simplest form of DELETE eliminates all rows of a table.

Command: Deleting all rows from the CUSTOMER table.

```
DELETE FROM CUSTOMER_T;
```

This form of the command should be used very carefully!

Deletion must also be done with care when rows from several relations are involved. For example, if we delete a CUSTOMER_T row, as in the previous query, before deleting associated ORDER_T rows, we will have a referential integrity violation, and the DELETE command will not execute. (Note: Including the ON DELETE clause with a field definition can mitigate such a problem. Refer back to the Creating Data Integrity Controls section in this chapter if you've forgotten about the ON clause.) SQL will actually eliminate the records selected by a DELETE command. Therefore, always execute a SELECT command first to display the records that would be deleted and visually verify that only the desired rows are included.

Updating Database Contents

To update data in SQL, we must inform the DBMS what relation, columns, and rows are involved. If an incorrect price is entered for the dining table in the PRODUCT_T table, the following SQL UPDATE statement would establish the correction.

Command: To modify unit price of product 7 in the PRODUCT table to 775.

```
UPDATE PRODUCT_T
SET UNIT PRICE = 775
      WHERE PRODUCT_ID = 7;
```

The SET command can also change a value to NULL; the syntax is SET columnname = NULL. As with DELETE, the WHERE clause in an UPDATE command may contain a subquery, but the table being updated may not be referenced in the subquery. Subqueries are discussed in Chapter 8.

The SQL:2003 standard has included a new keyword, MERGE, that makes updating a table easier. Many database applications need to update master tables with new data. A PURCHASES table, for example, might include rows with data about new products and rows that change the standard price of existing products. Updating PRODUCT_T can be accomplished by using INSERT to add the new products and

UPDATE to modify Standard_Price in an SQL-92 or SQL:1999 DBMS. SQL:2003 compliant DBMSs can accomplish the update and the insert in one step by using MERGE:

```
MERGE INTO PRODUCT_T AS PROD
USING
         (SELECT PRODUCT_ID, PRODUCT_DESCRIPTION, PRODUCT_FINISH,
         STANDARD_PRICE, PRODUCT_LINE_ID FROM PURCHASES_T) AS PURCH
            ON (PROD.PRODUCT_ID = PURCH.PRODUCT_ID)
WHEN MATCHED THEN UPDATE
         PROD.STANDARD_PRICE = PURCH.STANDARD_PRICE
WHEN NOT MATCHED THEN INSERT
         (PRODUCT_ID, PRODUCT_DESCRIPTION, PRODUCT_FINISH,
         STANDARD_PRICE, PRODUCT_LINE_ID)
         VALUES (PURCH.PRODUCT_ID, PURCH.PRODUCT_DESCRIPTION,
         PURCH.PRODUCT_FINISH, PURCH.STANDARD_PRICE,
         PURCH.PRODUCT_LINE_ID);
```

INTERNAL SCHEMA DEFINITION IN RDBMSS

The internal schema of a relational database can be controlled for processing and storage efficiency. Some techniques used to tune the operational performance of the relational database internal data model include:

1. Choosing to index primary and/or secondary keys to increase the speed of row selection, table joining, and row ordering. Dropping indexes to increase speed of table updating. You may want to review the section in Chapter 6 on selecting indexes.

2. Selecting file organizations for base tables that match the type of processing activity on those tables (e.g., keeping a table physically sorted by a frequently used reporting sort key).

3. Selecting file organizations for indexes, which are also tables, appropriate to the way the indexes are used and allocating extra space for an index file so that an index can grow without having to be reorganized.

4. Clustering data so that related rows of frequently joined tables are stored close together in secondary storage to minimize retrieval time.

5. Maintaining statistics about tables and their indexes so that the DBMS can find the most efficient ways to perform various database operations.

Not all of these techniques are available in all SQL systems. Indexing and clustering are typically available, however, so we discuss these in the following sections.

Creating Indexes

Indexes are created in most RDBMSs to provide rapid random and sequential access to base-table data. Because the ISO SQL standards do not generally address performance issues, no standard syntax for creating indexes is included. The examples given here use Oracle syntax and give a feel for how indexes are handled in most RDBMSs. Note that although users do not directly refer to indexes when writing any SQL command, the DBMS recognizes which existing indexes would improve query performance. Indexes can usually be created for both primary and secondary keys and both single and concatenated (multiple-column) keys. In some systems, users can choose between ascending or descending sequences for the keys in an index.

For example, an alphabetical index on CUSTOMER_NAME in the CUS-TOMER_T column in Oracle is created here.

Command: To create an alphabetical index on customer name in the CUS-TOMER table.

CREATE INDEX NAME_IDX ON CUSTOMER_T (CUSTOMER_NAME);

Indexes may be created or dropped at any time. If data already exist in the key column(s), index population will automatically occur for the existing data. If an index is defined as UNIQUE (using the syntax CREATE UNIQUE INDEX . . .) and the existing data violate this condition, the index creation will fail. Once an index is created, it will be updated as data are entered, updated, or deleted.

When we no longer need tables, views, or indexes, we use the associated DROP statements. For example, the NAME_IDX index from the previous example is dropped here.

Command: To remove the index on the customer name in the CUSTOMER table.

DROP INDEX NAME_IDX;

Although it is possible to index every column in a table, use caution when deciding to create a new index. Each index consumes extra storage space and also requires overhead maintenance time whenever indexed data change value. Together, these costs may noticeably slow retrieval response times and cause annoying delays for online users. A system may use only one index even if several are available for keys in a complex qualification. The database designer must know exactly how indexes are used by the particular RDBMS to make wise choices about indexing. Oracle includes an explain plan tool that can be used to look at the order in which an SQL statement will be processed and at the indexes that will be used. The output also includes a cost estimate that can be compared with estimates from running the statement with different indexes to determine which is most efficient.

PROCESSING SINGLE TABLES

Four data manipulation language commands are used in SQL. We have talked briefly about three of them (UPDATE, INSERT, and DELETE) and have seen several examples of the fourth, SELECT. Although the UPDATE, INSERT, and DELETE commands allow modification of the data in the tables, it is the SELECT command, with its various clauses, that allows users to query the data contained in the tables and ask many different questions or create ad hoc queries. The basic construction of an SQL command is fairly simple and easy to learn. Don't let that fool you; SQL is a powerful tool that enables users to specify complex data analysis processes. However, because the basic syntax is relatively easy to learn, it is also easy to write SELECT queries that are syntactically correct but do not answer the exact question that is intended. Before running queries against a large production database, always test queries carefully on a small test set of data to be sure that they are returning the correct results. In addition to checking the query results manually, it is often possible to parse queries into smaller parts, examine the results of these simpler queries, and then recombine them. This will ensure that they act together in the expected way. We begin by exploring SQL queries that affect only a single table. In Chapter 8, we join tables and use queries that require more than one table.

Clauses of the SELECT Statement

Most SQL data retrieval statements include the following three clauses:

SELECT Lists the columns (including expressions involving columns) from base tables or views to be projected into the table that will be the result of the command.

FROM Identifies the tables or views from which columns will be chosen to appear in the result table, and includes the tables or views needed to join tables to process the query.

WHERE Includes the conditions for row selection within a single table or view and the conditions between tables or views for joining. Because SQL is considered a set manipulation language, the WHERE clause is important in defining the set of rows being manipulated.

The first two clauses are required, and the third is necessary when only certain table rows are to be retrieved or multiple tables are to be joined. Most examples for this section are drawn from the data shown in Figure 7-3. As an example, we can display product name and quantity on hand from the PRODUCT view for all products that have a standard price of less than $275.

Query: Which products have a standard price of less than $275?

```
SELECT PRODUCT_DESCRIPTION, STANDARD_PRICE
   FROM PRODUCT_V
         WHERE STANDARD_PRICE < 275;
```

Result:

PRODUCT_DESCRIPTION	STANDARD_PRICE
End Table	175
Computer Desk	250
Coffee Table	200

Every SELECT statement returns a result table (a set of rows) when it executes. Two special keywords can be used along with the list of columns to display: DISTINCT and *. If the user does not wish to see duplicate rows in the result, SELECT DISTINCT may be used. In the preceding example, if the other computer desk carried by Pine Valley Furniture had also cost less than $275, the results of the query would have duplicate rows. SELECT DISTINCT PRODUCT_DESCRIPTION would display a result table without the duplicate rows. SELECT *, where * is used as a wildcard to indicate all columns; it displays all columns from all the tables or views in the FROM clause.

Also, note that the clauses of a SELECT statement must be kept in order, or syntax error messages will occur and the query will not execute. It may also be necessary to qualify the names of the database objects according to the SQL version being used. If there is any ambiguity in an SQL command, you must indicate exactly from which table or view the requested data are to come. For example, in Figure 7-3 CUSTOMER_ID is a column in both CUSTOMER_T and ORDER_T. When you own the database being used (i.e., the user created the tables) and you want the CUSTOMER_ID to come from CUSTOMER_T, specify it by asking for CUSTOMER_T.CUSTOMER_ID. If you want CUSTOMER_ID to come from ORDER_T, then ask for ORDER_T.CUSTOMER_ID. Even if you don't care which table CUSTOMER_ID comes from, it must be specified because SQL can't resolve the ambiguity without user direction. When using data created by someone else, you must also specify the owner of the table by adding the owner's user ID. Now a request to SELECT the CUSTOMER_ID from CUSTOMER_T may look like OWNER_ID.CUSTOMER_T.CUSTOMER_ID. The examples in this book assume that the reader owns the tables or views being used, as the SELECT statements will be easier to read without the qualifiers. Qualifiers will be included where necessary and may always be included in statements if desired. Problems may occur when qualifiers are left out, but no problems will occur when they are included.

If typing the qualifiers and column names is wearisome, or if the column names will not be meaningful to those who are reading the reports, establish aliases for columns, tables, or views that will then be used for the rest of the query. SQL:1999 does not include aliases or synonyms, but they are widely implemented and aid in readability and simplicity in query construction.

Query: What is the address of the customer named Home Furnishings? Use an alias, NAME, for customer name (AS clauses bolded for emphasis only).

```
SELECT CUST.CUSTOMER_NAME AS NAME, CUST.CUSTOMER_ADDRESS
   FROM ownerid.CUSTOMER_V AS CUST
      WHERE NAME = 'Home Furnishings';
```

This retrieval statement using the CUSTOMER_V view will give the following result in many versions of SQL. In Oracle's SQL*Plus, the alias for the column cannot be used in the rest of the SELECT statement, except in a HAVING clause, so CUSTOMER_NAME would have to be used in the last line rather than NAME in order to run. Notice that the column header prints as NAME rather than CUSTOMER_NAME, and that the view alias may be used in the SELECT clause even though it is not defined until the FROM clause.

Result:

NAME	CUSTOMER_ADDRESS
Home Furnishings	1900 Allard Ave.

When using the SELECT clause to pick out the columns for a result table, the columns can be rearranged so that they will be ordered differently in the result table than they were in the original table. In fact, they will be displayed in the same order as they are included in the SELECT statement. Look back at PRODUCT_T in Figure 7-3 to see the different ordering of the base table from the result table for this query.

Query: List the unit price, product name, and product ID for all products in the PRODUCT table.

```
SELECT STANDARD_PRICE, PRODUCT_DESCRIPTION, PRODUCT_ID
   FROM PRODUCT_T;
```

Result:

STANDARD_PRICE	PRODUCT_DESCRIPTION	PRODUCT_ID
175	End Table	1
200	Coffee Table	2
375	Computer Desk	3
650	Entertainment Center	4
325	Writer's Desk	5
750	8-Drawer Desk	6
800	Dining Table	7
250	Computer Desk	8

Using Expressions

Several other things can be done with the basic SELECT . . . FROM . . . WHERE clauses with a single table. You can create expressions, which are mathematical manipulations of the data in the table, or take advantage of stored functions, such as

SUM or AVG, to manipulate the chosen rows of data from the table. Perhaps you would like to know the average standard price of each inventory item. To get the average value, use the AVG stored function. Name the resulting expression AVERAGE. Using SQL*Plus, here are the query and the results.

Query: What is the average standard price for each product in inventory?

```
SELECT AVG (STANDARD_PRICE) AS AVERAGE
      FROM PRODUCT_V;
```

SQL:1999 stored functions included ANY, AVG, COUNT, EVERY, GROUPING, MAX, MIN, SOME, and SUM. SQL:2003 adds LN, EXP, POWER, SQRT, FLOOR, CEILING, and WIDTH_BUCKET.

Mathematical manipulations can be constructed by using the "+" for addition, "–" for subtraction, "*" for multiplication, and "/" for division. These operators can be used with any numeric columns. Some systems also have an operand called modulo, usually indicated by "%." A modulo is the integer remainder that results from dividing two integers. For example, 14 % 4 is 2 because 14/4 is 3 with a remainder of 2. The standard supports year–month and day–time intervals, which make it possible to perform date and time arithmetic. Notice that the result from the previous query on the PRODUCT_V view now shows the expression AVERAGE.

Result:

AVERAGE
440.625

The precedence rules for the order in which complex expressions are evaluated are the same as those used in other programming languages and in algebra. Expressions in parentheses will be calculated first. When parentheses do not establish order, multiplication and division will be completed first, from left to right, followed by addition and subtraction, also left to right. To avoid confusion, use parentheses to establish order. Where parentheses are nested, the innermost calculations will be completed first.

Using Functions

Functions such as COUNT, MIN, MAX, SUM, and AVG of specified columns in the column list of a SELECT command may be used to specify that the resulting answer table is to contain aggregated data instead of row-level data. Using any of these aggregate functions will give a one-row answer.

Query: How many different items were ordered on order number 1004?

```
SELECT COUNT (*)
  FROM ORDER_LINE_V
       WHERE ORDER_ID = 1004;
```

Result:

COUNT (*)
2

It seems that it would be simple enough to list order number 1004 by changing the query.

Query: How many different items were ordered on order number 1004, and what are they?

```
SELECT PRODUCT_ID, COUNT (*)
  FROM ORDER_LINE_V
       WHERE ORDER_ID = 1004;
```

But in Oracle, here is the result.

Result:

ERROR at line 1:
ORA-00937: not a single-group group function

And in MS SQL Server, the result is as follows.

Result:

Column 'order_line_v.Product_ID' is invalid in the select list because it is not contained in an Aggregate function and there is no GROUP BY clause.

The problem is that PRODUCT_ID returns two values, 6 and 8, for the two rows selected, whereas COUNT returns one aggregate value, 2, for the set of rows with ID =1004. In most implementations, SQL cannot return both a row value and a set value; users must run two separate queries, one that returns row information and one that returns set information.

Also, it is easy to confuse the functions COUNT (*) and COUNT. The function COUNT (*), used in the previous query, counts all rows selected by a query regardless of whether any of the rows contain null values. COUNT tallies only those rows that contain a value; it ignores all null values.

SUM and AVG can only be used with numeric columns. COUNT, COUNT (*), MIN, and MAX can be used with any data type. Using MIN on a text column, for example, will find the lowest value in the column, the one whose first column is closest to the beginning of the alphabet. SQL implementations interpret the order of the alphabet differently. For example, some systems may start with A–Z, then a–z, then 0–9 and special characters. Others treat upper- and lowercase letters as being equivalent. Still others start with some special characters, then proceed to numbers, letters, and other special characters. Here is the query to ask for the first PRODUCT_NAME in PRODUCT_T alphabetically, which was done using the AMERICAN character set in Oracle 10g.

Query: Alphabetically, what is the first product name in the PRODUCT table?

```
SELECT MIN (PRODUCT_DESCRIPTION)
   FROM PRODUCT_T;
```

It gives the following result, which demonstrates that numbers are sorted before letters in this character set. (Note: The following result is from Oracle. MS SQL Server returns the same result, but labels the column (No column name) in SQL Query Analyzer, unless the query specifies a name for the result.)

Result:

MIN(PRODUCT_DESCRIPTION)
8-Drawer Desk

Using Wildcards

The use of the asterisk (*) as a wildcard in a SELECT statement has been previously shown. Wildcards may also be used in the WHERE clause when an exact match is not possible. Here, the keyword LIKE is paired with wildcard characters and usually a string containing the characters that are known to be desired matches. The wildcard character, %, is used to represent any collection of characters. Thus, using LIKE '%Desk' when searching PRODUCT_DESCRIPTION will find all different types of desks carried by Pine Valley Furniture. The underscore ,_, is used as a wildcard character to represent exactly one character, rather than any collection of characters. Thus, using LIKE ' _-drawer' when searching PRODUCT_NAME will find any products with specified drawers, such as 3-, 5-, or 8-drawer dressers.

Using Comparison Operators

With the exception of the very first SQL example in this section, we have used the equality comparison operator in our WHERE clauses. The first example used the greater (less) than operator. The most common comparison operators for SQL implementations are listed in Table 7-3. You are used to thinking about using comparison operators with numeric data, but you can also use them with character data and dates in SQL. The query shown here asks for all orders placed after 10/24/2006.

Table 7-3 Comparison Operators in SQL

Operator	Meaning
=	Equal to
>	Greater than
>=	Greater than or equal to
<	Less than
<=	Less than or equal to
<>	Not equal to
!=	Not equal to

Query: Which orders have been placed since 10/24/2006?

```
SELECT ORDER_ID, ORDER_DATE
   FROM ORDER_V
          WHERE ORDER_DATE > '24-OCT-2006';
```

Notice that the date is enclosed in single quotes and that the format of the date is different from that shown in Figure 7-3, which was taken from Microsoft Access. The query was run in SQL*Plus.

Result:

ORDER_ID	ORDER_DATE
1007	27-OCT-06
1008	30-OCT-06
1009	05-NOV-06
1010	05-NOV-06

Query: What furniture does Pine Valley carry that isn't made of cherry?

```
SELECT PRODUCT_DESCRIPTION, PRODUCT_FINISH
   FROM PRODUCT_V
          WHERE PRODUCT_FINISH != 'Cherry';
```

Result:

PRODUCT	PRODUCT_FINISH
Coffee Table	Natural Ash
Computer Desk	Natural Ash
Entertainment Center	Natural Maple
8-Drawer Desk	White Ash
Dining Table	Natural Ash
Computer Desk	Walnut

Using Boolean Operators

More complex questions can be answered by adjusting the WHERE clause further. The Boolean or logical operators AND, OR, and NOT can be used to good purpose.

AND   Joins two or more conditions and returns results only when all conditions are true.

OR   Joins two or more conditions and returns results when any conditions are true.

NOT   Negates an expression.

If multiple Boolean operators are used in an SQL statement, NOT is evaluated first, then AND, then OR. For example, consider the following query.

Query A: List product name, finish, and unit price for all desks and all tables that cost more than $300 in the PRODUCT view.

Figure 7-8
Boolean query without use of parentheses
(a) Venn diagram of Query A logic, first process (AND)

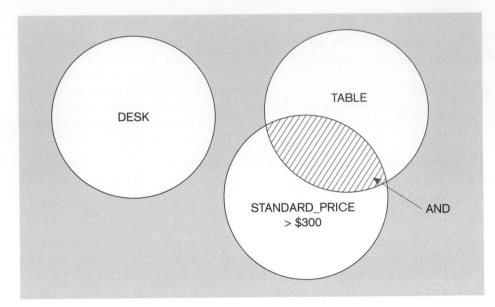

(b) Venn diagram of Query A logic, second process (OR)

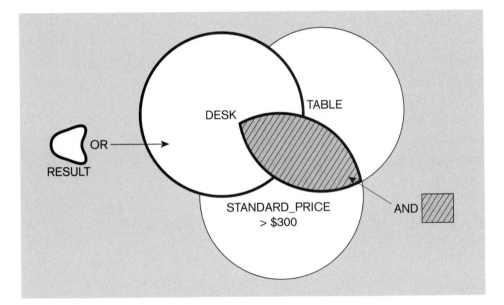

SELECT PRODUCT_DESCRIPTION, PRODUCT_FINISH, STANDARD_PRICE
   FROM PRODUCT_V
       WHERE PRODUCT_DESCRIPTION LIKE '%Desk'
       OR PRODUCT_DESCRIPTION LIKE '%Table'
       AND STANDARD_PRICE > 300;

All of the desks are listed, even the computer desk that costs less than $300. Only one table is listed; the less expensive ones that cost less than $300 are not included. Looking at the query, the AND will be processed first, returning all tables with a unit price greater than $300 (Figure 7-8a). Then the OR is processed, returning all desks, regardless of cost, and all tables costing more than $300 (Figure 7-8b). This is the area surrounded by the thick 'OR' line in Figure 7-8b.

Result:

PRODUCT_DESCRIPTION	PRODUCT_FINISH	STANDARD_PRICE
Computer Desk	Natural Ash	375
Writer's Desk	Cherry	325
8-Drawer Desk	White Ash	750
Dining Table	Natural Ash	800
Computer Desk	Walnut	250

If we had wanted to return only desks and tables costing more than $300, we should have put parentheses after the WHERE and before the AND, as shown in Query B. Figures 7-9a and 7-9b show the difference in processing caused by the

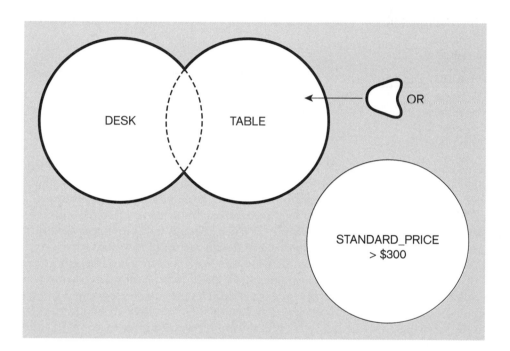

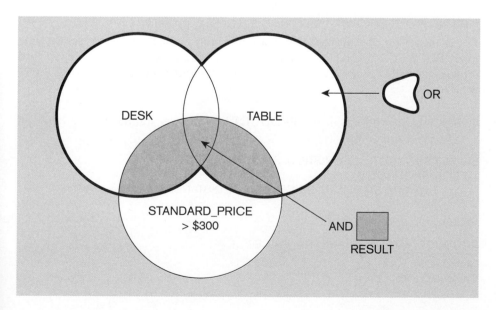

Figure 7-9
Boolean query with use of parentheses
(a) Venn diagram of Query B logic, first process (OR)

(b) Venn diagram of Query B logic, second process (OR)

judicious use of parentheses in the query. The result is all desks and tables with a standard price of more than $300, indicated by the filled area with horizontal lines. The walnut computer desk has a standard price of $250 and is not included.

> **Query B:** List product name, finish, and unit price for all desks and tables in the PRODUCT view that cost more than $300.

```
SELECT PRODUCT_DESCRIPTION, PRODUCT_FINISH, STANDARD_PRICE
   FROM PRODUCT_V
          WHERE (PRODUCT_DESCRIPTION LIKE '%Desk'
             OR PRODUCT_DESCRIPTION LIKE '%Table')
          AND STANDARD_PRICE > 300;
```

The results follow. Only products with unit price greater than $300 are included.

Result:

PRODUCT_DESCRIPTION	PRODUCT_FINISH	STANDARD_PRICE
Computer Desk	Natural Ash	375
Writer's Desk	Cherry	325
8-Drawer Desk	White Ash	750
Dining Table	Natural Ash	800

This example illustrates why SQL is considered a set-oriented, not a record-oriented language (C, Java, and Cobol are examples of record-oriented languages because they must process one record, or row, of a table at a time). To answer this query, SQL will find the set of rows that are Desk products, then union (i.e., merge) that set with the set of rows that are Table products. Finally, it will intersect (i.e., find common rows) the resultant set from this union with the set of rows that have a standard price above $300. If indexes can be used, the work is done even faster, because SQL will create sets of index entries that satisfy each qualification and do the set manipulation on those index entry sets, each of which takes up less space and can be manipulated much quicker. You will see in Chapter 8 even more dramatic ways in which the set-oriented nature of SQL works for more complex queries involving multiple tables.

Using Ranges for Qualification

The comparison operators < and > are used to establish a range of values. The keywords BETWEEN or NOT BETWEEN can also be used. For example, to find those products with a standard price between $200 and $300, the following query could be used.

> **Query:** Which products in the PRODUCT view have a standard price between $200 and $300?

```
SELECT PRODUCT_DESCRIPTION, STANDARD_PRICE
   FROM PRODUCT_V
          WHERE STANDARD_PRICE > 199 AND STANDARD_PRICE < 301;
```

Result:

PRODUCT_NAME	STANDARD_PRICE
Coffee Table	200
Computer Desk	250

The same result will be returned by this query.

Query: Which products in the PRODUCT view have a standard price between $200 and $300?

```
SELECT PRODUCT_DESCRIPTION, STANDARD_PRICE
  FROM PRODUCT_V
        WHERE STANDARD_PRICE BETWEEN 200 AND 300;
```

Result: Same as previous query.

Adding NOT before BETWEEN in this query will return all the other products in PRODUCT_V because their prices are less than $200 or more than $300.

Using Distinct Values

Sometimes when returning rows that don't include the primary key, duplicate rows will be returned. For example, look at this query and the results that it returns.

Query: What are the order numbers included in the ORDER_LINE table?

```
SELECT ORDER_ID
  FROM ORDER_LINE_T;
```

Eighteen rows are returned, and many of them are duplicates because many orders were for multiple items.

Result:

ORDER_ID
1001
1001
1001
1002
1003
1004
1004
1005
1006
1006
1006
1007
1007
1008
1008
1009
1009
1010

18 rows selected.

If, however, we add the keyword DISTINCT, then only one occurrence of each ORDER_ID will be returned, one for each of the ten orders represented in the table.

Query: What are the distinct order numbers included in the ORDER_LINE table?

```
SELECT DISTINCT ORDER_ID
  FROM ORDER_LINE_V;
```

Result:

ORDER_ID
1001
1002
1003
1004
1005
1006
1007
1008
1009
1010

10 rows selected.

DISTINCT and its counterpart, ALL, can only be used once in a SELECT statement. It comes after SELECT and before any columns or expressions are listed. If a SELECT statement projects more than one column, only rows that are identical for every column will be eliminated. Thus, if the previous statement also includes QUANTITY, fourteen rows are returned because there are now only four duplicate rows rather than eight. For example, both items ordered on ORDER_ID 1004 were for two items, so the second pairing of 1004 and 2 will be eliminated.

> **Query:** What are the unique combinations of order number and order quantity included in the ORDER_LINE table?

SELECT DISTINCT ORDER_ID, ORDERED_QUANTITY
   FROM ORDER_LINE_V;

Result:

ORDER_ID	QUANTITY
1001	1
1001	2
1002	5
1003	3
1004	2
1005	4
1006	1
1006	2
1007	2
1007	3
1008	3
1009	2
1009	3
1010	10

14 rows selected.

Using IN and NOT IN with Lists

To match a list of values, consider using IN.

Query: List all customers who live in warmer states.

SELECT CUSTOMER_NAME, CUSTOMER_CITY, CUSTOMER_STATE
   FROM CUSTOMER_V
       WHERE CUSTOMER_STATE IN ('FL', 'TX', 'CA', 'HI');

Results:

CUSTOMER_NAME	CUSTOMER_CITY	CUSTOMER_STATE
Contemporary Casuals	Gainesville	FL
Value Furniture	Plano	TX
Impressions	Sacramento	CA
California Classics	Santa Clara	CA
M and H Casual Furniture	Clearwater	FL
Seminole Interiors	Seminole	FL
Kaneohe Homes	Kaneohe	HI

7 rows selected.

IN is particularly useful in SQL statements that use subqueries, which will be covered in Chapter 8. The use of IN is also very consistent with the set nature of SQL. In fact, some SQL programmers always use IN even when the set in parentheses after IN includes only one item.

Sorting Results: The ORDER BY Clause

Looking at the preceding results, it may seem that it would make more sense to list the California customers, followed by the Floridians, Hawaiians, and Texans. That brings us to the other three basic parts of the SQL statement:

ORDER BY	Sorts the final results rows in ascending or descending order.
GROUP BY	Groups rows in an intermediate results table where the values in those rows are the same for one or more columns.
HAVING	Can only be used following a GROUP BY and acts as a secondary WHERE clause, returning only those groups which meet a specified condition.

So, we can order the customers by adding an ORDER BY clause.

Query: List customer, city, and state for all customers in the CUSTOMER view whose address is Florida, Texas, California, or Hawaii. List the customers alphabetically by state, and alphabetically by customer within each state.

```
SELECT CUSTOMER_NAME, CUSTOMER_CITY, CUSTOMER_STATE
   FROM CUSTOMER_V
       WHERE CUSTOMER_STATE IN ('FL', 'TX', 'CA', 'HI')
           ORDER BY CUSTOMER_STATE, CUSTOMER_NAME;
```

Now the results are easier to read.

Result:

CUSTOMER_NAME	CUSTOMER_CITY	CUSTOMER_STATE
California Classics	Santa Clara	CA
Impressions	Sacramento	CA
Contemporary Casuals	Gainesville	FL
M and H Casual Furniture	Clearwater	FL
Seminole Interiors	Seminole	FL
Kaneohe Homes	Kaneohe	HI
Value Furniture	Plano	TX

7 rows selected.

Notice that all customers from each state are listed together, and within each state, customer names are alphabetized. The sorting order is determined by the order in which the columns are listed in the ORDER BY clause; in this case, states were alphabetized first, then customer names were. If sorting from high to low, use DESC as a keyword placed after the column used to sort.

How are NULLS sorted? Null values may be placed first or last, before or after columns that have values. Where the NULLS will be placed will depend upon the SQL implementation.

Categorizing Results: The GROUP BY Clause

Scalar aggregate: A single value returned from an SQL query that includes an aggregate function.

Vector aggregate: Multiple values returned from an SQL query that includes an aggregate function.

GROUP BY is particularly useful when paired with aggregate functions, such as SUM or COUNT. GROUP BY divides a table into subsets (by groups); then an aggregate function can be used to provide summary information for that group. The single value returned by the previous aggregate function examples is called a **scalar aggregate**. When aggregate functions are used in a GROUP BY clause and several values are returned, they are called **vector aggregates**.

Query: Count the number of customers with addresses in each state to which we ship.

```
SELECT CUSTOMER_STATE, COUNT (CUSTOMER_STATE)
   FROM CUSTOMER_V
       GROUP BY CUSTOMER_STATE;
```

Result:

CUSTOMER_STATE	COUNT(CUSTOMER_STATE)
CA	2
CO	1
FL	3
HI	1
MI	1
NJ	2
NY	1
PA	1
TX	1
UT	1
WA	1

11 rows selected.

It is also possible to nest groups within groups; the same logic is used as when sorting multiple items.

Query: Count the number of customers with addresses in each city to which we ship. List the cities by state.

```
SELECT CUSTOMER_STATE, CUSTOMER_CITY, COUNT (CUSTOMER_CITY)
   FROM CUSTOMER_V
       GROUP BY CUSTOMER_STATE, CUSTOMER_CITY;
```

Although the GROUP BY clause seems straightforward, it can produce unexpected results if the logic of the clause is forgotten. When a GROUP BY is included, the columns allowed to be specified in the SELECT clause are limited. Only those columns with a single value for each group can be included. In the previous query, each group consists of a city and its state. The SELECT statement includes both the 'city' and 'state' columns. This works because each combination of city and state is one value. But, if the SELECT clause of the first query in this section had also included 'city', that statement would fail because the GROUP BY is only by state. Because states can have more than one city, the requirement that each value in the SELECT clause have only one value in the GROUP BY group is not met, and SQL will not be able to present the city information so that it makes sense. In general, each column referenced in the SELECT statement must be referenced in the GROUP BY clause, unless the column is an argument for an aggregate function included in the SELECT clause.

Qualifying Results by Categories: The HAVING Clause

The HAVING clause acts like a WHERE clause, but it identifies groups that meet a criterion, rather than rows. Therefore, you will usually see a HAVING clause following a GROUP BY clause.

Query: Find only states with more than one customer.

```
SELECT STATE, COUNT (CUSTOMER_STATE)
    FROM CUSTOMER_V
         GROUP BY CUSTOMER_STATE
              HAVING COUNT (CUSTOMER_STATE) > 1;
```

This query returns a result that has removed all those states with one customer. Remember that using WHERE here would not work because WHERE doesn't allow aggregates; further, WHERE qualifies a set of rows, whereas HAVING qualifies a set of groups.

Result:

CUSTOMER_STATE	COUNT(CUSTOMER_STATE)
CA	2
FL	3
NJ	2

To include more than one condition in the HAVING clause, use AND, OR, and NOT just as in the WHERE clause. In summary, here is one last command that includes all of the six clauses; remember that they must be used in this order.

Query: List the product finish and average standard price for each finish for selected finishes where the average standard price is less than 750.

```
SELECT PRODUCT_FINISH, AVG (STANDARD_PRICE)
    FROM PRODUCT_V
         WHERE PRODUCT_FINISH IN ('Cherry', 'Natural Ash', 'Natural Maple', 'White Ash')
              GROUP BY PRODUCT_FINISH
                  HAVING AVG (STANDARD_PRICE) < 750
                      ORDER BY PRODUCT_FINISH;
```

Result:

PRODUCT_FINISH	AVG(UNIT_PRICE)
Cherry	250
Natural Ash	458.333333
Natural Maple	650

Figure 7-10
SQL statement processing order
(adapted from van der Lans, p. 100)

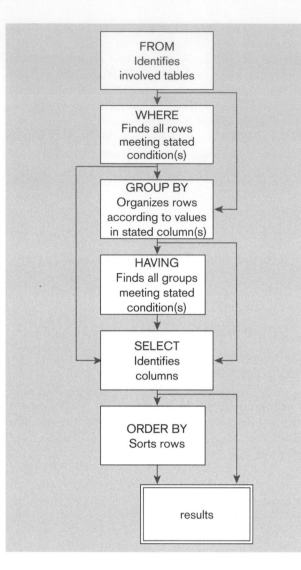

Base table: A table in the relational data model containing the inserted raw data. Base tables correspond to the relations that are identified in the database's conceptual schema.

Virtual table: A table constructed automatically as needed by a DBMS. Virtual tables are not maintained as real data.

Dynamic view: A virtual table that is created dynamically upon request by a user. A dynamic view is not a temporary table. Rather, its definition is stored in the system catalog and the contents of the view are materialized as a result of an SQL query that uses the view. It differs from a materialized view, which may be stored on a disk and refreshed at intervals or when used, depending on the RDBMS.

Figure 7-10 shows the order in which SQL processes the clauses of a statement. Arrows indicate the paths that may or may not be followed. Remember, only the SELECT and FROM clauses are mandatory. Notice that the processing order is different from the order of the syntax used to create the statement. As each clause is processed, an intermediate results table is produced that will be used for the next clause. Users do not see the intermediate results tables; they see only the final results. A query can be debugged by remembering the order shown in Figure 7-10. Take out the optional clauses, then add them back in one at a time in the order that they will be processed. In this way, intermediate results can be seen and problems often can be spotted.

Using and Defining Views

The SQL syntax shown in Figure 7-6 demonstrates the creation of four **base tables** in a database schema using Oracle 10g SQL. These tables, which are used to store data physically in the database, correspond to entities in the conceptual schema. Using SQL queries, it is possible to create **virtual tables**, or **dynamic views**, whose contents materialize when referenced. These views may often be manipulated in the same way as a base table can be manipulated, through SQL SELECT queries.

Table 7-4   Pros and Cons of Using Dynamic Views

Positive Aspects	Negative Aspects
Simplify query commands	Use processing time re-creating view each time it is referenced
Help provide data security and confidentiality	
Improve programmer productivity	May or may not be directly updateable
Contain most current base table data	
Use little storage space	
Provide a customized view for a user	
Establish physical data independence	

Materialized views, which are stored physically on a disk and refreshed at appropriate intervals or events, may also be used.

The often-stated purpose of a view is to simplify query commands, but a view may also provide valuable data security and significantly enhance programming consistency and productivity for a database. To highlight the convenience of a view, consider Pine Valley Invoice processing. Construction of their invoice requires access to the four tables from the Pine Valley database of Figure 7-3: CUSTOMER_T, ORDER_T, ORDER_LINE_T, and PRODUCT_T. A novice database user may make mistakes or be unproductive in properly formulating queries involving so many tables. A view allows us to predefine this association into a single virtual table as part of the database. With this view, a user who wants only customer invoice data does not have to reconstruct the joining of tables to produce the report or any subset of it. Table 7-4 summarizes the pros and cons of using views.

A view, INVOICE_V, is defined by specifying an SQL query (SELECT . . . FROM . . . WHERE) that has the view as its result. If you decide to try this query as is, without selecting additional attributes, remove the comma after ORDERED_QUANTITY. The example assumes you will elect to include additional attributes in the query.

> **Query:** What are the data elements necessary to create an invoice for a customer? Save this query as a view named INVOICE_V.

```
CREATE VIEW INVOICE_V AS
    SELECT CUSTOMER_T.CUSTOMER_ID, CUSTOMER_ADDRESS,
    ORDER_T.ORDER_ID, PRODUCT_T.PRODUCT_ID,STANDARD_PRICE,
    ORDERED_QUANTITY, and other columns as required
        FROM CUSTOMER_T, ORDER_T, ORDER_LINE_T, PRODUCT_T
            WHERE CUSTOMER_T.CUSTOMER_ID = ORDER_T.CUSTOMER_ID
            AND ORDER_T.ORDER_ID = ORDER_LINE_T.ORDER_ID
            AND PRODUCT_T.PRODUCT_ID = ORDER_LINE_T.PRODUCT_ID;
```

The SELECT clause specifies, or projects, what data elements (columns) are to be included in the view table. The FROM clause lists the tables and views involved in the view development. The WHERE clause specifies the names of the common columns used to join CUSTOMER_T to ORDER_T to ORDER_LINE_T to PRODUCT_T. Because a view is a table, and one of the relational properties of tables is that the order of rows is immaterial, the rows in a view may not be sorted. But queries that refer to this view may display their results in any desired sequence.

We can see the power of such a view when building a query to generate an invoice for order number 1004. Rather than having to specify the joining of four tables, the query can include all relevant data elements from the view table, INVOICE_V.

Materialized view: Copies or replicas of data based on SQL queries created in the same manner as dynamic views are. However, a materialized view exists as a table and thus care must be taken to keep it synchronized with its associated base tables.

Query: What are the data elements necessary to create an invoice for order number 1004?

```
SELECT CUSTOMER_ID, CUSTOMER_ADDRESS, PRODUCT_ID,
    ORDERED_QUANTITY, and other columns as required
    FROM INVOICE_V
        WHERE ORDER_ID = 1004;
```

A dynamic view is a virtual table; it is constructed automatically as needed by the DBMS, and is not maintained as persistent data. Any SQL SELECT statement may be used to create a view. The persistent data are stored in base tables, those that have been defined by CREATE TABLE commands. A dynamic view always contains the most current derived values and is thus superior in terms of data currency to constructing a temporary real table from several base tables. Also, in comparison to a temporary real table, a view consumes very little storage space. A view is costly, however, because its contents must be calculated each time they are requested. Materialized views are now available and address this drawback.

A view may join multiple tables or views together and may contain derived (or virtual) columns. For example, if a user of the Pine Valley Furniture database only wants to know the total value of orders placed for each furniture product, a view for this can be created from INVOICE_V in Oracle SQL*Plus.

Query: What is the total value of orders placed for each furniture product?

```
CREATE VIEW ORDER_TOTALS_V AS
    SELECT PRODUCT_ID PRODUCT, SUM (STANDARD_PRICE*QUANTITY) TOTAL
    FROM INVOICE_V
        GROUP BY PRODUCT_ID;
```

We can assign a different name (an alias) to a view column rather than use the associated base table or expression column name. Here, PRODUCT is a renaming of PRODUCT_ID, local to only this view. TOTAL is the column name given the expression for total sales of each product. The expression can now be referenced via this view in subsequent queries as if it were a column, rather than a derived expression. Defining views based on other views can cause problems. For example, if we redefine INVOICE_V so that STANDARD_PRICE is not included, then ORDER_TOTALS_V will no longer work because it will not be able to locate unit prices.

Views can also help to establish security. Tables and columns that are not included will not be obvious to the user of the view. Restricting access to a view with GRANT and REVOKE statements adds another layer of security. For example, granting some users access rights to aggregated data, such as averages, in a view but denying them access to base table, detailed data will not allow them to display the base table data. SQL security commands are explained further in Chapter 12.

Privacy and confidentiality of data can be achieved by creating views that restrict users to working with only the data they need to perform their assigned duties. If a clerical worker needs to work with employees' addresses but should not be able to access their compensation rates, they may be given access to a view that does not contain compensation information.

Some people advocate the creation of a view for every single base table, even if that view is identical to the base table. They suggest this approach because views can contribute to greater programming productivity as databases evolve. Consider a situation in which fifty programs all use the CUSTOMER_T table. Suppose that the Pine Valley Furniture Company database evolves to support new functions that require the CUSTOMER_T table to be renormalized into two tables. If these fifty programs refer directly to the CUSTOMER_T base table, they will all have to be modified to refer to one of the two new tables or to joined tables. But if these programs all use the view on this base table, then only the view has to be recreated, saving considerable reprogramming effort. However, dynamic views require considerable run-time computer processing because the virtual table of a view is recreated each time the view is referenced. Therefore, referencing a base table through a view rather than directly can add considerable time to query processing. This additional operational cost must be balanced against the potential reprogramming savings from a view.

Updating data directly from a view rather than from base tables is possible with certain limitations. In general, update operations to data in a view are permitted as long as the update is unambiguous in terms of data modification in the base table. But when the CREATE VIEW statement contains any of the following situations, that view may not be updated directly.

1. The SELECT clause includes the keyword DISTINCT. (SELECT clauses are covered in detail later in this chapter in the section titled Processing Single Tables.)

2. The SELECT clause contains expressions, including derived columns, aggregates, statistical functions, and so on.

3. The FROM clause, or a subquery, or a UNION clause references more than one table.

4. The FROM clause or a subquery references another view that is not updateable.

5. The CREATE VIEW command contains a GROUP BY or HAVING clause.

It could happen that an update to an instance would result in the instance disappearing from the view. Let's create a view named EXPENSIVE_STUFF_V, which lists all furniture products that have a UNIT_PRICE over $300. That view will include PRODUCT_ID 5, a writer's desk, which has a unit price of $325. If we update data using EXPENSIVE_STUFF_V and reduce the unit price of the writer's desk to $295, then the writer's desk will no longer appear in the EXPENSIVE_STUFF_V virtual table because its unit price is now less than $300. In Oracle, if you desire to track all merchandise with an original price over $300, include a WITH CHECK OPTION clause after the SELECT clause in the CREATE VIEW command. The WITH CHECK OPTION will cause UPDATE or INSERT statements to be rejected when those statements would cause updated or inserted rows to be removed from the view. This option can only be used with updateable views.

Here is the CREATE VIEW statement for EXPENSIVE_STUFF_V.

Query: List all furniture products that have ever had a UNIT_PRICE over $300.

```
CREATE VIEW EXPENSIVE_STUFF_V
AS
SELECT PRODUCT_ID, PRODUCT_DESCRIPTION, STANDARD_PRICE
        FROM PRODUCT_T
            WHERE STANDARD_PRICE > 300
            WITH CHECK OPTION;
```

When attempting to update the unit price of the writer's desk to $295 using the following Oracle SQL*Plus syntax

```
UPDATE EXPENSIVE_STUFF_V
SET STANDARD_PRICE = 295
        WHERE PRODUCT_ID = 5;
```

... Oracle gives the error message shown:

```
ERROR at line 1:
ORA-01402: view WITH CHECK OPTION where-clause violation
```

A price increase on the writer's desk to $350 will take effect with no error message because the view is updateable and the conditions specified in the view are not violated.

Information about views will be stored in the systems tables of the DBMS. In Oracle 10g, for example, the text of all views is stored in DBA_VIEWS. Users with system privileges can find this information.

Query: List some information that is available about the view named EXPEN-SIVE_STUFF_V. (Note that EXPENSIVE_STUFF_V is stored in upper case and must be entered in upper case to execute correctly.)

```
SELECT OWNER,VIEW_NAME,TEXT_LENGTH FROM DBA_VIEWS
    WHERE VIEW_NAME = 'EXPENSIVE_STUFF_V';
```

Result:

OWNER	VIEW_NAME	TEXT_LENGTH
MPRESCOTT	EXPENSIVE_STUFF_V	110

Materialized Views   Like dynamic views, materialized views can be constructed in different ways for various purposes. Tables may be replicated in whole or in part and refreshed on a predetermined time interval or triggered when the table needs to be accessed. Materialized views can be based on queries from one or more tables. In Oracle 10g, it is possible to create summary tables based on aggregations of data. Copies of remote data that use distributed data may be stored locally as materialized views. Maintenance overhead will be incurred to keep the local view synchronized with the remote base tables or data warehouse, but the use of materialized views may improve the performance of distributed queries, especially if the data in the materialized view are relatively static and do not have to be refreshed very often.

Summary

This chapter has introduced the SQL language for relational database definition (DDL), manipulation (DML), and control (DCL), commonly used to define and query relational database management systems (RDBMSs). This standard has been criticized as having many flaws. In reaction to these criticisms and to increase the power of the language, extensions are constantly under review by the ANSI X3H2 committee and ISO/IEC JTC1/SC 21/WG3 DBL. The current standard is known as SQL:2003.

The establishment of SQL standards and conformance certification tests has contributed to relational systems being the dominant form of new database development. Benefits of the SQL standards include reduced training costs, improved productivity, application portability and longevity, reduced dependence on single vendors, and improved cross-system communication.

The SQL environment includes an instance of an SQL DBMS along with accessible databases and associated users and programs. Each database is included in a catalog and

has a schema that describes the database objects. Information contained in the catalog is maintained by the DBMS itself, rather than by the users of the DBMS.

The DDL commands of SQL are used to define a database, including its creation and the creation of its tables, indexes, and views. Referential integrity is also established through DDL commands. The DML commands of SQL are used to load, update, and query the database through use of the SELECT command. DCL commands are used to establish user access to the database.

SQL commands may directly affect the base tables, which contain the raw data, or they may affect a database view that has been created. Changes and updates made to views may or may not be passed on to the base tables. The basic syntax of an SQL SELECT statement contains the following keywords: SELECT, FROM, WHERE, ORDER BY, GROUP BY, and HAVING. SELECT determines which attributes will be displayed in the query results table. FROM determines which tables or views will be used in the query. WHERE sets the criteria of the query, including any joins of multiple tables that are necessary. ORDER BY determines the order in which the results will be displayed. GROUP BY is used to categorize results and may return either scalar aggregates or vector aggregates. HAVING qualifies results by categories.

Understanding the basic SQL syntax presented in this chapter should enable the reader to start using SQL effectively, and to build a deeper understanding of the possibilities for more complex querying with continued practice. Advanced SQL topics are covered in Chapter 8.

CHAPTER REVIEW

Key Terms

Base table
Catalog
Data control language (DCL)
Data definition language (DDL)

Data manipulation language (DML)
Dynamic view
Materialized view
Referential integrity

Relational DBMS (RDBMS)
Scalar aggregate
Schema
Vector aggregate

Review Questions

1. Define each of the following terms:
   a. base table
   b. data definition language
   c. data manipulation language
   d. dynamic view
   e. materialized view
   f. referential integrity
   g. relational DBMS (RDBMS)
   h. schema

2. Match the following terms to the appropriate definitions.

   ____ view
   ____ referential integrity
   ____ dynamic view
   ____ materialized view
   ____ SQL:2003
   ____ null value
   ____ scalar aggregate
   ____ vector aggregate
   ____ catalog
   ____ schema
   ____ host language

   a. list of values
   b. description of a database
   c. view materialized as result of SQL query that uses the view
   d. logical table
   e. missing or nonexistent value
   f. descriptions of database objects of a database
   g. third-generation programming language in which SQL commands are embedded
   h. established in relational data models by use of foreign keys
   i. view that exists as a table
   j. standard relational query and definition language
   k. single value

3. Contrast the following terms.
   a. base table; view
   b. dynamic view; materialized view
   c. catalog; schema

4. What are SQL-92, SQL:1999 and SQL:2003? Briefly describe how SQL:2003 differs from SQL;1999.

5. Describe a relational DBMS (RDBMS), its underlying data model, its data storage structures, and how data relationships are established.

6. List six potential benefits of achieving an SQL standard that is widely accepted.

7. Describe the components and structure of a typical SQL environment.

8. Distinguish among data definition commands, data manipulation commands, and data control commands.

9. Explain how referential integrity is established in databases that are SQL:1999 compliant. Explain how the ON UPDATE RESTRICT, ON UPDATE CASCADE, and ON UPDATE SET NULL clauses differ. What happens if the ON DELETE CASCADE clause is set?

10. Explain some possible purposes of creating a view using SQL. In particular, explain how a view can be used to reinforce data security.

11. Explain why it is necessary to limit the kinds of updates performed on data when referencing data through a view.

12. Describe a set of circumstances for which using a view can save reprogramming effort.

13. Drawing on material covered in prior chapters, explain the factors to be considered in deciding whether to create a key index for a table in SQL.

14. Explain and provide at least one example of how one qualifies the ownership of a table in SQL.

15. How is the order in which attributes appear in a result table changed? How are the column heading labels in a result table changed?

16. What is the difference between COUNT, COUNT DISTINCT, and COUNT(*) in SQL? When will these three commands generate the same and different results?

17. What is the evaluation order for the Boolean operators (AND, OR, NOT) in an SQL command? How can one be sure that the operators will work in the desired order rather than in this prescribed order?

18. If an SQL statement includes a GROUP BY clause, the attributes that can be requested in the SELECT statement will be limited. Explain that limitation.

19. Describe a situation in which you would need to write a query using the HAVING clause.

20. What other SQL operator can be used to perform the same operation as the IN operator?

21. If a DBMS product claims to be compliant with Core SQL:1999, can it also claim to be Core SQL:2003 compliant? Why or why not?

22. When would the use of the LIKE keyword with the CREATE TABLE command be helpful?

23. What is an identity column? Explain the benefits of using the identity column capability in SQL.

24. SQL:2003 has a new keyword, MERGE. Explain how using this keyword allows one to accomplish updating and merging data into a table in one command rather than two.

Problems and Exercises

Problems and Exercises 1 through 9 are based on the class schedule ERD depicted in Figure 4-19 in Chapter 4. The 3NF relations along with some sample data are repeated in Figure 7-11. For Problems and Exercises 4 through 9, draw an instance diagram and mark it to show the data you expect your query to return in the results.

1. Write a database description for each of the relations shown, using SQL DDL (shorten, abbreviate, or change any data names as needed for your SQL version). Assume the following attribute data types:

   STUDENT_ID (integer, primary key)
   STUDENT_NAME (25 characters)
   FACULTY_ID (integer, primary key)
   FACULTY_NAME (25 characters)
   COURSE_ID (8 characters, primary key)
   COURSE_NAME (15 characters)
   DATE_QUALIFIED (date)
   SECTION_NO (integer, primary key)
   SEMESTER (7 characters)

2. Use SQL to define the following view:

Student_ID	Student_Name
38214	Letersky
54907	Altvater
54907	Altvater
66324	Aiken

3. Before any row can be entered into the SECTION table, the COURSE_ID to be entered must already exist in the COURSE table (referential integrity). Write an SQL assertion that will enforce this constraint.

4. Write SQL definition commands for each of the following queries:

   a. How would you add an attribute, CLASS, to the STUDENT table?

   b. How would you remove the REGISTRATION table?

   c. How would you change the field for FACULTY_NAME from twenty-five characters to forty characters?

5. Write SQL commands for the following:

   a. Create two different forms of the INSERT command to add a student with a student ID of 65798 and last name Lopez to the STUDENT table.

   b. Now write a command that will remove Lopez from the STUDENT table.

   c. Create an SQL command that will modify the name of course ISM 4212 from 'Database' to 'Introduction to Relational Databases'.

6. Write SQL queries to answer the following questions:

   a. Which students have an ID number that is less than 50000?

   b. What is the name of the faculty member whose ID is 4756?

   c. What is the smallest section number used in the first semester of 2001?

7. Write SQL queries to answer the following questions:

   a. How many students are enrolled in Section 2714 in the first semester of 2001?

   b. Which faculty members have qualified to teach a course since 1993? List the faculty ID, course, and date of qualification.

8. Write SQL queries to answer the following questions:

   a. Which students are enrolled in Database and Networking? (Hint: Use the SECTION_NO for each class so you can determine the answer from the REGISTRATION table by itself.)

   b. Which instructors cannot teach both Syst Analysis and Syst Design?

9. Write SQL queries to answer the following questions:

   a. What are the courses included in the SECTION table? List each course only once.

STUDENT (STUDENT_ID, STUDENT_NAME)

STUDENT_ID	STUDENT_NAME
38214	Letersky
54907	Altvater
66324	Aiken
70542	Marra
...	

QUALIFIED (FACULTY_ID, COURSE_ID, DATE_QUALIFIED)

FACULTY_ID	COURSE_ID	DATE_QUALIFIED
2143	ISM 3112	9/1988
2143	ISM 3113	9/1988
3467	ISM 4212	9/1995
3467	ISM 4930	9/1996
4756	ISM 3113	9/1991
4756	ISM 3112	9/1991
...		

FACULTY (FACULTY_ID, FACULTY_NAME)

FACULTY_ID	FACULTY_NAME
2143	Birkin
3467	Berndt
4756	Collins
...	

SECTION (SECTION_NO, SEMESTER, COURSE_ID)

SECTION_NO	SEMESTER	COURSE_ID
2712	I-2006	ISM 3113
2713	I-2006	ISM 3113
2714	I-2006	ISM 4212
2715	I-2006	ISM 4930
...		

COURSE (COURSE_ID, COURSE_NAME)

COURSE_ID	COURSE_NAME
ISM 3113	Syst Analysis
ISM 3112	Syst Design
ISM 4212	Database
ISM 4930	Networking
...	

REGISTRATION (STUDENT_ID, SECTION_NO, SEMESTER)

STUDENT_ID	SECTION_NO	SEMESTER
38214	2714	I-2006
54907	2714	I-2006
54907	2715	I-2006
66324	2713	I-2006
...		

Figure 7-11
Class scheduling relations (missing ASSIGNMENT)

b. List all students in alphabetical order by STUDENT_NAME.

c. List the students who are enrolled in each course in Semester I, 2001. Group the students by the sections in which they are enrolled.

d. List the courses available. Group them by course prefix. (ISM is the only prefix shown but there are many others throughout the university.)

Problems and Exercises 10 through 31 are based on the entire ("big" version) Pine Valley Furniture Company database. Note:

Depending on what DBMS you are using, some field names may have changed due to reserved words for the DBMS. When you first use the DBMS, check the table definitions to see what the exact field names are for the DBMS you are using.

10. Modify the PRODUCT_t table by adding an attribute QTY_ON_HAND that can be used to track the finished goods inventory. The field should be an integer field of five characters and should accept only positive numbers.

11. Enter sample data of your own choosing into QTY_ON HAND in the PRODUCT_t table. Test the modification you

made in Problem and Exercise 10 by attempting to update a product by changing the inventory to 10,000 units. Now test it again by changing the inventory for the product to −10 units. If you do not receive error messages and are successful in making these changes, then you did not establish appropriate constraints in Problem and Exercise 10.

12. Add an order to the ORDER_t table and include a sample value for every attribute.

    a. First, look at the data in the CUSTOMER_t table and enter an order from any one of those customers.

    b. Now, enter an order from a new customer. Unless you have also inserted information about the new customer in the CUSTOMER_t table, your entry of the order data should be rejected. Referential integrity constraints should prevent you from entering an order if there is no information about the customer.

13. Use the Pine Valley Database to answer the following questions:

    a. How many work centers does Pine Valley have?

    b. Where are they located?

14. What products have some sort of ash finish?

15. List the customers who live in California or Washington. Order them by zip code, from high to low.

16. Determine the average standard price of each product line.

17. List the employees whose last name begins with an 'L.'

18. Which employees were hired during 1999?

19. For every product that has been ordered, determine the total quantity that has been ordered. List the most popular product first and the least popular last.

20. For each customer, list the customer_id and total number of orders placed.

21. For each customer, list the customer_id and the total number of orders placed in 2006.

22. For each customer who had more than two orders, list the customer_id and the total number of orders placed.

23. List all sales territories (territory_id) that have more than one salesperson.

24. List all raw materials that are made of cherry and that have dimensions (thickness and width) of 12 by 12.

25. List the material_id, material_name, material, standard_price, and thickness for all raw materials made of cherry, pine, or walnut. Order the listing by material, standard_price, and thickness.

26. Which product is ordered most frequently?

27. Which product has the highest quantity ordered?

28. For each salesperson, list the total number of orders.

29. For each salesperson, list the total number of orders by month for the year 2003. (Hint: If you are using Access, use the Month function. If you are using Oracle, convert the date to a string using the to-char function with a format string of 'Mon' [i.e., to_char(order_date,'MON')].

30. For each salesperson, display a list of customer_ids.

31. List the number of customers in each state.

Field Exercises

1. Arrange an interview with a database administrator in an organization in your area. When you interview the database administrator, familiarize yourself with one application that is actively used in the organization. Focus your interview questions toward determining end users' involvement with the application and understanding the extent to which end users must be familiar with SQL. For example, if end users are using SQL, what training do they receive? Do they use an interactive form of SQL for their work or do they use embedded SQL?

2. Arrange an interview with a database administrator in your area. Focus the interview toward understanding the environment within which SQL is used in the organization. Inquire about the version of SQL that is used and determine whether the same version is used at all locations. If different versions are used, explore any difficulties that the DBA has had in administering the database. Also inquire about any proprietary languages, such as Oracle's PL*SQL, that are being used. Again, learn about possible differences in versions used at different locations and explore any difficulties that occur if different versions are installed.

3. Talk with a database developer at a local organization. Explore the developer's use of SQL in his or her work. Does the developer use any code-generation facilities or does the developer write all the SQL code without the help of code-generation tools? Is there a CASE tool, such as Designer 2000, that the developer has at his or her disposal? If possible, get the database developer to demonstrate any CASE tool that is being used.

References

Arvin, T. 2005. "Comparison of different SQL implementations." Available at troels.arvin.dk/db/rdbms.

Codd, E. F. 1970. "A Relational Model of Data for Large Shared Data Banks." *Communications of the ACM* 13,6 (June): 77–87.

Date, C. J., and H. Darwen. 1997. *A Guide to the SQL Standard.* Reading, MA: Addison-Wesley.

Eisenberg, A., J. Melton, K. Kulkarni, J. E. Michels, and F. Zemke. 2004. "SQL:2003 Has Been Published." *SIGMOD Record* 33,1 (March):119–126.

Gorman, M. M. 2001. "Is SQL a Real Standard Anymore?" The Data Administration Newsletter (July). Available at **www.tdan.com/ i016hy01.htm.**

Gulutzan, P. 2002. "Standard SQL. Do IBM, Microsoft, and Oracle support the SQL:1999 standard? And will they support the SQL:2003 standard as well?" Available at **www.dbazine.com/ gulutzan3.html.**

Tekrati Inc. 2005. "Worldwide RDBMS Market Recovers, as Vendors Gear Up for Middle Market Battle, Says IDC." Available at **www.tekrati.com/T2/Analyst_Research/ResearchAnnounce- mentsDetails.asp?Newsid=4607** (from *The Industry Analyst Reporter*, March 7, 2005.

Further Reading

Bordoloi, B. and D. Bock. 2004. *Oracle SQL*. Upper Saddle River, NJ: Pearson Education, Inc. Prentice Hall.

Bowman, J. S., S. L. Emerson, and M. Darnovsky. 1996. *The Practical SQL Handbook*, 3rd ed. Reading, MA: Addison-Wesley.

Celko, J. 1997. Joe Celko's SQL *Puzzles & Answers*. San Francisco: Morgan Kaufmann.

Gruber, M. 2000. *Mastering SQL*. Alameda, CA: SYBEX.

Guerrero, F. G., and C. E. Rojas. 2001. *Microsoft SQL Server 2000 Programming by Example*. Indianapolis: QUE Corporation.

Gulutzan, P., and T. Petzer. 1999. *SQL-99 Complete*, Really. Lawrence, KS: R&D Books.

Melton, J. 1997. "A Case for SQL Conformance Testing." *Database Programming & Design* 10,7 (July): 66–69.

Nielsen, P. 2003. *Microsoft SQL Server 2000 Bible*. New York: Wiley Publishing, Inc.

Olagson, C. W. 2003. Worldwide Enterprise Database Management Systems Software Competitive Analysis 2003: 2002 Market Shares and Current Outlook. Available at **www.idc.com.**

van der Lans, R. F. 1993. *Introduction to SQL*, 2d ed. Workingham, England: Addison-Wesley.

Web Resources

www.ansi.org Information on ANSI and the latest national and international standards.

www.cramsession.com/certifications/products/list-study-guides.asp A non-Oracle site that offers self-help for Oracle certification. Currently offering courses for 8i and 9i certifications.

www.iso.ch "Welcome to ISO Online" provides information about the International Organization for Standardization. Copies of current standards may be purchased here.

www.mysql.com This site is the official home page for MySQL and includes many free downloadable components for working with MySQL.

www.ncits.org "Welcome to NCITS" is the homepage of the International Committee for Information Technology Standards, which used to be the National Committee for Information Technology Standards, which used to be the Accredited Standard Committee X3.

www.sqlcourse.com/ "SQL Interpreter and Tutorial," a subset of ANSI SQL with practice database.

standards.ieee.org This site is the homepage of the IEEE Standards Organization.

Troels.arvin.dk/db/rdbms Detailed comparison of different SQL implementations, including DB2, MS SQL, MySQL, Oracle and PostgreSQL.

www.teradatastudentnetwork.com Your instructor may have created some course environments for you to use Teradata SQL Assistant, Web Edition, with one or more of the Pine Valley Furniture and Mountain View Community Hospital data sets for this text.

www.wiscorp.com/SQLStandards.html Whitemarsh Information Systems Corp is a good source of information about SQL Standards, including SQL:2003 information.

MOUNTAIN VIEW COMMUNITY HOSPITAL

Case

This case segment uses the physical designs you constructed for Mountain View Community Hospital in Chapter 6 to complete the case questions and case exercises.

CASE QUESTIONS

1. What version of SQL and what RDBMS will you use to do the case exercises?

2. Which CASE tools are available for completing the case exercises? Can the CASE tool you are using generate the database schema from the physical data model(s) you created?

3. Can you suggest an easy way to populate your tables if you wanted to create a large set of test data?

4. How do the actual values you are using help you to test the functionality of your database?

CASE EXERCISES

1. In Case Exercise 1 from Chapter 6, you created the physical data model for Dr. "Z's" database that keeps track of patients checking in. You may recall that Dr. "Z." decided to use SQL Server.

   a. Using that design, create the database and tables using SQL. Be sure to create the SQL assertions necessary to accomplish referential integrity and other constraints.

   b. Populate the database with sample data (MVCH Figure 5-5 in Chapter 5 provides some sample data, but you would need a few more patients and visits for the queries in part c.).

   c. Write and test some queries that will work using your sample data. Write queries that:

      i. Select information from only one of the tables (e.g., an alphabetical listing of all patients, an alphabetical listing of all the patients assigned to one of the social workers, etc.).

      ii. Aggregate information from one attribute in a table (e.g., How often has patient 8766 visited the

MS Center at MVCH in a given month? How many patients are assigned to each social worker?)

      iii. Try out the various functions such as MIN, MAX, and AVG (e.g., What is the average level of pain reported by Dr. "Z's" patients? What is the worst level of pain his patients have experienced?)

2. Complete Case Exercise 1 using Teradata's RDBMS accessible at www.teradatastudentnetwork.com.

3. Using the MVCH database files accompanying this textbook (implemented in either MS Access or Teradata), write and test SQL queries that:

   a. Select information from only one of the tables;

   b. Aggregate information from one attribute in a table;

   c. Try out the various functions such as MIN, MAX, and AVG;

   d. Qualify results by category.

PROJECT ASSIGNMENTS

P1. Use the physical data model you created in Chapter 6 to guide you in writing the SQL statements for creating the Mountain View Community Hospital database for the relational schema you created in Chapter 5.

   a. Write the SQL statements for creating the tables, specifying data types and field lengths, establishing primary keys and foreign keys, and implementing other constraints you identified.

   b. Following the examples in Chapter 6, write the SQL statements that create the indexes.

P2. Select a portion of your database and populate it with sample data. Be prepared to defend the sample test data that you insert into your database.

P3. Write and execute a variety of queries based on the introduction to SQL in Chapter 7 to test the functionality of your database. Ensure that your queries are correct and produce the results you expected.

Chapter 8

Advanced SQL

LEARNING OBJECTIVES

After studying this chapter, you should be able to:

- Concisely define each of the following key terms: **join, equi-join, natural join, outer join, correlated subquery, user-defined data type, Persistent Stored Modules (SQL/PSM), trigger, function, procedure, embedded SQL,** and **dynamic SQL.**

- Write single and multiple table queries using SQL commands.

- Define three types of join commands and use SQL to write these commands.

- Write noncorrelated and correlated subqueries and know when to write each.

- Establish referential integrity using SQL.

- Understand common uses of database triggers and stored procedures.

- Discuss the SQL:1999 standard and explain its enhancements and extensions of SQL-92.

INTRODUCTION

The previous chapter introduced SQL and explored its capabilities for querying one table. The real power of the relational model derives from its storage of data in many related entities. Taking advantage of this approach to data storage requires establishing the relationships and constructing queries that use data from multiple tables. This chapter demonstrates multiple-table queries in some detail. Different approaches to getting results from more than one table are demonstrated, including the use of subqueries, inner and outer joins, and union joins.

Once an understanding of basic SQL syntax is gained, it is important to understand how SQL is used in the creation of applications. Triggers, small modules of code that include SQL, execute automatically when a particular condition, defined in the trigger, exists. Procedures are similar modules of code, but must be called before they execute. SQL commands are often embedded within modules written in a host language, such as C or Java. Dynamic SQL creates SQL statements on the fly, inserting parameter values as needed, and is essential to Web applications. Brief introductions and examples of each of these methods are included in this chapter. Some of the enhancements and extensions to SQL included in SQL:2003 are also covered.

Completion of this chapter gives the student an overview of SQL and some of the ways in which it may be used. Many additional features, often referred to as "obscure" in more detailed SQL texts, will be needed in particular situations. Practice with the syntax included in this chapter will give the student a good start toward mastery of SQL.

PROCESSING MULTIPLE TABLES

Now that we have explored some of the possibilities for working with a single table, we will work with multiple tables simultaneously. The power of RDBMS is realized when working with multiple tables. When relationships exist among tables, they can be linked together in queries. Remember from Chapter 5 that these relationships are established by including a common column(s) in each table where a relationship is needed. Often this is accomplished by setting up a primary key–foreign key relationship, where the foreign key in one table references the primary key in another, and the values in both come from a common domain. We can use these columns to establish the link between two tables by finding common values in the columns. For example, in Figure 7-3, Customer_ID in Order_t matches Customer_ID in Customer_t. When we compare them, we learn that Contemporary Casuals placed orders 1001 and 1010 because Contemporary Casuals' Customer_ID is 1, and Order_t shows that Order_ID 1001 and 1010 were placed by customer 1. In a relational system, data from related tables are combined into one result table or view and then displayed or used as input to a form or report definition.

The linking of related tables varies among different types of relational systems. In SQL, the WHERE clause of the SELECT command is also used for multiple table operations. In fact, SELECT can include references to two, three, or more tables in the same command. As illustrated below, SQL has two ways to use SELECT for combining data from related tables.

Join: A relational operation that causes two tables with a common domain to be combined into a single table or view.

The most frequently used relational operation, which brings together data from two or more related tables into one resultant table, is called a **join**. Originally, SQL specified a join implicitly by referring in a WHERE clause to the matching of common columns over which tables were joined. Since SQL-92, joins may also be specified in the FROM clause, too. In either case, two tables may be joined when each contains a column that shares a common domain with the other. As mentioned above, a primary key from one table and a foreign key that references the table with the primary key will share a common domain and are frequently used to establish a join. Occasionally, joins will be established using columns that share a common domain but not the primary-foreign key relationship, and that will also work. The result of a join operation is a single table. Selected columns from all the tables are included. Each row returned contains data from rows in the different input tables where values for the common columns match.

Explicit JOIN...ON commands are included in the FROM clause. The following join operations are included in the standard, though each RDBMS product is likely to support only a subset of the keywords: INNER, OUTER, FULL, LEFT, RIGHT, CROSS, and UNION. NATURAL is an optional keyword. There should be one ON specification for each pair of tables being joined. Thus, if two tables are to be combined, one ON condition would be necessary, but if three tables (A, B, and C) are to be combined, then two ON conditions would be necessary because there are two pairs of tables (A-B and B-C), and so forth. Most systems support up to 10 pairs of tables within one SQL command. CROSS JOINs, UNION JOINs, FULL [OUTER] JOINS or use of the keyword NATURAL are not core SQL at this time. Knowing that should help you understand why you may not find these implemented in the RDBMS you are using. Since they are included in the SQL:2003 standard and are useful, expect to find them becoming more widely available.

Join commands within the WHERE clause are implicit. That is, the keywords JOIN … ON are not included. However, just as when specifying the join within the FROM clause, there should be one equality condition within the WHERE clause for each pair of tables being joined.

Each type of join is described in the following sections.

Equi-join

With an **equi-join**, the joining condition is based on *equality* between values in the common columns. For example, if we want to know the names of customers who have placed orders, that information is kept in two tables, CUSTOMER_T and ORDER_T. It is necessary to match customers with their orders and then collect the information about name and order number in one table in order to answer our question.

Equi-join: A join in which the joining condition is based on equality between values in the common columns. Common columns appear (redundantly) in the result table.

Query: What are the names of all customers who have placed orders?

```
SELECT CUSTOMER_T.CUSTOMER_ID, ORDER_T.CUSTOMER_ID,
CUSTOMER_NAME, ORDER_ID
  FROM CUSTOMER_T, ORDER_T
      WHERE CUSTOMER_T.CUSTOMER_ID = ORDER_T.CUSTOMER_ID;
```

Result:

CUSTOMER_ID	CUSTOMER_ID	CUSTOMER_NAME	ORDER_ID
1	1	Contemporary Casuals	1001
8	8	California Classics	1002
15	15	Mountain Scenes	1003
5	5	Impressions	1004
3	3	Home Furnishings	1005
2	2	Value Furniture	1006
11	11	American Euro Lifestyles	1007
12	12	Battle Creek Furniture	1008
4	4	Eastern Furniture	1009
1	1	Contemporary Casuals	1010

10 rows selected.

The redundant CUSTOMER_ID columns, one from each table, demonstrate that the customer IDs have been matched, and that matching gives one row for each order placed. The importance of achieving the match between tables can be seen if the WHERE clause is omitted. That query will return all combinations of customers and orders, or 150 rows, and includes all possible combinations of the rows from the two tables. In this case, this join does not reflect the relationships that exist between the tables and is not a useful or meaningful result. The number of rows is equal to the number of rows in each table, multiplied together (10 orders × 15 customers = 150 rows). This is called a Cartesian join. In the case that a Cartesian join is desired, omit the pairings in the WHERE clause. A Cartesian join may be explicitly created by using the phrase CROSS JOIN in the FROM statement. FROM

CUSTOMER_T CROSS JOIN ORDER_T would create a Cartesian product of all customers with all orders.

The keywords INNER JOIN...ON are used to establish an equi-join in the FROM clause: While the syntax demonstrated here is Microsoft Access SQL syntax, note that some systems, such as ORACLE, treat the keyword JOIN by itself without the word INNER to establish an equi-join:

Query: What are the names of all customers who have placed orders?

```
SELECT CUSTOMER_T.CUSTOMER_ID, ORDER_T.CUSTOMER_ID,
CUSTOMER_T.CUSTOMER_NAME, ORDER_T.ORDER_ID
FROM CUSTOMER_T INNER JOIN ORDER_T ON
CUSTOMER_T.CUSTOMER_ID = ORDER_T.CUSTOMER_ID;
```

Result: Same as previous query.

Simplest of all would be to use the new JOIN...USING syntax. If the database designer thought ahead and used identical column names for the primary and foreign keys, such as has been done above with CUSTOMER_ID in the CUSTOMER_T and ORDER_T tables, the syntax could be:

```
SELECT CUSTOMER_T.CUSTOMER_ID, ORDER_T.CUSTOMER_ID,
CUSTOMER_T.CUSTOMER_NAME, ORDER_T.ORDER_ID
FROM CUSTOMER_T INNER JOIN ORDER_T USING CUSTOMER_ID;
```

Notice that the WHERE clause now functions only as a filter. Since the FROM clause is generally evaluated prior to the WHERE clause, some users express a preference for the newer syntax in the FROM clause. Thus, a smaller record set, which meets the join conditions is all that must be evaluated by the remaining clauses, and performance may be improved. All DBMS products support the traditional method of defining joins within the WHERE clause. MS SQL Server supports the INNER JOIN...ON syntax, Oracle has supported it since 9i and MySQL has supported it since 3.23.17.

We again emphasize that SQL is a set-oriented language. Thus, this join example above is produced by taking the CUSTOMER table and the ORDER table as two sets and appending together those rows from CUSTOMER with rows from ORDER that have equal CUSTOMER_ID values. This is a set intersection operation, which is followed by appending matching rows.

Natural Join

Natural join: Same as equi-join except one of the duplicate columns is eliminated in the result table.

A **natural join** is the same as an equi-join except that it is performed over matching columns that have been defined with the same name, and one of the duplicate columns is eliminated. The natural join is the most commonly used form of join operation. The SQL command to find customer names and order numbers leaves out one CUSTOMER_ID. Notice that CUSTOMER_ID must still be qualified because there is still ambiguity; CUSTOMER_ID exists in both CUSTOMER_T and ORDER_T, and therefore it must be specified from which table CUSTOMER_ID should be picked. NATURAL is an optional keyword when the join is defined in the FROM clause.

Query: For each customer who has placed an order, what is the customer's name and order number?

```
SELECT CUSTOMER_T.CUSTOMER_ID, CUSTOMER_NAME, ORDER_ID
FROM CUSTOMER_T NATURAL JOIN ORDER_T ON
    CUSTOMER_T.CUSTOMER_ID = ORDER_T.CUSTOMER_ID;
```

Note that the order of table names in the FROM clause is immaterial. The query optimizer of the DBMS will decide in which sequence to process each table. Whether indexes exist on common columns will influence the sequence in which tables are processed, as will which table is on the 1 and which is on the M side of *1:M* relationships. If a query takes significantly different amounts of time depending on the order in which tables are listed in the FROM clause, the DBMS does not have a very good query optimizer.

Outer Join

In joining two tables, we often find that a row in one table does not have a matching row in the other table. For example, several CUSTOMER_ID numbers do not appear in the ORDER_T table. Figure 8-1 shows the Customer and Order tables. Pointers have been drawn from each customer to their order(s). Contemporary Casuals has placed two orders. Furniture Gallery, Period Furniture, M & H Casual Furniture, Seminole Interiors, Heritage Furnishings, and Kaneohe Homes have not placed an order in this small example. We can assume this is because those customers have not placed orders since 10/21/2006, or their orders are not included in our very short sample ORDER_T table. As a result, the equi-join and natural join shown previously do not include all of the customers shown in CUSTOMER_T.

Of course, the organization may be very interested in identifying those customers who have not placed orders. They may want to contact them to encourage new orders, or they may be interested in analyzing these customers to discern why they are not ordering. Using an **outer join** produces this information: Rows that do not have matching values in common columns are also included in the result table. Null values appear in columns where there is not a match between tables.

Outer join: A join in which rows that do not have matching values in common columns are nevertheless included in the result table.

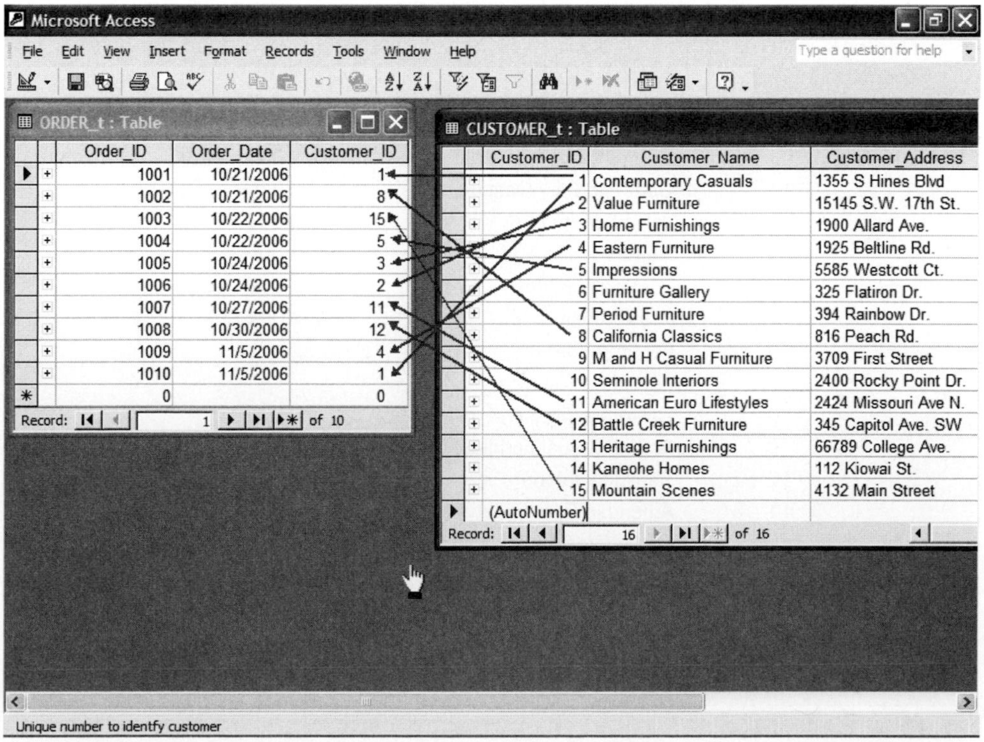

Figure 8-1

Pine Valley Furniture Company Customer and Order tables with pointers from customers to their orders

Outer joins can be handled by the major RDBMS vendors, but the syntax used to accomplish an outer join still varies across vendors. The example given here uses ANSI standard syntax. When an outer join is not available explicitly, use UNION and NOT EXISTS (discussed later in this chapter) to carry out an outer join. Here is an outer join.

Query: List customer name, identification number, and order number for all customers listed in the CUSTOMER table. Include the customer identification number and name even if there is no order available for that customer.

```
SELECT CUSTOMER_T.CUSTOMER_ID, CUSTOMER_NAME, ORDER_ID
    FROM CUSTOMER_T LEFT OUTER JOIN ORDER_T
        WHERE CUSTOMER_T.CUSTOMER_ID = ORDER_T.CUSTOMER_ID;
```

The syntax LEFT OUTER JOIN was selected because the CUSTOMER_T table was named first, and it is the table from which we wish all rows returned, regardless of whether there is a matching order in the ORDER_T table. Had we reversed the order in which the tables were listed, the same results would be obtained by requesting a RIGHT OUTER JOIN. It is also possible to request a FULL OUTER JOIN. In that case, all rows would be matched and returned, including any rows that do not have a match in the other table. INNER JOINs are much more common than OUTER JOINs are, because outer joins are necessary only when the user needs to see data from all rows, even those that have no matching row in another table.

It should also be noted that the OUTER JOIN syntax does not apply easily to a join condition of more than two tables. The results returned will vary according to the vendor, so be sure to test any outer join syntax that involves more than two tables until you understand how it will be interpreted by the DBMS being used.

Also, the results table from an outer join may indicate NULL as the values for columns in the second table where no match was achieved. If those columns could have NULL as a data value, you cannot know whether the row returned is a matched row or an unmatched row unless you run another query that checks for null values in the base table or view. And, a column that is defined as NOT NULL may be assigned a NULL value in the results table of an OUTER JOIN.

Result:

CUSTOMER_ID	CUSTOMER_NAME	ORDER_ID
1	Contemporary Casuals	1001
1	Contemporary Casuals	1010
2	Value Furniture	1006
3	Home Furnishings	1005
4	Eastern Furniture	1009
5	Impressions	1004
6	Furniture Gallery	
7	Period Furnishings	
8	California Classics	1002
9	M & H Casual Furniture	
10	Seminole Interiors	
11	American Euro Lifestyles	1007
12	Battle Creek Furniture	1008
13	Heritage Furnishings	
14	Kaneohe Homes	
15	Mountain Scenes	1003

16 rows selected.

It may help you to glance back at Figure 8-1. With an INNER JOIN of CUSTOMER_T and ORDER_T, only the 10 rows that have arrows drawn in will be returned. With an OUTER JOIN on CUSTOMER_T, all of the customers are returned along with the orders they have placed, and customers are returned even if they have not placed orders. Since Customer 1, Contemporary Casuals, has placed two orders, a total of 16 rows are returned because rows are returned for both orders placed by Contemporary Casuals.

The advantage of the outer join is that information is not lost. Here, all customer names were returned whether or not they had placed an order. Requesting a RIGHT OUTER join would return all orders. (Because referential integrity requires that every order be associated with a valid customer ID, that right outer join would only ensure that referential integrity is being enforced.) Customers who had not placed orders would not be included in the result.

Query: List customer name, identification number, and order number for all orders listed in the ORDER table. Include the order number even if there is no customer name and identification number available.

```
SELECT CUSTOMER_T.CUSTOMER_ID, CUSTOMER_NAME, ORDER_ID
    FROM CUSTOMER_T RIGHT OUTER JOIN ORDER_T ON
        CUSTOMER_T.CUSTOMER_ID = ORDER_T.CUSTOMER_ID;
```

Union Join

SQL:1999 and by extension SQL:2003 also allows for a UNION JOIN, which has not yet been implemented in all DBMS products. The results of a UNION JOIN will be a table that includes all data from each table that is joined. The results table will contain all columns from each table and will contain an instance for each row of data included from each table. Thus, a UNION JOIN of the CUSTOMER_T table (15 customers and 6 attributes) and the ORDER_T table (10 orders and 3 attributes) will return a results table of 25 rows (15 + 10) and 9 columns (6 + 3). Assuming that each original table contained no nulls, each customer row in the results table will contain three attributes with assigned null values, and each order row will contain six attributes with assigned null values.

UNION JOINs may not include the keyword NATURAL, an ON clause or a USING clause. Each of these implies an equivalence that would conflict with the UNION JOIN's inclusion of all the data from each table that is joined. Do not confuse this command with the UNION command that joins multiple SELECT statements and is covered later in this chapter.

Sample Multiple Join Involving Four Tables

Much of the power of the relational model comes from its ability to work with the relations among the objects in the database. Designing a database so that data about each object is kept in separate tables simplifies maintenance and data integrity. The capability to relate the objects to each other by joining the tables provides critical business information and reports to employees. Although the examples provided in Chapters 7 and 8 are simple and constructed only to provide a basic understanding of SQL, it is important to realize that these commands can be built into much more complex queries that provide exactly the information needed for a report or process.

Here is a sample join query that involves a four-table join. This query produces a result table that includes the information needed to create an invoice for order number 1006. We want the customer information, the order and order line information, and the product information, so we will need to join four tables.

Query: Assemble all information necessary to create an invoice for order number 1006.

```
SELECT CUSTOMER_T.CUSTOMER_ID, CUSTOMER_NAME,
CUSTOMER_ADDRESS, CUSTOMER_CITY, CUSTOMER_STATE, POSTAL_CODE,
ORDER_T.ORDER_ID, ORDER_DATE, ORDERED_QUANTITY,
PRODUCT_DESCRIPTION, STANDARD_PRICE,
(ORDERED_QUANTITY * STANDARD_PRICE)
  FROM CUSTOMER_T, ORDER_T, ORDER_LINE_T, PRODUCT_T
       WHERE CUSTOMER_T.CUSTOMER_ID = ORDER_T.CUSTOMER_ID
           AND ORDER_T.ORDER_ID = ORDER_LINE_T.ORDER_ID
           AND ORDER_LINE_T.PRODUCT_ID = PRODUCT_T.PRODUCT_ID
           AND ORDER_T.ORDER_ID = 1006;
```

The results of the query are shown in Figure 8-2. Traditional syntax is used. Remember, because the join involves four tables, there will be three column join conditions.

1. CUSTOMER_T.CUSTOMER_ID=ORDER_T.CUSTOMER_ID links the customer with their orders.

2. ORDER_T.ORDER_ID=ORDER_LINE_T.ORDER_ID links each order with the details of the items ordered.

3. ORDER_LINE_T.PRODUCT_ID=PRODUCT_T.PRODUCT_ID links each order detail record with the product description for that order line.

Subqueries

The preceding SQL examples illustrate one of the two basic approaches for joining two tables: the joining technique. SQL also provides the subquery technique, which involves placing an inner query (SELECT, FROM, WHERE) within a WHERE or HAVING clause of another (outer) query. The inner query provides values for the search condition of the outer query. Such queries are referred to as subqueries or nested subqueries. Subqueries can be nested multiple times. Subqueries are prime examples of why SQL is a set-oriented language.

Sometimes, either the joining or the subquery technique can be used to accomplish the same result, and different people will have different preferences about which technique to use. Other times, only a join or a subquery will work. The joining technique is useful when data from several relations are to be retrieved and displayed and the relationships are not necessarily nested. Let's compare two queries that return the same result. Both answer the question, what is the name and address of the customer who placed order number 1008? First, we will use a join query.

Query: What is the name and address of the customer who placed order number 1008?

Figure 8-2
Results from a four-table join (edited for readability)

```
SELECT CUSTOMER_NAME, CUSTOMER_ADDRESS, CUSTOMER_CITY,
CUSTOMER_STATE, POSTAL_CODE
```

CUSTOMER_ID	CUSTOMER_NAME	CUSTOMER_ADDRESS	CUSTOMER_CITY	CUSTOMER_ST	POSTAL_CODE
2	Value Furniture	15145 S.W. 17th St.	Plano	TX	75094 7743
2	Value Furniture	15145 S.W. 17th St.	Plano	TX	75094 7743
2	Value Furniture	15145 S.W. 17th St.	Plano	TX	75094 7743

ORDER_ID	ORDER_DATE	ORDERED_QUANTITY	PRODUCT_NAME	STANDARD_PRICE	(QUANTITY* STANDARD_PRICE)
1006	24-OCT-06	1	Entertainment Center	650	650
1006	24-OCT-06	2	Writer's Desk	325	650
1006	24-OCT-06	2	Dining Table	800	1600

```
FROM CUSTOMER_T, ORDER_T
     WHERE CUSTOMER_T.CUSTOMER_ID = ORDER_T.CUSTOMER_ID AND
          ORDER_ID = 1008;
```

In set-processing terms, this query finds the subset of the ORDER_T table for ORDER_ID=1008 and then matches the row(s) in that subset with the rows in the CUSTOMER_T table that have the same CUSTOMER_ID values. In this approach, it is not necessary that only one order have the ORDER_ID value of 1008. Now, look at the equivalent query using the subquery technique.

Query: What is the name and address of the customer who placed order number 1008?

```
SELECT CUSTOMER_NAME, CUSTOMER_ADDRESS, CUSTOMER_CITY,
CUSTOMER_STATE, POSTAL_CODE
    FROM CUSTOMER_T
         WHERE CUSTOMER_T.CUSTOMER_ID =
              (SELECT ORDER_T.CUSTOMER_ID
                  FROM ORDER_T
                     WHERE ORDER_ID = 1008);
```

Notice that the subquery, shaded in aqua and enclosed in parentheses, follows the form learned for constructing SQL queries and could stand on its own as an independent query. That is, the result of the subquery, as with any query, is a set of rows, in this case, a set of CUSTOMER_ID values. We know that only one value will be in the result. (There is only one CUSTOMER_ID for the order with ORDER_ID 1008.) To be safe, we can, and probably should, use the IN operator rather than "=" when writing subqueries. *The subquery approach may be used for this query because we need to display data from only the table in the outer query.* The value for ORDER_ID does not appear in the query result; it is used as the selection criterion in the inner query. To include data from the subquery in the result, use the join technique, because data from a subquery cannot be included in the final results.

As noted previously, we know in advance that the preceding subquery will return at most one value, the CUSTOMER_ID associated with ORDER_ID 1008. The result will be empty if an order with that ID does not exist. A subquery can also return a list (set) of values (with zero, one, or many entries) by using the keyword IN. *Because the result of the subquery is used to compare with one attribute (CUS-TOMER_ID in the query), the select list of a subquery may include only one attribute.* For example, which customers have placed orders? Here is a query that will answer that question.

Query: Which customers have placed orders?

```
SELECT CUSTOMER_NAME
    FROM CUSTOMER_T
         WHERE CUSTOMER_ID IN
              (SELECT DISTINCT CUSTOMER_ID
                  FROM ORDER_T);
```

This query produces the following result. As required, the subquery select list contains only the one attribute, CUSTOMER_ID, needed in the WHERE clause of the outer query. Distinct is used in the subquery because we do not care how many orders a customer has placed, just as long as they have placed an order. For each customer identified in the ORDER_T table, that customer's name has been returned from CUSTOMER_T. (You will study this query again in Figure 8-3a.)

CHAPTER 8 ADVANCED SQL

Result:

CUSTOMER_NAME
Contemporary Casuals
Value Furniture
Home Furnishings
Eastern Furniture
Impressions
California Classics
American Euro Lifestyles
Battle Creek Furniture
Mountain Scenes

9 rows selected.

The qualifiers NOT, ANY, and ALL may be used in front of IN or with logical operators such as =, >, and <. Because IN works with zero, one, or many values from the inner query, many programmers simply use IN instead of = for all queries, even if the equal sign would work. The next example shows the use of NOT, and it also demonstrates that a join can be used in an inner query.

Query: Which customers have not placed any orders for computer desks?

```
SELECT CUSTOMER_NAME
  FROM CUSTOMER_T
      WHERE CUSTOMER_ID NOT IN
          (SELECT CUSTOMER_ID
              FROM ORDER_T, ORDER_LINE_T, PRODUCT_T
              WHERE ORDER_T.ORDER_ID =
                    ORDER_LINE_T.ORDER_ID AND
                    ORDER_LINE_T.PRODUCT_ID =
                    PRODUCT_T.PRODUCT_ID
                    AND PRODUCT_DESCRIPTION =
                    'Computer Desk');
```

Result:

CUSTOMER_NAME
Value Furniture
Home Furnishings
Eastern Furniture
Furniture Gallery
Period Furniture
M & H Casual Furniture
Seminole Interiors
American Euro Lifestyles
Heritage Furnishings
Kaneohe Homes

10 rows selected.

The result shows that ten of our customers have not yet ordered computer desks. The inner query returned a list (set) of all customers who had ordered computer desks. The outer query listed the names of those customers who were not in the list returned by the inner query.

Two other conditions associated with using subqueries are EXISTS and NOT EXISTS. These keywords are included in an SQL query at the same location where IN would be, just prior to the beginning of the subquery. EXISTS will take a value of *true* if the subquery returns an intermediate results table that contains one or more rows (i.e., a nonempty set), and *false* if no rows are returned (i.e., an empty set). NOT EXISTS will take a value of *true* if no rows are returned, and *false* if one or more rows are returned. Consider the following SQL statement, which includes EXISTS.

Query: What are the order IDs for all orders that have included furniture finished in natural ash?

```
SELECT DISTINCT ORDER_ID FROM ORDER_LINE_T
WHERE EXISTS
    (SELECT *
        FROM PRODUCT_T
            WHERE PRODUCT_ID = ORDER_LINE_T.PRODUCT_ID
            AND PRODUCT_FINISH = 'Natural Ash');
```

The subquery checks for each order line to see if the finish for the product on that order line is natural ash. If this is true (EXISTS), the main query displays the order ID for that order. The outer query checks this for every row in the set of referenced rows (the ORDER_LINE_T table). There have been seven such orders, as the result shows. (We discuss this query further in Figure 8-3b.)

Result:

ORDER_ID
1001
1002
1003
1006
1007
1008
1009

7 rows selected.

When EXISTS or NOT EXISTS is used in a subquery, the select list of the subquery will usually just select all columns (SELECT *) as a placeholder because it does not matter which columns are returned. The purpose of the subquery is to test whether any rows fit the conditions, not to return values from particular columns for comparison purposes in the outer query. The columns that will be displayed are determined strictly by the outer query. The EXISTS subquery illustrated above, like almost all EXISTS subqueries, is a correlated subquery, which is described next. Queries containing the keyword NOT EXISTS will return a results table when no rows are found that satisfy the subquery.

In summary, use the subquery approach when qualifications are nested or when qualifications are easily understood in a nested way. Most systems allow pairwise joining of *one and only one column* in an inner query with one column in an outer query. An exception to this is when a subquery is used with the EXISTS keyword. Data can be displayed only from the table(s) referenced in the outer query. Up to sixteen levels of nesting are typically supported. Queries are processed inside out, although another type of subquery, a correlated subquery, is processed outside in.

Correlated Subqueries

In the first subquery example, it was necessary to examine the inner query before considering the outer query. That is, the result of the inner query was used to limit the processing of the outer query. In contrast, **correlated subqueries** use the result of the outer query to determine the processing of the inner query. That is, the inner query is somewhat different for each row referenced in the outer query. In this case, the inner query must be computed for *each* outer row, whereas in the earlier examples, the inner query was computed *only once* for all rows processed in the outer query. The EXISTS subquery example in the prior section had this characteristic, in which the inner query was executed for each ORDER_LINE_T row, and each time it was executed, the inner query was for a different PRODUCT_ID value—the one from the ORDER_LINE_T row in the outer query. Figure 8-3a and 8-3b depict the

Correlated subquery: In SQL, a subquery in which processing the inner query depends on data from the outer query.

```
SELECT CUSTOMER_NAME
        FROM CUSTOMER_T
            WHERE CUSTOMER_ID IN

                                            (SELECT DISTINCT CUSTOMER_ID
                                             FROM ORDER_T);
```

1. The subquery (shown in the box) is processed first and an intermediate results table created:

CUSTOMER_ID
———————
1
8
15
5
3
2
11
12
4
9 rows selected.

2. The outer query returns the requested customer information for each customer included in the intermediate results table:

CUSTOMER_NAME
———————————————————————————————————
Contemporary Casuals
Value Furniture
Home Furnishings
Eastern Furniture
Impressions
California Classics
American Euro Lifestyles
Battle Creek Furniture
Mountain Scenes
9 rows selected.

(a)

Figure 8-3
Subquery processing
(a) Processing a noncorrelated
subquery

different processing order for each of the examples from the previous section on subqueries.

Look at this query, which lists the details of the product that has a higher unit price than any other product in PRODUCT_T.

Query: List the details about the product with the highest unit price.

```
SELECT PRODUCT_DESCRIPTION, PRODUCT_FINISH,STANDARD_PRICE
    FROM PRODUCT_T PA
        WHERE STANDARD_PRICE > ALL
            (SELECT STANDARD_PRICE FROM PRODUCT_T PB
                WHERE PB.PRODUCT_ID ! = PA.PRODUCT_ID);
```

Here is the result; the dining table has a higher unit price than any other product.

Result:

PRODUCT_DESCRIPTION	PRODUCT_FINISH	STANDARD_PRICE
Dining Table	Natural Ash	800

The logic of this SQL statement is that the subquery will be executed once for each product to be sure that no other product has a higher standard price. Notice that we are comparing rows in a table to themselves and that we are able to do this by giving

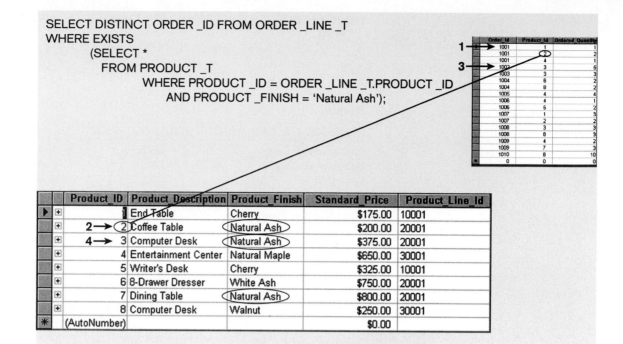

```
SELECT DISTINCT ORDER _ID FROM ORDER _LINE _T
WHERE EXISTS
        (SELECT *
            FROM PRODUCT _T
                WHERE PRODUCT _ID = ORDER _LINE _T.PRODUCT _ID
                    AND PRODUCT _FINISH = 'Natural Ash');
```

1. The first order ID is selected from ORDER _LINE _T: ORDER _ID =1001.

2. The subquery is evaluated to see if any product in that order has a natural ash finish. Product 2 does, and is part of the order. EXISTS is valued as *true* and the order ID is added to the result table.

3. The next order ID is selected from ORDER _LINE _T: ORDER _ID =1002.

4. The subquery is evaluated to see if the product ordered has a natural ash finish. It does. EXISTS is valued as true and the order ID is added to the result table.

5. Processing continues through each order ID. Orders 1004, 1005, and 1010 are not included in the result table because they do not include any furniture with a natural ash finish. The final result table is shown in the text on page 334.

(b)

Figure 8-3 (Continued)
(b) Processing a correlated subquery

the table two aliases, PA and PB. First, PRODUCT_ID 1, the end table, will be considered. When the subquery is executed, it will return a set of values, which are the standard prices of every product except the one being considered in the outer query (product 1 for the first time it is executed). Then, the outer query will check to see if the standard price for the product being considered is greater than all of the standard prices returned by the subquery. If it is, it will be returned as the result of the query. If not, the next standard price value in the outer query will be considered, and the inner query will return a list of all the standard prices for the other products. The list returned by the inner query changes as each product in the outer query changes; that makes it a correlated subquery. Can you identify a special set of standard prices for which this query will not yield the desired result?

Using Derived Tables

Subqueries are not limited to inclusion in the WHERE clause. They may also be used in the FROM clause, creating a temporary derived table (or set) that is used in the query. Creating a derived table that has an aggregate value in it, such as MAX, AVG, or MIN, allows the aggregate to be used in the WHERE clause. Here, pieces of furniture that exceed the average standard price are listed.

Query: Which products have a standard price that is higher than the average standard price?

```
SELECT PRODUCT_DESCRIPTION, STANDARD_PRICE, AVGPRICE
   FROM
            (SELECT AVG(STANDARD_PRICE) AVGPRICE FROM PRODUCT_T),
         PRODUCT_T
            WHERE STANDARD_PRICE > AVGPRICE;
```

Result:

PRODUCT_DESCRIPTION	STANDARD_PRICE	AVGPRICE
Entertainment Center	650	440.625
8-Drawer Dresser	750	440.625
Dining Table	800	440.625

Combining Queries

The UNION clause is used to combine the output (union the set of rows) from multiple queries together into a single result table. To use the UNION clause, each query involved must output the same number of columns, and they must be UNION compatible. This means that the output from each query for each column should be of compatible data types. Acceptance as a compatible data type varies among the DBMS products. When performing a union where output for a column will merge two different data types, it is safest to use the CAST command to control the data type conversion yourself. For example, the DATE data type in ORDER_T might need to be converted into a text data type. The SQL command to accomplish this would be:

SELECT **CAST(ORDER_DATE AS CHAR)** FROM ORDER_T;

The following example query determines the customer(s) who has purchased the largest quantity of any Pine Valley product and the customer(s) who has purchased the smallest quantity and returns the results in one table.

Query:

```
SELECT C1.CUSTOMER_ID,CUSTOMER_NAME,ORDERED_QUANTITY,
'Largest Quantity' QUANTITY
   FROM CUSTOMER_T C1,ORDER_T O1, ORDER_LINE_T Q1
         WHERE C1.CUSTOMER_ID =O1.CUSTOMER_ID
         AND O1.ORDER_ID =Q1.ORDER_ID
         AND ORDERED_QUANTITY =
               (SELECT MAX(ORDERED_QUANTITY)
               FROM ORDER_LINE_T)

UNION
SELECT C1.CUSTOMER_ID,CUSTOMER_NAME,ORDERED_QUANTITY,
'Smallest Quantity'
   FROM CUSTOMER_T C1,ORDER_T O1, ORDER_LINE_T Q1
         WHERE C1.CUSTOMER_ID =O1.CUSTOMER_ID
         AND O1.ORDER_ID =Q1.ORDER_ID
         AND ORDERED_QUANTITY =
               (SELECT MIN(ORDERED_QUANTITY)
               FROM ORDER_LINE_T)
ORDER BY ORDERED_QUANTITY;
```

Notice that an expression QUANTITY has been created in which the strings 'Smallest Quantity' and 'Largest Quantity' have been inserted for readability. The ORDER BY clause has been used to organize the order in which the rows of output are listed:

Result:

CUSTOMER_ID	CUSTOMER_NAME	ORDERED_QUANTITY	QUANTITY
1	Contemporary Casuals	1	Smallest Quantity
2	Value Furniture	1	Smallest Quantity
1	Contemporary Casuals	10	Largest Quantity

Conditional Expressions

Establishing IF-THEN-ELSE logical processing within an SQL statement can now be accomplished by using the CASE keyword in a statement. Figure 8-4 gives the CASE syntax, which actually has four forms. The CASE form can be constructed using either an expression that equates to a value or a predicate. The predicate form is based on three-value logic (true, false, don't know), but allows for more complex operations. The value-expression form requires a match to the value expression. NULLIF and COALESCE are the keywords associated with the other two forms of the CASE expression.

CASE could be used in constructing a query that asks, "What products are included in Product_Line 1?"

Query:

```
SELECT CASE
       WHEN PRODUCT_LINE = 1 THEN PRODUCT_DESCRIPTION
       ELSE '####'
END AS PRODUCT_DESCRIPTION
FROM PRODUCT_T;
```

Result:

```
PRODUCT_DESCRIPTION
End Table
####
####
####
Writers Desk
####
####
####
```

Gulutzan & Pelzer (1999, p. 573) indicate that "It's possible to use CASE expressions this way as retrieval substitutes, but the more common applications are (a) to make up for SQL's lack of an enumerated <data type>, (b) to perform complicated if/then calculations, (c) for translation, and (d) to avoid exceptions. We find CASE expressions to be indispensable, and it amazes us that in pre SQL-92 DBMSs they didn't exist."

```
{CASE expression
{WHEN expression
THEN {expression | NULL}} ...
| {WHEN predicate
THEN {expression | NULL}} ...
[ELSE {expression  NULL}]
END }
| ( NULLIF (expression, expression) }
| ( COALESCE (expression ...) }
```

Figure 8-4
CASE conditional syntax

More Complicated SQL Queries

The examples used in Chapters 7 and 8 have been very simple to make it easier for you to concentrate on the piece of SQL syntax being introduced. It is important to understand that real production databases may contain hundreds and even thousands of tables, and many of those contain hundreds of columns. While it is difficult to come up with complicated queries from the four tables used in Chapter 7 and 8, the text comes with a larger version of Pine Valley Furniture Company, which allows for somewhat more complex queries. This version is available at **www.prenhall.com/hoffer** and here are two samples drawn from that database:

Question 1: For each salesperson, list his or her biggest selling product.

Query:
First, we will define a view called tsales:

```
CREATE VIEW TSALES AS
SELECT SALESPERSON_T.SALESPERSON_NAME,
    PRODUCT_T.PRODUCT_DESCRIPTION,
    SUM(ORDER_LINE_T.ORDERED_QUANTITY) AS TOTORDERS
        FROM SALESPERSON_T, ORDER_LINE_T, PRODUCT_T, ORDER_T
            WHERE SALESPERSON_T.SALESPERSON_ID=
            ORDER_T.SALESPERSON_ID AND
            ORDER_T.ORDER_ID=ORDER_LINE_T.ORDER_ID AND
            ORDER_LINE_T.PRODUCT_ID=PRODUCT_T.PRODUCT_ID
                GROUP BY SALESPERSON_T.SALESPERSON_NAME,
                PRODUCT_T.PRODUCT_DESCRIPTION;
```

Next, write a correlated subquery using the view:

```
SELECT SALESPERSON_NAME, PRODUCT_DESCRIPTION
        FROM TSALES AS A
            WHERE TOTORDERS = (SELECT MAX(TOTORDERS)
            FROM TSALES B
            WHERE B.SALESPERSON_NAME = A.SALESPERSON_NAME);
```

Notice that it took two queries to answer the question: first a view that could be used in the second correlated subquery had to be built.

Question 2: Write an SQL query to list all salespersons who work in the territory where the most end tables have been sold.

Query:
First, we will create a query called topterritory using the following SQL statement:

```
SELECT TOP 1 TERRITORY_T.TERRITORY_ID,
SUM(ORDER_LINE_T.ORDERED_QUANTITY) AS TOTSALES
        FROM TERRITORY_T INNER JOIN (PRODUCT_T INNER JOIN
            (((CUSTOMER_T INNER JOIN DOES_BUSINESS_IN_T ON
            CUSTOMER_T.CUSTOMER_ID =
            DOES_BUSINESS_IN_T.CUSTOMER_ID)
            INNER JOIN ORDER_T ON CUSTOMER_T.CUSTOMER_ID =
            ORDER_T.CUSTOMER_ID) INNER JOIN ORDER_LINE_T ON
            ORDER_T.ORDER_ID = ORDER_LINE_T.ORDER_ID) ON
            PRODUCT_T.PRODUCT_ID = ORDER_LINE_T.PRODUCT_ID) ON
            TERRITORY_T.TERRITORY_ID =
            DOES_BUSINESS_IN_T.TERRITORY_ID
                WHERE ((PRODUCT_T.PRODUCT_DESCRIPTION)=
                "End Table")
                GROUP BY TERRITORY_T.TERRITORY_ID
                ORDER BY SUM(ORDER_LINE_T.ORDERED_QUANTITY) DESC;
```

This will give us the territory number of the top producing territory for sales of end tables.

Next, we will write a query using this query:

```
SELECT SALESPERSON_T.SALESPERSON_ID,
       SALESPERSON_T.SALESPERSON_NAME
       FROM TERRITORY_T INNER JOIN SALESPERSON_T ON
           TERRITORY_T.TERRITORY_ID = SALESPERSON_T.TERRITORY_ID
       WHERE SALESPERSON_T.TERRITORY_ID IN
           (SELECT TERRITORY_ID FROM TOPTERRITORY);
```

ENSURING TRANSACTION INTEGRITY

RDBMSs are no different from other types of database managers in that one of their primary responsibilities is to ensure that data maintenance is properly and completely handled. Data maintenance is defined in units of work called transactions, which involve one or more data manipulation commands. A transaction is the complete set of closely related update commands that must all be done, or none of them done, for the database to remain valid. Consider Figure 8-5. For example, when an order is entered into the Pine Valley database, all of the items ordered should be entered at the same time. Thus, either all ORDER_LINE_T rows from this form are to be entered, along with all the information in ORDER_T, or none of them should be entered. Here, the business transaction is the complete order, not the individual items that are ordered. What we need are commands to define the boundaries of a transaction, to commit the work of a transaction as a permanent change to the database, and to abort a transaction on purpose and correctly, if necessary. In addition, we need data recovery services to clean up after abnormal termination of database processing in the middle of a transaction. Perhaps the order form is accurate, but in the middle of entering the order, the computer system malfunctions or loses power. In this case, we do not want some of the changes made and not others. It's all or nothing at all if we want a valid database.

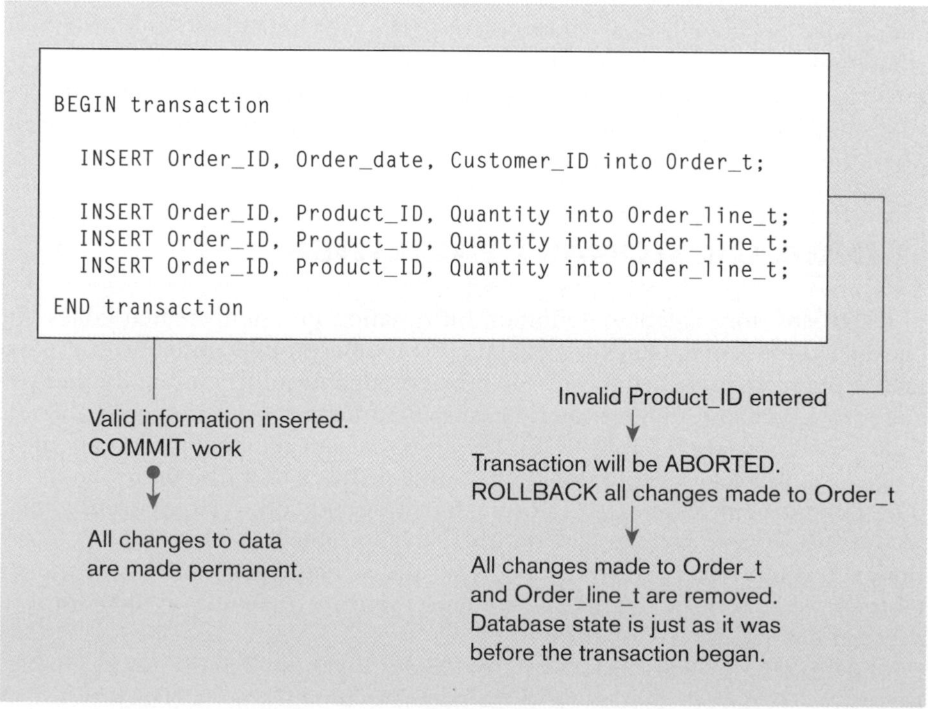

Figure 8-5
An SQL transaction sequence (in pseudocode)

```
BEGIN transaction

   INSERT Order_ID, Order_date, Customer_ID into Order_t;

   INSERT Order_ID, Product_ID, Quantity into Order_line_t;
   INSERT Order_ID, Product_ID, Quantity into Order_line_t;
   INSERT Order_ID, Product_ID, Quantity into Order_line_t;

END transaction
```

Valid information inserted.
COMMIT work

All changes to data
are made permanent.

Invalid Product_ID entered

Transaction will be ABORTED.
ROLLBACK all changes made to Order_t

All changes made to Order_t
and Order_line_t are removed.
Database state is just as it was
before the transaction began.

When a single SQL command constitutes a transaction, some RDBMSs will automatically commit or rollback after the command is run. With a user-defined transaction, however, where multiple SQL commands need to be run and either entirely committed or entirely rolled back, explicit commands to manage the transaction are needed. Many systems will have BEGIN TRANSACTION and END TRANSACTION commands, which are used to mark the boundaries of a logical unit of work. BEGIN TRANSACTION creates a log file and starts recording all changes (insertions, deletions, and updates) to the database in this file. END TRANSACTION or COMMIT WORK takes the contents of the log file and applies them to the database, thus making the changes permanent, and then empties the log file. ROLLBACK WORK asks SQL to empty the log file. Some RDBMSs also have an AUTOCOMMIT (ON/OFF) command that specifies whether changes are made permanent after each data modification command (ON) or only when work is explicitly made permanent (OFF) by the COMMIT WORK command.

User-defined transactions can improve system performance because transactions will be processed as sets rather than as individual transactions, thus reducing system overhead. When AUTOCOMMIT is set to OFF, changes will not be made automatically until the end of a transaction is indicated. When AUTOCOMMIT is set to ON, changes will be made automatically at the end of each SQL statement; this would not allow for user-defined transactions to be committed or rolled back only as a whole.

SET AUTOCOMMIT is an interactive command, therefore a given user session can be dynamically controlled for appropriate integrity measures. Each SQL INSERT, UPDATE, and DELETE command typically works on only one table at a time. Some data maintenance requires updating of multiple tables for the work to be complete. Therefore, these transaction-integrity commands are important in clearly defining whole units of database changes that must be completed in full for the database to retain integrity.

Further, some SQL systems have concurrency controls that handle the updating of a shared database by concurrent users. These can journalize database changes so that a database can be recovered after abnormal terminations in the middle of a transaction. They can also undo erroneous transactions. For example, in a banking application, the update of a bank account balance by two concurrent users should be cumulative. Such controls are transparent to the user in SQL; no user programming is needed to ensure proper control of concurrent access to data. To ensure the integrity of a particular database, be sensitive to transaction integrity and recovery issues and make sure that application programmers are appropriately informed of when these commands are to be used.

DATA DICTIONARY FACILITIES

RDBMSs store database definition information in system-created tables; we can consider these system tables as a data dictionary. Becoming familiar with the systems tables for any RDBMS being used will provide valuable information, whether you are a user or a database administrator. Because the information is stored in tables, it can be accessed by using SQL SELECT statements that can generate reports about system usage, user privileges, constraints, and so on. Further, a user who understands the systems-table structure can extend existing tables or build other tables to enhance built-in features (e.g., to include data on who is responsible for data integrity). A user is, however, often restricted from modifying the structure or contents of the system tables directly, because the DBMS maintains them and depends on them for its interpretation and parsing of queries.

Each RDBMS keeps various internal tables for these definitions. In Oracle 10g, there are 522 data dictionary views for database administrators (DBA) to use. Many of these views, or subsets of the DBA view (that information relevant to an individual user), are also available to users who do not possess DBA privileges. Those tables' names begin with USER or ALL rather than DBA. Here is a list of some of the tables (accessible to DBAs) that keep information about tables, clusters, columns, and security. There are also tables related to storage, objects, indexes, locks, auditing, exports, and distributed environments.

DBA_TABLES	Describes all tables in the database
DBA_TAB_COMMENTS	Comments on all tables in the database
DBA_CLUSTERS	Describes all clusters in the database
DBA_TAB_COLUMNS	Describes columns of all tables, views, and clusters
DBA_COL_PRIVS	Includes all grants on columns in the database
DBA_COL_COMMENTS	Comments on all columns in tables and views
DBA_CONSTRAINTS	Constraint definitions on all tables in the database
DBA_CLU_COLUMNS	Maps table columns to cluster columns
DBA_CONS_COLUMNS	Information about all columns in constraint definitions
DBA_USERS	Information about all users of the database
DBA_SYS_PRIVS	Describes system privileges granted to users and to roles
DBA_ROLES	Describes all roles that exist in the database
DBA_PROFILES	Includes resource limits assigned to each profile
DBA_ROLE_PRIVS	Describes roles granted to users and to other roles
DBA_TAB_PRIVS	Describes all grants on objects in the database

To give an idea of the type of information found in the system tables, consider DBA_USERS. DBA_USERS contains information about the valid users of the database; its 12 attributes include user name, user ID, encrypted password, default tablespace, temporary tablespace, date created, and profile assigned. DBA_TAB_COLUMNS has 31 attributes, including owner of each table, table name, column name, data type, data length, precision, and scale, among others. An SQL query against DBA_TABLES to find out who owns PRODUCT_T follows.

Query: Who is the owner of the PRODUCT table?

```
SELECT OWNER, TABLE_NAME
   FROM DBA_TABLES
      WHERE TABLE_NAME = 'PRODUCT_T';
```

Result:

OWNER	TABLE_NAME
MPRESCOTT	PRODUCT_T

Every RDBMS contains a set of tables in which metadata of the sort described for Oracle 10g is contained. The system-table design for Microsoft SQL Server 2000 differs from Oracle's. SQL Microsoft Server has 19 server system tables, all of which are named beginning with SYS, just as Oracle tables begin with DBA, USER, or ALL. Microsoft SQL Server 2000 also has 20 system-schema views that enable users to examine schema information about the database they are using according to the access privileges they have been assigned.

Here are a few of the Microsoft SQL Server 2000 server system tables:

SYSCOLUMNS	Table and column definitions
SYSDEPENDS	Object dependencies based on foreign keys
SYSINDEXES	Table index information

SYSINDEXKEYS	Primary key information
SYSMEMBERS	Users assigned to roles
SYSOBJECTS	Database objects listing
SYSPERMISSIONS	Access permissions granted to users, groups, and roles
SYSPROPERTIES	Master database only; currently running processes information
SYSUSERS	Database users, either Windows or SQL Server users

A command such as SELECT * FROM SYSUSERS returns information about every user account that has been established, including its creation date, update dates, password, and so forth.

System views such as TABLES, VIEWS, ROUTINES, KEY_COLUMN_USAGE can be accessed through the Information Schema views in Microsoft SQL Server 2000. For example, to obtain a listing of all tables and their type contained in a database, run this SELECT command:

```
SELECT * FROM INFORMATION_SCHEMA.TABLES
```

Once you know the names of the tables in the database, you can use the other views to examine them. For example, try:

```
SELECT * FROM INFORMATION_SCHEMA.KEY_COLUMN_USAGE
```

This query will return information about constraints established in the database, including primary keys and foreign keys. Similarly, SELECT * FROM INFORMA-TION_SCHEMA.TABLE_PRIVILEGES returns information about table ownership and user permissions.

SQL:2003 ENHANCEMENTS AND EXTENSIONS TO SQL

The previous sections of Chapters 7 and 8 have demonstrated the power and simplicity of SQL. However, readers with a strong interest in business analysis may well have wondered about the limited set of statistical functions available. Programmers familiar with other languages may have wondered how variables will be defined, flow control established, or **user-defined data types (UDTs)** created. And, as programming becomes more object oriented, how is SQL going to adjust? SQL:1999 extended SQL by providing more programming capabilities. SQL:2003 has standardized additional statistical functions. With time, the SQL standard will be modified to encompass object-oriented concepts. Other notable additions in SQL:2003 include three new data types and a new part, SQL/XML. The first two areas, additional statistical functions within the WINDOW clause, and the new datatypes, are discussed here. SQL/XML is discussed in Chapter 10.

User-defined data type (UDT): SQL:1999 allows users to define their own data type by making it a subclass of a standard type or creating a type that behaves as an object. UDTs may also have defined functions and methods.

Analytical Functions

SQL:2003 added a set of analytical functions, referred to as OLAP (on-line analytical processing) functions, as SQL language extensions. Most of the functions already have been implemented in Oracle, DB2, and Teradata. Including these functions in the standard addresses the needs for analytical capabilities within the database engine. Linear regressions, correlations, and moving averages may now be calculated without moving the data outside the database. As SQL:2003 is imple-

Table 8-1   Some Built-in Functions Added in SQL:2003

CEILING	Computes the least integer greater than or equal to its argument, i.e., CEIL(100) or CEILING(100)
FLOOR	Computes the greatest integer less than or equal to its argument, for example, FLOOR(25)
SQRT	Computes the square root of its argument, for example, SQRT(36)
RANK	Computes the ordinal rank of a row within its window. Implies that if duplicates exist, there will be gaps in the ranks assigned. The rank of the row is defined as 1 plus the number of rows preceding the row that are not peers of the row being ranked.
DENSE_RANK	Computes the ordinal rank of a row within its window. Implies that if duplicates exist, there will be no gaps in the ranks assigned. The rank of the row is the number of distinct rows preceding the row and itself.

mented, vendor implementations will adhere strictly to the standard and become more similar.

Table 8-1 lists a few of the newly standardized functions. Both statistical and numeric functions are included. Functions such as ROW_NUMBER and RANK will allow the developer to work much more flexibly with an ordered result. For database marketing or customer relationship management applications, the ability to consider only the top n rows or to subdivide the result into groupings by percentile is a welcome addition. Users can expect to achieve more efficient processing, too, as the functions are brought into the database engine and optimized. Once they are standardized, application vendors can depend on them, including their use in their applications and avoiding the need to create their own functions outside of the database.

SQL:1999 was amended to include an additional clause, the WINDOW clause. The WINDOW clause improves SQL's numerical analysis capabilities. It allows a query to specify that an action is to be performed over a set of rows (the window). This clause consists of a list of window definitions, each of which defines a name and specification for the window. Specifications include partitioning, ordering, and aggregation grouping.

Here is a sample query from the paper that proposed the amendment (Zemke et al., 1999, p. 4):

```
SELECT SH.TERRITORY, SH.MONTH, SH.SALES,
AVG (SH.SALES) OVER W1 AS MOVING_AVERAGE
      FROM SALES_HISTORY AS SH
        WINDOW W1 AS (PARTITION BY (SH.TERRITORY)
              ORDER BY (SH.MONTH ASC)
              ROWS 2 PRECEDING);
```

The window name is W1 and is defined in the WINDOW clause that follows the FROM clause. The PARTITION clause partitions the rows in SALES_HISTORY by TERRITORY. Within each territory partition, the rows will be ordered in ascending order by month. Last, an aggregation group is defined as the current row and the two preceding rows of the partition, following the order imposed by the ORDER BY clause. Thus, a moving average of the sales for each territory will be returned as MOVING_AVERAGE. Although proposed, MOVING_AVERAGE was not included in SQL:1999 or SQL:2003, but is anticipated for inclusion in SQL:2005. Though SQL is not the preferred way to perform numerical analyses on data sets, inclusion of the WINDOW clause has made many OLAP analyses easier. Several new WINDOW functions were approved in SQL:2003. Of these new window functions, RANK and DENSE_RANK are included in Table 8-1. Previously included aggregate functions such as AVG, SUM, MAX and MIN can also be used in WINDOW clause.

New Data Types

SQL:2003 includes three new data types and removed two traditional data types. The data types that were removed are BIT and BIT VARYING. Eisenberg et al. (2004) indicate that BIT and BIT VARYING were removed because they had not been widely supported by RDBMS products and were not expected to support those data types.

The three new data types are BIGINT, MULTISET, and XML. BIGINT is an exact numeric type of scale 0, meaning it is an integer. The precision of BIGINT is greater than that of either INT or SMALLINT, but its exact definition is implementation specific. However, BIGINT, INT and SMALLINT must have the same radix, or base system. All operations that can be performed using INT and SMALLINT can be performed using BIGINT, too.

MULTISET is a new collection data type. The previous collection data type is ARRAY, a noncore SQL data type. MULTISET differs from ARRAY because it can contain duplicates. This also distinguishes a table defined as MULTISET data from a relation, which is a set and cannot contain duplicates. MULTISET is unordered, and all elements are of the same element type. The elements can be any other supported data type. INTEGER MULTISET, for example, would define a multiset where all the elements are INTEGER data type. The values in a multiset may be created through INSERT or through a SELECT statement. An example of the INSERT approach would be MULTISET (2,3,5,7) and of the SELECT approach MULTISET (SELECT PRODUCT_DESCRIPTION FROM PRODUCT WHERE STANDARD_PRICE > 200;. MULTISET) reflects the real-world circumstance that some relations may contain duplicates that are acceptable when a subset is extracted from a table.

Other Enhancements

In addition to the enhancements to windowed tables described above, the CREATE TABLE command has been enhanced by the expansion of CREATE TABLE LIKE options. CREATE TABLE LIKE allows one to create a new table that is similar to an existing table, but in SQL:1999 information such as default values, expressions used to generate a calculated column, and so forth, could not be copied to the new table. Now a general syntax of CREATE TABLE LIKE … INCLUDING has been approved. INCLUDING COLUMN DEFAULTS, for example, will pick up any default values defined in the original CREATE TABLE command and transfer it to the new table by using CREATE TABLE LIKE … INCLUDING. It should be noted that use of this command creates a table that seems similar to a materialized view. However, tables created using CREATE TABLE LIKE are independent of the table that was copied. Once the table is populated, it will not be automatically updated if the original table is updated.

An additional approach to updating a table can now be taken by using the new SQL:2003 command, MERGE. In a transactional database, it is an everyday need to be able to add new orders, new customers, new inventory, and so forth, to existing order, customer, and inventory tables. If changes that require updating information about a customer and adding new customers are stored in a transaction table, to be added to the base customer table at the end of the business day, adding a new customer used to require an INSERT command, and changing information about an existing customer used to require an UPDATE command. The MERGE command allows both actions to be accomplished using only one query.

```
MERGE INTO CUSTOMER_T as CUST
   USING (SELECT CUSTOMER_ID, CUSTOMER_NAME, CUSTOMER_ADDRESS,
        CITY, STATE, POSTAL_CODE FROM CUST_TRANS_T)
          AS CT
     ON (CUST.CUSTOMER_ID = CT.CUSTOMER_ID)
WHEN MATCHED THEN UPDATE
```

```
        SET CUST.CUSTOMER_NAME = CT.CUSTOMER_NAME,
            CUST.CUSTOMER_ADDRESS = CT.CUSTOMER_ADDRESS,
            CUST.CITY = CT.CITY,
            CUST.STATE = CT.STATE,
            CUST.POSTAL_CODE = CT.POSTAL_CODE
    WHEN NOT MATCHED THEN INSERT
        (CUSTOMER_ID, CUSTOMER_NAME, CUSTOMER_ADDRESS, CITY, STATE,
            POSTAL_CODE)
            VALUES (CT.CUSTOMER_ID, CT.CUSTOMER_NAME,
                CT.CUSTOMER_ADDRESS, CT.CITY, CT.STATE, CT.POSTAL_CODE);
```

Programming Extensions

SQL-92 and earlier standards developed the capabilities of SQL as a data retrieval and manipulation language, and not as an application language. As a result, SQL has been used in conjunction with computationally complete languages such as C or Java to create business application programs, procedures, or functions. SQL:1999, however, extended SQL by adding programmatic capabilities in Core SQL, SQL/PSM, and SQL/OLB. These capabilities have been carried forward and included in SQL:2003.

The extensions that make SQL computationally complete include flow control capabilities, such as IF-THEN, FOR, WHILE statements, and loops, which are contained in a package of extensions to the essential SQL specifications. This package, called **Persistent Stored Modules (SQL/PSM)**, is so named because the capabilities to create and drop program modules are stored in it. Persistent means that a module of code will be stored until dropped, thus making it available for execution across user sessions, just as the base tables are retained until explicitly dropped. Each module is stored in a schema as a schema object. A schema does not have to have any program modules, or it may have multiple modules.

Persistent Stored Modules (SQL/PSM): Extensions defined in SQL:1999 that include the capability to create and drop modules of code stored in the database schema across user sessions.

Each module must have a name, an authorization ID, association with a particular schema, indication of the character set to be used, and any temporary table declarations that will be needed when the module executes. Every module must contain one or more SQL procedures, named programs that each execute one SQL statement when called. Each procedure must also include an SQLSTATE declaration that acts as a status parameter and indicates whether an SQL statement has been successfully executed.

SQL/PSM can be used to create applications or to incorporate procedures and functions using SQL data types directly. Using SQL/PSM introduces procedurality to SQL, because statements are processed sequentially. Remember that SQL by itself is a nonprocedural language and that no statement execution sequence is implied. SQL/PSM includes several SQL-control statements, including:

CASE	A statement that executes different sets of SQL sequences according to a comparison of values or the value of a WHEN clause using either search conditions or value expressions. The logic is similar to an SQL CASE expression, but ends with END CASE rather than END, and has no equivalent to the ELSE NULL clause.
IF	If a predicate is TRUE, an SQL statement will be executed. The statement ends with an ENDIF and contains ELSE and ELSEIF statements to manage flow control for different conditions.
LOOP	Causes a statement to be executed repeatedly until a condition exists that results in an exit.
LEAVE	Statement used to set a condition that results in exiting from a loop.

FOR	Statement that will execute once for each row of a results set.
WHILE	A statement that will be executed as long as a particular condition exists. Incorporates logic that functions as a LEAVE statement.
REPEAT	Similar to the WHILE statement, but the condition is tested after execution of the SQL statement.
ITERATE	Statement used to restart a loop.

SQL/PSM brings the promise of addressing several widely noted deficiencies of essential SQL. It is still too soon to know if programmers are going to embrace SQL/PSM or continue to use host languages, invoking SQL through embedded SQL or via CLI. But, the standard makes it possible to:

- Create procedures and functions within SQL, thus making it possible to accept input and output parameters and to return a value directly
- Detect and handle errors within SQL, rather than having to handle errors through another language
- Create variables using the DECLARE statement that stay in scope throughout the procedure, method, or function in which they are contained
- Pass groups of SQL statements rather than individual statements, thus improving performance
- Handle the impedance-mismatch problem, where SQL processes sets of data while procedural languages process single rows of data within modules

SQL/PSM has not yet been widely implemented, and therefore we have not included extensive syntax examples in this chapter. Oracle's PL/SQL bears some resemblance to the new standard with its modules of code, BEGIN ... END, LOOP, and WHILE statements. Although SQL/PSM is not yet widely popular, this situation could change quickly.

TRIGGERS AND ROUTINES

Prior to the issuance of SQL:1999, no support for user-defined functions or procedures was included in the SQL standards. Commercial products, recognizing the need for such capabilities, have provided them for some time, and we expect to see their syntax change over time to be in line with the SQL:1999 requirements, just as we expect to see inclusion of SQL/PSM standards.

Trigger: A named set of SQL statements that are considered (triggered) when a data modification (INSERT, UPDATE, DELETE) occurs. If a condition stated within the trigger is met, then a prescribed action is taken.

Triggers and routines are very powerful database objects because they are stored in the database and controlled by the DBMS. Thus, the code required to create them is stored in only one location and is administered centrally. This promotes stronger data integrity and consistency of use within the database. Because they are stored only once, code maintenance is also simplified (Mullins, 1995).

Both triggers and routines consist of blocks of procedural code. Routines are stored blocks of code that must be called to operate (see Figure 8-6). They do not run automatically. In contrast, trigger code is stored in the database and runs automatically whenever the triggering event, such as an UPDATE, occurs. Triggers are a special type of stored procedure and run only in response to an INSERT, UPDATE, or DELETE command. Trigger syntax and functionality vary from RDBMS to RDBMS. A trigger written to work with an Oracle database will need to be rewritten if the database is ported to Microsoft SQL Server, and vice versa. For example, ORACLE triggers can be written to fire once per INSERT, UPDATE, or DELETE command or to fire once per row affected by the command. Microsoft SQL Server triggers can fire only once per DML command, not once per row.

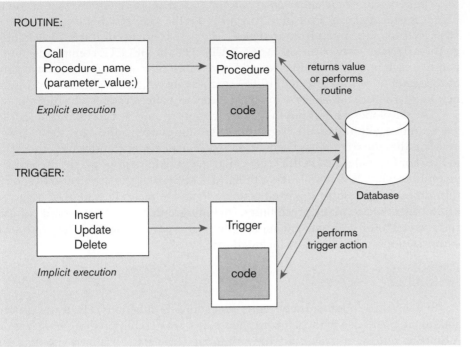

Figure 8-6
Triggers contrasted with stored procedures (adapted from Mullins, 1995)

Triggers

Because triggers are stored and executed in the database, they execute against all applications that access the database. Triggers can also cascade, causing other triggers to fire. Thus, a single request from a client can result in a series of integrity or logic checks being performed on the server without causing extensive network traffic between client and server. Triggers can be used to ensure referential integrity, enforce business rules, create audit trails, replicate tables, or activate a procedure (Rennhackkamp, 1996).

Constraints can be thought of as a special case of triggers. They also are applied (triggered) automatically as a result of data modification commands, but their precise syntax is determined by the DBMS and does not have the flexibility of a trigger.

Triggers have three parts, the *event*, the *condition*, and the *action*, and these parts are reflected in the coding structure for triggers. (See Figure 8-7 for a simplified trigger syntax.) Consider the following example: Perhaps the manager in charge of maintaining inventory needs to know when an inventory item's standard price is updated in the PRODUCT_T table. After creating a new table, Price_update_t, a trigger can be written that enters each product when it is updated, the date that the change was made, and the new standard price that was entered. The trigger is named standard_price_update. The code for this trigger follows:

```
CREATE TRIGGER STANDARD_PRICE_UPDATE
AFTER UPDATE OF STANDARD_PRICE ON PRODUCT_T
FOR EACH ROW
INSERT INTO PRICE_UPDATES_T VALUES ('PRODUCT_DESCRIPTION, SYSDATE,
     STANDARD_PRICE');
```

```
CREATE TRIGGER trigger_name
     {BEFORE | AFTER | INSTEAD OF} {INSERT | DELETE | UPDATE} ON
     table_name
     [FOR EACH {ROW | STATEMENT}] [WHEN (search condition)]
     <triggered SQL statement here>;
```

Figure 8-7
Simplified trigger syntax, SQL:2003

Triggers may occur either *before, after* or *instead of* the statement that aroused the trigger is executed. An "instead of" trigger is not the same as a before trigger, but executes instead of the intended transaction, which does not occur if the "instead of" trigger fires Triggers may occur on INSERT, UPDATE, or DELETE commands. And they may fire each time a *row* is affected, or they may fire only once per *statement,* regardless of the number of rows affected. In the case just shown, the trigger should insert the new standard price information into Price_update_t after Product_t has been updated.

The developer who wishes to include triggers should be careful. Because triggers fire automatically, unless the trigger includes a message to the user, the user will be unaware that the trigger has fired. Also, triggers can cascade and cause other triggers to fire. For example, a BEFORE UPDATE trigger could require that a row be inserted in another table. If that table has a BEFORE INSERT trigger, it will also fire, possibly with unintended results. It is even possible to create an endless loop of triggers! So, while triggers have many possibilities, including enforcement of complex business rules, creation of sophisticated auditing logs, and enforcement of elaborate security authorizations, they should be included with care.

Routines

Function: A stored subroutine that returns one value and has only input parameters.

Procedure: A collection of procedural and SQL statements that are assigned a unique name within the schema and stored in the database.

SQL-invoked routines can be either procedures or functions. The terms procedure and function are used in the same manner as they are in other programming languages. A **function** returns one value and has only input parameters. You have already seen the many built-in functions included in SQL, including the newest functions listed in Table 8-1. A **procedure** may have input parameters, output parameters, and parameters that are both input and output parameters. You may declare and name a unit of procedural code using proprietary code of the RDBMS product being used or invoke a host-language library routine. SQL products had developed their own versions of routines prior to the issuance of SQL:1999, so be sure to become familiar with the syntax and capabilities of any product you use. Some of these proprietary languages, such as Microsoft Sequel Server's Transact-SQL and Oracle's PL/SQL, are in wide use and will continue to be available. To give you an idea of how much stored procedure syntax has varied across products, Table 8-2 examines the CREATE PROCEDURE syntax used by three vendors. This table comes directly from http://www.tdan.com/i023fe03.htm by Peter Gulatzan.

Table 8-2 Comparison of Vendor Syntax Differences in Stored Procedures (Gulatzan & Pelzer, viewed at www.tdan.com/i023fe03.htm, July 28, 2005)

The vendors' syntaxes differ in stored procedures more than in ordinary SQL. For an illustration, here is a chart to show what CREATE PROCEDURE looks like in three dialects. I use one line for each significant part, so you can compare dialects by reading across the line.

SQL:1999/ IBM	Microsoft / Sybase	Oracle
CREATE PROCEDURE	CREATE PROCEDURE	CREATE PROCEDURE
Sp_proc1	Sp_proc1	Sp_proc1
(param1 INT)	@param1 INT	(param1 IN OUT INT)
MODIFIES SQL DATA BEGIN		
DECLARE num1 INT;	AS DECLARE @num1 INT	AS num1 INT; BEGIN
IF param1 <> 0	IF @param1 <> 0	IF param1 <> 0
THEN SET param1 = 1;	SELECT @param1 = 1;	THEN param1 :=1;
END IF		END IF;
UPDATE Table1 SET	UPDATE Table1 SET	UPDATE Table1 SET
column1 = param1;	column1 = @param1	column1 = param1;
END		END;

Data from SQL Performance Tuning *(Gulutzan and Pelzer, Addison-Wesley, 2002)*

```
{CREATE PROCEDURE | CREATE FUNCTION} routine_name
([parameter [{,parameter} . . .]])
[RETURNS data_type result_cast]    /* for functions only */
[LANGUAGE {ADA | C | COBOL | FORTRAN | MUMPS | PASCAL | PLI | SQL}]
[PARAMETER STYLE {SQL | GENERAL}]
[SPECIFIC specific_name]
[DETERMINISTIC | NOT DETERMINISTIC]
[NO SQL | CONTAINS SQL | READS SQL DATA | MODIFIES SQL DATA]
[RETURNS NULL ON NULL INPUT | CALLED ON NULL INPUT]
[DYNAMIC RESULT SETS unsigned_integer]      /* for procedures only */
[STATIC DISPATCH]                           /* for functions only */
[NEW SAVEPOINT LEVEL I OLD SAVEPOINT LEVEL]
routine_body
```

Figure 8-8
Create routine syntax, SQL:2003

The advantages of SQL-invoked routines include:

- *Flexibility* Routines may be used in more situations than constraints or triggers, which are limited to data-modification circumstances. Just as triggers have more code options than constraints, routines have more code options than triggers.

- *Efficiency* Routines can be carefully crafted and optimized to run more quickly than slower, generic SQL statements.

- *Sharability* Routines may be cached on the server and made available to all users so that they do not have to be rewritten.

- *Applicability* Routines may apply to the entire database rather than be limited to one application. This advantage is a corollary to sharability.

The SQL:2003 syntax for procedure and function creation is shown in Figure 8-8. As you can see, the syntax is complicated, and we will not go into the details about each clause here. However, a simple procedure follows, which will give you an idea of how the code works.

A procedure is a collection of procedural and SQL statements that are assigned a unique name within the schema and stored in the database. When it is needed to run the procedure, it is called by its name. When called, all of the statements in the procedure will be executed. This characteristic of procedures helps to reduce network traffic, because all of the statements are transmitted at one time, rather than sent individually.

To build a simple procedure that will set a sale price, the existing PRODUCT_T table is altered by adding a new column, SALE_PRICE, that will hold the sale price for the products:

```
ALTER TABLE PRODUCT_T
ADD (SALE_PRICE DECIMAL (6,2));
```

Result:

Table altered.

Our simple procedure will execute two SQL statements. Products with a STANDARD_PRICE of $400 or higher are discounted 10 percent, and products with a STANDARD_PRICE of less than $400 are discounted 15 percent. Here is the Oracle code module that will create and store the procedure named PRODUCT_LINE_SALE:

```
CREATE OR REPLACE PROCEDURE PRODUCT_LINE_SALE
   AS BEGIN
    UPDATE PRODUCT_T
      SET SALE_PRICE = .90 * STANDARD_PRICE
      WHERE STANDARD_PRICE > = 400;
```

```
UPDATE PRODUCT_T
    SET SALE_PRICE = .85 * STANDARD_PRICE
    WHERE STANDARD_PRICE < 400;
END;
```

Oracle returns a comment, Procedure created, if the syntax has been accepted. To run the procedure in Oracle, use this command:

```
SQL> EXEC PRODUCT_LINE_SALE
```

Oracle gives this response:

PL/SQL procedure successfully completed. Now PRODUCT_T contains:

PRODUCT_LINE	PRODUCT_ID	PRODUCT_DESCRIPTION	PRODUCT_FINISH	STANDARD_PRICE	SALE_PRICE
10001	1	End Table	Cherry	175	148.75
20001	2	Coffee Table	Natural Ash	200	170
20001	3	Computer Desk	Natural Ash	375	318.75
30001	4	Entertainment Center	Natural Maple	650	585
10001	5	Writers Desk	Cherry	325	276.25
20001	6	8-Drawer Dresser	White Ash	750	675
20001	7	Dining Table	Natural Ash	800	720
30001	8	Computer Desk	Walnut	250	212.5

EMBEDDED SQL AND DYNAMIC SQL

Embedded SQL: The process of including hard-coded SQL statements in a program written in another language, such as C or Java.

Dynamic SQL: The process of making an application capable of generating specific SQL code on the fly while the application is processing.

We have been using the interactive, or direct, form of SQL. With interactive SQL, one SQL command is entered and executed at a time. Each command constitutes a logical unit of work, or a transaction. The commands necessary to maintain a valid database, such as ROLLBACK and COMMIT, are transparent to the user in most interactive SQL situations. SQL was originally created to handle database access alone and did not have flow control or the other structures necessary to create an application. SQL/PSM, introduced in SQL:1999, provides for the types of programmatic extensions needed to develop a database application.

Prior to SQL/PSM, two other forms of SQL were widely used in creating applications on both clients and servers; they are referred to as **embedded SQL** and **dynamic SQL**. SQL commands can be embedded into 3GLs such as Ada, COBOL, C, or Java by placing the commands at appropriate locations in a 3GL host program. Oracle also offers PL/SQL, or Procedural Language SQL, a proprietary language that extends SQL by adding some procedural language features such as variables, types, control structures (including IF-THEN-ELSE loops), functions, and procedures. PL/SQL blocks of code can also be embedded within 3GL programs.

Dynamic SQL derives the precise SQL statement at run time. Programmers write to an application programming interface (API) to achieve the interface between languages. Embedded SQL and dynamic SQL will continue to be used. Programmers are used to them, and in many cases they are still an easier approach than attempting to use SQL as an application language in addition to using it for database creation, administration, and querying.

There are several reasons to consider embedding SQL in a 3GL:

1. It is possible to create a more flexible, accessible interface for the user. Using interactive SQL effectively requires a good understanding of both SQL and the database structure, understanding the typical application user may not have. Although many of the RDBMS come with form, report, and application generators (or such capabilities are available as add-ons), developers frequently envision capabilities that are not easily accomplished with these tools but that can be easily accomplished using a 3GL. Large, complex programs that require access to a relational database may best be programmed in a 3GL with embedded SQL calls to an SQL database.

2. It may be possible to improve performance by using embedded SQL. Using interactive SQL requires that each query be converted to executable machine code each time the query is processed. Or, the query optimizer, which runs automatically in a direct SQL situation, may not successfully optimize the query, causing it to run slowly. With embedded SQL, the developer has more control over database access and may be able to create significant performance improvements. Knowing when to rely on the SQL translator and optimizer and when to control it through the program depends on the nature of the problem, and making this trade-off is best accomplished through experience and testing.

3. Database security may be improved by using embedded SQL. Restricted access can be achieved by a DBA through the GRANT and REVOKE permissions in SQL and through the use of views. These same restrictions can also be invoked in an embedded SQL application, thus providing another layer of protection. Complex data integrity checks also may be more easily accomplished, including cross-field consistency checks.

A program that uses embedded SQL will consist of the host program written in a 3GL such as C or COBOL, but there will also be sections of SQL code sprinkled throughout. Each section of SQL code will begin with EXEC SQL, keywords used to indicate an embedded SQL command that will be converted to the host source code when run through the precompiler. You will need a separate precompiler for each host language that you plan to use. Be sure to determine that the 3GL compiler is compatible with your RDBMS's precompiler for each language.

When the precompiler encounters an EXEC SQL statement, it will translate that SQL command into the host program language. Some, but not all, precompilers will check for correct SQL syntax and generate any required error messages at this point. Others will not generate an error message until the SQL statement actually attempts to execute. Some products' precompilers (DB2, SQL/DS, Ingres) create a separate file of SQL statements that is then processed by a separate utility called a binder, which determines that the referenced objects exist, that the user possesses sufficient privileges to run the statement, and the processing approach that will be used. Other products (Oracle, Informix) interpret the statements at runtime rather than compiling them. In either case, the resulting program will contain calls to DBMS routines and the link/editor programs will link these routines into the program.

Here is a simple example using C as the host language that will give you an idea of what embedded SQL looks like in a program. This example uses a prepared SQL statement named 'getcust,' which will be compiled and stored as executable code in the database. Cust_ID is the primary key of the customer table. Getcust, the prepared SQL statement, returns customer information (c_name, c_address, city, state, postcode) for an order number. A placeholder is used for the order information, which is an input parameter. Customer information is output from the SQL query and stored into host variables using the *into* clause. This example assumes that only one row is returned from the query.

```
exec sql prepare getcust from
"select c_name, c_address, city, state, postcode
from customer_t, order_t
where customer_t.cust_id = order_t.cust_id and order_id = ?";
.
.

./* code to get proper value in theOrder */
exec sql execute getcust into :c_name, :c_address, :city, :state,
:postcode using theOrder;
.
.
.
```

If a prepared statement returns multiple rows, it is necessary to write a program loop using cursors to return a tuple at a time to be stored. Cursors help to eliminate the impedance mismatch between SQL's set-at-a-time processing and procedural languages' record-at-a-time processing.

Dynamic SQL is used to generate appropriate SQL code on the fly while an application is processing. Most programmers write to an API, such as ODBC, which can then be passed through to any ODBC-compliant database. Dynamic SQL is central to most Internet applications. The developer is able to create a more flexible application because the exact SQL query is determined at runtime, including the number of parameters to be passed, which tables will be accessed, and so forth. Dynamic SQL is very useful when an SQL statement shell will be used repeatedly, with different parameter values being inserted each time it executes.

Currently, the Open Database Connectivity (ODBC) standard is the most commonly used API. SQL:1999 includes the SQL Call Level Interface (SQL/CLI). Both are written in C, and both are based on the same earlier standard. Java Database Connectivity (JDBC) is an industry standard used for connecting from Java. It is not yet an ISO standard. No new functionality is added in SQL:2003.

As SQL:1999 is implemented more completely, the use of embedded and dynamic SQL will become more standardized, because the standard creates a computationally complete SQL language for the first time. Because most vendors have gone ahead and created these capabilities independently, though, the next few years will be a period in which SQL:1999 compliant products will exist side by side with older, but entrenched, versions. The user will need to be aware of these possibilities and deal with them.

Summary

This chapter continues from Chapter 7, which introduced the SQL language. Equi-joins, natural joins, outer joins, and union joins have been considered. Equi-joins are based on equal values in the common columns of the tables that are being joined and will return all requested results including the values of the common columns from each table included in the join. Natural joins return all requested results, but values of the common columns are included only once. Outer joins return all the values in one of the tables included in the join, regardless of whether a match exists in the other table or not. Union joins return a table that includes all data from each table that was joined.

Nested subqueries, where multiple SELECT statements are nested within a single query, are useful for more complex query situations. A special form of the subquery, a correlated subquery, requires that a value be known from the outer query before the inner query can be processed. Other subqueries process the inner query, return a result to the next outer query, and then process that outer query.

Other advanced SQL topics include the use of embedded SQL and the use of triggers and routines. SQL can be included within the context of many third-generation languages including COBOL, C, Fortran, and Ada. The use of embedded SQL allows for the development of more flexible interfaces, improved performance, and improved database security. User-defined functions that run automatically when records are inserted, updated, or deleted are called triggers. Procedures are user-defined code modules, which can be called to execute.

New analytical functions included in SQL:2003 are shown. Extensions already included in SQL:1999 made SQL computationally complete and included flow control capabilities in a set of SQL specifications known as Persistent Stored Modules (SQL/PSM). SQL/PSM can be used to create applications or to incorporate procedures and functions using SQL data types directly. SQL-invoked routines, including triggers, functions, and procedures, were also included in SQL:1999. Users must realize that these capabilities have been included as vendor-specific extensions and will continue to exist for some time.

Dynamic SQL is an integral part of Web-enabling databases and will be demonstrated in more detail in Chapter 10. This chapter has presented some of the more complex capabilities of SQL and has created awareness of the extended and complex capabilities of SQL that must be mastered to build database application programs.

CHAPTER REVIEW

Key Terms

Correlated subquery	Function	Persistent Stored Modules (SQL/PSM)
Dynamic SQL	Join	Procedure
Embedded SQL	Natural join	Trigger
Equi-join	Outer join	User-defined data type (UDT)

Review Questions

1. Define each of the following terms:
   a. dynamic SQL
   b. correlated subquery
   c. embedded SQL
   d. procedure
   e. join
   f. equi-join
   g. natural join
   h. outer join
   i. function
   j. Persistent Stored Modules (SQL/PSM)

2. Match the following terms to the appropriate definitions.

   ____ equi-join
   ____ natural join
   ____ outer join
   ____ trigger
   ____ procedure
   ____ embedded SQL
   ____ UDT
   ____ COMMIT
   ____ SQL/PSM
   ____ Dynamic SQL
   ____ ROLLBACK

   a. changes to a table are undone
   b. user-defined datatype
   c. SQL:1999 extension
   d. returns all records of designated table
   e. redundant columns are kept
   f. changes to a table are made permanent
   g. process that includes SQL statements within a host language
   h. process of making an application capable of generating specific SQL code on the fly
   i. redundant columns are not kept
   j. set of SQL statements that execute under stated conditions
   k. stored, named collection of procedural and SQL statements

3. When is an outer join used instead of a natural join?

4. Explain the processing order of a correlated subquery.

5. Explain the following statement regarding SQL: Any query that can be written using the subquery approach can also be written using the joining approach, but not vice-versa.

6. What is the purpose of the COMMIT command in SQL? How does commit relate to the notion of a business transaction (such as entry of a customer order or issuing a customer invoice)?

7. Care must be exercised when writing triggers for a database. What are some of the problems that could be encountered?

8. Explain the structure of a module of code that defines a trigger.

9. Under what conditions can a UNION clause be used?

10. Discuss the proposed Amendment 1 to SQL:1999.

11. Explain the purpose of SQL/PSM.

12. List four advantages of SQL-invoked routines.

13. When would you consider using embedded SQL? When would you use dynamic SQL?

14. When do you think that the CASE keyword in SQL would be useful?

15. Explain the use of derived tables.

16. Describe an example in which you would want to use a derived table.

17. What other Oracle object can be used in place of a derived table? Which approach do you think is better?

18. If two queries involved in a UNION operation contained columns that were data type incompatible, how would you recommend fixing this?

19. Can an outer join be easily implemented when joining more than two tables? Why or why not?

20. This chapter discusses the data dictionary views for Oracle 9i. Research another RDBMS, such as Microsoft SQL 2000, and report on its data dictionary facility and how it compares with Oracle.

Problems and Exercises

Problems and Exercises 1 through 5 are based on the class schedule ERD depicted in Figure 4-19 in Chapter 4. The 3NF relations along with some sample data are repeated in Figure 8-9. For Problems and Exercises 1 through 5, draw an instance diagram and mark it to show the data you expect your query to return in the results.

1. Write SQL retrieval commands for each of the following queries:

   a. Display the course ID and course name for all courses with an ISM prefix.

   b. Display all courses for which Professor Berndt has been qualified.

   c. Display the class roster, including student name, for all students enrolled in section 2714 of ISM 4212.

2. Write an SQL query to answer the following question: Which instructors are qualified to teach ISM 3113?

3. Write an SQL query to answer the following question: Is any instructor qualified to teach ISM 3113 and not qualified to teach ISM 4930?

4. Write SQL queries to answer the following questions:

   a. How many students are enrolled in section 2714 during semester I-2004?

   b. How many students are enrolled in ISM 3113 during semester I-2004?

5. Write an SQL query to answer the following question: Which students were not enrolled in any courses during semester I-2004?

Problems and Exercises 6 through 23 are based on the entire ("big" version) Pine Valley Furniture Company database. Note: depending on what DBMS you are using, some field names may have changed due to reserved words for the DBMS. When you first use the DBMS, check the table definitions to see what the exact field names are for the DBMS you are using.

6. Write an SQL command to display the order number, customer number, order date, and items ordered for order number 1001.

7. Write an SQL command to display each item ordered for order number 1001, its standard price, and the total price for each item ordered.

8. Write an SQL command to total the cost of order number 1001.

9. Write an SQL command that will find any customers who have not placed orders.

10. Write an SQL query to produce a list of all the products (i.e., product description) and the number of times each product has been ordered.

11. Write an SQL query to display customer number, name, and order number for all customers and their orders.

12. Write an SQL query to list the order number and order quantity for all customer orders for which the order quantity is greater than the average order quantity of that product. Hint: This involves a correlated subquery.

13. Write an SQL query to list each salesperson who has sold computer desks and the number of units sold by each salesperson.

14. Write an SQL query to list the salesperson who has sold the most computer desks.

15. Write an SQL query to list the supervisors who supervise employees with 12 in Bandsaw as a skill.

16. Write an SQL query to list all employees who have more than one skill.

17. Write an SQL query to list the territory_id and the territory_name of all territories where end tables have been sold.

18. Write an SQL query to list the number of end tables sold in each territory.

19. Write an SQL query to list the total number of sales for each product line.

20. Write an SQL query to list the total sales for each sales territory.

21. Write an SQL query to list the total sales for each sales territory by salesperson.

22. Write an SQL query to list what product lines each salesperson has sold.

23. Write an SQL query to list the total number of sales for each finish by salesperson. Order by finish and salesperson.

Field Exercises

1. Conduct a search of the Web to locate as many links as possible that discuss SQL standards.

2. Compare two versions of SQL to which you have access, such as Microsoft Access and Oracle SQL*Plus. Identify at least five similarities in the SQL code used and three dissimilarities. Do the dissimilarities cause results to differ?

STUDENT (STUDENT_ID, STUDENT_NAME)

STUDENT_ID	STUDENT_NAME
38214	Letersky
54907	Altvater
66324	Aiken
70542	Marra
...	

QUALIFIED (FACULTY_ID, COURSE_ID, DATE_QUALIFIED)

FACULTY_ID	COURSE_ID	DATE_QUALIFIED
2143	ISM 3112	9/1988
2143	ISM 3113	9/1988
3467	ISM 4212	9/1995
3467	ISM 4930	9/1996
4756	ISM 3113	9/1991
4756	ISM 3112	9/1991
...		

FACULTY (FACULTY_ID, FACULTY_NAME)

FACULTY_ID	FACULTY_NAME
2143	Birkin
3467	Berndt
4756	Collins
...	

SECTION (SECTION_NO, SEMESTER, COURSE_ID)

SECTION_NO	SEMESTER	COURSE_ID
2712	I-2006	ISM 3113
2713	I-2006	ISM 3113
2714	I-2006	ISM 4212
2715	I-2006	ISM 4930
...		

COURSE (COURSE_ID, COURSE_NAME)

COURSE_ID	COURSE_NAME
ISM 3113	Syst Analysis
ISM 3112	Syst Design
ISM 4212	Database
ISM 4930	Networking
...	

REGISTRATION (STUDENT_ID, SECTION_NO, SEMESTER)

STUDENT_ID	SECTION_NO	SEMESTER
38214	2714	I-2006
54907	2714	I-2006
54907	2715	I-2006
66324	2713	I-2006
...		

Figure 8-9
Class Scheduling Relations (missing ASSIGNMENT)

References

Eisenberg, A., J. Melton, K. Kulkarni, J. E. Michels, and F. Zemke. 2004. "SQL:2003 Has Been Published." *SIGMOD Record* 33,1 (March):119–126.

Gulutzan, P. and T. Pelzer 1999. *SQL-99 Complete, Really!* Lawrence, Kansas: R&D Books.

Mullins, C. S. 1995. "The Procedural DBA." *Database Programming & Design* 8,12 (December): 40–45.

Rennhackkamp, M. 1996. "Trigger Happy." *DBMS* 9,5 (May): 89–91, 95.

Zemke, F., K. Kulkarni, A. Witkowski, and B. Lyle. 1999. "Introduction to OLAP Functions." ISO/IEC JTC1/SC32 WG3: YGJ.068 ANSI NCITS H2-99-154r2.

Further Reading

American National Standards Institute. 2000. *ANSI Standards Action* 31,11 (June 2): 20.

Codd, E. F. 1970. "A Relational Model of Data for Large Shared Data Banks." *Communications of the ACM* 13,6 (June): 77–87.

Date, C. J., and H. Darwen. 1997. *A Guide to the SQL Standard*. Reading, MA: Addison-Wesley.

Kulkarni, K. 2004. "Overview of SQL:2003." Available at http://www.wiscorp.com/SQLStandards.html#keyreadings.

Melton, J. 1997. "A Case for SQL Conformance Testing." *Database Programming & Design* 10,7 (July): 66–69.

van der Lans, R. F. 1993. *Introduction to SQL*, 2nd ed. Workingham, England: Addison-Wesley.

Winter, R. 2000. "SQL-99's New OLAP Functions." *Intelligent Enterprise* 3,2 (January 20): 62, 64–65.

Winter, R. 2000. "The Extra Mile." *Intelligent Enterprise* 3,10 (June 26): 62–64.

See also Further Readings in Chapter 7.

Web Resources

www.ansi.org Site of the American National Standards Institute. Contains information on the ANSI federation and the latest national and international standards.

www.iso.ch "Welcome to ISO Online" provides information about the International Organization for Standardization. Copies of current standards may be purchased here.

standards.ieee.org.org This site is the homepage of the IEEE Standards Organization.

Troels.arvin.dk/db/rdbms Detailed comparison of different SQL implementations, including DB2, MS SQL, MySQL, Oracle and PostgreSQL.

www.teradatastudentnetwork.com Your instructor may have created some course environments for you to use Teradata SQL Assistant, Web Edition, with one or more of the Pine Valley Furniture and Mountain View Community Hospital data sets for this text.

MOUNTAIN VIEW COMMUNITY HOSPITAL

Case

Use the databases you implemented in Chapter 7 for Mountain View Community Hospital to complete the case questions and case exercises.

CASE QUESTIONS

1. Does your SQL-based DBMS support dynamic SQL, functions, triggers, stored procedures, and UDTs?

2. HIPAA's privacy and security rules mandate audit controls "that record and examine activity in information systems that contain or use electronic protected health information" (§164.312(b)). How can DDL triggers be used in support of that mandate?

CASE EXERCISES

1. Using the small sample database you created for Dr. "Z." in Case Exercise 1 in Chapter 7, write queries that illustrate the more complex queries covered in Chapter 8.

   a. Select information from two or more tables (e.g., all the details of all the visits of Patient 8766, etc.).

   b. Use subquery syntax (e.g., a listing of all the patients who reported pain that exceeded the average pain for all visits).

   c. Return a result table that could be used to produce a report, such as (in alphabetical order by patient name, or sorted by date) during a particular week or after a particular date, or a listing of patient visits for patients assigned to a specific social worker.

2. Using the MVCH database files accompanying this textbook (in MS Access or Teradata's RDBMS), write queries in SQL to determine the following. You may have to populate tables with more sample data to generate the required information:

   a. For a given physician, which treatments has that physician performed on each patient referred by that physician to the hospital?

   b. For the query in part a, also include physicians who have not referred patients to the hospital.

   c. For each patient, what is the average number of treatments performed on him or her by each physician who has treated that patient?

   d. List all patients who have received no treatments.

   e. For each nurse-in-charge, what is the total number of hours worked by all employees who work in the care center that that nurse supervises?

   f. Which technicians have more than one skill? Which technicians have no skills listed?

   g. Determine whether any outpatients were accidentally assigned to resident beds.

   h. Determine which item is consumed most.

   i. Determine which physicians prescribe the most expensive item.

   j. Return a result table that could be used to produce a hospital report, such as nursing staff assigned to each care center.

   k. Use the UNION statement to provide a combined listing of care center names and their locations as well as laboratories and their location. The list should be sorted by location in ascending order. (You should use aliases to rename the fields in this query.)

PROJECT ASSIGNMENTS

P1. Write and execute the queries for the five reports you identified in Chapter 6.

P2. Identify opportunities for triggers in your database and create at least one DDL trigger. For example, the claims manager at the hospital may need to know that a patient's health insurance has been updated.

Chapter 9

The Client/Server Database Environment

LEARNING OBJECTIVES

After studying this chapter, you should be able to:

- Concisely define each of the following key terms: **client/server systems, file server, fat client, database server, stored procedure, three-tier architecture, thin client, application partitioning, middleware, application program interface (API),** and **open database connectivity (ODBC) standard.**

- List several major advantages of the client/server architecture over other computing approaches.

- Explain the three components of application logic: data presentation services, processing services, and storage services.

- Suggest the range of possibilities for partitioning these services in various client/server architectures.

- Distinguish among a file server, a database server, a three-tiered, and an n-tiered architecture.

- Describe middleware and explain how middleware facilitates client/server architectures.

- Explain how to link external data tables to an application in a client/server environment using ODBC or JDBC.

LOCATION, LOCATION, LOCATION!

When looking for property to buy, at least one of your friends will say, "It's all about location, location, location." Storing data and applications comes down to making location decisions, too. No, we aren't talking about giving data an ocean view with hot tub and proximity to good schools. But, good database design is built on picking the right location to store data.

You already studied the location concept for storing data on storage devices in Chapter 6 with such concepts as denormalization, partitioning, and RAID. In addition, multitiered computer architectures offer storage possibilities at each tier, and there is no right answer for all situations. That's the beauty of the client/server approach; it can be tailored to optimize performance. As with most major steps forward in computerization, the first client-server applications were tried in noncritical situations. By the mid 90s, success stories began to be publicized, and the client/server approach moved up to handle business-critical applications. Now client/server has become old hat, and you may feel that this chapter is the most mundane one in the whole book. That may be, but you are urged to pay close attention anyway, because the client/server approach continues to drive the newest directions in database computing. You will read about Web-enabled databases in Chapter 10 and learn about some of the newest acronyms, including Service Oriented Architecture (SOA) and Web services. In some of your outside reading, authors will write as though these newest approaches are somehow different and beyond client/server technology. Actually, the clients may be fat or thin, and the servers connected in different ways, but the basic concepts included in this chapter underlie the newest approaches to distributed computing (for Web applications, in Chapter 10, and distributed databases, in Chapter 13).

And, it's mostly about location: what must be located on the client (think cell phone), what is stored on the server, and how much information should be moved from the server to the cell phone when a request for data (think SQL query) is made (think about locating a restaurant when you're traveling). Part of the answer to optimizing a particular architecture lies not in location, but in moving the information from one location to another location quickly. These issues are critically important to mobile applications, such as cell phones. In addition to transmitting voice data, phone services may now include text messaging, content browsing, object/image downloading, and business applications. Just as we can make a voice phone call from any phone in the world to any other phone, we expect to use these newer services in the same way, and we want immediate response times. Addressing these problems requires a good understanding of the client/server principles you will learn in this chapter.

There are other critical issues in the mobile applications area, too. The need to create open standards, protocols, and interfaces that will allow interoperability, regardless of operating system or application, reminds one of the original definition of a relational database. The Open Mobile Architecture initiative merged with the WAP forum in 2002 to form the Open Mobile Alliance (OMA). OMA has attracted over 300 businesses and organizations who are dedicated to making this environment a reality. The first critical enablers have been identified by OMA as XHTML, Java, and Multi-Messaging Service (MMS). OMA members have committed to implementation and interoperability testing across these enablers. OMA's Web site is **www.openmobilealliance.org**, if you are interested in exploring mobile architecture directions further. The size of the alliance and the organizations that have joined it should help to convince you of the importance of this area in the future.

INTRODUCTION

Client/server systems operate in networked environments, splitting the processing of an application between a front-end client and a back-end processor. Generally, the client process requires some resource, which the server provides to the client. Clients and servers can reside in the same computer, or they can be on different computers that are networked together. Both clients and servers are intelligent and programmable, so the computing power of both can be used to devise effective and efficient applications.

It is difficult to overestimate the impact that client/server applications have had in the last 15 years. Advances in personal computer technology and the rapid evolution of graphical user interfaces (GUIs), networking, and communications have

Client/server systems: A networked computing model that distributes processes between clients and servers, which supply the requested services. In a database system, the database generally resides on a server that processes the DBMS. The clients may process the application systems or request services from another server that holds the application programs.

changed the way businesses use computing systems to meet ever more demanding business needs. Electronic commerce requires that client browsers be able to access dynamic Web pages attached to databases that provide real-time information. Personal computers linked through networks that support workgroup computing are the norm. Mainframe applications have been rewritten to run in client/server environments and take advantage of the greater cost-effectiveness of networks of personal computers and workstations. The need for strategies that fit specific business environments is being filled by client/server solutions because they offer flexibility, scalability (the ability to upgrade a system without having to redesign it), and extensibility (the ability to define new data types and operations). As businesses become more global in their operations, they must devise distributed systems (these will be covered in Chapter 13); their plans often include client/server architectures.

In this chapter, we review developments in multiuser database management environments that have led to the development of various client/server strategies for data processing. These include LAN-based DBMSs, client/server DBMSs (including three-tiered architectures), parallel computing architectures, Internet and intranet DBMSs, and middleware.

Driving the trend toward these database technologies are a variety of new opportunities and competitive pressures. In one sense, the network has become the computer as users share data through network drives and turn to the Internet to access the information and data they require. Corporate restructurings, such as mergers, acquisitions, and consolidations, make it necessary to connect, integrate, or replace existing stand-alone applications. One consequence of corporate downsizing is that individual managers have broader control, necessitating access to a wider range of data. Applications are being downsized from expensive mainframes to networked microcomputers and workstations that are much more user-friendly and sometimes more cost-effective. Handling network traffic, which may become excessive with some architectures, is a key issue in developing successful client/server applications, especially as organizations place mission-critical applications in distributed environments. Establishing a good balance between centralized and decentralized systems is a matter of much current discussion, as organizations strive to gain maximum benefits from both client/server and mainframe-based DBMSs.

CLIENT/SERVER ARCHITECTURES

Client/server environments use a local area network (LAN) to support a network of personal computers, each with its own storage, that are also able to share common devices (such as a hard disk or printer) and software (such as a DBMS) attached to the LAN. Each PC and workstation on a LAN is typically within 100 feet of the others; all PCs are usually within one mile of one another. A LAN may be hardwired or it may be wireless. At least one PC is designated as a file server, on which the shared database is stored. The LAN modules of a DBMS add concurrent access controls, possibly extra security features, and query- or translation-queuing management to support concurrent access from multiple users of a shared database.

The several client/server architectures that have evolved can be distinguished by the distribution of application logic components across clients and servers. There are three components of application logic (see Figure 9-1). The first is the input/output (I/O), or presentation logic, component. This component is responsible for formatting and presenting data on the user's screen or other output device and for managing user input from a keyboard or other input device. The second component is the processing component. It handles data processing logic, business rules logic, and data management logic. Data processing logic includes such activities as data validation and identification of processing errors. Business rules that have not been coded at the DBMS level may be coded in the processing component. Data management

Figure 9-1
Application logic components

Presentation Logic
    Input
    Output

Processing Logic
    I/O processing
    Business rules
    Data management

Storage Logic
    Data storage and
    retrieval

logic identifies the data necessary for processing the transaction or query. The third component is storage, the component responsible for data storage and retrieval from the physical storage devices associated with the application. Activities of a DBMS occur in the storage component logic.

File Server Architectures

The first client/server architectures developed were file servers. In a basic file server environment (see Figure 9-2), all data manipulation occurs at the workstations where data are requested. The client handles the presentation logic, processing logic, and much of the storage logic (that part associated with a DBMS). One or

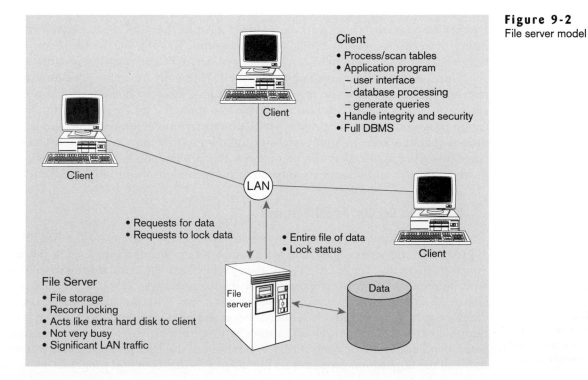

Figure 9-2
File server model

Client
• Process/scan tables
• Application program
  – user interface
  – database processing
  – generate queries
• Handle integrity and security
• Full DBMS

Client

Client

LAN

• Requests for data
• Requests to lock data

• Entire file of data
• Lock status

Client

File Server
• File storage
• Record locking
• Acts like extra hard disk to client
• Not very busy
• Significant LAN traffic

File server

Data

File server: A device that manages file operations and is shared by each of the client PCs attached to the LAN.

more file servers are attached to the LAN. A **file server** is a device that manages file operations and is shared by each of the client PCs attached to the LAN. Each of these file servers acts as an additional hard disk for each of the client PCs. For example, your PC might recognize a logical F: drive, which is actually a disk volume stored on a file server on the LAN. Programs on your PC refer to files on this drive by the typical path specification involving this drive and any directories, as well as the file name. With a file server, each client PC may be called a **fat client**, one where most processing occurs on the client rather than on a server.

In a file server environment, each client PC is authorized to use the DBMS when a database application program runs on that PC. Thus, there is one database but many concurrently running copies of the DBMS, one on each of the active PCs. The primary characteristic of file server architecture is that all data manipulation is performed at the client PCs, not at the file server. The file server acts simply as a shared data storage device. Software at the file server queues access requests, but it is up to the application program at each client PC, working with the copy of the DBMS on that PC, to handle all data management functions. For example, data security checks and file and record locking are initiated at the client PCs in this environment.

Fat client: A client PC that is responsible for processing presentation logic, extensive application and business rules logic, and many DBMS functions.

Limitations of File Servers

There are three limitations when using file servers on LANs. First, considerable data movement is generated across the network. For example, when an application program running on a client PC in Pine Valley Furniture wants to access the oak products, the whole Product table is transferred to the client PC and then scanned by the client to find the few desired records. Thus, the server does very little work, the client is busy with extensive data manipulation, and the network is transferring large blocks of data. Consequently, a client-based LAN places considerable burden on the client PC to do functions that have to be performed on all clients and creates a high network traffic load.

Second, each client workstation must devote memory to a full version of the DBMS. This means that there is less room in memory for application programs on the client PC. Increasing RAM on the PC will improve performance by increasing the total amount of data that can reside on the PC while a transaction is being processed. Further, because the client workstation does most of the work, each client must be rather powerful to provide a suitable response time. In contrast, the file server does not need much RAM and need not be a very powerful PC, because it does little work.

Third, and possibly most important, the DBMS copy in each workstation must manage the shared database integrity. In addition, each application program must recognize, for example, locks and take care to initiate the proper locks. Thus, application programmers must be rather sophisticated and understand various subtle conditions that can arise in a multiple-user database environment. They must understand how their application will interact with the DBMS's concurrency, recovery, and security controls and sometimes must program such controls into their applications.

Database Server Architectures

Database server: A computer that is responsible for database storage, access, and processing in a client/server environment. Some people also use this term to describe a two-tier client/server environment.

Two-tiered approaches to client/server architectures followed the file server approach. In this system, the client workstation is responsible for managing the user interface, including presentation logic, data processing logic, and business rules logic, and the **database server** is responsible for database storage, access, and processing. Figure 9-3 shows a typical database server architecture. With the DBMS placed on the database server, LAN traffic is reduced, because only those records that match the requested criteria are transmitted to the client station, rather than entire data files. Some people refer to the central DBMS functions as the back-end functions, whereas they call the application programs on the client PCs the front-end programs.

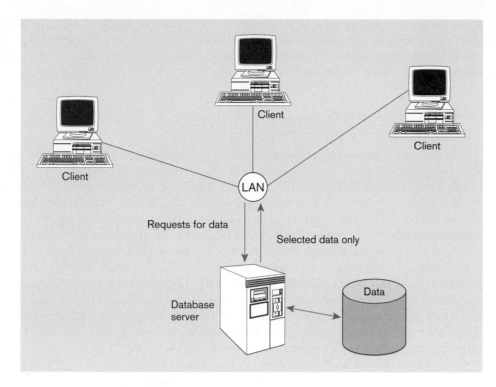

Figure 9-3
Database server architecture (two-tier architecture)

Moving the DBMS to the database server has several advantages. With this architecture, only the database server requires processing power adequate to handle the database, and the database is stored on the server, not on the clients. Therefore, the database server can be tuned to optimize database-processing performance. Because less data are sent across the LAN, the communication load is reduced. User authorization, integrity checking, data dictionary maintenance, and query and update processing are all performed at one location, on the database server.

Client/server projects that use file server and database server architectures tend to be departmental applications, supporting a relatively small number of users. Such applications are not mission critical and have been most successful where transaction volumes are low, immediate availability is not critical, and security is not of the highest concern. As companies have sought to gain expected benefits from client/server projects, such as scalability, flexibility, and lowered costs, they have had to develop new approaches to client/server architectures.

The use of **stored procedures**, modules of code that implement application logic, which are included on the database server, pushed the database server architecture toward being able to handle more critical business applications (Quinlan, 1995). As pointed out by Quinlan, stored procedures have the following advantages:

- Performance improves for compiled SQL statements.
- Network traffic decreases as processing moves from the client to the server.
- Security improves if the stored procedure is accessed rather than the data, and code is moved to the server, away from direct end-user access.
- Data integrity improves as multiple applications access the same stored procedure.
- Stored procedures result in a thinner client and a fatter database server.

However, writing stored procedures takes more time than using Visual Basic or PowerBuilder to create an application. Also, the proprietary nature of stored procedures reduces their portability and may make it difficult to change DBMSs without having to rewrite the stored procedures. And, each client must be loaded with the

Stored procedure: A module of code, usually written in a proprietary language such as Oracle's PL/SQL or Sybase's Transact-SQL, that implements application logic or a business rule and is stored on the server, where it runs when it is called.

applications that will be used at that location. Performance tends to degrade as the number of online users increases. Upgrades to an application require that each client be upgraded separately. These drawbacks to database server architectures have led to the popularity of three-tier architectures.

THREE-TIER ARCHITECTURES

Three-tier architecture: A client/ server configuration that includes three layers: a client layer and two server layers. Although the nature of the server layers differs, a common configuration contains an application server.

In general, a **three-tier architecture** includes another server layer in addition to the client and database server layers previously mentioned (see Figure 9-4a). Such configurations are also referred to as n-tier, multitier, or enhanced client/server architectures. The additional server in a three-tier architecture may be used for different purposes. Often, application programs reside on the additional server, in which case it is referred to as an application server. Or the additional server may hold a local database while another server holds the enterprise database. Each of these configurations is likely to be referred to as a three-tier architecture, but the functionality of each differs, and each is appropriate for a different situation. Advantages of the three-tier compared with the two-tier architecture, such as increased scalability, flexibility, performance, and reusability, have made three-layer architectures a popular choice for Internet applications and net-centric information systems. These advantages are discussed in more detail below.

In some three-tier architectures, most application code is stored on the application server. This case realizes the same benefits as those that come from putting stored procedures on the database server in a two-tier architecture. Using an application server can also improve performance through the use of true machine code, easier portability of the application code to other platforms, and less reliance on proprietary languages such as SQL/PLUS (Quinlan, 1995). In many situations, most business processing occurs on the application server rather than on the client workstation or database server, resulting in a **thin client**. The use of Internet browsers on clients for accessing the Web provides a contemporary example of a thin client architecture. Applications that reside on a server and execute on that server without

Thin client: A PC configured for handling user interfaces and some application processing, usually with no or limited local data storage.

Figure 9-4
Three-tier architecture
(a) Generic three-tier architecture

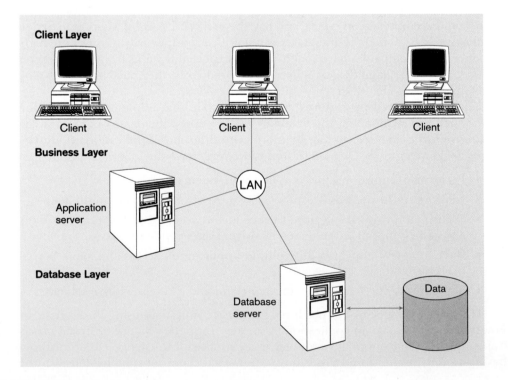

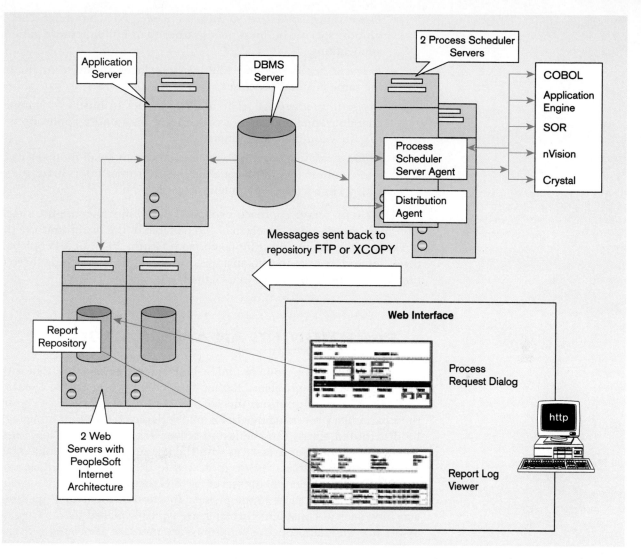

Figure 9-4 (Continued)
(b) Sample PeopleSoft Financials three-tier configuration (Source: Groth, 2003)

downloading to the client are becoming more common. Thus, upgrading application programs requires loading the new version only on the application server, rather than on client workstations.

Three-tier architectures can provide several benefits (Thompson, 1997):

- *Scalability* Three-tier architectures are more scalable than two-tier architectures. For example, the middle tier can be used to reduce the load on a database server by using a transaction processing (TP) monitor to reduce the number of connections to a server, and additional application servers can be added to distribute application processing. A TP monitor is a program that controls data transfer between clients and servers to provide a consistent environment for online transaction processing (OLTP).

- *Technological flexibility* It is easier to change DBMS engines, although triggers and stored procedures will need to be rewritten, with a three-tier architecture. The middle tier can even be moved to a different platform. Simplified presentation services make it easier to implement various desired interfaces such as Web browsers or kiosks.

- *Lower long-term costs* Use of off-the-shelf components or services in the middle tier can reduce costs, as can substitution of modules within an application rather than an entire application.

- *Better match of systems to business needs* New modules can be built to support specific business needs rather than building more general, complete applications.
- *Improved customer service* Multiple interfaces on different clients can access the same business processes.
- *Competitive advantage* The ability to react to business changes quickly by changing small modules of code rather than entire applications can be used to gain a competitive advantage.
- *Reduced risk* Again, the ability to implement small modules of code quickly and combine them with code purchased from vendors limits the risk assumed with a large-scale development project.

The client/server approach expanded our ability to configure systems to match a business' needs more closely than was possible in the mainframe era that preceded it. Look at the sample diagram taken from Groth, 2003, of a PeopleSoft Financials three-tier architecture to gain an appreciation of how the generic three-tier architecture might actually be set up (see Figure 9-4b).

PARTITIONING AN APPLICATION

Clearly, there is no one optimal client/server architecture that is the best solution for all business problems. Rather, the flexibility inherent in client/server architectures offers organizations the possibility of tailoring their configurations to fit their particular processing needs. Figure 9-1 depicted the computing logics that must be distributed across the client and server(s). Presentation logic resides on the client, where the user interfaces with the system. Processing logic may be divided across client and servers, as was indicated in the previous discussion of file server, two-tier, and three-tier client/server architectures. Storage logic usually resides on the database server, close to the physical location of the data. Data integrity control activities, such as constraint checking, are typically placed there. Triggers, which will always fire when appropriate conditions are met, are associated with insert, modify, update, and delete commands. As these commands affect the data directly, triggers are also usually stored on the database server. Stored procedures that use the data directly are usually stored on the database server. Those that work with a query result may be stored on an application server or on the client. Depending on the nature of the business problem being addressed, these general rules may not be followed in order to achieve optimum throughput and performance.

Application partitioning: The process of assigning portions of application code to client or server partitions after it is written to achieve better performance and interoperability (ability of a component to function on different platforms).

Application partitioning helps in this tailoring. It gives developers the opportunity to write application code that they can later place either on a client workstation or on a server, depending on which location will give the best performance. It is not necessary to include the code that will place the process being partitioned or to write the code that will establish the connections to the process. Those activities are handled by application partitioning tools.

The objects created by using object-oriented programming are very appropriate for application partitioning. Programmers have tremendous control over each object's content, and it is easier to separate user interface code, business rules, and data. This separation supports today's rapidly developing n-tier systems. The strong business push toward Internet and e-commerce business solutions is causing application partitioning to develop more rapidly and in new ways. Web applications must be multitiered and partitioned. They require components that can be assembled on the fly, as they are requested by the browser, and they need to be compatible with different operating systems, user interfaces, and databases. Effective application partitioning is necessary in the Web environment to achieve desired performance along with acceptable maintainability, data integrity, and security in an unpredictable distributed environment.

The application code can be developed and tested on a client workstation, and decisions about partitioning that code and placing it can be made later. This capability is likely to increase developers' productivity. Application modules can be placed on a client or server late in the design phase. However, the developer must understand how and where each process will need to run in order to synchronize each process or transaction correctly across databases and platforms. Decisions about placing code on the application or database server will depend partly on the DBMS's capabilities. For example, a DBMS that supports static SQL (completely prewritten SQL code) through stored procedures and triggers that are located on the database server may create a performance decrement if dynamic SQL code (SQL code created at runtime) is located on the application server. Each dynamic SQL statement will generate a dynamic bind (or linkage to database objects) at the database server as it is processed. The performance impact will depend on how intensively dynamic SQL statements are used. Whether to concentrate processing on the application server or the database server is a decision that must be made by the developer, who understands the hardware environment available, the interactions of the hardware and DBMS software, and the demands of the application.

It is also possible to add transaction processing monitors to client/server systems to improve performance. Where multiple application servers and database servers are available, TP monitors can balance the workload, directing transactions to servers that are not busy. TP monitors are also useful in distributed environments, where distributed transactions from a single unit of work can be managed across a heterogeneous environment.

Partitioning the environment to create a two-, three-, or n-tier architecture means that decisions must be made about the placement of the processing logic. In each case, storage logic (the database engine) is handled by the server, and presentation logic is handled by the client.

Figure 9-5a depicts some possible two-tier systems, placing the processing logic on the client (creating a fat client), on the server (creating a thin client), or partitioned across both the server and the client (a distributed environment). It is the placement of the processing logic that is emphasized in the three scenarios. In the fat client, the application processing occurs entirely on the client, whereas in the thin client, this processing occurs on the server. In the distributed example, application processing is partitioned between the client and the server.

Figure 9-5b presents a typical three-tier architecture and an n-tier architecture. Again, some processing logic could be placed on the client, if desired. But, a typical client in a Web-enabled client/server environment will be a thin client, using a browser for its presentation logic. The middle tiers are typically coded in a portable

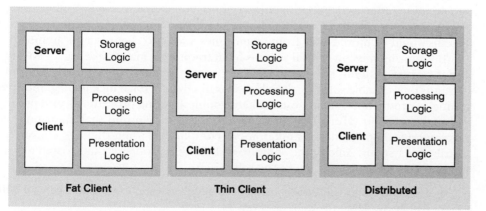

Figure 9-5 (Continues)
Common logic distributions
(a) Two-tier client server environments

Figure 9-5 (Continued)
(b) *n*-tier client/server environments
(There are many possibilities: these are
just samples.)

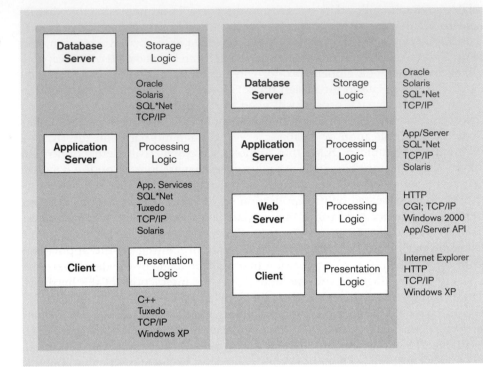

language such as C or Java. The flexibility and easier manageability of the n-tier approaches account for its increasing popularity, in spite of the increased complexity of managing communication among the tiers. The fast-paced, distributed, and heterogeneous environment of the Internet and e-commerce initiatives have also led to the development of many n-tier architectures.

The client, then, is responsible for the presentation logic. Users interface with the rest of the system through their browser, an application, or a programming interface.

ROLE OF THE MAINFRAME

The role of the mainframe has been uncertain over the last decade as distributed, client/server, and PC computing capabilities have developed. As mentioned in the previous section, mission-critical systems, which were resident on mainframe systems a decade ago, have tended to remain on mainframe systems. Less mission-critical, frequently workgroup-level, systems have been developed using client/server architectures. The popularity of client/server architectures and businesses' strong desire to achieve more effective computing in more distributed environments as their perspectives became broader and more global led to their expectation that mission-critical systems would be moved away from mainframes and onto client/server architectures.

But moving mission-critical systems from traditional mainframe legacy systems to client/server systems has been challenging. Successful distributed computing depends on workable software distribution, effective performance management, and tuning of production systems, established troubleshooting procedures, and proactive code management (Hurwitz, 1996). Organizations have found that managing these mission-critical applications is much more complicated when they are converted to distributed systems. Among the software distribution problems that exist in a distributed processing environment are the following:

- Determining which code must be placed on which workstations and which will be available through a server

- Identifying potential conflicts with code from other applications
- Ensuring that sufficient resources are available at all locations to handle the anticipated load

Unless developers anticipate scalability issues and address them as they develop code, moving mission-critical applications to client/server distributed environments is likely to cause serious problems in the transition from pilot phase to production. This has slowed the development of mission-critical client/server systems. Now, Internet applications are causing an upsurge in the need for applications to be interoperable. Troubleshooting such interactions is difficult, and many organizations may not be prepared to undertake such troubleshooting. Increasing use of component libraries (files of shared application modules) increases the need to manage interdependencies that will inevitably develop as these component libraries are shared across applications.

Supporting distributed environments is a very complex undertaking. Understanding the dynamics of different locations' environments and creating a distributed computing network can be very complex. The difficulties of managing distributed computing environments have caused IT managers to rethink their push to move mission-critical systems to client/server solutions. Powerful parallel processing equipment (discussed on the book's Web site in the Performance Optimization section) is becoming more readily available, thus making it more attractive to remain centralized on an application or database server.

The difficulties of moving complex, mission-critical applications to a distributed environment using client/server architectures have discouraged many IT managers, and some have withdrawn completely from client/server initiatives, returning to a mainframe environment. However, we expect that each organization will need to achieve a balance between mainframe and client/server platforms, between centralized and distributed solutions, that is closely tailored to the nature of their data and location of business users of the data. As Hurwitz (1996) suggests, data that do not need to be moved often can be centralized on a mainframe. Data to which users need frequent access, complex graphics, and the user interface should be kept close to the users' workstations.

Enterprise resource planning (ERP) systems have faced many challenges. During the 1990s, ERP systems, such as those of SAP, Baan, Oracle, and J.D. Edwards, convinced many companies dealing with large amounts of data that buying integrated financial, human resources, manufacturing, and procurement systems would be more efficient and cost-effective. Moving to a Y2K compliant suite of applications was more appealing than rewriting millions of lines of code in existing applications. However, the ERP systems were developed as strictly controlled, closed systems. Incorporating legacy systems, where the organization's historical data resides, often on a mainframe, has been a challenge. Now in the 2000s, attention has turned to achieving efficient supply chain management (SCM), customer relationship management (CRM), and business-to-business (B2B) procurement through e-commerce solutions. ERP systems establish an integrated infrastructure for companies' internal management needs, but they must also have e-commerce capabilities. Classic ERP systems are being rearchitected and positioned to compete in an ever more distributed and flexible environment. At this time, most companies involved in implementing ERP systems are continuing to improve their functionality, taking greater advantage of the capabilities of the large systems to which they are committed.

USING MIDDLEWARE

Middleware is often referred to as the glue that holds together client/server applications. It is a term that is commonly used to describe any software component between the PC client and the relational database in n-tier architectures. Simply put,

Middleware: Software that allows an application to interoperate with other software without requiring the user to understand and code the low-level operations necessary to achieve interoperability.

middleware is any of several classes of software that allow an application to interoperate with other software without requiring the user to understand and code the low-level operations required to achieve interoperability (Hurwitz, 1998). Middleware has existed for decades; examples are IBM's transaction-processing middleware, CICS, or BEA Systems' Tuxedo for UNIX machines. But the advent of client/server technologies, and now Web-oriented development, has stimulated new development of commercially available middleware. Universal middleware, one magical software package that could integrate and connect every type of system, would be ideal, of course. At this time, however, such a middleware package is not available. Most organizations use several different middleware packages, sometimes even within one application. The development of e-business requires that computers be able to communicate with each other over the Web. The middleware necessary to achieve that communication has come to be known as Web services, and is covered in the next chapter.

Another consideration is whether the communication involved is synchronous or asynchronous. With synchronous systems, the requesting system waits for a response to the request in real time. An online banking system where the teller checks an account balance before cashing a check is an example of a synchronous system. Asynchronous systems send a request but do not wait for a response in real time. Rather, the response is accepted whenever it is received. Electronic mail is an example of an asynchronous system.

Attempting to classify middleware has proved challenging. Classification by functions performed, such as operating system connectivity, programming language connectivity, or communication connectivity have been suggested. Other dimensions such as synchronization, time, and space might be used to develop a classification system. Hurwitz (1998) has provided a helpful six-category classification system that organizes the many types of middleware that are currently available. Her classifications are based on scalability and recoverability:

1. *Asynchronous remote procedure call (RPC)* The client requests services but does not wait for a response. It will typically establish a point-to-point connection with the server and perform other processing while it waits for the response. If the connection is lost, the client must reestablish the connection and send the request again. This type of middleware has high scalability but low recoverability, and has been largely replaced by synchronous RPC since 1998.

2. *Synchronous RPC* A distributed program using synchronous RPC may call services available on different computers. This middleware makes it possible to establish this facility without undertaking the detailed coding usually necessary to write an RPC. Examples include Microsoft's Transaction Server and IBM's CICS. The Java equivalent of an RPC is a Remote Method Invocation (RMI).

3. *Publish/subscribe* This type of middleware monitors activity and pushes information to subscribers. It is asynchronous; the clients, or subscribers, perform other activities between notifications from the server. The subscribers notify the publisher of information that they wish to receive, and when an event occurs that contains such information, it is sent to the subscriber, who can then elect to receive the information or not. For example, you can supply electronic bookstores with keywords of topics that interest you. Whenever the bookstore adds a book title that is keyword coded with one of your keywords, information about that title will be automatically forwarded to you for consideration. This type of middleware is very useful for monitoring situations where actions need to be taken when particular events occur.

4. *Message-oriented middleware (MOM)* MOM is also asynchronous software, sending messages that are collected and stored until they are acted upon,

while the client continues with other processing. Workflow applications such as insurance policy applications, which often involve several processing steps, can benefit from MOM. The queue where the requests are stored can be journalized, thus providing some recoverability.

5. *Object request broker (ORB)* This type of middleware makes it possible for applications to send objects and request services in an object-oriented system. The ORB tracks the location of each object and routes requests to each object. Current ORBs are synchronous, but asynchronous ORBs are being developed.

6. *SQL-oriented data access* Connecting applications to databases over networks is achieved by using SQL-oriented data access middleware. This middleware also has the capability to translate generic SQL into the SQL specific to the database. Database vendors and companies that have developed multidatabase access middleware dominate this middleware segment.

While the preceding classifications provide an elementary understanding of the functional variations in middleware, many hybrid products combine these capabilities. For example, SQL-oriented and RPC middleware add awareness of objects, and ORBs are adding transaction, queuing, and messaging services. Object transaction monitors promise to combine the functionality of distributed objects, currently handled by CORBA or DCOM, and transaction monitors, which provide transaction management for applications, helping to reduce I/O bottlenecks.

In client/server systems, database-oriented middleware provides some sort of **application program interface (API)** access to a database. APIs are sets of routines that an application program uses to direct the performance of procedures by the computer's operating system. For example, in achieving access to a database, an API calls library routines that transparently route SQL commands from the front-end client application to the database server. An API might work with existing front-end software, such as a third-generation language or custom report generator, and it might include its own facilities for building applications. When APIs exist for several program development tools, then you have considerable independence to develop client applications in the most convenient front-end programming environment yet still draw data from a common server database. Such middleware makes it possible for developers to link an application easily to popular databases.

Open database connectivity (ODBC) is similar to API, but is for Windows-based client/server applications. It is most useful for accessing relational data, and not well suited for accessing other types of data, such as ISAM files (LaRue, 1997). Even though ODBC is difficult to program and implement, it has been well accepted because it allows programmers to make connections to almost any vendor's database without learning proprietary code specific to that database. For a more detailed discussion of ODBC and establishing Internet database connectivity, see Chapter 10. Microsoft's OLE-DB adds value to the ODBC standard by providing a single point of access to multiple databases (Linthicum, 1997). Microsoft is planning to make OLE-DB a universal data access standard and has added OLE-DB for data mining applications and OLE-DB for OLAP. Access to legacy data while moving to client/server systems can be achieved by products such as EDA/SQL, which attempt to support many different operating systems, networks, and databases.

Java Database Connectivity (JDBC) classes can be used to help an applet access any number of databases without understanding the native features of each database. JDBC defines a call-level interface (CLI) for Java development and borrows from ODBC conventions. Establishing a common language to define interfaces between components and a mechanism to mediate will facilitate the development of universal middleware (Keuffel, 1997). The Object Management Group (OMG), established in 1989, is an industry coalition that has produced the Common Object Request Broker Architecture (CORBA), which sets the specification of object-oriented universal

Application program interface (API): Sets of routines that an application program uses to direct the performance of procedures by the computer's operating system.

middleware. Microsoft has developed a competing model, Distributed Component Object Model (DCOM), but CORBA is a more robust specification because it has been developed to handle many different platforms. Interoperability between the two standards is slowly emerging. Such standards are particularly important on the World Wide Web because of the diversity of the platforms that are connecting.

CLIENT/SERVER ISSUES

There is no question that the establishment of client/server architectures has affected the database computing environment. But, too often, one hears of client/server implementation failures and disillusioned users. To succeed, client/server projects should address a specific business problem with well-defined technology and cost parameters. Certain areas should be carefully addressed to improve the chances for building a successful client/server application (Linthicum, 1996):

- *Accurate business problem analysis* Just as is the case with other computing architectures, it is critical to develop a sound application design and architecture for a new client/server system. Developers' tendencies to pick the technology and then fit the application to it seem to be more pronounced in the strong push toward client/server environments that has occurred in the last decade. It is more appropriate to define the scope of the problem accurately, determine requirements, and then use that information to select the technology.

- *Detailed architecture analysis* It is also important to specify the details of the client/server architecture. Building a client/server solution involves connecting many components, which may not work together easily. One of the often touted advantages of client/server computing, the ability to accept an open systems approach, can be very detrimental if the heterogeneous components chosen are difficult to connect. Besides specifying the client workstations, server(s), network, and DBMS, analysts also should specify network infrastructure, the middleware layer, and the application development tools to be used. At each juncture, analysts should take steps to ensure that the tools will connect with the middleware, database, network, and so forth.

- *Avoiding tool-driven architectures* As above, determine project requirements before choosing software tools, and not the reverse. Choosing a tool first and then applying it to the problem risks having a poor fit between problem and tool. Tools selected this way are likely to have been chosen based on an emotional appeal rather than on the appropriate functionality of the tool.

- *Achieving appropriate scalability* A multitier solution allows client/server systems to scale to any number of users and handle diverse processing loads. But multitiered solutions are significantly more expensive and difficult to build. The tools to develop a multitier environment are still limited, too. Architects should avoid moving to a multitier solution when it is not really needed. Usually, multitier makes sense in environments of more than 100 concurrent users, high-volume transaction processing systems, or for real-time processing. Smaller, less intense environments can frequently run more efficiently on traditional two-tier systems, especially if triggers and procedures are used to manage the processing.

- *Appropriate placement of services* Again, a careful analysis of the business problem being addressed is important when making decisions about the placement of processing services. The move toward thin clients and fat servers is not always the appropriate solution. Moving the application logic to a server, thus creating a fat server, can affect capacity, as end users all attempt to use the application now located on the server. Sometimes it is possible to achieve better scaling by moving application processing to the client. Fat servers do tend to reduce network load because the processing takes place close to the data, and fat servers do lessen the need for powerful clients. Understanding the business problem intimately should help the architect to distribute the logic appropriately.

- *Network analysis* The most common bottleneck in distributed systems is still the network. Therefore, architects ignore at their peril the bandwidth capabilities of the network that the system must use. If the network is insufficient to handle the amount of information that must pass between client and server, response time will suffer badly, and the system is likely to fail.

- *Be aware of hidden costs* Client/server implementation problems go beyond the analysis, development, and architecture problems listed here (Atre, 1995). For example, systems that are intended to use existing hardware, networks, operating systems, and DBMSs are often stymied by the complexities of integrating these heterogeneous components to build the client/server system. Training is a significant and recurring expense that is often overlooked. The complexities of working in a multivendor environment can be very costly.

- *Establishing client/server security* The distributed nature of client/server database computing means that security issues are more complex than those encountered in a centralized environment. Both server security and network security must be established. The Web-enabled database environment raises additional security issues. Recent invasions of organizational databases and the resulting loss of sensitive customer information has made people much more aware of the potential threats that exist. These security issues are addressed in Chapter 12.

If these issues are addressed appropriately, there are benefits to be won from moving to client/server architectures (Atre, 1995):

- Functionality can be delivered in stages to the end users. Thus, it arrives more quickly as the first pieces of the project are deployed.

- The graphic user interfaces common in client/server environments encourage users to use the applications' functionality.

- The flexibility and scalability of client/server solutions facilitate business process reengineering.

- More processing can be performed close to the source of data being processed, thereby improving response times and reducing network traffic.

- Client/server architectures allow the development of Web-enabled applications, facilitating the ability of organizations to communicate effectively internally and to conduct external business over the Internet.

USING ODBC TO LINK EXTERNAL TABLES STORED ON A DATABASE SERVER

The **open database connectivity (ODBC) standard** was developed in the early 1990s by the X/Open and SQL Access Group committees. It proposed several levels of standards that RDBMSs could attain, thus enabling any application program to access them using a common API for accessing and processing. Such RDBMSs are said to be ODBC-compliant. The standard has gained wide acceptance, originally propelled by Microsoft's implementation of ODBC for their products. ODBC is also important for Internet applications because it allows for the development of applications that access different database products. To achieve this capability, ODBC uses the ANSI standard generic SQL statements presented in Chapter 8, but it is unable to take advantage of the extensions and special features that each vendor has given its engine.

Open database connectivity (ODBC) standard: An application programming interface that provides a common language for application programs to access and process SQL databases independent of the particular RDBMS that is accessed.

The ODBC specification allows drivers to conform to various levels of the specification, and that affects the level of functionality of the drivers. Differences in the way the drivers themselves are written may affect the performance achieved. Each vendor desiring to have an ODBC-compliant database provides an ODBC driver that can be installed on Windows machines. Thus, each Windows application can communicate, through the appropriate driver, with the desired version of the database server. For example, a Microsoft Access application can be connected to operate with an Oracle database server. The database tables are linked to the Microsoft Access application through the ODBC link and remain in the Oracle database. They are not brought into the Microsoft Access database.

You may hear the Oracle database server referred to as the database server, but it may also be called the remote server, the back-end server, or the SQL server. Because Microsoft's back-end server is called SQL Server, a reference to SQL Server may be a reference to a type of server or to a particular vendor database server. This can be confusing.

Five parameters must be defined in order to establish an ODBC connection:

1. Specific ODBC *driver* needed
2. Back-end *server* name to connect to
3. *Database* name to connect to
4. *User ID* to be granted access to database
5. *Password* of user ID

Additional information may be provided, if desired:

- Data source name (DSN)
- Windows client computer name
- Client application program's executable name

These parameters may be defined from different locations. They may be included in the program, or through the DSN, or by the user when prompted. Including all of the parameters in the program will make it possible for the program to connect directly to the database with no further communication. Of course, the program would have to be modified and new parameter values inserted to port the program to another server or RDBMS. Including the DSN, which includes some of the parameter values, in the program will allow local administrators to place the database and select an RDBMS. The user can provide the user ID and password when he or she logs on to use the application.

Figure 9-6 is a schematic of the typical ODBC architecture. The client application requests that a connection be established with a data source. The request is han-

Figure 9-6
Open database connectivity (ODBC)
architecture

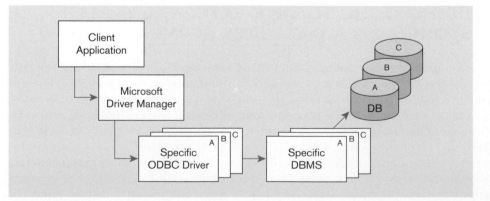

dled by Microsoft's driver manager, which identifies the appropriate ODBC driver to use. Remember that these drivers are supplied by the vendors, so there may be an SQL Server driver, an Oracle driver, an Informix driver, and so forth. Initialization requests, format validation, and ODBC request management are also handled by the driver manager. The driver selected will process the request received from the client and submit queries to the selected RDBMS couched in that particular RDBMS's SQL syntax. The amount of processing required to create that query depends on the capability of the RDBMS being accessed.

Also, the ODBC conformance level will be determined by the capabilities of the driver that has been supplied by the vendor. There are three defined levels of conformance: Core API, Level-1 API, and Level-2 API. These levels have been defined by the standards committees mentioned earlier in this section. Most drivers provide both Core API and Level-1 API functionalities, which include:

- Ability to connect to data sources with driver-specific information
- Prepare and execute SQL statements
- Retrieve data from a result set
- Commit or rollback transactions
- Retrieve error and catalog information
- Send and receive partial results
- Retrieve information about drivers

Distinguishing characteristics of Level-2 API capabilities include:

- Ability to browse potential data sources and connections
- Retrieve native (back-end dialect) SQL
- Call a translation library
- Process and display a scrollable cursor

Applications determine the level of API support available when they call the driver. If Level-2 API is needed and the application is only Level-1 API, then the execution sequence can be terminated in a controlled fashion, so that no corruption of the data occurs. Some applications are written to function at either Level 1 or Level 2, depending on the capabilities of the driver for the particular RDBMS being used.

USING JDBC TO LINK EXTERNAL TABLES STORED ON A DATABASE SERVER

The Java Database Connectivity (JDBC) API enables Java programs to execute SQL statements and connect to database servers. JDBC is similar to ODBC, but it is designed specifically for Java applications. ODBC is language independent. Java is a good language to use for client/server computing because it is network oriented, strong in security, and portable. Oracle has embraced Java and made it relatively easy to use Oracle's proprietary language, PL/SQL, or Java to provide the additional programming functionality needed beyond SQL to build database applications.

The JDBC standard is similar in concept to Microsoft's ODBC. Based on the X/Open SQL Call Level Interface, JDBC consists of two main layers. One layer, the JDBC API, supports communications from a Java application to the JDBC driver manager. The other layer, JDBC Driver API, supports communications from the JDBC driver manager directly to JDBC drivers and to network drivers and ODBC-based drivers.

SQLJ, which stands for SQL-Java, is an ANSI-approved standard for using SQL with Java. It was developed by a consortium of database vendors and Sun Microsystems. It has three parts:

Part 0: Embedded SQL in Java. Supports static SQL statements embedded in Java. Dynamic statements use JDBC. It is allowed to embed both static and dynamic SQL statements within a Java program.

Part 1: SQL routines using Java. Allows the use of Java methods to be invoked by SQL code. The DBMS needs a Java Virtual Machine associated with it.

Part 2: SQL Types using Java. Defines SQL extensions for using Java classes as data types in SQL.

LOOKING FORWARD WITH CLIENT/SERVER IN MIND

Understanding multitiered environments and optimizing them for specific circumstances will continue to be a challenge for information systems professionals in the coming decade. Web services have begun to attract attention, as businesses find that programming and development effort time may be cut by as much as 60 percent by using them and Services Oriented Architecture (SOA) methodologies. SOA is the software development methodology that supports the loose connection of services to implement business processes. The term services implies a server, doesn't it? And, services will be accessed and used by the client, whether it is a PC workstation, a cell phone, or a mobile laptop. The services may be written in any language, including Java and C#, but must use common communication protocols such as XML and SOAP. Chapter 10 will look at these areas in more detail.

Summary

Client/server architectures have offered businesses opportunities to better fit their computer systems to their business needs. Establishing the appropriate balance between client/server and mainframe DBMSs is a matter of much current discussion. Client/server architectures are prominent in providing Internet applications, including dynamic data access. Several client/server architectures are discussed in this chapter, including file server architectures, where the file server manages file operations and is shared by each client PC that is attached to its LAN. File servers create a heavy network load, require a full version of the DBMS on each client, and require complex programming to manage shared database integrity.

Another approach, the database server architecture, makes the client manage the user interface while the database server manages database storage and access. This architecture reduces network traffic, reduces the power required for each client, and centralizes user authorization, integrity checking, data dictionary mainte-

nance, and query and update processing on the database server.

Three-tier architectures, which include another server in addition to the client and database server layers, allow application code to be stored on the additional server. This approach allows business processing to be performed on the additional server, resulting in a thin client. Advantages of the three-tier architecture can include scalability, technological flexibility, lower long-term costs, better matching of systems to business needs, improved customer service, competitive advantage, and reduced risk. But, higher short-term costs, advanced tools and training, shortages of experienced personnel, incompatible standards, and lack of end-user tools are currently problems with using three-tier or n-tier architectures.

Application partitioning assigns portions of application code to client or server partitions after it is written in order to achieve better performance and interoperability. Application developer productivity is expected to increase as a result of using application partitioning, but the developer must understand each process intimately to place it correctly.

Although the hype associated with the widespread adoption of client/server architectures has led some to predict the demise of the mainframe, mission-critical applications have tended to remain on the mainframe. Converting these complex applications to distributed client/server environments has not been easy. The availability of parallel processing solutions is making it more attractive to remain centralized on an application or database server.

Middleware is any of several classes of software that allow an application to interoperate with other software without requiring the user to understand and code the low-level operations required to achieve interoperability. Six categories of middleware, based on scalability and recoverability, are discussed. These middleware types are

asynchronous remote procedure call (RPC), publish/subscribe, message-oriented middleware (MOM), object-request broker (ORB), SQL-oriented data access middleware, and synchronous RPC. Database-oriented middleware includes open database connectivity (ODBC) and Java database connectivity (JDBC).

Client/server issues that should be addressed to improve the chances for building a successful client/server application include accurate business problem analysis, detailed architecture analysis, avoidance of tool-driven architectures, appropriate scalability, appropriate placement of services, adequate network analysis, and awareness of potential hidden costs.

Benefits that may be gained by moving to a client/server environment include deliverance of functionality in stages, flexibility, scalability, less network traffic, and development of Web-enabled applications.

CHAPTER REVIEW

Key Terms

Application partitioning
Application program
  interface (API)
Client/server systems
Database server
Fat client

File server
Middleware
Open database
  connectivity (ODBC)
  standard
Stored procedure

Thin client
Three-tier architecture

Review Questions

1. Define each of the following terms:
   a. application partitioning
   b. application program interface (API)
   c. client/server system
   d. fat client
   e. file server
   f. middleware
   g. stored procedure
   h. three-tier architecture
   i. Java Database Connectivity (JDBC)
   j. Remote procedure call (RPC)

2. Match each of the following terms with the most appropriate definition:

   _____ client/server system

   _____ application program interface (API)

   _____ fat client

   _____ database server

   _____ file server

   _____ middleware

   a. a client that is responsible for processing, including application logic and presentation logic

   b. a PC configured for handling the presentation layer and some business logic processing for an application

   c. software that facilitates interoperability, reducing programmer coding effort

   d. responsible for database storage and access

_____ three-tiered architecture

_____ thin client

e. systems where the application logic components are distributed

f. responsible for managing file operations; shared by all attached clients

g. software that facilitates communication between front-end programs and back-end database servers

h. three-layer client/server configuration

3. List several major advantages of the client/server architecture compared with other computing approaches.

4. Contrast the following terms:
   a. file server; database server; three-tier architecture
   b. client/server computing; mainframe computing
   c. fat client; thin client
   d. ODBC; JDBC

5. Describe the limitations of file servers.

6. Describe the advantages and disadvantages of database servers.

7. Describe the advantages and disadvantages of three-tier and n-tier architectures.

8. How can application partitioning help developers tailor an application to a particular business situation?

9. Describe six categories of middleware.

10. How is the Web changing data distribution patterns?

11. What is the purpose of the ODBC specification?

12. If you were charged with developing a client/server application, how would you ensure success?

13. Search the Web for information on CORBA. A good resource is the OMG Web site (**www.omg.org**/). Discuss CORBA's advantages and disadvantages.

14. Research the Web for information on trends in migrating from mainframe systems to client/server architecture. What percentage of U.S. companies have migrated? Highlight success stories that you encounter, as well as difficulties. A good Web site to start with is www.educause.edu/content.asp?page_id=666&ID=CMR9710&bhcp=1.

Problems and Exercises

1. You have been asked to prepare a report that evaluates possible client/server solutions to handle a new customer application system for all branch offices. What business characteristics would you evaluate? What technology characteristics would you evaluate? Why?

2. What managerial issues do you feel are going to be important when introducing a new client/server architecture?

3. How is the Web affecting client/server database systems?

4. Why is ODBC important? What other connectivity standards are being developed?

5. Historically, what types of applications have moved quickly to client/server database systems? What types have moved more slowly and why? What do you think will happen in the future to the balance of client/server database systems and mainframe database systems?

6. What are the advantages and drawbacks of middleware that is used in connection with database systems?

Field Exercises

1. Investigate the computing architecture of your university. Trace the history of computing at your university and determine what path the university followed to get to its present configurations. Some universities started early with mainframe environments; others started when PCs became available. Can you tell how your university's initial computing environment has affected today's computing environment?

2. On a lesser scale, investigate the computing architecture of one department within your university. Try to find out how well the current system is meeting the department's information-processing needs.

3. Interview a systems professional at an organization in your location that you know has offices in other locations. Determine the computing architecture of that organization and find out how well the current system is meeting the department's information-processing needs.

4. Locate three sites on the Web that have interactive database systems attached to the site. Evaluate the functionality of the site and discuss how the interactive database system is likely to affect that functionality. If you're not sure where to start, try **www.amazon.com**.

5. Locate two similar small businesses in your area that use different computer systems for keeping their records. Compare the functionality and the ease of use of the two systems.

6. Contact a database analyst or systems developer in an organization with which you are familiar. Investigate the use of personal computer and server database systems by that organization. What factors were considered in choosing the platform for the database? Does the organization use a mixed platform, in which client-based application modules are written in one language (e.g., QBE) and server application modules are written in another (e.g., SQL)? Why or why not?

References

Atre, S. 1995. "The Hidden Costs of Client/Server." *DBMS* 8,7 (June): 71, 72, 74.

Groth, R. 2003. "Secrets to Achieving Peak Performance of PeopleSoft ERP Applications." dataWarehouse.com (March 13) and DMReview.com. viewed at **www.datawarehouse.com/article/?articleid=3136** (August 11, 2005).

Hurwitz, J. 1996. "Managing Complexity." *DBMS* 9,5 (May): 12, 80.

Hurwitz, J. 1998. "Sorting Out Middleware." *DBMS* 11,1 (January): 10–12.

Keuffel, W. 1997. "CORBA Masterminds Object Management." *DBMS* 10,3 (March): 42–50, 71.

LaRue, M. 1997. "Database Doorways." *Database Programming & Design* 10,12 (December): 62–67.

Linthicum, D. S. 1996. "Client/Server Collapse." *DBMS* 9,13 (December): 24, 26, 28.

Linthicum, D. S. 1997. "Next-Generation Middleware." *DBMS* 10,10 (October): 69–78.

Quinlan, T. 1995. "The Second Generation of Client/Server." *Database Programming & Design* 8,5 (May): 31–39.

Thompson, C. 1997. "Committing to Three-Tier Architecture." *Database Programming & Design* 10,8 (August): 26–33.

Further Reading

Anderson, G., and B. Armstrong. 1995. "Client/Server: Where Are We Really?" *Health Management Technology* 16,6 (May): 34, 36, 38, 40, 44.

Frazer, W. D. 1998. "Object/Relational Grows Up." *Database Programming & Design* 11,1 (January): 22–28.

Mason, J. N., and M. Hofacker. 2001. "Gathering Client-server Data." *Internal Auditor* 58:6 (December): 27–29.

Web Resources

www.orafaq.com/faqodbc.htm "Oracle ODBC Connectivity FAQ" by Frank Naudé.

www.javaworld.com/javaworld/jw-05-1996/jw-05-shah.html "Integrating Databases with Java via JDBC" by Rawn Shah.

www.javacoffeebreak.com/articles/jdbc "Getting Started with JDBC" by David Reilly.

www.dbmsmag.com/9805d14.html "The Middleware Muddle" by David Ritter.

www.openmobilealliance.org Open Mobile Architecture Initiative (OMA).

Case

In the Chapter 2 segment, you learned of the Mountain View Community Hospital special study team that is developing a long-term strategic plan, including an information systems plan for the Hospital. In assessing the future technology needs of the hospital, the planning team of Mr. Heller, Mr. Lopez, Dr. Jefferson, and a consultant has taken a close look at issues with existing systems as well as trends in the healthcare IT industry.

You may recall that MVCH has systems for many different areas including patient accounting, administrative services, and financial management. Most of the computer applications are implemented using relational database and client/server technology. Some systems were developed internally, while others were acquired from outside vendors. Responding to a recent survey of healthcare CIOs, Mr. Heller chose the term "limited integration" to describe the hospital's current IT infrastructure: best-in-class systems in some areas, stand-alone systems in other areas, and some processes still manual or paper-based. Such limited integration is affecting virtually all of the hospital's stakeholders.

Physicians often have to log on to multiple applications to retrieve patient-related information or read e-mail. Some doctors have also expressed an interest in being able to access clinical systems remotely while working outside of the hospital. Patients must negotiate a maze of health plans, administrators, physicians, and clinics in their encounters with the hospital. The hospital's heterogeneous environment of platforms and applications, and the paper-based systems, has made exchange of patient data between the clinical systems and administrative/financial applications a challenge. At the same time, the managed care environment and the needs to contain costs and simultaneously improve clinical outcomes, patient satisfaction, and efficiency require that MVCH closely tracks and analyzes its clinical and financial data related to patient care services and provides that data to its administrative and clinical decision makers. Oftentimes, accurate data needs to be available in real time.

In addition to these concerns, there are important developments in the healthcare IT industry that factor into the study team's analysis. One is the trend to electronic medical record systems that require various clinical information systems to work together to provide a complete patient record. Hospitals, concerned about moving patients through the hospital more efficiently and effectively, have begun adopting workflow automation (or business process management) technology. Then there are Web technologies that are making inroads. Web portals, for example, allow both patients and physicians to communicate online. Health care alliances are extending their member and patient services beyond their organizational boundaries, to the workplace, schools, and homes. Health plan members can check their claim status, send messages to service representatives, and review coverage. Patients can even make their own appointments by accessing appointment schedules.

Given these issues and trends, the study team has concluded that better and more centralized access to operational, financial, and clinical information should be a top priority for the hospital. Specifically, the team would like Mountain View to implement a system that integrates all of these data—data from health plans, physicians, and hospital systems—so that accurate real-time information would be available. In determining the best approach to integrating information throughout the hospital, the team is considering several strategies:

1. *Leverage existing systems and advances in new technology and move toward an integrated environment based on a three-tier architecture* with both thick and thin clients and continued connection to the hospital's databases and legacy systems. This solution might also include replacing some of the individual clinical applications with software from one vendor.

2. *Abandon the current best-of-breed approach altogether, and look for a single, integrated solution* such as an ERP system that uses a centralized data repository. One ERP system the study team looked at is Global Care Solutions' Hospital 2000 system, a fully integrated hospital information system (HIS). The system is based on a multitiered network design that uses PC-based servers and workstations in combination with RAID 5 hard disks. Advantages of the Hospital 2000 solution

are the use of MS SQL Server as the database management system and the possibility of integrating with existing systems that are following certain standards. That would allow for an incremental implementation approach, giving the team a chance to better evaluate its existing systems, and decide which ones to keep, and which ones to replace.

3. *Go the Web-enabled route.* Vendors, including Siemens and its Soarian solution, for example, provide server-based HIS that use thin client Web technology. Using a Web browser would enable access to information 24/7 across the entire enterprise. Mr. Heller also sees Web services as an efficient means of making the hospital's diverse systems work together and exchange data with other organizations.

4. *Connect to a data warehouse.* As the team works on the long-range plan, the need for data warehousing technologies is becoming apparent. Consequently, the team wants to plan the infrastructure now so that the establishment of a data warehouse will be as easy as possible.

When analyzing the various integration approaches in greater detail, the team realizes that further research is needed to properly evaluate Web-based solutions (see MVCH Chapter 10) and data warehousing possibilities (see MVCH Chapter 11). Therefore, the Case Questions and Exercises are limited to the client/server concepts covered in this chapter and do not directly address at this point the Web-enabled and data warehousing issues that must be considered by MVCH as the adoption of a more integrated approach is evaluated.

CASE QUESTIONS

1. Do you think that Mountain View IT staff under Mr. Heller should and could undertake the project of moving MVCH toward an integrated environment? Should Mountain View outsource such a project? Why or why not?

2. Can you see any other approaches that the study team has not considered? If so, which ones?

3. Why would systems integration be important in terms of addressing HIPAA's privacy and security concerns?

CASE EXERCISES

1. Outline both advantages and risks/disadvantages of moving toward an integrated environment based on a three-tier architecture. What do you think would be the most significant challenges with this integration approach? Which specific technologies would you recommend for implementing this solution?

2. What advantages do you see from adopting a fully integrated health information/ERP system? What do you

think would be the most significant challenges with this integration approach?

3. Using the information developed in the first two case exercises, indicate which solution you feel Mountain View Community Hospital should pursue. Defend your answer. Indicate what additional information you would like to have to help you with your recommendation.

4. Obtain material about hospital ERP systems including the ones addressed in the case description. Investigate the capabilities of each system, the number of installations, the operating systems used, cost, and so on. Which of the systems you have found and learned about might be of interest to a community hospital such as Mountain View?

5. Outline some of the benefits of using thin clients in a hospital setting such as Mountain View Community Hospital. Which thin client devices would be most beneficial? Would thin client hardware make it easier to comply with the privacy and security requirements of HIPAA? Why or why not? Would you recommend that Mountain View Community Hospital pursue a thin client strategy?

6. How is the Internet affecting thin client computing?

PROJECT ASSIGNMENTS

P1. Assume that the MVCH hospital database you developed in SQL Server (or other DBMS designated by your instructor) will be made available to several client applications at the hospital.

   a. What client and connectivity components are needed in order for the applications to access the database?

   b. What types of client applications can access the database? How do the different types of clients connect to the database server?

   c. Which APIs are supported for building database applications?

   d. What client management tools are available? What is their function?

   e. What client tools are available? Describe their function.

   f. Would you use more than one database server? For what purposes? How would you add another server?

P2. Assume Dr. "Z.'s" MS Management System uses the same RDBMS that you used for your MVCH database but is currently located on a different database server.

   a. How could you establish a link to that database?

   b. What would you need to do to place the database on the same server as the MVCH database you created? How would client applications access the MS Management database?

Chapter **10**

The Internet Database Environment

LEARNING OBJECTIVES

After studying this chapter, you should be able to:

- Concisely define each of the following key terms: **World Wide Web Consortium (W3C), XHTML, XSL, XSLT, XML Schema, RELAX NG, Document Structure Description (DSD), Common Gateway Interface (CGI), server-side extension, Java servlet, domain name server (DNS) balancing, software and hardware load balancing, reverse proxy, plug-ins, ActiveX, cookie, Web services, Universal Description, Discovery, and Integration (UDDI), Web Services Description Language (WSDL), Simple Object Access Protocol (SOAP), Service-Oriented Architecture (SOA),** and **Semantic Web.**

- Explain the importance of attaching a database to a Web page.

- Describe the basic environment that must be set up to establish Internet and intranet database-enabled connectivity.

- Use Internet-related terminology appropriately.

- Explain the purpose and accomplishments of the World Wide Web Consortium.

- Explain the purpose of server-side extensions.

- Describe Web services and the issues associated with their successful deployment in electronic commerce.

- Compare and contrast Web server interfaces, including Common Gateway Interface (CGI), API, and Java servlets.

- Describe three methods for balancing Web server loads.

- Explain plug-ins.

- Explain the purpose of XML and its uses in standardizing data interpretation across the Web.

INTRODUCTION

As use of the World Wide Web (WWW) has escalated, the importance of databases to this growth has become ever more evident. Electronic commerce (e-commerce), business conducted over the Internet, has been a significant cause of this escalation in use. It seems that every business from AT&T to Rose's Flower Shoppe has stepped up to the challenge of adapting its business to take advantage of the global network that we call the Internet. The use of Internet technology within companies to build intranets has also been widely adopted.

The public Internet and private intranets can be thought of as vast client/server architectures with very thin clients (browsers) and fat servers. The servers store information in databases to be sent to the browsers on request. It is necessary to access databases for current information, such as inventory availability, and to record information, such as the data items associated with an order, in these applications. However, attaching a database to a Web application may open up access to that database in unintended ways if the developer is not data-security conscious. Problems with a new online shopping site will be evident to customers throughout the world very quickly. Database professionals must know how to establish, operate, and administer Web interfaces to databases prudently.

In this chapter, we will build an understanding of the fit of databases with Internet applications, cover various Internet database architectures, illustrate the use of PHP to Web-enabled databases, and discuss management issues associated with these topics.

THE INTERNET AND DATABASE CONNECTION

Several characteristics of the Web environment have supported the rapid adoption and implementation of Internet and intranet business applications. First, the simplicity and functional similarities of the browser interfaces have significantly reduced traditional barriers to adoption, such as complexity. Just as using Microsoft Windows conventions has made it easier for people to learn new Windows-based applications, the most popular browser interfaces have similarities in functionality that make it easy for users to switch among browsers and among businesses' Web sites. Toolbars with functionality similar to Windows toolbars are often displayed at the top of the screen and can be used to print or to copy and paste information from the pages displayed. Most browsers support e-mail, instant messaging, bookmarking of Web sites, and Web site addressing and searching. Use of HTML, XML, and JavaScript result in a uniformity of presentation and function that make it easy to switch from site to site.

Second, the hardware and software independence of browsers has eased the sharing of information across platforms and has resolved many previously thorny cross-platform issues of access. In particular, wide access to database information has become possible. Through the Internet network, location independence has been achieved. Companies can access their data both locally and remotely, making some information publicly available while protecting critical information from public access by placing it behind a firewall or on a different server. The movement of data files and updates to databases through the Internet is now commonplace. Most recently, the development of Web services, XML-based protocols that help to automate communication among computers over the Web, has begun to ease the programming effort involved in establishing this movement of data. Once security protocols, reliability, and transaction speed issues have been resolved, Web services are expected to affect the development of e-commerce very positively.

Last, development costs and time have been reduced. Inexpensive or even free development and deployment tools are available, making the barriers to entry very low. Newborn babies have their own Web sites managed by proud parents. One expects any business to have a Web site, and although the functionality and timeliness of that Web site still varies widely, it is rare not to be able to find a Web site for any particular business you seek. At the same time, functionality and processing speed of each site may vary widely, and the bandwidth available on the Internet plays a part in how quickly Web pages display and load. Transactions abort with alarming frequency, and displays freeze at the most inconvenient times. In addition, the navigation logic used at each site differs and is not always apparent.

Many sites do not have a database attached to them. They provide static information that is coded using HTML, JavaScript, CGI, or other scripting languages. Common to many of the sites, however, is the need to extract or deposit information into a database that is attached to the site. Some sites are simply repositories of information that can be queried by the site visitor. The user can request information and read it, but not change it in any manner. In Hillsborough County, Florida, for example, anyone can find out who owns land in the county and details about a property, such as valuation for taxation and past purchase prices. The information is stored in a database that the site visitor can query. Information can be accessed by property record designation, street address, or owner's name. Other sites contain product inventory information, again stored in a database. These sites are able to provide information about particular products or classes of products because of the site visitor's query. Any set of data that lends itself to storage in a relational database can be attached to a site, and casual exploration of Web sites will convince the reader that the possibilities are almost endless. Data stored in numeric, character, or graphic formats are all widely used.

Other sites provide more interactivity between the user and the database in that the user can send back information to a database that is attached to a site. This capability has supported the explosive growth of electronic commerce, as orders may be placed online by customers. The customer is frequently able to determine prior to placing an order whether a desired product is in stock or not and how long it should take to receive it. Applications that enable electronic commerce include the capability to both display and load databases attached to a site.

Potential advantages of e-business that organizations foresee are better supply chain management, improved customer service, faster time to market, lower costs, and increased sales. Companies have been able to achieve some of these goals more easily than others. Problems with supply chain management when sites have been swamped with orders have received much negative press. Improved customer service has proved costly to implement, and probably most readers of this book have sent requests for information or support to companies that have gone unanswered. Profitability has been elusive.

THE INTERNET ENVIRONMENT

Common Internet architectures will be covered in more detail later; this section establishes a basic understanding of the Internet environment. Figure 10-1 depicts the basic environment needed to set up both intranet and Internet database-enabled connectivity. In the box on the right-hand side of the diagram is a depiction of an intranet. The client/server nature of the architecture is evident from the labeling. The network that connects the client workstations, Web server, and database server follows TCP/IP protocols. While multitier intranet structures are also used, Figure 10-1 depicts a simpler architecture, where a request from a client browser will be sent through the network to the Web server, which stores pages scripted in HTML to be returned and displayed through the client browser. If the request requires that data be obtained from the database, the Web server constructs a query and sends it to the database server, which processes the query and returns the results set when the query is run against the database. Similarly, data entered at the client station can be passed through and stored in the database by sending it to the Web server, which passes it on to the database server, which commits the data to the database.

The processing flow just described is similar when attaching to an extranet. This is the case whether the connection is available only to a particular customer or supplier or to any workstation connected to the Web. However, opening up the Web server to the outside world requires that additional data security measures be in place. This issue is central to the deployment of Web services, and will be discussed in more detail in Chapter 12.

Internally, access to data is typically controlled by the database management system, with the database administrator setting the permissions that determine employee access to data. Firewalls limit external access to the company's data and the movement of company data outside the company's boundaries. All communication is routed through a proxy server outside of the organization's network. The proxy server controls the passage of messages or files through to the organization's network.

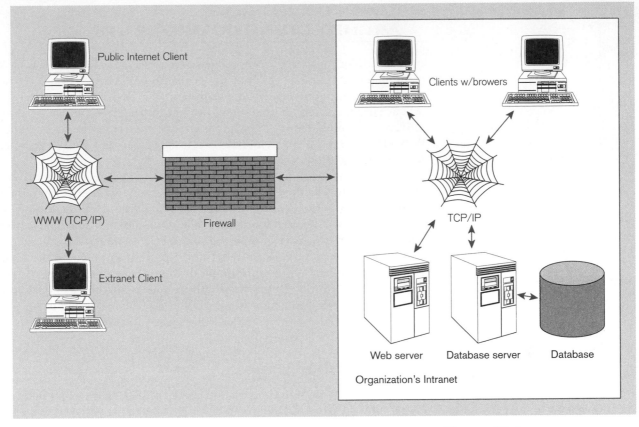

Figure 10-1
Database-enabled intranet/Internet environment

It can also improve a site's performance by caching frequently requested pages that can then be displayed without having to attach to the Web server.

Most intranets provide the following services:

- *Web server*   Used to process client requests and return HTML pages to the client.

- *Database-enabled services*   Database access through the Web server and database server are provided. Web-to-host access can provide access to legacy data stored on a mainframe computer.

- *Directory, security, and authentication services*   Used to prevent unauthorized access from within the corporate network and to provide accountability.

- *Electronic mail*   Provides the capability to transfer messages between computers in the intranet, extranet, or Internet.

- *File Transfer Protocol (FTP)*   Provides the capability to copy files between computers in the intranet, extranet, or Internet. The user needs an FTP client, and the remote system needs an FTP server.

- *Firewalls and proxy servers*   Used to provide security against unauthorized incursion from outside of the organization's intranet.

- *News or discussion groups*   Provides the capability to post information on shared bulletin boards for public access. Threaded discussions related to a subject indicated in the original posting's subject line help to organize the content of the bulletin boards.

- *Document search*   Provides the capability to search Web site content.

- *Load balancing and caching*   Distribution of heavy traffic flows to improve operating performance.

COMMON INTERNET ARCHITECTURE COMPONENTS

A bewildering array of technologies and tools, many identified by acronyms, has come together to create the Internet environment. This section discusses the most common components of that environment. We begin with the various languages that are used, sometimes in tandem, to create Web pages. Several resources operate as Web server middleware. These process requests either going to or coming from the Web server. We classify them into server-side extensions and Web server interfaces. Web servers and client-side extensions are also discussed.

Although Figure 10-1 gives an overview of the architecture required, there is no one right way to take the components and put them together. Rather, there are many possible configurations, using redundant tools. Often, Web technologies within the same category can be used interchangeably. One tool may solve the same problem as well as another tool. We will show the use of PHP to attach a database to a Web site, but other products such as ASP.NET and ColdFusion perform the same function. The need to adhere to organizational development standards may determine the tool selected. Begin by being sure that you understand the category in which each tool is useful, so that you know when you should be considering it. After that, a good reference manual for the product will provide you with its syntax and guide you through the interface issues that surface.

Internet-Related Languages

World Wide Web Consortium (W3C): An international consortium of companies working to develop open standards that foster the development of Web conventions so that Web documents can be consistently displayed across all platforms.

The **World Wide Web Consortium**, known as **W3C**, is the chief standards body for HTTP and HTML. Founded in 1994 by Tim Berners-Lee, W3C is an international consortium of companies. W3C's intent is to develop open standards that foster the development of Web conventions so that Web documents can be consistently displayed across all platforms. The consortium organizes its work into four domains, each of which reports its current activities on the W3C Website (**www.w3.org**). The four domains are Architecture, Interaction, Technology and Society, and the Web Accessibility Initiative.

The fundamental authoring language used to create documents for the Web is HTML, an acronym for Hypertext Markup Language. HTML is similar to SGML, or Standard Generalized Markup Language, which states the rules for tagging elements of a document so that they can be formatted in a standard way. HTML tag conventions are based on SGML rules. HTML is a scripting language, intended to define Web document structure and layout for display purposes, using a variety of tags and attributes. For example, an HTML document starts with the tags (document subject is entered here). The information to be displayed and additional formatting tags follow, and the document will end with the tags.

XML is a rapidly developing scripting language, also based on SGML, that may, in conjunction with XHTML, replace HTML. XML is an acronym for Extensible Markup Language, a specification developed by the W3C. Designed especially for Web documents, XML allows the creation of customized tags. These tags can be used across organizations, enabling the definition, transmission, validation, and interpretation of data between applications and between organizations. XML has also proved useful for attaching legacy data to the Web, because the XML tags can be used to define data as it is formatted in the legacy data store, thus eliminating the need to reformat it. Because XML is so rapidly becoming a standard for e-commerce content, it is covered more extensively in the next section.

XHTML: A hybrid scripting language that extends HTML code to make it XML compliant.

W3C has issued specifications for a hybrid scripting language, **XHTML**, which extends HTML code to make it XML compliant. XHTML uses three XML namespaces that correspond to three HTML 4.0 data type definitions (DTDs). These are Strict, Transitional, and Frameset. Because the modules used in XHTML conform to certain standards, layout and presentation remain consistent over any platform. The W3C wants XHTML to replace HTML as the standard scripting language. It is recommended that the reader visit the W3C Web site to learn how close they are to accomplishing this objective. The 300-plus members of OMA have designated XHTML as a critical enabler for mobile computing applications; this means they have agreed that the applications they develop will be tested for XHTML compliance.

The languages mentioned thus far have been scripting or markup languages, intended for handling layout and display of documents (or, in the case of XML, handling data definition and interpretation), rather than to program functions or activities. A general-purpose programming language, Java, is well suited for use on the Web. Small Java programs, Java applets, download from a Web server to the client and run in a Java-compatible Web browser, such as Netscape Navigator or Microsoft Internet Explorer. Java is an object-oriented language and is simpler than C++. It was designed by Sun Microsystems, whose intention was to create a language that caused fewer common programming errors. Java source code files compile into a format called bytecode that are executed by a Java interpreter. Java interpreters and run-time environments, known as Java Virtual Machines (JVMs), exist for most operating systems, allowing compiled Java code to run on most systems. Bytecode can also be converted directly into machine-language instructions.

Although JavaScript shares many of the features and structures of the full Java language, Netscape developed it independently. Web authors use JavaScript to achieve interactivity and introduce dynamic content. For example, mouse rollovers, automatic notices that content has been updated, and error handling can be accomplished through JavaScripting embedded in the HTML code. When an event occurs, such as the mouse rolling over a button, the JavaScript will be activated. JavaScript is an open language and does not require a license. It is supported by current Netscape, Microsoft, and Mozilla browsers.

VBScript is similar to JavaScript. Just as JavaScript is based on Java but is simpler, VBScript is based on Visual Basic, but it also is simpler. VBScript can be used to add buttons, scrollbars, and other interactive controls to a Web page. Microsoft developed this scripting language, and it is supported by the Microsoft Explorer browser.

Cascading Style Sheets (CSS) are another feature developed by the W3C and being added to HTML. With CSS, designers and users create style sheets that define the appearance of different elements, such as headers and links. A style sheet can then be applied to any Web page. In fact, multiple style sheets can be applied to a Web page. Two W3C recommendations (CSS1 and CSS2) have been published. CSS2.1 and CSS3 are currently being developed. These recommendations are now implemented in most browsers, but they are not consistently implemented.

XSL is a language used to develop style sheets from XML documents. An XSL style sheet is a file that describes how an XML document will be displayed. **XSLT**, originally a transformation language for transforming complex XML documents such as tables of contents or indexes, has also come into wide use for creating HTML pages from XML documents (W3C Web site, August 2005,**www.w3.org/Style/XSL/WhatIsXSL.html**).

XSL: A language used to develop style sheets. An XSL style sheet is similar to CSS but describes how an XML document will be displayed.

XSLT: Language used to transform complex XML documents and also used to create HTML pages from XML documents.

XML Overview

Whereas HTML documents govern the display of information in a Web browser, XML addresses the structuring and manipulation of the data involved. Thus, XML makes it possible to store data items that are consistently defined across businesses, and XML is becoming the standard for e-commerce data exchange. XML does not replace HTML, but works with HTML to facilitate the transfer, exchange, and manipulation of data. The X in XML stands for eXtensible; while a user may take advantage of commonly defined XML tags, a user may also define new tags in SML if necessary. Thus, all types of content can be managed using XML, including sound files and image files.

Data that need to be shared outside the organization should adhere to publicly defined XML schemas. Internal data may be defined ideosyncratically in XML.

New XML-based languages, such as Extensible Business Reporting Language (XBRL) and Structured Product Labeling (SPL) are emerging as open standards that will allow meaningful and unambiguos comparisons that could not be made easily previously. Financial organizations that adhere to XBRL may record up to 2000 financial data points, such as cost, assets, and net income, using standard XBRL tag definitions. These data points may then be combined or compared across institutions' financial reports. As products that enable easier use of XBRL come to market, large financial institutions expect to spend much less time cleansing and normalizing their data, and exchanging data with business partners. Smaller institutions anticipate improved and more affordable access to financial analysis (Henschen, 2005). SPL, used to record the information provided on drug labels, will soon be required by the FDA for both prescription and over-the-counter drugs.

XML uses tags, short descriptions enclosed in angle brackets, to characterize data. The use of angle brackets is similar to their use for HTML tags. But HTML tags are used to describe the appearance of content, and XML tags are used to describe the content itself. In addition to these element tags, the XML language uses XML Schemas, document type declarations (DTDs), comments, and entity references. Understanding each of these components makes it possible to read XML documents.

The XML Schema standard was published in May 2001 by W3C. It defines the data model and establishes data types for the document data. The W3C XML Schema Definition Language (XSD) uses a custom XML vocabulary to describe XML documents. It represents a step forward from using DTDs because it allows data types to be denoted. Here is a very simple XML Schema that describes the structure, data typing, and validation of a salesperson record. Notice the tags: xsd stands for **XML Schema Definition** and what follows until the matching /xsd tag defines a type of XML document. The W3C standard supports namespaces. Within a namespace, all elements and attributes must have unique names. The same name may safely be used in another namespace. The tag, xmlns, seen below, identifies the namespace that will be used for this XML Schema, and its value must be a URI address.

```
<xsd:schema xmlns:xsd="http:///www.w3.org/2001/XMLSchema">
    <xsd:element name="Salesperson" type="SalespersonType"/>
    <xsd:complexType name="SalespersonType">
        <xsd:sequence>
        <xsd:element name="SalespersonID" type="xsd:integer"/>
        <xsd:element name="SalespersonName" type="xsd:string"/>
        <xsd:element name="SalespersonTelephone" type="xsd:string"/>
            <pattern value="(?\d{3})?-?\d{3}-?\d{4}"/>
                <xsd:element name="SalespersonFax" type="xsd:string"/>
            <pattern value="(?\d{3})?-?\d{3}-?\d{4}"/>
            <xsd:sequence>
    </xsd:complexType>
</xsd:schema>
```

DTDs were included in the first XML but have some limitations. DTDs are not able to specify data types and are written in their own language, not in XML. DTDs do not support some newer features of XML, such as namespaces. A namespace contains definitions of identifiers. By specifying a particular namespace, a developer can be confident that the definition of the identifier will be exactly as specified within that namespace. An identifier with the same name stored in a different namespace may have a different definition, but it will not conflict because it is contained in a different namespace that is not accessed.

Three newer XML schema languages are now being used more frequently than DTDs. **XML Schema** or XML Schema Definition (XSD) was granted Recommendation status by the W3C in May 2001. XML Schema provides for backward compatibility with

XML Schema (XSD): Language used for defining XML databases that has been recommended by W3C.

DTDs by including traditional XML types such as ID and ENTITY. **RELAX NG** (Regular Language for XML Next Generation) is another schema language for XML that is an ISO international standard. **Document Structure Description (DSD)** is another alternative to using XML Schema and is considered by some to be the most expressive of the major schema languages, and easy to use.

An XML document that conforms to the schema listed above follows. As SalespersonFax was defined as optional, denoted by the "?" after SalespersonFax in the XMLSchema, it is not necessary to include a data value for SalespersonFax here.

RELAX NG: Language used for defining XML database that is an ISO international standard.

Document Structure Description (DSD): Language used for defining XML databases noted for ease of use and expressiveness.

```
<salesperson>
xmlns:xsi=http://www.w3.org/2001/XMLSchema-instance"
xsi:noNamespaceSchemaLocation="Salesman.xsd"
      <SalespersonID>1</SalespersonID>
      <SalespersonName>Doug Henny</SalespersonName>
      <SalespersonTelephone>813-444-5555</SalespersonTelephone>
</Salesperson>
```

Notice that these XML examples have provided little information about how data elements are to be displayed. Rather, they have concentrated on modeling the data. It is possible to set up your own XML vocabulary, as we have just done. However, a wide variety of public XML vocabularies already exists and can be used to mark up your data. Many are listed at **http://wdvl.com/Authoring/Languages/XML/Specifications. html** and **http://www.service-architecture.com/xml/articles/xml_vocabularies.html**. Selecting the best XML vocabulary to use to describe a database is very important. More libraries of external XML schemas should become available, but for now Web searches and word of mouth may lead you most directly to appropriate schemas. Such libraries make it easier for an organization to exchange data with other organizations without having to engage in individual agreements with each business partner.

Some sites are making standardization with their site easier for outside developers. For example, developers can use the eBay API via XML to display eBay listings on any third-party site. In addition, after downloading a developer's kit, creating an account, and obtaining a license key, developers can use Google APIs to query its database from within their own Web pages and applications. It is beyond the scope of this text to provide the reader with an in-depth understanding of XML. Nevertheless, the functionality provided by eBay and Google already make it clear that XML is an area that melds closely with traditional database content as e-commerce continues to develop.

Server-Side Extensions

To handle a request from a client that requires access to a database, the Web server's capabilities must be increased or extended, because Web servers understand only HTML-formatted pages. A **server-side extension** is a program that interacts directly with a Web server to handle requests. For example, the Web server's capabilities must be extended so that it can support database requests. The process is shown in Figure 10-2. Initially, a request for information is submitted from a browser via the Web to the Web server. The SQL query will be included in the script, but cannot be directly interpreted by the Web server. Instead, the Web-to-database middleware identifies the query and prepares it to be passed to the database management system and the database, where the data items are stored. The result set returned by the query is returned to the middleware, which converts the result so that it will display correctly when the Web page is returned to the client browser.

Server-side extensions allow for a high degree of flexibility. The network administrator can select any Web server, perhaps Apache, Netscape Fast Track Server, or Microsoft Internet Information Server. Any ODBC-compliant database that has SQL capability, such as Oracle, Sybase, or Microsoft Access can be used, and the

Server-side extension: A software program that interacts directly with a Web server to handle requests.

Figure 10-2
Web-to-database middleware

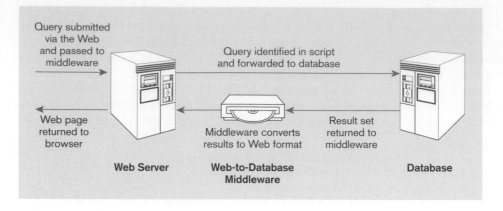

middleware will connect them both. ColdFusion and Netscape Application Server are examples of middleware.

Web Server Interfaces

For a Web server to interact with an external program, a mechanism to establish the interface must be in place. Whether one uses the term interface, interoperability, or interactivity, this need to be able to communicate between the Web server and the client or the database is often necessary. Static Web pages do not require this type of interface because all information to be displayed is contained in the HTML document that will be shown. However, dynamic Web pages determine some of their content at the time that the client browser requests a page. For example, displaying updated information of some sort, such as the current inventory level for a product, will require a Web server interface. The following are two common Web server interfaces:

Common Gateway Interface (CGI):
A Web server interface that specifies the transfer of information between a Web server and a CGI program.

- **Common Gateway Interface (CGI)**
- Application Program Interface (API)

CGI specifies the transfer of information between a Web server and a CGI program. CGI programs are designed to accept and return data and may be written in any language that produces executable files, including C or C++, Perl, Java, or Visual Basic. The data must conform to the CGI specification. CGI programs are commonly used to accept data from forms that are displayed in a browser and filled in by the user. They may also be used to accept data from a legacy system, perhaps from an existing database or other body of documents. Remember, the gateway programs are executable programs and can be run under different information servers interchangeably.

CGI programs are a common way for Web servers to interact dynamically with user requests. Some other client-side approaches will be covered shortly. CGI scripts are stored on the Web server and must be executed each time a user makes a request that uses that CGI script. In a situation where many users are sending requests that require the CGI scripts, performance can be slowed noticeably. Therefore, some client-side solutions, such as Java scripts and applets and ActiveX controls, have been devised, and they will be discussed later in the Client-Side Extensions section.

Java servlet: A small program that executes from within another application rather than from the operating system and is stored on the server rather than with an application on a client.

Java servlets are used as an alternative to CGI programs. Like applets, servlets are programs that execute from within another application rather than from the operating system, but they are stored on the server rather than with an application on a client. Servlets allow a client program to upload additional program code to a server, where it executes. Because servlets are small in file size and cross-platform compatible, they are ideal for small Internet applications that are accessible from a browser. Java servlets are persistent; once started, they remain in active memory and

401

can fulfill multiple requests. A CGI program closes after it runs. Thus, Java servlets are more efficient because they are persistent, and server performance is less likely to be noticeably affected.

APIs are also more efficient than CGI scripts are. They are implemented as shared code or dynamic link libraries (DLLs). This means that the code is resident in memory and can be called dynamically as needed. No external program need be executed for each request. An API is a set of routines, protocols, and tools that an application program uses to direct the operating system's performance of procedures. APIs can also use a shared connection to a database, rather than having to establish a new link each time a connection is requested. However, APIs do have some negatives. Because APIs reside on the Web server, an API error can cause a server to crash. APIs are specific to the operating system and Web server on which they reside and must be rewritten to run with other systems.

Web Servers

There is an interesting Web site (**www.netcraft.com/survey/**) that provides a monthly survey of the Web servers on the Internet that it can identify. In 1995, its first survey located 3,428 sites. In August 2003, it located 42,807,275 sites. In August 2005, it located 70,392,567 sites. This exponential growth of sites has been supported by the ability to communicate with databases and offer dynamic pages that contain current information. Each of these sites provides an HTTP service, the protocol that allows Web browsers and Web servers to communicate. HTTP is a relatively simple protocol, passing plain text via a TCP connection. Originally, a new HTTP connection had to be established to the Web server for each object to be downloaded to a browser. Newer versions of HTTP support a persistent connection so that multiple objects can be transmitted in packets over a single TCP connection.

A Web server must be able to serve many users at a time, and this is accomplished by multithreading or multiprocessing. Web servers running on UNIX tend to use a form of multiprocessing. Others use multithreading, multiprocessing, or a hybrid of multiprocessing and multithreading. Multiprocessing uses multiple processors working in tandem to achieve faster processing. A thread is a process that is part of a larger program. Multithreading is the simultaneous running of processes that comprise more than one thread.

Popular Web sites receive more hits than can be managed by a single server, and multiple servers must be installed. Balancing the load to take advantage of the additional servers can be a challenge. Some sites use **DNS (domain name server) balancing** to handle more hits, placing multiple copies of the site on separate but identical physical servers. The DNS server for the hostname of the site returns multiple IP addresses for the site, either by returning more than one IP address for the hostname or by returning a different IP address for each DNS request received. Although this approach is simple, it does not guarantee that the load on the servers will be balanced because the IP addresses chosen may not be balanced.

DNS (domain name server) balancing: A load-balancing approach where the DNS server for the hostname of the site returns multiple IP addresses for the site.

Software and hardware load balancing can distribute the requests more evenly across the Web servers. Only one IP address is published for the site. Requests to this one IP address are distributed among the multiple servers hosting the Web site at the TCP/IP routing level. The load balancing achieved by using software and hardware load balancing is usually better than the DNS method. Some load balancers detect a Web server in the pool that is down and dynamically redirect the request to another Web server.

Software and hardware load balancing: A load-balancing approach where requests to one IP address are distributed among the multiple servers hosting the Website at the TCP/IP routing level.

A third method reduces the load on a Web site by intercepting requests from clients and caching the response on the Web server that sends it back to the client. This approach is called **reverse proxying**. The result is that the proxy can often serve a request from its own local cache rather than contacting the Web server, reducing the load on the Web server.

Reverse proxy: A load-balancing approach that intercepts requests from clients and caches the response on the Web server that sends it back to the client.

Some companies use global load-balancing techniques that distribute the work of sending data files all over the world. Typically, they use both DNS load balancing and software–hardware-based load balancing. By determining where a client is located, files located closest to the user are served to that user.

The distinction between Web servers and application servers is now becoming somewhat blurred, as Web servers turn into application servers that serve XML data and HTML data. Moreover, application servers are configured to act as a simple Web server while still performing as an application server. Decisions about configuration will be determined by the expectations being placed on the Web site. For Web sites that are closely involved with delivering results from an application, it may be best to have both a Web server and an application server. For a site that delivers HTML pages without frequent reliance on an application, a Web server approach with application server capabilities may be best.

Client-Side Extensions

Extensions to the client-side add functionality to the browser. A few of the most popular are discussed briefly here, to give you a sense of client-side extensions. Plug-ins, ActiveX controls, and cookies reside on the client side and are discussed here.

Plug-ins: Hardware or software modules that extend the capabilities of a browser by adding a specific feature, such as encryption, animation, or wireless access.

Plug-ins are hardware or software modules that add a specific feature or service, extending the original capabilities of a browser. Downloading and installing a specific plug-in in a browser's plug-in folder provides the extension. For example, RealAudio creates the ability to listen to audio broadcasts over the Web. Shockwave plays animation files. Other capabilities include palmtop PC synchronization, wireless access, and encryption. Although plug-ins were originally devised to conform to Netscape Navigator specifications, they also work with Microsoft Internet Explorer and other browsers. Microsoft Explorer supports many Netscape Navigator plug-ins, but it also uses a different software standard, ActiveX, instead of plug-ins. ActiveX controls are discussed next. Netscape Navigator also supports some ActiveX controls.

Most plug-ins are free and download quickly because they are small files. Even so, users can be resistant to adding a plug-in program that may cause their browser or machine to behave in unexpected ways. Companies may opt not to use plug-ins on their site because of this resistance or because plug-ins may interfere with a company's ability to get their site selected by a search engine. As has happened with other externally developed functionality, the most popular plug-ins will probably be incorporated into future versions of the browsers.

ActiveX: A loosely defined set of technologies developed by Microsoft that extends browser capabilities and allows the manipulation of data inside the browser.

ActiveX is a loosely defined set of technologies developed by Microsoft. ActiveX follows from two other Microsoft technologies called *Object Linking and Embedding (OLE)* and *Component Object Model (COM)*. ActiveX controls extend browsers, allowing the manipulation of data inside the browser. They are the third version of OLE controls presented by Microsoft. They use COM technologies to provide interoperability with other types of COM components and services. For example, they allow users to identify the authors of controls before allowing them to execute, an important Web security feature. COM architecture works across all Microsoft products and creates objects that have a standard interface so that they can be used by any COM-aware program. ActiveX controls are most commonly written in C++; or Visual Basic.

Cookie: A block of data stored on a client by a Web server. When a user returns to a site, the contents of the cookie are sent back to the Web server and may be used to identify the user and return a customized Web page.

Cookies are used to identify a user when that user returns to a Web site. Often a Web site will request that a visitor fill out a form that asks for the user's name and e-mail and may ask for other information such as mailing address, phone, and interests related to the site. The information provided will be stored in a cookie and sent to the Web browser. When the user returns to the site later, the contents of the cookie are sent back to the server and may be used to customize the Web page that is returned. Cookies are persistent; they can be stored on the browser for a lengthy period of time. Users who object to providing such information may disable the storage of cookies in their Web browsers. Spyware programs such as Spy Sweeper may also be used to detect and remove cookies that have been stored as a user surfs the Internet, making it easier to retain desired cookies and remove undesired ones.

WEB-TO-DATABASE TOOLS

Many middleware applications now exist that ease the connection of databases to Web applications. PHP, Microsoft ASP.net, and ColdFusion remain among the more popular. Each organization selects a set of tools to accomplish this task. There are about six different components that must be used together to create a dynamic Web site.

1. *A DBMS.* You have read about many of them, including Oracle, Microsoft SQL Server, Informix, Sybase, DB2, Microsoft Access, and MySQL.
2. *A Web server.* The most commonly used Web server is Apache, but you are also likely to encounter Microsoft's IIS Web server. Some products, such as Coral Web Builder, a product included in the third component, are composite products and include Web server capabilities.
3. *Programming languages* and *development technologies* used for developing dynamic Web sites and Web-based applications. Examples include ASP.NET, ColdFusion, PHP, and Coral Web Builder, though there are other contenders to fill this component.

Some set of technologies that provides the functionalities listed above is necessary to build a dynamic Web site. In addition, development work will require two or three additional components:

1. A *Web browser.* Microsoft's Internet Explorer, Netscape's Navigator, Mozilla Firefox, Apple's Safari, and Opera are examples.
2. A *text editor.* Notepad, BBEdit, or vi will work. You might prefer a WYSIWYG application that is PHP–capable such as Macromedia's Dreamweaver. Another possibility would be an Integrated Development Environment (IDE). These are usually language specific, such as the Java IDE, and include a source code editor, a compiler and/or interpreter, and they build automation tools. They may also have a debugger.
3. *FTP* capabilities, if using a remote server. SmartFTP is available for free and FTP Explorer is available free for educational use. WS_FTP is another popular product.

As you can see, there is a bewildering collection of tools available to use for Web development. Your development environment is likely to be determined by your employer. When you know what environment you will be using, there are many alternatives available for becoming familiar and proficient with the tools. Your employer may send you to training classes or even hire a subject matter expert to work with you. You will find one or more books specific to each tool when you search online or in a bookstore. Each company provides a Web site and assistance. Manuals may be available from them online. Newsgroups and mailing lists will help you find answers to your most challenging questions. More general Web sites, such as **www.devshed.com** and **www.webmonkey.com,** include relevant articles. Figure 10-3 presents a visual depiction of the components necessary to create a dynamic Web site.

Database (May be on same machine
as Web server for development purposes)
(Oracle, MS SQL Server, Informix, Sybase,
DB2, MS Access, MySQL...)

Programming Languages (C, C#, Java, XML, XHTML, JavaScript...)
Development Technologies (ASP.NET, PHP, ColdFusion...)
Client side extensions (ActiveX, plug-ins, cookies)
Web browser (Internet Explorer, Navigator, Firefox...)
Text editor (Notepad, BBEdit, vi, Dreamweaver...)
FTP capabilities (SmartFTP, FTP Explorer, WS_FTP...)

Web server (Apache, MS-IIS)
Server side extensions (JavaScript Session
    Management Service & LiveWire
    Database Service, FrontPage Extensions...)
Web server interfaces (CGI, API,
    Java servlets)

Figure 10-3
Dynamic Web development
environment

For this section, we have selected a set of open source components. Thus, you can obtain each of these components and experiment with them at no cost to yourself, assuming you have a computer to use. The components are listed below, along with some information about each. Web sites that you may be interested in to help you get started are RB Software's WebServerXKit, a shareware package program that installs MySQL, Apache, and PHP on a Mac OS X operating system (available at **http://www.rbsoftware.net/?page=wsxk**). Phpteam.net offers a similar installer package for the Windows environment at **http://www.en.wampserver. com/index.php**.

1. *DMBS: MySQL*. Available from **www.mysql.com/downloads**. You will be able to select a version appropriate to your computing environment and download it there. The MySQL manual is also available at **www.mysql.com**. Mailing lists about specific MySQL topics may be reviewed and selected at **dev.mysql.com/doc/mysql/en/mailing-list.html**. Administrative tools in which you may be interested include mysql client, a command-line tool included in MySQL, and phpMyAdmin, a shareware program with a Web interface.

2. *Web server: Apache Web Server*. Available from **httpd.apache.org/download.cgi**. Documentation for the current recommended versions of Apache Web Server is also available at this site.

3. *Development language: PHP*. Available from **www.php.net/downloads.php**. An annotated PHP manual is at **www.php.net/manual/en**. There are many useful PHP sites beyond **www.php.net**. **www.zend.com** is the homepage of the creators of the PHP4 engine. For specific questions, try **www.phpbuilder.com**. **Pear.php.net** includes common libraries of code that you can use to learn to read and program in PHP and that you can use for your projects. Available mailing lists are at **www.php.net/mailing-lists.php**. There is also a newsgroup, **comp.lang.php**.

In addition to the discussion using open source resources, complete script files and instructions for setting up an ASP.NET shopping cart are available from the text

Web site, **www.prenhall.com/hoffer**. These sample files demonstrate pulling data from an attached database and do not actually store the order information or accept credit card information.

As indicated above, there are several suitable languages and development tools available with which to create dynamic Web pages. Java, C, C++, C#, and Perl are possible APIs that can be used with MySQL. However, PHP is one of the most popular for several reasons. Support for MySQL has been built into PHP since version 4 of PHP. It has a reputation for ease of use, short development time, and high performance. PHP5, recently released, is more object-oriented than PHP4, and includes several class libraries. It is considered to be relatively easy to learn. Intermediate level programmers will learn it quickly.

Figure 10-4 includes a sample script from Ullman (2003) that demonstrates the integration of PHP with a MySQL database and HTML code. The script accepts a guest's registration on a Web site, including first name, last name, email address, user name, and password. Once this information has been stored in the MySQL database, the database owner will want to retrieve it. Ullman also includes a sample script for retrieving the results and displaying them in good form. Reviewing Figure 10-4 will give you an overview of one approach to building a dynamic Web site with an attached database, and an appreciation for PHP's use of other language's syntax conventions that will make the script relatively easy for you to understand. As you review the figure, look for the embedded SQL code, necessary to establish a dynamic Web site.

Web Services

The Internet has served as a powerful driver to encourage the integration of communication between the providers of software applications and the users of those applications. As the Internet evolves as a distributed computing platform, a set of emerging standards is affecting software development and distribution practices. Easing the automatic communication of software programs through the use of XML coding and Internet protocols such as HTTP and e-mail, a set of protocols known as **Web services** are improving the ability of computers to communicate over the Internet automatically, thus aiding the development and deployment of applications within a company or across an industry. Existing methods of establishing communication, such as electronic data interchange (EDI) are still being used, but the Web services approach promises to make it much easier to create program application modules that execute in a distributed environment.

Some organizations have already attracted attention by their use of Web services. Both Amazon and Google, two companies with high profile Web presence, have used Web service approaches. Google began its program in April 2002, allowing developers to access their search database directly for noncommercial uses and to create their own interfaces to the data. Access to Amazon's inventory database was made available in July 2002. Combining the service with a Weblogger, API allows bloggers to create a link to a relevant Amazon product in one step. Programmers benefit from improved ease of access, customers conduct more efficient searches, and Amazon and Google continue to spread and support their brands. Just google on "Amazon Web services documentation" or "Google Web services documentation" to become more familiar with these free opportunities.

Others charge for using their Web services. .NET developers can use Microsoft's Map Point Web Service to provide location-based services (LBS) from their Web site. Map Point Web Service provides both location and mapping capabilities that may be accessed over any HTTPS connection. MapQuest offers similar capabilities. After paying a setup fee, users may elect to pay on an annual or monthly basis. Charges depend on transaction count. Microsoft's foray into Web services has been successful enough topographic, and satellite images available through TerraService (see **http://terraservice.net/webservices.aspx**).

Web services: Set of emerging standards that define protocols for automatic communication between software programs over the Web. Web services are XML-based and usually run in the background to establish transparent communication among computers.

```php
<?php # Script 6.6 - register.php

// Set the page title and include the HTML header.
$page_title = 'Register';
include ('templates/header.inc');

//Handle the form.
if (isset($_POST['submit'])) {

        // Create an empty new variable.
        $message = NULL;

        // Check for a first name.
        if (empty($_POST['first_name'])) {
                    $fn = FALSE;
                    $message .= '<p>You forgot to enter your first name!</p>';
        } else {
                    $fn = $_POST['first_name'];
        }

        // Check for a last name.
        if (empty($_POST['last_name'])) {
                    $ln = FALSE;
                    $message .= '<p>You forgot to enter your last name!</p>';
        } else {
                    $ln = $_POST['last_name'];
        }

        // Check for an email address.
        if (empty($_POST['email'])) {
                    $e = FALSE;
                    $message .= '<p>You forgot to enter your email address!</p>';
        } else {
                    $e = $_POST['email'];
        }

        // Check for a username.
        if (empty($_POST['username'])) {
                    $u = FALSE;
                    $message .= '<p>You forgot to enter your username!</p>';
        } else {
                    $u = $_POST['username'];
        }

        // Check for a password and match against the confirmed password.
        if (empty($_POST['password1'])) {
                    $p = FALSE;
                    $message .= '<p>You forgot to enter your password!</p>';
        } else {
                        if ($_POST['password1'] == $_POST['password2']) {
                                    $p = $_POST['password1'];
                        } else {
                                    $p = FALSE;
                                    $message .= '<p>Your password did not match
                                                the confirmed password!</p>';
                        }
        }
```

Callout annotations:
- PHP file named register.php begins.
- This file contains HTML code to set up a generic page, including its page title and header.
- Check whether to process form.
- Validate first name.
- Validate last name.
- Validate email address.
- Validate username.
- Validate the password.

Figure 10-4
Sample PHP script that accepts user
registration input
(Ullman, *PHP and MySQL for Dynamic
Web Sites,* 2003, Script 6.6)
a) PHP script initiation and input
validation

```php
//If everything's OK.
    if ($fn && $ln && $e && $u && $p) {

        // Register the user in the database.

        // Connect to the db.
        require_once ('../mysql_connect.php');

        // Make the query.
        $query = "INSERT INTO users (username, first_name, last_name, email, password,
        registration_date) VALUES ('$u', '$fn', '$ln', '$e', PASSWORD('$p'), NOW() )";

        //Run the query.
        $result = @mysql_query ($query);

        //If it ran OK.
        if ($result) {

            // Send an email, if desired.
            echo '<p><b>You have been registered!</b></p>';

            //Include the HTML footer.
            include ('templates/footer.inc');

            //Quit the script.
            exit();

        // If it did not run OK.
        } else {

            $message = '<p>You could not be registered due to a system error.
            We apologize for any inconvenience.</p><p>' . mysql_error() . '</p>';

        }

        //Close the database connection.
        mysql_close();

    } else {

        $message .= '<p>Please try again.</p>';

    }

// End of the main Submit conditional.
}
```

Callouts:
- If all user information has been validated, the data will be inserted into the MySQL database.
- Establish connection to database.
- SQL query with encrypted password and current date.
- mysql_query( ) function sends SQL to MySQL.
- $result contains value returned by mysql_query. If TRUE, message is displayed, footer is required, script is halted.
- If $result FALSE, assign value to $message.
- Close connection to MySQL database.
- Completion of registration conditional.
- Completion of submit conditional.

Figure 10-4 (Continues)
b) Adding user information to the database

The promise of Web services is the development of a standardized communication system using XML. Easier integration of applications is possible because developers need not be familiar with the technical details associated with the applications being integrated, nor must they learn the programming language of the application being integrated. Anticipation of increased business agility derived from significant reductions in the time and effort needed to establish enterprise application integration and B2B relationships is driving the interest in the Web services approach. Figure 10-5 demonstrates a very simple diagram of an order entry system that includes both internal Web services (Order Entry and Accounting) and Web services that are outsourced to companies that provide authentication and credit validation services over the Web (Newcomer, 2002).

```
// Print the message if there is one.          ◄──── [If an error message exists, display it.]
if (isset($message)) {
        echo '<font color="red">',$message, '</font>';
}
?>                          ◄──── [Begin HTML form.]

<form action="<?php echo $_SERVER['PHP_SELF']; ?>" method="post">
<fieldset><legend>Enter your information in the form below:</legend>


<p><b>First Name:</b> <input type="text" name="first_name" size="15" maxlength="15"
value="<?php if (isset($_POST['first_name'])) echo $_POST['first_name']; ?>" /></p>

<p><b>Last Name:</b> <input type="text" name="last_name" size="30" maxlength="30"
value="<?php if (isset($_POST['last_name'])) echo $_POST['last_name']; ?>" /></p>

<p><b>Email Address:</b> <input type="text" name="email" size="40" maxlength="40"
value="<?php if (isset($_POST['email'])) echo $_POST['email']; ?>" /> </p>

<p><b>User Name:</b> <input type="text" name="username" size="10" maxlength="20"
value="<?php if (isset($_POST['username'])) echo $_POST['username']; ?>" /></p>

<p><b>Password:</b> <input type="password" name="password1" size="20" maxlength="20"/></p>

<p><b>Confirm Password:</b> <input type="password" name="password2" size="20" maxlength="20"

/></p>
</fieldset>

<div align="center"><input type="submit" name="submit" value="Register" /></div>

</form><!-- End of Form -->

<?php
//Include the HTML footer.
include ('templates/footer.inc'); ?>          ◄──── [Use the HTML template for the page footer.]
```

Figure 10-4 (Continued)
c) Close PHP script and display HTML form

Concerns about adopting a Web services approach center around transaction speed, security, and reliability. The open system implied in establishing automatic communication among computers attached to the Web must be further developed before the security and reliability matches that of traditional business applications. Next, we present some terms associated with Web services and discuss a typical database/Web services protocol stack. Figure 10-6 depicts a common Web services protocol stack. There are additional approaches available within each layer, but that is beyond the scope of this chapter.

There is additional terminology associated with using Web services. The transformation and communication of data in and out of application programs and databases relies on a set of XML-related protocols. **Universal Description, Discovery, and Integration (UDDI)** is a technical specification for creating a distributed registry of Web services and businesses that are open to communicating through Web services. Using the UDDI specifications, Microsoft, IBM, and Ariba have led the development of the UDDI Project. This project, based on UDDI, is often compared to an American telephone book's white, yellow, and green pages (information about how to do e-business with an organization).

Universal Description, Discovery, and Integration (UDDI): A technical specification for creating a distributed registry of Web services and businesses that are open to communicating through Web services.

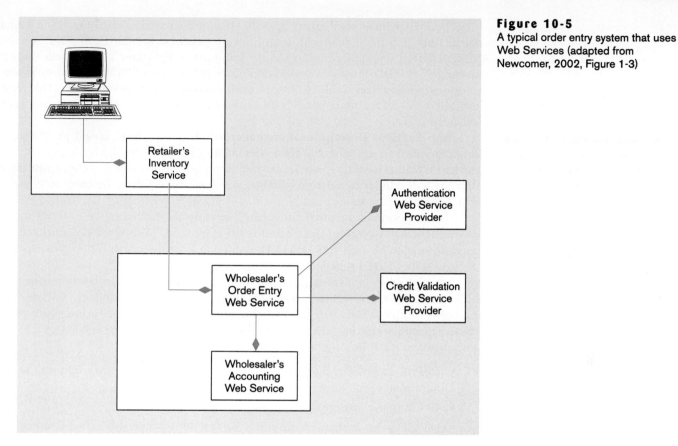

Figure 10-5
A typical order entry system that uses
Web Services (adapted from
Newcomer, 2002, Figure 1-3)

Publish, Find, Use Services	UDDI	**Universal Description, Discovery, Integration**
Describe Services	WSDL	**Web Services Description Language**
Service Interactions	SOAP	**Simple Object Access Protocol**
Data Format	XML	**eXtensible Markup Language**
Open Communications	Internet	

Figure 10-6
Web services protocol stack

The white pages category includes general company information, including business name, address, and so forth. The yellow pages category includes business classification data for companies and/or Web services offered. The green pages category includes technical information about a Web service, including pointers to the address for calling it up.

The UDDI Business Registry specification was turned over to OASIS, a global consortium that is the leader in establishing e-business standards, in 2002. Version 3.0.2 of UDDI was ratified as an OASIS standard in February 2005. If you want to investigate a UDDI business registry, explore **http://www-306.ibm.com/software/ solutions/webservices/uddi/** or **http://uddi.microsoft.com/default.aspx**. IBM, SAP, and Microsoft all maintain beta UDDI Version 3 sites that you may investigate freely once you register.

Web Services Description Language (WSDL) is an XML-based grammar or language used to describe a Web service and to specify a public interface for that service. WSDL is used to create a file that automatically generates a client interface, allowing a developer to attend to the business logic rather than the communications requirements of an application.

Web Services Description Language (WSDL): An XML-based grammar or language used to describe a Web service and specify a public interface for that service.

The definition of the public interface may indicate data types for XML messages, message format, location information for the specified Web service, and the transport protocol to be used (HTTP, HTTPS, or e-mail), and so forth. These descriptions are stored in a UDDI repository. Draft version 2.0 was released in May 2005 by W3C and is expected to become a recommendation. WSDL is used in combination with XML Schema and SOAP to provide Web services over the Internet. This version includes example WSDL code at **www.w3.org/TR/2005/WD-wsdl20-primer-20050803/ #basics-greath-scenario.** The code is for GreatH Hotel reservation service and demonstrates the following components of WSDL:

- Defining a WSDL 2 *target namespace*, analogous to an XML Schema target namespace.
- Defining the *message types* that the Web service will use.
- Defining the *interface* by defining the operations that will occur between the server and the client, and which message types will be used by each operation type.
- Specifying *bindings and defaults* for each operation. Information about message format and transmission protocols are specified.
- Defining a *service*, indicating where the service may be accessed. A service may only have one interface.
- *Documenting* the service.

Simple Object Access Protocol (SOAP) is an XML-based communication protocol used for sending messages between applications via the Internet. Because it is a language-independent platform, it enables communication between diverse applications. As SOAP moves toward becoming a W3C standard, it generalizes a capability that was previously established on an ad-hoc basis between specific programs. Many view it as the most important Web service. SOAP structures a message into three parts: an optional header, a required body, and optional attachments. The header can support in-transit processing, and thus deal with firewall security issues.

Simple Object Access Protocol (SOAP): An XML-based communication protocol used for sending messages between applications via the Internet.

Here is an example, adapted from an example displayed at **en.wikipedia.org/ wiki/SOAP**, of how Pine Valley Furniture Company might format a SOAP message requesting product information from one of their suppliers. PVFC needs to know which product corresponds to product ID 32879 of the supplier.

```
<soap:Envelope xmlns:soap=http://schemas.xmlsoap.org/soap/envelope/>
    <soap:Body>
        <getProductDetails xmlns=http://supplier.example.com/ws
            <productID>32879</productID>
        </getProductDetails>
    </soap:Body>
</soap:Envelope>
```

The supplier Web service could format its reply message, which contains the requested information about the product, in this way:

```
<soap:Envelope xmlns:soap=http://schemas.xmlsoap.org/soap/envelope/
   <soap:Body>
      <getProductDetailsResponse xmlns="suppliers.example.com/ws">
         <getProductDetailsResult>
            <productName>Dining Table</productName>
            <Finish>Natural Ash</Finish>
            <Price>800</Price>
            <inStock>True</inStock>
         </getProductDetailsResult>
      </getProductDetailsResponse>
   </soap:Body>
</soap:Envelope>
```

Figure 10-7 depicts the interaction of applications and systems with Web services. Note that as a transaction flows from one business to another or from a customer to a business, a SOAP processor creates the message envelope that allows the exchange of formatted XML data across the Web. Because SOAP messages connect remote sites, appropriate security measures must be implemented so that data integrity is maintained.

Web services, with their promise of automatic communication between businesses and customers, whether they are other businesses or individual retail customers, have generated much discussion and anticipation in the last few years. Two major issues must be resolved before the promise of Web services can be realized at an enterprise level for critical applications. Those issues are the development of accepted standards that enable the open communication desired between systems and the creation of strong security controls.

Lack of Mature Standards Progress has been made in addressing the need to develop Web services standards. SOAP and WSDL have been established as part of the core Web services standards. SOAP and WSDL specifications manage the movement of data between applications, but they do not standardize more sophisticated Web

Figure 10-7
Web services deployment (Adapted from Newcomer, 2002)

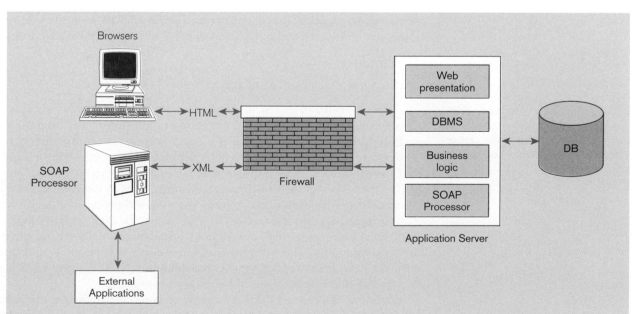

services, such as transaction verification. The UDDI Business Registry enables companies to announce the Web services they are using and to locate other companies with whom they can interface through common Web services.

Although it would be ideal to have Web services standards developed by a single group, four standardization bodies are active: OASIS, WS-I, W3C, and the Liberty Alliance. OASIS has moved to the forefront in the development of Web services standards since receiving the UDDI specifications and the UDDI Business Directory in 2002. Another OASIS contribution is the Security Assertion Markup Language (SAML), which is XML based and enables the exchange of authentication and authorization information. WS-I, the Web Services Interoperability Organization, is devoted to promoting Web services interoperability across platforms, operating systems, and programming languages. The W3C, with its focus on the development of the Web, provides a forum for the discussion of standards. The Liberty Alliance, a global consortium of vendors, businesses, and governmental units, released specifications in July 2002 that focuses on system interoperability and establishing opt-in account linking, session management, and simpler sign-on. The Alliance's work extends beyond establishing standard technical specifications. The Alliance also examines business issues associated with establishing wider trusted relationships, thus attempting to smooth the development of new services that require identity determination. Its work has been of particular interest to financial organizations, for which such standards are critical.

The need for more standardization so that Web services can flourish may be hampered by a lack of cooperation in developing more sophisticated standards. IBM and Microsoft have formed a joint initiative in an attempt to create industrywide standards, known as Business Process Execution Language for Web Services (BPEL4WS). Sun and Oracle, two other major companies with a strong interest in Web services, have not agreed to join in this joint initiative. However, before Web services can be developed to fully meet its expectations, security, connection, and enterprise standards must be developed further.

Lack of Security   Wider deployment of Web services is dependent on the continued development of Web services security standards. The promises of easier enterprise and supply-chain integration and Internet-based service distribution along with widespread vendor support and cooperation indicate that Web services will develop rapidly if businesses are confident that the security risks have been addressed.

The security risks to be considered are the same as those for Web traffic: authentication, authorization, and data encryption, discussed in Chapter 12. Yang (see **www.xwss.org/articlesThread.jsp?forum=34&thread=648** in the Web Resources section at the end of this chapter) has addressed these issues from a Web services perspective.

Service-Oriented Architecture (SOA)

Service-oriented architecture (SOA):
A collection of services that communicate with each other in some manner, usually by passing data or coordinating a business activity.

While **service-oriented architectures (SOA)** aren't new; they have received considerable attention recently because there are now some standard technologies, such as Web services, that make the approach easier to implement. Because Web services are now so often used in SOA approaches, you may get the false impression that implementing SQA requires the use of Web services. Rather, some previous SOAs were based on the CORBA specification. An SOA is a collection of services that communicate with each other in some manner, usually passing data or coordinating a business activity, but the services do not have to be Web services. SOAs differ from traditional object-oriented approaches in that the services are loosely coupled and very interoperable. The software components are very reusable and operate across different development platforms such as Java and .NET. The use of XML, SOAP, and WSDL ease the establishment of necessary connections.

Defining SOA as a collection of services is too restrictive, as the commitment to take an SOA approach should result in the establishment of a modeling, design, and software development process that supports the efficient development of applications. Organizations that have adopted such an approach have found their development time being reduced by at least 40 percent. Not only are the organizations experiencing shorter development time, they also hope to demonstrate more flexibility in responding to a rapidly changing business environment.

Semantic Web

There is a W3C project known as the **Semantic Web** project. The intent is to utilize metadata about the Web, automating the collection of the knowledge and structuring its storage in such a way that it may be understood relatively easily by both computers and people. The structuring is based on XML, Resource Description Framework (RDF) and Web Ontology Language (OWL). The RDF metadata model stores data in a subject-predicate-object format. The subject is the resource, or thing that is being described. The predicate is a trait or aspect of the resource. The object is the value of that trait. These three pieces can be stored in XML format, thus making it widely accessible. The resource or predicate in each RDF 'sentence' must be uniquely identifiable and is named by a Universal Resource Identifier (URI). URLs are one set of URIs that perform double duty; not only does a URL uniquely identify the resource, it also points to the resource's location on the Web. However, a resource does not have to be available on the Web, and therefore its URI does not have to be a URL. And it is possible that a resource may be described more than once within the Semantic Web. Realizing this lack of constraints is one of the interesting things about the Semantic Web project. When existing databases, including governmental ones, are recorded using RDF, the information becomes machine processable. Intelligent programs can then begin to fit the data together. Another W3C Working Group, the Web Ontology Working Group is working to further specify the meanings inherent in the RFD coding.

As the Semantic Web becomes more real and more complete, the uses that people will develop based on it will be diverse and exciting. Communication between your PDA, your laptop and even your car will be easier. Strategic decision making may be aided by previously unavailable automated analyses. Everyone will find it easier to find answers to their questions, and determining the trustworthiness of that answer will also be improved.

Semantic Web: A W3C project intended to automate Web metadata so that it may be utilized easily by both computers and people.

Internet Technology Rate-of-Change Issues

As you have seen in this chapter, changes in hardware, software, and telecommunication technologies are playing a major role in the way the Information Age is developing. Rarely over the last two decades have companies had opportunities to implement an information system and rely on it for an extended period. The rate and breadth of change have caught many companies off guard. As planning horizons shorten, competing in such a dynamic environment has been very challenging, and companies have had to reinvent themselves and attempt to equip their employees with the environment, experiences, and skills required to thrive in a transformed economy and culture.

Over the last two decades, the rate of change in information technology has accelerated. Throughout, implementing the conceptually simple and elegant vision of integrated but distributed systems has been elusive. The phrase "the devil is in the details" comes to mind. Information technology planning has moved from being an independent tactical activity to being central to organizations' strategic planning processes. Expectations of both employees and customers for relevant, easy-to-use systems have risen dramatically. Effective IT systems are now seen as a critical success factor in the marketplace. Database technology has been fundamental to meeting these expectations and supporting business strategy.

Progress toward creating a more integrated data management environment began when databases replaced flat files. Relational database technology made it possible to record an item of data in one place but use it in different applications. Object-oriented databases hold the promise of improving response time because objects do not have to be reconstituted when they are requested.

Now the long anticipated integration of computing and telecommunications is transforming the way people acquire and share information. Traditional technology boundaries are becoming blurred. Cell phones and personal digital assistants (PDAs) connect to the Internet. People answer their e-mail through their pagers, sometimes while sitting in meetings. Wi-Fi wireless networks allow properly equipped devices to access databases in public locations over radio waves that are easily intercepted. Television is delivered over airwaves, cables, and satellites. Integration of traditionally separate technologies has created new business opportunities and the need for new policies and laws to control public services such as airwaves and public networks. As new methods and locations for database access are established, database security issues come to the fore.

Concurrently, changes in organizational relationships also pressure database administrators to deal with new business forms. Models of competition have been supplemented by models of cooperation. As companies come together to work on a project, only to move apart when the project is completed, issues of shared database access never before raised must now be addressed.

Globalization of business is also increasing faster than ever before. Companies place work teams strategically around the world so that at least one team is always working. IT managers are assigned global management responsibilities, such as managing teams in upstate New York, Melbourne, and London. No longer is there available downtime for backing up and tuning databases; the database is expected to always be available.

In the face of this ever-increasing rate of change, database administrators must participate actively in accomplishing the alignment of organizational (IT) structure with business strategy. This requires an understanding of the business in addition to an understanding of the technology infrastructure and database architecture. Leadership skills, (including communication and listening skills), upward influence techniques, and employee management techniques must be highly developed. The successful IT manager can no longer depend on technical depth alone to navigate the rapid changes occurring in the business environment.

Summary

This chapter built an understanding of the fit of databases with Internet applications, covered various Internet database architectures and Web services, illustrated the use of PHP with Web-enabled databases, such as MySQL, and discussed management issues associated with these topics. Several characteristics of the Web environment have supported the rapid adoption and implementation of Internet and intranet business applications, including the simplicity and functional similarities of browser interfaces. The hardware and software independence of the browsers has eased the sharing of information across platforms. Development costs and time have been reduced.

The Internet environment is composed of a network that connects client workstations, Web servers, and database servers, following TCP/IP protocols. Every computer connected to the Internet must have a distinct IP address. In a simple architecture, a request from a client browser is sent through the network to the Web server. If the request requires that data be obtained from the database, the Web server constructs a query and sends it to the database server, which processes the query and returns the results. Firewalls are used to limit external access to the company's data.

Common components of Internet architecture are certain programming and markup languages, Web server middleware, including server-side extensions and Web services, Web servers, and client-side extensions. To aid understanding of connecting a database to a Web page, a simple sample of PHP and MySQL, along with its associated HTML, was included.

Some traditional database issues have taken on additional significance as databases have become more important to Internet applications. These issues include the increasingly rapid rate of change in both business and technology practices. The rate of change in information technology has accelerated, and all of us must struggle with keeping those changes strategically aligned with changes in business practices. Web services have gained prominence as they create more flexibility and ease Web-enabled development. Services Oriented Architecture (SOA) is a software development approach that frequently uses Web services.

Although in some respects databases have matured, their fundamental importance to the development of the Internet and electronic commerce have kept them at the forefront of technological change. This chapter has presented basic concepts of Web-enabled databases; the informed reader must turn to current outside reading to be completely abreast of recent opportunities in this area.

CHAPTER REVIEW

Key Terms

ActiveX
Application Program
   Interface (API)
Common Gateway
   Interface (CGI)
Cookie
DNS (domain name
   server) balancing
Document Structure
   Description (DSD)
Java servlet
Plug-ins
RELAX NG

Reverse proxy
Semantic Web
Server-side extension
Service-Oriented
   Architecture (SOA)
Simple Object Access
   Protocol (SOAP)
Software and hardware
   load balancing
Universal Description,
   Discovery and
   Integration (UDDI)
Web services

Web Services Description
   Language (WSDL)
World Wide Web
   Consortium (W3C)
XHTML
XML Schema
XSL
XSLT

Review Questions

1. Define each of the following key terms:
   a. XML Schema
   b. cookie
   c. DNS balancing
   d. electronic business
   e. API
   f. server-side extension
   g. Web services
   h. XSL
   i. SOAP

2. Match the following terms and definitions:

   _____ CGI
   _____ DSD
   _____ SOA
   _____ XHTML
   _____ servlet
   _____ reverse proxy
   _____ Semantic Web
   _____ W3C

   a. load-balancing approach for multiple Web servers
   b. World Wide Web Consortium
   c. Language used for defining XML databases
   d. A W3C project intended to automate Web metadata
   e. small program that executes from within another application and is stored on a server
   f. A Web server interface that specifies the transfer of information
   g. A collection of services that communicate with each other in some manner
   h. scripting language that extends HTML to make it XML compliant

3. Contrast the following terms:
   a. CGI; API
   b. Internet; intranet; extranet
   c. HTML; XML; XHTML
   d. DNS balancing; software and hardware load balancing; reverse proxy
   e. HTML; XML
   f. Web services; SOA

4. Explain why attaching a database to a Web page is important in the facilitation of e-business.

5. What environmental components are needed to establish Internet database-enabled connectivity?

6. Explain the purpose and accomplishments of the World Wide Web Consortium.

7. To what does the term Web services refer? Describe the potential benefits to widespread deployment of Web services of various types and the issues currently associated with that deployment.

8. What is the purpose of database middleware, such as ColdFusion and ASP.NET?

9. Compare and contrast Web server interfaces, including CGI, API, and Java servlets.

10. Describe three methods for balancing Web server loads.

11. Explain what a cookie is (as used in Internet terminology) and how it can be used.

12. What components is a PHP program that enables a dynamic Web site going to contain?

13. Explain why an XML Schema is a step forward from using Document Type Declarations (DTDs).

14. What is a plug-in? Provide an example of one that you have used.

15. Describe ActiveX controls.

16. Discuss some concerns that businesses have about adopting a Web-services approach.

17. Discuss UDDI. Compare and contrast it with the white, yellow, and green pages of the telephone book (if your telephone book does not have green pages, you will need to research this feature found in some telephone books).

18. Discuss why the development of Web services standards is being hampered. What standardization bodies currently exist?

Problems and Exercises

1. Explain the difference between a static Web site and a dynamic one. What are the characteristics of a dynamic Web site that enable it to better support the development of e-business?

2. Discuss some of the languages that are associated with Internet application development. Classify these languages according to the functionality they provide for each application. It is not necessary that you use the same classification scheme used in the chapter.

3. Discuss how Web services can be used to effectively integrate business applications and data. Search the Web for resources on current Web services that employ XML, SOAP, UDDI, and WSDL. Find at least three, and discuss how each is used, including examples from industry.

4. The chapter demonstrates using PHP and MySQL and Apache Web Server to create a dynamic Web site. Suggest two other combinations of products, not necessarily open source products, that could also be used.

5. Find some dynamic Web site code such as that included in Figure 10-3. Annotate the code, as is done in Figure 10-3, to explain each section, especially those elements that involve interaction with the database. (Hint: Googling on "PHP MySQL Examples" will give you a rich set of opportunities to explore to find sample code.)

6. Write PHP code, similar to that found in Figure 10-3, that accepts the e-mail address as input, queries the database with that e-mail address value, and returns for display the associated username.

Field Exercises

1. Consider your own personal computer. Determine the plug-ins you have downloaded and the purpose of each. Are any of these plug-ins related to manipulating or presenting data that is being returned from a database?

2. Find where cookies have been saved on your personal computer. Review them and organize them by category. Describe your decision process if you decide to delete any of the cookies. Were you surprised by the number of cookies stored on your machine? Have you protected your computer from spyware?

3. Determine what you would have to do to use ColdFusion or ASP.NET on a public Web site owned either by yourself or by the organization for which you work.

4. Outline the steps you would take to conduct a risk assessment for your place of employment with regard to attaching a database to the public site. If possible, help with the actual implementation of the risk assessment.

5. According to your own personal interests, use PHP and MySQL to attach a database to your personal Web site. Test it locally and then move it to your public site.

References

Henschen, D. 2005. "XBRL Offers a Faster Route to Intelligence." *Intelligent Enterprise 8, 8* (August): 12.

Newcomer, E. 2002. *Understanding Web Services, XML, WSDL, SOAP, and UDDI.* Boston: Addison-Wesley.

Ullman, L. 2003. *PHP and MySQL for Dynamic Web Sites.* Berkeley, CA: Peachpit Press.

Further Reading

Cerami, E. 2002. *Web Services Essentials.* Sebastopol, CA: O'Reilly & Associates, Inc.

Irwin, M. F., and C. N. Prague. 2002. *Microsoft Access 2002 Bible*, Gold Edition. New York: Wiley.

Morrison, M., and J. Morrison. 2003. *Database-Driven Web Sites*, 2nd ed. Cambridge, MA: Thomson-Course Technologies.

Morrison, M. 2001. *HTML & XML for Beginners*. Redmond, WA: Microsoft Press.

Web Resources

hoohoo.ncsa.uiuc.edu/cgi/ Information about and the complete CGI specification from NCSA.

www.w3.org/CGI/ W3C's homepage for CGI.

www.w3.org/MarkUp/ W3C's homepage for HTML and XHTML.

www.w3.org/XML/1999/XML-in-10-points W3C article "XML in 10 points" presents basic XML concepts.

www.netcraft.com/survey The Netcraft Web Server Survey tracks the market share of different Web servers and SSL site operating systems.

www.projectliberty.org The homepage of the Liberty Alliance. Open standards specifications and drafts of specifications may be downloaded here.

www.ws-i.org Homepage of the Web Services Interoperability Organization (WS-I).

www.oasis-open.org/home/index.php Homepage of the Organization for the Advancement of Structured Information Standards (OASIS).

xml.apache.org/cocoon/ The Cocoon project is a Java Web publishing framework that separates document content, style, and logic, allowing the independent design, creation, and management of each.

www.vbxml.com/xsl/tutorials/intro/default.asp Tutorial about XSLT, which allows the transformation of an XML file into an HTML file or other text-based format.

www.oracle.com/oramag/oracle/02-mar/index.html?o22industry.html "A Light, Clean Protocol" from Oracle Magazine. Offers information about SOAP.

www.gotdotnet.com/Community/UserSamples/ Try some applications built using Microsoft's .NET technology.

Case

Mountain View Community Hospital's planning committee believes the adoption of Web-based solutions may greatly improve the hospital's operations, extend customer service and marketing functions, speed up and improve the quality of patient care, and allow physicians to be more responsive to their patients. The committee specifically sees Web services as a way of addressing many of the hospital's challenges.

For one thing, given the widespread access to the Internet these days, patients are increasingly demanding online capabilities, such as making appointments, booking surgeries, making payments, and so on. In response, hospitals have begun to implement patient portals that can even provide patients with access to their medical records. Another issue at MVCH is the heterogeneous environment of platforms and applications. As stated in previous chapters, Mountain View Community Hospital has applications and software from many different vendors. Consequently, the IT department has been struggling to interface the many different systems, and exchange patient data between the clinical systems and software that is not health-care specific such as reporting and billing applications. Mr. Heller, MVCH's CIO, believes that Web services would provide an efficient means of making the diverse systems work together.

Such a solution would also be beneficial for the medical staff. Currently, physicians have to log on to multiple applications to retrieve diagnostic information such as radiology reports and digital images, access the latest medical literature regarding a patient condition, or read e-mail. Some doctors have also expressed an interest in accessing clinical systems remotely while working outside of the hospital. A physician's portal accessed from a standard Web browser could provide faster access to information regardless of location, and doctors could open and navigate multiple applications to extract information. Web services could even push relevant new information regarding a patient's condition. At a recent conference for healthcare CIOs, Mr. Heller also learned from presentations and conversations with peers that Web services could be rolled out in a relatively short time frame, 3 to 6 months potentially.

In considering where Web services and other Web-based solutions could be developed for Mountain View's health care systems, several issues have been raised.

- First, privacy and security concerns are of primary importance. Patient health information requires high levels of confidentiality because it is so sensitive by nature, and because of HIPAA's privacy and security mandates.

- Data entry questions are also significant. Doctors, nurses, and other health care workers must be able and willing to enter the data into any system that is provided.

- Given that Web services are built on a foundation of HTTP, system availability and reliability would be crucial if a decision is made to implement a Web-enabled system, particularly for key business processes.

- How easy or difficult would it be to integrate a browser-based system with existing or planned systems?

- Would Mountain View Community Hospital have the funding and staffing resources to go forward with a Web services project? Would it be necessary to hire an external service provider? Could it be done in-house with existing IT staff?

- How would Mountain View demonstrate that the proposed system is cost-effective?

- How will Mountain View predict and handle changes in work patterns that may occur?

- What organizational policies and procedures will need to be changed or modified as system changes are implemented?

CASE QUESTIONS

1. Discuss the extent and nature of security and privacy issues that the planning committee should consider when evaluating any decisions to provide more information that is critical to patients over the Web.

2. Apart from Web services, which other Web-based solutions might the hospital consider?

3. Discuss data entry issues that the planning committee should consider. Be sure to consider data entry by physicians, nurses, and other health care workers and propose possible approaches to address the issues you have raised.

4. The healthcare industry has not embraced Web services as quickly as other industries for integrating diverse systems. Why do you think that's the case? What would be critical success factors for making Web services solutions a success at Mountain View Community Hospital and others?

5. Should Mountain View Community Hospital treat the potential implementation of Web-based solutions and Web services as a technology or a strategy issue? Please explain.

CASE EXERCISES

1. Health care professionals want to engage patients more actively in their own health care. Locate at least five hospital and other health care Web sites that individuals can access. Compare and contrast the information and/or services that are available through each site. Suggest possible services that Mountain View could consider for their Web site that would involve patients more actively in their own health care.

2. The case description provided a brief overview of some of the possibilities of Web services, particularly within the hospital. Should the hospital utilize Web services to provide data exchange with external entities? Which ones? Do some research and describe in greater detail how a hospital, such as Mountain View, could utilize Web services.

3. Using the information you collected for Case Exercise 3, suggest how Mr. Heller could make a business case for Web services and demonstrate that it is cost-effective.

4. The Mountain View planning committee is considering several business functions to be accessed online via the Web: (1) submitting insurance claims online, (2) providing clinical information to patients online, (3) implementing supply chain management online, (4) providing medical records to other facilities, and (5) implementing an online medical knowledgebase. Which of these five possibilities do you recommend implementing first? Why? In your answer, address the following issues for each option being considered:

a. Security and confidentiality concerns: Who would need to access the data? How would access be restricted? How likely is the proposed security system to be compromised?

b. Data entry requirements: Which job functions would enter data? How much resistance is expected from each function, and how is this resistance to be handled?

c. The benefits that Mountain View could expect and the expected costs.

5. The following exercises use the Mountain View Community Hospital files for this textbook, which your instructor can provide.

a. Provide the PATIENT data as an XML file.

b. Provide a query related to the PATIENT table as an XML file.

c. Generate a report, and using MS Access XML capabilities (e.g., ReportML and an XSLT file), transform the report so that it can be displayed inside the browser view to look like the report in Access' Print Preview.

PROJECT ASSIGNMENTS

P1. Web-enable the MVCH database you developed earlier and develop one or more functionalities such as:

- Online patient registration (e.g., for ambulatory surgery, for Dr. "Z" MS Center, etc.)
- Online volunteer application
- Login for employees or physicians with a username and password

P2. Using the MVCH database you created earlier, identify one or two tables and provide the data as an XML file.

P3. Using the MVCH database you created earlier, identify one or two queries and return the data as an XML stream.

Chapter **11**

Data Warehousing

LEARNING OBJECTIVES

After studying this chapter, you should be able to:

- Concisely define each of the following key terms: **data warehouse, operational system, informational system, data mart, independent data mart, dependent data mart, enterprise data warehouse (EDW), operational data store (ODS), logical data mart, real-time data warehouse, reconciled data, derived data, event, transient data, periodic data, static extract, incremental extract, data scrubbing, refresh mode, update mode, data transformation, selection, joining, aggregation, star schema, grain, market basket analysis, conformed dimension, snowflake schema, OLAP, ROLAP, MOLAP, data mining,** and **data visualization.**
- Give two important reasons why an "information gap" often exists between the information manager's need and the information generally available.
- List two major reasons why most organizations today need data warehousing.
- Name and briefly describe the three levels in a data warehouse architecture.
- List the four main steps of data reconciliation.
- Describe the two major components of a star schema.
- Estimate the number of rows and total size in bytes of a fact table, given reasonable assumptions concerning the database dimensions.
- Design a data mart using various schemes to normalize and denormalize dimensions and to account for fact history and changing dimension attribute values.

INTRODUCTION

Everyone agrees that readily available high-quality information is vital in business today. Consider the following actual critical situation:

In September, 2004, Hurricane Frances was heading for the Florida Atlantic coast. Fourteen hundred miles away in Bentonville, Arkansas, Wal-Mart executives were getting ready. By analyzing 460 terabytes of data in their data warehouse, focusing on sales data from several weeks earlier when Hurricane Charley hit the Florida Gulf coast, the executives were able to predict what products people in Miami would want to buy. Sure, they needed flashlights, but Wal-Mart also discovered that people also bought strawberry Pop-Tarts and, yes, beer. Wal-Mart was able to stock their stores with plenty of the in-demand items, providing what people wanted and avoiding stockouts, thus gaining what would otherwise have been lost revenue. Beyond special circumstances like hurricanes, by studying a market basket of what individuals buy, Wal-Mart can set prices to attract customer who want to buy "loss leader" items because they will also likely put several higher-margin products in the same shopping cart. Detailed sales data also helps Wal-Mart determine how many cashiers are needed at different hours in different stores given the time of year, holidays, weather, pricing, and many other factors. Wal-Mart's data warehouse contains not only general sales data, sufficient to answer the questions for Hurricane Frances, but also they are able to match sales with many individual customer demographics when people use their credit and debit cards to pay for merchandise. At their Sam's Club chain, membership cards provide the same personal identification. With this identifying data, Wal-Mart can associate product sales with location, income, home prices, and other personal demographics. The data warehouse facilitates targeting marketing of the most appropriate products to individuals. Further, they use sales data to improve their supply chain by negotiating better terms with suppliers for delivery, price, and promotions. All of this is possible through an integrated, comprehensive, enterprise-wide data warehouse with significant analytical tools to make sense out of this mountain of data (adapted from Hays, *New York Times*, November 14, 2004).

In light of this strong emphasis on information and the recent advances in information technology, you might expect most organizations to have highly developed systems for delivering information to managers and other users. Yet this is often not the case. In fact, despite having mountains of data, and often many databases, few organizations have more than a fraction of the information they need. Managers are often frustrated by their inability to access or use the data and information they need.

Modern organizations are said to be drowning in data but starving for information. Despite the mixed metaphor, this statement seems to portray quite accurately the situation in many organizations. What is the reason for this state of affairs? Let's examine two important (and related) reasons why an information gap has been created in most organizations.

The first reason for the information gap is the fragmented way in which organizations have developed information systems—and their supporting databases—for many years. The emphasis in this text is on a carefully planned, architectural approach to systems development that should produce an integrated set of databases. However, in reality, constraints on time and resources cause most organizations to resort to a "one-thing-at-a-time" approach to developing islands of information systems. This approach inevitably produces a hodgepodge of uncoordinated and often inconsistent databases. Usually databases are based on a variety of hardware and software platforms. In this environment, it is extremely difficult, if not impossible, for managers to locate and use accurate information, which must be synthesized across these various systems of record.

The second reason for the information gap is that most systems are developed to support operational processing, with little or no thought given to the information or analytical tools needed for decision making. *Operational processing*, also called transaction processing, captures, stores, and manipulates data to support daily operations of the organization. It tends to focus database design on optimizing access to a small set of data related to a transaction. *Informational processing* is the analysis of data or other forms of information to support decision making. It needs large "swatches" of data from which to derive information. Most systems that are developed internally or purchased from outside vendors are designed to support operational processing, with little thought given to informational processing.

Bridging the information gap are *data warehouses* that consolidate and integrate information from many internal and external sources and arrange it in a meaningful format for making accurate and timely business decisions. They support executives, managers, and business analysts in making complex business decisions through applications such as the analysis of trends, target marketing, competitive analysis, customer relationship management, and so on. Data warehousing has evolved to meet these needs without disturbing existing operational processing.

The proliferation of Web-based customer interactions has made the situation much more interesting and more real-time. The activities of customers and suppliers on an organization's Web site provide a wealth of new clickstream data to help understand behaviors and preferences and create a unique opportunity to communicate the right message (e.g., product cross-sales message). Extensive details, such as time, IP address, pages visited, context from where the page request was made, links taken, elapsed time on page, and so forth, can be captured unobtrusively. These data, along with customer transaction, payment, product return, inquiry, and other history consolidated into the data warehouse from a variety of transaction systems, can be used to personalize pages. Such reasoned and active interactions can lead to satisfied customers and business partners and more profitable business relationships.

This chapter provides an overview of data warehousing. This exceptionally broad topic normally requires an entire text. In fact, most texts on the topic are devoted to just a single aspect, such as data warehouse design or administration. We focus on the two areas relevant to a text on database management: data architecture and database design. You will learn first how the data warehouse relates to existing operational systems. Described next is the three-tier data architecture, which is most appropriate for most data warehouse environments. Then we address the problem of extracting data from existing operational systems and loading them into a data warehouse. Next we show special database design elements frequently used in data warehousing. Finally, you will see how users interact with the data warehouse including online analytical processing, data mining, and data visualization.

BASIC CONCEPTS OF DATA WAREHOUSING

Data warehouse: A subject-oriented, integrated, time-variant, nonupdatable collection of data used in support of management decision-making processes.

A **data warehouse** is a subject-oriented, integrated, time-variant, nonupdatable collection of data used in support of management decision-making processes and business intelligence (Inmon and Hackathorn, 1994). The meaning of each of the key terms in this definition follows:

- *Subject-oriented* A data warehouse is organized around the key subjects (or high-level entities) of the enterprise. Major subjects may include customers, patients, students, products, and time.

- *Integrated* The data housed in the data warehouse are defined using consistent naming conventions, formats, encoding structures, and related characteristics gathered from several internal systems of record and also often from sources external to the organization. This means that the data warehouse holds the one version of "the truth."

- *Time-variant* Data in the data warehouse contain a time dimension so that they may be used to study trends and changes.

- *Nonupdatable* Data in the data warehouse are loaded and refreshed from operational systems, but cannot be updated by end users.

A data warehouse is not just a consolidation of all the operational databases in an organization. Because of its focus on business intelligence, external data, and time-variant data (not just current status), a data warehouse is a unique kind of database.

Data warehousing is the process whereby organizations create and maintain data warehouses and extract meaning and inform decision making from their informational assets through these data warehouses. Since its beginnings about 18 years ago, data warehousing has evolved so rapidly that data warehousing is now one of the hottest topics in information systems. Studies repeatedly show that over 90 percent of larger companies either have a data warehouse or are starting one. A

1996 study of 62 data warehousing projects showed an average return on investment of 321 percent, with an average payback period of 2.73 years. Studies have also shown that approximately 40 percent of data warehousing projects fail, primarily due to insufficient attention to organizational issues of data ownership and definition within an organization (Whiting, 2003). Thus, successful data warehousing requires following proven data warehousing practices, sound project management, strong organizational commitment, as well as making the right technology decisions.

A Brief History

Data warehousing emerged as a result of advances in the field of information systems over several decades. Some key advances were the following:

- Improvements in database technology, particularly the development of the relational data model and relational database management systems (RDBMSs)
- Advances in computer hardware, particularly the emergence of affordable mass storage and parallel computer architectures
- The emergence of end-user computing, facilitated by powerful, intuitive computer interfaces and tools
- Advances in middleware products that enable enterprise database connectivity across heterogeneous platforms (Hackathorn, 1993)

The key discovery that triggered the development of data warehousing was the recognition (and subsequent definition) of the fundamental differences between operational (or transaction processing) systems (sometimes called systems of record because their role is to keep the official, legal record of the organization) and informational (or decision-support) systems. In 1988, Devlin and Murphy (1988) published the first article describing the architecture of a data warehouse, based on this distinction. In 1992, Inmon published the first book describing data warehousing and has subsequently become one of the most prolific authors in this field.

The Need for Data Warehousing

Two major factors drive the need for data warehousing in most organizations today:

1. A business requires an integrated, companywide view of high-quality information.
2. The information systems department must separate informational from operational systems to improve performance dramatically in managing company data.

Need for a Companywide View   Data in operational systems are typically fragmented and inconsistent. They are also generally distributed on a variety of incompatible hardware and software platforms. For example, one file containing customer data may be located on a UNIX-based server running an Oracle DBMS, whereas another is located on an IBM mainframe running the DB2 DBMS. Yet, for decision-making purposes, it is often necessary to provide a single, corporate view of that information.

To understand the difficulty of deriving a single corporate view, look at the simple example shown in Figure 11-1. This figure shows three tables from three separate systems of record, each containing some student data. There is a STUDENT_DATA table from the class registration system, a STUDENT_EMPLOYEE table from the personnel system, and a STUDENT_HEALTH table from a health center system. Each table contains some unique data concerning students, but even common data (such as student names) are stored using different formats.

Figure 11-1
Examples of heterogeneous data

STUDENT_DATA

Student_No	Last_Name	MI	First_Name	Telephone	Status	• • •
123-45-6789	Enright	T	Mark	483-1967	Soph	
389-21-4062	Smith	R	Elaine	283-4195	Jr	

STUDENT_EMPLOYEE

Student_ID	Address	Dept	Hours	• • •
123-45-6789	1218 Elk Drive, Phoenix, AZ 91304	Soc	8	
389-21-4062	134 Mesa Road, Tempe, AZ 90142	Math	10	

STUDENT_HEALTH

Student_Name	Telephone	Insurance	ID	• • •
Mark T. Enright	483-1967	Blue Cross	123-45-6789	
Elaine R. Smith	555-7828	?	389-21-4062	

Suppose you want to develop a profile for each student, consolidating all data into a single file format. Some of the issues that you must resolve are as follows:

- *Inconsistent key structures* The primary key of the first two tables is some version of the student Social Security number, whereas the primary key of STUDENT_HEALTH is Student_Name.

- *Synonyms* In STUDENT_DATA, the primary key is named Student_No, whereas in STUDENT_EMPLOYEE it is named Student_ID (we discussed how to deal with synonyms in Chapter 5).

- *Free-form fields versus structured fields* In STUDENT_HEALTH, Student_Name is a single field. In STUDENT_DATA, Student_Name (a composite attribute) is broken into its component parts: Last_Name, MI, and First_Name.

- *Inconsistent data values* Elaine Smith has one telephone number in STUDENT_DATA, but a different number in STUDENT_HEALTH. Is this an error, or does this person have two telephone numbers?

- *Missing data* The value for Insurance is missing (or null) for Elaine Smith in the STUDENT_HEALTH table. How will this value be located?

This simple example illustrates the nature of the problem of developing a single corporate view but fails to capture the complexity of that task. A real-life scenario would likely have dozens (if not hundreds) of files and thousands (or millions!) of records.

Why do organizations need to bring data together from various systems of record? Ultimately, of course, the reason is to be more profitable, to be more competitive, or to grow by adding value for customers. This can be accomplished by increasing the speed and flexibility of decision making, improving business processes, or gaining a clearer understanding of customer behavior. For the previous student example, university administrators may want to investigate if the health or number of hours students work on campus is related to student academic performance, if taking certain courses is related to the health of students, or whether poor academic performers cost more to support, for example, due to increased health care as well as other costs. In general, certain trends in organizations encourage the need for data warehousing; these trends include the following:

- *No single system of record*   Almost no organization has one database. Seems odd, doesn't it? Remember our discussion in Chapter 1 about the reasons for a database compared to separate file-processing systems? Because of the heterogeneous needs for data in different operational settings, because of corporate mergers and acquisitions, and due to the sheer size of many organizations, multiple operational databases exist.

- *Multiple systems are not synchronized*   It is difficult, if not impossible, to make separate databases consistent. Even if the metadata are controlled and made the same by one data administrator (see Chapter 12), the data values for the same attributes will not agree. This is because of different update cycles and separate places where the same data are captured for each system. Thus, to get one view of the organization, the data from the separate systems must be periodically consolidated and synchronized into one additional database. We will see that there can be actually two such consolidated databases—one called an operational data store and the other called an enterprise data warehouse, both of which we include under the topic of data warehousing.

- *Organizations want to analyze the activities in a balanced way*   Many organizations have implemented some form of a balanced scorecard—metrics that show organization results in financial, human, customer satisfaction, product quality, and other terms simultaneously. To ensure that this multidimensional view of the organization shows consistent results, a data warehouse is necessary. When questions arise in the balanced scorecard, analytical software working with the data warehouse can be used to "drill down," "slice and dice," visualize, and in other ways mine business intelligence.

- *Customer relationship management*   Organizations in all sectors are realizing that there is value in having a total picture of their interactions with customers across all touch points. Different touch points (e.g., for a bank, these touch points include ATM, online banking, teller, electronic funds transfers, investment portfolio management, and loans) are supported by separate operational systems. Thus, without a data warehouse, a teller may not know to try to cross-sell a customer one of the bank's mutual funds if a large, atypical automatic deposit transaction appears on the teller's screen. A total picture of the activity with a given customer requires a consolidation of data from various operational systems.

- *Supplier relationship management*   Managing the supply chain has also become a critical element in reducing costs and raising product quality for many organizations. Organizations want to create strategic supplier partnerships based on a total picture of their activities with suppliers, from billing, to meeting delivery dates, to quality control, to pricing, to support. Data about these different activities can be locked inside separate operational systems (e.g., accounts payable, shipping and receiving, production scheduling, and maintenance). ERP systems have improved this situation by bringing many of these data into one database. However, ERP systems tend to be designed to optimize operational, not informational or analytical, processing, which we discuss next.

Operational system: A system that is used to run a business in real time, based on current data. Also called system of record.

Need to Separate Operational and Informational Systems   An **operational system** is a system that is used to run a business in real time, based on current data. Examples of operational systems are sales order processing, reservation systems, and patient registration. Operational systems must process large volumes of relatively simple read/write transactions, while providing fast response. Operational systems are also called *systems of record*.

Informational systems: Systems designed to support decision making based on historical point-in-time and prediction data for complex queries or data mining applications.

Informational systems are designed to support decision making based on historical point-in-time and prediction data. They are also designed for complex queries or data mining applications. Examples of informational systems are sales trend analysis, customer segmentation, and human resources planning.

The key differences between operational and informational systems are shown in Table 11-1. These two types of processing have very different characteristics in nearly every category of comparison. In particular, notice that they have quite different communities of users. Operational systems are used by clerks, administrators, salespersons, and others who must process business transactions. Informational systems are used by managers, executives, business analysts, and (increasingly) by customers who are searching for status information or who are decision makers.

The need to separate operational and informational systems is based on three primary factors:

1. A data warehouse centralizes data that are scattered throughout disparate operational systems and makes them readily available for decision support applications.

2. A properly designed data warehouse adds value to data by improving their quality and consistency.

3. A separate data warehouse eliminates much of the contention for resources that results when informational applications are confounded with operational processing.

Data Warehousing Success   "Build it and they will come" might work in classic baseball movies. Data warehousing success, however, is not guaranteed. Data warehousing projects still fail about 40 percent of the time (Whiting, 2003). Data warehousing is

Table 11-1 Comparison of Operational and Informational Systems

Characteristic	Operational Systems	Informational Systems
Primary purpose	Run the business on a current basis	Support managerial decision making
Type of data	Current representation of state of the business	Historical point-in-time (snapshots) and predictions
Primary users	Clerks, salespersons, administrators	Managers, business analysts, customers
Scope of usage	Narrow, planned, and simple updates and queries	Broad, ad hoc, complex queries and analysis
Design goal	Performance: throughput, availability	Ease of flexible access and use
Volume	Many, constant updates and queries on one or a few table rows	Periodic batch updates and queries requiring many or all rows

complex, involving cooperation across the organization. For example, when errors are discovered in data being loaded into the warehouse, the right place to fix the errors is in the source systems so erroneous data are not loaded again later. But, the errors may be acceptable in the source system or not even considered errors by the business unit for the source system.

Several professional organizations sponsor annual award programs to highlight the best data warehousing practices. One of the most prestigious is the Data Warehousing Institute Awards. The winners for 2003 illustrate many of the reasons success is becoming more common (Whiting, 2003). The following summarizes some of the 2003 award winners:

- *Continental Airlines—Best Enterprise Data Warehouse*   The Continental data warehouse has a real-time architecture and automated data transformations. This *simplifies consolidating data from different source systems.* A cross-business-unit steering committee develops *standard data definitions (metadata).* Uses of and changes to the warehouse must be *justified by revenue and profitability projections.*

- *Bank of America—Data Warehouse Integration*   Separate well-established data warehouses had to be integrated when NationsBank and Bank of America merged in 1998. Links between the existing data warehouses created significant *performance issues* and encouraged departments to create separate work-arounds, with *independent systems (called data marts)* negating the value of the data warehouse. Top leadership designated the *data warehouse consolidation as high priority, appropriate resources were allocated, and extensive user requirements planning was completed.*

- *International Truck—Business-Performance Management*   The data warehouse is the basis for the Key Business Indicators system, which is an information portal for the top 450 executives, managers, analysts, and other knowledge workers to view key performance measures. There are *many business values* that result from the use of the system, including a 10 to 12 percent speedier monthly closing process and lower operating costs, which results in a competitive advantage.

- *Toyota Motor Sales USA—Metadata Management*   A metadata repository improves the performance of Toyota's data warehouse by helping IT workers and business users *access the meaning of warehouse data,* and hence the meaning of information in reports generated from the warehouse. It also makes it easier to *identify the impact of changes to data specifications.*

- *Iowa Department of Revenue—Government or Nonprofit Organization*   The department managers felt that there were many companies and individuals who did not file tax returns or who under-reported earnings. The data to uncover such problems were buried in many different mainframe applications, file extracts, and twenty disparate systems. The data warehouse was *funded from business improvements* from the additional $10 million per year in tax revenue that it now generates.

Based on these award winners, success is more likely when there is high-level support, adequate resources are committed, real business value is apparent, well-managed metadata exist, the organization has an enterprise vision, and changes are anticipated and well managed. Technology is important, and high-performance technologies enable successful data warehousing. But the more organization-related factors outlined here are more important than technical factors. As one data warehousing executive from a consumer products company told the authors, "The technology is easy, it's the organizational issues that are tough." Thus, the tone of the rest of the chapter is to make sound database management decisions for the data warehouse within an organizational context.

DATA WAREHOUSE ARCHITECTURES

The basic architectures used most often with data warehouses are first, a generic two-level physical architecture for entry-level data warehouses; second, an expanded three-level architecture that is increasingly used in more complex environments; and finally, the three-level data architecture that is associated with a three-level physical architecture.

Generic Two-Level Architecture

A generic architecture for a data warehouse is shown in Figure 11-2. The two levels of this architecture are the source data systems and the consolidated data and metadata storage area. Building this architecture requires four basic steps (moving left to right in Figure 11-2):

1. Data are extracted from the various internal and external source system files and databases. In a large organization, there may be dozens or even hundreds of such files and databases.

2. The data from the various source systems are transformed and integrated before being loaded into the data warehouse. Transactions may be sent to the source systems to correct errors discovered in data staging.

3. The data warehouse is a database organized for decision support. It contains both detailed and summary data.

4. Users access the data warehouse by means of a variety of query languages and analytical tools. Results (e.g., predictions, forecasts) may be fed back to data warehouse and operational databases.

We will discuss in more detail in subsequent sections the important processes of extracting, transforming, and loading (ETL) data from the source systems into the data warehouse. We also overview in a subsequent section various end-user presentation tools.

Figure 11-2
Generic two-level data warehousing architecture

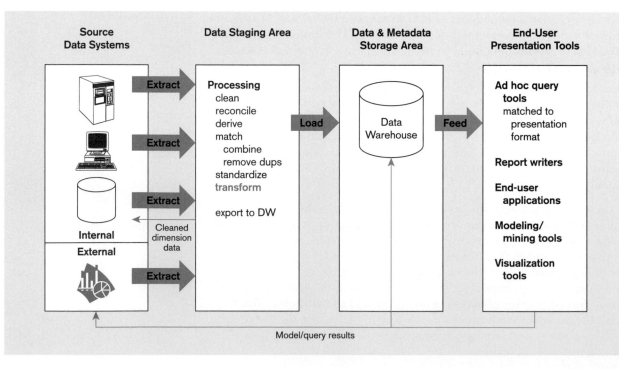

Extraction and loading happens on a periodic basis, sometimes daily, weekly, or monthly. Thus, the data warehouse often does not have, nor does it need to have, current data. Remember, the data warehouse is not (directly) supporting operational transaction processing, although it may contain transactional data (but more often summaries of transactions and snapshots of status variables such as account balances and inventory levels). For most data warehousing applications, users are not looking for a reaction to an individual transaction, but rather for trends and patterns in the state of the organization across a large subset of the data warehouse. At a minimum, five fiscal quarters of data are kept in a data warehouse so that at least annual trends and patterns can be discerned. Older data may be purged or archived. We will see later that one advanced data warehousing architecture, real-time data warehousing, is based on a different assumption about the need for current data.

Independent Data Mart Data Warehousing Environment

Contrary to many of the principles discussed so far in this chapter, some organizations do not create one data warehouse. Instead, they create many separate data marts, each based on data warehousing, not transactional processing, database technologies. A **data mart** is a data warehouse that is limited in scope, customized for the decision-making applications of a particular end-user group. Its contents are obtained either from independent ETL processes, as shown in Figure 11-3 for an **independent data mart**, or are derived from the data warehouse, which we will discuss in the next two sections. A data mart is designed to optimize the performance for well-defined and predicable uses, sometimes as few as a single or a couple of queries. For example, an organization may have a marketing data mart, a finance data mart, a supply chain data mart, and so on, to support known analytical processing.

We will provide a comparison of the various data warehousing architectures later, but you can see one obvious characteristic of the independent data mart strategy—the complexity for end users when they need to access data in separate data marts (evidenced by the crisscrossed lines connecting all the data marts to the end-user presentation tools). This complexity comes not only from having to access data from separate data mart databases, but also from possibly a new generation of inconsistent data systems—the data marts. If there is one set of metadata across all the data marts, and if data are made consistent across the data marts through the activities in the data staging area (e.g., by what is called "conform dimensions" in the data staging area box in Figure 11-3), then the complexity for users is reduced. Not so obvious in Figure 11-3 is the complexity for the ETL processes, because separate transformation and loads need to be built for each independent data mart.

Independent data marts are often created because an organization focuses on a series of short-term, expedient business objectives. The limited short-term objectives can be more compatible with the comparably lower cost (money and organizational capital) to implement yet one more independent data mart. However, designing the data warehousing environment around different sets of short-term objectives means that you lose flexibility for the long term and the ability to react to changing business conditions. And being able to react to change is critical for decision support. It can be organizationally and politically easier to have separate, small data warehouses than to get all organizational parties to agree to one view of the organization in a central data warehouse. Also, some data warehousing technologies have technical limitations for the size of the data warehouse they can support—what we will call later a scalability issue. Thus, technology, rather than the business, may dictate a data warehousing architecture if you first lock yourself into a particular data warehousing set of technologies before you understand your data

Data mart: A data warehouse that is limited in scope, whose data are obtained by selecting and summarizing data from a data warehouse or from separate extract, transform, and load processes from source data systems.

Independent data mart: A data mart filled with data extracted from the operational environment, without benefit of a data warehouse.

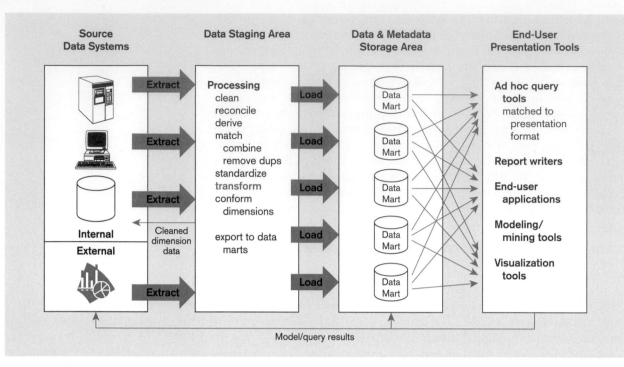

Figure 11-3
Independent data mart data
warehousing architecture

warehousing requirements. We discuss the pros and cons of the independent data mart architecture compared with its prime competing architecture in the next section.

Dependent Data Mart and Operational Data Store Architecture: A Three-Level Approach

The independent data mart architecture in Figure 11-3 has several important limitations (Meyer, 1997; Marco, 2003), including:

1. A separate ETL processes is developed for each data mart, which can yield costly redundant data and processing efforts.

2. Data marts may not be consistent with one another, because they are often developed with different technologies, and thus may not provide a clear enterprisewide view of data concerning important subjects such as customers, suppliers, and products.

3. There is no capability to drill down into greater detail or into related facts in other data marts or a shared data repository, so analysis is limited, or at best very difficult (e.g., doing joins across separate platforms for different data marts). Essentially, relating data across data marts is a task performed by users outside the data warehouse.

4. Scaling costs are excessive because every new application, which creates a separate data mart, repeats all the extract and load steps. Usually operational systems have limited time windows for batch data extracting, so at some point, the load on the operations systems may mean that new technology is needed, with additional costs.

5. If there is an attempt to make the separate data marts consistent, the cost to do so is quite high.

The value of independent data marts has been hotly debated. Kimball (1997) strongly supports the development of independent data marts as a viable strategy for a phased development of decision support systems. Armstrong (1997), Inmon (1997; 2000), and Marco (2003) point out the five fallacies above and many more. There are two debates as to the actual value of independent data marts:

1. One debate deals with the nature of the phased approach to implementing a data warehousing environment. The essence of this debate is whether each data mart should or should not evolve in a bottom-up fashion from a subset of enterprisewide decision support data.

2. The other debate deals with the suitable database architecture for analytical processing. This debate centers on the extent to which a data mart database should be normalized.

The essences of these two debates are addressed throughout this chapter. We provide an exercise at the end of the chapter for you to explore these debates in more depth.

One of the most popular approaches to address the independent data mart limitations raised earlier is to use a three-level approach represented by the dependent data mart and operational data store architecture (see Figure 11-4). Here the new level is the operational data store, and the data and metadata storage level is reconfigured. The first and second limitations are addressed by loading the **dependent data marts** from an **enterprise data warehouse (EDW)**, which is a central, integrated data warehouse that is the control point and single "version of the truth" made available to end users for decision support applications. Dependent data marts still have a purpose to provide a simplified and high-performance environment that is tuned to the decision-making needs of user groups. A user group can access its data mart, and then when other data are needed, users can access the EDW. Redundancy across dependent data marts is planned, and redundant data are consistent because each data mart is loaded in a synchronized way from one common source of data.

Dependent data mart: A data mart filled exclusively from the enterprise data warehouse and its reconciled data.

Enterprise data warehouse (EDW): A centralized, integrated data warehouse that is the control point and single source of all data made available to end users for decision support applications.

Figure 11-4
Dependent data mart and operational data store: a three-level architecture

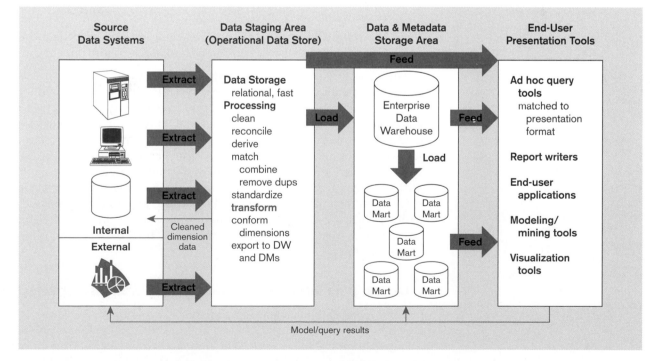

Operational data store (ODS) An integrated, subject-oriented, updatable, current-valued, enterprisewide, detailed database designed to serve operational users as they do decision support processing.

Integration of data is the responsibility of the IT staff managing the enterprise data warehouse; it is not the end users' responsibility to integrate data across independent data marts for each query or application. The dependent data mart and operational data store architecture is often called a "hub and spoke" approach, in which the EDW is the hub and the source data systems and the data marts are at the ends of input and output spokes.

The third limitation is addressed by providing an integrated source for all the operational data in an operational data store. An **operational data store (ODS)** is an integrated, subject-oriented, updatable, current-valued, organizationwide, detailed database designed to serve operational users as they do decision support processing (Imhoff, 1998; Inmon, 1998). An ODS is typically a relational database and normalized like databases in the systems of record, but it is tuned for decision-making applications. For example, indexes and other relational database design elements are tuned for queries that retrieve broad groups of data, rather than for transaction processing or querying individual and directly related records (e.g., a customer order). Because it has volatile, current data, the same query against an ODS very likely will yield different results at different times. An ODS typically does not contain history, whereas an EDW holds a history of snapshots of the state of the organization. An ODS may be fed from the database of an ERP application, but because most organizations do not have only one ERP database and do not run all operations against one ERP, an ODS is usually different from an ERP database. The ODS also serves as the staging area for loading data into the EDW. The ODS may receive data immediately or with some delay from the systems of record, whichever is practical and acceptable for the decision-making requirements that it supports.

The dependent data mart and operational data store architecture is also called a *corporate information factory (CIF)* (see Imhoff, 1999). It is considered to be a comprehensive view of organizational data in support of all user data requirements.

Different leaders in the field definitely endorse different approaches to data warehousing. Those that endorse the independent data mart approach argue that this approach has two significant benefits:

1. It allows for the concept of a data warehouse to be proved by working on a series of small projects.

2. The length of time until there is some benefit from data warehousing is reduced because the organization is not delayed until all data are centralized.

The advocates of the CIF (Inmon, 1999; Armstrong, 2000) raise serious issues with the independent approach; these issues include the five limitations of independent data marts outlined earlier. Inmon suggests that an advantage of physically separate *dependent* data marts is that they can be tuned to the needs of each community of users. In particular, he suggests the need for an *exploration warehouse*, which is a special version of the EDW optimized for data mining and business intelligence using advanced statistical, mathematical modeling, and visualization tools. Armstrong (2000) and others go further to argue that the benefits claimed by the independent data mart advocates really are benefits of taking a phased approach to data warehouse development. A phased approach can be accomplished within the CIF framework as well, and is facilitated by the final data warehousing architecture we review in the next section.

Logical Data Mart and Real-Time Data Warehouse Architecture

The logical data mart and real-time data warehouse architecture is practical for only moderate-sized data warehouses or when using high-performance data warehousing technology, such as the NCR Teradata system. As can be seen in Figure 11-5, this architecture has the following unique characteristics:

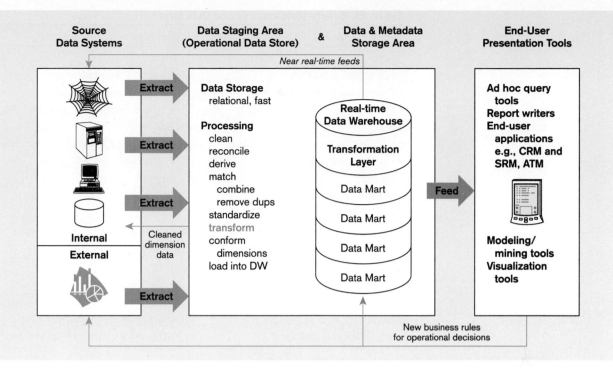

Figure 11-5
Logical data mart and real-time warehouse architecture

1. **Logical data marts** are not physically separate databases, but rather different relational views of one physical, slightly denormalized relational data warehouse. (Refer to Chapter 7 to review the concept of views.)

2. Data are moved into the data warehouse rather than to a separate staging area to utilize the high-performance computing power of the warehouse technology to perform the cleansing and transformation steps.

3. New data marts can be created quickly because no physical database or database technology needs to be created or acquired and no loading routines need to be written.

4. Data marts are always up to date because data in a view are created when the view is referenced; views can be materialized if a user has a series of queries and analysis that need to work off the same instantiation of the data mart.

Whether logical or physical, data marts and data warehouses play different roles in a data warehousing environment; these different roles are summarized in Table 11-2. Although limited in scope, a data mart may not be small. Thus, scalable technology is often critical. A significant burden and cost is placed on users when they themselves need to integrate the data across separate physical data marts (if this is even possible). As data marts are added, a data warehouse can be built in phases; the easiest way for this to happen is to follow the logical data mart and real-time data warehouse architecture.

The **real-time data warehouse** aspect of the architecture in Figure 11-5 means that the source data systems, decision support services, and the data warehouse *exchange* data and business rules at a near-real-time pace because there is a need for rapid response (that is, action) to a current, comprehensive picture of the organization. The purpose of real-time data warehousing is to know what is happening when it is happening. For example, a help desk professional answering questions and logging problem tickets will have a total picture of the customer's most recent sales contacts, billing and payment transactions, maintenance activities, and

Logical data marts: A data mart created by a relational view of a data warehouse.

Real-time data warehouse: An enterprise data warehouse that accepts near-real-time feeds of transactional data from the systems of record analyzes warehouse data, and in near-real-time relays business rules to the data warehouse and systems of record so that immediate action can be taken in response to business events.

Table 11-2 Data Warehouse Versus Data Mart

Data Warehouse	Data Mart
Scope	*Scope*
• Application independent	• Specific DSS application
• Centralized, possibly enterprise-wide	• Decentralized by user area
• Planned	• Organic, possibly not planned
Data	*Data*
• Historical, detailed, and summarized	• Some history, detailed, and summarized
• Lightly denormalized	• Highly denormalized
Subjects	*Subjects*
• Multiple subjects	• One central subject of concern to users
Sources	*Sources*
• Many internal and external sources	• Few internal and external sources
Other Characteristics	*Other Characteristics*
• Flexible	• Restrictive
• Data-oriented	• Project-oriented
• Long life	• Short life
• Large	• Start small, becomes large
• Single complex structure	• Multi, semi-complex structures, together complex

Adapted from Strange (1997)

orders. With this information, the system supporting the help desk can, based on operational decision rules created from a continuous analysis of up-to-date warehouse data, automatically generate a script for the professional to sell what the analysis has shown to be a likely and profitable maintenance contract, an upgraded product, or another product bought by customers with a similar profile. A critical event, such as entry of a new product order, can be considered immediately so that the organization knows at least as much about the relationship with its customer as does the customer.

Another example of real-time data warehousing (with real-time analytics) would be an express mail and package delivery service using frequent scanning of parcels to know exactly where a package is in their transportation system. Real-time analytics, based on this package data, as well as pricing, customer service level agreements, and logistics opportunities, could automatically reroute packages to meet delivery promises for their best customers. RFID technologies are allowing these kind of opportunities for real-time data warehousing (with massive amounts of data) coupled with real-time analytics to be used to greatly reduce the latency between event data capture and appropriate actions being taken.

The orientation is that each event, with say, a customer, is a potential opportunity for a customized, personalized, and optimized communication based on a strategic decision of how to respond to a customer with a particular profile. Thus, decision making, and the data warehouse, are actively involved in guiding operational processings, which is why some people call this active data warehousing. The goal is to shorten the cycle to:

- Capture customer data at the time of a business event (what did happen)
- Analyze customer behavior (why did something happen) and predict customer responses to possible actions (what will happen)
- Develop rules for optimizing customer interactions, including the appropriate response and channel that will yield the best results

- Take immediate *action* with customers at touch points based on best responses to customers as determined by decision rules in order to make desirable results happen

The idea is that the potential value of taking the right action decays the longer the delay from event to action. The real-time data warehouse is where all the intelligence comes together to reduce this delay. Thus, real-time data warehousing moves data warehousing from the back office to the front office. For a thorough status report on real-time data warehousing, see Hackathorn (2002). Other authors refer to real-time data warehousing as action-oriented or active (@ctive) data warehousing.

Some beneficial applications for real-time data warehousing include:

- Just-in-time transportation for rerouting deliveries based on up-to-date inventory levels
- E-commerce where, for instance, an abandoned shopping cart can trigger an e-mail promotional message before the user signs off
- Sales people who monitor key performance indicators for important accounts in real-time
- Fraud detection in credit card transactions, where an unusual pattern of transactions could alert a sales clerk or online shopping cart routine to take extra precautions

Such applications are often characterized by online user access 24 hours a day, 7 days a week, 365 days a year. For any of the data warehousing architectures, users may be employees, customers, or business partners.

With high-performance computers and data warehousing technologies, there may not be a need for a separate ODS from the enterprise data warehouse. When the ODS and EDW are one and the same, it is much easier for users to drill down and drill up when working through a series of ad hoc questions in which one question leads to another. It is also a simpler architecture, because one layer of the dependent data mart and operational data store architecture has been eliminated.

Three-Layer Data Architecture

Figure 11-6 shows a three-layer data architecture for a data warehouse:

1. Operational data are stored in the various operational systems of record throughout the organization (and sometimes in external systems).
2. Reconciled data are the type of data stored in the enterprise data warehouse and an operational data store.
3. Derived data are the type of data stored in each of the data marts.

Reconciled data are detailed, current data intended to be the single, authoritative source for all decision support applications. **Derived data** are data that have been selected, formatted, and aggregated for end-user decision support applications.

We discuss reconciled data and derived data in the next two sections. Two components shown in Figure 11-6 play critical roles in the data architecture; they are the enterprise data model and metadata.

Role of the Enterprise Data Model   In Figure 11-6, we show the reconciled data layer linked to the enterprise data model. Recall from Chapter 2 that the enterprise data model presents a total picture explaining the data required by an organization.

Reconciled data: Detailed, current data intended to be the single, authoritative source for all decision support applications.

Derived data: Data that have been selected, formatted, and aggregated for end-user decision support applications.

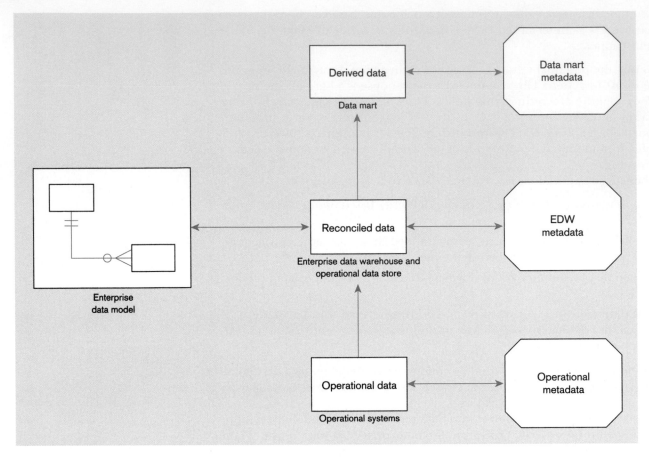

Figure 11-6
Three-layer data architecture for a data
warehouse

If the reconciled data layer is to be the single, authoritative source for all data required for decision support, it must conform to the design specified in the enterprise data model. Thus, the enterprise data model controls the phased evolution of the data warehouse. Usually the enterprise data model evolves as new problems and decision applications are addressed. It takes too long to develop the enterprise data model in one step, and the dynamic needs for decision making will change before the warehouse is built.

Role of Metadata   Figure 11-6 also shows a layer of metadata linked to each of the three data layers. Recall from Chapter 1 that metadata are technical and business data that describe the properties or characteristics of other data. Following is a brief description of the three types of metadata shown in Figure 11-6.

1. *Operational metadata*   describe the data in the various operational systems (as well as external data) that feed the enterprise data warehouse. Operational metadata typically exist in a number of different formats and unfortunately are often of poor quality.

2. *Enterprise data warehouse (EDW) metadata*   are derived from (or at least consistent with) the enterprise data model. EDW metadata describe the reconciled data layer as well as the rules for extracting, transforming, and loading operational data into reconciled data.

3. *Data mart metadata*   describe the derived data layer and the rules for transforming reconciled data to derived data.

For a thorough review of data warehouse metadata, see Marco (2000).

SOME CHARACTERISTICS OF DATA WAREHOUSE DATA

To understand the data in each of these layers, you need to learn some basic characteristics of data as they are stored in data warehouse databases.

Status Versus Event Data

The difference between status data and event data is shown in Figure 11-7. The figure shows a typical log entry recorded by a DBMS when processing a business transaction for a banking application. This log entry contains both status and event data: The "before image" and "after image" represent the status of the bank account before and then after a withdrawal. Data representing the withdrawal (or update event) are shown in the middle of the figure.

Transactions, which are discussed further in Chapter 12, are business activities that cause one or more business events to occur at a database level. An **event** is a database action (create, update, or delete) that results from a transaction. Notice that a transaction may lead to one or more events. The withdrawal transaction in Figure 11-7 leads to a single event, which is the reduction in the account balance from 750 to 700. On the other hand, the transfer of money from one account to another would lead to two events: a withdrawal event and a deposit event. Sometimes nontransactions, such as an abandoned online shopping cart, busy signal or dropped network connection, or an item put in a shopping cart and then taken out before checkout, can also be important events.

Event: A database action (create, update, or delete) that results from a transaction.

Both status data and event data can be stored in a database. However, in practice, most of the data stored in databases (including data warehouses) are status data. A data warehouse likely contains a history of snapshots of status data or a summary (say, an hourly total) of transaction or event data. Event data, which represent transactions, may be stored for a defined period but are then deleted or archived to save storage space. Both status and event data are typically stored in database logs (such as represented in Figure 11-7) for backup and recovery purposes. As will be explained later, the database log plays an important role in filling the data warehouse.

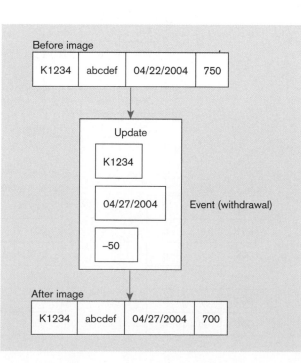

Figure 11-7
Example of DBMS log entry

Transient Versus Periodic Data

In data warehouses, it is typical to maintain a record of when events occurred in the past. This is necessary, for example, to compare sales or inventory levels on a particular date or during a particular period with the previous year's sales on the same date or during the same period.

Most operational systems are based on the use of transient data. **Transient data** are data in which changes to existing records are written over previous records, thus destroying the previous data content. Records are deleted without preserving the previous contents of those records.

You can easily visualize transient data by again referring to Figure 11-7. If the after image is written over the before image, the before image (containing the previous balance) is lost. However, because this is a database log, both images are normally preserved.

Periodic data are data that are never physically altered or deleted once added to the store. The before and after images in Figure 11-7 represent periodic data. Notice that each record contains a timestamp that indicates the date (and time, if needed) when the most recent update event occurred (we introduced the use of timestamps in Chapter 3).

> **Transient data:** Data in which changes to existing records are written over previous records, thus destroying the previous data content.

> **Periodic data:** Data that are never physically altered or deleted once they have been added to the store.

An Example of Transient and Periodic Data

A more detailed example comparing transient and periodic data is shown in Figures 11-8 and 11-9.

Transient Data Figure 11-8 shows a relation (Table X) that initially contains four rows. The table has three attributes: a primary key and two nonkey attributes, A and B. The values for each of these attributes on the date 10/05 are shown in the figure. For example, for record 001 the value of attribute A on this date is a.

On date 10/06, three changes are made to the table (changes to rows are indicated by arrows to the left of the table). Row 002 is updated, so the value of A is

Figure 11-8
Transient operational data

Table X (10/05)

Key	A	B
001	a	b
002	c	d
003	e	f
004	g	h

Table X (10/06)

Key	A	B
001	a	b
002	r	d
003	e	f
004	y	h
005	m	n

Table X (10/07)

Key	A	B
001	a	b
002	r	d
003	e	t
005	m	n

Table X (10/05)

Key	Date	A	B	Action
001	10/03	a	b	C
002	10/03	c	d	C
003	10/03	e	f	C
004	10/03	g	h	C

Table X (10/06)

Key	Date	A	B	Action
001	10/05	a	b	C
002	10/05	c	d	C
002	10/06	r	d	U
003	10/05	e	f	C
004	10/05	g	h	C
004	10/06	y	h	U
005	10/06	m	n	C

Table X (10/07)

Key	Date	A	B	Action
001	10/05	a	b	C
002	10/05	c	d	C
002	10/06	r	d	U
003	10/05	e	f	C
003	10/07	e	t	U
004	10/05	g	h	C
004	10/06	y	h	U
004	10/07	y	h	D
005	10/06	m	n	C

Figure 11-9
Periodic warehouse data

changed from c to r. Row 004 is also updated, so the value of A is changed from g to y. Finally, a new row (with key 005) is inserted into the table.

Notice that when rows 002 and 004 are updated, the new rows replace the previous rows. Therefore the previous values are lost; there is no historical record of these values. This is characteristic of transient data.

More changes are made to the rows on date 10/07 (to simplify the discussion, we assume that only one change can be made to a given row on a given date). Row 003 is updated, and row 004 is deleted. Notice that there is no record to indicate that row 004 was ever stored in the database. The way the data are processed in Figure 11-8 is characteristic of the transient data typical in operational systems.

Periodic Data   One typical objective for a data warehouse is to maintain a historical record of key events or to create a time series for particular variables such as sales. This often requires storing periodic data, rather than transient data. Figure 11-9 shows the table used in Figure 11-8, now modified to represent periodic data. The following changes have been made in Figure 11-9:

1. Two new columns have been added to Table X.
   a. The column named Date is a timestamp that records the most recent date when a row has been modified.
   b. The column named Action is used to record the type of change that occurred. Possible values for this attribute are C (Create), U (Update), and D (Delete).

2. Once a record has been stored in the table, that record is never changed. When an update operation occurs on a record, both the before image and the after image are stored in the table. Although a record may be *logically* deleted, a historical version of the deleted record is maintained in the database for as much history (at least five quarters) as needed to analyze trends.

Now let's examine the same set of actions that occurred in Figure 11-8. Assume that all four rows were created on the date 10/05, as shown in the first table.

In the second table (for 10/06), rows 002 and 004 have been updated. The table now contains both the old version (for 10/05) and the new version (for 10/06) for these rows. The table also contains the new row (005) that was created on 10/06.

The third table (for 10/07) shows the update to row 003, with both the old and new versions. Also, row 004 is deleted from this table. This table now contains three versions of row 004: the original version (from 10/05), the updated version (from 10/06), and the deleted version (from 10/07). The D in the last row for record 004 indicates that this row has been logically deleted, so that it is no longer available to users or their applications.

If you examine Figure 11-9, you can see why data warehouses tend to grow very rapidly. Storing periodic data can impose large storage requirements. A corollary is that users must choose very carefully the key data that require this form of processing.

Other Data Warehouse Changes   Besides the periodic changes to data values outlined above, there are six other kinds of changes to a warehouse data model that must be accommodated by data warehousing, which are as follows:

1. *New descriptive attributes*   For example, new characteristics of products or customers that are important to store in the warehouse must be accommodated. Later in the chapter we call these attributes of dimension tables. This change is fairly easily accommodated by adding columns to tables and allowing null values for existing rows (if historical data exist in source systems, null values do not have to be stored).

2. *New business activity attributes*   For example, new characteristics of an event already stored in the warehouse, such as a column C for the table in Figure 11-9, must be accommodated. This can be handled as in item 1, but is more difficult when the new facts are more refined, such as a data associated with days of the week, not just month and year, as in Figure 11-9.

3. *New classes of descriptive attributes*   This is equivalent to adding new tables to the database.

4. *Descriptive attributes become more refined*   For example, data about stores must be broken down by individual cash register to understand sales data. This change is in the grain of the data, an extremely important topic, which we discuss later in the chapter. This can be a very difficult change to accommodate.

5. *Descriptive data are related to one another*   For example, store data are related to geography data. This causes new relationships, often hierarchical, to be included in the data model.

6. *New source of data*   This is a very common change, in which some new business need causes data feeds from an additional source system or some new operational system is installed that must feed the warehouse. This change can cause almost any of the above changes, as well as the need for new extract, transform, and load processes.

It is usually not possible to go back and reload the data warehouse to accommodate all of these kinds of changes for the whole data history maintained. But, it is critical to accommodate such changes smoothly to enable the data warehouse to meet new business conditions and information and business intelligence needs. Thus, designing the warehouse for change is very important.

THE RECONCILED DATA LAYER

As indicated in Figure 11-6, we use the term reconciled data to refer to the data layer associated with the operational data store and enterprise data warehouse. This is the term used by IBM in 1993 describing data warehouse architectures. Although the term is not widely used, it accurately describes the nature of the data that should appear in the enterprise data warehouse and the way they are derived. More commonly, reconciled data are referred to as the result of the ETL process. An EDW or ODS usually is a normalized, relational database, because it needs the flexibility to support a wide variety of decision support needs.

Characteristics of Data after ETL

The goal of the extract, transform, and load process is to provide a single, authoritative source for data that support decision making. Ideally, this data layer is detailed, historical, normalized, comprehensive, timely, and quality controlled:

1. *Detailed* The data are detailed (rather than summarized), providing maximum flexibility for various user communities to structure the data to best suit their needs.

2. *Historical* The data are periodic (or point-in-time) to provide a historical perspective.

3. *Normalized* The data are fully normalized (i.e., third normal form or higher). (We discussed normalization in Chapter 5.) Normalized data provide greater integrity and flexibility of use than denormalized data do. Denormalization is not necessary to improve performance, because reconciled data are usually accessed periodically using batch processes. We will see, however, that some popular data warehouse data structures are denormalized.

4. *Comprehensive* Reconciled data reflect an enterprisewide perspective, whose design conforms to the enterprise data model.

5. *Timely* Except for real-time data warehousing, data need not be (near) real time, however, data must be current enough so that decision making can react in time.

6. *Quality controlled* Reconciled data must be of unquestioned quality and integrity, because they are summarized into the data marts and used for decision making.

Notice that these characteristics of reconciled data are quite different from the typical operational data from which they are derived. Operational data are typically detailed, but they differ strongly in the other four dimensions described earlier.

1. Operational data are transient, rather than historical.

2. They are not normalized. Depending on their roots, operational data may never have been normalized or may have been denormalized for performance reasons.

3. Rather than being comprehensive, operational data are generally restricted in scope to a particular application.

4. Operational data are often of poor quality, with numerous types of inconsistencies and errors.

The data reconciliation process is responsible for transforming operational data to reconciled data. Because of the sharp differences between these two types of data, data reconciliation clearly is the most difficult and technically challenging part of building a data warehouse. The Data Warehousing Institute supports this claim by finding that 60-80 percent of work on a business intelligence project, often the reason for data warehousing, is spent on ETL activities (Eckerson and White, 2003). Fortunately, several sophisticated software products are available to assist with this activity. (See Krudop, 2005, for a summary of why ETL tools are useful and how to successfully implement them in an organization.)

The ETL Process

Data reconciliation occurs in two stages during the process of filling the enterprise data warehouse.

1. An initial load, when the EDW is first created
2. Subsequent updates (normally performed on a periodic basis) to keep the EDW current and/or to expand it

Data reconciliation can be visualized as a process, shown in Figure 11-10, consisting of four steps: capture, scrub, transform, and load and index. In reality, the steps may be combined in different ways. For example, data capture and scrub might be combined as a single process, or scrub and transform might be combined. Typically, data rejected from the cleansing step cause messages to be sent to the appropriate operational systems to fix the data at the source and to be resent in a later extract. Figure 11-10 actually simplifies ETL considerably. Kimball (2004) outlines 38 subsystems of ETL. We do not have space to detail all of these subsystems. The fact that there are 38 subsystems highlights why so much time is spent on ETL for data warehousing, and why selecting ETL tools can be so important and difficult. We discuss capture, scrub, and load and index next, followed by a thorough discussion of transform.

Extract   Capturing the relevant data from the source files and databases used to fill the EDW is typically called extracting. Usually, not all data contained in the various operational source systems are required, but just a subset. Extracting the subset of data is based on an extensive analysis of both the source and target systems, which

Figure 11-10
Steps in data reconciliation

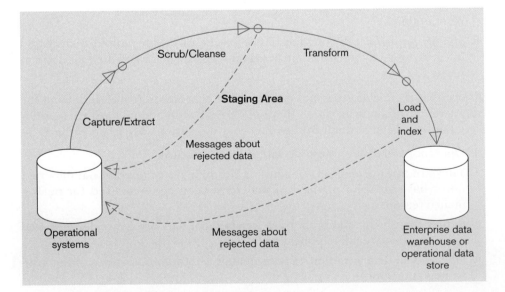

is best performed by a team directed by data administration and composed of both end users and data warehouse professionals.

A foundation for capturing data is a careful source-to-target mapping and definition of process flows of various computing jobs consistent with this mapping. The process flows take the source data through various steps of consolidation, merging, de-duping, and simply conversion into one consistent stream of jobs to feed the scrubbing and transformation steps. And to do this mapping, which involves selecting the most reliable source for data, one must have good metadata sufficient to understand fine differences between apparently the same data in multiple sources. Metadata are then created to explain the mapping and job flow process. The mapping may be conceived of as a simple spreadsheet that shows all possible source data elements as rows and data warehouse data elements as columns, with cell entries indicating which source data go into feeding which data warehouse data.

Technically, an alternative to this classical beginning to the ETL process is supported by a newer class of tools called Enterprise Application Integration (EAI). EAI tools enable event-driven (that is, real-time) data to be captured and used in an integrated way across disparate source systems. EAI can be used to capture data when they change not on a periodic basis, which is common of many ETL processes. So called "trickle feeds" are important for the real-time data warehouse architecture to support active business intelligence. EAI tools can also be used to feed ETL tools, which often have richer abilities for cleansing and transformation.

The two generic types of data extracts are static extract and incremental extract. Static extract is used to fill the data warehouse initially, and incremental extract is used for ongoing warehouse maintenance.

Static extract is a method of capturing a snapshot of the required source data at a point in time. The view of the source data is independent of the time at which it was created.

Static extract: A method of capturing a snapshot of the required source data at a point in time.

Incremental extract captures only the changes that have occurred in the source data since the last capture. The most common method is log capture. Recall that the database log contains after images that record the most recent changes to database records (see Figure 11-7). With log capture, only after images that are logged after the last capture are selected from the log.

Incremental extract: A method of capturing only the changes that have occurred in the source data since the last capture.

English (1999) and White (2000) address in detail the careful steps necessary to qualify which systems of record and other data sources to use for extraction into the staging area. A major criterion is the quality of the data in the source systems. Quality depends on the following:

- Clarity of data naming, so the warehouse designers know exactly what data exist in a source system

- Completeness and accuracy of business rules enforced by a source system, which directly affects the accuracy of data; also, the business rules in the source should match the rules to be used in the data warehouse

- Format of data (common formats across sources help to match related data)

It is also important to have agreements with the owners of source systems so that they will inform the data warehouse administrators when changes are made in the metadata for the source system. Because transaction systems frequently change to meet new business needs and to utilize new and better software and hardware technologies, managing changes in the source systems is one of the biggest challenges of the extraction process. Changes in the source system require a reassessment of data quality and the procedures for extracting and transforming data. These procedures map data in the source systems to data in the target data warehouse (or data marts). For each data element in the data warehouse a map says which data from which source systems to use to derive that data; transformation rules, which we address in a separate section, then state how to perform the derivation. For custom-built source systems, a data warehouse administrator has to develop customized maps and extraction routines; predefined map templates can be purchased for some packaged application software, such as ERP systems.

Extraction may be done by routines written with tools associated with the source system, say, a tool to export data. Data are usually extracted in a neutral data format, such as comma-delimited ANSI. Sometimes the SQL command SELECT . . . INTO can be used to create a table. Once the data sources have been selected and extraction routines written, data can be moved into the staging area, where the cleansing process begins.

Cleanse It is generally accepted that the role of the ETL process is to identify erroneous data, not fix them. Fixes should be made in the appropriate source systems, so such erroneous data, created by systematic procedural mistakes, do not reoccur. Rejected data are eliminated from further ETL steps and will be reprocessed in the next feed from the relevant source system.

Poor data quality is the bane of ETL. In fact, it is the bane of all information systems ("garbage in, garbage out"). Unfortunately, this has always been true and remains so. Eckerson and While (2003) found that ensuring adequate data quality was the number one challenge of ETL, followed closely by understanding source data, a highly related issue. Procedures should be in place to ensure data are captured "correctly" at the source. But, what is correct depends on the source system, so the cleansing step of ETL must, at a minimun, resolve differences between what each source believes is quality data. The issue may be timing; that is, one system is ahead of another on updating common or related data. (As you will see later, time is a very important factor in data warehouses, so it is important for data warehousing to understand the timestamp for a piece of data.) So, there is a need for further data quality steps to be taken during ETL. (We return to this important topic of data quality for database management in Chapter 12.)

Data in the operational systems are of poor quality or are inconsistent across source systems for many common reasons, including data entry errors by employees and customers, changes to the source systems, bad and inconsistent metadata, and system errors or corrupted data from the extract process. You cannot assume the data are clean even when the source system works fine (e.g., the source system used default, but inaccurate values). Some of the errors and inconsistencies typical of these data are as follows:

1. Misspelled names and addresses
2. Impossible or erroneous dates of birth
3. Fields used for purposes for which they were never intended
4. Mismatched addresses and area codes
5. Missing data
6. Duplicate data
7. Inconsistencies (e.g., different addresses) in values or formats across sources
8. Different primary keys across sources

Let's consider some examples of such errors. Customer names are often used as primary keys or as search criteria in customer files. However, these names are often misspelled or spelled in various ways in these files. For example, the name "The Coca-Cola Company" is the correct name for the soft-drink company. This name may be entered in customer records as "Coca-Cola," "Coca Cola," "TCCC," and so on. In one study, a company found that the name "McDonald's" could be spelled 100 different ways!

Another type of data pollution occurs when a field is used for purposes for which it was not intended. For example, in one bank a record field was designed to hold a telephone number. However, branch managers who had no such use for this field instead stored the interest rate in it. Another example, reported by a major UK bank, was even more bizarre. The data-scrubbing program turned up a customer on their files whose occupation was listed as "steward on the Titanic" (Devlin, 1997).

You may wonder why such errors are so common in operational data. The quality of operational data is largely determined by their value to the organization responsible for gathering them. Unfortunately, it often happens that the data-gathering organization places a low value on some data whose accuracy is important to downstream applications, such as data warehousing.

Given the common occurrence of errors, the worst thing a company can do is simply copy operational data to the data warehouse. Instead, it is important to improve the quality of the source data through a technique called data scrubbing. **Data scrubbing** (also called data cleansing) is a technique using pattern recognition and other techniques to upgrade the quality of raw data before transforming them and moving the data to the data warehouse. How to scrub each piece of data varies by attribute, so considerable analysis goes into the design of each ETL scrubbing step. And, the data scrubbing techniques must be reassessed each time there are changes made to the source system. Some scrubbing will outright reject data, when the data are obviously bad, and the source system will be sent a message to fix the erroneous data and get them ready for the next extract. Other results from scrubbing may flag the data for more detailed manual analysis (e.g., why did one salesperson sell more than three times any other salesperson?) before outright rejecting the data.

> **Data scrubbing:** A technique using pattern recognition and other artificial intelligence techniques to upgrade the quality of raw data before transforming and moving the data to the data warehouse. Also called data cleansing.

Successful data warehousing requires that a formal program in total quality management (TQM) be implemented. TQM focuses on defect prevention, rather than defect correction. Although data scrubbing can help upgrade data quality, it is not a long-term solution to the data quality problem. For a good discussion of TQM applied to data management, see English (1999).

The type of data cleansing required depends on the quality of data in the source system. Besides fixing the types of problems identified earlier, other common cleansing tasks include the following:

- Decoding data to make them understandable for data warehousing applications.

- Reformatting and changing data types and performing other functions to put data from each source into the standard data warehouse format ready for transformation.

- Adding timestamps to distinguish values for the same attribute over time.

- Converting between different units of measure.

- Generating primary keys for each row of a table. (We discuss the formation of data warehouse table primary and foreign keys later in this chapter.)

- Matching and merging separate extractions into one table or file and matching data to go into the same row of the generated table. (This can be a very difficult process when different keys are used in different source systems, when naming conventions are different, and when the data in the source systems are erroneous.)

- Logging errors detected, fixing those errors, and reprocessing corrected data without creating duplicate entries.

- Finding missing data to complete the batch of data necessary for subsequent loading.

The order in which different data sources are processed may matter. For example, it may be necessary to process customer data from a sales system before new customer demographic data from an external system can be matched to customers.

Once the data are cleansed in the staging area, data are ready for transformation. Before we discuss the transformation process in some detail, however, we briefly review in the next section the procedures used to load data into the data warehouse or data marts.

Refresh mode: An approach to filling the data warehouse that employs bulk rewriting of the target data at periodic intervals.

Update mode: An approach in which only changes in the source data are written to the data warehouse.

Load and Index   The last step in filling the enterprise data warehouse (see Figure 11-10) is to load the selected data into the target data warehouse and to create the necessary indexes. The two basic modes for loading data to the target EDW are refresh and update.

Refresh mode is an approach to filling the data warehouse that employs bulk rewriting of the target data at periodic intervals. That is, the target data are written initially to fill the warehouse. Then at periodic intervals the warehouse is rewritten, replacing the previous contents. This mode has become less popular.

Update mode is an approach in which only changes in the source data are written to the data warehouse. To support the periodic nature of warehouse data, these new records are usually written to the data warehouse without overwriting or deleting previous records (see Figure 11-9).

As you would expect, refresh mode is generally used to fill the warehouse when it is first created. Update mode is then generally used for ongoing maintenance of the target warehouse. Refresh mode is used in conjunction with static data capture, whereas update mode is used in conjunction with incremental data capture.

With both the refresh and update modes, it is necessary to create and maintain the indexes that are used to manage the warehouse data. Two types of indexing, called *bit-mapped indexing* and *join indexing* (see Chapter 6) are often used in a data warehouse environment.

Because a data warehouse keeps historical data, integrated from disparate source systems, it is often important to those who use the data warehouse to know where the data came from. Metadata may provide this information about specific attributes, but the metadata, too, must show history (e.g., the source may change over time). More detailed procedures may be necessary if there are multiple sources or if knowing which specific extract or load file placed the data in the warehouse or what transformation routine created the data. (This may be necessary for uncovering the source of errors discovered in the warehouse.) Variar (2002) outlines the intricacies of tracing the origins of warehouse data.

Westerman (2001), based on the highly publicized and successful data warehousing at Wal-Mart Corporation, discusses factors in determining how frequently to update the data warehouse. His guideline is to update the data warehouse as frequently as is practical. Infrequent updating causes massive loads and users to wait for new data. Near-real-time loads are necessary for active data warehousing, but may be inefficient and unnecessary for most data mining and analysis applications. Westerman suggests that daily updates are sufficient for most organizations. (Statistics show that 75 percent of organizations do daily updates.) However, daily updates make it impossible to react to some changing conditions, such as repricing or changing purchase orders for slow-moving items. Wal-Mart updates the data warehouse continuously, which is practical given the massively parallel data warehouse technology they use. The industry trend is toward updates several times a day and near-real time, and less use of more infrequent refresh intervals, such as monthly (Agosta, 2003).

Loading data into the warehouse typically means appending new rows to tables in the warehouse. It may also mean updating existing rows with new data (e.g., to fill in missing values from an additional data source), and it may mean purging identified data from the warehouse that have become obsolete due to age or that were incorrectly loaded in a prior load operation. Data may be loaded from the staging area into the warehouse by the following:

- SQL commands (e.g., INSERT or UPDATE)
- Special load utilities provided by the data warehouse or third-party vendor
- Custom-written routines coded by the warehouse administrators (a very common practice, which uses the above two approaches)

In any case, these routines must not only update the data warehouse but must also generate error reports to show rejected data (e.g., attempting to append a row with a duplicate key or updating a row that does not exist in a table of the data warehouse).

Load utilities may work in batch or continuous mode. With a utility, you write a script that defines the format of the data in the staging area and which staging area data maps to which data warehouse fields. The utility may be able to convert data types for a field in the staging area to the target field in the warehouse and may be able to perform IF . . . THEN . . . ELSE logic to handle staging area data in various formats or to direct input data to different data warehouse tables. The utility can purge all data in a warehouse table (DROP TABLE) before data loading (refresh mode) or can append new rows (update mode). The utility may be able to sort input data so that rows are appended before they are updated. The utility program runs as would any stored procedure for the DBMS, and ideally all the controls of the DBMS for concurrency as well as restart and recovery in case of a DBMS failure during loading will work. Because the execution of a load can be very time-consuming, it is critical to be able to restart a load from a checkpoint in case the DBMS crashes in the middle of executing a load. See Chapter 12 for a thorough discussion of restart and recovery of databases.

DATA TRANSFORMATION

Data transformation (or transform) is at the very center of the data reconciliation process. **Data transformation** is the component of data reconciliation that converts data from the format of the source operational systems to the format of the enterprise data warehouse. Data transformation accepts data from the data capture component (after data scrubbing, if it applies), then maps the data to the format of the reconciled data layer, and then passes them to the load and index component.

Data transformation may range from a simple change in data format or representation to a highly complex exercise in data integration. Following are three examples that illustrate this range:

Data transformation: The component of data reconciliation that converts data from the format of the source operational systems to the format of the enterprise data warehouse.

1. A salesperson requires a download of customer data from a mainframe database to her laptop computer. In this case, the transformation required is simply mapping the data from EBCDIC to ASCII representation, which can easily be performed by off-the-shelf software.

2. A manufacturing company has product data stored in three different legacy systems: a manufacturing system, a marketing system, and an engineering application. The company needs to develop a consolidated view of these product data. Data transformation involves several different functions, including resolving different key structures, converting to a common set of codes, and integrating data from different sources. These functions are quite straightforward, and most of the necessary software can be generated using a standard commercial software package with a graphical interface.

3. A large health care organization manages a geographically dispersed group of hospitals, clinics, and other care centers. Because many of the units have been acquired through acquisition over time, the data are heterogeneous and uncoordinated. For a number of important reasons, the organization

needs to develop a data warehouse to provide a single corporate view of the enterprise. This effort will require the full range of transformation functions described below, including some custom software development.

The functions performed in data scrubbing and the functions performed in data transformation blend together. In general, the goal of data scrubbing is to correct errors in data *values* in the source data, whereas the goal of data transformation is to convert the data *format* from the source to the target system. Note that it is essential to scrub the data before they are transformed because, if there are errors in the data before they are transformed, the errors will remain in the data after transformation.

Data Transformation Functions

Data transformation encompasses a variety of different functions. These functions may be classified broadly into two categories: record-level functions and field-level functions. In most data warehousing applications, a combination of some or even all of these functions is required.

Record-Level Functions   Operating on a set of records, such as a file or table, are the most important record-level functions: selection, joining, normalization, and aggregation.

Selection: The process of partitioning data according to predefined criteria.

Selection (also called subsetting) is the process of partitioning data according to predefined criteria. For data warehouse applications, selection is used to extract the relevant data from the source systems that will be used to fill the data warehouse. In fact, selection is typically a part of the capture function discussed earlier.

When the source data are relational, SQL SELECT statements can be used for selection. (See Chapter 7 for a detailed discussion.) For example, recall that incremental capture is often implemented by selecting after images from the database log that have been created since the previous capture. A typical after image was shown in Figure 11-7. Suppose that the after images for this application are stored in a table named ACCOUNT_HISTORY. Then the after images that have been created after 12/31/2004 can be selected with the following statements:

```
SELECT*
FROM ACCOUNT_HISTORY
WHERE Create_Date > 12/31/2004;
```

Joining: The process of combining data from various sources into a single table or view.

Joining combines data from various sources into a single table or view. Joining data is an important function in data warehouse applications, because it is often necessary to consolidate data from various sources. For example, an insurance company may have client data spread throughout several different files and databases. When the source data are relational, SQL statements can be used to perform a join operation. (See Chapter 7 for details.)

Joining is often complicated by factors such as the following:

- Often the source data are not relational (the extracts are flat files), in which case SQL statements cannot be used. Instead, procedural language statements must be coded or the data must first be moved into a staging area that uses a RDBMS.

- Even for relational data, primary keys for the tables to be joined are often from different domains (e.g., engineering part number versus catalog number). These keys must then be reconciled before a SQL join can be performed.

- Source data may contain errors, which makes join operations hazardous.

Normalization is the process of decomposing relations with anomalies to produce smaller, well-structured relations. (See Chapter 5 for a detailed discussion.) As indicated earlier, source data in operational systems are often denormalized (or simply not normalized). The data must therefore be normalized as part of data transformation.

Aggregation: The process of transforming data from a detailed to a summary level.

Aggregation is the process of transforming data from a detailed level to a summary level. For example, in a retail business, individual sales transactions can be summarized to produce total sales by store, product, date, and so on. Because (in our model) the enterprise data warehouse contains only detailed data, aggregation is not normally associated with this component. However, aggregation is an important function in filling the data marts, as explained below.

Because selection, joining, and aggregation can often be done in SQL, some data warehouse experts argue that transformation should be done in an operational data store or even in the data warehouse.

Field-Level Functions A field-level function converts data from a given format in a source record to a different format in a target record. Field-level functions are of two types: single-field and multifield.

A *single-field* transformation converts data from a single source field to a single target field. Figure 11-11a is a basic representation of this type of transformation

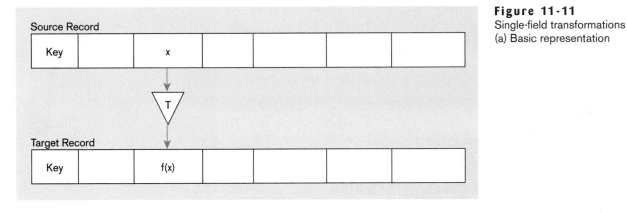

Figure 11-11
Single-field transformations
(a) Basic representation

(b) Algorithmic transformation

(c) Table look-up

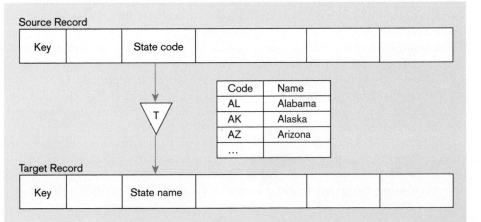

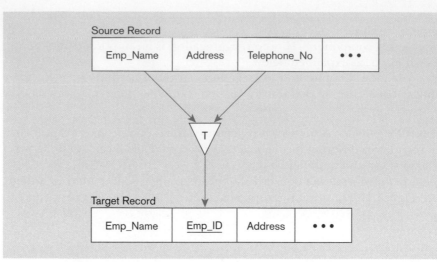

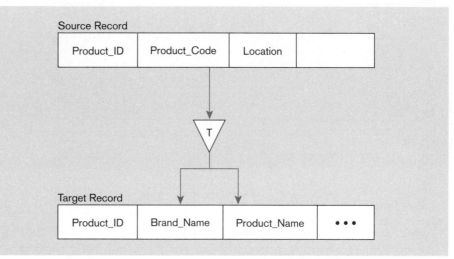

(designated by the letter "T" in the diagram). An example of a single-field transformation is converting a measurement from English to metric representation.

As shown in Figures 11-11b and 11-11c, there are two basic methods for performing a single-field transformation: algorithmic and table lookup. An algorithmic transformation is performed using a formula or logical expression. Figure 11-11b shows a conversion from Fahrenheit to Celsius temperature using a formula. When a simple algorithm does not apply, a lookup table can be used instead. Figure 11-11c shows the use of a table to convert state codes to state names. (This type of conversion is common in data warehouse applications.)

A *multifield* transformation converts data from one or more source fields to one or more target fields. This type of transformation is very common in data warehouse applications. Two multifield transformations are shown in Figure 11-12.

Figure 11-12a is an example of a many-to-one transformation. (In this case, two source fields are mapped to one target field.) In the source record, the combination of employee name and telephone number is used as the primary key. This combination is awkward and may not uniquely identify a person. Therefore, in creating a target record, the combination is mapped to a unique employee identification (Emp_ID). A lookup table would be created to support this transformation. A data scrubbing program might be employed to help identify duplicates in the source data.

Figure 11-12b is an example of a one-to-many transformation. (In this case, one source field has been converted to two target fields.) In the source record, a product code has been used to encode the combination of brand name and product name. (The use of such codes is common in operational data.) However, in the target record, it is desired to display the full text describing product and brand names. Again, a lookup table would be employed for this purpose.

More Complex Transformations   In Figure 11-12, the multifield transformations both involve only one source record and one target record. More generally, multi-field transformations may involve more than one source record and/or more than one target record. In the most complex cases, these records may even originate in different operational systems and in different time zones (Devlin, 1997).

Tools to Support Data Reconciliation

As you can readily see, data reconciliation is an extremely complex and challenging process. A variety of closely integrated software applications must be developed (or acquired) to support this process. Fortunately, a number of powerful software tools are available to assist organizations in developing these applications. In this section, we describe three categories of such tools: data quality, data conversion, and data cleansing. Table 11-3 summarizes some tools in each of these three categories. (There may be as many as 75 ETL tools on the market.)

Data Quality Tools   These tools are intended to assess the quality of data in existing systems and compare them to the requirements of the data warehouse. Features include data profiling, automatic generation of code to enforce quality control rules, parse and standardize source data into a common format, verify data against external data sources, and basic matching of data cross sources. Thus, the tools are useful during an early stage of warehouse development. One such tool listed in Table 11-3 is WizRule (WizSoft, Inc.). WizRule is a rules discovery tool that searches through records in existing tables and discovers the rules associated with the data. For example, a rule might state the following: "If Customer_Name is Able or Baker, then City is San Diego; probability 0.95. This rule exists in 50 records." The product also identifies records that deviate from the established rules. At a

Table 11-3 Tools to Support Data Reconciliation

Product Name	Company	Description
WizRule	WizSoft, Inc. **www.wizsoft.com**	Rules discovery
InfoRefiner	Computer Associates **www.ca.com**	Extract, transform, load, and index
DataBridger	Taurus Software, Inc. **www.taurus.com**	Extract, transform, load and index
Hummingbird Integration Suite	Hummingbird, Ltd. **www.hummingbird.com**	Extract, transform, enrich, load
Power Center	Informatica **www.informatica.com**	Extract, transform, load, and index
Trillium	Harte-Hanks **www.harte-hanks.com**	Quality analysis and data cleansing
Information Quality Suite	Firstlogic **www.firstlogic.com**	Quality analysis and data cleansing
Quality Stage	Ascential Software **www.ascential.com** (now part of IBM)	Family of products for quality analysis, data scrubbing

basic level, these types of tools profile data so that data modelers understand the properties of existing data. For example, showing a distribution of values for a column can identifier outliers that may indicate bad data or exceptional circumstances not previously known. Knowing data properties is essential for developing astute cleansing actions.

Data Conversion Tools   These tools generally perform three mainstream functions: extract, transform, and load and index. The tools in this category are basically program-generation tools. They accept as input the schema (or file descriptions) of the source and target files and the business rules that are to be used for data transformation. Typical business rules would include formulas, algorithms, and lookup tables, such as those shown in Figure 11-11. The tools then generate the program code necessary to perform the transformation functions on an ongoing basis.

Data Cleansing Tools   QualityStage (Ascential Software, now part of IBM), Trillium (Harte-Hanks), and Information Quality Suite (Firstlogic) are designed to perform data quality analysis, data cleansing, and data reengineering (i.e., discovering business rules and relationships among entities).

Selecting Tools   Because of the number and variety of tools, finding the right tool takes research. Meyer (2001) and Eckerson and White (2003) provide excellent guidelines on tool selection. Some of the critical factors in finding the right tool include the following: ease of use in the development environment, the ability to share metadata (e.g., transformation rules) with DBMS and data warehouse metadata tools, the number and types of distinct sources supported, input file size limitations, support for SQL extraction from source system using joins, the ability to do incremental updates, support for near-real-time data capture, code translation capabilities, support for slowing changing dimensions (to be discussed later in this chapter), testing and debugging support, version management, the number of simultaneous processes supported, the ability to define sequential job streams, the platforms supported, reporting capabilities, and the ability to handle restart and recovery of a data load with minimal reprocessing.

THE DERIVED DATA LAYER

We turn now to the derived data layer. This is the data layer associated with logical or physical data marts (see Figure 11-6). It is the layer with which users normally interact for their decision support applications. Ideally, the reconciled data level is designed first and is the basis for the derived layer, whether data marts are dependent, independent, or virtual. In this section, we first discuss the characteristics of the derived data layer and the way that it is derived from the reconciled data layer. We then introduce the star schema (or dimensional model), which is the data model most commonly used today to implement this data layer. A star schema is a specially designed denormalized relational data model. We emphasize that the derived data layer can use normalized relations in the enterprise data warehouse; however, most organizations still build many data marts.

Characteristics of Derived Data

Earlier we defined derived data as data that have been selected, formatted, and aggregated for end-user decision support applications. As shown in Figure 11-6, the source of the derived data is the reconciled data described earlier. Derived data in a data mart are generally optimized for the needs of particular user groups, such as departments, workgroups, or even individuals. A common mode of operation is to select the relevant data from the enterprise data warehouse on a daily basis, format and aggregate those data as needed, and then load and index those data in the target data marts.

The objectives that are sought with derived data are quite different from the objectives of reconciled data. Typical objectives are the following:

- Provide ease of use for decision support applications
- Provide fast response for predefined user queries or requests for information
- Customize data for particular target user groups
- Support ad-hoc queries and data mining applications

To satisfy these needs, we usually find the following characteristics in derived data:

- Both detailed data and aggregate data are present.
  a. Detailed data are often (but not always) periodic—that is, they provide a historical record.
  b. Aggregate data are formatted to respond quickly to predetermined (or common) queries.
- Data are distributed to departmental servers.
- The data model that is most commonly used for a data mart is the star schema, which is a relational-like model. Proprietary models are also sometimes used.

The Star Schema

A **star schema** is a simple database design (particularly suited to ad-hoc queries) in which dimensional data (describing how data are commonly aggregated) are separated from fact or event data (describing individual business transactions). Another name that is often used is the dimensional model (Kimball, 1996a). Although the star schema is suited to ad-hoc queries (and other forms of informational processing), it is not suited to online transaction processing, and therefore is not generally used in operational systems, operational data stores, or an EDW.

Star schema: A simple database design in which dimensional data are separated from fact or event data. A dimensional model is another name for star schema.

Fact Tables and Dimension Tables
A star schema consists of two types of tables: fact tables and dimension tables. *Fact tables* contain factual or quantitative data (measurements) about a business such as units sold, orders booked, and so on. *Dimension tables* hold descriptive data (context) about the subjects of the business. The dimension tables are usually the source of attributes used to qualify, categorize, or summarize facts in queries, reports, or graphs. The simplest star schema consists of one fact table surrounded by several dimension tables. Typical business dimensions (subjects) are Product, Customer, and Period. Period, or time, is always one of the dimensions. This structure is shown in Figure 11-13, which contains four dimension tables.

Each dimension table has a one-to-many relationship to the central fact table. Each dimension table generally has a simple primary key, as well as several nonkey attributes. The primary key, in turn, is a foreign key in the fact table (as shown in Figure 11-13). The primary key of the fact table is a composite key that consists of the concatenation of all of the foreign keys (four keys in Figure 11-13), plus possibly other components that do not correspond to dimensions. The relationship between each dimension table and the fact table provides a join path that allows users to query the database easily, using SQL statements for either predefined or ad-hoc queries.

By now you have probably recognized that the star schema is not a new data model, but instead a denormalized implementation of the relational data model. The fact table plays the role of a normalized n-ary associative entity that links the

Figure 11-13
Components of a star schema

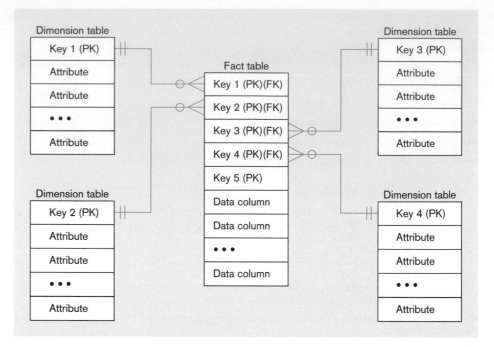

instances of the various dimensions, which are in second, but possibly not third, normal form. To review associative entities see Chapter 3, and for an example of the use of an associative entity, see Figure 3-11. The dimension tables are denormalized. Most experts view this denormalization as acceptable because dimensions are not updated and void costly joins; thus the star is optimized around certain facts and business objects.

Example Star Schema   A simple example of a star schema is shown in Figure 11-14. This example has three dimension tables: PRODUCT, PERIOD, and STORE, and one fact table, named SALES. The fact table is used to record three business facts: total units sold, total dollars sold, and total dollars cost. These totals are recorded for each possible value of product, period, and store.

Figure 11-14
Star schema example

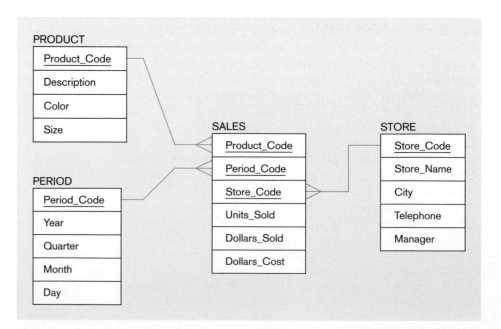

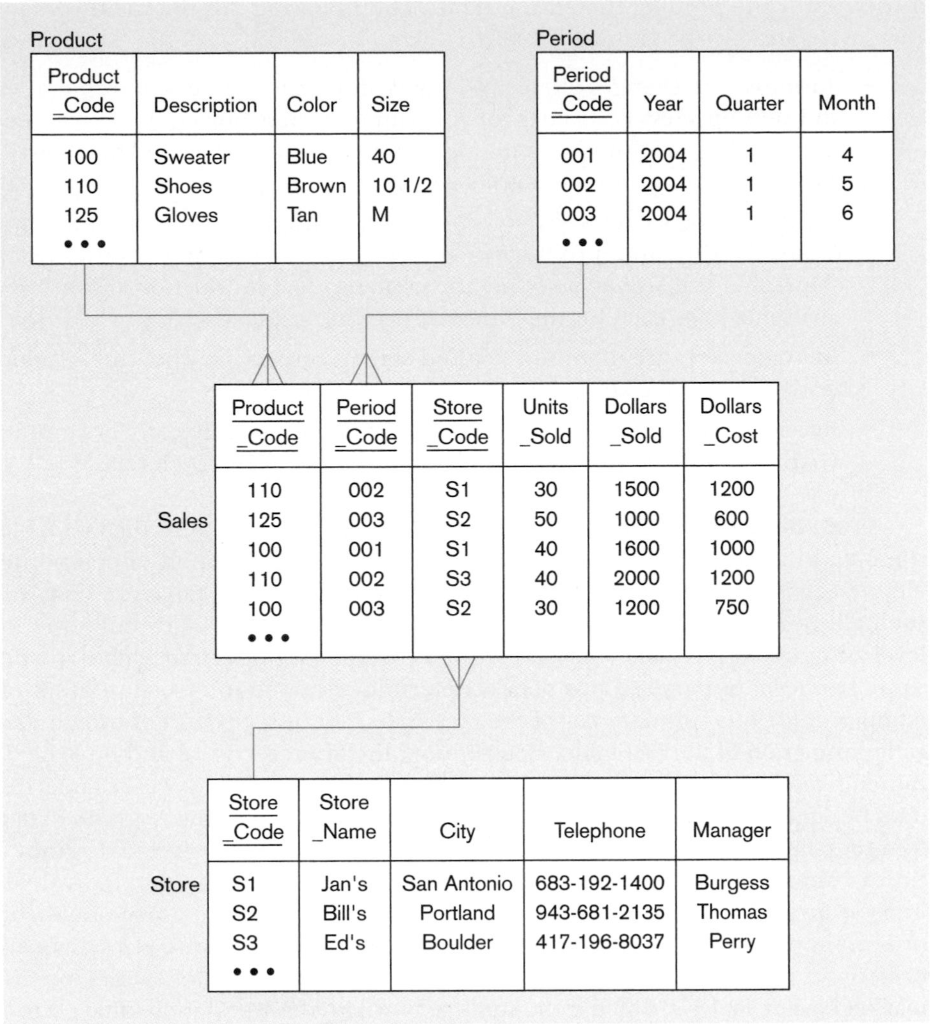

Figure 11-15
Star schema with sample data

Product

Product _Code	Description	Color	Size
100	Sweater	Blue	40
110	Shoes	Brown	10 1/2
125	Gloves	Tan	M
•••			

Period

Period _Code	Year	Quarter	Month
001	2004	1	4
002	2004	1	5
003	2004	1	6
•••			

Sales

Product _Code	Period _Code	Store _Code	Units _Sold	Dollars _Sold	Dollars _Cost
110	002	S1	30	1500	1200
125	003	S2	50	1000	600
100	001	S1	40	1600	1000
110	002	S3	40	2000	1200
100	003	S2	30	1200	750
•••					

Store

Store _Code	Store _Name	City	Telephone	Manager
S1	Jan's	San Antonio	683-192-1400	Burgess
S2	Bill's	Portland	943-681-2135	Thomas
S3	Ed's	Boulder	417-196-8037	Perry
•••				

Some sample data for this schema are shown in Figure 11-15. From the fact table, we find (for example) the following facts for product number 110 during period 002:

1. Thirty units were sold in store S1. The total dollar sale was 1500, and total dollar cost was 1200.

2. Forty units were sold in store S3. The total dollar sale was 2000, and total dollar cost was 1200.

Additional detail concerning the dimensions for this example can be obtained from the dimension tables. For example, in the PERIOD table, we find that period 002 corresponds to year 2004, quarter 1, month 5. Try tracing the other dimensions in a similar manner.

Surrogate Key Every key used to join the fact table with a dimension table should be a surrogate (nonintelligent or system assigned) key, not a key that uses a business value (sometimes called a natural, smart, or a production key). That is, in Figure 11-15, Product_Code, Store_Code, and Period_Code should all be surrogate keys in both the fact and dimension tables. If, for example, it is necessary to know the product catalog number, engineering number, or inventory item number for a product, these attributes would be stored along with Description, Color, and Size as attributes of the product dimension table. The following are the main reasons for this surrogate-key rule (Kimball, 1998a):

- Business keys change, often slowly, over time, and we need to remember old and new business key values for the same business object. As we will see in a later section on slowing changing dimensions, a surrogate key allows us to handle changing and unknown keys with ease.

- Using a surrogate key also allows us to keep track of different nonkey attribute values for the same production key over time. Thus, if a product package changes in size, we can associate the same product production key with several surrogate keys, each for the different package sizes.

- Surrogate keys are often simpler and shorter, especially when the production key is a composite key.

- Surrogate keys can be of the same length and format for all keys, no matter what business dimensions are involved in the database, even dates.

Grain: The level of detail in a fact table determined by the intersection of all the components of the primary key, including all foreign keys and any other primary key elements.

Market basket analysis: The study of buying behavior of individual customers.

Grain of Fact Table   The raw data of a star schema are kept in the fact table. All the data in a fact table are determined by the same combination of composite key elements; so, for example, if the most detailed data in a fact table are daily values, then all measurement data must be daily in that fact table. Determining the lowest level of detailed fact data stored is arguably the most important data mart design step. The level of detail of this data is determined by the intersection of all of the components of the primary key of the fact table. This intersection of primary keys is called the **grain** of the fact table. Determining the grain is critical and must be determined from business decision-making needs. There is always a way to summarize fact data by aggregating using dimension attributes, but there is no way in the data mart to understand business activity at a level of detail finer than the fact table grain.

A common grain would be each business transaction, such as an individual line item or an individual scanned item on a product sales receipt, a personnel change order, a line item on a material receipt, a claim against an insurance policy, a boarding pass, or an individual ATM transaction. A transactional grain allows users to perform **market basket analysis**, which is the study of buying behavior of individual customers. A grain higher than the transaction level might be all sales of a product on a given day, all receipts of a raw material in a given month at a specific warehouse, or the net effect of all ATM transactions for one ATM session. The finer the grain of the fact table, the more dimensions exist, the more fact rows exist, and often, the closer the data mart model is to a data model for the operational data store.

With the explosion of Web-based commerce, clicks become the possible lowest level of granularity. An analysis of Web site buying habits requires clickstream data (e.g., time spent on page, pages migrated from and to). Such an analysis can be used to understand Web site usability and to customize messages based on navigational paths taken.

Kimball (2001) and others recommend using the smallest grain possible, given the limitations of the data mart technology. Even when data mart user information requirements imply a certain level of aggregated grain, often after some use, users ask more detailed questions (drill down) as a way to explain why certain aggregated patterns exist. You cannot "drill down" below the grain of the fact tables (without going to other data sources, such as the EDW, ODS, or the original source systems, which may add considerable effort to the analysis).

Duration of the Database   Another important decision in the design of a data mart as well as the EDW or ODS is the amount of history to be kept; that is, the duration of the database. The natural duration is about 13 months or 5 calendar quarters, which is sufficient to see annual cycles in the data. Some businesses, such as financial institutions, have a need for longer durations. Older data may be difficult to source and cleanse if additional attributes are required from data sources. Even if sources of old data are available, it may be most difficult to find old values of dimension data, which are less likely than fact data to have been retained. Old fact data without associated dimension data at the time of the fact may be worthless.

Size of the Fact Table   As you would expect, the grain and duration of the fact table have a direct impact on the size of that table. We can estimate the number of rows in the fact table as follows:

1. Estimate the number of possible values for each dimension associated with the fact table (in other words, the number of possible values for each foreign key in the fact table).

2. Multiply the values obtained in the first step after making any necessary adjustments.

Let's apply this approach to the star schema shown in Figure 11-15. Assume the following values for the dimensions:

Total number of stores = 1,000
Total number of products = 10,000
Total number of periods = 24 (2 years' worth of monthly data)

Although there are 10,000 total products, only a fraction of these products are likely to record sales during a given month. Because item totals appear in the fact table only for items that record sales during a given month, we need to adjust this figure. Suppose that on average 50 percent (or 5,000) items record sales during a given month. Then an estimate of the number of rows in the fact table is computed as follows:

Total rows = 1,000 stores X 5,000 active products X 24 months
           = 120,000,000 rows (!)

Thus, in our relatively small example, the fact table that contains two years' worth of monthly totals can be expected to have well over 100 million rows. This example clearly illustrates that the size of the fact table is many times larger than the dimension tables. For example, the STORE table has 1,000 rows, the PRODUCT table 10,000 rows, and the PERIOD table 24 rows.

If we know the size of each field in the fact table, we can further estimate the size (in bytes) of that table. The fact table (named SALES) in Figure 11-15 has six fields. If each of these fields averages four bytes in length, we can estimate the total size of the fact table as follows:

Total size = 120,000,000 rows X 6 fields X 4 bytes/field
           = 2,880,000,000 bytes (or 2.88 gigabytes)

The size of the fact table depends on both the number of dimensions and the grain of the fact table. Suppose that after using the database shown in Figure 11-15 for a short period of time, the marketing department requests that *daily* totals be accumulated in the fact table. (This is a typical evolution of a data mart.) With the grain of the table changed to daily item totals, the number of rows is computed as follows:

Total rows = 1,000 stores X 2,000 active products X 720 days (2 years)
           = 1,440,000,000 rows

In the preceding calculation, we have assumed that 20 percent of all products record sales on a given day. The database can now be expected to contain well over 1 *billion* rows. The database size is calculated as follows:

Total size = 1,440,000,000 rows X 6 fields X 4 bytes/field
           = 34,560,000,000 bytes (or 34.56 gigabytes)

Many large retailers (such as Wal-Mart, Kmart, and Sears) and e-businesses (such as Travelocity.com and MatchLogic.com) now have data warehouses (or data marts).

Figure 11-16
Modeling dates

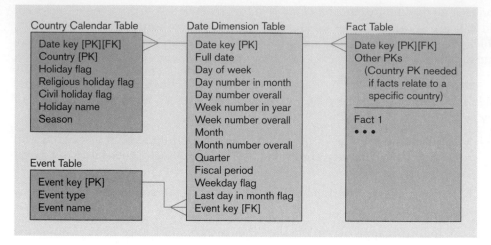

The size of most of these data warehouses is in the multiple-terabyte range and growing rapidly as marketing people continue to press for more dimensions and an ever-finer grain in the fact table.

Modeling Date and Time   Because data warehouses and data marts record facts about dimensions over time; date and time (henceforth simply called date) is always a dimension table, and a date surrogate key is always one of the components of the primary key of any fact table. Because a user may want to aggregate facts on many different aspects of date, a date dimension may have many nonkey attributes. Also, because some characteristics of dates are country or event specific (e.g., whether the date is a holiday or there is some standard event on a given day, such as a festival or football game), modeling the date dimension can be more complex than illustrated so far.

Figure 11-16 shows a typical design for the date dimension. As we have seen before, a date surrogate key appears as part of the primary key of the fact table and is the primary key of the date dimension table. The nonkey attributes of the date dimension table include all of the characteristics of dates that users use to categorize, summarize, and group facts that do not vary by country or event. For an organization doing business in several countries (or several geographical units in which dates have different characteristics), we have added a Country Calendar table to hold the characteristics of each date in *each country*. Thus, the Date key is a foreign key in the Country Calendar table, and each row of the Country Calendar table is unique by the combination of Date key and Country, which form the composite primary key for this table. A special event may occur on a given date. (We assume here, for simplicity, no more than one special event may occur on a given date.) We have normalized the Event data by creating an event table, so descriptive data on each event (e.g., the "Strawberry Festival" or the "Homecoming Game") are stored only once.

Variations of the Star Schema

The simple star schema introduced earlier is adequate for many applications. However, various extensions to this schema are often required to cope with more complex modeling problems. In this section, we briefly describe several such extensions: multiple fact tables with conformed dimensions and factless fact tables. For a discussion of additional extensions and variations, see subsequent sections, Poe (1996), and **www.ralphkimball.com**.

Multiple Fact Tables   It is often desirable for performance or other reasons to define more than one fact table in a given star schema. For example, suppose that various users require different levels of aggregation (in other words, a different table

Figure 11-17
Conformed dimensions

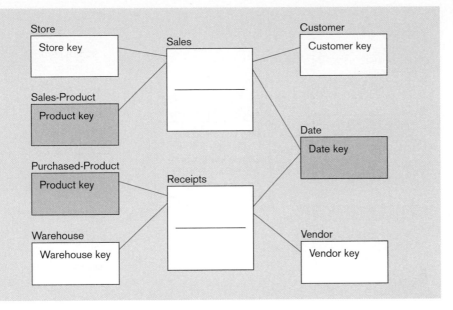

grain). Performance can be improved by defining a different fact table for each level of aggregation. The obvious trade-off is that storage requirements may increase dramatically with each new fact table. More commonly, multiple fact tables are needed to store facts for different combinations of dimensions.

Figure 11-17 illustrates a typical situation of multiple fact tables with two related star schemas. In this example, there are two fact tables, one at the center of each star:

1. Sales—facts about the sale of a product to a customer in a store on a date

2. Receipts—facts about the receipt of a product from a vendor to a warehouse on a date

As is common, data about one or more business subjects (in this case, Product and Date) need to be stored in dimension tables for each fact table. Two approaches have been adopted in this design to handle shared dimension tables. In one case, because the description of product is quite different for sales and receipts, two separate product dimension tables have been created. On the other hand, because users want the same descriptions of dates, one date dimension table is used. In each case, we have created a **conformed dimension**, meaning that the dimension means the same thing with each fact table, and hence, uses the same surrogate primary keys. Even when the two star schemas are stored in separate physical data marts, if dimensions are conformed, there is a potential for asking questions across the data marts (e.g., Do certain vendors recognize sales more quickly and are they able to supply replenishments with less lead time?). In general, conformed dimensions allow users to:

Conformed dimension: One or more dimension tables associated with two or more fact tables for which the dimension tables have the same business meaning and primary key with each fact table.

- Share nonkey dimension data
- Query across fact tables with consistency
- Work on facts and business subjects for which all users have the same meaning

Factless Fact Tables   There are applications for fact tables that do not have non-key data but do have foreign keys for the associated dimensions. The two general situations in which factless fact tables may apply are to track events (see Figure 11-18a) and to inventory the set of possible occurrences (called coverage) (see Figure 11-18b). The star schema in Figure 11-18a tracks which students attend which courses at which time in which facilities with which instructors. All that needs to be known is whether this event occurs, represented by the intersection of the five foreign keys.

Figure 11-18
Factless fact tables
(a) Factless fact table showing occurrence of an event

(b) Factless fact table showing coverage

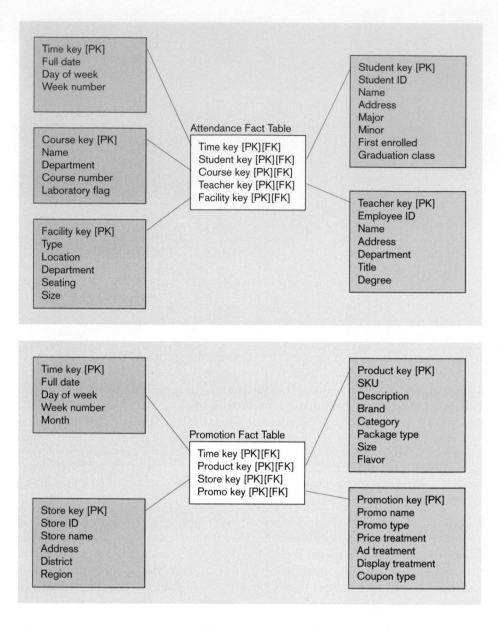

The star schema in Figure 11-18b shows the set of possible sales of a product in a store at a particular time under a given promotion. A second sales fact table, not shown in Figure 11-18b, could contain the dollar and unit sales (facts) for this same combination of dimensions (i.e., with the same four foreign keys as the Promotion fact table plus these two nonkey facts). With these two fact tables and four conformed dimensions, it is possible to discover which products that were on a specific promotion at a given time in a specific store did not sell (i.e., had zero sales), which can be discovered by finding a combination of the four key values in the promotion fact table, which are not in the sales fact table. The sales fact table, alone, is not sufficient to answer this question because it is missing rows for a combination of the four key values, which has zero sales.

Normalizing Dimension Tables

Fact tables are fully normalized because each fact depends on the whole composite primary key and nothing but the composite key. However, dimension tables may not be normalized. Most data warehouse experts find this acceptable for a data

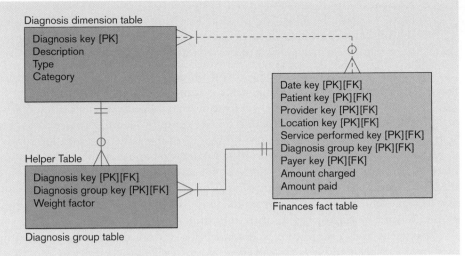

Figure 11-19
Multivalued dimension

mart optimized and simplified for a given user group, so that all the dimension data are only one join away from associated facts. Sometimes, as with any relational database, the anomalies of a denormalized dimension table cause add, update, and delete problems. In this section, we address various situations in which it makes sense or is essential to further normalize dimension tables.

Multivalued Dimensions   There may be a need for facts to be qualified by a set of values for the same business subject. For example, consider the hospital example in Figure 11-19. In this situation, a particular hospital charge and payment for a patient on a date (e.g., for all foreign keys in the Finances fact table) is associated with one or more diagnoses. (We indicate this with a dashed *M:N* relationship line between the Diagnosis and Finances tables.) We could pick the most important diagnosis as a component key for the Finances table, but that would mean we lose potentially important information about other diagnoses associated with a row. Or, we could design the Finances table with a fixed number of diagnosis keys, more than we think is ever possible to associate with one row of the Finances table, but this would create null components of the primary key for many rows, which violates a property of relational databases.

The best approach (the normalization approach) is to create a table for an associative entity between Diagnosis and Finances, in this case the Diagnosis group table (thus the dashed relationship is not needed). In the data warehouse database world, such an associative entity table is called a "helper table," and we will see more examples of helper tables as we progress through subsequent sections. A helper table may have nonkey attributes (as can any table for an associative entity); for example, the weight factor in the Diagnosis group table of Figure 11-19 indicates the relative role each diagnosis plays in each group, presumably normalized to a total of 100 percent for all the diagnoses in a group. Also note that it is not possible for more than one Finances row to be associated with the same Diagnosis group key; thus, the diagnosis group key is really a surrogate for the composite primary key of the Finances fact table.

Hierarchies   Many times a dimension in a star schema forms a natural hierarchy. For example, there are geographical hierarchies (e.g., markets with a state, states within a region, and regions within a country) and product hierarchies (packages or sizes within a product, products within bundles, and bundles within product groups). When a dimension participates in a hierarchy, the database designer has two basic choices:

1. Include all the information for each level of the hierarchy in a single denormalized dimension table for the most detailed level of the hierarchy, thus creating considerable redundancy and update anomalies.

2. Normalize the dimension into a nested set of tables with *1:M* relationships between them. It will still be possible to aggregate the fact data at any level of the hierarchy, but now the user will have to perform nested joins along the hierarchy or be given a view of the hierarchy that is prejoined.

Consider the example of a typical consulting company that invoices customers for specified time periods on projects. A revenue fact table in this situation might show how much revenue is billed and for how many hours on each invoice, which is for a particular time period, customer, service, employee, and project. Because consulting work may be done for different divisions of the same organization, if we want to understand the total role of consulting in any level of a customer organization, we need a customer hierarchy. This hierarchy is a recursive relationship between organizational units. As shown in Figure 5-17 for a supervisory hierarchy, the standard way to represent this in a normalized database is to put into the company row a foreign key of the Company key for its parent unit.

Recursive relationships implemented in this way are difficult for the typical end user because specifying how to aggregate at any level of the hierarchy requires complex SQL programming. A simpler and general alternative appear in Figure 11-20. Figure 11-20a shows how this hierarchy is typically modeled in a data warehouse using a helper table (Kimball, 1998b; Chisholm, 2000). Each customer organizational unit the consulting firm serves is assigned a different surrogate customer key and row in the Customer dimension table, and the customer surrogate key is used as a foreign key in

Figure 11-20
Representing hierarchical relationships within a dimension
(a) Use of a helper table

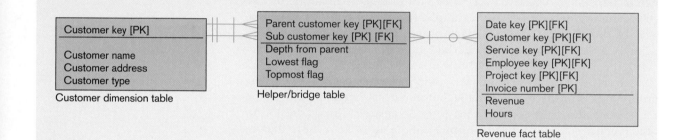

Customer dimension table   Helper/bridge table   Revenue fact table

(b) Example hierarchy with customer and helper tables

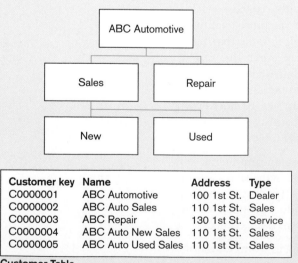

Parent key	Sub key	Depth	Lowest	Topmost
C0000001	C0000001	0	N	Y
C0000001	C0000002	1	N	N
C0000001	C0000003	1	N	N
C0000001	C0000004	2	Y	N
C0000001	C0000005	2	Y	N
C0000002	C0000002	0	N	N
C0000002	C0000004	1	Y	N
C0000002	C0000005	1	Y	N
C0000003	C0000003	0	Y	N
C0000004	C0000004	0	Y	N
C0000005	C0000005	0	Y	N

Hierarchy Helper Table

Customer key	Name	Address	Type
C0000001	ABC Automotive	100 1st St.	Dealer
C0000002	ABC Auto Sales	110 1st St.	Sales
C0000003	ABC Repair	130 1st St.	Service
C0000004	ABC Auto New Sales	110 1st St.	Sales
C0000005	ABC Auto Used Sales	110 1st St.	Sales

Customer Table

the Revenue fact table; this foreign key relates to the Sub customer key in the Helper table, because the revenue facts are associated at the lowest possible level of the organizational hierarchy. The problem with joining in a recursive relationship of arbitrary depth is that the user has to write code to join an arbitrary number of times (once for each level of subordination) and these joins in a data warehouse, because of its massive size, can be very time-consuming (except for some high-performance data warehouse technologies using parallel processing). To avoid this problem, the helper table flattens out the hierarchy by recording a row for each organizational subunit and each of its parent organizational units (including itself) all the way up to the top unit of the customer organization. Each row of this helper table has three descriptors: the number of levels the subunit is from its parent unit for *that* table row, a flag indicating whether this subunit is the lowest in the hierarchy, and a flag indicating whether this subunit is the highest in the hierarchy. Figure 11-20b depicts an example customer organizational hierarchy and the rows that would be in the helper table to represent that total organization. (There would be other rows in the helper table for the subunit-parent unit relationships within other customer organizations.)

The Revenue fact table in Figure 11-20a includes a primary key attribute of Invoice number. Invoice number is an example of what is called a *degenerative dimension*, which has no interesting dimension attributes (thus no dimension table exists and Invoice number is not part of the table's primary key). Invoice number also is not a fact that will be used for aggregation because mathematics on this attribute has no meaning. This attribute may be helpful if there is a need to explore an ODS or source systems to find additional details about the invoice transaction or to group together related fact rows (e.g., all the revenue line items on the same invoice).

When the dimension tables are further normalized by using helper tables (sometimes called *bridge* or *reference tables*), the simple star schema turns into a **snowflake schema**. A snowflake schema resembles a segment of an ODS or source database centered on the transaction tables summarized into the fact table and all of the tables directly and indirectly related to these transaction tables. Many data warehouse experts discourage the use of snowflake schemas because they are more complex for users and require more joins to bring the results together into one table. A snowflake may be desirable if the normalization saves significant redundant space (e.g., when there are many redundant, long textual attributes) or when users may find browsing through the normalized tables themselves useful.

An even simpler approach is taken when the depth of the hierarchy can be fixed, in which case each level of the hierarchy is a separate dimensional entity. Some hierarchies can more easily use this scheme than can others. Consider the product hierarchy in Figure 11-21. Here each product is part of a product family (e.g., Crest

Snowflake schema: An expanded version of a star schema in which dimension tables are normalized into several related tables.

Figure 11-21
Fixed product hierarchy

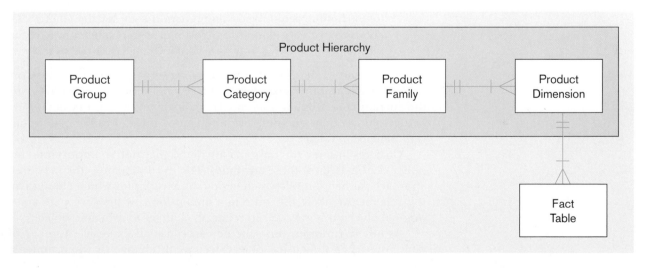

with Tartar Control is part of Crest), and a product family is part of a product category (e.g., toothpaste), and a category is part of a product group (e.g., health and beauty). This works well if every product follows this same hierarchy.

Slowly Changing Dimensions

Recall that data warehouses and data marts track business activities over time. The business does not remain static over time; products change size and weight, customers relocate, stores change layouts, and sales staff are assigned to different locations. Most systems of record keep only the current values for business subjects (e.g., the current customer address). But in a data warehouse or data mart, we need to know the history of values to match the history of facts with the correct dimensional descriptions at the time the facts happened. For example, we need to associate a sales fact with the description of the associated customer during the time period of the sales fact, which may not be the description of that customer today. Of course, business subjects change slowly compared with most transactional data (e.g., inventory level). Thus, dimensional data change, but change slowly.

We might handle changing dimension attributes in one of three ways (Kimball, 1996b and 1999):

1. Overwrite the current value with the new value, but this is unacceptable because it eliminates the description of the past that we need to interpret historical facts.

2. For each dimension attribute that changes, create a current value field and as many old value fields as we wish (i.e., a multivalued attribute with a fixed number of occurrences). This scheme might work if there were a predictable number of changes over the length of history retained in the data warehouse (e.g., if we keep 24 months of history and an attribute may change value at most monthly). However, this works only under this kind of restrictive assumption and cannot be generalized to any slowly changing dimension attribute.

3. Create a new dimension table row (with a new surrogate key) each time the dimension object changes; this new row contains all the dimension characteristics at the time of the change; the new surrogate key is the original surrogate key plus the start date for the period when these dimension values are in effect. A fact row is associated with the surrogate key whose attributes apply at the date/time of the fact (that is, the fact date/time falls between the start and end dates of a dimension row for the same original surrogate key). We likely also want to store in a dimension row the date/time the change ceases being in effect (which will be the maximum possible date or null for the current row for each dimension object) and a reason code for the change. This approach allows us to create as many dimensional object changes as necessary. However, it becomes unwieldy if rows frequently change or if the rows are very long.

A variation of the third approach creates two dimension tables: one table with only the current dimension rows and a second table with the history rows. Because the current table will likely be much smaller than the history table is, this may be a better solution than one dimension table is if most of the queries require only current dimension values.

Changes in some dimensional attributes may not be important. Hence, the first policy can be used for these attributes. The third scheme is the most frequently used approach for handling slowly changing dimensions for which changes matter. Under this scheme, we likely also store in a dimension row the surrogate key value for the original object; this way, we can relate all changes to the same object.

As noted, however, this scheme can cause an excessive number of dimension table rows when dimension objects frequently change or when dimension rows are

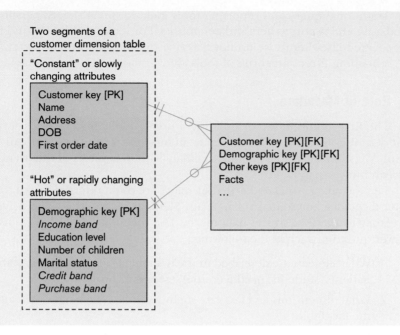

Figure 11-22
Dimension segmentation

large "monster dimensions." Figure 11-22 illustrates one approach, dimension segmentation, which handles this situation as well as the more general case of subsets of dimension attributes that change at different frequencies. In this example, the Customer dimension is segmented into two dimension tables; one segment may hold nearly constant or very slowly changing dimensions and other segments (we show only two in this example) hold clusters of attributes that change more rapidly and, for attributes in the same cluster, often change at the same time. These more rapidly changing attributes are often called "hot" attributes by data warehouse designers.

Another aspect of this segmentation is that for hot attributes, we changed individual dimension attributes, such as customer income (e.g., $75,400/year) into an attribute for a band, or range, of income values (e.g., $60,000–$89,999/year). Bands are defined as required by users and are as narrow or wide as can be useful, but certainly some precision is lost. Bands make the hot attributes less hot, because a change within a band does not cause a new row to be written. This design is more complex for users because they now may have to join facts with multiple dimension segments, depending on the analysis. See Kimball (2002) for additional ideas on handling slowly changing dimensions.

THE USER INTERFACE

Even a well-designed data mart or enterprise data warehouse, loaded with relevant data, may not be used unless users are provided with a powerful, intuitive interface that allows them to access and analyze those data easily. In this section, we provide a brief introduction to contemporary interfaces for data warehouses.

A variety of tools are available to query and analyze data stored in data warehouses and data marts. These tools may be classified as follows:

- Traditional query and reporting tools
- On-line analytical processing (OLAP), MOLAP, and ROLAP tools
- Data mining tools
- Data visualization tools

Traditional query and reporting tools include spreadsheets, personal computer databases, and report writers and generators. For reasons of space (and because they are covered elsewhere), we do not describe these tools in this chapter. We describe the remaining three categories of tools after discussing the role of metadata.

Role of Metadata

The first requirement for building a user-friendly interface is a set of metadata that describes the data in the data mart in business terms that users can easily understand. We show the association of metadata with data marts in the overall three-level data architecture in Figure 11-6.

The metadata associated with data marts are often referred to as a "data catalog," "data directory," or some similar term. Metadata serve as kind of a "yellow pages" directory to the data in the data marts. The metadata should allow users to easily answer questions such as the following:

1. What subjects are described in the data mart? (Typical subjects are customers, patients, students, products, courses, and so on.)

2. What dimensions and facts are included in the data mart? What is the grain of the fact table?

3. How are the data in the data mart derived from the enterprise data warehouse data? What rules are used in the derivation?

4. How are the data in the enterprise data warehouse derived from operational data? What rules are used in this derivation?

5. What reports and predefined queries are available to view the data?

6. What drill-down and other data analysis techniques are available?

7. Who is responsible for the quality of data in the data marts, and to whom are requests for changes made?

Querying Tools

The most common database query language, SQL (see Chapters 7 and 8), is being extended to support some types of calculations and querying needed for a data warehousing environment. In general, however, SQL is not an analytical language (Mundy, 2001). Recent versions of SQL do include some data warehousing extensions. Because many data warehousing operations deal with categories of objects, possibly ordered by date, the SQL standard includes a WINDOW clause to define dynamic sets of rows. For example, a WINDOW clause can be used to define three adjacent days as the basis for calculating moving averages. (Think of a window moving between the bottom and top of its window frame, giving you a sliding view of rows of data.) PARTITION within a WINDOW is similar to GROUP BY; PARTITION tells a WINDOW clause the basis for each set, an ORDER BY clause sequences the elements of a set, and the ROWS clause says how many rows in sequence to use in a calculation. The RANK windowing function calculates something that is very difficult to calculate in standard SQL, which is the row of a table in a specific relative position based on some criteria (e.g., the customer with the third-highest sales in a given period). In the case of ties, RANK will cause gaps (e.g., if there is a two way tie for third, then there is no rank of 4, rather the next rank is 5). DENSE_RANK works the same as RANK but creates no gaps. The CUME_DIST function finds the relative position of a specified value in a group of values; this function can be used to find the break point for percentiles (e.g., what value is the break point for the top 10 percent of sales or which customers are in the top 10 percent of sales?).

See the section Analytical Functions in Chapter 8 for an example of a WINDOW clause. Different DBMS vendors will implement some or all of the SQL:1999 OLAP extension commands and possibly others specific to their products. SQL:1999 still is not a full-featured data warehouse querying and analysis tool, but it is a start at recognizing the special querying needs of decision support systems.

Online Analytical Processing (OLAP) Tools

A specialized class of tools has been developed to provide users with multidimensional views of their data. Such tools also offer users a graphical interface so that they can easily analyze their data. In the simplest case, data are viewed as a simple three-dimensional cube.

Online analytical processing (OLAP) is the use of a set of graphical tools that provides users with multidimensional views of their data and allows them to analyze the data using simple windowing techniques. The term online analytical processing is intended to contrast with the more traditional term *online transaction processing (OLTP)*. The differences between these two types of processing were summarized in Table 11-1. The term *multidimensional analysis* is often used as a synonym for OLAP.

An example of a "data cube" (or multidimensional view) of data that is typical of OLAP is shown in Figure 11-22. This view corresponds quite closely to the star schema introduced in Figure 11-14. Two of the dimensions in Figure 11-23 correspond to the dimension tables (PRODUCT and PERIOD) in Figure 11-14, whereas the third dimension (named measures) corresponds to the data in the fact table (named SALES) in Figure 11-14.

OLAP is actually a general term for several categories of data warehouse and data mart access tools (Dyché, 2000). **Relational OLAP (ROLAP)** tools use variations of SQL and view the database as a traditional relational database, in either a star schema or other normalized or denormalized set of tables. ROLAP tools access the data warehouse or data mart directly. **Multidimensional OLAP (MOLAP)** tools load data into an intermediate structure, usually a three- or higher dimensional array. We illustrate MOLAP in the next few sections because of its popularity. It is important to note with MOLAP that the data are not simply viewed as a multidimensional array (cube for three dimensions), but rather a MOLAP data mart is created by extracting data from

Online analytical processing (OLAP): The use of a set of graphical tools that provides users with multidimensional views of their data and allows them to analyze the data using simple windowing techniques.

Relational OLAP (ROLAP): OLAP tools that view the database as a traditional relational database in either a star schema or other normalized or denormalized set of tables.

Multidimensional OLAP (MOLAP): OLAP tools that load data into an intermediate structure, usually a three-or higher dimensional array.

Figure 11-23
Slicing a data cube

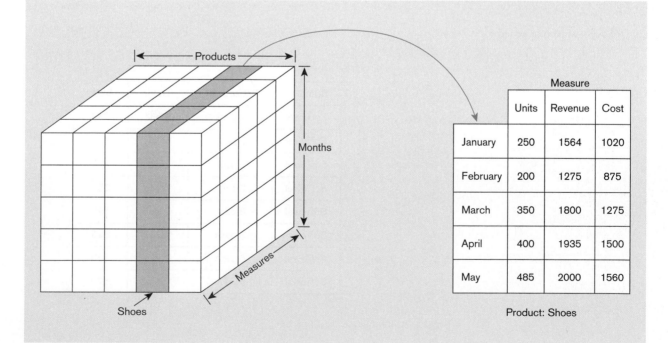

	Measure		
	Units	Revenue	Cost
January	250	1564	1020
February	200	1275	875
March	350	1800	1275
April	400	1935	1500
May	485	2000	1560

Product: Shoes

the data warehouse or data mart and then storing the data in a specialized separate data store through which data can be viewed only through a multidimensional structure. Other, less-common categories of OLAP tools are DOLAP (database OLAP), which includes OLAP functionality in the DBMS query language (there are proprietary, non-ANSI standard SQL systems that do this), and HOLAP (hybrid OLAP), which allows access via both multidimensional cubes or relational query languages.

Slicing a Cube   Figure 11-23 also shows a typical MOLAP operation: slicing the data cube to produce a simple two-dimensional table or view. In Figure 11-23, this slice is for the product named "shoes." The resulting table shows the three measures (units, revenues, and cost) for this product by period (or month). Other views can easily be developed by the user by means of simple "drag and drop" operations. This type of operation is often called *slicing and dicing* the cube.

Another operation closely related to slicing and dicing is data pivoting. This term refers to rotating the view for a particular data point to obtain another perspective. For example, Figure 11-23 shows sales of 400 units of shoes for April. The analyst could pivot this view to obtain (for example) the sales of shoes by store for the same month.

Drill-Down   Another type of operation often used in multidimensional analysis is *drill-down*—that is, analyzing a given set of data at a finer level of detail. An example of drill-down is shown in Figure 11-24. Figure 11-24a shows a summary report for the total sales of three package sizes for a given brand of paper towels: 2-pack, 3-pack,

Figure 11-24
Example of drill-down
(a) Summary report

Brand	Package size	Sales
SofTowel	2-pack	$75
SofTowel	3-pack	$100
SofTowel	6-pack	$50

(b) Drill-down with color added

Brand	Package size	Color	Sales
SofTowel	2-pack	White	$30
SofTowel	2-pack	Yellow	$25
SofTowel	2-pack	Pink	$20
SofTowel	3-pack	White	$50
SofTowel	3-pack	Green	$25
SofTowel	3-pack	Yellow	$25
SofTowel	6-pack	White	$30
SofTowel	6-pack	Yellow	$20

and 6-pack. However, the towels come in different colors, and the analyst wants a further breakdown of sales by color within each of these package sizes. Using an OLAP tool, this breakdown can be easily obtained using a "point-and-click" approach with a mouse device.

The result of the drill-down is shown in Figure 11-24b. Notice that a drill-down presentation is equivalent to adding another column to the original report. (In this case, a column was added for the attribute "color".)

Executing a drill-down (as in this example) may require that the OLAP tool "reach back" to the data warehouse to obtain the detail data necessary for the drill-down. This type of operation can be performed by an OLAP tool (without user participation) only if an integrated set of metadata is available to that tool. Some tools even permit the OLAP tool to reach back to the operational data if necessary for a given query.

Data Mining Tools

With OLAP, users are searching for answers to questions they have raised, for example, "Are health care costs greater for single or married persons?" With data mining, users are looking for patterns or trends in a collection of facts or observations. **Data mining** is knowledge discovery using a sophisticated blend of techniques from traditional statistics, artificial intelligence, and computer graphics (Weldon, 1996).

The goals of data mining are threefold:

1. *Explanatory*   To explain some observed event or condition, such as why sales of pickup trucks have increased in Colorado

2. *Confirmatory*   To confirm a hypothesis, such as whether two-income families are more likely to buy family medical coverage than single-income families

3. *Exploratory*   To analyze data for new or unexpected relationships, such as what spending patterns are likely to accompany credit card fraud

Data Mining Techniques   Several different techniques are commonly used for data mining. See Table 11-4 for a summary of the most common of these techniques. The choice of an appropriate technique depends on the nature of the data to be analyzed, as well as the size of the data set. Data mining can be performed against either the data marts or the enterprise data warehouse (or both).

Data Mining Applications   Data mining techniques have been successfully used for a wide range of real-world applications. A summary of some of the typical types of applications, with examples of each type, is presented in Table 11-5. Data mining applications are growing rapidly, for the following reasons:

Data mining: Knowledge discovery using a sophisticated blend of techniques from traditional statistics, artificial intelligence, and computer graphics.

Table 11-4   Data Mining Techniques

Technique	Function
Regression	Test or discover relationships from historical data
Decision tree induction	Test or discover if . . . Then rules for decision propensity
Clustering and signal processing	Discover subgroups or segments
Affinity	Discover things with strong mutual relationships
Sequence association	Discover cycles of events and behaviors
Case-based reasoning	Derives rules from real-world case examples
Rule discover	Searches for patterns and correlations in large data sets
Fractals	Compresses large databases without losing information
Neural nets	Develops predictive models based on principles modeled after the human brain

Table 11-5   Typical Data Mining Applications (Adapted from Zaitz, 1997, and Dyche, 2000)

Type of Application	Example
Profiling populations	Developing profiles of high-value customers, credit risks, and credit-card fraud.
Analysis of business trends	Identifying markets with above average (or below average) growth.
Target marketing	Identifying customers (or customer segments) for promotional activity.
Usage analysis	Identifying usage patterns for products and services.
Campaign effectiveness	Comparing campaign strategies for effectiveness.
Product affinity	Identifying products that are purchased concurrently, or the characteristics of shoppers for certain product groups.
Customer retention and churn	Examining the behavior of customers who have left for competitors to prevent remaining customers from leaving.
Profitability analysis	Determining which customers are profitable given the total set of activities the customer has with the organization.
Customer value analysis	Determining where valuable customers are at different stages in their life.
Up-selling	Identifying new products or services to sell to a customer based upon critical events and life-style changes.

- The amount of data in data warehouses and data marts is growing exponentially. Users need the type of automated techniques provided by data mining tools to mine the knowledge in these data.

- New data mining tools with expanded capabilities are continually being introduced.

- Increasing competitive pressures are forcing companies to make better use of the information and knowledge contained in their data.

Data Visualization

Data visualization: The representation of data in graphical and multimedia formats for human analysis.

Often the human eye can best discern patterns when data are represented graphically. **Data visualization** is the representation of data in graphical and multimedia formats for human analysis. Benefits of data visualization include the ability to better observe trends and patterns and to identify correlations and clusters. Data visualization is often used in conjunction with data mining and other analytical techniques.

S u m m a r y

Despite the vast quantities of data collected in organizations today, most managers have difficulty obtaining the information they need for decision making. Two major factors contribute to this "information gap." First, data are often heterogeneous and inconsistent as a result of the piecemeal system development approaches that have commonly been used. Second, systems are developed (or acquired) primarily to satisfy operational objectives, with little thought given to the information needs of managers.

There are major differences between operational and informational systems, and between the data that appear in those systems. Operational systems are used to run the business on a current basis, and the primary design goal is to provide high performance to users who process transactions and update databases. Informational systems are used to support managerial decision making, and the primary design goal is to provide ease of access and use for information workers.

The purpose of a data warehouse is to consolidate and integrate data from a variety of sources, and to format those data in a context for making accurate business decisions. A data warehouse is an integrated and consistent store of subject-oriented data obtained from a variety of sources and formatted into a meaningful context to support decision making in an organization.

Most data warehouses today follow a three-layer architecture. The first layer consists of data distributed throughout the various operational systems. The second layer is an enterprise data warehouse, which is a centralized, integrated data warehouse that is the control point and single source of all data made available to end users for decision support applications. The third layer is a series of data marts. A data mart is a data warehouse whose data are limited in scope for the decision-making needs of a particular user group. A data mart can be independent of an enterprise data warehouse (EDW), derived from the EDW, or a logical subset of the EDW.

The data layer in the enterprise data warehouse is called the reconciled data layer. The characteristics of this data layer (ideally) are the following: It is detailed, historical, normalized, comprehensive, and quality controlled. Reconciled data are obtained by filling the enterprise data warehouse or operational data store from the various operational systems. Reconciling the data requires four steps: capturing the data from the source systems; scrubbing the data (to remove inconsistencies); transforming the data (to convert it to the format required in the data warehouse); and loading and indexing the data in the data warehouse. Reconciled data are not normally accessed directly by end users.

The data layer in the data marts is referred to as the derived data layer. These are the data that are accessed by end users for their decision support applications.

Data are most often stored in a data mart using a variation of the relational model called the star schema, or dimensional model. A star schema is a simple database design where dimensional data are separated from fact or event data. A star schema consists of two types of tables: dimension tables and fact tables. The size of a fact table depends, in part, on the grain (or level of detail) in that table. Fact tables with over one billion rows are common in data warehouse applications today. There are several variations of the star schema, including models with multiple fact tables and snowflake schemas that arise when one or more dimensions have a hierarchical structure.

A variety of end-user interfaces are available to access and analyze decision support data. Online analytical processing (or OLAP) is the use of a set of graphical tools that provides users with multidimensional views of their data (data are normally viewed as a cube). OLAP facilitates data analysis operations such as slice and dice, data pivoting, and drill-down. Data mining is a form of knowledge discovery that uses a sophisticated blend of techniques from traditional statistics, artificial intelligence, and computer graphics.

CHAPTER REVIEW

Key Terms

Aggregation	Dependent data mart	Informational system
Conformed dimension	Derived data	Joining
Data mart	Enterprise data warehouse (EDW)	Logical data mart
Data mining		Market basket analysis
Data scrubbing	Event	Multidimensional OLAP (MOLAP)
Data transformation	Grain	
Data visualization	Incremental extract	Online analytical processing (OLAP)
Data warehouse	Independent data mart	

Operational data store
   (ODS)
Operational system
Periodic data
Real-time data warehouse

Reconciled data
Refresh mode
Relational OLAP
   (ROLAP)
Selection

Snowflake schema
Star schema
Static extract
Transient data
Update mode

Review Questions

1. Define each of the following terms:
   a. data warehouse
   b. data mart
   c. reconciled data
   d. derived data
   e. online analytical processing
   f. data mining
   g. star schema
   h. snowflake schema
   i. grain
   j. static extract
   k. incremental extract
   l. event

2. Match the following terms and definitions:

   _____ event
   _____ periodic data
   _____ data mart
   _____ star schema
   _____ data mining
   _____ reconciled data
   _____ dependent data mart
   _____ data visualization
   _____ transient data
   _____ snowflake schema
   _____ data transformation
   _____ data scrubbing

   a. previous data content is lost
   b. detailed, historical data
   c. converts data formats
   d. corrects errors in source data
   e. data are not altered or deleted
   f. a database action (e.g., create)
   g. data warehouse of limited scope
   h. dimension and fact tables
   i. form of knowledge discovery
   j. filled from data warehouse
   k. results from hierarchical dimensions
   l. data represented in graphical formats

3. Contrast the following terms:
   a. static extract; incremental extract
   b. transient data; periodic data
   c. data warehouse; data mart; operational data store
   d. data scrubbing; data transformation
   e. reconciled data; derived data
   f. fact table; dimension table
   g. star schema; snowflake schema
   h. independent data mart; dependent data mart; logical data mart

4. List the five major trends that necessitate data warehousing in many organizations today.

5. Briefly describe the major components of a data warehouse architecture.

6. List the three types of metadata that appear in a three-layer data warehouse architecture and briefly describe the purpose of each.

7. List five typical characteristics of reconciled data.

8. List and briefly describe four steps in the data reconciliation process.

9. List five errors and inconsistencies that are commonly found in operational data.

10. Briefly describe three types of operations that can easily be performed with OLAP tools.

11. Explain how the phrase extract, transform, and load relates to the data reconciliation process.

12. Explain the pros and cons (limitations) of independent data marts.

13. Explain how the volatility of a data warehouse is different from the volatility of a database for an operational information system.

14. Explain the pros and cons of logical data marts.

15. List common tasks performed during data cleansing.

16. Visit http://www.baseline-consulting.com/analytics/default.aspx?doc=analytics0705.htm and play the "Let's Play Post Office!" game. What did you learn about cleansing addresses in the USA from this game?

17. Describe the characteristics of a surrogate key as used in a data warehouse or data mart.

18. Why is time almost always a dimension in a data warehouse or data mart?

19. What is the purpose of conformed dimensions for different star schemas within the same data warehousing environment?

20. Can a fact table have no nonkey attributes? Why or why not?

21. In what ways are dimension tables often not normalized?

22. What is a hierarchy as it relates to a dimension table?

23. What is the meaning of the phrase "slowing changing dimension"?

24. Explain the most common approach used to handle slowly changing dimensions.

Problems and Exercises

1. Examine the three tables with student data shown in Figure 11-1. Design a single table format that will hold all of the data (nonredundantly) that are contained in these three tables. Choose column names that you believe are most appropriate for these data.

2. The following table shows some simple student data as of the date 06/20/2004:

Key	Name	Major
001	Amy	Music
002	Tom	Business
003	Sue	Art
004	Joe	Math
005	Ann	Engineering

The following transactions occur on 06/21/2004:

- Student 004 changes major from 'Math' to 'Business.'
- Student 005 is deleted from the file.
- New student 006 is added to the file: Name is 'Jim,' Major is 'Phys Ed.'

The following transactions occur on 06/22/2004:

- Student 003 changes major from 'Art' to 'History.'
- Student 006 changes major from 'Phys Ed' to 'Basket Weaving.'

Your assignment is in two parts:

a. Construct tables for 06/21/2004 and 06/22/2004 reflecting these transactions, assume that the data are transient (refer to Figure 11-8).

b. Construct tables for 06/21/2004 and 06/22/2004 reflecting these transactions, assume that the data are periodic (refer to Figure 11-9).

3. Millennium College wants you to help them design a star schema to record grades for courses completed by students. There are four dimension tables, with attributes as follows:

- **Course_Section**. Attributes: Course_ID, Section_Number, Course_Name, Units, Room_ID, Room_Capacity. During a given semester the college offers an average of 500 course sections.

- **Professor**. Attributes: Prof_ID, Prof_Name, Title, Department_ID, Department_Name.

- **Student**. Attributes: Student_ID, Student_Name, Major. Each course section has an average of forty students.

- **Period**. Attributes: Semester_ID, Year. The database will contain data for thirty periods (a total of 10 years).

The only fact that is to be recorded in the fact table is Course_Grade.

a. Design a star schema for this problem. See Figure 11-14 for the format you should follow.

b. Estimate the number of rows in the fact table, using the assumptions stated above.

c. Estimate the total size of the fact table (in bytes), assuming that each field has an average of five bytes.

d. Various characteristics of sections, professors, and students change over time. How do you propose designing the star schema to allow for these changes? Why?

4. Having mastered the principles of normalization described in Chapter 5, you recognize immediately that the star schema you developed for Millennium College (Problem and Exercise 3) is not in third normal form. Using these principles, convert the star schema to a snowflake schema. What impact (if any) does this have on the size of the fact table for this problem?

5. You are to construct a star schema for Simplified Automobile Insurance Company (see Kimball, 1996b, for a more realistic example). The relevant dimensions, dimension attributes, and dimension sizes are as follows:

- **Insured Party**. Attributes: Insured_Party_ID, Name. There is an average of two insured parties for each policy and covered item.

- **Coverage Item**. Attributes: Coverage_Key, Description. There is an average of ten covered items per policy.

- **Agent**. Attributes: Agent_ID, Agent_Name. There is one agent for each policy and covered item.

- **Policy**. Attributes: Policy_ID, Type. The company has approximately one million policies at the present time.

- **Period**. Attributes: Date_Key, Fiscal_Period.

Facts to be recorded for each combination of these dimensions are Policy_Premium, Deductible, and Number_of_Transactions.

a. Design a star schema for this problem. See Figure 11-14 for the format you should follow.

b. Estimate the number of rows in the fact table, using the assumptions stated above.

c. Estimate the total size of the fact table (in bytes), assuming an average of five bytes per field.

6. Simplified Automobile Insurance Company would like to add a Claims dimension to its star schema (see Problem and Exercise 5). Attributes of Claim are Claim_ID, Claim_Description, and Claim_Type. Attributes of the fact table are now Policy_Premium, Deductible, and Monthly_Claim_Total.

a. Extend the star schema from Problem and Exercise 5 to include these new data.

b. Calculate the estimated number of rows in the fact table, assuming that the company experiences an average of 2,000 claims per month.

7. Millennium College (see Problem and Exercise 3) now wants to include new data about course sections: the department offering the course, the academic unit to which the department reports, and the budget unit to which the department is assigned. Change your answer to Problem and Exercise 3 to accommodate these new data requirements. Explain why you implemented the changes in the star schema the way you did.

8. As mentioned in the chapter, Kimball (1997), Inmon (1997 and 2000), and Armstrong (2000) have debated the merits of independent and dependent data marts and normalized

versus denormalized data marts. Obtain copies of these articles from your library or from online sources and summarize the arguments made by each side of this debate. See also www.intelligententerprise.com/030917/615warehouse1_1. shtml for a recent article clarifying the Kimball position.

9. A food manufacturing company needs a data mart to summarize facts about orders to move goods. Some orders transfer goods internally, some are sales to customers, some are purchases from vendors, and some are returns of goods from customers. The company needs to treat customers, vendors, plants, and storage locations as distinct dimensions that can be involved at both ends of a movement event. For each type of destination or origin, the company wants to know the type of location (i.e., customer, vendor, etc.), name, city, and state. Facts about each movement include dollar volume moved, cost of movement, and revenue collected from the move (if any, and this can be negative for a return). Design a star-type schema to represent this data mart. Hint: After you design a typical star schema, think about how you might simplify the design through the use of generalization.

10. Visit www.ralphkimball.com and locate Kimball University Design Tip #37. Study this design tip and draw the dimensional model for the recommended design for a "pipeline" application for university admissions.

11. Visit www.teradatastudentnetwork.com and download the dimensional modeling tool located under the software section. Use this tool to draw your answers to Problems and Exercises 3, 5, 6, and 9. Write a report that comments on the usefulness of this modeling tool. What other features would you like the tool to have?

12. Visit the Problems and Exercises material on www.prenhall. com/hoffer for Chapter 11 and answer the data warehouse and processing questions located there. These questions deal with a data warehouse for Pine Valley Furniture; there are questions for you to design a data mart for Pine Valley and to write some queries against an instance of this data mart.

Problems 13–20 are based upon the Fitchwood Insurance Company case study, which is described below.

Fitchwood Insurance Company, which is primarily involved in the sales of annuity products, would like to design a data mart for its sales and marketing organization. Presently, the OLTP system is a legacy system residing on a Novell network consisting of approximately 600 different flat files. For the purposes of our case study, we can assume that thirty different flat files are going to be used for the data mart. Some of these flat files are transaction files that change constantly. The OLTP system is shut down overnight on Friday evening beginning at 6 PM for backup. During that time, the flat files are copied to another server, an extraction process is run, and the extracts are sent via FTP to a UNIX server. A process is run on the UNIX server to load the extracts into Oracle and rebuild the star schema. For the initial loading of the data mart, all information from the thirty files was extracted and loaded. On a weekly basis, only additions and updates will be included in the extracts.

Although the data contained in the OLTP system are broad, the sales and marketing organization would like to focus on the sales data only. After substantial analysis, the ERD shown in Figure 11-25 was developed to describe the data to be used to populate the data mart.

Figure 11-25
Fitchwood Insurance Company ERD

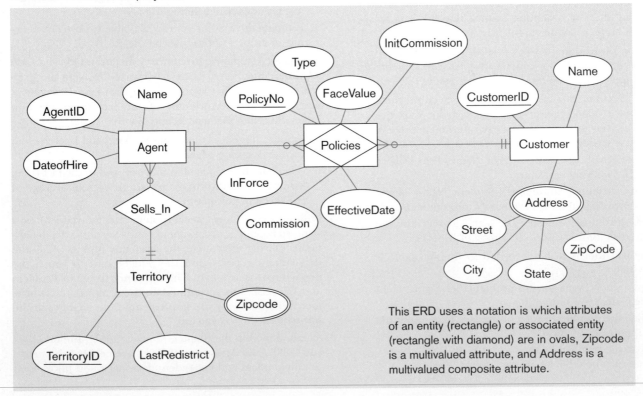

This ERD uses a notation is which attributes of an entity (rectangle) or associated entity (rectangle with diamond) are in ovals, Zipcode is a multivalued attribute, and Address is a multivalued composite attribute.

From this ERD, we get the set of relations shown in Figure 11-26. Sales and marketing is interested in viewing all sales data by territory, effective date, type of policy, and face value. In addition, the data mart should be able to provide reporting by individual agent on sales as well as commissions earned. Occasionally, the sales territories are revised (i.e., zip codes are added or deleted). The Last Redistrict attribute of the Territory table is used to store the date of the last revision. Some sample queries and reports are shown below:

- Total sales per month by territory by type of policy
- Total sales per quarter by territory by type of policy
- Total sales per month by agent by type of policy
- Total sales per month by agent by zip code
- Total face value of policies by month of effective date
- Total face value of policies by month of effective date by agent
- Total face value of policies by quarter of effective date
- Total number of policies in force by agent
- Total number of policies not in force by agent
- Total face value of all policies sold by an individual agent

- Total initial commission paid on all policies to an agent
- Total initial commission paid on policies sold in a given month by agent
- Total commissions earned by month by agent
- Top selling agent by territory by month

Commissions are paid to an agent upon the initial sale of a policy. The InitComm field of the policy table contains the percentage of the face value paid as an initial commission. The Commission field contains a percentage that is paid each month as long as a policy remains active or in force. Each month, commissions are calculated by computing the sum of the commission on each individual policy that is in force for an agent.

13. The OLTP system data for the Fitchwood Insurance Company is in a series of flat files. What process do you envision would be needed in order to extract the data and create the ERD shown above? How often should the extraction process be performed? Should it be a static extract or an incremental extract?

14. What types of data pollution problems might occur with the Fitchwood OLTP system data?

Figure 11-26
Relations for Fitchwood Insurance Company

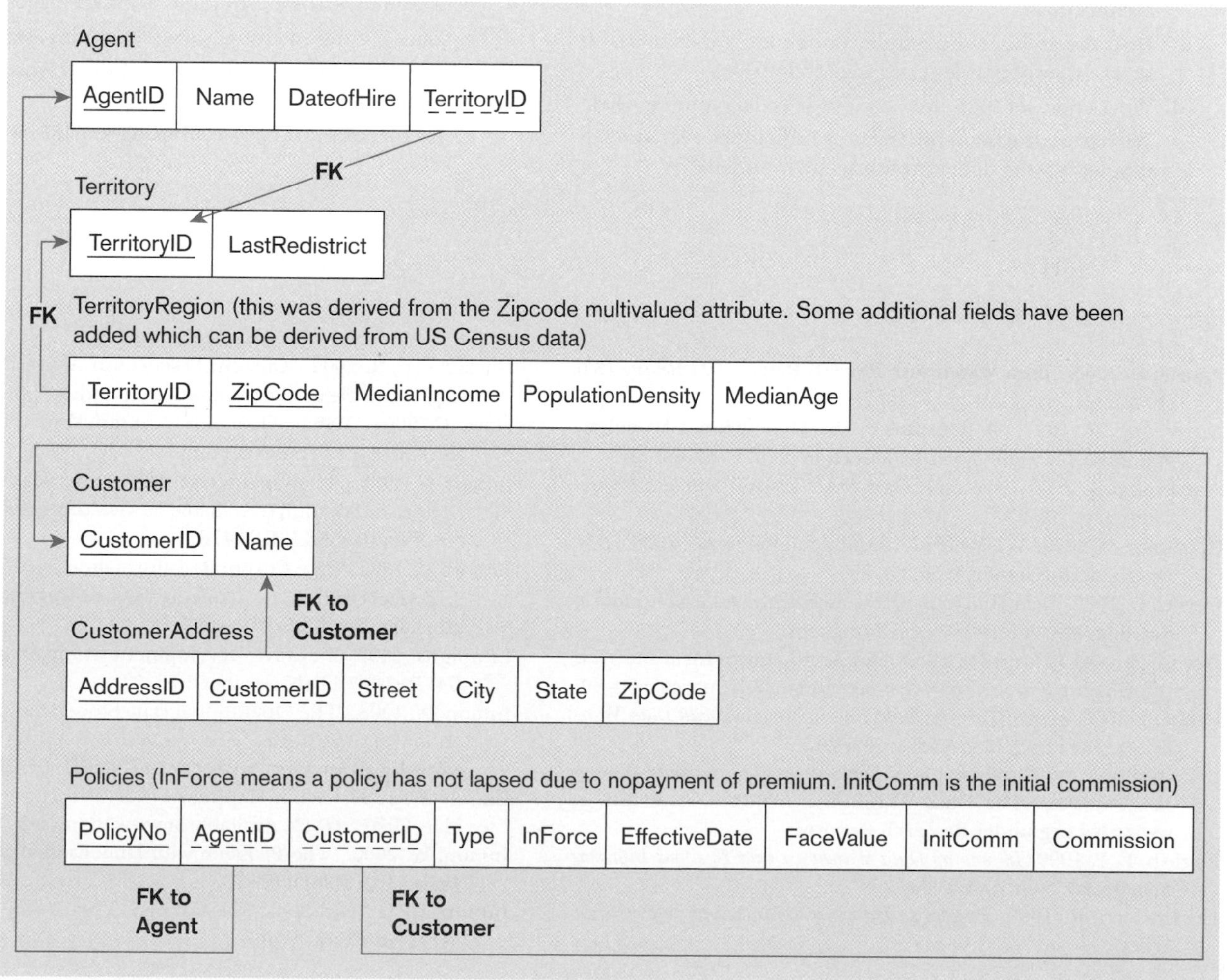

15. Research some tools that perform data scrubbing. What tool would you recommend for the Fitchwood Insurance Company?

16. What types of data transformations might be needed in order to build the Fitchwood data mart?

17. After some further analysis, you discover that the commission field in the Policies table is updated on a yearly basis to reflect changes in the yearly commission paid to agents on existing policies. Would this change the way in which you extract and load data into the data mart from the OLTP system?

18. Create a star schema for this case study. How did you handle the time dimension?

19. Management would like to use the data mart for drill-down online reporting. For example, a sales manager might want to view a report of total sales for an agent by month and then drill-down into the individual types of policies to see how sales were broken down by type of policy. What type of tool would you recommend for this? What additional tables, other than those required by the tool for administration, might need to be added to the data mart?

20. Do you see any opportunities for data mining using the Fitchwood data mart? Research data mining tools and recommend one or two for use with the data mart.

Field Exercises

1. Visit an organization that has developed a data warehouse and interview the data administrator or other key participant. Discuss the following issues:

   a. How satisfied are users with the data warehouse? In what ways has it improved their decision making?

   b. Does the warehouse employ a two-tier or three-tier architecture?

   c. Does the architecture employ one or more data marts? If so, are they dependent or independent?

   d. What end-user tools are employed? Is data mining used?

   e. What were the main obstacles or difficulties overcome in developing the data warehouse environment?

2. Visit the following Web sites. Browse these sites for additional information on data warehouse topics, including case examples of warehouse implementations, descriptions of the latest warehouse-related products, and announcements of conferences and other events.

   a. The Data Warehousing Institute: **www.tdwi.org**

   b. Knowledge Discovery Mine: **www.kdnuggets.com**

   c. Data Mining Institute: **www.datamining.org**

   d. Data Warehousing Knowledge Center: **www. dataware housing.org**

   e. An electronic data warehousing journal: **www.tdan.com**

References

Agosta, L. 2003. "Data Warehouse Refresh Rates." *DM Review* 13,6 (June): 49.

Armstrong, R. 1997. "A Rebuttal to the Dimensional Modeling Manifesto." A white paper produced by NCR Corporation.

Armstrong, R. 2000. "Avoiding Data Mart Traps." *Teradata Review* (Summer): 32–37.

Chisholm, M. 2000. "A New Understanding of Reference Data." *DM Review* 10,10 (October): 60, 84–85.

Devlin, B. 1997. *Data Warehouse: From Architecture to Implementation.* Reading, MA: Addison-Wesley Longman.

Devlin, B., and P. Murphy. 1988. "An Architecture for a Business Information System." *IBM Systems Journal* 27,1 (March): 60–80.

Dyché, J. 2000. *e-Data: Turning Data into Information with Data Warehousing.* Reading, MA: Addison-Wesley.

Eckerson, W., and C. White. 2003. *Evaluating ETL and Data Integration Platforms.* The Data Warehouse Institute. Available at **www.tdwi.org** under Research Reports.

English, L. P. 1999. *Improving Data Warehouse and Business Information Quality.* New York: Wiley.

Hackathorn, R. 1993. *Enterprise Database Connectivity.* New York: Wiley.

Hackathorn, R. 2002. "Current Practices in Active Data Warehousing." Available at **www.teradata.com** under White Papers.

Hays, C. 2004. "What They Know About You." *New York Times.* November 14: section 3, page 1.

Imhoff, C. 1998. "The Operational Data Store: Hammering Away." *DM Review* 8,7 (July): Available at **www.dmreview.com/master. cfm?NavID=55&EdID=470**.

Imhoff, C. 1999. "The Corporate Information Factory." *DM Review* 9,12 (December): Available at **www.dmreview.com/master. cfm?NavID=55&EdID=1667**.

Inmon, B. 1997. "Iterative Development in the Data Warehouse." *DM Review* 7,11 (November): 16, 17.

Inmon, W. 1998. "The Operational Data Store: Designing the Operational Data Store." *DM Review* 8,7 (July): Available at **www.dmreview.com/master.cfm?NavID=55&EdID=469**.

Inmon, W. 1999. "What Happens When You Have Built the Data Mart First?" *TDAN.* Available at **www.tdan.com/i012fe02.htm**.

Inmon, W. 2000. "The Problem with Dimensional Modeling." *DM Review* 10,5 (May): 68–70.

Inmon, W. H., and R. D. Hackathorn. 1994. *Using the Data Warehouse.* New York: Wiley.

Kimball, R. 1996a. *The Data Warehouse Toolkit.* New York: Wiley.

Kimball, R. 1996b. "Slowly Changing Dimensions." *DBMS* 9,4 (April): 18–20.

Kimball, R. 1997. "A Dimensional Modeling Manifesto." *DBMS* 10,9 (August): 59.

Kimball, R. 1998a. "Pipelining Your Surrogates." *DBMS* 11,6 (June): 18–22.

Kimball, R. 1998b. "Help for Hierarchies." *DBMS* 11,9 (September) 12–16.

Kimball, R. 1999. "When a Slowly Changing Dimension Speeds Up." *Intelligent Enterprise* 2,8 (August 3): 60–62.

Kimball, R. 2001. "Declaring the Grain." from Kimball University Design Tip #21 at **www.ralphkimball.com**.

Kimball, R. 2002. "What Changed?" *Intelligent Enterprise* 5,8 (August 12): 22, 24, 52.

Kimball, R. 2004. "The 38 Subsystems of ETL." *Intelligent Enterprise* 8,12 (December 4): 16, 17, 46.

Krudop, M. E. 2005. "Maximizing Your ETL Tool Investment." *DM Review* 15,3 (March): 26-28.

Marco, D. 2000. *Building and Managing the Meta Data Repository: A Full Life-Cycle Guide.* New York: Wiley.

Marco, D. 2003. "Independent Data Marts: Stranded on Islands of Data, Part 1." *DM Review* 13,4 (April): 30, 32, 63.

Meyer, A. 1997. "The Case for Dependent Data Marts." *DM Review* 7,7 (July–August): 17–24.

Meyer, S. 2001. "Which ETL Tool is Right for You?" *DM Review* 11,3 (March): 24, 26, 28, 63.

Mundy, J. 2001. "Smarter Data Warehouses." *Intelligent Enterprise* 4,2 (February 16): 24–29.

Poe, V. 1996. *Building a Data Warehouse for Decision Support.* Upper Saddle River, NJ: Prentice Hall.

Variar, G. 2002. "The Origin of Data." *Intelligent Enterprise* 5,2 (February 1): 37–41.

Weldon, J. L. 1996. "Data Mining and Visualization." *Database Programming & Design* 9,5 (May): 21–24.

Westerman, P. 2001. *Data Warehousing: Using the Wal-Mart Model.* San Francisco, CA: Morgan Kaufmann.

White, C. 2000. "First Analysis." *Intelligent Enterprise* 3,9 (June): 50–55.

Whiting, R. 2003. "The Data-Warehouse Advantage." *Information Week* Issue 648 (July 28): 63–66.

Further Reading

Bischoff, J., and T. Alexander. 1997. *Data Warehouse: Practical Advice from the Experts.* Upper Saddle River, NJ: Prentice Hall.

Gallo, J. 2002. "Operations and Maintenance in a Data Warehouse Environment." *DM Review* 12,12 (2003 Resource Guide): 12–16.

Goodhue, D., M. Mybo, and L. Kirsch. 1992. "The Impact of Data Integration on the Costs and Benefits of Information Systems." *MIS Quarterly* 16,3 (September): 293–311.

Jenks, B. 1997. "Tiered Data Warehouse." *DM Review* 7,10 (October): 54–57.

Web Resources

www.teradatareview.com *Teradata Review* contains articles on the technology and application of the NCR Teradata data warehouse system. (This magazine recently changed its name. Articles under the magazine's new and previous names can be found at **www.teradatamagazine.com.**)

www.dmreview.com *DM Review* is a monthly trade magazine that contains articles and columns about data warehousing.

www.tdan.com An electronic journal on data warehousing.

www.imoncif.com Bill Inmon is a leading authority on data management and data warehousing.

www.ralphkimball.com Ralph Kimball is a leading authority on data warehousing.

www.tdwi.org The Data Warehousing Institute is an industry group that focuses on data warehousing methods and applications.

www.datawarehousing.org The Data Warehousing Knowledge Center contains links to many vendors.

www.olapreport.com This site provides detailed information about OLAP products and applications.

www.information-quality.com See the IQ Forum under the IQ resources button for information about data quality and ETL processes.

www.teradatastudentnetwork.com A portal to resources for databases, data warehousing, and business intelligence. Data sets from this textbook are stored on the software site from which you can use SQL, data mining, dimensional modeling, and other tools.

Case

In most respects, Mountain View Community Hospital has followed a carefully planned approach to designing, selecting, and installing its information systems. The organization developed an enterprise data model to guide its database development (Chapters 3–8). The hospital installed computer systems to support most of the routine operations in the organization. For example, there are systems for patient accounting, administrative services, and financial management. Many systems were acquired from outside vendors after a careful selection process.

Despite this careful planning, management is aware that there are some deficiencies and limitations in the present hospital information systems. In addition to the challenge of interfacing systems in MVCH's heterogenous environment of platforms and applications, two further problems have been noted:

1. Data are often duplicated in different files and databases, in different formats, and even in different media. For example, one set of patient data (used for billing purposes) resides in a patient accounting system based on a relational database. On the other hand, many patient medical records are maintained in a manual system (one folder per patient), or other applications, such as Dr. "Z's" MS Management System.

2. The systems are designed primarily to support operational (or transaction) processing, but are not generally well suited to provide management information or to support analytical studies that are increasingly required for modern hospital management.

Management feels that these problems must be addressed, and that better and more centralized access to the hospital's operational, financial, and clinical information is a strategic necessity for two reasons. First, like many other hospitals, Mountain View Community Hospital is being driven by the trend to managed care and the resulting need to contain costs while maintaining or improving clinical outcomes. As a consequence, MVCH must closely track and analyze its clinical and financial data related to patient care services and provide that data to its administrative and clinical decision makers in a timely fashion. Secondly, Sarbanes-Oxley is beginning to

have an impact. Mountain View, as a not-for profit organization, is not a covered entity under SOX. However, both Mr. Lopez, MVCH's CFO, as well Ms. Baker, the hospital's CEO, have come under pressure from board members from the corporate world to certify the accuracy of financial statements, certify the accuracy of the hospital's annual information return file with the IRS, and provide timely reports. As a result, both Mr. Lopez and Ms. Baker have begun to demand more timely access to financial data for decision making, business intelligence, and financial reporting. The Board of Directors is also asking that reports include trend information and graphic presentations. In light of these issues, management wishes to investigate whether the techniques of data warehousing might be successfully applied in their organization.

A typical hospital data warehouse often contains four types of data: patient records; doctor, clinic, and hospital records; drug and pharmaceutical company records; and HMO and insurance company records. However, the small size of the hospital may not justify a large-scale data warehouse development project. Instead, several smaller data marts may be more feasible. After some investigation, Mountain View Community Hospital plans to test the concept with two small prototype data marts:

1. A data mart that will record summary information regarding tests and procedures performed by physicians at the hospital;

2. A more detailed data mart that will record the details of tests and procedures performed by physicians for individual patients.

CASE QUESTIONS

1. What are some of the advantages that a hospital such as Mountain View might realize from a data warehouse and/or data mart(s)? How can a data warehouse/data mart help with improving the following?

   - Operational efficiency
   - Treatment efficiency
   - Clinical outcomes

- Patient safety
- Clinical research

2. How could a data mart be used to improve the quality of emergency room care?

3. Should Mountain View Community Hospital consider developing data marts (such as those proposed) without an established data warehouse? What are the risks associated with that approach? Do you think that an organization can develop a prototype data mart to investigate "proof of concept" without an established data warehouse? Discuss some of the likely advantages and disadvantages of this approach.

4. Which data quality challenges may arise if Mountain View Community Hospital develops a data warehouse and/or data mart(s)? Do you think that there is a need for data scrubbing? If so, on all tables or just some?

5. How can a data warehouse help improve data quality at Mountain View Community Hospital?

6. How would you address concerns about security and HIPAA's privacy mandates that prohibit unauthorized use of patient-identifiable information?

7. If Mountain View Community Hospital was going to develop a data mart, do you think that OLAP tools should be used? If yes, which type (OLAP, ROLAP, or MOLAP)?

8. What types of data mining operations could be used (e.g., predictive modeling, cluster analysis, etc.)? For what purposes?

9. The case segment mentions the Sarbanes-Oxley Act (described in Chapter 6). How can a data warehouse or data mart help Ms. Baker and Mr. Lopez respond to pressures from the Board of Directors for the following:

   a. Ensuring the accuracy of financial data
   b. Providing reports in a timely manner
   c. Providing reports that include trend information and graphic presentations?

CASE EXERCISES

1. MVCH Table 11-1 provides some details regarding the two data marts MVCH is considering.

   a. Design a star schema for each data mart.
   b. Calculate the expected number of rows in each fact table and its estimated size (bytes).

   c. For the detailed data mart, why is it necessary to assume that a given treatment may be performed only once by a given physician for a given patient on a given day? Suggest a way to overcome this.
   d. Would you recommend that MVCH implement both data marts? Why or why not? If yes, then what should MVCH do to ensure consistency across the two data marts?
   e. Using SQL, create two star queries for each of the data marts.

2. After hearing about the data mart prototypes, Dr. Jefferson, Chief of Surgery, expresses an interest in a surgery data mart. Some of the reports he wishes to receive include number of surgeries by surgeon; the number of inpatient and outpatient surgeries per week and per month; the number of cancelled surgeries by reason, surgeon, and month; surgeries per week, operating room (MVCH has a suite of six operating rooms), and surgeon; mortality rates by surgeon; average surgery time by type of surgery; average surgery time by OR; and number of negative patient reactions to blood transfusions by surgeon and by patient gender and age. Dr. Jefferson also wishes to analyze surgeries in terms of the duration of anesthesia, total time in the operating room, and amount of time in the operating room before the start and after the end of the surgery. He wants to be able to slice and dice the surgery data by diagnosis, patient age, gender, insurance company, acuity code (patient acuity at MVCH is rated on a 5-point scale, with 1 reflecting the highest acuity and 5 the lowest acuity), operating room, and surgeon.

   Given this information, you have the following tasks:

   a. Identify the dimensions and facts for this data mart.
   b. Create the star schema.
   c. Use SQL to create three star queries that satisfy some of Dr. Jefferson information requirements.
   d. Develop a business case for this data mart.

3. Identify dimensions and facts for two other possible data marts at Mountain View Community Hospital: an emergency room data mart, and a data mart for Dr. "Z's" MS Center. Use MS Visio (or other similar tool) to draw the star schema.

MVCH Table 11-1   MVCH Prototype Data Mart Details

	Summary Data Mart	*Detailed Data Mart*
Physician dimension	Physician_ID (pk): 5 bytes Physician_Name: 10 bytes Specialty: 5 bytes Physician_Address: 10 bytes Physicain_Telephone: 5 bytes Physician_Address: 10 bytes Physician_Telephone: 5 bytes	Same as summary data mart
Treatment dimension	Treatment_ID (pk): 3 bytes Treatment_Description: 6 bytes	Same as summary data mart
Period dimension	Period_ID (pk): 2 bytes Month: 1 byte Year: 2 bytes	Period_ID (pk): 3 bytes Date: 5 bytes
Patient Dimension	none	Patient_ID (pk): 5 bytes Patient_Name: 10 bytes Patient_Address: 10 bytes Patient_Telephone: 5 bytes
Treatment (fact) table	*Grain: Monthly summary of treatments and average treatment costs, by physician and treatment* Monthly_Total: 3 bytes Average_Cost: 5 bytes	*Grain: Detail for each treatment occurrence administered to a patient by a physician* Treatment_Cost: 4 bytes Treatment_Result: 20 bytes
Assumptions	• Treatments: Approximately 500 different treatments are performed at the hospital. During a typical month, approximately 30 percent (or 150 different treatments) are performed. • Physicians: Each treatment is performed by one physician. • Periods: If a full-scale data mart is developed, it is anticipated that 36 periods (or 3 years) of data will be accumulated.	• Treatments: An average of 200 total treatments are performed for patients on a given day (this is based on an average patient census of 200, and an average of two treatments per patient per day). • Patients: Each treatment is performed for one patient. To simplify matters, assume that a given treatment may only be performed once by a given physician and for a particular patient on a given day. • Physicians: Each treatment is performed by one physician. • Periods: If a full-scale data mart is developed, it is anticipated that approximately 1,000 days (nearly 3 years) of data will be collected.

Part FIVE

Advanced Database Topics

in the primary end-user organization for the EDW, but this runs the risk of creating many data warehouses or marts, rather than leading to a true, scalable EDW.

Summary   The DA and DBA roles are some of the most challenging roles in any organization. The DA has renewed visiability with the recent enactment of financial control regulations and greater interest in data quality. The DBA is always expected to keep abreast of rapidly changing new technologies and is usually involved with mission-critical applications. A DBA must be constantly available to deal with problems, so the DBA is constantly on call. In return, the DBA position ranks among the best compensated in the IS profession. A search for open DA and DBA jobs shows that salaries range from $60,000 to $105,000.

It is expected that the DBA role will continue to evolve toward increased specialization, such as distributed database/network capacity planning DBAs, server programming DBAs, off-the-shelf customizing DBAs, or data warehousing DBAs (Dowgiallo et al., 1997). The ability to work with multiple databases, communication protocols, and operating systems will be highly valued. Those DBAs who gain broad experience and develop the ability to adapt quickly to changing environments will have many opportunities. It is possible that some current DBA activities, such as tuning, will be replaced by decision support systems able to tune systems by analyzing usage patterns. Some operational duties, such as backup and recovery, can be outsourced and off-shored with remote database administration services. Opportunities in large companies to continue working with very large databases (VLDBs) and opportunities in small and midsize companies to manage desktop and midrange servers should remain strong.

THE OPEN-SOURCE MOVEMENT

As was mentioned previously, one role of a DBA is to select the DBMS(s) to be used in the organization. Database administrators and systems developers in all kinds of organizations have new alternatives when selecting a DBMS. Increasingly, organizations of all sizes are seriously considering open-source DBMSs, such as MySQL and PostgreSQL, as viable choices along with Oracle, DB2, Microsoft SQL Server, Informix, and Teradata. This interest is spurred by the success of the Linux operating system and the Apache Web server. The open-source movement began in roughly 1984 with the start of the Free Software Foundation. Today, the Open Source Initiative (www.opensource.org) is a nonprofit organization dedicated to managing and promoting the open-source movement.

Why has open-source software become so popular? It's not all about cost. Advantages of open-source software include the following:

- A large pool of volunteer testers and developers facilitate the construction of reliable, low-cost software in a relatively short amount of time (but, be aware that only the most widely used open-source software comes close to achieving this advantage).

- The availability of the source code allows people to make modifications to add new features, which are easily inspected by others. (In fact, the agreement is that you do share all modifications for the good of the community.)

- Because the software is not proprietary to one vendor, you do not become locked into the product development plans of only one vendor, which might not be adding the features you need for your environment.

- Distributing application code dependent on and working with the open-source software does not incur any additional costs for copies or licenses (so, deploying software across multiple servers even within the same organization has no marginal cost for the DBMS).

Part FIVE

Advanced Database Topics

An Overview of Part F I V E

Parts II through IV have prepared you to develop useful and efficient databases. Part V introduces some additional important database design and management issues. These issues include database security, backup, recovery, controlling concurrent access to data, and preserving data quality and availability, (including complying with regulations for accuracy of data reporting), and advanced topics in database performance tuning (Chapter 12); distributed databases (Chapter 13); and object-oriented databases (Chapters 14 and 15). Chapter 12 is included in its entirety in the printed text; full versions of Chapters 13–15 are included on the textbook's Web site while summaries of these chapters are included in the printed text. Following Part V are four appendices, covering alternative E-R notations (complementing Chapters 3 and 4), advanced normal forms (supplementing Chapter 5), data structures (supplementing Chapter 6), and the object-relational data model (complementing Chapters 5 and 14).

You are likely to conclude from reading this text that data are a corporate asset, just like personnel, physical resources, and financial resources. As such, data and information are resources that are too valuable to be managed casually. In Chapter 12 (Data and Database Administration), you will learn about the meaning of open-source DBMSs, concurrency control, deadlock, encryption, information repository, locking, recovery, system catalog, transaction, and versioning—all core topics today for managing the data resource. You will learn about the roles of the following:

- A *data administrator*—the person who takes overall responsibility for data, metadata, and policies about data use
- A *database administrator*—the person who is responsible for physical database design and for dealing with the technical issues, such as security enforcement, database performance, and backup and recovery, associated with managing a database.

Specialized data and database administrator roles for Web-based, data warehouses, and mobile systems are defined in Chapter 12.

In larger organizations, databases may be distributed across multiple computers and locations. Special issues arise when an organization tries to manage distributed data as one database rather than many decentralized, separate databases. In Chapter 13 (Distributed Databases), you learn about homogeneous and heterogeneous distributed databases, the objectives and trade-offs for distributed databases, and several alternative architectures for such databases. You learn about the important concept of data replication and partitioning and how to synchronize multiple instances of the same data across a distributed database. You also study the special features of a distributed DBMS, including distributed transaction controls (such as commit protocols). There is a review of the evolution of distributed DBMSs and of the range of distributed DBMS products.

Chapter 14 (Object-Oriented Data Modeling) introduces an alternative to E-R modeling. Object-oriented models of data and other system aspects are becoming increasingly popular because of their ability to represent complex ideas using highly related modeling notations. This chapter uses the Unified Modeling Language (UML), a standard in this field. In the UML, an object is an entity that has three properties: state, behavior, and identity. The behavior of an object is determined by one or more operations that are encapsulated in the object. Associations, generalization, inheritance, and polymorphism are important concepts. This chapter presents an object-oriented version (in the form of a class diagram) of the Pine Valley Furniture Company case from Chapter 3.

Chapter 15 (Object-Oriented Database Development) demonstrates the transformation of class diagrams into schemas that can be implemented using object database management systems (ODBMSs). The object definition language (ODL) and object query language (OQL) are introduced. You learn how to create object-oriented database definitions in the ODL, including how to define objects, attributes, operations, and relationships, and the basics of the SQL-like OQL, including single- and multiple-table queries.

Chapter **12**

Data and Database Administration

LEARNING OBJECTIVES

After studying this chapter, you should be able to:

- Concisely define each of the following key terms: **data administration, database administration, open-source DBMS, database security, authorization rules, user-defined procedures, encryption, smart card, database recovery, back-up facilities, journalizing facilities, transaction, transaction log, database change log, before-image, after-image, checkpoint facility, recovery manager, restore/rerun, transaction boundaries, backward recovery (rollback), forward recovery (rollforward), aborted transaction, database destruction, concurrency control, inconsistent read problem, locking, locking level (lock granularity), shared lock (S lock, read lock), exclusive lock (X lock, write lock), deadlock, deadlock prevention, two-phase locking protocol, deadlock resolution, versioning, data steward, data dictionary, system catalog, information repository, Information Repository Dictionary System (IRDS), data archiving,** and **heartbeat query.**

- List several major functions of data administration and of database administration.

- Describe the changing roles of the data administrator and database administrator in the current business environment.

- Describe the role of data dictionaries and information repositories and how they are used by data administration.

- Compare the optimistic and pessimistic systems of concurrency control.

- Describe the problem of database security and list five techniques that are used to enhance security.

- Describe the problem of database recovery and list four basic facilities that are included with a DBMS to recover databases.

- Describe the problem of tuning a database to achieve better performance and list five areas where changes may be made when tuning a database.

- Describe the importance of data quality and list several measures to improve quality.

- Describe the importance of data availability and list several measures to improve availability.

INTRODUCTION

ChoicePoint: More ID theft warnings: ID company says criminals able to obtain almost 140,000 names, addresses and other information.

ChoicePoint Inc., a national provider of identification and credential verification services, says it will send an additional 110,000 statements to people informing them of possible identity theft after a group of well-organized criminals was able to obtain personal information on almost 140,000 consumers through the company.

According to a statement on the ChoicePoint Web site, the incident was not the result of its systems being hacked but rather caused by criminals posing as legitimate businesses seeking to gain access to personal information.

ChoicePoint said the criminals may have gained access to people's names, addresses, Social Security numbers and credit reports.

The company said Tuesday it sent warning letters to 30,000 to 35,000 consumers in California, the only state that requires companies to disclose security breaches.

Although the company knew about the fraud last fall, it said it did not reveal the information until now at the request of authorities, who said it would jeopardize the investigation.

ChoicePoint said 35,000 California residents have already been notified and another 110,000 people outside of California will receive notice soon.

Alpharetta, Ga.-based ChoicePoint maintains personal profiles of nearly every U.S. consumer, which it sells to employers, landlords, marketing companies and about 35 U.S. government agencies.

ChoicePoint's databases contain 19 billion public records, including driving records, sex-offender lists, and FBI lists of wanted criminals and suspected terrorists.

The company says its records enable law enforcers to track down serial killers and have helped find 822 missing children. (Source: *CNN Money* Web site, February 17, 2005)

The critical importance of data to organizations is widely recognized. Data are a corporate asset, just as personnel, physical resources, and financial resources are corporate assets. Like these other assets, data and information are too valuable to be managed casually. The development of information technology has made effective management of corporate data far more possible, but data are also vulnerable to accidental and malicious damage and misuse. Data and database administration activities have been developed to help achieve organizations' goals for the effective management of data.

Ineffective data administration, on the other hand, leads to poor data quality and utilization and can be characterized by the following conditions, which are all too common in organizations:

1. Multiple definitions of the same data entity and/or inconsistent representations of the same data elements in separate databases, making integration of data across different databases hazardous

2. Missing key data elements, whose loss eliminates the value of existing data

3. Low data quality levels due to inappropriate sources of data or timing of data transfers from one system to another, thus reducing the reliability of the data

4. Inadequate familiarity with existing data, including awareness of data location and meaning of stored data, thus reducing the capability to use the data to make effective strategic or planning decisions

5. Poor and inconsistent query response time, excessive database downtime, and either stringent or inadequate controls to ensure agreed upon data privacy and security

Many of these conditions put the organization at risk for failing to comply with regulations, such as Sarbanes-Oxley (SOX), Health Insurance Portability and Accountability Act (HIPAA), and Gramm-Leach-Bliley for adequate internal controls and procedures in support of financial control, data transparency, and data privacy. Manual processes for data control are discouraged, so organizations need to implement automated controls, in part through the DBMS (such as sophisticated data validation controls, security features, triggers, and stored procedures), to prevent and detect accidental damage of data and fraudulent activities. Databases must be backed-up and recovered to prevent permanent data loss. The who, what, when, and where of data must be documented in metadata repositories for auditor review. Data stewardship programs, aimed at reviewing data quality control procedures, are becoming popular. Collaboration across the organization is needed so data consolidation across distributed databases is accurate. Breaches of data accuracy or security must be communicated to executives and managers.

Organizations have responded to these data management issues with different strategies. Some have created a function called *data administration*. The person who heads this function is called the data administrator (DA), or information resource manager, and takes responsibility for the overall management of data resources. A second function, that of *database administration*, has been regarded as being responsible for physical database design and for dealing with the technical issues, such as security enforcement, database performance, and backup and recovery, associated with managing a database. Other organizations combine the data administration and database administration functions. The rapidly changing pace of business has caused the roles of the data administrator and the database administrator (DBA) to change, in ways that are discussed below.

THE ROLES OF DATA AND DATABASE ADMINISTRATORS

Several new technologies and trends are driving the changes in the data administration and database administration roles (Mullins, 2001):

1. The proliferation of proprietary and open-source technologies and databases on diverse platforms that must be managed concurrently in many organizations

2. Rapid growth in the size of databases, fueled by the storage of complex data types and the business intelligence needs of today's organizations

3. The embedding of business rules in databases in the form of triggers, stored procedures, and user-defined functions

4. The explosion of e-business applications that require linking corporate databases to the Internet and tracking Internet activity, thus making databases more open for unauthorized access from outside the organization

Against the background of these changes, it is important to understand traditional role distinctions. This will help us understand the ways in which the roles are being blended in organizations that have different information technology architectures.

Traditional Data Administration

Databases are shared resources that belong to the entire enterprise; they are not the property of a single function or individual within the organization. Data administration is the custodian of the organization's data, in much the same sense that the controller is custodian of the financial resources. Like the controller, the data administrator must develop procedures to protect and control the resource. Also, data administration must resolve disputes that may arise when data are centralized and shared among users and must play a significant role in deciding where data will be stored and managed. **Data administration** is a high-level function that is responsible for the overall management of data resources in an organization, including maintaining corporatewide data definitions and standards.

Data administration: A high-level function that is responsible for the overall management of data resources in an organization, including maintaining corporatewide definitions and standards.

Selecting the data administrator and organizing the function are extremely important organizational decisions. The data administrator must be a highly skilled manager capable of eliciting the cooperation of users and resolving differences that normally arise when significant change is introduced into an organization. The data administrator should be a respected, senior-level manager selected from within the organization, rather than a technical computer expert or a new individual hired for the position. However, the data administrator must have sufficient technical skills to interact effectively with technical staff members such as database administrators, systems administrators, and programmers.

Following are some of the core roles of traditional data administration:

- *Data policies, procedures, and standards* Every database application requires protection established through consistent enforcement of data policies, procedures, and standards. Data policies are statements that make explicit the goals of data administration, such as, "Every user must have a valid password." Data procedures are written outlines of actions to be taken to perform a certain activity. Back-up and recovery procedures, for example, should be communicated to all involved employees. Data standards are explicit conventions and behaviors that are to be followed and that can be used to help evaluate database quality. Naming conventions for database objects should be standardized for programmers, for example. Increased use of external data sources and increased access to organizational databases from outside the organization have increased the importance of employees' understanding of data policies, procedures, and standards. Such policies and procedures need to be well documented to comply with the transparency requirements of financial reporting, security, and privacy regulations.

- *Planning* A key administration function is providing leadership in developing the organization's information architecture. Effective administration requires both an understanding of the needs of the organization for data and information and the ability to lead the development of an information architecture that will meet the diverse needs of the typical organization.

- *Data conflict resolution* Databases are intended to be shared and usually involve data from several different departments of the organization. Ownership of data is a ticklish issue at least occasionally in every organization. Those in data administration are well placed to resolve data ownership issues because they are not typically associated with a certain department. Establishing procedures for resolving such conflicts is essential. If the administration function has been given sufficient authority to mediate and enforce the resolution of the conflict, they may be very effective in this capacity.

- *Managing the information repository* Repositories contain the metadata that describe an organization's data and data processing resources. Information repositories are replacing data dictionaries in many organizations. Whereas data dictionaries are simple data element documentation tools, information repositories are used by data administrators and other information specialists to manage the total information processing environment. An information repository serves as an essential source of information and functionality for each of the following:

  1. Users who must understand data definitions, business rules, and relationships among data objects

  2. Automated CASE tools that are used to specify and develop information systems

  3. Applications that access and manipulate data (or business information) in the corporate databases

  4. Database management systems, which maintain the repository and update system privileges, passwords, object definitions, and so on

- *Internal marketing* While the importance of data and information to the organization has become more widely recognized within the organization, it is not necessarily true that an appreciation for data management issues, such as information architecture, data modeling, metadata, data quality, and data standards, has also evolved. The importance of following established procedures and policies must be proactively instituted through data (and database) administrators. Effective internal marketing may reduce resistance to change and data ownership problems.

When the data administration role is not separately defined in an organization, the above roles are assumed by database administration and/or others in the IT organization.

Traditional Database Administration

Typically, the role of database administration is taken to be a hands-on, physical involvement with the management of a database or databases. **Database administration** is a technical function responsible for logical and physical database design and for dealing with technical issues, such as security enforcement, database performance, backup and recovery, and database availability. The database administrator (DBA) must understand the data models built by data administration and be capable of transforming them into efficient and appropriate logical and physical database designs (Mullins, 2002). The DBA implements the standards and procedures established by the data administrator, including enforcing programming standards, data standards, policies, and procedures.

Just as the data administrator needs a wide variety of job skills, so does the DBA. A broad technical background, including a sound understanding of current hardware and software (operating system and networking) architectures and capabilities and a solid understanding of data processing are essential. An understanding of the database development life cycle, including traditional and prototyping approaches, is also necessary. Strong design and data modeling skills are essential, especially at the logical and physical levels. But managerial skills are also critical; the DBA must manage other information systems (IS) personnel while the database is analyzed, designed, and implemented, and the DBA must also interact with and provide support for the end users who are involved with the design and use of the database.

Following are some of the core roles assumed by database administration:

- *Selecting DBMS and related software tools* The evaluation and selection of hardware and software is critical to an organization's success. The database administration group must establish policies regarding the DBMS and related system software (such as compilers, system monitors, etc.) that will be supported within the organization. This requires evaluating vendors and their software products, performing benchmarks, and so on.

- *Installing and upgrading the DBMS* Once the DBMS is selected, it must be installed. Before installation, benchmarks of the workload against the database on a computer supplied by the DBMS vendor should be run. Benchmarking anticipates issues that must be addressed during the actual installation. A DBMS installation can be a complex process of making sure all the correct versions of different modules are in place, all the proper device drivers are present, and the DBMS works correctly with any third-party software products. DBMS vendors periodically update package modules; planning for, testing, and installing upgrades to ensure existing applications still work properly can be time-consuming and intricate. Once the DBMS is installed, user accounts must be created and maintained.

- *Tuning database performance* Because databases are dynamic, it is improbable that the initial design of the database will be sufficient to achieve the best processing performance for the life of the database. The performance of the database (query and update processing time as well as data storage utilization)

Database administration: A technical function that is responsible for physical database design and for dealing with technical issues, such as security enforcement, database performance, and backup and recovery.

needs to be constantly monitored. The design of a database must be frequently changed to meet new requirements and to overcome the degrading effects of many content updates. Periodically, the database must be rebuilt, reorganized, and reindexed to recover wasted space and to correct poor data allocation and fragmentation with the new size and use of the database.

- *Improving database query processing performance*   The workload against a database most certainly will expand over time as more users find more ways to use the growing amount of data in a database. Thus, some queries that originally ran quickly against a small database may need to be rewritten in a more efficient form to run in a satisfactory time against a fully populated database. Indexes may need to be added or deleted to balance performance across all queries. Data may need to be relocated to different devices to allow better concurrent processing of queries and updates. Arguably, the vast majority of the time spent by a DBA will be for tuning database performance and improving database query processing time.

- *Managing data security, privacy, and integrity*   Protecting the security, privacy, and integrity of the organizational databases rests with the database administration function. More detailed explanations of the ways in which privacy, security, and integrity are ensured are included later in the chapter. Here it is important to realize that the advent of the Internet and intranets to which databases are attached, along with the possibilities for distributing data and databases to multiple sites, have complicated the management of data security, privacy, and integrity.

- *Data backup and recovery*   The DBA must ensure that back-up procedures are established that will allow the recovery of all necessary data should a loss occur through application failure, hardware failure, physical or electrical disaster, or human error or malfeasance. Common back-up and recovery strategies are also discussed later in this chapter. These strategies must be fully tested and evaluated at regular intervals.

Reviewing these data and database administration functions should convince any reader of the importance of proper administration, both at the organizational and the project level. Failure to take the proper steps can greatly reduce an organization's ability to operate effectively and may even result in its going out of business. Pressures to reduce application development time must always be reviewed to be sure that necessary quality is not being forgone in order to react more quickly, for such shortcuts are likely to have very serious repercussions. Figure 12-1 summarizes how these data and database administration functions are typically viewed with respect to the steps of the systems development life cycle.

Evolving Approaches to Data Administration

As we indicated early in this chapter, rapidly changing business conditions are driving new approaches in data and database administration. In this section, we describe some of these new roles and approaches.

Blending Data and Database Administration   Many organizations now have blended together the data administration and database administration roles. These organizations emphasize the capability to build a database quickly, tune it for maximum performance, and restore it to production quickly when problems develop. These databases are more likely to be departmental, client/server databases that are developed quickly using newer development approaches, such as prototyping, which allow changes to be made more quickly. The blending of data administration and database administration roles also means that DBAs in such organizations must be able to create and enforce data standards and policies.

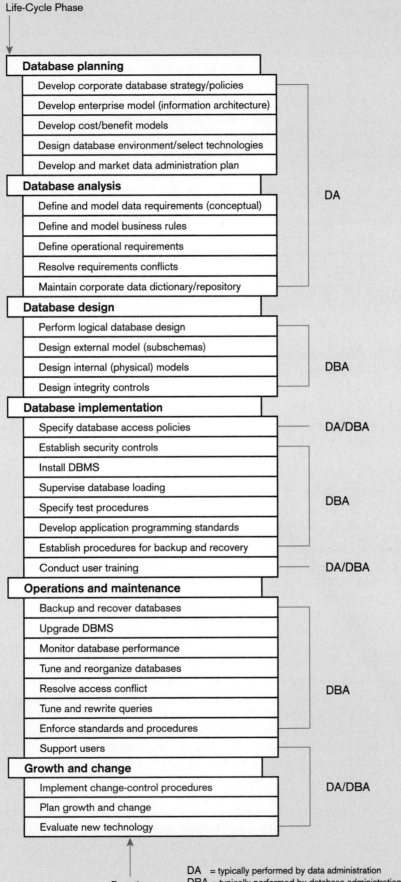

Life-Cycle Phase

Database planning
- Develop corporate database strategy/policies
- Develop enterprise model (information architecture)
- Develop cost/benefit models
- Design database environment/select technologies
- Develop and market data administration plan

Database analysis
- Define and model data requirements (conceptual)
- Define and model business rules
- Define operational requirements
- Resolve requirements conflicts
- Maintain corporate data dictionary/repository

DA

Database design
- Perform logical database design
- Design external model (subschemas)
- Design internal (physical) models
- Design integrity controls

DBA

Database implementation
- Specify database access policies — DA/DBA
- Establish security controls
- Install DBMS
- Supervise database loading
- Specify test procedures
- Develop application programming standards
- Establish procedures for backup and recovery

DBA

- Conduct user training — DA/DBA

Operations and maintenance
- Backup and recover databases
- Upgrade DBMS
- Monitor database performance
- Tune and reorganize databases
- Resolve access conflict
- Tune and rewrite queries
- Enforce standards and procedures
- Support users

DBA

Growth and change
- Implement change-control procedures
- Plan growth and change
- Evaluate new technology

DA/DBA

Function

DA = typically performed by data administration
DBA = typically performed by database administration

Fast-Track Development   Quinlan (1996) has suggested some changes in data administration and database administration practices that can be made at each stage of the traditional database development life cycle to reduce development times:

- *Database planning*   Improve selection of technology by selectively evaluating possible products. Be sure to consider each technology's fit with the enterprise data model and seek ways to reduce time required in later stages as a result of careful selection of technology at the database planning stage.

- *Database analysis*   Try to work on physical design in parallel with development of the logical and physical models. Prototyping the application now may well lead to changes in the logical and physical data models earlier in the development process.

- *Database design*   Prioritize application transactions by volume, importance, and complexity. These transactions are going to be most critical to the application. Specifications for them should be reviewed as quickly as the transactions are developed. Logical data modeling, physical database modeling, and prototyping may occur in parallel. DBAs should strive to provide adequate control of the database environment while allowing the developers space and opportunity to experiment.

- *Database implementation*   Institute database change-control procedures so that development and implementation are supported rather than slowed. Wherever possible, segment the model into modules that can be analyzed and implemented more quickly. Find ways to test the system more quickly without compromising quality. Testing may be moved earlier in the development; use testing and change control tools to build and manage the test and production environments.

- *Operation and maintenance*   Review all timesaving measures that have been taken to ensure that database quality has not been compromised. Consider using third-party tools and utilities wherever possible to save work; other tools such as Lotus Notes may reduce the need for meetings, thus saving time.

New DBA Roles   To cope with the new challenges described earlier in this chapter, several new, specialized DBA roles are emerging. Some of these roles are discussed in the following list:

- *Procedural DBAs*   Features such as triggers, stored procedures, and Persistent Stored Modules (all described in Chapter 8) provide the ability to define business rules to the DBMS, rather than in separate application programs. Once developers begin to rely on the use of these objects, the DBA must address the issues of quality, maintainability, performance, and availability. The procedural DBA is responsible for ensuring that all such procedural database logic is effectively planned, tested, implemented, shared, and reused (Mullins, 2002). The person filling this role will typically come from the ranks of application programming and be capable of working closely with that group.

- *e-DBA*   When a business goes online, it never closes. People expect the site to be available and fully functional on a 24 × 7 × 365 basis. The e-DBA is a person with a full range of DBA skills who, in addition, is capable of managing applications and databases that are Internet enabled (Mullins, 2001). Major priorities in this role include high (24 × 7 × 365) data availability, integration of legacy data with Web-based applications, tracking of Web activity, and performance engineering for the Internet.

- *The PDA DBA*   Use of PDAs in organizations is exploding. Most DBMS vendors (such as Oracle, IBM, and Sybase) offer small-footprint versions of their products to run on PDAs. (This is an example of the personal databases described in Chapter 1.) A small amount of critical data is typically stored on the PDA, which is periodically synchronized with data stored on the enterprise data servers. DBAs will often be asked questions about how to design these personal databases (or how to rescue users when they get in trouble). However, the greater issue is how to manage data synchronization from hundreds (or possibly thousands) of PDAs while maintaining data integrity. The PDA DBA role may be created to support mobile workers with this new technology.

- *Data warehouse administration* The significant growth in data warehousing (see Chapter 11) in the past five years has caused a new role to emerge, that of a data warehouse administrator (DWA). Inmon (1999), in several articles on his Web site, has outlined the duties of the DWA. As you might expect, two generalizations are true about the DWA role:

  1. A DWA plays many of the same roles as do DAs and DBAs for the data warehouse and data mart databases for the purpose of supporting decision-making applications (rather than transaction-processing applications for the typical DA and DBA).

  2. The role of a DWA emphasizes integration and coordination of metadata and data (extraction agreements, operational data stores, and enterprise data warehouses) across many data sources, not necessarily the standardization of data across these separately managed data sources outside the control and scope of the DWA.

  Specifically, Inmon suggests that a DWA has a unique charter to perform the following functions:

- Build and administer an environment supportive of decision support applications. Thus, a DWA is more concerned with the time to make a decision than with query response time.

- Build a stable architecture for the data warehouse. A DWA is more concerned with the effect of data warehouse growth (scalability in the amount of data and number of users) than with redesigning existing applications. Inmon refers to this architecture as the Corporate Information Factory. For a detailed discussion of this architecture see Chapter 11 and Inmon, Imhoff, and Sousa (2001).

- Develop service level agreements with suppliers and consumers of data for the data warehouse. Thus, a DWA works more closely with end users and operational systems administrators to coordinate vastly different objectives and to oversee the development of new applications (data marts, ETL procedures, and analytical services) than do DAs and DBAs.

These responsibilities are in addition to the responsibilities typical of any DA or DBA, such as selecting technologies, communicating with users about data needs, making performance and capacity decisions, and budgeting and planning data warehouse requirements.

Inmon has estimated that every 100 gigabytes of data in the EDW necessitates another DWA. Another metric is that a DWA is needed for each year of data kept in the EDW. The use of custom-built tools for ETL usually increases the number of DWAs needed.

Data warehouse administrators typically report through the IT unit of an organization but have strong relationships with marketing and other business areas that depend on the EDW for applications, such as customer or supplier relationship management, sales analysis, channel management, and other analytical applications. DWAs should not be part of traditional systems development organizations, as are many DBAs, because data warehousing applications are developed differently than operational systems are and need to be viewed as independent from any particular operational system. Alternatively, DWAs can be placed in the primary end-user organization for the EDW, but this runs the risk of creating many data warehouses or marts, rather than leading to a true, scalable EDW.

Summary   The DA and DBA roles are some of the most challenging roles in any organization. The DA has renewed visiability with the recent enactment of financial control regulations and greater interest in data quality. The DBA is always expected to keep abreast of rapidly changing new technologies and is usually involved with mission-critical applications. A DBA must be constantly available to deal with problems, so the DBA is constantly on call. In return, the DBA position ranks among the best compensated in the IS profession. A search for open DA and DBA jobs shows that salaries range from $60,000 to $105,000.

It is expected that the DBA role will continue to evolve toward increased specialization, such as distributed database/network capacity planning DBAs, server programming DBAs, off-the-shelf customizing DBAs, or data warehousing DBAs (Dowgiallo et al., 1997). The ability to work with multiple databases, communication protocols, and operating systems will be highly valued. Those DBAs who gain broad experience and develop the ability to adapt quickly to changing environments will have many opportunities. It is possible that some current DBA activities, such as tuning, will be replaced by decision support systems able to tune systems by analyzing usage patterns. Some operational duties, such as backup and recovery, can be outsourced and off-shored with remote database administration services. Opportunities in large companies to continue working with very large databases (VLDBs) and opportunities in small and midsize companies to manage desktop and midrange servers should remain strong.

THE OPEN-SOURCE MOVEMENT

As was mentioned previously, one role of a DBA is to select the DBMS(s) to be used in the organization. Database administrators and systems developers in all kinds of organizations have new alternatives when selecting a DBMS. Increasingly, organizations of all sizes are seriously considering open-source DBMSs, such as MySQL and PostgreSQL, as viable choices along with Oracle, DB2, Microsoft SQL Server, Informix, and Teradata. This interest is spurred by the success of the Linux operating system and the Apache Web server. The open-source movement began in roughly 1984 with the start of the Free Software Foundation. Today, the Open Source Initiative (www.opensource.org) is a nonprofit organization dedicated to managing and promoting the open-source movement.

Why has open-source software become so popular? It's not all about cost. Advantages of open-source software include the following:

- A large pool of volunteer testers and developers facilitate the construction of reliable, low-cost software in a relatively short amount of time (but, be aware that only the most widely used open-source software comes close to achieving this advantage).

- The availability of the source code allows people to make modifications to add new features, which are easily inspected by others. (In fact, the agreement is that you do share all modifications for the good of the community.)

- Because the software is not proprietary to one vendor, you do not become locked into the product development plans of only one vendor, which might not be adding the features you need for your environment.

- Distributing application code dependent on and working with the open-source software does not incur any additional costs for copies or licenses (so, deploying software across multiple servers even within the same organization has no marginal cost for the DBMS).

There are, however, some risks or disadvantages:

- Often the absence of complete documentation (although for-fee services might provide quite sufficient documentation).

- Systems with specialized or proprietary needs across organizations do not have the commodity nature that makes open-source software viable, so not all kinds of software lend themselves to being provided via an open-source arrangement (however, DBMSs are viable).

- There are different types of open-source licenses, so not all open-source software is available under the same terms; thus, you have to know the ins and outs of each type of license (see Michaelson, 2004).

An **open-source DBMS** is free or nearly free database software whose source code is publicly available. (Some people refer to open source as "sharing with rules.") The free DBMS is sufficient to run a database, but vendors provide additional fee-based components and support services that make the product more full featured and comparable to the more traditional product leaders. Because many vendors often provide the additional fee-based components, use of an open-source DBMS means that an organization is not tied to one vendor's proprietary product.

A core open-source DBMS is not competitive with IBM's DB2, Oracle, or Teradata, but it is more than competitive against Microsoft Access and other PC-oriented packages. As of the writing of this chapter, the commercial version of MySQL cost $440, compared to $5,000–$40,000 for Oracle, DB2, or Microsoft SQL Server, depending on the edition chosen. According to Hall (2003), a typical Oracle database annual license is $300,000, and a comparable MySQL annual would be $4,000.

Open-source DBMSs are improving rapidly to include more powerful features, such as the transaction controls described later in this chapter, needed for mission critical applications. The open-source DBMSs are fully SQL compliant and run on most popular operating systems. For organizations that cannot afford to spend a lot on software or staff (e.g., small businesses, nonprofits, and educational institutions), an open-source DBMS can be an ideal choice. For example, MySQL and PHP, an open-source alternative to the ASP Web coding environment (see Chapter 10), power many Web sites with database back ends. Visit **www.postgresql.com, www.postgresql.org,** and **www.mysql.com** for details on the two leading open-source DBMSs.

When choosing an open-source (or really any DBMS), you need to consider the following types of factors:

- *Features*   Does the DBMS include capabilities you need, such as subqueries, stored procedures, views, and transaction integrity controls?

- *Support*   How widely is the DBMS used and what alternatives exist for helping you solve problems, and provide documentation, and ancillary tools?

- *Ease-of-use*   This often depends on the availability of tools that make any piece of system software, like a DBMS, easier to use through things like a GUI interface.

- *Stability*   How frequently and how seriously does the DBMS malfunction over time or with high volume use?

- *Speed*   How rapid is the response time to queries and transactions with proper tuning of the database? (Because open-source DBMSs are often not as fully loaded with advanced, obscure features, their performance can be attractive.)

- *Training*   How easy is it for developers and users to learn to use the DBMS?

- *Licensing*   What are the terms of the open-source license and are there commercial licenses that would provide the types of support you need?

Open-source DBMS: Free DBMS source code software that provides the core functionality of an SQL-compliant DBMS.

MODELING ENTERPRISE DATA

As you consider the various responsibilities of data and database administration outlined earlier in this chapter, you discover that data modeling and database design are key responsibilities. In this section, we describe the roles of each of these two groups, as well as the role of an information systems architecture in imposing a discipline on the modeling and design processes.

Organizational Roles

Typical responsibilities are shown in Figure 12-2, assuming that both DA and DBA functions exist in the organization. In simplest terms, data administration is responsible for data modeling, whereas database administration is responsible for database design. Notice that data administration is primarily concerned with metadata (data about data), whereas database administration is more concerned with data.

Although the roles shown in Figure 12-2 are quite well defined, it is important that each group not only understand but participate in the activities of the other group. Thus, it would be counterproductive for data administration to develop the conceptual data model in isolation, then "throw the design over the wall" to database administration. There is also the potential for feedback; for example, detailed logical design work can lead to expansion of the conceptual data model.

Role of an Information Systems Architecture

In the current business environment, DBAs are pressured to adapt to change while providing high-quality systems quickly. Key to meeting these expectations is developing an enterprise architecture or Information Systems Architecture, as described briefly in Chapter 2. The author of ISA (Zachman, 1987) sees the development of information systems to be similar to other complex product development and manufacturing processes. He has studied those processes to apply their principles and procedures to development of an information systems enterprise architecture. Building an enterprise architecture enables an organization to make the step from business strategy to implementation more effectively. Zachman (1997, p. 48) defines an enterprise architecture as "that set of descriptive representations (that is, models) that are relevant for describing an enterprise such that it (the enterprise) can be produced to management's requirements (quality) and maintained over the period of its useful life (change)." Data models are one class of such models.

All too often in systems development, the enterprise view has been deemphasized as developers concentrated on building a piece of the enterprise system. It has

Figure 12-2
Data modeling responsibilities

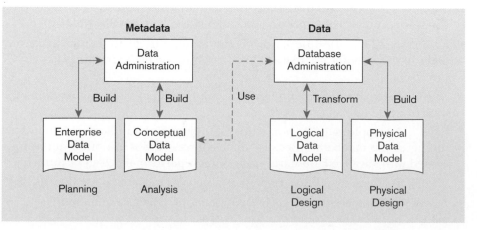

often been problematic to fit together these pieces into a smoothly functioning enterprise system. Some systems are no longer relevant when completed, or do not remain relevant for long. System maintenance is a major portion of the overall cost of a new system. Problems such as the Year 2000 problem, estimated to have cost $400 billion worldwide, arise from past failures to address data element definitions within the enterprise architecture.

Ideally, every database development project should fit within the enterprise architecture. This means developing conceptual data models that are congruent with the needs of the business and that are then translated into logical data models, physical data models, and implemented systems. But the conceptual data models must also fit across Zachman's framework, meshing with the business process model, business network logistics, work flow models within the enterprise, the enterprise master schedule, and the enterprise business plan. The enterprisewide impacts of execution of each component must be considered, and problems and discontinuities resolved.

Organizations that articulate an enterprise architecture and develop standards and procedures to ensure that systems development projects fit within that enterprise architecture should experience tangible benefits. Code can be reused, systems meshed together rather than conflicting with each other, and business objectives met. As the articulation and incorporation of business rules becomes more sophisticated, those organizations with an articulated enterprise architecture should be able to implement those business rules more consistently and more quickly than similar organizations that have not developed an enterprise architecture. Such possibilities provide obvious strategic benefits to organizations in today's competitive environment.

MANAGING DATA SECURITY

The goal of **database security** is the protection of data from accidental or intentional threats to their integrity and access. The database environment has grown more complex, with distributed databases located on client/server architectures and personal computers as well as on mainframes. Access to data has become more open through the Internet and corporate intranets and from mobile computing devices. As a result, managing data security effectively has become more difficult and time-consuming. Some security procedures for client/server and Web-based systems were introduced in Chapter 9.

Database security: Protection of the data against accidental or intentional loss, destruction, or misuse.

Because data are a critical resource, all persons in an organization must be sensitive to security threats and take measures to protect the data within their domains. For example, computer listings or computer disks containing sensitive data should not be left unattended on desktops. Data administration is often responsible for developing overall policies and procedures to protect databases. Database administration is typically responsible for administering database security on a daily basis. The facilities that database administrators have to use in establishing adequate data security are discussed later, but first it is important to review potential threats to data security.

Threats to Data Security

Threats to data security may be direct threats to the database. For example, those who gain unauthorized access to a database may then browse, change, or even steal the data to which they have gained access. (See the news story at the beginning of this chapter for a good example.) Focusing on database security alone, however, will not ensure a secure database. All parts of the system must be secure, including the database, the network, the operating system, the building(s) in which the database resides physically, and the personnel who have any opportunity to access the system.

Figure 12-3
Possible locations of data security
threats

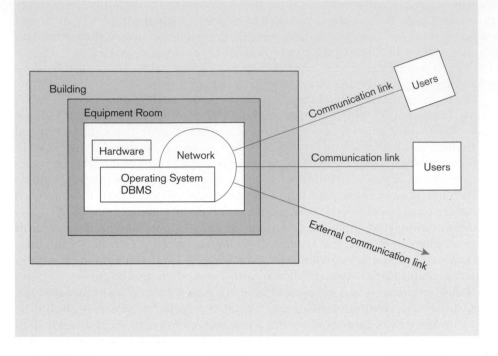

Figure 12-3 diagrams many of the possible locations for data security threats. Accomplishing this level of security requires careful review, establishment of security procedures and policies, and implementation and enforcement of those procedures and policies. The following threats must be addressed in a comprehensive data security plan:

- *Accidental losses, including human error, software, and hardware-caused breaches* Establishing operating procedures such as user authorization, uniform software installation procedures, and hardware maintenance schedules are examples of actions that may be taken to address threats from accidental losses. As in any effort that involves human beings, some losses are inevitable, but well–thought-out policies and procedures should reduce the amount and severity of losses. Of potentially more serious consequence are the threats that are not accidental.

- *Theft and fraud* These activities are going to be perpetrated by people, quite possibly through electronic means, and may or may not alter data. Attention here should focus on each possible location shown in Figure 12-3. For example, physical security must be established so that unauthorized persons are unable to gain access to rooms where computers, servers, telecommunications facilities, or computer files are located. Physical security should also be provided for employee offices and any other locations where sensitive data are stored or easily accessed. Establishment of a firewall to protect unauthorized access to inappropriate parts of the database through outside communication links is another example of a security procedure that will hamper people who are intent on theft or fraud.

- *Loss of privacy or confidentiality* Loss of privacy is usually taken to mean loss of protection of data about individuals, whereas loss of confidentiality is usually taken to mean loss of protection of critical organizational data that may have strategic value to the organization. Failure to control privacy of information may lead to blackmail, bribery, public embarrassment, or stealing of user passwords. Failure to control confidentiality may lead to loss of competitiveness. State and federal laws now exist to require some types of organizations to create and communicate policies to ensure privacy of customer and client data.

Security mechanisms must enforce these policies, and failure to do so can mean significant financial and reputation loss.

- *Loss of data integrity*   When data integrity is compromised, data will be invalid or corrupted. Unless data integrity can be restored through established back-up and recovery procedures, an organization may suffer serious losses or make incorrect and expensive decisions based on the invalid data.

- *Loss of availability*   Sabotage of hardware, networks, or applications may cause the data to become unavailable to users, which again may lead to severe operational difficulties. This category of threat includes the introduction of viruses intended to corrupt data or software or to render the system unusable. It is important to counter this threat by always installing the most current antivirus software, as well as educating employees on the sources of viruses. We discuss data availability later in this chapter.

As noted earlier, data security must be provided within the context of a total program for security. Two critical areas that strongly support data security are client/server security and Web site security. We address these two topics next before outlining approaches aimed more directly at data security.

Establishing Client/Server Security

Database security is only as good as the security of the whole computing environment. Client/server database computing implies the existence of a network that connects the client/server components. In this distributed environment, establishing database security is more complex than in a centralized environment. Networks are susceptible to breaches of security through eavesdropping, unauthorized connections, or unauthorized retrieval of packets of information that are traversing the network. Thus, client/server architectures are more susceptible to security threats than centralized systems.

Security measures that should be taken in a client/server environment include measures that are common to securing all systems, but should also include measures to secure the more distributed environment of client/server architectures. Physical security, logical security, and change control security must be established across all components of the client/server environment, including the servers, the client workstations, the network and its related components, and the users.

Server Security   Multiple servers, including database servers, need to be protected. Each should be located in a secure area, accessible only to authorized administrators and supervisors. Logical access controls, including server and administrator passwords, provide layers of protection against intrusion. Security standards should include guidelines for password lengths, password naming conventions, frequency of password changes, and so on for each component of the client/server environment. Password management utilities should be included as part of the network and operating systems.

Most client/server DBMSs have database-level password security that is similar to system-level password security. It is also possible to pass authentication information through from the operating system authentication capability, but this reduces the number of password security layers. Reliance on operating system authentication should not be encouraged. Other systems, such as Oracle and SQL Server, provide database administrators with considerable capabilities that can provide aid in establishing data security, including the capability to limit each user's access and activity permissions (such as *select, update, insert,* or *delete*) to tables within the database.

Network Security   Securing client/server systems includes securing the network between client and server. The encryption of data so that attackers cannot read a data packet that is being transmitted is obviously an important part of network security. (We discuss encryption later in the chapter.) Because networks are more vulnerable to attack than the other components of the client/server system are, security measures in place for those components help to keep the network secure. For example, authentication of the client workstation that is attempting to access the server also helps to enforce network security, and application authentication gives the user confidence that the server being contacted is the real server needed by the user. Audit trails of attempted accesses can help administrators identify unauthorized attempts to use the system. Other system components, such as routers, can also be configured to restrict access to authorized users, IP addresses, and so forth.

Client/Server Security Issues for Web-Enabled Databases

The explosion of Web sites that make current data accessible to viewers through their Internet connections raises new issues that go beyond the traditional client/server security issues just addressed. The dynamic creation of a Web page from a database requires access to the database, and if the database is not properly protected, it is vulnerable to inappropriate access by any user. This is a new point of vulnerability that was previously avoided by specialized client access software. Also of interest is privacy. Companies are able to collect information about those who access their Web sites. If they are conducting e-commerce activities, selling products over the Web, they can collect information about their customers that has value to other businesses. If a company sells customer information without those customers' knowledge or if a customer believes that may happen, ethical and privacy issues are raised that must be addressed.

Figure 12-4 illustrates a typical environment for Web-enabled databases. The Web farm includes Web servers and database servers supporting Web-based applications.

Web Security If an organization wishes only to make static HTML pages available, protection must be established for the HTML files stored on a Web server. Creation of a static Web page with extracts from a database uses traditional client/server tools such as Visual Basic or PowerBuilder, and thus their creation can be controlled by using standard methods of database access control. If some of the

Figure 12-4
Establishing Internet security

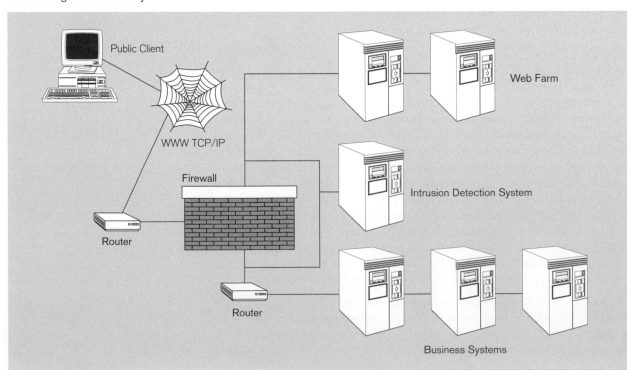

HTML files loaded on the Web server are sensitive, they can be placed in directories that are protected using operating system security or they may be readable but not published in the directory. Thus, the user must know the exact filename to access the sensitive HTML page. It is also common to segregate the Web server and limit its contents to publicly browsable Web pages. Sensitive files may be kept on another server accessible through an organization's intranet.

Security measures for dynamic Web page generation are different. Dynamic Web pages are stored as a template into which the appropriate and current data are inserted from the database once the query(ies) associated with the page is run. This means that the Web server must be able to access the database. To function appropriately, the connection usually requires full access to the database. Thus, establishing adequate server security is critical to protecting the data. The server that owns the database connection should be physically secure, and execution of programs and common gateway interface (CGI) scripts should be controlled.

Access to data can also be controlled through another layer of security: user-authentication security. Use of an HTML login form will allow the database administrator to define each user's privileges. Each session may be tracked by storing a piece of data, or "cookie," on the client machine. This information can be returned to the server and provide information about the login session. CGI scripts or other means must be established to perform the necessary authentication routines.

Session security must also be established to ensure that private data are not compromised during a session, because information is broadcast across a network for reception by a particular machine and is thus susceptible to being intercepted. TCP/IP is not a very secure protocol, and encryption systems, such as the ones discussed later in this chapter, are essential. A standard encryption method, Secure Sockets Layer (SSL), is used by many developers to encrypt all data traveling between client and server during a session. URLs that begin with https:// use SSL for transmission.

Additional methods of Web security include ways to restrict access to Web servers:

- Restrict the number of users on the Web server as much as possible. Of those users, give as few as possible superuser or administrator rights. Only those given these privileges should also be allowed to load software or edit or add files.

- Restrict access to the Web server, keeping a minimum number of ports open. Try to open a minimum number of ports, and preferably only http and https ports.

- Remove any unneeded programs that load automatically when setting up the server. Demo programs are sometimes included that can provide a hacker with the access desired. Compilers and interpreters such as Perl should not be on a path that is directly accessible from the Internet. CGI has potential security issues and should only be run if necessary. Restrict all CGI scripts to one subdirectory.

If running on UNIX, be sure that the default operating system install as root was not used. Instead, install from a user's account that has only the minimum access.

Web Privacy   Protection of individual privacy when using the Internet has become an important issue. E-mail, e-commerce and marketing, and other online resources have created new computer-mediated communication paths. Many groups have an interest in people's Internet behavior, including employers, governments, and businesses. Applications that return individualized responses require that information be collected about the individual, but at the same time proper respect for the privacy and dignity of employees, citizens, and customers should be observed.

Individuals must guard their privacy rights and must be aware of the privacy implications of the tools they are using. For example, when using a browser, users may elect to allow cookies to be placed on their machines or they may reject that option. To make a decision with which they would be comfortable, they must know several things. They must be aware of cookies, understand what they are, evaluate their own desire to receive customized information versus their wish to keep their browsing behavior to themselves, and learn how to set their machine to accept or reject cookies. Browsers and Web sites have not been quick to help users understand all of these aspects. Abuses of privacy, such as selling customer information collected in cookies, has helped increase general awareness of the privacy issues that have developed as use of the Web for communication, shopping, and other uses has developed.

At work, the individual needs to realize that communication executed through their employer's machines and networks is not private. Courts have upheld the rights of employers to monitor all employee electronic communication.

On the Internet itself, privacy of communication is not guaranteed. Encryption products, anonymous remailers, and built-in security mechanisms in commonly used software help to preserve privacy. Protecting the privately owned and operated computer networks that now make up a very critical part of our information infrastructure is essential to the further development of electronic commerce, banking, health care, and transportation applications over the Web.

The W3C has created a standard, the Platform for Privacy Preferences (P3P), that will communicate a Web site's stated privacy policies and compare that statement with the user's own policy preferences. P3P uses XML code on Web site servers that can be fetched automatically by any browser or plug-in equipped for P3P. The client browser or plug-in can then compare the site's privacy policy with the user's privacy preferences and inform the user of any discrepancies. P3P addresses the following aspects of online privacy:

- Who is collecting the data?
- What information is being collected and for what purpose?
- Which information will be shared with others and who are those others?
- Can users make changes in the way their data will be used by the collector?
- How are disputes resolved?
- What policies are followed for retaining data?
- Where can the site's detailed policies be found in readable form?

Anonymity is another important facet of Internet communication that has come under pressure. Although U.S. law protects a right to anonymity, chat rooms and e-mail forums have been required to reveal the names of people who have posted messages anonymously. A 1995 European Parliament directive that would cut off data exchanges with any country lacking adequate privacy safeguards has led to an agreement that the United States will provide the same protection to European customers as European businesses do. This may lead Congress to establish legislation that is more protective than that previously enacted.

Database Software Data Security Features

A comprehensive data security plan will include establishing administrative policies and procedures, physical protections, and data management software protections. Physical protections, such as securing data centers and work areas, disposing of obsolete media, and protecting portable devices from theft, are not covered here. We discuss administrative policies and procedures later in this section. All the elements of a data security plan work together to achieve the desired level of security. Some industries, for example health care, have regulations that set standards for the security plan and, hence, put requirements on data security. (See Anderson, 2005 for a discussion of the HIPAA security guidelines.) The most important security features of data management software follow:

1. Views or subschemas, which restrict user views of the database
2. Domains, assertions, checks, and other integrity controls defined as database objects, which are enforced by the DBMS during database querying and updating

3. Authorization rules, which identify users and restrict the actions they may take against a database

4. User-defined procedures, which define additional constraints or limitations in using a database

5. Encryption procedures, which encode data in an unrecognizable form

6. Authentication schemes, which positively identify persons attempting to gain access to a database

7. Back-up, journaling, and checkpointing capabilities, which facilitate recovery procedures

Views

In Chapter 7, we defined a view as a subset of the database that is presented to one or more users. A view is created by querying one or more of the base tables, producing a dynamic result table for the user at the time of the request. Thus, a view is always based on the current data in the base tables from which it is built. The advantage of a view is that it can be built to present only the data (certain columns and/or rows) to which the user requires access, effectively preventing the user from viewing other data that may be private or confidential. The user may be granted the right to access the view, but not to access the base tables upon which the view is based. So, confining a user to a view may be more restrictive for that user than allowing him or her access to the involved base tables.

PINE VALLEY FURNITURE

For example, we could build a view for a Pine Valley employee that provides information about materials needed to build a Pine Valley furniture product without providing other information, such as unit price, that is not relevant to the employee's work. This command creates a view that will list the wood required and the wood available for each product:

```
CREATE VIEW MATERIALS_V
     AS
     SELECT PRODUCT_T.PRODUCT_ID, PRODUCT_NAME, FOOTAGE,
     FOOTAGE_ON_HAND
          FROM PRODUCT_T, RAW_MATERIALS_T, USES_T
               WHERE PRODUCT_T.PRODUCT_ID = USES_T.PRODUCT_ID
               AND RAW_MATERIALS_T.MATERIAL_ID =
               USES_T.MATERIAL_ID;
```

The contents of the view created will be updated each time the view is accessed, but here are the current contents of the view, which can be accessed with the SQL command:

```
SELECT * FROM MATERIALS_V;
```

PRODUCT_ID	PRODUCT_NAME	FOOTAGE	FOOTAGE_ON_HAND
1	End Table	4	1
2	Coffee Table	6	11
3	Computer Desk	15	11
4	Entertainment Center	20	84
5	Writer's Desk	13	68
6	8-Drawer Desk	16	66
7	Dining Table	16	11
8	Computer Desk	15	9

8 rows selected.

The user can write SELECT statements against the view, treating it as though it were a table. Although views promote security by restricting user access to data, they are not adequate security measures, because unauthorized persons may gain knowledge of or access to a particular view. Also, several persons may share a particular view; all may have authority to read the data, but only a restricted few may be authorized to update the data. Finally, with high-level query languages, an unauthorized person may gain access to data through simple experimentation. As a result, more sophisticated security measures are normally required.

Integrity Controls

Integrity controls protect data from unauthorized use and update. Often, integrity controls limit the values a field may hold and the actions that can be performed on data, or trigger the execution of some procedure, such as placing an entry in a log to record which users have done what with which data.

One form of integrity control is a domain. In essence, a domain is a way to create a user-defined data type. Once a domain is defined, any field can be assigned that domain as its data type. For example, the following PriceChange domain (defined in SQL) can be used as the data type of any database field, such as PriceIncrease and PriceDiscount, to limit the amount standard prices can be augmented in one transaction:

```
CREATE DOMAIN PriceChange AS DECIMAL
    CHECK (VALUE BETWEEN .001 and .15);
```

Then, in the definition of, say, a pricing transaction table, we might have the following:

```
PriceIncrease PriceChange NOT NULL,
```

One advantage of a domain is that, if it ever has to change, it can be changed in one place—the domain definition—and all fields with this domain will be changed automatically. Alternatively, the same CHECK clause could be included in a constraint on both the PriceIncrease and PriceDiscount fields, but in this case if the limits of the check were to change, a DBA would have to find every instance of this integrity control and change it in each place separately.

Assertions are powerful constraints that enforce certain desirable database conditions. Assertions are checked automatically by the DBMS when transactions are run involving tables or fields on which assertions exist. For example, assume that an employee table has fields of EmpID, EmpName, SupervisorID, and SpouseID. Suppose that a company rule is that no employee may supervise his or her spouse. The following assertion enforces this rule:

```
CREATE ASSERTION SpousalSupervision
    CHECK (SupervisorID < > SpouseID);
```

If the assertion fails, the DBMS will generate an error message.

Assertions can become rather complex. Suppose that Pine Valley Furniture has a rule that no two salespersons can be assigned to the same territory at the same time. Suppose a Salesperson table includes fields of SalespersonID and TerritoryID. This assertion can be written using a correlated subquery as follows:

```
CREATE ASSERTION TerritoryAssignment
    CHECK (NOT EXISTS
        (SELECT * FROM Salesperson SP WHERE SP.TerritoryID IN
            (SELECT SSP.TerritoryID FROM Salesperson SSP WHERE
                SSP.SalespersonID < > SP.SalespersonID)));
```

Finally, *triggers* can be used for security purposes. Triggers were defined and illustrated in Chapter 8. A trigger, which includes an event, condition, and action, is potentially more complex than an assertion. For example, a trigger can do the following:

- Prohibit inappropriate actions (e.g., changing a salary value outside of the normal business day)

- Cause special handling procedures to be executed (e.g., if a customer invoice payment is received after some due date, a penalty can be added to the account balance for that customer)

- Cause a row to be written to a log file to echo important information about the user and a transaction being made to sensitive data, so that the log can be reviewed by human or automated procedures for possible inappropriate behavior (e.g., the log can record which user initiated a salary change for which employee)

As with domains, a powerful benefit of a trigger, like any stored procedure, is that the DBMS enforces these controls for all users and all database activities. The control does not have to be coded into each query or program. Thus, individual users and programs cannot circumvent the necessary controls.

Assertions, triggers, stored procedures, and other forms of integrity controls may not stop all malicious or accidental use or modification of data. Thus, it is recommended (Anderson, 2005) that a change audit process be used in which all user activities are logged and monitored to check that all policies and constraints are enforced. Following this recommendation means that every database query and transaction is logged to record characteristics of all data use, especially modifications: who accessed the data, when it was accessed, what program or query was run, where in the computer network the request was generated, and other parameters that can be used to investigate suspicious activity or actual breaches of security and integrity.

Authorization Rules

Authorization rules are controls incorporated in the data management system that restrict access to data and also restrict the actions that people may take when they access data. For example, a person who can supply a particular password may be authorized to read any record in a database but cannot necessarily modify any of those records.

Fernandez et al. (1981) have developed a conceptual model of database security. Their model expresses authorization rules in the form of a table (or matrix) that includes subjects, objects, actions, and constraints. Each row of the table indicates that a particular subject is authorized to take a certain action on an object in the database, perhaps subject to some constraint. Figure 12-5 shows an example of such an authorization matrix. This table contains several entries pertaining to records in an accounting database. For example, the first row in the table indicates that anyone in the Sales Department is authorized to insert a new customer record in the database, provided that the customer's credit limit does not exceed $5,000. The last row indicates that the program AR4 is authorized to modify order records without restriction. Data administration is responsible for determining and implementing authorization rules that are implemented at the database level. Authorization schemes can also be implemented at the operating system level or the application level.

Authorization rules: Controls incorporated in the data management systems that restrict access to data and also restrict the actions that people may take when they access data.

Subject	Object	Action	Constraint
Sales Dept.	Customer record	Insert	Credit limit LE $5000
Order trans.	Customer record	Read	None
Terminal 12	Customer record	Modify	Balance due only
Acctg. Dept.	Order record	Delete	None
Ann Walker	Order record	Insert	Order aml LT $2000
Program AR4	Order record	Modify	None

Figure 12-5
Authorization matrix

Figure 12-6
Implementing authorization rules
(a) Authorization table for subjects
(salespersons)

	Customer records	Order records
Read	Y	Y
Insert	Y	Y
Modify	Y	N
Delete	N	N

(b) Authorization table for objects
(order records)

	Salespersons (password BATMAN)	Order entry (password JOKER)	Accounting (password TRACY)
Read	Y	Y	Y
Insert	N	Y	N
Modify	N	Y	Y
Delete	N	N	Y

Most contemporary database management systems do not implement an authorization matrix such as the one shown in Figure 12-5; they normally use simplified versions. There are two principal types: authorization tables for subjects and authorization tables for objects. Figure 12-6 shows an example of each type. In Figure 12-6a, for example, we see that salespersons are allowed to modify customer records but not delete these records. In Figure 12-6b, we see that users in Order Entry or Accounting can modify order records, but salespersons cannot. A given DBMS product may provide either one or both of these types of facilities.

Authorization tables, such as those shown in Figure 12-6, are attributes of an organization's data and their environment; they are therefore properly viewed as metadata. Thus, the tables should be stored and maintained in the repository. Because authorization tables contain highly sensitive data, they themselves should be protected by stringent security rules. Normally, only selected persons in data administration have authority to access and modify these tables.

For example, in Oracle, the privileges included in Figure 12-7 can be granted to users at the database or table level. INSERT and UPDATE can be granted at the column level. Where many users, such as those in a particular job classification, need similar privileges, roles may be created that contain a set of privileges, and then all the privileges can be granted to a user simply by granting the role. To grant the ability to read the product table and update prices to a user with the login ID of SMITH, the following SQL command may be given:

GRANT SELECT, UPDATE (unit_price) ON PRODUCT_T TO SMITH;

There are eight data dictionary views that contain information about privileges that have been granted. In this case, DBA_TAB_PRIVS contains users and objects for every user who has been granted privileges on objects, such as tables. DBA_COL_PRIVS contains users who have been granted privileges on columns of tables.

Figure 12-7
Oracle privileges

Privilege	Capability
SELECT	Query the object.
INSERT	Insert records into the table/view.
	Can be given for specific columns.
UPDATE	Update records in table/view.
	Can be given for specific columns.
DELETE	Delete records from table/view.
ALTER	Alter the table.
INDEX	Create indexes on the table.
REFERENCES	Create foreign keys that reference the table.
EXECUTE	Execute the procedure, package, or function.

User-Defined Procedures

Some DBMS products provide user exits (or interfaces) that allow system designers or users to create their own **user-defined procedures** for security, in addition to the authorization rules we have just described. For example, a user procedure might be designed to provide positive user identification. In attempting to log on to the computer, the user might be required to supply a procedure name in addition to a simple password. If valid password and procedure names are supplied, the system then calls the procedure, which asks the user a series of questions whose answers should be known only to that password holder (such as mother's maiden name).

User-defined procedures: User exits (or interfaces) that allow system designers to define their own security procedures in addition to the authorization rules.

Encryption

Data encryption can be used to protect highly sensitive data such as customer credit card numbers or account balances. **Encryption** is the coding or scrambling of data so that humans cannot read them. Some DBMS products include encryption routines that automatically encode sensitive data when they are stored or transmitted over communications channels. For example, encryption is commonly used in electronic funds transfer (EFT) systems. Other DBMS products provide exits that allow users to code their own encryption routines.

Encryption: The coding or scrambling of data so that humans cannot read them.

Any system that provides encryption facilities must also provide complementary routines for decoding the data. These decoding routines must be protected by adequate security, or else the advantages of encryption are lost. They also require significant computing resources.

Two common forms of encryption exist: one key and two key. With a one-key method, also called data encryption standard (DES), both the sender and the receiver need to know the key that is used to scramble the transmitted or stored data. A two-key method, also called asymmetric encryption, employs a private and a public key. Two-key methods are especially popular in e-commerce applications to provide secure transmission and database storage of payment data, such as credit card numbers.

A simplified illustration of the two-key method is shown in Figure 12-8. With this method, all users who can transmit an encrypted message possess the public key. This key is used by the encryption algorithm to transform a plain-text message into a

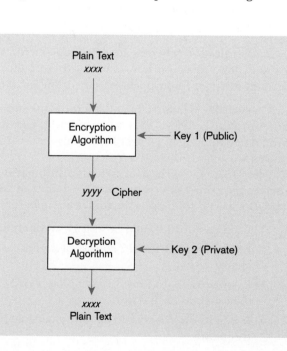

Figure 12-8
Basic two-key encryption

cipher (or encrypted message), as shown in the figure. The private key is used by the decryption algorithm to convert the cipher back to plain text. However, only a person (or persons) who is allowed to receive the plain-text message may possess the private key.

You may understand two-key encryption better by means of a (somewhat contrived) analogy. Suppose that you have ten friends who are traveling in Italy. You and each of your friends have an English-to-Italian dictionary in your possession, because none of you understand much Italian. You decide to write a letter to each of your friends in Italian, to encourage their learning the language. To write the letter, you translate English words into Italian words using the dictionary, which fills the role of a public key in this example. When they receive your letter, your friends are a little frustrated because they can't read the Italian and the English-to-Italian dictionary is of little use because it is much too cumbersome to work backwards. You then realize that one of your friends will probably never translate the letter on his own initiative, so you send him an Italian-to-English dictionary but ask him not to share it with the others. With this dictionary (which functions as a private key) your friend is able to translate your letter into English quickly and amaze the others.

A popular implementation of the two-key method is the Secure Sockets Layer (SSL), developed by Netscape Communications Corporation. SSL is built into most major browsers and Web servers. It provides data encryption, server authentication, and other services in a TCP/IP connection. For example, the U.S. banking industry uses a 128-bit version of SSL (the most secure level in current use) to secure online banking transactions. (Online banking is the fastest-growing Internet application at the present time.)

Authentication Schemes

A long-standing problem in computer circles is how to identify positively persons who are trying to gain access to a computer or its resources. In an electronic environment, a user can prove his or her identity by supplying one or more of the following factors:

1. Something the user knows, usually a password or personal identification number (PIN)

2. Something the user possesses, such as a smart card or token

3. Some unique personal characteristic, such as a fingerprint or retinal scan

Authentication schemes are called one-factor, two-factor, or three-factor authentication, depending on how many of these factors are employed. Authentication becomes stronger in proportion to the number of factors that are used.

Passwords   The first line of defense is the use of passwords, which is a one-factor authentication scheme. That is, anyone who can supply a valid password can log on to the database system. (A user ID may also be required, but user IDs are typically not secured.)

The DBA (or perhaps a systems administrator) is responsible for managing schemes for issuing or creating passwords for the DBMS and/or specific applications. The DBA should follow several guidelines in creating passwords:

1. Each password should be at least eight characters long.

2. Each password should consist of a combination of alphabetic and numeric characters.

3. Passwords should not be complete words and should not embed personal data such as birth dates.

4. Initial passwords should be random values, and passwords should be changed frequently.

Although passwords are a good starting point for authentication, it is well known that they have a number of deficiencies. People assigned passwords for different devices quickly devise ways to remember these passwords, ways that tend to compromise the password scheme. The passwords get written down, where others may find them. They get shared with other users; it is not unusual for an entire department to use one common password for access. Passwords get included in automatic logon scripts, which removes the inconvenience of remembering them and typing them but also eliminates their effectiveness. And passwords usually traverse a network in cleartext, not encrypted, so if intercepted they may be easily interpreted. Also, passwords cannot, by themselves, ensure the security of a computer and its databases because they give no indication of who is trying to gain access. Thus, for example, a log should be kept and analyzed of attempted logons with incorrect passwords.

Strong Authentication   More reliable authentication techniques have become a business necessity, with the rapid advances in e-commerce and increased security threats in the form of hacking, identity theft, and so on.

Two-factor authentication schemes require two of the three factors: something the user has (usually a card or token) and something the user knows (usually a PIN). You are already familiar with this system from using automated teller machines (ATMs). To use the ATM you must insert your bankcard (something you have) into the machine; then at the prompt you must key in your valid PIN (something you hopefully know). This scheme is much more secure than simple passwords because (barring carelessness) it is quite difficult for an unauthorized person to obtain both factors at the same time.

Although an improvement, two-factor schemes are not infallible. Cards can be lost or stolen, and PINs can be intercepted. For sensitive applications, such as e-commerce and online banking, stronger security is desirable or mandatory. *Three-factor authentication* schemes add an important third factor: a biometric attribute that is unique for each individual user. Personal characteristics that are commonly used include fingerprints, voiceprints, eye pictures, or signature dynamics. The use of retina prints has declined because of concerns about possible damaging effects to the eye by the laser optics used to capture a retina print.

Three-factor authentication is normally implemented with a high-tech card called a smart card (or smart badge). A **smart card** is a credit-card sized plastic card with an embedded microprocessor chip with the ability to store, process, and output electronic data in a secure manner. Smart cards are replacing the familiar magnetic-stripe-based cards we have used for decades. The microprocessor is embedded in a module that provides an interface to external devices such as ATMs, personal computer card readers, mobile phones, and so on. When properly handled and distributed, smart cards are considered to be secure mechanisms. Some manufacturers encode each smart card with a unique serial number for card control. Sensitive data are stored on the cards in encrypted form, so the cards are highly tamper resistant.

Smart card: A credit-card sized plastic card with an embedded microprocessor chip with the ability to store, process, and output electronic data in a secure manner.

Three-factor authentication is implemented with smart cards in two stages. When the card is first issued to its owner, it is personalized with that owner's data. This data might include a digitized photograph, as well as the person's name, address, and so on. The user selects (or is assigned) a PIN, which is encrypted and stored on the chip. Assuming fingerprint identification will be used, the person's fingerprint is scanned and a digital representation of the print is securely stored on the chip.

Each time the user attempts to log on to his (or her) computer, the user must insert the smart card into a card reader attached to the computer (normally a USB or serial port is used). The computer prompts the user for his PIN, which must match the one stored on the chip. The user is next prompted to place his finger into a scanning device which is attached to (or integral with) the reader. The digital representation of this fingerprint scan must match that stored on the chip. Notice that an imposter who tries to use a lost or stolen card will be rejected because he or she will not have the correct PIN (first line of defense) or will certainly fail the fingerprint ID.

Smart cards can be a very strong means to authenticate a database user. In addition, smart cards can themselves be database storage devices; today smart cards can store well over 100,000 bytes of data, and this number is increasing rapidly. Smart cards can provide secure storage of personal data such as medical records or a summary of medications taken.

Smart cards can be only as secure as the process that is used to issue them. Before issuing a new card to an employee or other person, the issuing agency must validate beyond any reasonable doubt the identity of that person. Often paper documents are used in this process—birth certificates, passports, driver's licenses, and so on. These types of documents are notoriously unreliable because they can be easily copied, forged, and so on. Notice that if a smart card is issued and personalized to an imposter (either carelessly or deliberately), it can be used freely by that person.

Mediated Authentication   Another approach is the use of third-party mediated authentication systems, which establish user authenticity through a trusted authentication agent, such as Kerberos. Developed at MIT, Kerberos is primarily used in application-level protocols, such as TELNET or FTP, to provide user-to-host security. Kerberos works by providing a secret key (Kerberos ticket) to a qualified user that can then be embedded in any other network protocol. Any process that implements that protocol can then be certain of the source of the request. Sun Microsystems also has an authentication mechanism, called DES Authentication, which is based on the sender encrypting a timestamp when the message is sent, which is then checked against the receiver's internal clock. This requires agreement between the agents as to the current time and both must be using the same encryption key. Liability issues have kept third-party authentication schemes from achieving widespread acceptance. Public key, certificate-based authentication schemes, which issue parties identification certificates that they can then exchange without further involvement of a third party, are also being used. Such digital certificates will be used extensively in e-commerce transactions involving credit card or digital cash purchases.

A last piece of the authentication problem is establishing nonrepudiation. That is, after a message has been sent, the user should not be able to repudiate having sent the message, or say that it was not sent. Biometric devices coupled with the sending of messages are used to establish nonrepudiation.

Security Policies and Procedures

We have described numerous features of data management software that organizations should use to secure their databases and other computing resources. Organizations must also establish administrative policies and procedures that serve as a context for effectively implementing these measures. Four types of security policies and procedures are the following: personnel controls, physical access controls, maintenance controls, and data privacy controls.

Personnel Controls   Adequate controls of personnel must be developed and followed, for the greatest threat to business security is often internal rather than external. In addition to the security authorization and authentication procedures just discussed, organizations should develop procedures to ensure a selective hiring process that validates potential employees' representations about their backgrounds and capabilities. Monitoring to ensure that personnel are following established practices, taking regular vacations, working with other employees, and so forth should be followed. Employees should be trained in those aspects of security and quality that are relevant to their jobs and encouraged to be aware of and follow standard security and data quality measures. Standard job controls, such as separating duties so no one employee has responsibility for an entire business process or keeping application developers from having access to production systems, should also be enforced. Should an employee need to be let go, there should be an orderly set of procedures to remove authorizations and authentications and to notify other employees of the status change.

Physical Access Controls   Limiting access to particular areas within a building is usually a part of controlling physical access. Swipe or proximity access cards can be used to gain access to secure areas, and each access can be recorded in a database with timestamps. Guests should be issued badges and escorted into secure areas. This includes vendor maintenance representatives. Sensitive equipment, including hardware and peripherals, such as printers (which may be used to print classified reports) can be controlled by placement in secure areas. Other equipment may be locked to a desk or cabinet or may have an alarm attached. Back-up data tapes should be kept in fireproof data safes and/or kept off-site at a safe location. Procedures that make explicit the schedules for moving media and disposing of media, and that establish labeling and indexing of all materials stored, and so forth, must be established.

Placement of computer screens so that they cannot be seen from outside the building may also be important. Control procedures for areas external to the office building should also be developed. Companies frequently use security guards to control access to their buildings or use a card swipe system or handprint recognition system (smart badges) to automate employee access to the building. Visitors should be issued an identification card and required to be accompanied throughout the building.

New concerns are raised by the increasingly mobile nature of work. Laptop computers are very susceptible to theft, which puts data on the laptop at risk. Encryption and multiple-factor authentication can protect data in the event of theft. Antitheft devices (e.g., security cables, geographical tracking chips) can deter theft or quickly recover stolen laptops on which critical data are stored.

Maintenance Controls   An area of control that helps to maintain data quality and availability but that is often overlooked is maintenance control. Organizations should review external maintenance agreements for all hardware and software they are using to ensure that appropriate response rates are agreed to for maintaining system quality and availability. It is also important to consider reaching agreements with the developers of all critical software so that the organization can get access to source code should the developer go out of business or stop supporting the programs. One way to accomplish this is by having a third party hold the source code, with an agreement that it will be released if such a situation develops. Controls should be in place to protect data from inappropriate access and use by outside maintenance staff and other contract workers.

Data Privacy Controls   As mentioned earlier in the section on Web security issues for databases, concerns about the rights of individuals to not have personal information collected and disseminated casually or recklessly have intensified as more of the population has become familiar with computers and as communications among computers have proliferated. Information privacy legislation generally gives individuals the right to know what data have been collected about them and to correct any errors in those data. As the amount of data exchanged continues to grow, the need is also growing to develop adequate data protection. Also important are adequate provisions to allow the data to be used for legitimate legal purposes so that organizations that need the data can access them and rely on their quality. Individuals need to be given the opportunity to state with whom data retained about them may be shared, and then these wishes must be enforced; enforcement is more reliable if access rules based on privacy wishes are developed by the DBA staff and handled by the DBMS.

DATABASE BACKUP AND RECOVERY

Database recovery: Mechanisms for restoring a database quickly and accurately after loss or damage.

Database recovery is database administration's response to Murphy's law. Inevitably, databases are damaged or lost or become unavailable because of some system problem that may be caused by human error, hardware failure, incorrect or invalid data, program errors, computer viruses, network failures, conflicting transactions, or natural catastrophes. It is the responsibility of the DBA to ensure that all critical data in the database are protected and can be recovered in the event of loss. Because the organization depends so heavily on its databases, the DBA must be able to minimize downtime or other disruptions while the database is being backed up or recovered. To achieve these objectives, the database management system must provide mechanisms for backing up data with as little disruption of production time as possible and restoring a database quickly and accurately after loss or damage.

Basic Recovery Facilities

A database management system should provide four basic facilities for backup and recovery of a database:

1. *Back-up facilities*, which provide periodic back-up copies of portions of or the entire database

2. *Journalizing facilities*, which maintain an audit trail of transactions and database changes

3. A *checkpoint facility*, by which the DBMS periodically suspends all processing and synchronizes its files and journals to establish a recovery point

4. A *recovery manager*, which allows the DBMS to restore the database to a correct condition and restart processing transactions

Back-up facilities: A DBMS COPY utility that produces a backup copy (or save) of the entire database or a subset of the database.

Back-up Facilities   The DBMS should provide **back-up facilities** that produce a back-up copy (or save) of the entire database plus control files and journals. Each DBMS normally provides a COPY utility for this purpose. In addition to the database files, the back-up facility should create a copy of related database objects including the repository (or system catalog), database indexes, source libraries, and so on. Typically, a back-up copy is produced at least once per day. The copy should be stored in a secured location where it is protected from loss or damage. The back-up copy is used to restore the database in the event of hardware failure, catastrophic loss, or damage.

Some DBMSs provide back-up utilities for the DBA to use to make backups; other systems assume the DBA will use the operating system commands, export commands, or SELECT . . . INTO SQL commands to perform backups. Because performing the nightly backup for a particular database is repetitive, creating a script that automates regular backups will save time and result in fewer back-up errors.

With large databases, regular full backups may be impractical, because the time required to perform the backup may exceed that available. Or, a database may be a critical system that must always remain available; so, a cold backup, where the database is shut down, is not practical. As a result, backups may be taken of dynamic data regularly (a so-called hot backup in which only a selected portion of the database is shut down from use), but backups of static data, which don't change frequently, may be taken less often. Incremental backups, which record changes made since the last full backup, but which do not take so much time to complete, may also be taken on an interim basis, allowing for longer periods of time between full backups. Thus, determining back-up strategies must be based on the demands being placed on the database systems.

Figure 12-9
Database audit trail

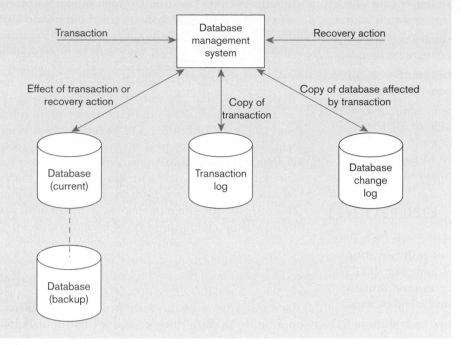

Journalizing Facilities

Journalizing Facilities   A DBMS must provide **journalizing facilities** to produce an audit trail of **transactions** and database changes. In the event of a failure, a consistent database state can be reestablished using the information in the journals together with the most recent complete backup. As Figure 12-9 shows, there are two basic journals, or logs. The first is the **transaction log**, which contains a record of the essential data for each transaction that is processed against the database. Data that are typically recorded for each transaction include the transaction code or identification, action or type of transaction (e.g., insert), time of the transaction, terminal number or user ID, input data values, table and records accessed, records modified, and possibly the old and new field values.

The second kind of log is the **database change log**, which contains before- and after-images of records that have been modified by transactions. A **before-image** is simply a copy of a record before it has been modified, and an **after-image** is a copy of the same record after it has been modified.

Some systems also keep a security log, which can alert the DBA to any security violations that occur or are attempted.

The recovery manager uses these logs to undo and redo operations, which we explain later in this chapter. These logs may be kept on disk or tape; because they are critical to recovery, they, too, must be backed up.

Checkpoint Facility

Checkpoint Facility   A **checkpoint facility** in a DBMS periodically refuses to accept any new transactions. All transactions in progress are completed, and the journal files are brought up-to-date. At this point, the system is in a quiet state, and the database and transaction logs are synchronized. The DBMS writes a special record (called a checkpoint record) to the log file, which is like a snapshot of the state of the database. The checkpoint record contains information necessary to restart the system. Any dirty data blocks (pages of memory that contain changes that have not yet been written out to disk) are written from memory to disk storage, thus ensuring that all changes made prior to taking the checkpoint have been written to long-term storage.

A DBMS may perform checkpoints automatically (which is preferred) or in response to commands in user application programs. Checkpoints should be taken frequently (say, several times an hour). When failures do occur, it is often possible to

Journalizing facilities: An audit trail of transactions and database changes.

Transaction: A discrete unit of work that must be completely processed or not processed at all within a computer system. Entering a customer order is an example of a transaction.

Transaction log: A record of the essential data for each transaction that is processed against the database.

Database change log: Before- and after-images of records that have been modified by transactions.

Before-image: A copy of a record (or page of memory) before it has been modified.

After-image: A copy of a record (or page of memory) after it has been modified.

Checkpoint facility: A facility by which the DBMS periodically refuses to accept any new transactions. The system is in a quiet state, and the database and transaction logs are synchronized.

resume processing from the most recent checkpoint. Thus, only a few minutes of processing work must be repeated, compared with several hours for a complete restart of the day's processing.

Recovery manager: A module of the DBMS that restores the database to a correct condition when a failure occurs and then resumes processing user questions.

Recovery Manager   The **recovery manager** is a module of the DBMS that restores the database to a correct condition when a failure occurs and then resumes processing user requests. The type of restart used depends on the nature of the failure. The recovery manager uses the logs shown in Figure 12-9 (as well as the backup copy, if necessary) to restore the database.

Recovery and Restart Procedures

The type of recovery procedure that is used in a given situation depends on the nature of the failure, the sophistication of the DBMS recovery facilities, and operational policies and procedures. Following is a discussion of the techniques that are most frequently used.

Disk Mirroring   To be able to switch to an existing copy of the database, the database must be mirrored. That is, at least two copies of the database must be kept and updated simultaneously. When a media failure occurs, processing is switched to the duplicate copy of the database. This strategy allows for the fastest recovery and has become increasingly popular for applications requiring high availability as the cost of long-term storage has dropped. Level 1 RAID systems implement mirroring. A damaged disk can be rebuilt from the mirrored disk with no disruption in service to the user. Such disks are referred to as being *hot-swappable*. This strategy does not protect against loss of power or catastrophic damage to both databases, though. See Chapter 6 for a more detailed discussion of RAID.

Restore/rerun: A technique that involves reprocessing the day's transactions (up to the point of failure) against the backup copy of the database.

Restore/Rerun   The **restore/rerun** technique involves reprocessing the day's transactions (up to the point of failure) against the back-up copy of the database or portion of the database being recovered. First, the database is shut down, and then the most recent copy of the database or file to be recovered (say, from the previous day) is mounted, and all transactions that have occurred since that copy (which are stored on the transaction log) are rerun. This may also be a good time to make a back-up copy and clear out the transaction, or redo, log.

The advantage of restore/rerun is its simplicity. The DBMS does not need to create a database change journal, and no special restart procedures are required. However, there are two major disadvantages. First, the time to reprocess transactions may be prohibitive. Depending on the frequency with which back-up copies are made, several hours of reprocessing may be required. Processing new transactions will have to be deferred until recovery is completed, and if the system is heavily loaded, it may be impossible to catch up. The second disadvantage is that the sequencing of transactions will often be different from when they were originally processed, which may lead to quite different results. For example, in the original run, a customer deposit may be posted before a withdrawal. In the rerun, the withdrawal transaction may be attempted first and may lead to sending an insufficient funds notice to the customer. For these reasons, restore/rerun is not a sufficient recovery procedure and is generally used only as a last resort in database processing.

Maintaining Transaction Integrity   A database is updated by processing transactions that result in changes to one or more database records. If an error occurs during the processing of a transaction, the database may be compromised, and some form of database recovery is required. Thus, to understand database recovery, we must first understand the concept of transaction integrity.

A business transaction is a sequence of steps that constitute some well-defined business activity. Examples of business transactions are "Admit Patient" in a hospital and "Enter Customer Order" in a manufacturing company. Normally, a business transaction requires several actions against the database. For example, consider the transaction "Enter Customer Order." When a new customer order is entered, the following steps may be performed by an application program:

1. Input order data (keyed by user).
2. Read CUSTOMER record (or insert record if a new customer).
3. Accept or reject the order. If Balance Due plus Order Amount does not exceed Credit Limit, accept the order; otherwise, reject it.
4. If the order is accepted, Increase Balance Due by Order Amount. Store the updated CUSTOMER record. Insert the accepted ORDER record in the database.

When processing transactions, the DBMS must ensure that the transactions follow four well-accepted properties, called the ACID properties:

1. Atomic, meaning that the transaction cannot be subdivided, and hence, it must be processed in its entirety or not at all. Once the whole transaction is processed, we say that the changes are committed. If the transaction fails at any midpoint, we say that it has aborted. For example, suppose that the program accepts a new customer order, increases Balance Due, and stores the updated CUSTOMER record. However, suppose that the new ORDER record is not inserted successfully (perhaps due to a duplicate Order Number key or insufficient physical file space). In this case, we want none of the parts of the transaction to affect the database.
2. Consistent, meaning any database constraints that must be true before the transaction must also be true after the transaction. For example, if the inventory on-hand balance must be the difference between total receipts minus total issues, this will be true both before and after an order transaction, which depletes the on-hand balance to satisfy the order.
3. Isolated, meaning changes to the database are not revealed to users until the transaction is committed. For example, this property means that other users do not know what the on-hand inventory is until an inventory transaction is complete; this property then usually means that other users are prohibited from simultaneously updating and possibly even reading data that are in the process of being updated. We discuss this topic in more detail later under concurrency controls and locking. A consequence of transactions being isolated from one another is that concurrent transactions (i.e., several transactions in some partial state of completion) all affect the database as if they were presented to the DBMS in serial fashion.
4. Durable, meaning changes are permanent. Thus, once a transaction is committed, no subsequent failure of the database can reverse the effect of the transaction.

To maintain transaction integrity, the DBMS must provide facilities for the user or application program to define **transaction boundaries**—that is, the logical beginning and end of a transaction. In SQL, the BEGIN TRANSACTION statement is placed in front of the first SQL command within the transaction, and the COMMIT command is placed at the end of the transaction. Any number of SQL commands may come in between these two commands; these are the database processing steps that perform some well-defined business activity, as explained earlier. If a command such as ROLLBACK is processed after a BEGIN TRANSACTION is executed and before a COMMIT is executed, the DBMS aborts the transaction and undoes the effects of the SQL statements processed so far within the transaction boundaries. The application would likely be programmed to execute a ROLLBACK when the DBMS generates an error message performing an UPDATE or INSERT command in the middle of the transaction. The

Transaction boundaries: The logical beginning and end of transactions.

DBMS thus commits (makes durable) changes for successful transactions (those that reach the COMMIT statement) and effectively rejects changes from transactions that are aborted (those that encounter a ROLLBACK). Any SQL statement encountered after a COMMIT or ROLLBACK and before a BEGIN TRANSACTION is executed as a single statement transaction, automatically committed if it executed without error, aborted if any error occurs during its execution.

Although conceptually a transaction is a logical unit of business work, such as a customer order or receipt of new inventory from a supplier, you may decide to break the business unit of work into several database transactions for database processing reasons. For example, because of the isolation property, a transaction that takes many commands and a long time to process may prohibit other uses of the same data at the same time, thus delaying other critical (possibly read-only) work. Some database data are used frequently, so it is important to complete transactional work on these so-called hotspot data as quickly as possible. For example, a primary key and its index for bank account numbers will likely need to be accessed by every ATM transaction, so the database transaction must be designed to use and release this data quickly. Also, remember, all the commands between the boundaries of a transaction must be executed, even those commands seeking input from an online user. If a user is slow to respond to input requests within the boundaries of a transaction, other users may encounter significant delays. Thus, if possible, collect all user input before beginning a transaction. Also, to minimize the length of a transaction, check for possible errors, such as duplicate keys or insufficient account balance, as early in the transaction as possible, so portions of the database can be released as soon as possible for other users if the transaction is going to be aborted. Some constraints (such as balancing the number of units of an item received with the number placed in inventory less returns) cannot be checked until many database commands are executed, so the transaction must be long to ensure database integrity. Thus, the general guideline is to make a database transaction as short as possible while still maintaining the integrity of the database.

Backward recovery (rollback): The back out, or undo, of unwanted changes to the database. Before-images of the records that have been changed are applied to the database, and the database is returned to an earlier state. Used to reverse the changes made by transactions that have been aborted or terminated abnormally.

Backward Recovery   With **backward recovery** (also called **rollback**), the DBMS backs out of or undoes unwanted changes to the database. As Figure 12-10a shows, before-images of the records that have been changed are applied to the database. As a result, the database is returned to an earlier state; the unwanted changes are eliminated.

Backward recovery is used to reverse the changes made by transactions that have aborted, or terminated abnormally. To illustrate the need for backward recovery (or UNDO), suppose that a banking transaction will transfer $100 in funds from the account for customer A to the account for customer B. The following steps are performed:

1. The program reads the record for customer A and subtracts $100 from the account balance.

2. The program then reads the record for customer B and adds $100 to the account balance. Now the program writes the updated record for customer A to the database. However, in attempting to write the record for customer B, the program encounters an error condition (such as a disk fault) and cannot write the record. Now the database is inconsistent—record A has been updated but record B has not—and the transaction must be aborted. An UNDO command will cause the recovery manager to apply the before-image for record A to restore the account balance to its original value. (The recovery manager may then restart the transaction and make another attempt.)

Forward recovery (rollforward): A technique that starts with an earlier copy of the database. After-images (the results of good transactions) are applied to the database, and the database is quickly moved forward to a later state.

Forward Recovery   With **forward recovery** (also called **rollforward**), the DBMS starts with an earlier copy of the database. Applying after-images (the results of good transactions) quickly moves the database forward to a later state (see Figure 12-10b). Forward recovery is much faster and more accurate than restore/rerun, for the following reasons:

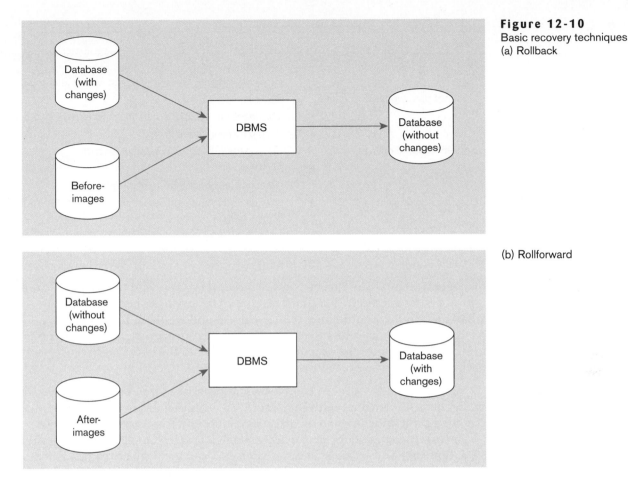

Figure 12-10
Basic recovery techniques
(a) Rollback

(b) Rollforward

- The time-consuming logic of reprocessing each transaction does not have to be repeated.
- Only the most recent after-images need to be applied. A database record may have a series of after-images (as a result of a sequence of updates), but only the most recent, "good" after-image is required for rollforward.

The problem of different sequencing of transactions is avoided, because the results of applying the transactions (rather than the transactions themselves) are used.

Types of Database Failure

A wide variety of failures can occur in processing a database, ranging from the input of an incorrect data value to complete loss or destruction of the database. Four of the most common types of problems are aborted transactions, incorrect data, system failure, and database loss or destruction. Each of these types of problems is described in the following sections, and possible recovery procedures are indicated (see Table 12-1).

Aborted Transactions   As we noted earlier, a transaction frequently requires a sequence of processing steps to be performed. An **aborted transaction** terminates abnormally. Some reasons for this type of failure are human error, input of invalid data, hardware failure, and deadlock (covered in the next section). A common type of hardware failure is the loss of transmission in a communications link when a transaction is in progress.

When a transaction aborts, we want to "back out" the transaction and remove any changes that have been made (but not committed) to the database. The recovery

Aborted transaction: A transaction in progress that terminates abnormally.

Table 12-1   Responses to Database Failure

Type of Failure	Recovery Technique
Aborted transaction	Rollback (preferred)
	Rollforward/rerun transactions to state just prior to abort
Incorrect data (update inaccurate)	Rollback (preferred)
	Reprocess transactions without inaccurate data updates
	Compensating transactions
System failure (database intact)	Switch to duplicate database (preferred)
	Rollback
	Restart from checkpoint (rollforward)
Database destruction	Switch to duplicate database (preferred)
	Rollforward
	Reprocess transactions

manager accomplishes this by backward recovery (applying before-images for the transaction in question). This function should be accomplished automatically by the DBMS, which then notifies the user to correct and resubmit the transaction. Other procedures, such as rollforward or transaction reprocessing, could be applied to bring the database to the state it was in just prior to the abort occurrence, but rollback is the preferred procedure in this case.

Incorrect Data   A more complex situation arises when the database has been updated with incorrect, but valid, data. For example, an incorrect grade may be recorded for a student, or an incorrect amount input for a customer payment.

Incorrect data are difficult to detect and often lead to complications. To begin with, some time may elapse before an error is detected and the database record (or records) corrected. By this time, numerous other users may have used the erroneous data, and a chain reaction of errors may have occurred as various applications made use of the incorrect data. In addition, transaction outputs (such as documents and messages) based on the incorrect data may be transmitted to persons. An incorrect grade report, for example, may be sent to a student or an incorrect statement sent to a customer.

When incorrect data have been processed, the database may be recovered in one of the following ways:

- If the error is discovered soon enough, backward recovery may be used. (However, care must be taken to ensure that all subsequent errors have been reversed.)

- If only a few errors have occurred, a series of compensating transactions may be introduced through human intervention to correct the errors.

- If the first two measures are not feasible, it may be necessary to restart from the most recent checkpoint before the error occurred, and subsequent transactions processed without the error.

Any erroneous messages or documents that have been produced by the erroneous transaction will have to be corrected by appropriate human intervention (letters of explanation, telephone calls, etc.).

System Failure   In a system failure, some component of the system fails, but the database is not damaged. Some causes of system failure are power loss, operator error, loss of communications transmission, and system software failure.

When the system crashes, some transactions may be in progress. The first step in recovery is to back out those transactions using before-images (backward recovery). Then, if the system is mirrored, it may be possible to switch to the mirrored data and rebuild the corrupted data on a new disk. If the system is not mirrored, it may not be possible to restart because status information in main memory has been lost or damaged. The safest approach is to restart from the most recent checkpoint before the system failure. The database is rolled forward by applying after-images for all transactions that were processed after that checkpoint.

Database Destruction   In the case of **database destruction**, the database itself is lost, or destroyed, or cannot be read. A typical cause of database destruction is a disk drive failure (or head crash).

Again, using a mirrored copy of the database is the preferred strategy for recovering from such an event. If there is no mirrored copy, a backup copy of the database is required. Forward recovery is used to restore the database to its state immediately before the loss occurred. Any transactions that may have been in progress when the database was lost are restarted.

Disaster Recovery   Every organization requires contingency plans for dealing with disasters that may severely damage or destroy their data center. Such disasters may be natural (e.g., floods, earthquakes, tornadoes, and hurricanes) or man-made (e.g., wars, sabotage, and terrorist attacks). For example, the 2001 terrorist attacks on the World Trade Center resulted in the complete destruction of several data centers and widespread loss of data.

Planning for disaster recovery is an organization-wide responsibility. Database administration is responsible for developing plans for recovering the organization's data and for restoring data operations. Following are some of the major components of a recovery plan (Mullins, 2002):

- Develop a detailed, written disaster recovery plan. Schedule regular tests of the plan.

- Choose and train a multidisciplinary team to carry out the plan.

- Establish a back-up data center at an off-site location. This site must be located at a sufficient distance from the primary site so that no foreseeable disaster will disrupt both sites. If an organization has two or more data centers, each site may serve as a backup for one of the others. If not, the organization may contract with a disaster recovery service provider.

- Send back-up copies of databases to the back-up data center on a scheduled basis. Database backups may be sent to the remote site by courier or transmitted by replication software.

> **Database destruction:** The database itself is lost, or destroyed, or cannot be read.

CONTROLLING CONCURRENT ACCESS

Databases are shared resources. Database administrators must expect and plan for the likelihood that several users will attempt to access and manipulate data at the same time. With concurrent processing involving updates, a database without **concurrency control** will be compromised due to interference between users. There are two basic approaches to concurrency control: a pessimistic approach (involving locking) and an optimistic approach (involving versioning). We summarize both of these approaches in the following sections.

Most DBMSs run in a multiuser environment, with the expectation that users will be able to share the data contained in the database. If users are only reading data, no data integrity problems will be encountered, because no changes will be made in the database. However, if one or more users are updating data, then potential problems with maintaining data integrity arise. When more than one transaction is being processed against a database at the same time, the transactions are considered to be concurrent. The actions that must be taken to ensure that data integrity is maintained are called currency control actions. Although these actions are implemented

> **Concurrency control:** The process of managing simultaneous operations against a database so that data integrity is maintained and the operations do not interfere with each other in a multiuser environment.

Figure 12-11
Lost update (no concurrency control in effect)

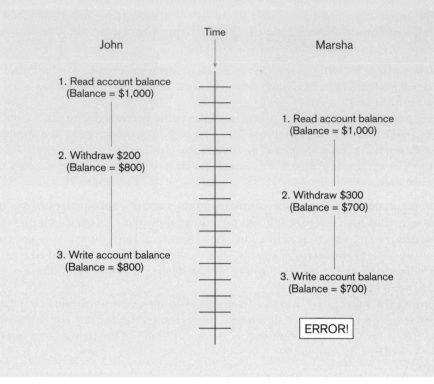

by the DBMS, the database administrator must understand these actions and may expect to make certain choices governing their implementation.

Remember that the CPU can process only one instruction at a time. As new transactions are submitted while other processing is occurring against the database, the transactions are usually interleaved, with the CPU switching among the transactions so that some portion of each transaction is performed as the CPU addresses each transaction in turn. Because the CPU is able to switch among transactions so quickly, most users will not notice that they are sharing CPU time with other users.

The Problem of Lost Updates

The most common problem encountered when multiple users attempt to update a database without adequate concurrency control is that of lost updates. Figure 12-11 shows a common situation. John and Marsha have a joint checking account and both want to withdraw some cash at the same time, each using an ATM terminal in a different location. Figure 12-11 shows the sequence of events that might occur in the absence of a concurrency control mechanism. John's transaction reads the account balance (which is $1,000) and he proceeds to withdraw $200. Before the transaction writes the new account balance ($800), Marsha's transaction reads the account balance (which is still $1,000). She then withdraws $300, leaving a balance of $700. Her transaction then writes this account balance, which replaces the one written by John's transaction. The effect of John's update has been lost due to interference between the transactions, and the bank is unhappy.

Another, similar type of problem that may occur when concurrency control is not established is the **inconsistent read problem**. This problem occurs when one user reads data that have been partially updated by another user. The read will be incorrect, and is sometimes referred to as a dirty read or an unrepeatable read. The lost update and inconsistent read problems arise when the DBMS does not isolate transactions, part of the ACID transaction properties.

Inconsistent read problem: An unrepeatable read, one that occurs when one user reads data that have been partially updated by another user.

Serializability

Concurrent transactions need to be processed in isolation so that they do not interfere with each other. If one transaction were entirely processed at a time before another transaction, no interference would occur. Procedures that process transactions so that the outcome is the same as this are called *serializable*. Processing transactions using a serializable schedule will give the same results as if the transactions had been processed one after the other. Schedules are designed so that transactions that will not interfere with each other can still be run in parallel. For example, transactions that request data from different tables in a database will not conflict with each other and can be run concurrently without causing data integrity problems. Serializability is achieved by different means, but locking mechanisms are the most common type of concurrency control mechanism. With **locking**, any data that are retrieved by a user for updating must be locked, or denied to other users, until the update is complete or aborted. Locking data is much like checking a book out of the library; it is unavailable to others until the borrower returns it.

Locking: Any data that are retrieved by a user for updating must be locked, or denied to other users, until the update is completed or aborted.

Locking Mechanisms

Figure 12-12 shows the use of record locks to maintain data integrity. John initiates a withdrawal transaction from an ATM. Because John's transaction will update

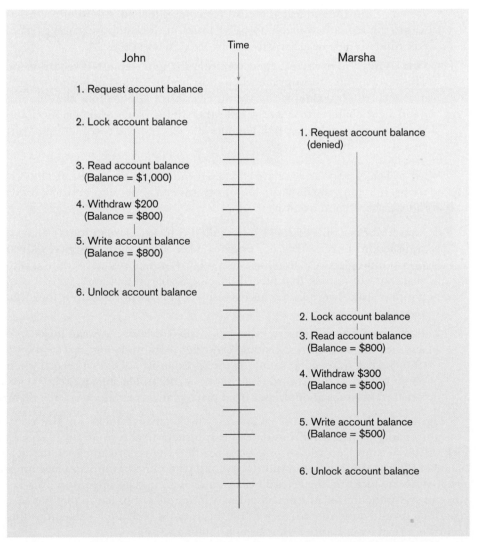

Figure 12-12
Updates with locking (concurrency control)

this record, the application program locks this record before reading it into main memory. John proceeds to withdraw $200, and the new balance ($800) is computed. Marsha has initiated a withdrawal transaction shortly after John, but her transaction cannot access the account record until John's transaction has returned the updated record to the database and unlocked the record. The locking mechanism thus enforces a sequential updating process that prevents erroneous updates.

Locking Level   An important consideration in implementing concurrency control is choosing the locking level. The **locking level** (also called **lock granularity**) is the extent of the database resource that is included with each lock. Most commercial products implement locks at one of the following levels:

Locking level (lock granularity): The extent of the database resource that is included with each lock.

- *Database*   The entire database is locked and becomes unavailable to other users. This level has limited application, such as during a backup of the entire database (Rodgers, 1989).
- *Table*   The entire table containing a requested record is locked. This level is appropriate mainly for bulk updates that will update the entire table, such as giving all employees a 5 percent raise.
- *Block or page*   The physical storage block (or page) containing a requested record is locked. This level is the most commonly implemented locking level. A page will be a fixed size (4K, 8K, etc.) and may contain records of more than one type.
- *Record*   Only the requested record (or row) is locked. All other records, even within a table, are available to other users. It does impose some overhead at run time when several records are involved in an update.
- *Field*   Only the particular field (or column) in a requested record is locked. This level may be appropriate when most updates affect only one or two fields in a record. For example, in inventory control applications the quantity-on-hand field changes frequently, but other fields (such as description and bin location) are rarely updated. Field-level locks require considerable overhead and are seldom used.

Types of Locks   So far, we have discussed only locks that prevent all access to locked items. In reality, the database administrator can generally choose between two types of locks: shared and exclusive.

Shared lock (S lock or read lock): A technique that allows other transactions to read but not update a record or other resource.

1. **Shared locks**   Shared locks (also called **S locks**, or **read locks**) allow other transactions to read (but not update) a record or other resource. A transaction should place a shared lock on a record or data resource when it will only read but not update that record. Placing a shared lock on a record prevents another user from placing an exclusive lock, but not a shared lock, on that record.

Exclusive lock (X lock or write lock): A technique that prevents another transaction from reading and therefore updating a record until it is unlocked.

2. **Exclusive locks**   Exclusive locks (also called **X locks**, or **write locks**) prevent another transaction from reading (and therefore updating) a record until it is unlocked. A transaction should place an exclusive lock on a record when it is about to update that record (Descollonges, 1993). Placing an exclusive lock on a record prevents another user from placing any type of lock on that record.

Figure 12-13 shows the use of shared and exclusive locks for the checking account example. When John initiates his transaction, the program places a read lock on his account record, because he is reading the record to check the account balance. When John requests a withdrawal, the program attempts to place an exclusive lock (write lock) on the record because this is an update operation. However, as you can see in the figure, Marsha has already initiated a transaction that has placed a read lock on the same record. As a result, his request is denied; remember that if a record is a read lock, another user cannot obtain a write lock.

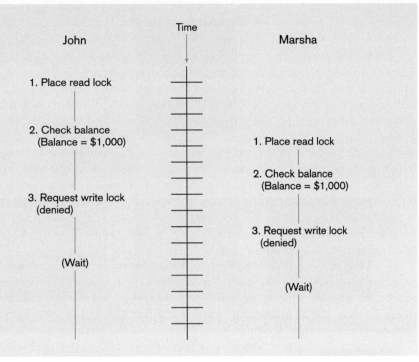

Figure 12-13
The problem of deadlock

Deadlock   Locking solves the problem of erroneous updates but may lead to another problem, called **deadlock**: an impasse that results when two or more transactions have locked a common resource, and each must wait for the other to unlock that resource. Figure 12-13 shows a simple example of deadlock. John's transaction is waiting for Marsha's transaction to remove the read lock from the account record, and vice versa. Neither person can withdraw money from the account, even though the balance is more than adequate.

Figure 12-14 shows a slightly more complex example of deadlock. In this example, user A has locked record X and user B has locked record Y. User A then requests

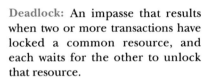

Deadlock: An impasse that results when two or more transactions have locked a common resource, and each waits for the other to unlock that resource.

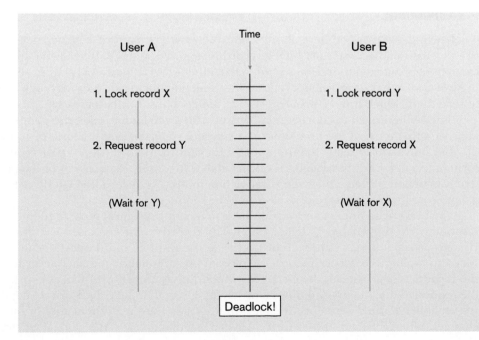

Figure 12-14
Another example of deadlock

record Y (intending to update), and user B requests record X (also intending to update). Both requests are denied, because the requested records are already locked. Unless the DBMS intervenes, both users will wait indefinitely.

Deadlock prevention: User programs must lock all records they require at the beginning of a transaction (rather than one at a time).

Two-phase locking protocol: A procedure for acquiring the necessary locks for a transaction where all necessary locks are acquired before any locks are released, resulting in a growing phase, when locks are acquired, and a shrinking phase, when they are released.

Managing Deadlock There are two basic ways to resolve deadlocks: deadlock prevention and deadlock resolution. When **deadlock prevention** is employed, user programs must lock all records they will require at the beginning of a transaction, rather than one at a time. In Figure 12-14, user A would have to lock both records X and Y before processing the transaction. If either record is already locked, the program must wait until it is released. Where all locking operations necessary for a transaction occur before any resources are unlocked, a **two-phase locking protocol** is being used. Once any lock obtained for the transaction is released, no more locks may be obtained. Thus, the phases in the two-phase locking protocol are often referred to as a growing phase (where all necessary locks are acquired) and a shrinking phase (where all locks are released). Locks do not have to be acquired simultaneously. Frequently, some locks will be acquired, processing will occur, and then additional locks will be acquired as needed.

Locking all the required records at the beginning of the transaction (called conservative two-phase locking) prevents deadlock. Unfortunately, it is often difficult to predict in advance what records will be required to process a transaction. A typical program has many processing parts and may call other programs in varying sequences. As a result, deadlock prevention is not always practical.

Two-phase locking in which each transaction must request records in the same sequence (i.e., serializing the resources) also prevents deadlock, but again this may not be practical.

Deadlock resolution: An approach that allows deadlocks to occur but builds mechanisms into the DBMS for detecting and breaking the deadlocks.

The second, and more common, approach is to allow deadlocks to occur but to build mechanisms into the DBMS for detecting and breaking the deadlocks. Essentially, these **deadlock resolution** mechanisms work as follows. The DBMS maintains a matrix of resource usage, which, at a given instant, indicates what subjects (users) are using what objects (resources). By scanning this matrix, the computer can detect deadlocks as they occur. The DBMS then resolves the deadlocks by "backing out" one of the deadlocked transactions. Any changes made by that transaction up to the time of deadlock are removed, and the transaction is restarted when the required resources become available. We will describe the procedure for backing out shortly.

Versioning

Locking, as described here, is often referred to as a pessimistic concurrency control mechanism, because each time a record is required, the DBMS takes the highly cautious approach of locking the record so that other programs cannot use it. In reality, in most cases other users will not request the same documents, or they may only want to read them, which is not a problem (Celko, 1992). Thus, conflicts are rare.

Versioning: Each transaction is restricted to a view of the database as of the time that transaction started, and when a transaction modifies a record, the DBMS creates a new record version instead of overwriting the old record. Hence, no form of locking is required.

A newer approach to concurrency control, called **versioning**, takes the optimistic approach that most of the time other users do not want the same record, or if they do, they only want to read (but not update) the record. With versioning, there is no form of locking. Each transaction is restricted to a view of the database as of the time that transaction started, and when a transaction modifies a record, the DBMS creates a new record version instead of overwriting the old record.

The best way to understand versioning is to imagine a central records room, corresponding to the database (Celko, 1992). The records room has a service window. Users (corresponding to transactions) arrive at the window and request documents (corresponding to database records). However, the original documents never leave the records room. Instead, the clerk (corresponding to the DBMS) makes copies of the requested documents and timestamps them. Users then take their private copies (or versions) of the documents to their own workplace and read them and/or make changes. When finished, they return their marked-up copies to the clerk. The clerk

Figure 12-15
The use of versioning

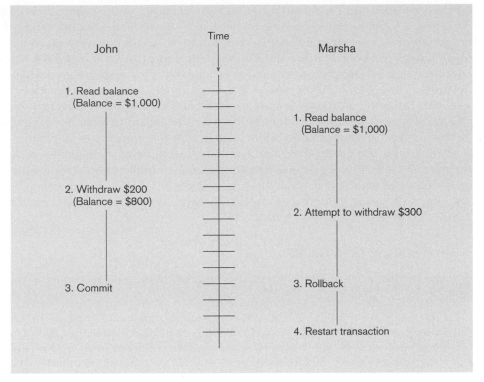

merges the changes from marked-up copies into the central database. When there is no conflict (e.g., when only one user has made changes to a set of database records), that user's changes are merged directly into the public (or central) database.

Suppose instead that there is a conflict; for example, two users have made conflicting changes to their private copy of the database. In this case, the changes made by one of the users are committed to the database. (Remember that the transactions are time-stamped, so that the earlier transaction can be given priority.) The other user must be told that there was a conflict, and his work cannot be committed (or incorporated into the central database). He must check out another copy of the data records and repeat the previous work. Under the optimistic assumption, this type of rework will be the exception rather than the rule.

Figure 12-15 shows a simple example of the use of versioning for the checking account example. John reads the record containing the account balance, successfully withdraws $200, and the new balance ($800) is posted to the account with a COMMIT statement. Meanwhile, Marsha has also read the account record and requested a withdrawal, which is posted to her local version of the account record. However, when the transaction attempts to COMMIT it discovers the update conflict, and her transaction is aborted (perhaps with a message such as, "Cannot complete transaction at this time"). She can then restart the transaction, working from the correct starting balance of $800.

The main advantage of versioning over locking is performance improvement. Read-only transactions can run concurrently with updating transactions, without loss of database consistency.

MANAGING DATA QUALITY

High-quality data, that is, data that are accurate, consistent, and available in a timely fashion are essential to the management of organizations today. Organizations must strive to identify the data that are relevant to their decision making to develop business policies and practices that ensure the accuracy and completeness of the data, and to facilitate enterprisewide data sharing. Managing the quality of data is an organizationwide responsibility, with data administration often playing a leading role in planning and coordinating the efforts. This and prior chapters have already addressed many approaches to improving data quality, such as thorough analysis and documentation of all business rules in E-R diagram and other documentation, field level data integrity constraints, security controls, and back-up and recovery methods. This section motivates the need for a comprehensive data quality control program in an organization and introduces additional procedures to improve data quality.

What, then, are quality data? Redman (2004) summarizes data quality as "fit for their intended uses in operations, decision making, and planning." This means that data are free of defects (accessible, accurate, timely, complete, and consistent across sources) and possess desirable features (relevant, comprehensive, proper level of detail, easy to read, and easy to interpret).

The State of Data Quality

The importance of high quality data cannot be overstated. According to Brauer (2002):

> Critical business decisions and allocation of resources are made based on what is found in the data. Prices are changed, marketing campaigns created, customers are communicated with, and daily operations evolve around whatever data points are churned out by an organization's various systems. The data that serves as the foundation of these systems *must be good data*. Otherwise we fail before we ever begin. It doesn't matter how pretty the screens are, how intuitive the interfaces are, how high the performance rockets, how automated the processes are, how innovative the methodology is, and how far-reaching the access to the system is, *if the data are bad—the systems fail*. Period. And if the systems fail, or at the very least provide inaccurate information, every process, decision, resource allocation, communication, or interaction with the system will have a damaging, if not disastrous impact on the business itself.

This quote is in essence a restatement of the old IT adage *garbage-in, garbage-out* (GIGO), but with increased emphasis on the dramatically higher stakes in today's environment.

Unfortunately, there are strong indications that the state of data quality is problematic, or even unacceptable, in many organizations today. Consider the following assessments:

- Experts estimate that up to 70 percent of data warehousing projects fail because users reject the data as unreliable (Dubois, 2002).
- A survey by The Data Warehouse Institute (Eckerson, 2002) determined that only one in four U.S. companies has implemented data quality initiatives
- It has been estimated that bad data can cost a business as much as 10 to 20 percent of total operating budgets through lost revenues. Further, as much as 40 to 50 percent of an IT department budget may be spent correcting errors caused by bad data (English 1999)
- Experts say two percent of records in a customer file become obsolete in one month because customers die, divorce, marry, or move (Betts, 2002).

Following are three important reasons (among others) why the quality of data in organizational databases has deteriorated in the past few years.

External Data Sources Much of the data originates outside the organization, where there is less control over the data sources. For example, a company receives a flood of data via the Internet from Web forms filled out by users. Such data are often inaccurate or incomplete, or even purposely wrong (have you ever entered a wrong phone number in a Web-based form because a phone number was required and you didn't want to divulge your actual phone number?). Other data for B2B transactions arrive via XML channels, and this data may also contain inaccuracies. Also, organizations often purchase data files or databases from external organizations, and these sources may contain data that are inaccurate or incompatible with internal data.

Redundant Data Storage   Many organizations have allowed the uncontrolled proliferation of spreadsheets, desktop databases, legacy databases, data marts, data warehouses, and other repositories of data. Much of this data are redundant and filled with inconsistencies and incompatibilities.

Lack of Organizational Commitment   For a variety of reasons, many organizations simply have not made the commitment or invested the resources to improve their data quality. Some organizations are simply in denial that they have problems with data quality. Others realize they have a problem but fear that the solution will be too costly or that they cannot quantify the return on investment.

Data Quality Improvement

Implementing a successful quality improvement program will require the active commitment and participation of all members of the organization. Following is a brief outline of some of the key steps in such a program.

Conduct a Data Quality Audit   An organization without an established data quality program should begin with an audit of data to understand the extent and nature of data quality problems. A data quality audit includes many procedures, but one simple task is to statistically profile all files. A profile documents the set of values for each field. By inspection, obscure and unexpected extreme values can be identified. Patterns of data (distribution) can be analyzed to see if the distribution makes sense. (An unexpected high frequency of one value may indicate that users are entering an easy number or a default is often being used, thus accurate data are not being recorded.) Data can be checked against relevant business rules to be sure that controls that are in place are effective and somehow not being bypassed (e.g., some systems allow users to override warning messages that data entered violates some rule; if this happens too frequently, it can be a sign of lax enforcement of business rules). Data quality software, such as those mentioned in Chapter 11 for ETL processes, can be used to check for valid addresses, and find redundant records due to insufficient methods for matching customer or other subjects across different sources, and violations of specified business rules.

An audit will thoroughly review all process controls on data entry and maintenance. Procedures for changing sensitive data should likely involve actions by at least two people with separated duties and responsibilities. Primary keys and important financial data fall into this category. Proper edit checks should be defined and implemented for all fields. Error logs from processing data from each source (e.g., user, work station, or source system) should be analyzed to identify patterns or high frequencies of errors and rejected transactions, and actions should be taken to improve the ability of the sources to provide high quality data. For example, users should be prohibited from entering data into fields for which they are not intended. Some users, who do not have a use for a certain data may use that field to store data they need but for which there is not appropriate field. This can confuse other users who do use these fields and see unintended data.

Establish a Data Stewardship Program   The Sarbanes-Oxley Act of 2002 has made it imperative that organizations undertake actions to ensure data accuracy, timeliness, and consistency (Laurent, 2005). Although not mandated by regulations, many organizations require the CIO as well as the CEO and CFO to sign off on financial statements, recognizing the role of IT to build procedures to ensure data quality. Establishment of a business information advisory committee consisting of representatives from each major business unit who have the authority to make business policy decisions can contribute to the establishment of high data quality (Moriarty, 1996; Carlson, 2002). These committee members act as liaisons between IT and their business unit, and consider not only their functional unit's data needs but also enterprisewide data needs. The members are subject-matter experts for the data they steward, and hence need to have a strong interest in managing information as a corporate resource, an in-depth understanding of the business of the organization, and good negotiation skills. Such members (typically high-level managers) are sometimes referred to as **data stewards**, people who have the responsibility to ensure that organizational applications properly support the organization's enterprise goals. Data stewards are held accountable for the quality of the data for which they are responsible. They must also ensure that the data that are captured are accurate and consistent throughout the organization, so that users throughout the organization can rely on the data. Data stewardship is a role, not a job; as such, data stewards do not own the data and data stewards usually have other duties inside and usually outside the data administration area.

Seiner (2005) outlines a comprehensive set of roles and responsibilities for data stewards. Roles include oversight of the data stewardship program, managers of data subject areas (such as customer, product, etc.), stewards for data definitions of each subject, stewards for accurate and efficient production/maintenance of data for each subject, and stewards for proper use of data for each subject area.

Data stewards: A person assigned the responsibility of ensuring that organizational applications properly support the organization's enterprise goals for data quality.

Apply TQM Principles and Practices

Leading organizations are applying Total Quality Management (TQM) to improve data quality, just as in other business areas. Some of the principles of TQM that apply are defect prevention (rather than correction), continuous improvement, and the use of enterprise data standards. For example, where data in legacy systems is found defective, it is better to correct the legacy systems that generate that data than to attempt to correct the data when moving it to a data warehouse. For an in-depth discussion of applying TQM to data quality improvement see English (1999).

Overcome Organizational Barriers

Establishing enterprisewide data quality standards is not easy, and there are even some business structures and practices that tend to inhibit data quality (Moriarty, 1996). Where organizations establish strategic business units that compete with each other within the enterprise, data sharing may be difficult as each strategic business unit strives to protect its competitive position. Regulated industries such as banking and telecommunications may be legally limited in the amount of data that can be shared. Another threat to maintaining high data quality may occur when data entry is conducted under an incentive plan or quota system that is based on volume of work completed. Then, achieving high speeds of data entry may override concerns about accuracy of data entry. Where data that need to be shared are collected from more than one business unit, the potential for inaccurate and inconsistent data skyrockets. Policies must be developed to handle each of these concerns. An organization must establish a discipline for data quality that includes assigning responsibilities (which are included in job descriptions) to each person and creating and following supporting procedures.

Apply Modern Data Management Technology

Powerful software is now available from vendors that can assist users with the technical aspects of data quality improvement. This software often employs advanced techniques such as pattern matching, fuzzy logic, and expert systems. These programs can be used to analyze current data for quality problems, identify and eliminate redundant data, integrate data from multiple sources, and so on. Some of these programs were discussed in Chapter 11 under the topic of data extract, transform, and load.

Estimate Return on Investment

With the competing demands for resources today, management must be convinced that a data quality program will yield a sufficient return on investment (ROI). Fortunately (or unfortunately) this is not difficult to do in most organizations today. There are two general types of benefits from such a program: cost avoidance and avoidance of opportunity losses.

Consider a simple example. Suppose a bank has 500,000 customers in its customer file. The bank plans to advertise a new product to all of its customers by means of a direct mailing. Suppose the error rate in the customer file is 10 percent, including duplicate customer records, obsolete addresses, and so on (such an error rate is not unusual). If the direct cost of mailing is $5.00 (including postage and materials), the expected loss due to bad data is: 500,000 customers $\times$ .10 $\times$ $5, or $250,000.

Often, the opportunity loss associated with bad data is greater than direct costs. For example, suppose the average bank customer generates $2,000 revenue annually from interest charges, service fees, and so on. This equates to $10,000 over a five-year period. Suppose the bank implements an enterprisewide data quality program that improves its customer relationship management, cross-selling, and other related activities. If this program results in a net increase of only 2 percent new business (an educated guess), the results over five years will be remarkable: 500,000 customers $\times$ $10,000 $\times$ .02, or $50 million. This is why it is sometimes stated that "quality is free."

DATA DICTIONARIES AND REPOSITORIES

In Chapter 1, we defined metadata as data that describe the properties or characteristics of end-user data and the context of that data. To be successful, any organization must develop sound strategies to collect, manage, and utilize their metadata. These strategies should address identifying the types of metadata that need to be collected and maintained and developing methods for the orderly collection and storage of that metadata. Data administration is usually responsible for the overall direction of the metadata strategy.

Metadata must be stored and managed using DBMS technology. The collection of metadata is referred to as a data dictionary (an older term) or a repository (a modern term). We describe each of these terms in this section.

Data Dictionary

An integral part of relational DBMSs is the **data dictionary**, which stores metadata, or information about the database, including attribute names and definitions for each table in the database. The data dictionary is usually a part of the **system catalog** that is generated for each database. The system catalog describes all database objects, including table-related data such as table names, table creators or owners, column names and data types, foreign keys and primary keys, index files, authorized users, user access privileges, and so forth. The system catalog is created and maintained automatically by the database management system, and the information is stored in systems tables, which may be queried in the same manner as any other data table, if the user has sufficient access privileges.

Data dictionaries may be either active or passive. An *active* data dictionary is managed automatically by the database management software. Active systems are always consistent with the current structure and definition of the database because they are maintained by the system itself. Most relational database management systems now contain active data dictionaries that can be derived from their system catalog. A passive data dictionary is managed by the user(s) of the system and is modified whenever the structure of the database is changed. Because this modification must be performed manually by the user, it is possible that the data dictionary will not be current with the current structure of the database. However, the passive data dictionary may be maintained as a separate database. This may be desirable during the design phase, because it allows developers to remain independent from using a particular RDBMS for as long as possible. Also, passive data dictionaries are not limited to information that can be discerned by the database management system. Because passive data dictionaries are

Data dictionary: Repository of information about a database that documents data elements of a database.

System catalog: A system-created database that describes all database objects, including data dictionary information, and also includes user access information.

maintained by the user, they may be extended to contain information about organizational data that is not computerized.

Repositories

Whereas data dictionaries are simple data element documentation tools, information repositories are used by data administrators and other information specialists to manage the total information processing environment. The **information repository** is an essential component of both the development environment and the production environment. In the application development environment, people (either information specialists or end users) use CASE tools, high-level languages, and other tools to develop new applications. CASE tools may tie automatically to the information repository. In the production environment, people use applications to build databases, keep the data current, and extract data from databases. To build a data warehouse and develop business intelligence applications, it is absolutely essential that an organization build and maintain a comprehensive repository.

As indicated previously, CASE tools often generate information that should be a part of the information repository, as do documentation tools, project management tools, and, of course, the database management software itself. When they were first developed, the information recorded by each of these products was not easily integrated. Now, however, there has been an attempt to make this information more accessible and shareable. The **Information Repository Dictionary System (IRDS)** is a computer software tool that is used to manage and control access to the information repository. It provides facilities for recording, storing, and processing descriptions of an organization's significant data and data processing resources (Lefkovitz, 1985). When systems are compliant with IRDS, it is possible to transfer data definitions among the data dictionaries generated by the various products. IRDS, which has been adopted as a standard by the International Standards Organization (1990), includes a set of rules for storing data dictionary information and for accessing it.

Figure 12-16 shows the three components of a repository system architecture (Bernstein, 1996). First is an information model. This model is a schema of the infor-

Information repository: A component that stores metadata that describe an organization's data and data processing resources, manages the total information processing environment, and combines information about an organization's business information and its application portfolio.

Information Repository Dictionary System (IRDS): A computer software tool that is used to manage and control access to the information repository.

Figure 12-16
Three components of repository system architecture (Adapted from Bernstein, 1996)

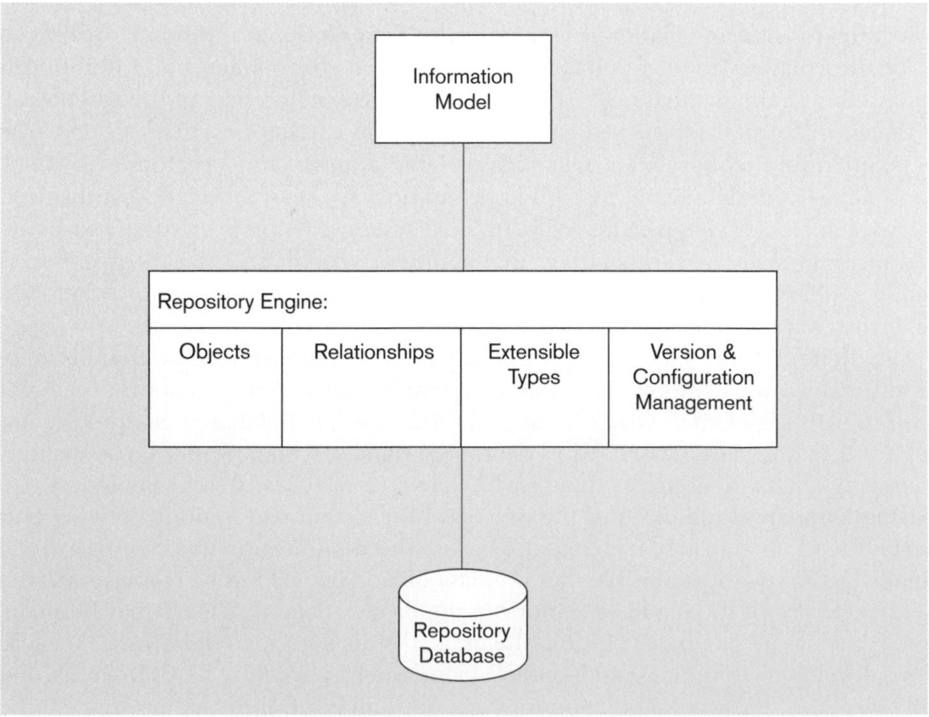

mation stored in the repository, which can then be used by the tools associated with the database to interpret the contents of the repository. Next is the repository engine, which manages the repository objects. Services, such as reading and writing repository objects, browsing, and extending the information model, are included. Last is the repository database, in which the repository objects are actually stored. Notice that the repository engine supports five core functions (Bernstein, 1996):

1. *Object management*   Object-oriented repositories store information about objects. As databases become more object oriented, developers will be able to use the information stored about database objects in the information repository. The repository can be based on an object-oriented database or it can add the capability to support objects.

2. *Relationship management*   The repository engine contains information about object relationships that can be used to facilitate the use of software tools that attach to the database.

3. *Dynamic extensibility*   The repository information model defines types, which should be easy to extend, that is, to add new types or to extend the definitions of those that already exist. This capability can make it easier to integrate a new software tool into the development process.

4. *Version management*   During development, it is important to establish version control. The information repository can be used to facilitate version control for software design tools. Version control of objects is more difficult to manage than version control of files, because there are many more objects than files in an application, and each version of an object may have many relationships.

5. *Configuration management*   It is also necessary to group the versioned objects into configurations that represent the entire system, which are also versioned. It may help you to think of a configuration as similar to a file directory, except configurations can be versioned and they contain objects rather than files. Repositories often use checkout systems to manage objects, versions, and configurations. A developer who wishes to use an object checks it out, makes the desired changes, and then checks the object back in. At that time, a new version of the object will be created and the object will become available to other developers.

As object-oriented database management systems become more available, and as object-oriented programming associated with relational databases increases, the importance of the information repository is also going to increase, because object-oriented development requires the use (and reuse) of the metadata contained in the information repository. Also, the metadata and application information generated by different software tools will be more easily integrated into the information repository now that the IRDS standard has been accepted. Although information repositories have already been included in the enterprise-level development tools, the increasing emphasis on object-oriented development and the explosion of data warehouse solutions are leading to more widespread use of information repositories.

OVERVIEW OF TUNING THE DATABASE FOR PERFORMANCE

Effective database support results in a reliable database where performance is not subject to interruption from hardware, software, or user problems and where optimal performance is achieved. Tuning a database is not an activity that is undertaken at the time of DBMS installation and/or at the time of implementation of a new application and then disregarded. Rather, performance analysis and tuning is an ongoing part of managing any database, as hardware and software configurations change and as user activity changes. Five areas of DBMS management that should be addressed when trying to maintain a well-tuned database are addressed here: installation of the DBMS, memory and storage space usage, input/output contention, CPU usage, and application tuning. The extent to which the database administrator can affect each of these areas will vary across DBMS products. Oracle 9i will be used as the exemplar DBMS throughout this section, but it should be noted that each product has its own set of tuning capabilities.

Tuning a database application requires familiarity with the system environment, the DBMS, the application, and the data used by the application. It is here that the skills of even an experienced database administrator are tested. Achieving a quiet environment, one that is reliable and allows users to secure desired information in a timely manner, requires skills and experience that are obtained by working with databases over time. The areas discussed below are quite general and are intended to provide an initial understanding of the scope of activities involved in tuning a database rather than providing the type of detailed understanding necessary to tune a particular database application.

Installation of the DBMS

Correct installation of the DBMS product is essential to any environment. Products often include README files, which may include detailed installation instructions, revisions of procedures, notification of increased disk space needed for installation, and so on. A quick review of any README files may save time during the installation process and result in a better installation. Failing to review general installation instructions may result in default parameter values being set during installation that are not optimal for the situation. Some possible considerations are listed here.

Before beginning installation, the database administrator should ensure that adequate disk space is available. You will need to refer to manuals for the specific DBMS to be able to translate logical database size parameters (such as field length, number of table rows, and estimated growth) into actual physical space requirements. It is possible that the space allocation recommendations are low, as changes made to a DBMS tend to make it larger, but the documentation may not reflect that change. To be safe, allocate at least 20 percent more space than suggested by standard calculations. After installation, review any log files generated during the installation process. Their contents will reveal installation problems that were not noticed or provide assurance that the installation proceeded as expected.

Allocation of disk space for the database should also receive consideration. For example, some UNIX back-up systems have trouble with data files that exceed a gigabyte in size. Keeping data files under one gigabyte will avoid possible problems. Allocation of data files in standard sizes will make it easier to balance I/O, because data file locations can be swapped more easily should a bottleneck need to be resolved.

Memory and Storage Space Usage

Efficient usage of main memory involves understanding how the DBMS uses main memory, what buffers are being used, and what needs the programs in main memory have. For example, Oracle has many background processes that reside in memory and handle database management functions when a database is running. Some operating systems require a contiguous chunk of memory to be able to load Oracle, and a system with insufficient memory will have to free up memory space first. Oracle maintains in main memory a data dictionary cache that ideally should be large enough so that at least 90 percent of the requests to the data dictionary can be located in the cache rather than having to retrieve information from disk. Each of these is an example of typical memory management issues that should be considered when tuning a database.

Storage space management may include many activities, some of which have already been discussed in this book, such as denormalization and partitioning. One other activity is **data archiving**. Any database that stores history, such as transaction history or a time series of values for some field, will eventually include obsolete data—data that no longer has any use. Database statistics showing loc access frequencies for records or pages can be a clue that data no longer has a purpose. Business rules may also indicate that data older than some value (e.g., seven years) does not need to be kept for active processing. However, there may be legal reasons or infrequently needed business intelligence queries that suggest data should simply not be discarded. Thus, database administrations should develop a program of archiving inactive data. Data may be archived to separate database tables (thus making active tables more compact and, hence, more likely to be more quickly processed) or to files stored outside the database (possibly on magnetic tape or optical storage). Archive files may also be compressed to save space. Methods also need to be developed to restore, in an acceptable time, archived data to the database if and when they are needed. (Remember, archived data are inactive, not totally obsolete.) Archiving reclaims disk space, saves disk storage costs, and may improve database performance by allowing the active data to be stored is less expansive space.

Data archiving: The process of moving inactive data to another storage location where it can be accessed when needed.

Input/Output (I/O) Contention

Database applications are very I/O intensive; a production database will usually both read and write large amounts of data to disk as it works. While CPU clock speeds have increased dramatically, I/O speeds have not increased proportionately, and increasingly complex distributed database systems have further complicated I/O functioning.

Understanding how data are accessed by end users is critical to managing I/O contention. When hot spots (physical disk locations that are accessed repeatedly) develop, understanding the nature of the activity that is causing the hot spot affords the database administrator a much better chance of reducing the I/O contention being experienced. Oracle allows the DBA to control the placement of tablespaces, which contain data files. The DBA's in-depth understanding of user activity facilitates her or his ability to reduce I/O contention by separating data files that are being accessed together. Where possible, large database objects that will be accessed concurrently may be striped across disks to reduce I/O contention and improve performance. An overall objective of distributing I/O activity evenly across disks and controllers should guide the DBA in tuning I/O.

CPU Usage

Most database operations are going to require CPU work activity. Because of this, it is important to evaluate CPU usage when tuning a database. Using multiple CPUs allows query processing to be shared when the CPUs are working in parallel, and performance may be dramatically improved. DBAs need to maximize the performance of their existing CPUs while planning for the gains that may be achieved with each new generation of CPUs.

Monitoring CPU load so that typical load throughout a 24-hour period is known provides DBAs with basic information necessary to begin to rebalance CPU loading. The mixture of online and background processing may need to be adjusted for each environment. For example, establishing a rule that all jobs that can be run in off-hours must be run in off-hours will help to unload the machine during peak working hours. Establishing user accounts with limited space will help manage the CPU load also.

Application Tuning

The previous sections have concentrated on activities to tune the DBMS. Examining the applications that end users are using with the database may also increase performance. While normalization to at least 3NF is expected in many organizations that are using relational data models, carefully planned denormalization (see Chapter 6) may improve performance, often by reducing the number of tables that must be joined when running an SQL query.

Examination and modification of the SQL code in an application may also lead to performance improvement. Queries that do full table scans should be avoided, for example, because they are not selective and may not remain in memory very long. This necessitates more retrievals from long-term storage. Multitable joins should be actively managed when possible with the DBMS being used, because the type of join can dramatically affect performance, especially if a join requires a full table join. A general rule of thumb is that any query whose ratio of CPU to I/O time exceeds 13:1 is probably poorly designed. Active monitoring of queries by the DBMS can be used to actually terminate a query of job that exhibits exceeding this ratio. Alternatively, such queries may be put into a "penalty box" to wait until the job scheduler determines that sufficient CPU time is available to continue processing the query.

Similarly, statements containing views and those containing subqueries should be actively reviewed. Tuning of such statements so that components are resolved in the most efficient manner possible may achieve significant performance gains. Chapter 6 discussed a variety of techniques a DBA could use to tune application processing speed and disk space utilization (such as reindexing, overriding automatic query plans, changing data block sizes, reallocating files across storage devices, and guidelines for more efficient query design). A DBA plays an important role in advising programmers and developers which techniques will be the most effective.

The same database activity may take vastly different amounts of time depending on the workload mix at the time the query or program is run. Some DBMS have job schedulers that look at statistics about the history of running queries and will schedule batch jobs to achieve a desirable mix of CPU usage and I/O. A DBA can actively monitor query processing times by running so called "**heartbeat**" or "canary" **queries**. A heartbeat query is a very simple query (possibly SELECT * FROM table WHERE some condition) that is run many times during the day by the DBA to monitor variations in processing times. When heartbeat queries are taking extraordinarily long to run, then there probably is either an inappropriate mix of jobs running or some inefficient queries are consuming too many DBMS resources. A heartbeat query may also be exactly like certain regularly run user queries for which there are service level agreements (SLAs) with users on maximum response times. In this case, the heartbeat query is run periodically to make sure that if the user were to submit this query, the SLA goals would be met.

Another aspect of application tuning is setting realistic user expectations. Users should be trained to realize that more complex queries, especially if submitted ad hoc, will take more processing and response time. Users should also be trained to submit queries first using the EXPLAIN or similar function that will not actually run the query but rather estimate the time for query processing from database statistics. This way many poorly written queries can be avoided. For this to be effective, the DBA needs to specify to the DBMS that database statistics (such as number of table rows and distribution of values for certain fields often used for

Heatbeat query: A query submitted by the DBA to test the current performance of the database or to predict the response time for queries that have promised response times. Also called a canary query.

qualifications) need to be recalculated frequently. Recalculation of statistics should occur at least after every batch load of a table, and more frequently for tables that are constantly being updated online. Statistics affect the query optimizer, so reasonable up-to-date statistics are essential for the DBMS to develop a very good query processing plan (i.e., which indexes to use and in which order to execute joins).

The preceding description of potential areas where database performance may be affected should convince you of the importance of effective database management and tuning. As a DBA achieves an in-depth understanding of a DBMS and the applications for which responsibility is assigned, the importance of tuning the database for performance should become apparent. Hopefully this brief section on database tuning will whet your appetite for learning more about one or more database products in order to develop tuning skills.

DATA AVAILABILITY

Ensuring the availability of databases to their users has always been a high-priority responsibility of database administrators. However, the growth of e-business has elevated this charge from an important goal to a business imperative. An e-business must be operational and available to its customers 24 hours a day, 7 days a week, every day of the year. Studies have shown that if an online customer does not get the service he or she expects within a few seconds, the customer will take his or her business to a competitor.

Costs of Downtime

The costs of downtime (when databases are unavailable) include several components: lost business during the outage, costs of catching up when service is restored, inventory shrinkage, legal costs, and permanent loss of customer loyalty. These costs are often difficult to estimate accurately and vary widely from one type of business to another. Table 12-2 shows the estimated *hourly* costs of downtime for several business types (Mullins, 2002).

The task of the database administrator is to balance the costs of downtime with the costs of achieving the desired availability level. Unfortunately it is seldom (if ever) possible to provide 100-percent service levels. Failures may occur (as discussed earlier in this chapter) that may interrupt service. Also, it is necessary to perform periodic database reorganizations or other maintenance activities that may cause service interruptions. It is the responsibility of database administration to minimize the impact of these interruptions. The goal is to provide a high level of availability that balances the various costs involved. Table 12-3 shows several availability levels (stated

Table 12-2   Cost of Downtime by Type of Business (Source: Mullins, 2002, p. 226)

Type of business	Estimated hourly cost
Retail brokerage	$6.45 million
Credit card sales authorization	$2.6 million
Home shopping channel	$113,750
Catalog sales centers	$90,000
Airline reservation centers	$89,500
Package shipping service	$28,250
ATM service fees	$14,500

Table 12-3 Cost of Downtime by Availability (Source: Mullins, 2002, p. 226)

Availability	Downtime per year		Cost per year
	Minutes	Hours	
99.999%	5	.08	$8,000
99.99%	53	.88	$88,000
99.9%	526	8.77	$877,000
99.5%	2,628	43.8	$4,380,000
99%	5,256	87.6	$8,760,000

as percentages) and, for each level, the approximate downtime per year (in minutes and hours). Also shown is the annual cost of downtime for an organization whose hourly cost of downtime is $100,000 (say a shopping network or online auction). Notice that the annual costs escalate rapidly as the availability declines, yet in the worst case shown in the table the downtime is only 1 percent.

Measures to Ensure Availability

A new generation of hardware, software, and management techniques has been developed (and continues to be developed) to assist database administrators achieve the high availability levels expected in today's organizations. We have already discussed many of these techniques in this chapter or in earlier ones, so in this section we provide only a brief summary of potential availability problems and measures for coping with them.

Hardware Failures   Any hardware component, such as a database server, disk subsystem, power supply, or network switch, can become a point of failure that will disrupt service. The usual solution is to provide redundant or standby components that replace a failing system. For example, with clustered servers, the workload of a failing server can be reallocated to another server in the cluster.

Loss or Corruption of Data   Service can be interrupted when data are lost or become inaccurate. Mirrored (or back-up) databases are almost always provided in high-availability systems. Also, it is important to use the latest back-up and recovery systems (discussed earlier in this chapter).

Maintenance Downtime   Historically, the greatest source of database downtime was attributed to planned database maintenance activities. Databases were taken off-line during periods of low activity (nights, weekends) for database reorganization, backup, and other activities. This luxury is no longer available for high-availability applications. New database products are now available that automate maintenance functions. For example, some utilities (called *nondisruptive utilities*) allow routine maintenance to be performed while the systems remain operational for both read and write operations, without loss of data integrity.

Network-Related Problems   High-availability applications nearly always depend on the proper functioning of both internal and external networks. Both hardware and software failures can result in service disruption. However, the Internet has spawned new threats that can also result in interruption of service. For example, a hacker can mount a denial-of-service attack by flooding a Web site with computer-generated messages. To counter these threats, an organization should carefully monitor its traffic volumes and develop a fast-response strategy when there is a sudden spike in activity. An organization also must employ the latest firewalls, routers, and other network technologies.

Summary

The importance of managing data was emphasized in this chapter. The functions of data administration, which takes responsibility for the overall management of data resources, include developing procedures to protect and control data, resolving data ownership and use issues, conceptual data modeling, and developing and maintaining corporatewide data definitions and standards. The functions of database administration, on the other hand, are those associated with the direct management of a database or databases, including DBMS installation and upgrading, database design issues, and technical issues such as security enforcement, database performance, data availability, and backup and recovery. The data administration and database administration roles are changing in today's business environment, with pressure being exerted to maintain data quality while building high-performing systems quickly. Key to achieving these expectations is developing an enterprise architecture (ISA) and performing adequate database planning.

Threats to data security include accidental losses, theft and fraud, loss of privacy, loss of data integrity, and loss of availability. A comprehensive data security plan will address all of these potential threats, partly through the establishment of views, authorization rules, user-defined procedures, and encryption procedures.

Database recovery and back-up procedures are another set of essential database administration activities. Basic recovery facilities that should be in place include backup facilities, journalizing facilities, checkpoint facilities, and a recovery manager. Depending on the type of problem encountered, backward recovery (rollback) or forward recovery (rollforward) may be needed.

The problems of managing concurrent access in multiuser environments must also be addressed. The DBMS must ensure that database transactions possess the ACID properties: atomic, consistent, isolated, and durable. Proper transaction boundaries must be chosen to achieve these properties at an acceptable performance. If concurrency controls on transactions are not established, lost updates may occur, which will cause data integrity to be impaired. Locking mechanisms, including shared and exclusive locks, can be used. Deadlocks may also occur in multiuser environments and may be managed by various means, including using a two-phase locking protocol or other deadlock-resolution mechanism. Versioning is an optimistic approach to concurrency control.

Ensuring the quality of data that enters databases and data warehouses is essential if users are to have any confidence in their systems. Ensuring data quality is also now mandated by regulations such as Sarbanes-Oxley and the Basel II Accord. Many organizations today do not have proactive data quality programs, and poor quality data is a widespread problem. A proactive data quality program will employ the use of data stewards, apply proven TQM principles and practices, address persistent organizational barriers, apply modern data management software technology, and use appropriate return on investment calculations.

Managing the data dictionary, which is part of the system catalog in most relational database management systems, and the information repository help the DBA maintain high-quality data and high-performing database systems. The establishment of the Information Repository Dictionary System (IRDS) standard has helped with the development of repository information that can be integrated from multiple sources, including the DBMS itself, CASE tools, and software development tools.

Ensuring the availability of databases to users has become a high priority for the modern DBA. Use of batch windows to perform periodic maintenance (such as database reorganization) is no longer permissible for mission-critical applications. A new generation of hardware, software, and management techniques is being introduced to assist the DBA in managing data availability.

Effective data administration is not easy and encompasses all of the areas summarized here. Increasing emphasis on object-oriented development methods and rapid development are changing the data administration function, but better tools to achieve effective administration and database tuning are becoming available.

CHAPTER REVIEW

Key Terms

Aborted transaction	Back-up facilities	Before-image
After-image	Backward recovery	Checkpoint facility
Authorization rules	(rollback)	Concurrency control

Data archiving
Data administration
Data dictionary
Data steward
Database administration
Database change log
Database destruction
Database recovery
Database security
Deadlock
Deadlock prevention
Deadlock resolution
Encryption
Exclusive lock (X lock
   write lock)

Forward recovery
   (rollforward)
Heartbeat query
Inconsistent read
   problem
Information repository
Information Repository
   Dictionary System
   (IRDS)
Journalizing facilities
Locking
Locking level (lock
   granularity)
Open-source DBMS
Recovery manager

Restore/rerun
Shared lock (S lock, read
   lock)
Smart card
System catalog
Transaction
Transaction boundaries
Transaction log
Two-phase locking
   protocol
User-defined procedures
Versioning

Review Questions

1. Define each of the following terms:

   a. data administration

   b. database administration

   c. data steward

   d. information repository

   e. locking

   f. versioning

   g. deadlock

   h. transaction

   i. encryption

   j. data availability

   k. data archiving

   l. heartbeat query

2. Match the following terms to the appropriate definitions.

   ____ back-up facilities

   ____ biometric device

   ____ checkpoint facility

   ____ database recovery

   ____ database security

   ____ granularity

   ____ recovery manager

   ____ rollback

   ____ rollforward

   ____ system catalog

   a. protects data from loss or misuse

   b. reversal of abnormal or aborted transactions

   c. describes all database objects

   d. automatically produces a saved copy of an entire database

   e. application of after-images

   f. might analyze your signature

   g. restoring a database after a loss

   h. DBMS module that restores a database after a failure

   i. extent to which a database is locked for transaction

   j. records database state at moment of synchronization

3. Compare and contrast the following terms:

   a. data administration; database administration

   b. repository; data dictionary

   c. deadlock prevention; deadlock resolution

   d. backward recovery; forward recovery

   e. active data dictionary; passive data dictionary

   f. optimistic concurrency control; pessimistic concurrency control

   g. shared lock; exclusive lock

   h. before-image; after-image

   i. two-phase locking protocol; versioning

   j. authorization; authentication

   k. data backup; data archiving

4. What is the function of a data steward?

5. Indicate whether data administration or database administration is typically responsible for each of the following functions:

   a. Managing the data repository

   b. Installing and upgrading the DBMS

   c. Conceptual data modeling

   d. Managing data security and privacy

   e. Database planning

   f. Tuning database performance

   g. Database backup and recovery

   h. Running heartbeat queries

6. Describe the changing roles of the data administrator and database administrator in the current business environment.

7. List four common problems of ineffective data administration.

8. List four job skills necessary for data administrators. List four job skills necessary for database administrators.

9. Briefly describe four new specialized DBA roles that are emerging today.

10. What changes can be made in data administration at each stage of the traditional database development life cycle to deliver high-quality, robust systems more quickly?

11. List and discuss five areas where threats to data security may occur.

12. Explain how creating a view may increase data security. Also explain why one should not rely completely on using views to enforce data security.

13. List and briefly explain how integrity controls can be used for database security.

14. What is the difference between an authentication scheme and an authorization scheme?

15. What is the advantage of optimistic concurrency control compared with pessimistic concurrency control?

16. What is the difference between shared locks and exclusive locks?

17. What is the difference between deadlock prevention and deadlock resolution?

18. Briefly describe four DBMS facilities that are required for database backup and recovery.

19. What is transaction integrity? Why is it important?

20. List and describe four common types of database failure.

21. Briefly describe four threats to high data availability and at least one measure that can be taken to counter each of these threats.

22. What is an Information Resource Dictionary System (IRDS)?

23. List and briefly explain the ACID properties of a database transaction.

24. Explain the two common forms of encryption.

25. Briefly describe four components of a disaster recovery plan.

26. Explain the purpose of heartbeat queries.

Problems and Exercises

1. Fill in the two authorization tables for Pine Valley Furniture Company below, based on the following assumptions (enter Y for yes or N for no):

Authorizations for Inventory Clerks

	Inventory Records	Receivables Records	Payroll Records	Customer Records
Read				
Insert				
Modify				
Delete				

Authorizations for Inventory Records

	Salespersons	A/R Personnel	Inventory Clerks	Carpenters
Read				
Insert				
Modify				
Delete				

- Salespersons, managers, and carpenters may read inventory records but may not perform any other operations on these records.
- Persons in Accounts Receivable and Accounts Payable may read and/or update (insert, modify, delete) receivables records and customer records.
- Inventory clerks may read and/or update (modify, delete) inventory records. They may not view receiv-

ables records or payroll records. They may read but not modify customer records.

2. Five recovery techniques are listed below. For each situation described, decide which of the following recovery techniques is most appropriate.
- Backward recovery
- Forward recovery (from latest checkpoint)
- Forward recovery (using backup copy of database)

- Reprocessing transactions
- Switch

a. A phone disconnection occurs while a user is entering a transaction.

b. A disk drive fails during regular operations.

c. A lightning storm causes a power failure.

d. An incorrect amount is entered and posted for a student tuition payment. The error is not discovered for several weeks.

e. Data entry clerks have entered transactions for two hours after a full database backup when the database becomes corrupted. It is discovered that the journalizing facility of the database has not been activated since the backup was made.

3. Whitlock Department Stores runs a multiuser DBMS on a LAN file server. Unfortunately, at the present time, the DBMS does not enforce concurrency control. One Whitlock customer had a balance due of $250.00 when the following three transactions related to this customer were processed at about the same time:

- Payment of $250.00
- Purchase on credit of $100.00
- Merchandise return (credit) of $50.00

Each of the three transactions read the customer record when the balance was $250.00 (i.e., before any of the other transactions were completed). The updated customer record was returned to the database in the order shown above.

a. What balance will be included for the customer after the last transaction was completed?

b. What balance should be included for the customer after the three transactions have been processed?

4. For each of the situations described below, indicate which of the following security measures is most appropriate:

- Authorization rules
- Encryption
- Authentication schemes

a. A national brokerage firm uses an electronic funds transfer (EFT) system to transmit sensitive financial data between locations.

b. An organization has set up an off-site computer-based training center. The organization wishes to restrict access to the site to authorized employees. Because each employee's use of the center is occasional, the center does not wish to provide the employees with keys to access the center.

c. A manufacturing firm uses a simple password system to protect its database but finds it needs a more comprehensive system to grant different privileges (such as read, versus create or update) to different users.

d. A university has experienced considerable difficulty with unauthorized users who access files and databases by appropriating passwords from legitimate users.

5. Metro Marketers, Inc. wants to build a data warehouse for storing customer information that will be used for data marketing purposes. Building the data warehouse will require much more capacity and processing power than they have previously needed, and they are considering Oracle and Red Brick as their database and data warehousing products. As part of their implementation plan, Metro has decided to organize a data administration function. At present, they have four major candidates for the data administrator position:

a. Monica Lopez, a senior database administrator with five years of experience as an Oracle database administrator managing a financial database for a global banking firm, but no data warehousing experience.

b. Gerald Bruester, a senior database administrator with six years of experience as an Informix database administrator managing a marketing-oriented database for a Fortune 1000 food products firm. Gerald has been to several data warehousing seminars over the last twelve months and is interested in being involved with a data warehouse.

c. Jim Reedy, currently project manager for Metro Marketers. Jim is very familiar with Metro's current systems environment and is well respected by his co-workers. He has been involved with Metro's current database system but does not have any data warehousing experience.

d. Marie Weber, a data warehouse administrator with two years of experience using a Red Brick-based application that tracks accident information for an automobile insurance company.

Based on this limited information, rank the four candidates for the data administration position. Support your rankings by indicating your reasoning.

6. Referring to Problem and Exercise 5, rank the four candidates for the position of data warehouse administrator at Metro Marketing. Again, support your rankings.

7. Referring to Problem and Exercise 5, rank the four candidates for the position of database administrator at Metro Marketing. Again, support your rankings.

8. What concerns would you have if you accept a job as a database administrator and discover that the database users are entering one common password to log on to the database each morning when they arrive for work? You also learn that they leave their workstations connected to the database all day, even when they are away from their machines for an extended period of time.

9. An organization has a database server with three disk devices. The accounting and payroll applications share one of these disk devices and are experiencing performance problems. You have been asked to investigate the problem and tune the databases. What might you suggest to reduce I/O contention?

10. You take a new job as a database administrator at an organization that has a globally distributed database. You are asked to analyze the performance of the database, and as part of your analysis, you discover that all of the processing for regional monthly sales reports is being conducted at the corporate headquarters location. Operations are categorized by

five regions: Eastern United States, Western United States, Canada, South America, and Mexico. Data for each region are kept on a server located at the regional headquarters. What would you try to improve the time needed to create the monthly sales reports?

11. An e-business operates a high-volume catalog sales center. Through the use of clustered servers and mirrored disk drives, the data center has been able to achieve a data availability of 99.9 percent. Although this exceeds industry norms, the organization still receives periodic customer complaints that the Web site is unavailable (due to data outages). A vendor has proposed several software upgrades as well as expanded disk capacity to improve data availability. The cost of these proposed improvements would be about $25,000 per month. The vendor estimates that the improvements should improve availability to 99.99 percent.

   a. If this company is typical for a catalog sales center, what is the current annual cost of system unavailability? (You will need to refer to Tables 12-2 and 12-3 to answer this question.)

   b. If the vendor's estimates are accurate, can the organization justify the additional expenditure?

12. Review the tables for data availability (Tables 12-2 and 12-3). For the retail brokerage firm shown in Table 12-2, calculate the expected annual cost of downtime for the following availability levels: 99.9 percent and 99.5 percent. Do you think that either of these levels are acceptable for this organization?

13. The mail order firm described in Problem and Exercise 11 has about one million customers. The firm is planning a mass mailing of its spring sales catalog to all of its customers. The unit cost of the mailing (postage and catalog) is $6.00. The error rate in the database (duplicate records, erroneous addresses, etc.) is estimated to be 12 percent. Calculate the expected loss of this mailing due to bad quality data.

14. The average annual revenue per customer for the mail order firm described in Problems and Exercises 11 and 13 is $100. The organization is planning a data quality improvement program that it hopes will increase the average revenue per customer by five percent per year. If this estimate proves accurate, what will be the annual increase in revenue due to improved quality?

15. Referring to the Fitchwood Insurance Company case study at the end of Chapter 11, what types of security issues would you expect to encounter when building a data warehouse? Would there be just one set of security concerns related to user access to the data warehouse, or would you also need to be concerned with security of data during the extracting, cleansing, and loading processes?

16. How would Fitchwood's security have to be different if the data mart was made available to customers via the Internet?

17. What security and data quality issues need to be addressed when developing a B2B application using Web services?

18. Research available data quality software. Describe in detail at least one technique employed by one of these tools (such as an expert system).

19. Visit some of the Web sites for open-source databases, such as **www.postgresql.org** and **www.mysql.com**. What do you see as major differences in administration between open-source databases, such as MySQL, and commercial database products, such as Oracle? How might these differences come into play when choosing a database platform? Summarize the DBA functions of MySQL versus PostgresSQL.

20. Compare the concurrency issues that must be dealt with when developing an OLTP system versus a data warehouse.

Field Exercises

1. Visit an organization that has implemented a database approach. Evaluate each of the following:

   a. The organizational placement of data administration, database administration, and data warehouse administration

   b. The assignment of responsibilities for each of the functions listed in part a

   c. The background and experience of the person chosen as head of data administration

   d. The status and usage of an information repository (passive, active-in-design, active-in-production)

2. Visit an organization that has implemented a database approach and interview an MIS department employee who has been involved in disaster recovery planning. Before you go for the interview, think carefully about the relative probabilities of various disasters for the organization you are visiting. For example, is the area subject to earthquakes, tornadoes, or other natural disasters? What type of damage might the physical plant be subject to? Or, what is the background and

training of the employees who must use the system? Find out about the organization's disaster recovery plans and ask specifically about any potential problems you have identified.

3. Visit an organization that has implemented a database approach and interview them about the security measures that they take routinely. Evaluate each of the following:

   a. Database security measures

   b. Network security measures

   c. Operating system security measures

   d. Physical plant security measures

   e. Personnel security measures

4. Identify an organization that handles large, sporadic data loads. For example, organizations that have implemented data warehouses may have large data loads as they populate their data warehouses. Determine what measures the organization has taken to handle these large loads as part of their capacity planning.

5. Databases tend to grow larger over time, not smaller, as new transaction data are added. Interview at least three companies who use databases extensively and identify their criteria and procedures for purging or archiving old data. Find out how often data are purged and what type of data are purged. Identify the data each organization archives and how long those data are archived.

6. Visit an organization that relies heavily on e-commerce applications. Interview the database administrator (or a senior person in that organization) to determine the following:

   a. What is the organizational goal for system availability? (Compare with Table 12-3.)

   b. Has the organization estimated the cost of system downtime (\$/hour)? If not, use Table 12-2 and select a cost for a similar type of organization.

   c. What is the greatest obstacle to achieving high data availability for this organization?

   d. What measures has the organization taken to ensure high availability? What measures are planned for the future?

7. Visit an organization that uses an open-source DBMS. Why did they choose open-source software? Do they have other open-source software besides a DBMS? Have they purchased any fee-based components or services? Do they have a DA or DBA staff, and, if so, how do these people evaluate the open-source DBMS they are using? (This could be especially insightful if the organization also has some traditional DBMS products such as Oracle or DB2.)

References

Anderson, D. 2005. "HIPAA Security and Compliance." Published on **www.tdan.com,** July, 2005.

Bernstein, P. A. 1996. "The Repository: A Modern Vision." *Database Programming & Design* 9,12 (December): 28–35.

Betts, M. 2002. "Data Quality: The Cornerstone of CRM." *Computerworld* (February 18) available at **http://www.computerworld. com/softwaretopics/crm/story/0,10801,68270,00.html.**

Brauer, B. 2002. "Data Quality-Spinning Straw into Gold," Available at **www.dataflux.com/data/spinning.pdf** (no longer available at this address).

Carlson, D. 2002. "Data Stewardship Action." *DM Review* 12,5 (May): 37, 62.

Celko, J. 1992. "An Introduction to Concurrency Control." *DBMS* 5,9 (September): 70–83.

Descollonges, M. 1993. "Concurrency for Complex Processing." *Database Programming & Design* 6,1 (January): 66–71.

Dowgiallo, E., H. Fosdick, Y. Lirov, A. Langer, T. Quinlan, and C. Young. 1997. "DBA of the Future." *Database Programming & Design* 10,6 (June): 33–41.

Dubois, L. "Business Intelligence: The Dirty (and Costly) Little Secret of Bad Data." *DM Review Business Intelligence Report* (September) available at **www.dmreview.com/master.cfm?NavID=198&EdID=5786.**

Eckerson, W. 2002. "Data Quality and the Bottom Line." *Application Development Trends* available at **www.adtmag.com/article.asp?id= 6303.**

English, Larry. 1999. *Business Information Quality: Methods for Reducing Costs and Improving Profits.* New York: Wiley.

Fernandez, E. B., R. C. Summers, and C. Wood. 1981. *Database Security and Integrity.* Reading, MA: Addison-Wesley.

Hall, M. 2003. "MySQL Breaks Into the Data Center" available at **www.computerworld.com/printthis/2003/0,4814,85900,00.html.**

Inmon, W. H. 1999. "Data Warehouse Administration." Available at **www.billinmon.com/library/other/dwadmin.asp.**

Inmon, W. H., C. Imhoff, and R. Sousa. 2001. *Corporate Information Factory,* 2nd ed. New York: Wiley.

Laurent, W. 2005. "The Case for Data Stewardship." *DM Review* 15,2 (February): 26-28.

Lefkovitz, H. C. 1985. *Proposed American National Standards Information Resource Dictionary System.* Wellesley, MA: QED Information Sciences.

Michaelson, J. 2004. "What Every Developer Should Know About Open Source Licensing." *Queue* 2,3 (May): 41–47. (Note: This whole issue of *Queue* was devoted to the open-source movement, and contains many interesting articles.)

Moriarty, T. 1996. "Better Business Practices." *Database Programming & Design* 9,7 (September): 59–61.

Mullins, C. 2001. "Modern Database Administration, Part 1." *DM Review* 11,9 (September): 31, 55–57.

Mullins, C. 2002. *Database Administration: The Complete Guide to Practices and Procedures.* Boston: Addison-Wesley.

Quinlan, T. 1996. "Time to Reengineer the DBA?" *Database Programming & Design* 9,3 (March): 29–34.

Redman, T. 2004. "Data: An Unfolding Quality Disaster." *DM Review* 14,8 (August): 21–23, 57.

Rodgers, U. 1989. "Multiuser DBMS Under UNIX." *Database Programming & Design* 2,10 (October): 30–37.

Seiner, R. 2005. "Data Steward Roles & Responsibilities." Published on **www.tdan.com,** July, 2005.

Zachman, J. A. 1987. "A Framework for Information Systems Architecture." *IBM Systems Journal* 26,3 (March): 276–92.

Zachman, J. A. 1997. "Enterprise Architecture: The Issue of the Century." *Database Programming & Design* 10,3 (March): 44–53.

Further Reading

Loney, K. 2000. "Protecting Your Database." *Oracle Magazine.* 14,3 (May/June): 101–106.

Surran, M. 2003. "Making the Switch to Open Source Software." *T.H.E. Journal.* 31,2 (September): 36–41. (This journal available at **www.thejournal.com.**)

Web Resources

www.bionetrix.com and **www.keyware.com** BioNetrix Systems and Keyware Technologies are leaders in biometric technologies. Their Web sites explain the diversity of biometric devices available for various applications.

www.isi.edu/gost/brian/security/kerberos.html This document is a guide to the Kerberos method of user authentication.

www.abanet.org/scitech/ec/isc/dsg-tutorial.html The American Bar Association Section of Science and Technology, Information Security Committee has prepared this excellent guide to digital signatures.

tpc.org TPC is a nonprofit corporation founded to define transaction processing and database benchmarks and to disseminate objective, verifiable transaction processing performance data to the industry. This is an excellent site to learn more about evaluating DBMSs and database designs through technical articles on database benchmarking.

MOUNTAIN VIEW COMMUNITY HOSPITAL

Case

At the end of Chapter 2, you learned of the Mountain View Community Hospital special study team that is developing a long-term strategic and information systems plan for the next five years. The team composed of Mr. Heller, Mr. Lopez, Dr. Jefferson, and a consultant is trying to devise a plan that will meet the hospital's goals of high-quality health care, cost containment, and expansion into new services, such as Dr. Browne's anticipated Geriatric Medicine department. Mr. Heller, MVCH's CIO, is a member of the Healthcare Information and Management Systems Society (HIMMS) and regularly reads IT-related magazines to keep up with developments and new technologies (e.g., *Computerworld, CIO Magazine, Health Management Technology, Health Data Management,* and *Healthcare Informatics*). He also attends healthcare IT conferences that allow him to interact with his peers and find out what's new.

In response to issues with existing systems and recent trends in healthcare IT (e.g. electronic medical records systems or EMRs, work flow automation, etc.), the study team has been evaluating various options for integrating the hospital's operational, clinical, and financial information (see MVCH Chapter 9). An EMR system would allow physicians to access all medical information for a patient, even though that information is from different systems and locations, including various physician, hospital, laboratory, and insurance records. As part of a transition from the paper chart to EMRs, and as a way of addressing medical errors, hospitals, including Mountain View, are also beginning to take a closer look at computerized physician order entry (CPOE) systems. (You may recall that the enterprise model developed by the study team included an ORDER entity.) Primarily implemented in large metropolitan areas and leading government hospitals at the present time, CPOE allows physicians to electronically enter their orders for labs, medications, radiology, and so on. CPOE not only eliminates problems stemming from illegible handwriting, but also provides decision support capabilities, intercepting medication errors at the time of order, or alerting a physician to potential interactions with other medications a patient may be taking.

EMR and CPOE systems, however, represent a significant change in the way health care information is collected and used. And change is often difficult. After a conversation with Dr. "Z.", who worked at a large hospital that used a CPOE system prior to joining Mountain View, Mr. Heller realizes that physicians may not readily embrace such a system. For example, a physician who wants to prescribe an antibiotic for 10 days or 2 weeks may find that the default in the computer is one week. The physician would then have to manually override the default. Not only would this extra step consume extra time, it would also require greater knowledge of the computerized order system on the part of the physician. A handwritten order would have been more convenient. And, according to Dr. "Z.", this example is just one of a million little things that would be more difficult. While advocating the technology, Dr. "Z." believes that CPOE's steep learning curve and need for relearning can make the practice of medicine harder. Dr. "Z.'" also remembers a situation where the pharmacy went into the system and unilaterally changed one of his orders.

In addition to his involvement with the hospital's special study team, Mr. Heller is facing a number of data management issues as a result of HIPAA's security rules to protect patient information. Contingency planning is one of them. HIPAA's contingency plan standard has five components: a data back-up plan, a disaster recovery plan, an emergency mode operation plan, testing and revision procedures, and applications and data criticality analysis. The latter involves identifying all potential data security threats, and determining their level of risk. HIPAA also has audit trail requirements that were briefly described in the Chapter 8 case segment.

Password management has become a huge issue lately. MVCH upgraded its security policies in response to HIPAA's information access management requirements. Users must have unique names and passwords for many applications and are required to change their passwords regularly. Physicians in particular are complaining about the many passwords they have to keep track of, and the problems they have with logging onto an application when they forget a password. As a result, Mr. Heller's staff is working on making single sign-on (SSO) a reality at Mountain View Community Hospital.

Other data management issues of concern to Mr. Heller include the hospital's data storage needs and data quality. Storage needs at MVCH continue to grow at an unprecedented rate as data (clinical and nonclinical) and diagnostic images are being created. HIPAA and other new regulations are increasing data volumes even more. HIPPA, for example, requires that some types of medical information be retained for many years, and beyond the lifetime of a patient. The study team's discussions of data warehousing technologies (see MVCH Chapter 11) have also brought data quality to the forefront. At one of the team's meetings, Mr. Lopez, the hospital's CFO, wanted to know just how much poor quality data cost the hospital every year. He had read that poor data quality costs account for approximately 4 percent of a hospital's expenses.[1] Given the need for cost containment, Mr. Heller is beginning to feel the pressure to shift away from the current focus on fixing after the fact and moving towards proactively preventing data quality problems and building quality into the process.

CASE QUESTIONS

1. Do EMR and CPOE systems seem to have the potential to help Mountain View achieve its goals of achieving high-quality care and cost containment? Support your answers with examples of how you think these goals may or may not be achieved.

2. In light of HIPAA and other regulations, securing and protecting patient records is a primary requirement for MVCH.

   a. What data security issues would you expect Mountain View to encounter if an EMR system is implemented that is accessible by physicians in the community, by laboratories, and by healthcare organizations?

   b. What data security techniques described in this chapter could be used to address these issues?

   c. Examine the organization chart for Mountain View Community Hospital in Chapter 2 (MVCH Figure 2-1). Who would be the best choice for a data steward for patient data? Please explain your answer.

3. If MVCH decides to implement a CPOE system, how could access problems such as the one that Dr. "Z." experienced at another hospital be prevented?

4. Given that the Mountain View database you developed in SQL Server already includes tables for physicians, orders, and so on, do you think a full-fledged CPOE system could or should be developed internally? Why or why not?

5. Dr. "Z." indicated that physicians might resist the implementation of a CPOE system. Do you think that would also be true for an EMR system? Why or why not? What would be critical success factors for implementing an electronic medical record at MVCH?

6. Should Mountain View Community Hospital adopt a continuous data protection (CDP) system? Why or

why not? What other back-up strategies might the hospital pursue?

7. Do you think data storage at Mountain View Community should be treated as a strategic issue? Why or why not?

8. Do you think that data quality at Mountain View Community Hospital is a strategic issue? Why or why not?

9. Which data and database administration issues described in Chapter 12 should be addressed by Mountain View Community Hospital's special study team as part of the long-range business and information systems plan? Why?

CASE EXERCISES

1. List all the possible types of users that would need authorization to use (a) an ERM system, and (b) a CPOE system at Mountain View Community Hospital. Include user groups external to the hospital that may need to be included.

2. For each user type you listed in Case Exercise 1, indicate what permissions (read, insert, delete, modify) you would grant.

3. Investigate how a hospital such as Mountain View could use RFID in connection with an EMR system. How would that affect data storage requirements?

4. In light of HIPAA's security rules (data back up, access to data, data retention, etc.), and the tremendous growth of data at MVCH, outline the pros and cons of various data storage options that the hospital may be using? Are there storage media that can potentially lead to violations under HIPAA? Which ones? Why?

5. Access HIPAA's security requirements online and outline a contingency plan for Mountain View Community Hospital.

6. Investigate data quality management in greater detail, then outline a data quality strategy that would address the issues raised in the case description. What should be the first step? What would be considered high-quality data at MVCH? How could data quality be built into the process? Who should be part of it? What would be the ROI of a data quality initiative?

PROJECT ASSIGNMENTS

P1. Password protect the MVCH database you created in SQL Server (or other database management systems required by your instructor).

P2. Create a matrix to indicate the permissions (read, insert, delete, modify) you would grant to different users of the database you identify.

P3. Create at least two different users and implement their permissions using SQL statements.

---

[1] Barlow, R. D. (2005). "Routine Database Maintenance Can Lead To Hospital Treasure", *Health Care Purchasing News*, 29:1 (January), 48–51.

Chapter 13

Overview: Distributed Databases

LEARNING OBJECTIVES

After studying this chapter, you should be able to:

- Concisely define each of the following key terms: **distributed database, decentralized database, location transparency, local autonomy, synchronous distributed database, asynchronous distributed database, local transaction, global transaction, replication transparency, transaction manager, failure transparency, commit protocol, two-phase commit, concurrency transparency, timestamping,** and **semijoin.**

- Explain the business conditions that are drivers for the use of distributed databases in organizations.

- Describe the salient characteristics of the variety of distributed database environments.

- Explain the potential advantages and risks associated with distributed databases.

- Explain four strategies for the design of distributed databases, options within each strategy, and the factors to consider in selection among these strategies.

- State the relative advantages of synchronous and asynchronous data replication and partitioning as three major approaches for distributed database design.

- Outline the steps involved in processing a query in a distributed database and several approaches used to optimize distributed query processing.

- Explain the salient features of several distributed database management systems.

A complete version of this chapter is available on the textbook's Web site. The following is a brief overview.

OVERVIEW

When an organization is geographically dispersed, it may choose to store its databases on a central computer or to distribute them to local computers (or a combination of both). A **distributed database** is a single logical database that is spread physically across computers in multiple locations that are connected by a data communications network. We emphasize that a distributed database is truly a database, not a loose collection of files. The distributed database is still centrally administered as a corporate resource while providing local flexibility and customization. The network must allow the users to share the data; thus a user (or program) at location A must be able to access (and perhaps update) data at location B. The sites of a distributed system may be spread over a large area (such as the United States or the world) or over a small area (such as a building or campus). The computers may range from microcomputers to large-scale computers or even supercomputers.

A distributed database requires multiple database management systems running at each remote site. The degree to which these different DBMSs cooperate, or work in partnership, and whether there is a master site that coordinates requests involving data from multiple sites distinguish different types of distributed database environments.

Various business conditions encourage the use of distributed databases: Distribution and autonomy of business units, data sharing, data communications costs and reliability, multiple application vendor environments, database recovery, and the satisfying of both transaction and analytical processing.

> **Distributed database:** A single logical database that is spread physically across computers in multiple locations that are connected by a data communication link.

Objectives and Trade-Offs

A major objective of distributed databases is to provide ease of access to data for users at many different locations. To meet this objective, the distributed database system must provide what is called **location transparency**, which means that a user (or user program) using data for querying or updating need not know the location of the data. Any request to retrieve or update data from any site is automatically forwarded by the system to the site or sites related to the processing request. Ideally, the user is unaware of the distribution of data, and all data in the network appear as a single logical database stored at one site. In this ideal case, a single query can join data from tables in multiple sites as if the data were all in one site.

> **Location transparency:** A design goal for a distributed database, which says that a user (or user program) using data need not know the location of the data.

A second objective of distributed databases is **local autonomy**, which is the capability to administer a local database and to operate independently when connections to other nodes have failed (Date, 1995). With local autonomy, each site has the capability to control local data, administer security, log transactions, recover when local failures occur, and provide full access to local data to local users when any central or coordinating site cannot operate. In this case, data are locally owned and managed, even though they are accessible from remote sites. This implies that there is no reliance on a central site.

> **Local autonomy:** A design goal for a distributed database, which says that a site can independently administer and operate its database when connections to other nodes have failed.

Compared with centralized databases, either form of a distributed database has numerous advantages. The most important are the following: increased reliability and availability, local control, modularity, lower communication costs, and faster response. A distributed database system also faces certain costs and disadvantages: software cost and complexity, processing overhead, data integrity, and slow response (if the data are not distributed properly).

Options for Distributing a Database

How should a database be distributed among the sites (or nodes) of a network? We discussed this important issue of physical database design in Chapter 6, which introduced an analytical procedure for evaluating alternative distribution strategies. In that chapter, we noted that there are four basic strategies for distributing databases: data replication, horizontal partitioning, vertical partitioning, and combinations of the above.

There are many forms of *data replication*, which are discussed in detail in the complete chapter. There are five advantages to data replication: reliability, fast response, possible avoidance of complicated distributed transaction integrity routines, node decoupling, and reduced network traffic at prime time. Replication has two primary disadvantages: storage requirements, complexity, and cost of updating.

With *horizontal partitioning* (see Chapter 6 for a description of different forms of table partitioning), some of the rows of a table (or relation) are put into a base relation at one site, and other rows are put into a base relation at another site. More generally, the rows of a relation are distributed to many sites. Horizontal partitions for a distributed database have four major advantages: efficiency, local optimization, security, and ease of querying. Thus, horizontal partitions are usually used when an organizational function is distributed, but each site is concerned with only a subset of the entity instances (frequently based on geography). Horizontal partitions also have two primary disadvantages: *inconsistent access speed* and *backup vulnerability*.

Distributed DBMS

To have a distributed database, there must be a database management system that coordinates the access to data at the various nodes. We will call such a system a *distributed DBMS*. Although each site may have a DBMS managing the local database at that site, a distributed DBMS will perform the following functions (Buretta, 1997; Elmasri and Navathe, 1989):

1. Keep track of where data are located in a distributed data dictionary. This means, in part, presenting one logical database and schema to developers and users.

2. Determine the location from which to retrieve requested data and the location at which to process each part of a distributed query without any special actions by the developer or user.

3. If necessary, translate the request at one node using a local DBMS into the proper request to another node using a different DBMS and data model and return data to the requesting node in the format accepted by that node.

4. Provide data management functions, such as security, concurrency and deadlock control, global query optimization, and automatic failure recording and recovery.

5. Provide consistency among copies of data across the remote sites (e.g., by using multiphase commit protocols).

6. Present a single logical database that is physically distributed. One ramification of this view of data is global primary key control, meaning that data about the same business object are associated with the same primary key no matter where in the distributed database the data are stored, and different objects are associated with different primary keys.

7. Be scalable. Scalability is the ability to grow, reduce in size, and become more heterogeneous as the needs of the business change. Thus, a distributed database must be dynamic and be able to change within reasonable limits and without having to be redesigned. Scalability also means that there are easy ways for new sites to be added (or to subscribe) and to be initialized (e.g., with replicated data).

8. Replicate both data and stored procedures across the nodes of the distributed database. The need to distribute stored procedures is motivated by the same reasons as those for distributing data.

9. Transparently use residual computing power to improve the performance of database processing. This means, for example, the same database query may be processed at different sites and in different ways when submitted at different times, depending on the particular workload across the distributed database at the time of query submission.

10. Permit different nodes to run different DBMSs. Middleware (see Chapter 9) can be used by the distributed DBMS and each local DBMS to mask the differences in query languages and nuances of local data.

11. Allow different versions of application code to reside on different nodes of the distributed database. In a large organization with multiple, distributed servers, it may not be practical to have each server/node running the same version of software.

Replication transparency: A design goal for a distributed database, which says that although a given data item may be replicated at several nodes in a network, a programmer or user may treat the data item as if it were a single item at a single node. Also called fragmentation transparency.

Failure transparency: A design goal for a distributed database, which guarantees that either all the actions of each transaction are committed or else none of them is committed.

Concurrency transparency: A design goal for a distributed database, with the property that although a distributed system runs many transactions, it appears that a given transaction is the only activity in the system. Thus, when several transactions are processed concurrently, the results must be the same as if each transaction were processed in serial order.

Commit protocol: An algorithm to ensure that a transaction is successfully completed or else it is aborted.

The distributed DBMS provides location transparency (defined earlier), **replication transparency, failure transparency,** and **concurrency transparency**. The distributed DBMS uses a **commit protocol** to ensure data integrity for real-time, distributed update operations. The most common commit protocol is **two-phase commit** (which is detailed in the complete chapter).

Two-phase commit: An algorithm for coordinating updates in a distributed database.

Query Optimization

With distributed databases, the response to a query may require the DBMS to assemble data from several different sites (although with location transparency, the user is unaware of this need). A major decision for the DBMS is how to process a query, which is affected by both the way a user formulates a query and the intelligence of the distributed DBMS to develop a sensible plan for processing. Several plausible query-processing strategies are detailed in the complete chapter. Depending on the choice of strategy, the time required to satisfy the query ranges from one second to 2.3 days!

One technique used to make processing a distributed query more efficient is to use what is called a **semijoin** operation (Elmasri and Navathe, 1989). In a semijoin, only the joining attribute is sent from one site to another, and then only the required rows are returned. If only a small percentage of the rows participate in the join, then the amount of data being transferred is minimal.

Semijoin: A joining operation used with distributed databases in which only the joining attribute from one site is transmitted to the other site, rather than all the selected attributes from every qualified row.

CHAPTER REVIEW

For coverage of key terms, review questions, problems and exercises, and field questions, see the complete chapter on the textbook's Web site. The following are the full set of references for the chapter followed by information about additional sources of information on distributed databases.

References

Bell, D., and J. Grimson. 1992. *Distributed Database Systems.* Reading, MA: Addison-Wesley.

Buretta, M. 1997. *Data Replication: Tools and Techniques for Managing Distributed Information.* New York: Wiley.

Date, C. J. 1983. *An Introduction to Database Systems*, Vol. 2. Reading, MA: Addison-Wesley.

Date, C. J. 1995. *An Introduction to Database Systems*, 6th ed. Reading, MA: Addison-Wesley.

Edelstein, H. 1993. "Replicating Data." *DBMS* 6,6 (June): 59–64.

Edelstein, H. 1995a. "The Challenge of Replication, Part I." *DBMS* 8,3 (March): 46–52.

Elmasri, R., and S. B. Navathe. 1989. *Fundamentals of Database Systems.* Menlo Park, CA: Benjamin/Cummings.

Froemming, G. 1996. "Design and Replication: Issues with Mobile Applications—Part 1." *DBMS* 9,3 (March): 48–56.

Koop, P. 1995. "Replication at Work." *DBMS* 8,3 (March): 54–60.

McGovern, D. 1993. "Two-Phased Commit or Replication." *Database Programming & Design* 6,5 (May): 35–44.

Özsu, M. T., and P. Valduriez. 1992. "Distributed Database Systems: Where Were We?" *Database Programming & Design* 5,4 (April): 49–55.

Thé, L. 1994. "Distribute Data Without Choking the Net." *Datamation* 40,1 (January 7): 35–38.

Thompson, C. 1997. "Database Replication: Comparing Three Leading DBMS Vendors' Approaches to Replication." *DBMS* 10,5 (May): 76–84.

Further Reading

Edelstein, H. 1995. "The Challenge of Replication, Part II." *DBMS* 8,4 (April): 62–70, 103.

Web Resources

www.wide.ad.jp The WIDE project is a research and development project that is concerned with extending the technology of distributed and active databases in order to provide added value to advanced, application-oriented software products implementing workflow techniques. These problems have been tackled by a consortium involving partners from organizations in Spain, Italy, and the Netherlands.

www.compapp.dcu.ie This site, maintained by Dublin City University, has a variety of material on several important aspects of distributed databases.

databases.about.com This Web site contains a variety of news and reviews about various database technologies, including distributed databases.

Chapter 14

Overview: Object-Oriented Data Modeling

LEARNING OBJECTIVES

After studying this chapter, you should be able to:

- Concisely define each of the following key terms: **class, object, state, behavior, object class, class diagram, object diagram, operation, encapsulation, constructor operation, query operation, update operation, scope operation, association, association role, multiplicity, association class, abstract class, concrete class, class-scope attribute, abstract operation, method, polymorphism, overriding, multiple classification, aggregation,** and **composition.**

- Describe the activities in the different phases of the object-oriented development life cycle.

- State the advantages of object-oriented modeling vis-à-vis structured approaches.

- Compare and contrast the object-oriented model with the E-R and EER models.

- Model a real-world application by using a UML class diagram.

- Provide a snapshot of the detailed state of a system at a point in time using a UML (Unified Modeling Language) object diagram.

- Recognize when to use generalization, aggregation, and composition relationships.

- Specify different types of business rules in a class diagram.

A complete version of this chapter is available on the textbook's Web site. The following is a brief overview.

OVERVIEW

In Chapters 3 and 4, you learned about data modeling using the E-R and EER models. In those chapters, you learned how to model the data needs of an organization using entities, attributes, and a wide variety of relationships. In this chapter, you will be introduced to the object-oriented model, which is becoming increasingly popular because of its ability to thoroughly represent complex relationships, as well as to represent data and data processing in a consistent notation. Fortunately, most of the concepts you learned in those chapters correspond to concepts in object-oriented modeling, but, as you will see, the object-oriented model has even more features than the EER model.

An object-oriented model is built around *objects*, just as the E-R model is built around entities. An object *encapsulates* both data *and* behavior, implying that we can use the object-oriented approach not only for data modeling, but also for process modeling. To thoroughly model any real-world application, you need to model both the data and the processes that act on the data (recall the discussion in Chapter 2 about information planning objects). By allowing you to capture them together within a common representation, and by offering benefits such as *inheritance* and code reuse, the object-oriented modeling approach provides a powerful environment for developing complex systems.

Coad and Yourdon (1991b) identify several motivations and benefits of object-oriented modeling, which follow: the ability to tackle more challenging problem domains; improved communication between the users, analysts, designers, and programmers; increased consistency among analysis, design, and programming activities; explicit representation of commonality among system components; robustness of systems, reusability of analysis, design, and programming results; and increased consistency among all the models developed during object-oriented analysis, design, and programming.

In this chapter, we present object-oriented data modeling as a high-level conceptual activity. As you will learn in Chapter 15, a good conceptual model is invaluable for designing and implementing an object-oriented database application.

The Unified Modeling Language

The Unified Modeling Language (UML) is "a language for specifying, visualizing, and constructing the artifacts of software systems, as well as for business modeling" (*UML Document Set*, 1997). For representing a complex system effectively, it is necessary that the model you develop has a small set of independent views or perspectives. UML allows you to represent multiple perspectives of a system by providing different types of graphical diagrams, such as the use-case diagram, class diagram, state diagram, interaction diagram, component diagram, and deployment diagram. The underlying model integrates those views so that the system can be analyzed, designed, and implemented in a complete and consistent fashion.

Because this text is about databases, we will describe only the *class diagram*, which addresses the data, as well some behavioral, aspects of a system. We will not describe the other diagrams because they provide perspectives that are not directly related to a database system, for example, the dynamic aspects of a system. But keep in mind that a database system is usually part of an overall system, whose underlying model should encompass all the different perspectives. For a discussion of other UML diagrams, see Hoffer et al. (2005) and George et al. (2005).

Object-Oriented Data Modeling

A **class** is an entity that has a well-defined role in the application domain about which the organization wishes to maintain state, behavior, and identity. A class is a concept, abstraction, or thing that makes sense in an application context (Rumbaugh et al., 1991). A class could be a tangible or visible entity (e.g., a person, place, or thing); it could be a concept or event (e.g., Department, Performance, Marriage, Registration, etc.); or it could be an artifact of the design process (e.g., User Interface, Controller, Scheduler, etc.). An **object** is an instance of a class (e.g., a particular person, place, or thing) that encapsulates the data and behavior we need to maintain about that object. A class of objects shares a common set of attributes and behaviors.

The **state** of an object encompasses its properties (attributes and relationships) and the values those properties have, and its **behavior** represents how an object acts and reacts (Booch, 1994). An object's state is determined by its attribute values and links to other objects. An object's behavior depends on its state and the operation being performed. An operation is simply an action that one object performs on

Class: An entity that has a well-defined role in the application domain about which the organization wishes to maintain state, behavior, and identity.

Object: An instance of a class that encapsulates data and behavior.

State: Encompasses an object's properties (attributes and relationships) and the values those properties have.

Behavior: Represents how an object acts and reacts.

Figure 14-2
UML class and object diagrams
(a) Class diagram showing two classes

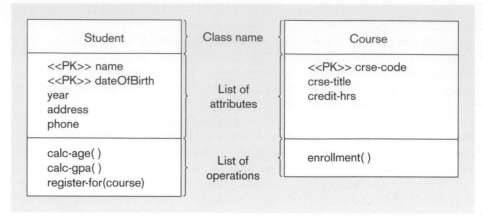

another to get a response. You can think of an operation as a service provided by an object (supplier) to its clients. A client sends a message to a supplier, which delivers the desired service by executing the corresponding operation.

Consider an example of the student class and a particular object in this class, Mary Jones. The state of this object is characterized by its attributes, say, name, date of birth, year, address, and phone, and the values these attributes currently have. For example, name is "Mary Jones," year is "junior," and so on. Its behavior is expressed through operations such as calc-gpa, which is used to calculate a student's current grade point average. The Mary Jones object, therefore, packages both its state and its behavior together. All objects have a persistent identity; that is, no two objects are the same, and an object maintains its own identity over its life. For example, if Mary Jones gets married and changes her name, address, and phone, she will still be represented by the same object.

You can depict the classes graphically in a class diagram as in Figure 14-2a. (Note: figure numbers are not continuous in this summary because only selected figures from the complete chapter on the textbook's Web site are included in this summary). A **class diagram** shows the static structure of an object-oriented model: the object classes, their internal structure, and the relationships in which they participate. The figure shows two classes, Student and Course, along with their attributes and operations. All students have in common the properties of name, date of birth, year, address, and phone. They also exhibit common behavior by sharing the calc-age, calc-gpa, and register-for(course) operations.

An **operation**, such as calc-gpa in Student (see Figure 14-2a), is a function or a service that is provided by all the instances of a class. It is only through such operations that other objects can access or manipulate the information stored in an object. The operations, therefore, provide an external interface to a class; the interface presents the outside view of the class without showing its internal structure or how its operations are implemented. This technique of hiding the internal implementation details of an object from its external view is known as **encapsulation**, or information hiding. So although we provide the abstraction of the behavior common to all instances of a class in its interface, we encapsulate within the class its structure and the secrets of the desired behavior.

Parallel to the definition of a relationship for the E-R model, an **association** is a named relationship between or among instances of object classes. In Figure 14-3, we use examples from Figure 3-12 to illustrate how the object-oriented model can be used to represent association relationships of different degrees. The end of an association where it connects to a class is called an **association role** (*UML Notation Guide*, 1997). A role may be explicitly named with a label near the end of an association (see the "manager" role in Figure 14-3a).

Class diagram: Shows the static structure of an object-oriented model: the object classes, their internal structure, and the relationships in which they participate.

Operation: A function or a service that is provided by all the instances of a class.

Encapsulation: The technique of hiding the internal implementation details of an object from its external view.

Association: A named relationship between or among object classes.

Association role: The end of an association where it connects to a class.

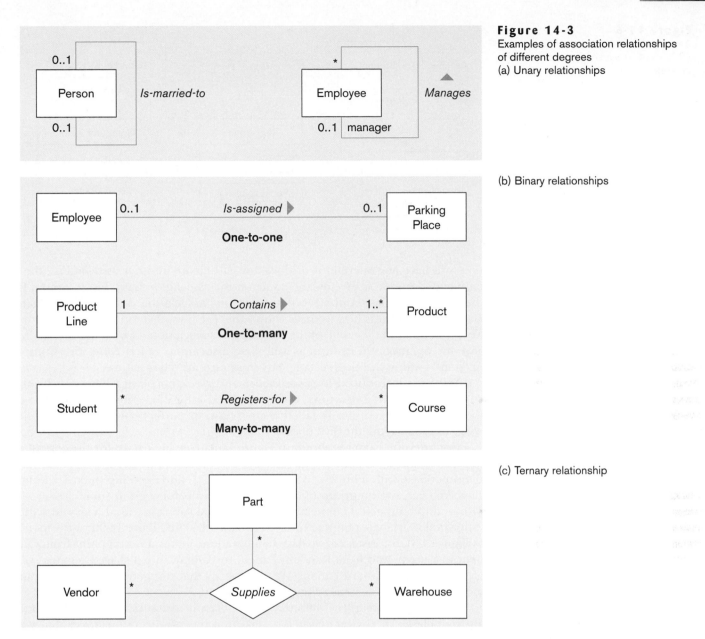

Figure 14-3
Examples of association relationships of different degrees
(a) Unary relationships

(b) Binary relationships

(c) Ternary relationship

Each role has a **multiplicity**, which indicates how many objects participate in a given relationship. In a class diagram, a multiplicity specification is shown as a text string representing an interval (or intervals) of integers in the following format:

Multiplicity: A specification that indicates how many objects participate in a given relationship.

lower-bound..upper-bound

In addition to integer values, the upper bound of a multiplicity can be a star character (*), which denotes an infinite upper bound. If a single integer value is specified, it means that the range includes only that value.

When an association itself has attributes or operations of its own, or when it participates in relationships with other classes, it is useful to model the association as an **association class** (just as we used an "associative entity" in Chapter 3). For example, in Figure 14-6a, the attributes term and grade and the operation checkEligibility really belong to the many-to-many association between Student and Course.

Association class: An association that has attributes or operations of its own or that participates in relationships with other classes.

You have the option of showing the name of an association class on the association path, or the class symbol, or both. When an association has only attributes, but

Figure 14-6
Association class and link object
(a) Class diagram showing association classes

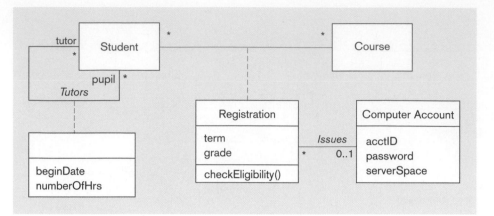

does not have any operations or does not participate in other associations, the recommended option is to show the name on the association path, but to omit it from the association class symbol, to emphasize its "association nature" (*UML Notation Guide,* 1997). That is how we have shown the *Tutors* association. On the other hand, we have displayed the name of the Registration association—which has two attributes and one operation of its own, as well as an association called *Issues* with Computer Account—within the class rectangle to emphasize its "class nature."

You were introduced to *generalization* and *specialization* in Chapter 4. In object data modeling, the classes that are generalized are called subclasses, and the class they are generalized into is called a superclass, in perfect correspondence to subtypes and supertypes for EER diagramming.

Consider the example shown in Figure 14-9a (see Figure 4-8 for the corresponding EER diagram). A generalization path is shown as a solid line from the subclass to the superclass, with a hollow triangle at the end of, and pointing toward, the superclass. You can show a group of generalization paths for a given superclass as a tree with multiple branches connecting the individual subclasses, and a shared segment with a hollow triangle pointing toward the superclass. In Figure 14-9b (corresponding to Figure 4-3), for instance, we have combined the generalization paths from Outpatient to Patient, and from Resident Patient to Patient, into a shared segment with a triangle pointing toward Patient. We also specify that this generalization is dynamic, meaning that an object may change subtypes.

Notice that in Figure 14-9b the *Patient* class is in italics, implying that it is an abstract class. An **abstract class** is a class that has no direct instances, but whose descendants may have direct instances (Booch, 1994; Rumbaugh et al., 1991). (Note: You can additionally write the word *abstract* within braces just below the class name. This is especially useful when you generate a class diagram by hand.) A class that can have direct instances (e.g., Outpatient or Resident Patient) is called a **concrete class**. In this example, therefore, Outpatient and Resident Patient can have direct instances, but *Patient* cannot have any direct instances of its own.

In Figures 14-9a and 14-9b, the words "complete," "incomplete," and "disjoint" have been placed within braces, next to the generalization. They indicate semantic constraints among the subclasses (complete corresponds to total specialization in the EER notation, whereas incomplete corresponds to partial specialization). Any of the following UML keywords for contraints may be used: overlapping, disjoint, complete, and incomplete, corresponding to overlapping, disjoint, total, and partial from EER modeling.

In Figure 14-11, we represent both graduate and undergraduate students in a model developed for student billing. The calc-tuition operation computes the tuition a student has to pay; this sum depends on the tuition per credit hour (tuitionPerCred), the courses taken, and the number of credit hours (creditHrs) for each of those courses. The tuition per credit hour, in turn, depends on whether the student is a

Abstract class: A class that has no direct instances, but whose descendants may have direct instances.

Concrete class: A class that can have direct instances.

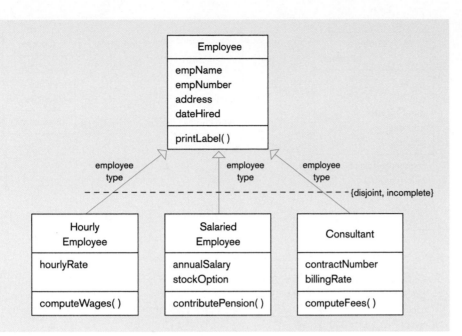

Figure 14-9
Examples of generalization, inheritance, and constraints
(a) Employee superclass with three subclasses

(b) Abstract Patient class with two concrete subclasses

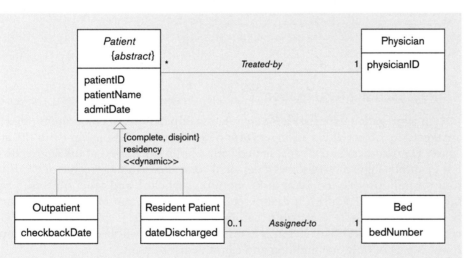

graduate or an undergraduate student. In this example, that amount is $300 for all graduate students and $250 for all undergraduate students. To denote that, we have underlined the tuitionPerCred attribute in each of the two subclasses, along with its value. Such an attribute is called a **class-scope attribute**, which specifies a value common to an entire class, rather than a specific value for an instance (Rumbaugh et al., 1991).

It is important to note that although the Graduate Student and Undergraduate Student classes share the same calc-tuition operation, they might implement the operation in quite different ways. For example, the method that implements the operation for a graduate student might add a special graduate fee for each course the student takes. The fact that the same operation may apply to two or more classes in different ways is known as polymorphism, a key concept in object-oriented systems. The enrollment operation in Figure 14-11 illustrates another example of **polymorphism**. While the enrollment operation within Course Offering computes the enrollment for a particular course offering or section, an operation with the same name within Course computes the combined enrollment for all sections of a given course.

Class-scope attribute: An attribute of a class that specifies a value common to an entire class, rather than a specific value for an instance.

Polymorphism: The same operation may apply to two or more classes in different ways.

Figure 14-11
Polymorphism, abstract operation,
class-scope attribute, and ordering

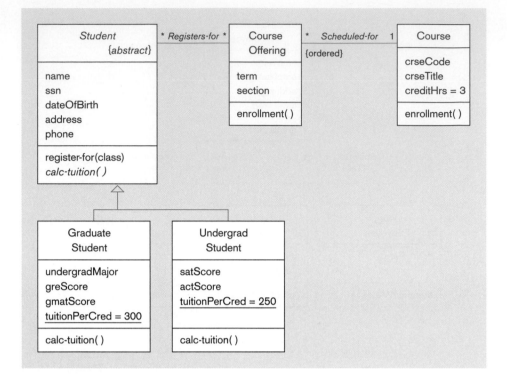

Representing Aggregation

Aggregation: A part-of relationship between a component object and an aggregate object.

An **aggregation** expresses a *Part-of* relationship between a component object and an aggregate object. It is a stronger form of association relationship (with the added "part-of" semantics) and is represented with a hollow diamond at the aggregate end. For example, Figure 14-14 shows a personal computer as an aggregate of CPU (up to four for multiprocessors), hard disks, monitor, keyboard, and other objects (a typical bill-of-materials structure). It is also possible for component objects to exist without being part of a whole (e.g., there can be a Monitor that is not part of any PC). In **composition**, a part object belongs to one and only one whole object; for example, a room is part of only one building and cannot exist by itself.

Composition: A part object that belongs to only one whole object and that lives and dies with the whole object.

Figure 14-14
Example of aggregation

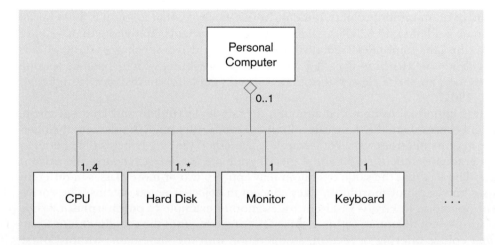

CHAPTER REVIEW

For coverage of key terms, review questions, problems and exercises, and field questions, see the complete chapter on the textbook's Web site. The following are the full set of references for the chapter followed by information about additional sources of information on object data modeling.

References

Booch, G. 1994. *Object-Oriented Analysis and Design with Applications,* 2nd ed. Redwood City, CA: Benjamin/Cummings.

Coad, P., and E. Yourdon. 1991. *Object-Oriented Design.* Upper Saddle River, NJ: Prentice Hall.

Fowler, M. 2000. *UML Distilled: A Brief Guide to the Standard Object Modeling Language,* 2nd ed. Reading, MA: Addison Wesley Longman.

George, J., D. Batra, J. Valacich, and J. Hoffer. 2005. *Object Oriented Systems Analysis and Design.* Upper Saddle River, NJ: Prentice Hall.

Hoffer, J., J. George, and J. Valacich. 2005. *Modern Systems Analysis and Design.* Upper Saddle River, NJ: Prentice Hall.

Jacobson, I., M. Christerson, P. Jonsson, and G. Overgaard. 1992. *Object-Oriented Software Engineering: A Use Case Driven Approach.* Reading, MA: Addison-Wesley.

Quatrani, T. 2000. *Visual Modeling with Rational Rose 2000 and UML.* Upper Saddle River, NJ: Addison-Wesley.

Rumbaugh, J., M. Blaha, W. Premerlani, F. Eddy, and W. Lorensen. 1991. *Object-Oriented Modeling and Design.* Upper Saddle River, NJ: Prentice Hall.

UML Document Set. 1997. Version 1.0 (January). Santa Clara, CA: Rational Software Corp.

UML Notation Guide. 1997. Version 1.0 (January). Santa Clara, CA: Rational Software Corp.

Further Reading

Eriksson, H., and M. Penker. 1998. *UML Toolkit.* New York: Wiley.

Linthicum, D. 1996. "Objects Meet Data." *DBMS* 9,9 (September): 72–78.

See also Appendix D.

Web Resources

www.omg.org This is the Web site of the Object Management Group, a leading industry association concerned with object-oriented analysis and design.

Chapter 15

Overview: Object-Oriented

Database Development

LEARNING OBJECTIVES

After studying this chapter, you should be able to:

- Concisely define each of the following key terms: **atomic literal, collection literal, set, bag, list, array, dictionary, structured literal,** and **extent.**
- Create logical object-oriented database schemas using the object definition language (ODL).
- Transform conceptual UML class diagrams to logical ODL schemas by mapping classes (abstract and concrete), attributes, operations (abstract and concrete), association relationships (one-to-one, one-to-many, and many-to-many), and generalization relationships.
- Identify the type specifications for attributes, operation arguments, and operation returns.
- Create objects and specify attribute values for those objects.
- Understand the steps involved in implementing object-oriented databases.
- Understand the syntax and semantics of the object query language (OQL).
- Use OQL commands to formulate various types of queries.
- Gain an understanding of the types of applications to which object-oriented databases have been applied.

A complete version of this chapter is available on the textbook's Web site. The following is a brief overview.

OVERVIEW

In Chapter 14, we introduced you to object-oriented data modeling. You learned how to conceptually model a database using UML class diagrams. In this chapter, we will describe how such conceptual object-oriented models can be transformed into logical schemas that can be directly implemented using an object database management system (ODBMS).

Although relational databases are effective for traditional business applications, they have severe limitations (in the amount of programming required and DBMS performance) when it comes to storing and manipulating complex data and relationships. In this chapter, we will show how to implement applications within an object-oriented database environment. In

Appendix D, you will learn about object-relational databases, which are the most popular way object-oriented principles are implemented in DBMSs.

In this chapter, we will adopt the Object Model proposed by the Object Database Management Group (ODMG) (see **www.odmg.org**) for defining and querying an object-oriented database (OODB). For developing logical schemas, we will specifically use the object definition language (ODL), and for data manipulation language (DML) we will use the object query language (OQL).

Object Definition Language

In ODL, a class is specified using the class keyword, and an attribute is specified using the *attribute* keyword. Student and Course classes might be defined as follows:

```
class Student {
    attribute string name;
    attribute Date dateOfBirth;
    attribute string address;
    attribute string phone;
// plus relationship and operations . . .
};
class Course {
    attribute string crse_code;
    attribute string crse_title;
    attribute short credit_hrs;
// plus relationships and operation . . .
};
```

An attribute's value is either a literal or an *object identifier*. As we discussed in Chapter 14, each object has a unique identifier. Because an object retains its identifier over its lifetime, the object remains the same despite changes in its state. In contrast, literals do not have identifiers and, therefore, cannot be individually referenced like objects can. Literals are embedded inside objects. You can think of literal values as constants. For example, the string Mary Jones, the character C, and the integer 20 are all literal values.

In addition to the standard data types provided by ODL, you can define structures yourself by using the *struct* keyword. For example, you can define a structure called Address that consists of four components—street_address, city, state, and zip—all of which are string attributes.

```
struct Address {
    string street_address;
    string city;
    string state;
    string zip;
};
```

In ODL, you specify an operation using parentheses after its name. The ODL definition for Student is now as follows:

```
class Student {
    attribute string name;
    attribute Date dateOfBirth;
//user-defined structured attributes
    attribute Address address;
    attribute Phone phone;
//plus relationship
//operations
    short age( );
    float gpa( );
    boolean register_for(string crse, short sec, string term);
};
```

We have defined above three operations age, gpa, and register_for. The first two are query operations. The register_for operation is an update operation that registers a student for a section (sec) of a course (crse) in a given term. Each of these arguments, shown within parentheses, is preceded by its type. We also have to specify the return type for each operation. For example, the return types for age and gpa are short (short integer) and float (real number), respectively. The return type for the register_for operation is boolean (true or false), indicating if the registration was successfully completed or not. If the operation does not return any value, the return type is declared as void.

Each type of object has certain predefined operations. For example, a set object has a predefined "is_subset_of" operation, and a data object (attribute) has a predefined boolean operation "days_in_year." See Cattell et al. (2000) for a thorough coverage of predefined object operations.

The ODMG Object Model supports only unary and binary relationships. For example, we name a relationship between Student and Course Offering *Takes* when traversing from the former to the latter and *Taken by* when traversing in the reverse direction. We use the ODL keyword relationship to specify a relationship.

```
class Student {
    attribute string name;
    attribute Date dateOfBirth;
    attribute Address address;
    attribute Phone phone;
// relationship between Student and CourseOffering
    relationship set <CourseOffering> takes inverse CourseOffering::taken_by;
// operations
    short age( );
    float gpa( );
    boolean register_for(string crse, short sec, string term);
};
```

Within the Student class, we have defined the "takes" relationship, using the relationship keyword. The name of the relationship is preceded by the class the relationship targets: CourseOffering. Because a student can take multiple course offerings, we have used the keyword "set" to indicate that a Student object is related to a set of CourseOffering objects (and the set is unordered). This relationship specification represents the traversal path from Student to CourseOffering.

The ODMG Object Model requires that a relationship be specified in both directions. In ODL, the *inverse* keyword is used to specify the relationship in the reverse direction. The inverse of "takes" is "taken_by" from CourseOffering to Student. In the class definition for Student, we have named this traversal path (taken_by), preceded by the name of the class from where the path originates (CourseOffering), along with a double colon (::). In the class definition for CourseOffering shown below, the relationship is specified as "taken_by," with the inverse being "takes" from Student. Because a course offering can be taken by many students, the relationship links a set of Student objects to a given CourseOffering object. For a many-to-many relationship such as this, therefore, you must specify a collection (set, list, bag, or array) of objects on both sides.

```
class CourseOffering {
    attribute string term;
    attribute enum section {1, 2, 3, 4, 5, 6, 7, 8};
// many-to-many relationship between CourseOffering and Student
    relationship set <Student> taken_by inverse Student::takes;
// one-to-many relationship between CourseOffering and Course
    relationship Course belongs_to inverse Course::offers;
// operation
    short enrollment( );
};
```

Many-to-many relationships and multivalued attributes may also be defined in ODL; see the complete chapter on the textbook Web site for illustrations.

ODL allows you to represent generalization relationships using the *extends* keyword. Suppose three subclasses—Hourly Employee, Salaried Employee, and Consultant—are generalized into a superclass called Employee. The ODL schema corresponding to the class diagram might be as follows:

```
class Employee {
(extent employees)
   attribute short empName;
   attribute string empNumber;
   attribute Address address;
   attribute Date dateHired;
   void printLabel( );
};
class HourlyEmployee extends Employee {
(extent hrly_emps)
   attribute float hourlyRate;
   float computeWages( );
};
class SalariedEmployee extends Employee {
(extent salaried_emps)
   attribute float annualSalary;
   attribute boolean stockOptions;
   void contributePension( );
};
class Consultant extends Employee {
(extent consultants)
   attribute short contractNumber;
   attribute float billingRate;
   float computeFees( );
};
```

The subclasses HourlyEmployee, SalariedEmployee, and Consultant extend the more general Employee class by introducing new features. For example, Hourly-Employee has two special features, hourlyRate and computeWages, in addition to the common set of features inherited from Employee. All the classes, including Employee, are concrete, implying that they can have direct instances. Employee is a concrete class because the subclasses are incomplete.

Creating Object Instances

When a new instance of a class is created, a unique object identifier is assigned. You may specify an object identifier with one or more unique tag names. Suppose you want to create a new student object and initialize some of its attributes.

Cheryl **student** (**name:** "Cheryl Davis", **dateOfBirth:** 4/5/77);

This creates a new student object with a tag name of Cheryl and initializes the values of two attributes.

For a multivalued attribute, you can specify a set of values. For example, you can specify the skills for an employee called Dan Bellon as follows:

Dan **employee** (**emp_id:** 3678, **name:** "Dan Bellon",
skills: {"Database design", "OO Modeling"});

Establishing links between objects for a given relationship is also easy. Suppose you want to store the fact that Cheryl took three courses in fall 1999. You can write

Cheryl **student** (**takes:** {OOAD99F, Telecom99F, Java99F});

where OOAD99F, Telecom99F, and Java99F are tag names for three course-offering objects. This definition creates three links for the "takes" relationship, from the object tagged Cheryl to each of the course offering objects.

Consider another example. To assign Dan to the TQM project, we write

assignment (**start_date:** 2/15/2001, **allocated_to:** Dan, for TQM);

Notice that we have not specified a tag name for the assignment object. Such objects will be identified by the system-generated object identifiers. The assignment object has a link to an employee object (Dan) and another link to a project object (TQM).

When an object is created, it is assigned a lifetime, either transient or persistent. A transient object exists only while some program or session is in operation. A persistent object exists until it is explicitly deleted. Database objects are almost always persistent.

Object Query Language

In OQL you can write a simple query such as

Jack.dateOfBirth

. . . which returns Jack's birth date, a literal value, or

Jack.address

. . . which returns a structure with values for street address, city, state, and zip. If instead we want to simply find in which city Jack resides, we can write

Jack.address.city

Like SQL, OQL uses a select-from-where structure to write more complex queries. Suppose we want to find the title and credit hours for a course, MBA 664. Parallel to SQL, those attributes are specified in the select clause, and the *extent* of the class that has those attributes is specified in the from clause. In the where clause, we specify the condition that has to be satisfied. For example,

```
select c.crse_title, c.credit_hrs
from courses c
where c.crse_code = "MBA 664"
```

Because we are dealing with only one extent, we could have left out the variable c without any loss in clarity. However, as with SQL, if you are dealing with multiple classes that have common attributes, you must bind the extents to variables so that the system can unambiguously identify the classes for the selected attributes. The result of this query is a bag with two attributes.

We can invoke operations in an OQL query similar to the way we specify attributes. For example, to find the age of John Marsh, a student, we invoke the age operation in the select clause.

```
select s.age
from students s
where s.name = "John Marsh"
```

Or, the query

```
select s
from students s
where s.gpa >= 3.0
```

. . . returns a collection (bag) of student objects for which the gpa is greater than or equal to 3.0. Notice that we have used the gpa operation in the where clause.

In an OQL query, you can join classes in the where clause as in SQL. This is necessary when the relationship that is the basis for the join has not been defined in the object data model. When the relationship has been defined, you can traverse the paths for the relationships defined in the schema. The following query finds the course codes of all courses that were offered in fall 2005.

```
select distinct y.crse_code
from courseofferings x,
x.belongs_to y
where x.term = "Fall 2005"
```

You can use a select statement within a select statement (subqueries). To select course codes, course titles, and course offerings for which the enrollment is less than twenty, you can write the following OQL command:

```
select distinct struct (code: c.crse_code, title: c_crse_title,
    (select x
    from c.offers x
    where x.enrollment < 20 ))
    from courses c
```

We have illustrated in this section only a subset of the capabilities of OQL. See the complete chapter on the textbook Web site as well as Cattell et al. (2000) and Chaudhri and Zicari (2001) for more standard OQL features and how OQL is implemented in various ODBMSs.

CHAPTER REVIEW

For coverage of key terms, review questions, problems and exercises, and field questions, see the complete chapter on the textbook's Web site. The following are the full set of references for the chapter followed by information about additional sources of information on object data modeling.

References

Bertino, E., and L. Martino. 1993. *Object-Oriented Database Systems: Concepts and Architectures.* Wokingham, England: Addison-Wesley.

Cattell, R. G. G., D. Barry, D. Bartels, M. Berler, J. Eastman, S. Gamerman, D. Jordan, A. Springer, H. Strickland, and D. Wade. (Eds.) 2000. *The Object Database Standard: ODMG 3.0.* San Francisco: Morgan Kaufmann.

Chaudhri, A. B., and R. Zicari. 2001. *Succeeding with Object Databases.* New York: Wiley.

King, N. H. 1997. "Object DBMSs: Now or Never." *DBMS* 10,7 (July): 42–99.

Watterson, K. 1998. "When It Comes to Choosing a Database, the Object Is Value." *Datamation* 44,1 (December–January): 100–107.

Further Reading

Atkinson, M, F. Bacnilhon, D. DeWitt, K. Dittich, D. Maier, and S. Zdonik. 1995. " The Object-Oriented Database System Manifesto." Available at **http://www.cs.cmu.edu/People/clamen/ OODBMS/Manifesto/htManifesto/Manifesto.html.**

Leavitt Communications. 2003. "Whatever Happened to Object-Oriented Databases." Available at **www.leavcom.com/db_08_00. htm.**

Web Resources

www.cai.com/products/jasmine/analyst/idc/14821Eat.htm This bulletin discusses the changes and innovations currently shaping database technology and related products. It includes a summary of 1996 when a trend toward multimedia-type database product rollouts and a new extended version of relational database technology emerged that was dubbed the "object relational" database management system (ORDBMS). The ORDBMS technology (see Appendix D) is compared with the relational databases from which ORDBMS is evolving and with the pure object databases that they will never replace. What challenges did you face in completing this task?

A p p e n d i x   A

Data Modeling Tools and Notation

Chapters 3 and 4 present several common notations for representing data models. Depending on the software tool available for depicting a data model, your ability to replicate these notations will vary. Just as business rules and policies are not universal, neither are the symbols and notation used in the various data modeling tools. Each uses different graphical constructs and methodologies that may or may not be able to convey the meaning of a particular business rule.

This appendix is intended to help you compare the book's notations with your modeling tool's notation. Four commonly used tools are covered: Computer Associates' AllFusion ERwin Data Modeler 4.1 SP1, Oracle Designer 10g, Sybase PowerDesigner 11.1, and Visio Pro 2003. Table A-1a and Table A-1b chart samples of the notation used in each tool for entities, relationships, attributes, rules, constraints, and so forth. In addition, a screen capture for each tool is included in Figures A-3 through A-6, depicting each tool's interface.

Figure 3-22, a data modeling diagram for Pine Valley Furniture Company (PVFC), is the basis for the examples pictured in this appendix. That figure shows the data model drawn from the narrative of PVFC business rules included in Chapter 3, using the text's notation system. Figure 3-22 has been drawn using Visio Pro matched to Hoffer, Prescott, McFadden notation as closely as possible. Table A-1 allows a comparison of this notation with that available in the four software tools.

COMPARING E-R MODELING CONVENTIONS

As can be seen from Table A-1, modeling tools differ significantly in the notation available to create a data model. While not intended as an in-depth comparison of the various tools, the following explanation provides a means to analyze the tools' differences using the PVFC data model depicted in Figure 3-22. Pay particular attention to differences in depicting many-to-many relationships, cardinalities and/or optionalities, foreign keys, and supertype/subtype relationships. Each tool offers multiple sets of notation. We have chosen entity/relationship sets of symbols for each tool. We have included the symbols as the tool will draw them, whereas Figure 3-22, drawn in Visio, includes modifications to match Hoffer, Prescott, McFadden notation. Note, in particular, how associative entities are drawn; the foreign key relationships are included.

Visio Professional 2003 Notation

The Professional version of Visio includes a database diagramming tool for modeling a conceptual or physical diagram. Visio provides three database modeling

Table A-1 A Comparison of Hoffer, Prescott, and McFadden Modeling Notation with Four Software Tools (Continues)

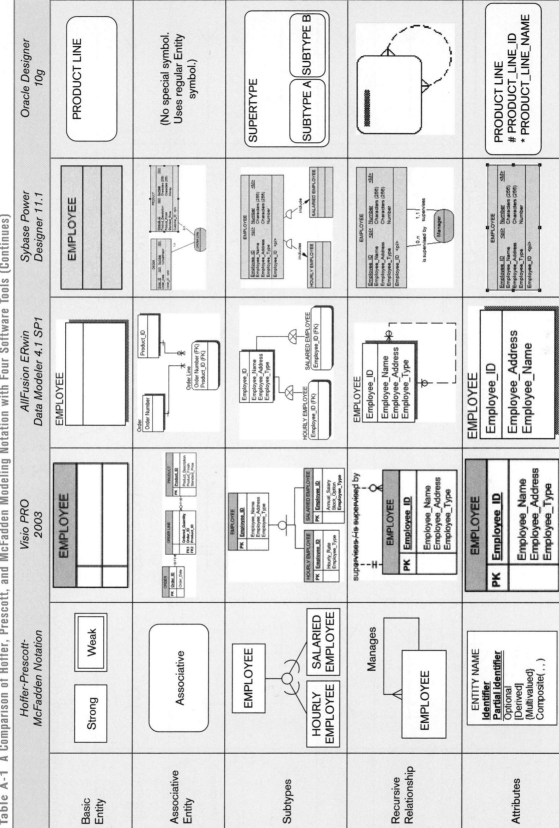

(a) Common modeling tools, notations

563

	Hoffer-Prescott-McFadden Notation	Visio PRO 2003	AllFusion ERwin Data Modeler 4.1	Sybase Power Designer 11.1	Oracle Designer 10g
1:1		(Not available without cardinality)	(Not available without cardinality)	0,1 0,1	
1:M		(Not available without cardinality)	(Not available without cardinality)	0,1 0,n	
M:N		(Not allowed)		0,n 0,n	
Mandatory 1:1			1	Not available in E/R notation symbols. Use iDEF1X.	
Mandatory 1:M			P	Not available in E/R notation symbols. Use iDEF1X.	
Optional 1:M				0,1 0,n	

Table A-1 (Continued)

(b) Common modeling tools' cardinality/optionality notations templates. Selecting Database Model Diagram for a new data model allows a further choice of relational or IDEF1X symbols. Both of these choices allow reverse engineering of existing physical databases. The two other template choices are Express-G and ORM, which allow you to use the notation associated with each of those methods, and do not provide for reverse engineering unless you are using Visio Enterprise. Each template may be customized to indicate primary key (PK), foreign keys (FK), secondary indexes, nonkey fields, data types, and so on. You can also elect to display the primary key fields at the top of each entity or in their actual physical order. This text uses the relational template.

Entities All entities are depicted as square rectangles with optional horizontal and vertical lines used to partition entity information. In Figure A-1, associative entities, such as Produced In are named in mixed case to distinguish them from other entities, which are named using capital letters. Keys (primary, alt, foreign), nonkey attributes, referential integrity, and so on can be optionally displayed within the entity box. Subtype/supertype connectors are available.

Relationships Lines can be labeled in one or both directions or neither, and the relationship types are either identifying (solid line) or nonidentifying (dashed line). Cardinality and optionality notation differ according to the symbol set chosen, relational or IDEF1X. Notation samples for the relational symbol set chosen for our diagram can be seen in Table A-1b. This tool provides a helpful "range" option where a minimum and a maximum value can also be set for cardinality. When identifying or nonidentifying relationships are established, keys are automatically migrated above or below, respectively, the entity's horizontal separator line. The recursive Supervises relationship shows the business rule that a supervisor may supervise none or any number of employees, but cannot show that the president has no supervisor, only that each employee has exactly one supervisor. A many-to-many relationship between two entities cannot be established—a new (associative) entity must be added to resolve it. The many and varied line connectors provided by the tool can be used to draw a many-to-many relationship, but these connector objects do not establish the functional relationship within the tool.

AllFusion ERwin Data Modeler 4.1 SP1 Notation

Here, for physical or logical modeling, one has the choice among IDEF1X, IE (Information Engineering), or DM (Dimensional Modeling) notation. The examples used here demonstrate IE.

Entities An independent entity is represented as a box with a horizontal line and square corners. If an entity is a child (weak) entity in an identifying relationship, it appears as a dependent entity—a box with rounded corners. Associative entity symbols are also represented this way. ERwin determines the entity type based on the relationship in which it is involved. For example, when you initially place an entity in a model, it displays as an independent entity. When you connect it to another entity using a relationship, ERwin determines if the entity is independent or dependent based on the relationship type selected.

Relationships ERwin represents a relationship as a solid or dashed line connecting two entities. Depending on the notation you choose, the symbols at either end of the line may change. Cardinality options are flexible and may be specified unambiguously. A parent may be connected to "Zero, One, or More," signified by a blank space; "One or More," signified by a P; "Zero or One," signified by a Z; or "Exactly," some number of instances, which will appear on the ERD. Many-to-many relationships can be depicted or the user may opt to automatically resolve them. Figure A-2 illustrates several many-to-many relationships that correspond to the PVFC diagram in Figure 3-22. We opted to allow ERwin to automatically resolve one

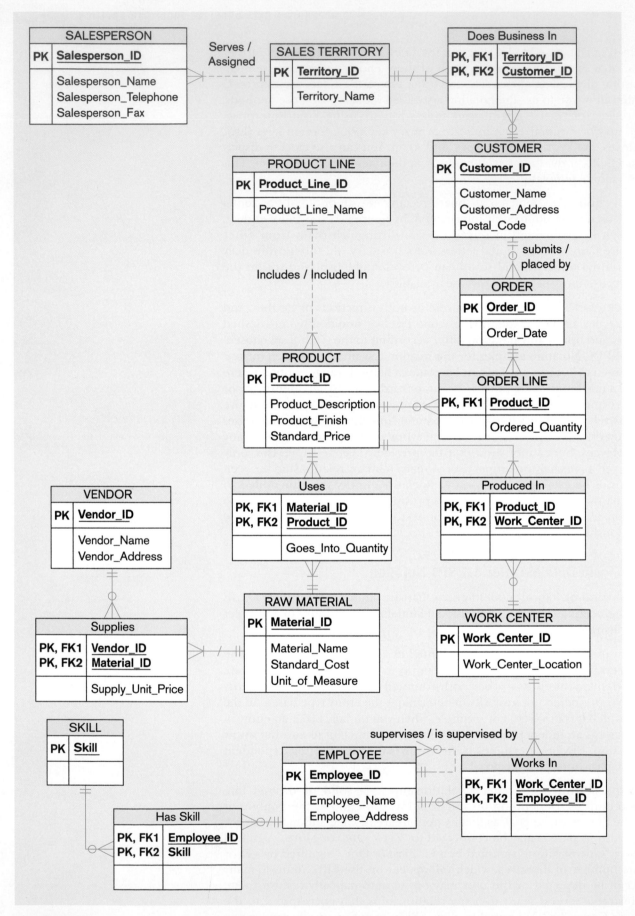

Figure A-1
Visio PRO 2003 model

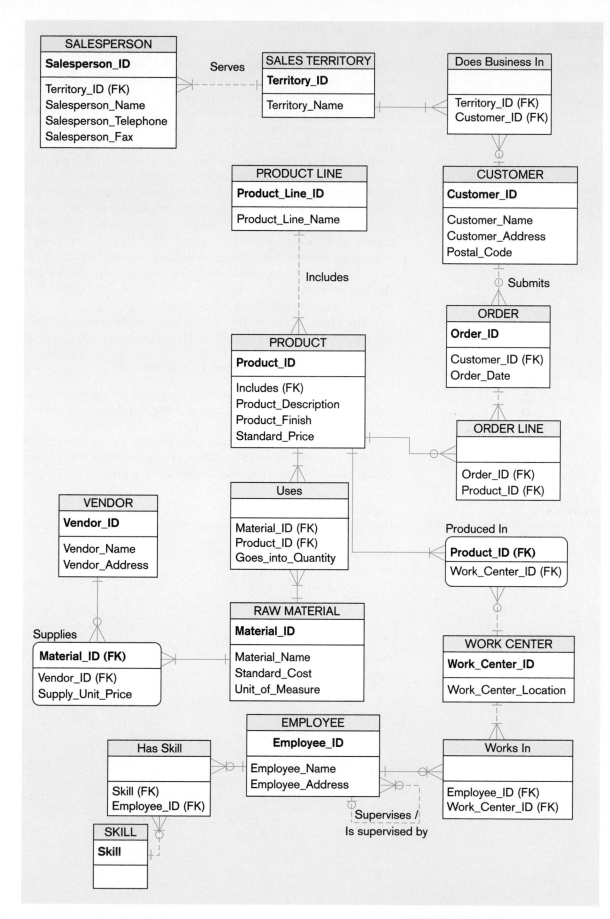

Figure A-2
AllFusion ERwin Data Modeler 4.1
SP1 model

of these relationships for illustrative purposes—the many-to-many "supplies" relationship between Vendor and Raw Materials. The user selects a "Show Association Entity" option on the relationship line which then automatically eliminates the many-to-many relationship, establishes new ones with cardinality and optionality notations, creates the associative entity, and allows the "Supply Unit Price" attribute for the "supplies" relationship to be displayed in the diagram. The recursive nonidentifying relationship, where parent and child are shown as the same entity, shows that an Employee (a Supervisor) may supervise many employees, but not all employees are supervisors. The notation also indicates that nulls are allowed, which shows that a supervisor may have no employees and an employee (the president) may have no supervisor. Keys migrate automatically when relationships are established, and foreign keys are notated "FK." In an identifying relationship, the FK migrates above the horizontal line in the entity and becomes part of the primary key of the child entity. In a nonidentifying relationship, the foreign key migrates below the line and becomes a nonkey attribute in the child entity. In ERwin, a dashed line represents a nonidentifying relationship.

The chart captured from ERwin's online help and shown in Figure A-3 depicts the range of cardinality symbols that may be used from this product.

Sybase Power Designer 11.1 Notation

Power Designer projects are contained within a workspace that may be customized and includes a hierarchy of folders and models. Links to model files, report files, and external files are also stored in the workspace. Where a data modeler is working on multiple projects or on a part of a project with different requirements, multiple workspaces may be defined as needed. Each is kept locally and is reusable. It is only possible to work in one workspace at a time.

Figure A-3
ERwin cardinality/optionality symbols

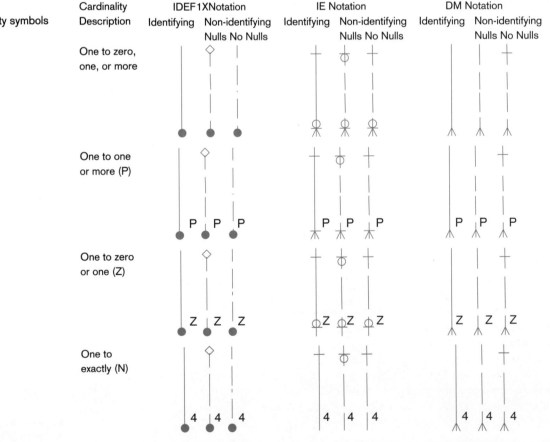

The examples in this appendix use the Conceptual Data Model graphics. Any of the following modeling conventions may be chosen when using Power Designer:

- The Conceptual Data Model (CDM)
- The Business Process Model (BPM)
- The Free Model (FEM)
- The Object-Oriented Model (OOM)
- The Physical Data Model (PDM)
- The XML Model (XSM)
- The Information Liquidity Model (ILM)
- The Requirements Model (RQM)

Entities   The amount of detail that is displayed in the data model is selected by the modeler and may include primary identifiers, a predetermined number of attributes, data type, optionality, and/or domain. A double-click of the entity allows access to the entity's property sheet. Properties shown include name, technical code name, a comment field that contains a descriptive label if desired, stereotype (subclassification of entity), estimated number of occurrences, and the possibility of generating a table in the physical data model. Additional entity properties include attributes, identifiers, and rules. Each of these properties has its own property sheet.

Relationships   Power Designer uses a solid line between entities to establish any relationship. Crows foot notation is used to establish cardinality and the circle and line establish optionality, similar to the Hoffer notation. Dashed lines are not available in CDM. It is possible to model a many-to-many relationship without breaking it down to include the associative entity. If desired, however, an associative entity may be modeled and displayed. Recursive relationships may be modeled easily, and subtypes may also be presented.

Oracle Designer Notation

Diagrams drawn using Oracle Designer's Entity Relationship Diagrammer tool can be set to show only the entity names, the entity names *and* the primary key, or the entity names *and* all of the attribute labels.

Entities   No specific symbols exist for the different entity types, including associative entities and supertypes or subtypes. All entities are depicted as rounded rectangles, and attributes can be displayed within the box. Unique identifiers are preceded by a "#" sign and must be mandatory; mandatory attributes are tagged with "*," whereas optional attributes are tagged with "7."

Relationships   Lines must be labeled in *both* directions, not just one direction, and are challenging to manipulate and align. Cardinality is read by picking up the cardinality sign attached to the other entity. Thus, a Customer *may* place an order or not, but when an order is placed, it must be related to a particular customer. Looking at the EMPLOYEE entity, the recursive supervisory relationship is depicted by the "pig's ear" attached to the entity. It shows that an Employee *may* supervise one or more employees and that an employee *must* be supervised by one employee, or supervisor. It is ambiguous as to whether the multiple cardinality is zero, one, or many.

When working with Oracle Designer, it is important to sketch your data model carefully and completely before attempting to use the tool. Editing the model can be challenging, and deleting an object from the diagram does not automatically delete it from the Repository.

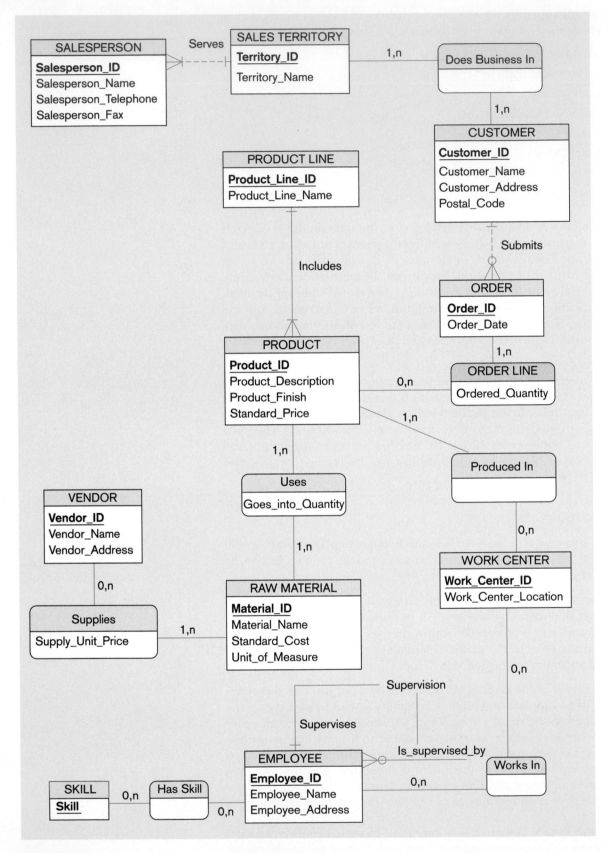

Figure A-4
Sybase Power Designer 11.1 model

COMPARISON OF TOOL INTERFACES AND E-R DIAGRAMS

For each of the software modeling tools included in Table A-1, the data model for Figure 3-22 is included here. These figures should give you a better idea of what the symbol notation looks like in actual use. Figure A-1 was drawn using Visio PRO 2003 and its relational template. Figure A-2 was drawn using AllFusion ERwin Data Modeler 4.1 SP1 and the Information Engineering (IE) option. Foreign keys are included in this diagram. Figure A-4 shows Sybase PowerDesigner 11.1 using the Conceptual Data Model template. Figure A-5 was drawn using Oracle Designer 10g with the Information Engineering (IE) option selected.

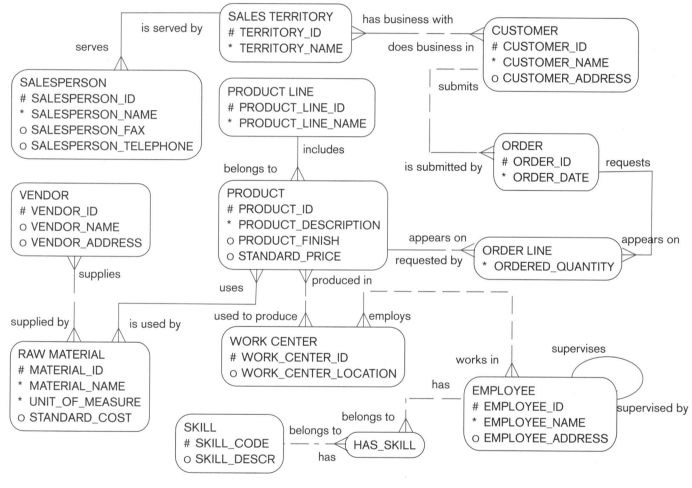

Figure A-5
Oracle Designer 10g model

Appendix B

Advanced Normal Forms

In Chapter 5, we introduced the topic of normalization and described first through third normal forms in detail. Relations in third normal form (3NF) are sufficient for most practical database applications. However, 3NF does not guarantee that all anomalies have been removed. As indicated in Chapter 5, several additional normal forms are designed to remove these anomalies: Boyce-Codd normal form, fourth normal form, and fifth normal form (see Figure 5-22). We describe Boyce-Codd normal form and fourth normal form in this appendix.

BOYCE-CODD NORMAL FORM

When a relation has more than one candidate key, anomalies may result even though that relation is in 3NF. Foar example, consider the STUDENT_ADVISOR relation shown in Figure B-1. This relation has the following attributes: SID (student ID), Major, Advisor, and Maj_GPA. Sample data for this relation are shown in Figure B-1a, and the functional dependencies are shown in Figure B-1b.

Figure B-1
Relation in 3NF, but not in BCNF
(a) Relation with sample data

STUDENT_ADVISOR

SID	Major	Advisor	Maj_GPA
123	Physics	Hawking	4.0
123	Music	Mahler	3.3
456	Literature	Michener	3.2
789	Music	Bach	3.7
678	Physics	Hawking	3.5

(b) Functional dependencies in STUDENT_ADVISOR

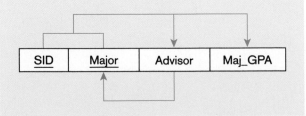

As shown in Figure B-1b, the primary key for this relation is the composite key consisting of SID and Major. Thus, the two attributes Advisor and Maj_GPA are functionally dependent on this key. This reflects the constraint that although a given student may have more than one major, for each major a student has exactly one advisor and one GPA.

There is a second functional dependency in this relation: Major is functionally dependent on Advisor. That is, each advisor advises in exactly one major. Notice that this is not a transitive dependency. In Chapter 5, we defined a transitive dependency as a functional dependency between two nonkey attributes. In contrast, in this example a key attribute (Major) is functionally dependent on a nonkey attribute (Advisor).

Anomalies in STUDENT_ADVISOR

The STUDENT_ADVISOR relation is clearly in 3NF, because there are no partial functional dependencies and no transitive dependencies. Nevertheless, because of the functional dependency between Major and Advisor, there are anomalies in this relation. Consider the following examples:

1. Suppose that in Physics the advisor Hawking is replaced by Einstein. This change must be made in two (or more) rows in the table (update anomaly).

2. Suppose we want to insert a row with the information that Babbage advises in Computer Science. This, of course, cannot be done until at least one student majoring in Computer Science is assigned Babbage as an advisor (insertion anomaly).

3. Finally, if student number 789 withdraws from school, we lose the information that Bach advises in Music (deletion anomaly).

Definition of Boyce-Codd Normal Form (BCNF)

The anomalies in STUDENT_ADVISOR result from the fact that there is a determinant (Advisor) that is not a candidate key in the relation. R. F. Boyce and E. F. Codd identified this deficiency and proposed a stronger definition of 3NF that remedies the problem. We say a relation is in **Boyce-Codd normal form (BCNF)** if and only if every determinant in the relation is a candidate key. STUDENT_ADVISOR is not in BCNF because although the attribute Advisor is a determinant, it is not a candidate key (only Major is functionally dependent on Advisor).

Boyce-Codd normal form (BCNF): A relation in which every determinant is a candidate key.

Converting a Relation to BCNF

A relation that is in 3NF (but not BCNF) can be converted to relations in BCNF using a simple two-step process. This process is shown in Figure B-2.

In the first step, the relation is modified so that the determinant in the relation that is not a candidate key becomes a component of the primary key of the revised relation. The attribute that is functionally dependent on that determinant becomes a nonkey attribute. This is a legitimate restructuring of the original relation because of the functional dependency.

The result of applying this rule to STUDENT_ADVISOR is shown in Figure B-2a. The determinant Advisor becomes part of the composite primary key. The attribute Major, which is functionally dependent on Advisor, becomes a nonkey attribute.

If you examine Figure B-2a, you will discover that the new relation has a partial functional dependency (Major is functionally dependent on Advisor, which is just one component of the primary key). Thus the new relation is in first (but not second) normal form.

The second step in the conversion process is to decompose the relation to eliminate the partial functional dependency, as we learned in Chapter 5. This results in two

Figure B-2
Converting a relation to BCNF relations
(a) Revised STUDENT_ADVISOR relation (2NF)

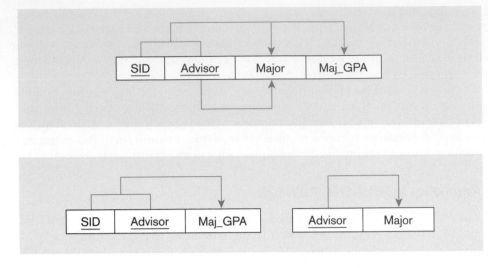

(b) Two relations in BCNF

(c) Relations with sample data

relations, as shown in Figure B-2b. These relations are in 3NF. In fact, the relations are also in BCNF, because there is only one candidate key (the primary key) in each relation. Thus, we see that if a relation has only one candidate key (which therefore becomes the primary key), then 3NF and BCNF are equivalent.

The two relations (now named STUDENT and ADVISOR) with sample data are shown in Figure B-2c. You should verify that these relations are free of the anomalies that were described for STUDENT_ADVISOR. You should also verify that you can recreate the STUDENT_ADVISOR relation by joining the two relations STUDENT and ADVISOR.

Another common situation in which BCNF is violated is when there are two (or more) overlapping candidate keys of the relation. Consider the relation in Figure B-3a. In this example, there are two candidate keys, (SID,COURSE_ID) and (SNAME,COURSE_ID), in which COURSE_ID appears in both candidate keys. The problem with this relationship is that we cannot record student data (SID and SNAME) unless the student has taken a course. Figure B-3b shows two possible solutions, each of which creates two relations that are in BCNF.

FOURTH NORMAL FORM

When a relation is in BCNF, there are no longer any anomalies that result from functional dependencies. However, there may still be anomalies that result from multivalued dependencies (defined below). For example, consider the user view

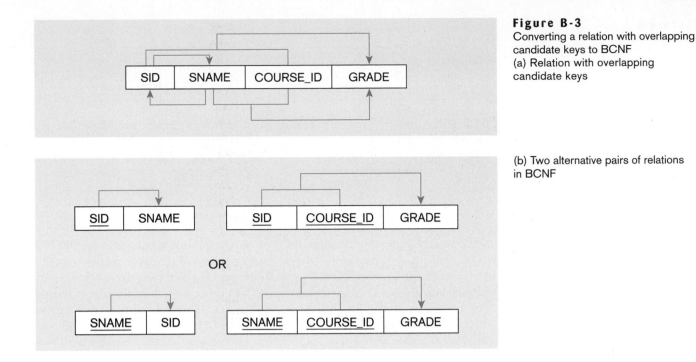

Figure B-3
Converting a relation with overlapping
candidate keys to BCNF
(a) Relation with overlapping
candidate keys

(b) Two alternative pairs of relations
in BCNF

shown in Figure B-4a. This user view shows for each course the instructors who teach that course and the textbooks that are used. (These appear as repeating groups in the view.) In this table view, the following assumptions hold:

1. Each course has a well-defined set of instructors (e.g., Management has three instructors).

2. Each course has a well-defined set of textbooks that are used (e.g., Finance has two textbooks).

3. The textbooks that are used for a given course are independent of the instructor for that course (e.g., the same two textbooks are used for Management regardless of which of the three instructors is teaching Management).

In Figure B-4b, this table view has been converted to a relation by filling in all of the empty cells. This relation (named OFFERING) is in first normal form. Thus, for

Figure B-4
Data with multivalued dependencies

COURSE STAFF AND BOOK ASSIGNMENTS

Course	Instructor	Textbook
Management	White Green Black	Drucker Peters
Finance	Gray	Jones Chang

(a) View of courses, instructors, and textbooks

OFFERING

Course	Instructor	Textbook
Management	White	Drucker
Management	White	Peters
Management	Green	Drucker
Management	Green	Peters
Management	Black	Drucker
Management	Black	Peters
Finance	Gray	Jones
Finance	Gray	Chang

(b) Relation in BCNF

Figure B-5
Relations in 4NF

TEACHER	
Course	Instructor
Management	White
Management	Green
Management	Black
Finance	Gray

TEXT	
Course	Textbook
Management	Drucker
Management	Peters
Finance	Jones
Finance	Chang

each course, all possible combinations of instructor and text appear in OFFERING. Notice that the primary key of this relation consists of all three attributes (Course, Instructor, and Textbook). Because there are no determinants other than the primary key, the relation is actually in BCNF. Yet it does contain much redundant data that can easily lead to update anomalies. For example, suppose that we want to add a third textbook (author: Middleton) to the Management course. This change would require the addition of three new rows to the relation in Figure B-4b, one for each Instructor (otherwise that text would apply to only certain instructors).

Multivalued Dependencies

Multivalued dependency: The type of dependency that exists when there are at least three attributes (e.g., A, B, and C) in a relation, with a well-defined set of B and C values for each A value, but those B and C values are independent of each other.

The type of dependency shown in this example is called a **multivalued dependency**, which exists when there are at least three attributes (e.g., A, B, and C) in a relation, and for each value of A there is a well-defined set of values of B and a well-defined set of values of C. However, the set of values of B is independent of set C, and vice versa.

To remove the multivalued dependency from a relation, we divide the relation into two new relations. Each of these tables contains two attributes that have a multi-valued relationship in the original relation. Figure B-5 shows the result of this decomposition for the OFFERING relation of Figure B-4b. Notice that the relation called TEACHER contains the Course and Instructor attributes, because for each course there is a well-defined set of instructors. Also, for the same reason, TEXT contains the attributes Course and Textbook. However, there is no relation containing the attributes Instructor and Course because these attributes are independent.

Fourth normal form (4NF): A relation in BCNF that contains no multivalued dependencies.

A relation is in **fourth normal form (4NF)** if it is in BCNF and contains no multivalued dependencies. You can easily verify that the two relations in Figure B-5 are in 4NF and are free of the anomalies described earlier. Also, you can verify that you can reconstruct the original relation (OFFERING) by joining these two relations. In addition, notice that there are fewer data in Figure B-5 than in Figure B-4b. For simplicity, assume that Course, Instructor, and Textbook are all of equal length. Because there are twenty-four cells of data in Figure B-4b and sixteen cells of data in Figure B-5, there is a space savings of 25 percent for the 4NF tables.

HIGHER NORMAL FORMS

At least two higher-level normal forms have been defined: fifth normal form (5NF) and domain-key normal form (DKNF). Fifth normal form deals with a property called "lossless joins." According to Elmasri and Navathe (2000), fifth normal form is not of practical significance because lossless joins occur very rarely and are difficult to detect. For this reason (and also because fifth normal form has a complex definition), we do not describe 5NF in this text.

Domain-key normal form is an attempt to define an "ultimate normal form" that takes into account all possible types of dependencies and constraints (Elmasri and Navathe, 2000). Although the definition of DKNF is quite simple, its practical value is minimal. For this reason, we do not describe DKNF in this text.

For more information concerning these two higher normal forms see Elmasri and Navathe (2000) and Dutka and Hanson (1989).

APPENDIX REVIEW

Key Terms

Boyce-Codd normal
  form (BCNF)

Fourth normal
  form (4NF)

Multivalued dependency

References

Dutka, A., and H. Hanson. 1989. *Fundamentals of Data Normalization.* Reading, MA: Addison-Wesley.

Elmasri, R., and S. Navathe. 2000. *Fundamentals of Database Systems,* 3rd ed. Reading, MA: Addison-Wesley.

Web Resources

http://www.bkent.net/Doc/simple5.htm A simple but understandable guide to first through fifth normal forms.

Data Structures

Data structures are the basic building blocks of any physical database architecture. No matter what file organization or DBMS you use, data structures are used to connect related pieces of data. Although many modern DBMSs hide the underlying data structures, the tuning of a physical database requires understanding the choices a database designer can make about data structures. This appendix addresses the fundamental elements of all data structures and overviews some common schemes for storing and locating physical elements of data.

POINTERS

A pointer was introduced in Chapter 6. As described in that chapter, a pointer is used generically as any reference to the address of another piece of data. In fact, there are three types of pointers, as illustrated in Figures C-1:

1. *Physical address pointer* Contains the actual, fully resolved disk address (device, cylinder, track, and block number) of the referenced data. A physical pointer is the fastest way to locate another piece of data, but it is also the most restrictive: If the address of the referenced data changes, all pointers to it must also be changed. Physical pointers are commonly used in legacy database applications with network and hierarchical database architectures.

2. *Relative address pointer* Contains the relative position (or "offset") of the associated data from some base, or starting, point. The relative address could be a byte position, a record, or a row number. A relative pointer has the advantage that when the whole data structure changes location, all relative references to that structure are preserved. Relative pointers are used in a wide variety of DBMSs; a common use is in indexes in which index keys are matched with row identifiers (a type of relative pointer) for the record(s) with that key value.

3. *Logical key pointer* Contains meaningful data about the associated data element. A logical pointer must be transformed into a physical or relative pointer by some table lookup, index search, or mathematical calculation to actually locate the referenced data. Foreign keys in a relational database are often logical key pointers.

Table C-1 summarizes the salient features of each of these three types of pointers. A database designer may be able to choose which type of pointer to use in different

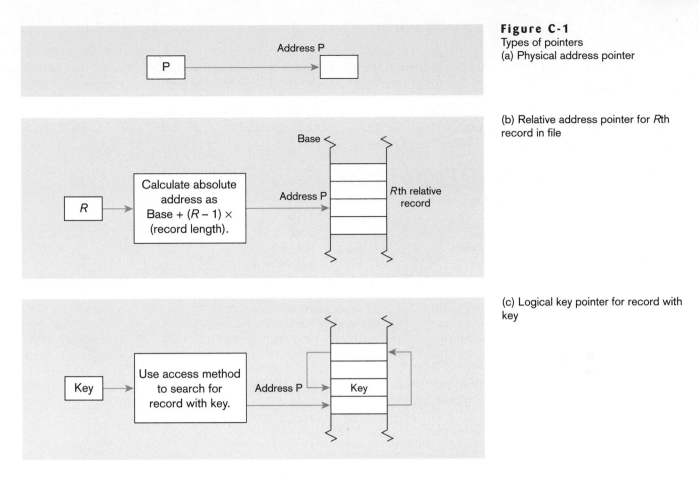

Figure C-1
Types of pointers
(a) Physical address pointer

(b) Relative address pointer for *R*th record in file

(c) Logical key pointer for record with key

situations in a database. For example, a foreign key in a relation can be implemented using any of these three types of pointers. In addition, when a database is damaged, a database administrator who understands what types of pointers are used may be able to rebuild broken links between database contents.

DATA STRUCTURE BUILDING BLOCKS

All data structures are built from several alternative basic building blocks for connecting and locating data. Connecting methods allow movement between related elements of data. Locating methods allow data within a structure to first be placed or stored and then found.

Table C-1 Comparison of Types of Pointers

Characteristic	Type of Pointer		
	Physical	**Relative**	**Logical**
Form	Actual secondary memory (disk) address	Offset from reference point (beginning of file)	Meaningful business data
Speed of access	Fastest	Medium	Slowest
Sensitivity to data movement	Most	Only sensitive to relative position changes	Least
Sensitivity to destruction	Vary	Vary	Often can be easily reconstructed
Space requirement	Fixed, usually short	Varies, usually shortest	Varies, usually longest

There are only two basic methods for connecting elements of data:

1. *Address-sequential connection* A successor (or related) element is placed and located in the physical memory space immediately following the current element (see Figures C-2a and C-2c). Address-sequential connections perform

Figure C-2
Basic location methods

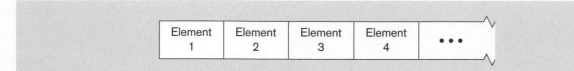

(a) Address sequential connection (sequential)

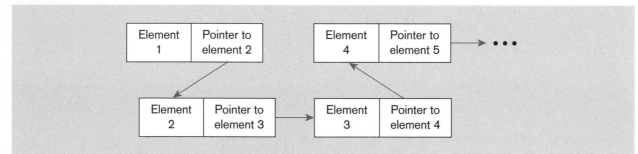

(b) Pointer sequential connection (simple chain or linear list)

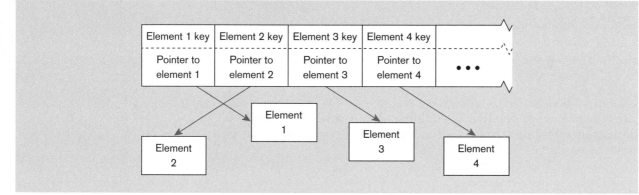

(c) Address sequential, data indirect connection (key index)

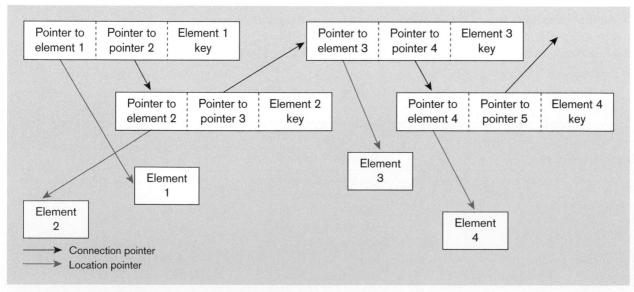

(d) Pointer sequential, data indirect connection (chain key index) best for reading the entire set of data or reading the next record in the stored sequence. In contrast, address-sequential structures are inefficient for retrieving arbitrary records and data update (add, delete, and change) operations. Update operations are also inefficient because the physical order must be constantly maintained, which usually requires immediate reorganization of the whole set of data.

2. *Pointer-sequential connection*   A pointer (or pointers) is stored with one data element to identify the location of the successor (or related) data element (see Figures C-2b and C-2d). Pointer sequential is more efficient for data update operations because data may be located anywhere as long as links between related data are maintained. Another major feature of pointer-sequential schemes is the ability to maintain many different sequential linkages among the same set of data by using several pointers. We review various common forms of pointer-sequential schemes (linear data structures) shortly.

Also, there are two basic methods for *placement* of data relative to the connection mechanism:

1. *Data-direct placement*   The connection mechanism links an item of data directly with its successor (or related) item (see Figures C-2a and C-2b). Direct placement has the advantage of immediately finding the data once a connection is traversed. The disadvantage is that the actual data are spread across large parts of disk storage because space for the actual data must be allocated among the connection elements.

2. *Data-indirect placement*   The connection mechanism links pointers to the data, not the actual data (see Figures C-2c and C-2d). The advantage of indirect placement is that scanning a data structure for data with specified characteristics is usually more efficient because the scanning can be done through compact entries of key characteristics and pointers to the associated data. Also, the connection and placement of data are decoupled, so the physical organization of the data records can follow the most desirable scheme (e.g., physically sequential for a specified sorting order). The disadvantage is the extra access time required to retrieve both references to data and the data, and the extra space required for pointers.

Any data structure, file organization, or database architecture uses a combination of these four basic methods.

LINEAR DATA STRUCTURES

Pointer-sequential data structures have been popular for storing highly volatile data, typical of what is found in operational databases. Transactional data (such as customer orders or personnel change requests) and historical data (such as product price quotes and student class registrations) make up a large portion of operational databases. Also, because users of operational databases want to view data in many different sequences (e.g., customer orders in sequence by order date, product numbers, or customer numbers), the ability to maintain several chains of pointers running through the same data can support a range of user needs with one set of data.

The ability of a linear data structure (a pointer-sequential structure that maintains a sorted sequence on the data) to handle data updates is illustrated in Figure C-3. Figure C-3a shows how easy it is to insert a new record into a linear (or chain) structure. This figure illustrates a file of product records. For simplicity, we represent each product record by only the product number and a pointer to the next product record in

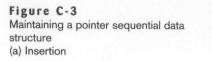

Figure C-3
Maintaining a pointer sequential data structure
(a) Insertion

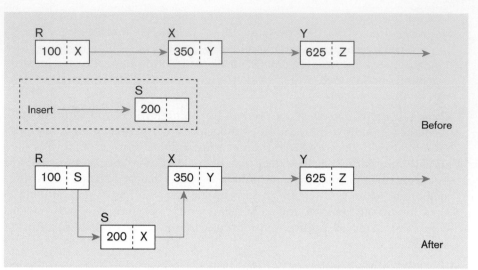

(b) Deletion

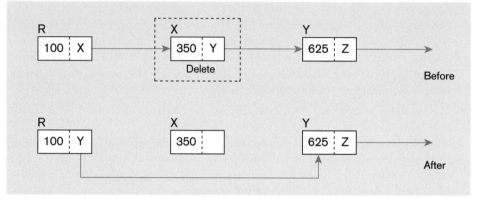

sequence by product number. A new record is stored in an available location (S) and patched into the chain by changing pointers associated with the records in locations R and S. In Figure C-3b the act of deleting a record is equally easy, as only the pointer for the record in location R is changed. Although there is extra space to store the pointers, this space is minimal compared to what may be hundreds of bytes needed to store all the product data (product number, description, quantity on hand, standard price, and so forth). It is easy to find records in product number order given this structure, but the actual time to retrieve records in sequence can be extensive if logically sequential records are stored far apart on disk.

With this simple introduction to linear data structures, we now consider four specific versions of such structures: stacks, queues, sorted lists, and multilists. We conclude this section with some cautions about linear, chain data structures.

Stacks

A stack has the property that all record insertions and deletions are made at the same end of the data structure. Stacks exhibit a last-in-first-out (LIFO) property. A common example of a stack is a vertical column of plates in a cafeteria. In business information systems, stacks are used to maintain unprioritized or unsorted records (e.g., the line items associated with the same customer order).

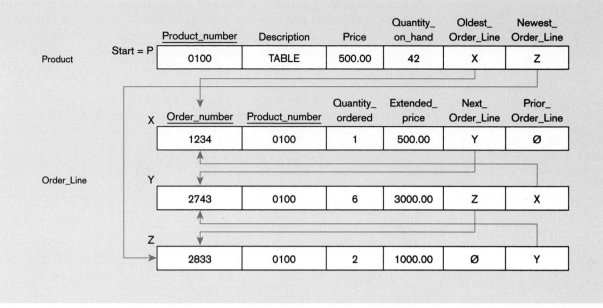

Figure C-4
Example of a queue with bidirectional pointers

Queues

A queue has the property that all insertions occur at one end and all deletions occur at the other end. A queue exhibits a first-in-first-out (FIFO) property. A common example of a queue is a checkout lane at a grocery store. In business information systems, queues are used to maintain lists of records in chronological order of insertion. For example, Figure C-4 illustrates a chained queue of Order Line records kept in order of arrival for a common Product record in Pine Valley Furniture.

In this example, the Product record acts as the head-of-chain node in the data structure. The value of the Oldest_order_line field is a pointer to the oldest (first entered) Order Line record for product 0100. The Next_order_line field in the Order_Line record contains the pointers to the next record in reverse chronological sequence. The value Ø in a pointer is called a null pointer and signifies the end of the chain.

This example also introduces the concept of a bidirectional chain, which has both forward and backward pointers. The benefit of next and prior pointers is that data in the records can be retrieved and presented in either forward or backward order, and the code to maintain the chain is easier to implement than with single-directional chains.

Sorted Lists

A sorted list has the property that insertions and deletions may occur anywhere within the list; records are maintained in logical order based on a key field value. A common example of a sorted list is a telephone directory. In business information systems, sorted lists occur frequently. Figure C-5a illustrates a single-directional, pointer sequential sorted list of Order records related to a Customer record, in which records are sorted by Delivery_date.

Maintaining a sorted list is more complex than maintaining a stack or a queue because insertion or deletion can occur anywhere in a chain, which may have zero or many existing records. To guarantee that insertions and deletions always occur in the interior of the chain, "dummy" first and last records are often included (see Figure C-5b). Figure C-5c shows the result of inserting a new Order into the sorted list of Figure C-5b. To perform the insertion, the list is scanned starting from the address in the pointer First_order. Once the proper position in the chain is found, there must be a rule for deciding where to store a record with a duplicate key value, if duplicates are allowed, as in this example. Usually this location for a duplicate record will be first among the duplicates because this requires the least scanning.

If you use a file organization or DBMS that supports chains, and in particular sorted lists, you will not have to write the code to maintain lists. Rather, this code will exist within the technology you use. Your program will simply issue an insert, delete, or update command, and the support software will do the chain maintenance.

Figure C-5
Example of a sorted list
(a) Before new Order record insertion and without dummy first and dummy last Order records

(b) Before new Order record insertion and with dummy first and dummy last Order records

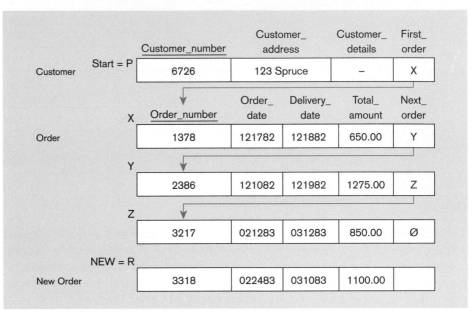

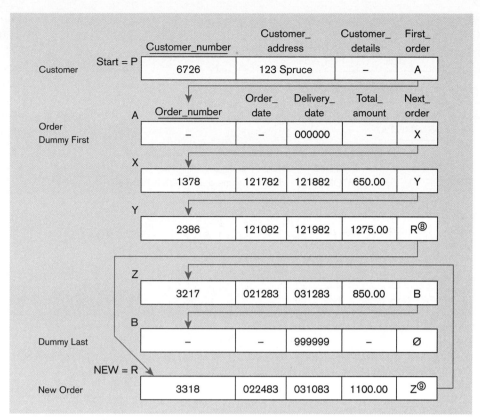

Figure C-5 (Continued)
(c) After new Order record insertion
(Circled numbers next to pointers
indicate the step number in the
associated maintenance procedure of
Figure C-6 that changes pointer value.)

Figure C-6 contains an outline of the code needed to insert a new record in the sorted list of Figure C-5b. In this outline, position variables PRE and AFT are used to hold the values of the predecessor and successor, respectively, of the new Order record. Step 7 is included in brackets to show where a check for duplicate keys would appear if required. The symbol ; means replace the value of the variable on the left with the value of the variable on the right. Steps 8 and 9, which change pointer values in Figure C-5, show exactly which pointers would change for the example of this figure. You may want to desk check this routine by manually executing it to see how variables' values are set and changed.

Multilists

A multilist data structure is one for which more than one sequence is maintained among the same records. Thus, multiple chains are threaded through the same

```
/*    Establish position variables beginning values */
1     PRE ← First_order(START)
2     AFT ← Next_order(PRE)
/*    Skip/scan through chain until proper position is found */
3     DO WHILE Delivery_date(AFT) < Delivery_date(NEW)
4        PRE ← AFT
5        AFT ← Next_order(AFT)
6     ENDO
7     [If Delivery_date(AFT) = Delivery_date(NEW) then indicate a Duplicate Error and
      terminate procedure]
/*    Weld in new chain element */
8     Next_order(PRE) ← NEW
9     Next_order(NEW) ← AFT
```

Figure C-6
Outline of record insertion code

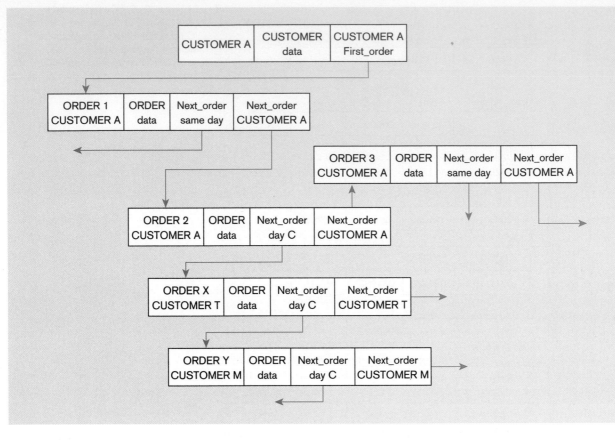

Figure C-7
Example of multilist structures

records, and records can be scanned in any of the maintained sequences without duplicating the data records. The trade-off for this flexible accessing is the extra storage space and maintenance for each chain. With a multilist, it is possible to walk through one association and in the middle decide to follow another. For example, while accessing the Order records for a given Customer (one list), we could find all the Orders to be delivered on the same day of delivery for a given Order record. Such a multilist is depicted in Figure C-7.

A multilist provides some of the same benefits of multiple indexes (see Chapter 6 for a discussion of primary and secondary key indexes). The major disadvantages of multilists, and the main reasons they are not used in relational DBMSs, is that the cost to scan a list is high compared with accessing an index, and there is no quick way to respond to multiple key qualifications with multilists (e.g., find all the orders for customers in the Northwest region and products in the Paper product line). For this and other reasons, indexes have generally replaced linear data structures in modern database technologies. However, legacy applications may still use technologies employing single- and multilist structures.

HAZARDS OF CHAIN STRUCTURES

Besides the limitation of chains that prohibits their use in quickly responding to multiple-key qualifications, chains also have the following hazards and limitations:

1. Long chains can take an enormous amount of time to scan because records in sequence are not necessarily stored physically close to one another.

2. Chains are vulnerable to being broken. If an abnormal event occurs in the middle of a chain maintenance routine, the chain can be partially updated, and the chain becomes incomplete or inaccurate. Some safety measures can be taken to cope with such mistakes, but these measures add extra storage or processing overhead.

TREES

The problem that a linear data structure may become long, and hence time-consuming to scan, is an inherent issue with any linear structure. Fortunately, nonlinear structures, which implement a divide-and-conquer strategy, have been developed. A popular type of nonlinear data structure is a tree. A tree (see Figure C-8) is a data structure that consists of a set of nodes that branch out from a node at the top of the tree (thus the tree is upside down!). Trees have a hierarchical structure. The root node is the node at the top of a tree. Each node in the tree, except the root node, has exactly one parent and may have zero, one, or more than one child nodes. Nodes are defined in terms of levels: the root is level zero, and the children of this node are at level one, and so on.

A leaf node is a node in a tree that has no child nodes (e.g., nodes J, F, C, G, K, L, and I in Figure C-8). A subtree of a node consists of that node and all the descendants of that node.

Balanced Trees

The most common use of trees in database management systems today is as a way to organize the entries within a key index. As with linear data structures, the database programmer does not have to maintain the tree structure because this is done by the DBMS software. However, a database designer may have the opportunity to control the structure of an index tree to tune the performance of index processing.

The most common form of tree used to build key indexes is a balanced tree, or B-tree. In a B-tree, all leaves are the same distance from the root. For this reason, B-trees have a predictable efficiency. B-trees support both random and sequential

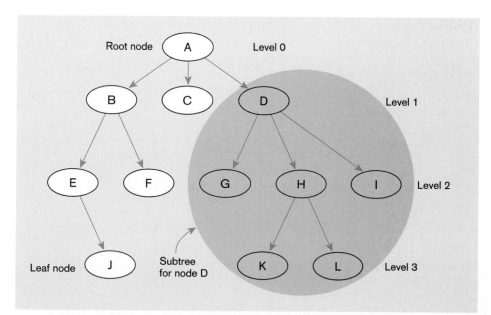

Figure C-8
Example of a tree data structure

retrieval of records. The most popular form of B-tree is the B+-tree. A B+-tree of degree *m* has the following special balanced tree property:

- Every node has between $m/2$ and m children (*m* is an integer greater than or equal to 3 and usually odd), except the root (which does not obey this lower bound).

It is this property that leads to the dynamic reorganization of nodes, which we illustrate later in this section.

Virtual sequential access method (VSAM), a data access method supported by many operating systems, is based on the B+-tree data structure. VSAM is a more modern version of indexed sequential access method (ISAM). There are two primary differences between ISAM and VSAM: (1) the location of index entries under ISAM are limited by the physical boundaries of a disk drive, whereas in VSAM index entries may span the physical boundaries, and (2) an ISAM file needs to be occasionally rebuilt when its structure becomes inefficient after many key additions and deletions, whereas in VSAM the index is dynamically reorganized in incremental ways when segments of the index become unwieldy.

An example of a B+-tree (of degree 3) appears in Figure C-9 for the Product file of Pine Valley Furniture Company. In this diagram, each vertical arrow represents the path followed for values that are equal to the number to the left of the arrow, but less than the number to the right of the arrow. For example, in the nonleaf node that contains the values 625 and 1000, the middle arrow leaving the bottom of this node is the path followed for values equal to 625 but less than 1000. Horizontal arrows are used to connect the leaf nodes so that sequential processing can occur without having to move up and down through the levels of the tree.

Suppose you wanted to retrieve the data record for product number 1425. Notice that the value in the root node is 1250. Because 1425 is greater than 1250, you follow the arrow to the right of this node down to the next level. In this node you find the target value (1425), so you follow the middle arrow down to the leaf node that contains the value 1425. This node contains a pointer to the data record for product number 1425, so this record can now be retrieved. You should trace a similar path to locate the record for product number 1000. Because the data records are stored outside the index, multiple B+-tree indexes can be maintained on the same data.

A B+-tree also easily supports the addition and deletion of records. Any necessary changes to the B+-tree structure are dynamic and retain the properties of a B+-tree. Consider the case of adding a record with key 1800 to the B+-tree in Figure C-9. The result of this addition is shown in Figure C-10a. Because node 1 still has only three

Figure C-9
Example of a B+-tree of degree 3

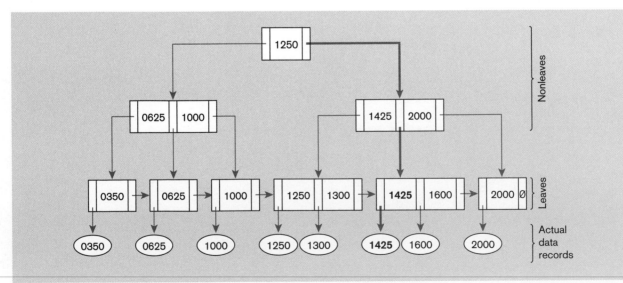

Figure C-10
Inserting records in a B+-tree

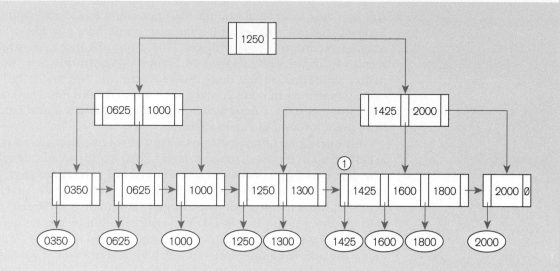

(a) Insertion of record 1800

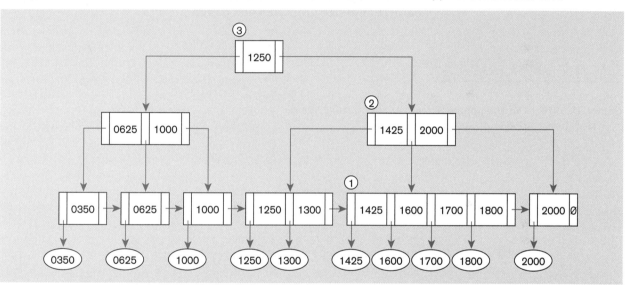

(b) Initial attempt to insert record 1700

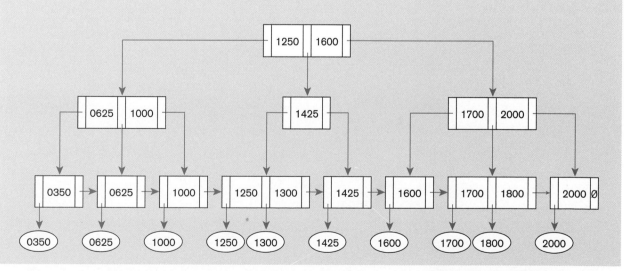

(c) Final B+-tree after insertion of record 1700

children (the horizontal pointer does not count as a child pointer), the B+-tree in Figure C-10a still satisfies all B+-tree properties. Now consider the effect of adding another record, this time with key 1700, to the B+-tree in Figure C-10a. An initial result of this insertion appears in Figure C-10b. In this case, node 1 violates the degree limitation, so this node must be split into two nodes. Splitting node 1 will cause a new entry in node 2, which then will make this node have four children, one too many. So, node 2 must also be split, which will add a new entry to node 3. The final result is shown in Figure C-10c.

An interesting situation occurs when the root becomes too large (has more than m children). In this case, the root is split, which adds an additional level to the tree. The deletion of a record causes an entry in a leaf to be eliminated. If this elimination causes a leaf to have fewer than $m/2$ children, that leaf is then merged with an adjacent leaf; if the merged leaf is too large (more than m children), the merged leaf is split, resulting simply in a less skewed redistribution of keys across nodes. The result is that a B+-tree is dynamically reorganized to keep the tree balanced (equal depth along any path from the root) and with a limited number of entries per node (which controls the business, or width, of the tree).

If you are interested in learning more about B-trees, see Comer (1979), a classic article on B-tree properties and design.

References

Comer, D. 1979. "The Ubiquitous B-tree." *ACM Computing Surveys* 11,2 (June): 121–37.

Appendix D

Object-Relational Databases

In this textbook, we have described the two models most widely used for the design and implementation of databases: relational and object-oriented. The relational model (with its associated relational database management systems) is the model most often used for implementing mainstream business applications today. Some of the strengths of this model are:

- Data independence, described in Chapter 1
- A powerful query language (SQL), described in Chapter 7
- Mature relational database management system technology, including features such as online backup and recovery and flexible concurrency control (described in Chapter 12)

Despite these strengths, we noted in Chapter 14 (as well as in other chapters) that the relational data model is not well suited to handling complex data types such as images, audio, video, and spatial (or geographical) data. Thus, the object-oriented data model was introduced primarily to manage these complex data types. (This model is described in Chapters 14 and 15.) The market for object-oriented database management systems has grown slowly, yet the technology is extremely promising for applications such as Web servers that incorporate multimedia data types. The weaknesses of object-oriented database systems (at least until recently) have been the lack of important features found in relational systems such as query capability, online backup and recovery, and flexible concurrency control.

In summary, relational and object-oriented database systems each have certain strengths as well as certain weaknesses. In general, the weaknesses of one type of system tend to be a strength of the other (and vice versa). This has led the industry to develop a new generation of hybrid database system—the object-relational system—that seeks to combine the best features of both models (Stonebraker et al., 1990). Most of the major DBMS vendors have released a version of an object-relational database system. These systems handle objects and rules, encapsulation, polymorphism, and inheritance and are compatible with RDBMSs. In this appendix, we present a brief description of this type of system, including its advantages and disadvantages.

BASIC CONCEPTS AND DEFINITIONS

An **object-relational database management system (ORDBMS)** is a database engine that supports both relational and object-oriented features in an integrated fashion (Frank, 1995). Thus, the user can (at least ideally) define, manipulate, and

Object-relational database management system (ORDBMS): A database engine that supports both relational and object-oriented features in an integrated fashion.

591

query both relational data and objects while using common interfaces (such as SQL). The underlying data model of the DBMS is relational, but with some extensions. Thus, whereas the database may appear to a programmer to be object-oriented, the storage and process is relational; hence, there is an overhead to map between relational and objects.

Two other terms that are used for object-relational databases are extended relational and universal server. The term *extended relational* (an older term) derives from the fact that the first versions of these types of systems were developed by adding object-oriented features onto existing relational DBMSs. The term *universal server* (a more contemporary term) is based on the stated objective of managing any type of data (including user-defined data types) with the same server technology.

Features of an ORDBMS

As indicated above, the intent with ORDBMS is to combine the best features of the relational and object database models. Following are the main features usually included in an ORDBMS:

1. An enhanced version of SQL (similar to SQL3) that can be used to create and manipulate both relational tables and object types or classes

2. Support for traditional object-oriented functions including generalization, inheritance, polymorphism and overloading, rich data types (such as large objects, images, geographic coordinates) and user-defined (or abstract) data types, storage of methods in relations, and navigational access

3. Support for some nonstandard data types within a relation: multivalued attributes, nested tables (multidimensional arrays of multivalued attributes within a relation), aggregation, and object identifiers

See Chapter 14 for a description of these object-oriented terms.

Complex Data Types

There are three main categories of data types in SQL: NUMERIC, CHARACTER, and TEMPORAL. NUMERIC types include DECIMAL and INTEGER, whereas TEMPORAL types include DATE and TIME (Celko, 1995).

Modern business applications often require storing and manipulating complex data types that are not easily handled by relational systems. Some of the more common of these complex data types are shown in Table D-1. For each data type, this table provides a brief description and one or more typical applications. For example, the Graphic data type consists of geometric objects such as points, lines, and circles; typical applications are for computer-assisted design (CAD), computer-assisted manufacturing (CAM), computer-assisted software engineering (CASE) tools, and presentation graphics (such as charts and graphs).

Table D-1 Complex Data Types

Data type	Description	Example applications
Image	Bit-mapped representation	Documents, photographs, medical images, fingerprints
Graphic	Geometric objects	CAD, CAM, CASE, presentation graphics
Spatial	Geographic objects	Maps
Recursive	Nested objects	Bills of materials
Audio	Sound clips	Music, animation, games
Video	Video segments, movies	Training films, product demonstrations, movies
Array	Subscripted variables	Time series, multidimensional data, multivalued attribute
Computational-intensive	Data requiring extensive-computations	Data mining, financial instruments (e.g., derivatives)

An ORDBMS allows a composite attribute to be defined as a separate data type that can be used to specify the type of any database attribute. For example, the following SQL command [see George et al. (2005) for more examples of this and other commands shown below] defines a composite attribute as a user-defined data type called NAME_TYPE:

```
Create or replace type NAME_TYPE as object (
        LASTNAME VARCHAR2(25),
        FIRSTNAME VARCHAR2(25),
        MIDDLEINIT CHAR(1)
);
```

This user-defined data type can then be used to define other user-defined attributes, and eventually attributes of any table, such as in the following:

```
Create or replace type PERSON_TYPE as object (
        NAME NAME_TYPE,
        ADDRESS ADDRESS_TYPE,
        DATEBIRTH DATE,
        PHONE VARCHAR2(12)
);
Create table EMPLOYEE (
        EMPID NUMBER(8) not null primary key,
        EMP PERSON_TYPE
);
```

An ORDBMS also supports supertype–subtype hierarchies, such as that shown in Figure 4-2 for employees. A portion of this hierarchy might be defined in an ORDBMS as follows:

```
create type EMP_TYPE as object (
  empNo number,
  empName varchar2(50),
  empAddress varchar2(100)
)
not final;
  create type HOURLY_EMP_TYPE under EMP_TYPE (
  hourlyRate number
);
create table HOURLY_EMP of HOURLY_EMP_TYPE;
```

As is seen in Chapter 5 and Appendix B, the approach in normalization for handling repeating data (e.g., multiple addresses for a customer or multiple majors for a student) is to separate out the repeating data into another relation using foreign keys to tie the related data together. This is often ideal, because the data separated out has an identity of its own and is often related to other data (e.g., data about a student's majors may also be related to data about advisors or curricula). In contrast, the repeating addresses for a customer are just related to the associated customer. An ORDBMS allows you to define an attribute as multivalued (e.g., an arbitrary list of a student's majors) and tables within tables (nested tables or an array of multivalued attributes). The object-relational data model also allows a customer and its related addresses in aggregate to be logically all in the same table row. Physically, the nested table rows are stored in a separate table. In each case, the repeating data are defined as in the above examples as an independent data type, and then multivalued attributes of tables are assigned this data type.

ENHANCED SQL

The most powerful feature of an ORDBMS is that it uses an extended version of a relational query language (such as SQL3) to define, fetch, and manipulate data (Cattell, 1994; Chaudhri and Zicari, 2001).

Figure D-1
Relation with complex object

Emp_ID	Name	Address	Date_of_Birth	Emp_Photo
12345	Charles	112 Main	04/27/1973	
34567	Angela	840 Oak	08/12/1967	
56789	Thomas	520 Elm	10/13/1975	

A Simple Example

Suppose that an organization wants to create a relation named EMPLOYEE to record employee data (see Figure D-1). Traditional relational attributes in this table are the following: Emp_ID, Name, Address, and Date_of_Birth. In addition, the organization would like to store a photograph of each employee that will be used for identification purposes. This attribute (whose type is defined by an object) is named Emp_Photo in Figure D-1. When the data for a particular employee are retrieved, the employee photo will be displayed with the remaining data.

As shown above, SQL3 will provide statements to create both tables and data types (or object classes). For example, the SQL CREATE TABLE statement for EMPLOYEE might appear as follows:

```
CREATE TABLE EMPLOYEE
    Emp_ID INTEGER NOT NULL,
    Name CHAR(20) NOT NULL,
    Address CHAR(20),
    Date_of_Birth DATE NOT NULL,
    Emp_Photo IMAGE);
```

In this example IMAGE is a data type (or class), and Emp_Photo is an object of that class. IMAGE may be either a predefined class or a user-defined class. If it is a user-defined class (as was NAME_TYPE above), a SQL CREATE TYPE or CREATE CLASS statement is used to define the class. The user can also define methods that operate on the data defined in a class. For example, one method of IMAGE is Scale( ), which can be used to expand or reduce the size of the photograph. The method would be coded in Java, C++, or Smalltalk and would be encapsulated with the IMAGE CLASS. Methods can be used in the select list of queries just like attributes.

Content Addressing

One of the most powerful features of the relational SQL language is the ability to select a subset of the records in a table that satisfy stated qualifications. For example, in the EMPLOYEE relation a simple SQL statement will select records for all employees whose date of birth is on or before 12/31/1940 (see Chapter 7 for examples). In contrast, "pure" object database systems do not have this query capability. Instead, access to objects is navigational—that is, each object has a unique object identifier (see Chapter 14).

Content addressing: The facility that allows a user to query a database to select all records and/or objects that satisfy a given set of qualifications.

The ORDBMS products extend relational's content addressibility to complex objects (Norman and Bloor, 1996). **Content addressing** is the facility that allows a user to query a database (or database table) to select all records and/or objects that satisfy a given set of qualifications.

SQL3 includes extensions for content addressing with complex data types. Let's see how content addressing might be applied in the EMPLOYEE table. Remember that each employee record contains (or is at least linked to) a photo of that employee. A user might want to pose the following query: given a photograph of a person, scan the EMPLOYEE table to determine whether there is a close match for any employee to that photo; then display the data (including the photograph) of the employee or employees selected (if any). Suppose the electronic image of a photograph is stored in a location called My_Photo. A simple query for this situation might appear as follows:

```
SELECT *
    FROM EMPLOYEE
    WHERE My_Photo LIKE Emp_Photo;
```

Content addressing in an ORDBMS is a very powerful feature that allows users to search for matches to multimedia objects such as images, audio or video segments, and documents. One obvious application for this feature is searching databases for fingerprint or voiceprint matches.

ADVANTAGES OF THE OBJECT-RELATIONAL APPROACH

For applications that require complex processing or significant query activity on large datasets, the object-relational approach offers several advantages compared with relational database systems (Moxon, 1997):

1. *Reduced network traffic*   Queries that employ methods to scan data can be executed entirely on the server, without the need to send large quantities of data back to the clients.

2. *Application and query performance*   The methods that process large datasets can exploit large parallel servers to significantly improve performance.

3. *Software maintenance*   The fact that data and methods are stored together on the server greatly simplifies the task of software maintenance.

4. *Integrated data and transaction management*   All transaction integrity, concurrency, and backup and recovery are handled within the database engine.

ORDBMS VENDORS AND PRODUCTS

A list of the major vendors and the ORDBMS products they provide is shown in Table D-2. The table also shows the extender technology (or framework) that is provided by each vendor that allows users to define their own data types, as well as the methods that manipulate those data.

Table D-2 Selected ORDBMS Vendors and Products

Vendor	ORDBMS Product	Extender technology	Website
IBM	DB2 Universal Database	none	http://www-03.ibm.com/servers/eserver/iseries/db2/
Informix	Dynamic Server	Data Blades	http://www-306.ibm.com/software/data/informix/blades/index.html
Oracle	Oracle 10g	Data Cartridges	www.oracle.com/technology/products/database/ application_development/pdf/Oracle_Database_ 10g_Extensibility_Framework.pdf
PostgreSQL Inc	PostgreSQL	eRServer	http://www.pgsql.com

APPENDIX REVIEW

Key Terms

Content addressing
Object-relational database
  management system
  (ORDBMS)

References

Cattell, R. 1994. *Object Data Management: Object-Oriented and Extended Relational Database Systems.* Reading, MA: Addison-Wesley.

Celko, J. 1995. *Instant SQL Programming.* Chicago: Wrox Press.

Chaudhri, A. B., and R. Zicari. 2001. *Succeeding with Object Databases.* New York: Wiley.

Frank, M. 1995. "Object-Relational Hybrids." *DBMS* 8,7 (July): 46–56.

George, J., D. Batra, J. Valacich, and J. Hoffer. 2005. *Object-Oriented Systems Analysis and Design.* Upper Saddle River, NJ: Prentice Hall.

Moxon, B. 1997. "Database Out of This Universe." *DB2 Magazine* 2,3 (Fall): 9–16.

Norman, M., and R. Bloor. 1996. "To Universally Serve." *Database Programming & Design* 9,7 (July): 26–35.

Stonebraker, M., L. Rowe, B. Lindsay, J. Gray, M. Carey, M. Brodie, P. Bernstein, and D. Beech 1990. "Third-Generation Database System Manifesto—The Committee for Advanced DBMS Function." *SIGMOD Record* 19,3 (September): 31–44.

Web Resources

www.service-architecture.com/object-relational-mapping/ This site from Barry & Associates, Inc. compares the features of many object-relational DBMSs and stores many articles and other resources on mapping object-relational structures into relations.

Glossary of Acronyms

ACID	Atomic, Consistent, Isolated, and Durable	**DBD**	Database Description
ACM	Association for Computing Machinery	**DBMS**	Database Management System
AITP	Association of Information Technology Professionals	**DB2**	Data Base2 (an IBM Relational DBMS)
ANSI	American National Standards Institute	**DCL**	Data Control Language
API	Application Program Interface	**DCOM**	Distributed Component Object Model
ASCII	American Standards Code for Information Interchange	**DDL**	Data Definition Language
		DES	Data Encryption Standard
ASP	Active Server Pages	**DFD**	Data Flow Diagram
ATM	Automated Teller Machine	**DK/NF**	Domain-Key Normal Form
BCNF	Boyce-Codd Normal Form	**DML**	Data Manipulation Language
BOM	Bill of Materials	**DNS**	Domain Name Server
BPEL4WS	Business Process Execution Language for Web Services	**DSD**	Documents Structure Description
		DSS	Decision Support System
B2B	Business-to-Business	**DTD**	Data Type Definitions
B2C	Business-to-Consumer	**DWA**	Data Warehouse Administrator
CAD/CAM	Computer-Aided Design/Computer-Aided Manufacturing	**EDI**	Electronic Data Interchange
		EDW	Enterprise Data Warehouse
CASE	Computer-Aided Software Engineering	**EER**	Extended Entity-Relationship
CD-ROM	Compact Disk-Read-Only Memory	**EFT**	Electronic Funds Transfer
CEO	Chief Executive Officer	**E-R**	Entity-Relationship
CGI	Common Gateway Interface	**ERD**	Entity-Relationship Diagram
CIF	Corporate Information Factory	**ERP**	Enterprise Resource Planning
CLI	Call-Level Interface	**ETL**	Extract-Transform-Load
COM	Component Object Model	**FDA**	Food and Drug Administration
COO	Chief Operating Officer	**FK**	Foreign Key
CPU	Central Processor Unit	**FTP**	File Transfer Protocol
CRM	Customer Relationship Management	**GPA**	Grade Point Average
C/S	Client/Server	**GUI**	Graphical User Interface
CSF	Critical Success Factor	**HIPAA**	Health Insurance Portability and Accountability Act
CSS	Cascading Style Sheets		
DA	Data Administrator (or Data Administration)	**HTML**	Hypertext Markup Language
		HTTP	Hypertext Transfer Protocol
DBA	Database Administrator (or Database Administration)	**IBM**	International Business Machines

I-CASE	Integrated Computer-Aided Software Engineering
ID	Identifier
IDE	Integrated Development Environment
IE	Information Engineering
INCITS	InterNational Committee for Information Technology Standards
I/O	Input/Output
IP	Internet Protocol
IRDS	Information Repository Dictionary System
IRM	Information Resource Management
IS	Information System
ISA	Information Systems Architecture
ISAM	Indexed Sequential Access Method
ISO	International Standards Organization
IT	Information Technology
ITAA	Information Technology Association of America
J2EE	Java 2 Enterprise Edition
JDBC	Java Database Connectivity
JSP	Java Server Pages
LAN	Local Area Network
LDB	Logical Database
LDBR	Logical Database Record
MB	Million Bytes
MIS	Management Information System
M:N	Many-to-Many
M:1	Many-to-One
MOLAP	Multidimensional On-line Analytical Processing
MMS	Multi-Messaging Service
MOM	Message-oriented Middleware
MRN	Medical Record Number
MRP	Materials Requirements Planning
MS	Microsoft
MVCH	Mountain View Community Hospital
NIST	National Institute of Standards and Technology
NUPI	Nonunique Primary Index
NUSI	Nonunique Secondary Index
ODBC	Open Database Connectivity
ODBMS	Object Database Management System
ODL	Object Definition Language
ODS	Operational Data Store
OLAP	On-line Analytical Processing
OLE	Object Linking and Embedding
OLTP	On-line Transaction Processing
OMA	Open Mobile Alliance

OO	Object-Oriented
OODM	Object-Oriented Data Model
OQL	Object Query Language
O/R	Object/Relational
ORB	Object Request Broker
ORDBMS	Object-Relational Database Management System
OSAM	Overflow Sequential Access Method
OWL	Web Ontology Library
P3P	Platform for Privacy Preferences
PC	Personal Computer
PDA	Personal Data Assistant
PIN	Personal Identification Number
PK	Primary Key
PL/SQL	Programming Language/SQL
PVF	Pine Valley Furniture
PVFC	Pine Valley Furniture Company
QBE	Query-by-Example
RAD	Rapid Application Development
RAID	Redundant Array of Inexpensive Disks
RAM	Random Access Memory
RDBMS	Relational Database Management System
RDF	Resource Description Framework
ROLAP	Relational On-line Analytical Processing
RPC	Remote Procedure Call
SAML	Security Assertion Markup Language
SDLC	Systems Development Life Cycle
SGML	Standard Generalized Markup Language
SOA	Service Oriented Architecture
SOAP	Simple Object Access Protocol
SOX	Sarbanes-Oxley
SPL	Structured Product Labeling
SQL	Structured Query Language
SQL/CLI	SQL/Call Level Interface
SQL/DS	Structured Query Language/Data System (an IBM relational DBMS)
SQLJ	SQL-Java
SQL/PSM	SQL/Persistent Stored Modules
SSL	Secure Sockets Layer
TCP/IP	Transmission Control Protocol/Internet Protocol
TDWI	The Data Warehousing Institute
TQM	Total Quality Management
UDDI	Universal Description, Discovery, and Integration
UDF	User-Defined Function

UDT	User-Defined Data Type	**XHTML**	Extensible Hypertext Markup Language
UML	Unified Modeling Language	**XML**	Extensible Markup Language
UPI	Unique Primary Index	**XSL**	Extensible Style Language
URI	Universal Resource Identifier	**XSLT**	XML Style Language Transformation
URL	Uniform Resource Locator	**1:1**	One-to-One
USI	Unique Secondary Index	**1:M**	One-to-Many
VLDB	Very Large Database	**1NF**	First Normal Form
W3C	World Wide Web Consortium	**2NF**	Second Normal Form
WSDL	Web Services Description Language	**3GL**	Third-Generation Language
WYSIWYG	What You See Is What You Get	**3NF**	Third Normal Form
WWW	World Wide Web	**4NF**	Fourth Normal Form
XBRL	Extensible Business Reporting Language	**5NF**	Fifth Normal Form

Glossary of Terms

Aborted transaction A transaction in progress that terminates abnormally. (12)

Abstract class A class that has no direct instances, but whose descendants may have direct instances. (14)

Abstract operation Defines the form or protocol of the operation, but not its implementation. (14)

Action An operation, such as create, delete, update, or read, which may be performed on data objects. (4)

Action assertion A statement of a constraint or control on the actions of the organization. (4)

ActiveX A loosely defined set of technologies developed by Microsoft that extends browser capabilities and allows the manipulation of data inside the browser. (10)

After-image A copy of a record (or page of memory) after it has been modified. (12)

Aggregation The process of transforming data from a detailed to a summary level. (11). A part-of relationship between a component object and an aggregate object. (14)

Alias An alternative name used for an attribute. (5)

Anchor object A business rule (a fact) on which actions are limited. (4)

Anomaly An error or inconsistency that may result when a user attempts to update a table that contains redundant data. The three types of anomalies are insertion, deletion, and modification. (5)

Application partitioning The process of assigning portions of application code to client or server partitions after it is written in order to achieve better performance and interoperability (ability of a component to function on different platforms). (9)

Application program interface (API) Sets of routines that an application program uses to direct the performance of procedures by the computer's operating system. (9)

Array A dynamically sized ordered collection of elements that can be located by position. (15)

Association A named relationship between or among object classes. (14)

Association class An association that has attributes or operations of its own or that participates in relationships with other classes. (14)

Association role The end of an association where it connects to a class. (14)

Associative entity An entity type that associates the instances of one or more entity types and contains attributes that are peculiar to the relationship between those entity instances. (3)

Asynchronous distributed database A form of distributed database technology in which copies of replicated data are kept at different nodes so that local servers can access data without reaching out across the network. (13)

Atomic literal A constant that cannot be decomposed into any further components. (15)

Attribute A property or characteristic of an entity type that is of interest to the organization. (3)

Attribute inheritance A property by which subtype entities inherit values of all attributes of the supertype. (4)

Authorization rules Controls incorporated in the data management systems that restrict access to data and also restrict the actions that people may take when they access data. (12)

Backup facilities A DBMS COPY utility that produces a backup copy (or save) of the entire database or a subset of the database. (12)

Backward recovery (rollback) The back out, or undo, of unwanted changes to the database. Before-images of the records that have been changed are applied to the database, and the database is returned to an earlier state. Used to reverse the changes made by transactions that have been aborted or terminated abnormally. (12)

Bag An unordered collection of elements that may contain duplicates. (15)

Base table A table in the relational data model containing the inserted raw data. Base tables correspond to the relations that are identified in the database's conceptual schema. (7)

Before-image A copy of a record (or page of memory) before it has been modified. (12)

Behavior Represents how an object acts and reacts. (14)

Binary relationship A relationship between the instances of two entity types. (3)

Bitmap index A table of bits in which each row represents the distinct values of a key and each column is a bit, which when on indicates that the record for that bit column position has the associated field value. (6)

Blocking factor The number of physical records per page. (6)

Boyce-Codd normal form (BCNF)   A relation in which every determinant is a candidate key. (B)

Business function   A related group of business processes that support some aspects of the mission of an enterprise. (2)

Business rule   A statement that defines or constrains some aspect of the business. It is intended to assert business structure or to control or influence the behavior of the business. (3)

Candidate key   An attribute, or combination of attributes, that uniquely identifies a row in a relation. (5)

Cardinality constraint   Specifies the number of instances of one entity that can (or must) be associated with each instance of another entity. (3)

Catalog   A set of schemas that, when put together, constitute a description of a database. (7)

Checkpoint facility   A facility by which the DBMS periodically refuses to accept any new transactions. The system is in a quiet state, and the database and transaction logs are synchronized. (12)

Class   An entity that has a well-defined role in the application domain about which the organization wishes to maintain state, behavior, and identity. (14)

Class diagram   Shows the static structure of an object-oriented model: the object classes, their internal structure, and the relationships in which they participate. (14)

Class-scope attribute   An attribute of a class that specifies a value common to an entire class, rather than a specific value for an instance. (14)

Client/server architecture   A LAN–based environment in which database software on a server (called a database server or database engine) performs database commands sent to it from client workstations, and application programs on each client concentrate on user interface functions. (2)

Client/server systems   A networked computing model that distributes processes between clients and servers, which supply the requested services. In a database system, the database generally resides on a server that processes the DBMS. The clients may process the application systems or request services from another server that holds the application programs. (9)

Collection literal   A collection of literals or object types. (15)

Commit protocol   An algorithm to ensure that a transaction is successfully completed or else it is aborted. (13)

Common Gateway Interface (CGI)   A Web server interface that specifies the transfer of information between a Web server and a CGI program. (10)

Completeness constraint   A type of constraint that addresses the question whether an instance of a supertype must also be a member of at least one subtype. (4)

Composite attribute   An attribute that can be broken down has meaningful component parts. (3)

Composite identifier   An identifier that consists of a composite attribute. (3)

Composite key   A primary key that consists of more than one attribute. (5)

Composition   A part object that belongs to only one whole object and that lives and dies with the whole object. (14)

Computer-aided software engineering (CASE)   Software tools that provide automated support for some portion of the systems development process. (2)

Conceptual schema   A detailed, technology-independent specification of the overall structure of organizational data. (2)

Concrete class   A class that can have direct instances. (14)

Concurrency control   The process of managing simultaneous operations against a database so that data integrity is maintained and the operations do not interfere with each other in a multiuser environment. (12)

Concurrency transparency   A design goal for a distributed database, with the property that although a distributed system runs many transactions, it appears that a given transaction is the only activity in the system. Thus, when several transactions are processed concurrently, the results must be the same as if each transaction were processed in serial order. (13)

Conformed dimension   One or more dimension tables associated with two or more fact tables for which the dimension tables have the same business meaning and primary key with each fact table. (11)

Constraint   A rule that cannot be violated by database users. (1)

Constructor operation   An operation that creates a new instance of a class. (14)

Content addressing   The facility that allows a user to query a database to select all records and/or objects that satisfy a given set of qualifications. (D)

Cookie   A block of data stored on a client by a Web server. When a user returns to a site, the contents of the cookie are sent back to the Web server and may be used to identify the user and return a customized Web page. (10)

Correlated subquery   In SQL, a subquery in which processing the inner query depends on data from the outer query. (8)

Corresponding object   A business rule (a fact) that influences the ability to perform an action on another business rule. (4)

Data   Stored representations of objects and events that have meaning and importance in the user's environment. (1)

Data administration   A high-level function that is responsible for the overall management of data resources in an organization, including maintaining corporatewide definitions and standards. (12)

Data archiving   The process of moving inactive data to another storage location where it can be accessed when needed. (12)

Database   An organized collection of logically related data. (1)

Database administration   A technical function that is responsible for physical database design and for dealing with technical issues, such as security enforcement, database performance, and backup and recovery. (12)

Database application   An application program (or set of related programs) that is used to perform a series of database activities (create, read, update, and delete) on behalf of database users. (1)

Database change log   Before- and after-images of records that have been modified by transactions. (12)

Database destruction   The database itself is lost or destroyed or cannot be read. (12)

Database Management System (DBMS): A software system that is used to create, maintain, and provide controlled access to user databases. (1)

Database recovery Mechanisms for restoring a database quickly and accurately after loss or damage. (12)

Database security Protection of the data against accidental or intentional loss, destruction, or misuse. (12)

Database server A computer that is responsible for database storage, access, and processing in a client/server environment. Some people also use this term to describe a two-tier client/server environment. (9)

Data control language (DCL) Commands used to control a database, including administering privileges and the committing (saving) of data. (7)

Data definition language (DDL) Those commands used to define a database, including creating, altering, and dropping tables and establishing constraints. (7)

Data dictionary Repository of information about a database that documents data elements of a database. (12)

Data independence The separation of data descriptions from the application programs that use the data. (1)

Data manipulation language (DML) Those commands used to maintain and query a database, including updating, inserting, modifying, and querying data. (7)

Data mart A data warehouse that is limited in scope, whose data are obtained by selecting and summarizing data from a data warehouse or from separate extract, transform, and load processes from source data systems. (11)

Data mining Knowledge discovery using a sophisticated blend of techniques from traditional statistics, artificial intelligence, and computer graphics. (11)

Data model Graphical systems used to capture the nature and relationships among data. (1)

Data scrubbing A technique using pattern recognition and other artificial intelligence techniques to upgrade the quality of raw data before transforming and moving the data to the data warehouse. Also called data cleansing. (11)

Data steward A person assigned the responsibility of ensuring that organizational applications properly support the organization's enterprise goals for data quality. (12)

Data transformation The component of data reconciliation that converts data from the format of the source operational systems to the format of the enterprise data warehouse. (11)

Data type A detailed coding scheme recognized by system software, such as a DBMS, for representing organizational data. (6)

Data visualization The representation of data in graphical and multimedia formats for human analysis. (11)

Data warehouse An integrated decision support database whose content is derived from the various operational databases. (1). A subject-oriented, integrated, time-variant, nonupdatable collection of data used in support of management decision-making processes. (11)

Deadlock An impasse that results when two or more transactions have locked a common resource, and each waits for the other to unlock that resource. (12)

Deadlock prevention User programs must lock all records they require at the beginning of a transaction (rather than one at a time). (12)

Deadlock resolution An approach that allows deadlocks to occur but builds mechanisms into the DBMS for detecting and breaking the deadlocks. (12)

Decentralized database A database that is stored on computers at multiple locations; these computers are not interconnected by network and database software that make the data appear in one logical database. (13)

Degree The number of entity types that participate in a relationship. (3)

Denormalization The process of transforming normalized relations into unnormalized physical record specifications. (6)

Dependent data mart A data mart filled exclusively from the enterprise data warehouse and its reconciled data. (11)

Derivation A statement derived from other knowledge in the business. (4)

Derived attribute An attribute whose values can be calculated from related attribute values. (3)

Derived data Data that have been selected, formatted, and aggregated for end-user decision support applications. (11)

Derived fact A fact that is derived from business rules using an algorithm or inference. (4)

Determinant The attribute on the left-hand side of the arrow in a functional dependency. (5)

Dictionary An unordered sequence of key-value pairs without any duplicates. (15)

Disjointness constraint A constraint that addresses the question whether an instance of a supertype may simultaneously be a member of two (or more) subtypes. (4)

Distributed database A single logical database that is spread physically across computers in multiple locations that are connected by a data communication link. (13)

DNS (domain name server) balancing A load-balancing approach where the DNS server for the hostname of the site returns multiple IP addresses for the site. (10)

Document structure description Language used for defining XML databases noted for ease of use and expressiveness. (10)

Dynamic SQL The process of making an application capable of generating specific SQL code on the fly while the application is processing. (8)

Dynamic view A virtual table that is created dynamically upon request by a user. A dynamic view is not a temporary table. Rather, its definition is stored in the system catalog, and the contents of the view are materialized as a result of an SQL query that uses the view. It differs from a materialized view, which may be stored on a disk and refreshed at intervals or when used, depending on the RDBMS. (7)

Embedded SQL The process of including hard-coded SQL statements in a program written in another language, such as C or Java. (8)

Encapsulation The technique of hiding the internal implementation details of an object from its external view. (14)

Encryption The coding or scrambling of data so that humans cannot read them. (12)

Enhanced entity-relationship (EER) model The model that has resulted from extending the original E-R model with new modeling constructs. (4)

Enterprise data model A graphical model that shows the high-level entities for the organization and the relationships among those entities. (1)

Enterprise data modeling The first step in database development, in which the scope and general contents of organizational databases are specified. (2)

Enterprise data warehouse (EDW) A centralized, integrated data warehouse that is the control point and single source of all data made available to end users for decision support applications. (11)

Enterprise key A primary key whose value is unique across all relations. (5)

Enterprise resource planning (ERP) systems A business management system that integrates all functions of the enterprise, such as manufacturing, sales, finance, marketing, inventory, accounting, and human resources. ERP systems are software applications that provide the data necessary for the enterprise to examine and manage its activities. (1)

Entity A person, place, object, event, or concept in the user environment about which the organization wishes to maintain data. (1, 3)

Entity cluster A set of one or more entity types and associated relationships grouped into a single abstract entity type. (4)

Entity instance A single occurrence of an entity type. (3)

Entity integrity rule No primary key attribute (or component of a primary key attribute) can be null. (5)

Entity-relationship diagram (E-R diagram) A graphical representation of an entity-relationship model. (3)

Entity-relationship model (E-R model) A logical representation of the data for an organization or for a business area. (3)

Entity type A collection of entities that share common properties or characteristics. (3)

Equi-join A join in which the joining condition is based on equality between values in the common columns. Common columns appear (redundantly) in the result table. (8)

Event A database action (create, update, or delete) that results from a transaction. (11)

Exclusive lock (X lock or write lock) A technique that prevents another transaction from reading and therefore updating a record until it is unlocked. (12)

Extent Relates to physical database design. A contiguous section of disk storage space. (6). Relates to object-oriented databases. The set of all instances of a class within the database. (15)

Fact An association between two or more terms. (3)

Failure transparency A design goal for a distributed database, which guarantees that either all the actions of each transaction are committed or else none of them is committed. (13)

Fat client A client PC that is responsible for processing presentation logic, extensive application and business rules logic, and many DBMS functions. (9)

Field The smallest unit of named application data recognized by system software. (6)

File organization A technique for physically arranging the records of a file on secondary storage devices. (6)

File server A device that manages file operations and is shared by each of the client PCs attached to the LAN. (9)

Firewall A hardware/software security component that limits external access to company data. (10)

First normal form A relation that has a primary key and in which there are no repeating groups. (5)

Foreign key An attribute in a relation of a database that serves as the primary key of another relation in the same database. (5)

Forward recovery (rollforward) A technique that starts with an earlier copy of the database. After-images (the results of good transactions) are applied to the database, and the database is quickly moved forward to a later state. (12)

Fourth normal form (4NF) A relation in BCNF that contains no multivalued dependencies. (B)

Function A stored subroutine that returns one value and has only input parameters. (8)

Functional decomposition An iterative process of breaking down the description of a system into finer and finer detail in which one function is described in greater detail by a set of other, supporting functions. (2)

Functional dependency A constraint between two attributes in which the value of one attribute is determined by the value on another attribute. (5)

Generalization The process of defining a more general entity type from a set of more specialized entity types. (4)

Global transaction In a distributed database, a transaction that requires reference to data at one or more nonlocal sites to satisfy the request. (13)

Grain The level of detail in a fact table determined by the intersection of all the components of the primary key, including all foreign keys and any other primary key elements. (11)

Hashed file organization A storage system in which the address for each record is determined using a hashing algorithm. (6)

Hash index table A file organization that uses hashing to map a key into a location in an index, where there is a pointer to the actual data record matching the hash key. (6)

Hashing algorithm A routine that converts a primary key value into a relative record number (or relative file address). (6)

Heartbeat query A query submitted by the DBA to test the current performance of the database or to predict the response time for queries that have promised response times. Also called a canary query. (12)

Homonym An attribute that may have more than one meaning. (5)

Horizontal partitioning Distributing the rows of a table into several separate files. (6)

Identifier An attribute (or combination of attributes) that uniquely distinguishes individual instances of an entity type. (3)

Identifying owner (owner) The entity type on which the weak entity type depends. (3)

Identifying relationship The relationship between a weak entity type and its owner. (3)

Inconsistent read problem   An unrepeatable read, one that occurs when one user reads data that have been partially updated by another user. (12)

Incremental commitment   A strategy in systems development projects in which the project is reviewed after each phase and continuation of the project is rejustified in each of these reviews. (2)

Incremental extract   A method of capturing only the changes that have occurred in the source data since the last capture. (11)

Independent data mart   A data mart filled with data extracted from the operational environment, without benefit of a data warehouse. (11)

Index   A table or other data structure used to determine the location of rows in a file that satisfy some condition. (6)

Indexed file organization   The storage of records either sequentially or nonsequentially with an index that allows software to locate individual records. (6)

Information   Data that have been processed in such a way as to increase the knowledge of the person who uses the data. (1)

Information engineering   A formal, top-down methodology that uses a data orientation to create and maintain information systems. (2)

Information repository   A component that stores metadata that describe an organization's data and data processing resources, manages the total information processing environment, and combines information about an organization's business information and its application portfolio. (12)

Information Repository Dictionary System (IRDS)   A computer software tool that is used to manage and control access to the information repository. (12)

Information systems architecture (ISA)   A conceptual blueprint or plan that expresses the desired future structure for the information systems in an organization. (2)

Informational systems   Systems designed to support decision making based on historical point-in-time and prediction data for complex queries or data mining applications. (11)

Java servlet   A small program that executes from within another application rather than from the operating system and is stored on the server rather than with an application on a client. (10)

Join   A relational operation that causes two tables with a common domain to be combined into a single table or view. (8)

Join index   An index on columns from two or more tables that come from the same domain of values. (6)

Joining   The process of combining data from various sources into a single table or view. (11)

Journalizing facilities   An audit trail of transactions and database changes. (12)

List   An ordered collection of elements of the same type. (15)

Local autonomy   A design goal for a distributed database, which says that a site can independently administer and operate its database when connections to other nodes have failed. (13)

Local transaction   In a distributed database, a transaction that requires reference only to data that are stored at the site where the transaction originates. (13)

Location transparency   A design goal for a distributed database, which says that a user (or user program) using data need not know the location of the data. (13)

Locking   Any data that are retrieved by a user for updating must be locked, or denied to other users, until the update is completed or aborted. (12)

Locking level (lock granularity)   The extent of the database resource that is included with each lock. (12)

Logical data marts   A data mart created by a relational view of a data warehouse. (11)

Logical schema   The representation of a database for a particular data management technology. (2)

Market basket analysis   The study of buying behavior of individual customers. (11)

Materialized view   Copies or replicas of data based on SQL queries created in the same manner as dynamic views. However, a materialized view exists as a table and thus care must be taken to keep it synchronized with its associated base tables. (7)

Maximum cardinality   The maximum number of instances of one entity that may be associated with each instance of another entity. (3)

Metadata   Data that describe the properties or characteristics of end-user data, and the context of that data. (1)

Method   The implementation of an operation. (14)

Middleware   Software that allows an application to interoperate with other software without requiring the user to understand and code the low-level operations necessary to achieve interoperability. (9)

Minimum cardinality   The minimum number of instances of one entity that may be associated with each instance of another entity. (3)

Multidimensional OLAP (MOLAP)   OLAP tools that load data into an intermediate structure, usually a three- or higher-dimensional array. (11)

Multiple classification   An object is an instance of more than one class. (14)

Multiplicity   A specification that indicates how many objects participate in a given relationship. (14)

Multivalued attribute   An attribute that may take on more than one value for a given entity (or relationship) instance. (3)

Multivalued dependency   The type of dependency that exists when there are at least three attributes (e.g., A, B, and C) in a relation, with a well-defined set of B and C values for each A value, but those B and C values are independent of each other. (B)

Natural join   Same as equi-join except one of the duplicate columns is eliminated in the result table. (8)

Normal form   A state of a relation that results from applying simple rules regarding functional dependencies (or relationships between attributes) to that relation. (5)

Normalization   The process of decomposing relations with anomalies to produce smaller, well-structured relations. (5)

Null   A value that may be assigned to an attribute when no other value applies or when the applicable value is unknown. (5)

Object An instance of a class that encapsulates data and behavior. (14)

Object diagram A graph of instances that are compatible with a given class diagram. (14)

Object-relational database management system (ORDBMS) A database engine that supports both relational and object-oriented features in an integrated fashion. (D)

Online analytical processing (OLAP) The use of a set of graphical tools that provides users with multidimensional views of their data and allows them to analyze the data using simple windowing techniques. (11)

Open database connectivity (ODBC) standard An application programming interface that provides a common language for application programs to access and process SQL databases independent of the particular RDBMS that is accessed. (9)

Open-source DBMS Free DBMS source code software that provides the core functionality of an SQL-compliant DBMS. (12)

Operation A function or a service that is provided by all the instances of a class. (14)

Operational data store (ODS) An integrated, subject-oriented, updatable, current-valued, enterprisewide, detailed database designed to serve operational users as they do decision support processing. (11)

Operational system A system that is used to run a business in real time based on current data. Also called system of record. (11)

Optional attribute An attribute that may not have a value for every entity (or relationship) instance. (3)

Outer join A join in which rows that do not have matching values in common columns are nevertheless included in the result table. (8)

Overriding The process of replacing a method inherited from a superclass by a more specific implementation of that method in a subclass. (14)

Page The amount of data read or written by an operating system in one secondary memory (disk) input or output (I/O) operation. For I/O with a magnetic tape, the equivalent term is record block. (6)

Partial functional dependency A functional dependency in which one or more nonkey attributes are functionally dependent on part (but not all) of the primary key. (5)

Partial specialization rule Specifies that an entity instance of the supertype is allowed not to belong to any subtype. (4)

Periodic data Data that are never physically altered or deleted once they have been added to the store. (11)

Persistent Stored Modules (SQL/PSM) Extensions defined in SQL:1999 that include the capability to create and drop modules of code stored in the database schema across user sessions. (8)

Physical file A named portion of secondary memory (a magnetic tape or hard disk) allocated for the purpose of storing physical records. (6)

Physical record A group of fields stored in adjacent memory locations and retrieved and written together as a unit by a DBMS. (6)

Physical schema Specifications for how data from a logical schema are stored in a computer's secondary memory by a database management system. (2)

Plug-ins Hardware or software modules that extend the capabilities of a browser by adding a specific feature, such as encryption, animation, or wireless access. (10)

Pointer A field of data that can be used to locate a related field or record of data. (6)

Polymorphism The same operation may apply to two or more classes in different ways. (14)

Primary key An attribute (or combination of attributes) that uniquely identifies each row in a relation. (5)

Procedure A collection of procedural and SQL statements that are assigned a unique name within the schema and stored in the database. (8)

Project A planned undertaking of related activities to reach an objective that has a beginning and an end. (2)

Prototyping An iterative process of systems development in which requirements are converted to a working system that is continually revised through close work between analysts and users. (2)

Query operation An operation that accesses the state of an object but does not alter the state. (14)

Real-time data warehouse An enterprise data warehouse that accepts near-real-time feeds of transactional data from the systems of record, analyzes warehouse data, and in near-real-time relays business rules to the data warehouse and systems of record so that immediate action can be taken in response to business events. (11)

Reconciled data Detailed, current data intended to be the single, authoritative source for all decision support applications. (11)

Recovery manager A module of the DBMS that restores the database to a correct condition when a failure occurs and then resumes processing user questions. (12)

Recursive foreign key A foreign key in a relation that references the primary key values of that same relation. (5)

Redundant Array of Inexpensive Disks (RAID) A set, or array, of physical disk drives that appear to the database user (and programs) as if they form one large logical storage unit. (6)

Referential integrity An integrity constraint specifying that the value (or existence) of an attribute in one relation depends on the value (or existence) of a primary key in the same or another relation. (7)

Referential integrity constraint A rule that states that either each foreign key value must match a primary key value in another relation or the foreign key value must be null. (5)

Refresh mode An approach to filling the data warehouse that employs bulk rewriting of the target data at periodic intervals. (11)

Relation A named two-dimensional table of data. (5)

Relational database A database that represents data as a collection of tables in which all data relationships are represented by common values in related tables. (1)

Relational DBMS (RDBMS) A database management system that manages data as a collection of tables in which all data relationships are represented by common values in related tables. (7)

Relational OLAP (ROLAP)   OLAP tools that view the database as a traditional relational database in either a star schema or other normalized or denormalized set of tables. (11)

Relationship instance   An association between (or among) entity instances where each relationship instance includes exactly one entity from each participating entity type. (3)

Relationship type   A meaningful association between (or among) entity types. (3)

RELAX NG   Language used for defining XML database that is an ISO international standard. (10)

Replication transparency   A design goal for a distributed database, which says that although a given data item may be replicated at several nodes in a network, a programmer or user may treat the data item as if it were a single item at a single node. Also called fragmentation transparency. (13)

Repository   A centralized knowledge base of all data definitions, data relationships, screen and report formats, and other system components. (1)

Required attribute   An attribute of an entity that must have a value for each entity instance. (3)

Restore/rerun   A technique that involves reprocessing the day's transactions (up to the point of failure) against the backup copy of the database. (12)

Reverse proxy   A load-balancing approach that intercepts requests from clients and caches the response on the Web server that sends it back to the client. (10)

Scalar aggregate   A single value returned from an SQL query that includes an aggregate function. (7)

Schema   The structure that contains descriptions of objects created by a user, such as base tables, views, and constraints, as part of a database. (7)

Scope operation   An operation that applies to a class rather than an object instance. (14)

Secondary key   One field or a combination of fields for which more than one record may have the same combination of values. Also called a nonunique key. (6)

Second normal form (2NF)   A relation in first normal form in which every nonkey attribute is fully functionally dependent on the primary key. (5)

Selection   The process of partitioning data according to predefined criteria. (11)

Semantic Web   A W3C project intended to automate Web metadata so that it may be utilized easily by both computers and people. (10)

Semijoin   A joining operation used with distributed databases in which only the joining attribute from one site is transmitted to the other site, rather than all the selected attributes from every qualified row. (13)

Sequential file organization   The storage of records in a file in sequence according to a primary key value. (6)

Server-side extension   A software program that interacts directly with a Web server to handle requests. (10)

Service-oriented architecture (SOA)   A collection of services that communicate with each other in some manner, usually by passing data or coordinating a business activity. (10)

Set   An unordered collection of elements without any duplicates. (15)

Shared lock (S lock or read lock)   A technique that allows other transactions to read but not update a record or other resource. (12)

Simple (or atomic) attribute   An attribute that cannot be broken down into smaller components. (3)

Simple Object Access Protocol (SOAP)   An XML-based communication protocol used for sending messages between applications via the Internet. (10)

Smart card   A credit-card sized plastic card with an embedded microprocessor chip with the ability to store, process, and output electronic data in a secure manner. (12)

Snowflake schema   An expanded version of a star schema in which dimension tables are normalized into several related tables. (11)

Software and hardware load balancing   A load-balancing approach where requests to one IP address are distributed among the multiple servers hosting the Website at the TCP/IP routing level. (10)

Specialization   The process of defining one or more subtypes of the supertype and forming supertype/subtype relationships. (4)

Star schema   A simple database design in which dimensional data are separated from fact or event data. A dimensional model is another name for star schema. (11)

State   Encompasses an object's properties (attributes and relationships) and the values those properties have. (14)

Static extract   A method of capturing a snapshot of the required source data at a point in time. (11)

Stored procedure   A module of code, usually written in a proprietary language such as Oracle's PL/SQL or Sybase's Transact-SQL, that implements application logic or a business rule and is stored on the server, where it runs when it is called. (9)

Stripe   The set of pages on all disks in a RAID that are the same relative distance from the beginning of the disk drive. (6)

Strong entity type   An entity that exists independently of other entity types. (3)

Structural assertion   A statement that expresses some aspect of the static structure of the organization. (4)

Structured literal   A fixed number of named elements, each of which could be of literal or object type. (15)

Subtype   A subgrouping of the entities in an entity type that is meaningful to the organization and that shares common attributes or relationships distinct from other subgroupings. (4)

Subtype discriminator   An attribute of the supertype whose values determine the target subtype or subtypes. (4)

Supertype   A generic entity type that has a relationship with one or more subtypes. (4)

Supertype/subtype hierarchy   A hierarchical arrangement of supertypes and subtypes, where each subtype has only one supertype. (4)

Synchronous distributed database A form of distributed database technology in which all data across the network are continuously kept up to date so that a user at any site can access data anywhere on the network at any time and get the same answer. (13)

Synonyms Two (or more) attributes having different names but the same meaning, as when they describe the same characteristic of an entity. (5)

System catalog A system-created database that describes all database objects, including data dictionary information, and also includes user access information. (12)

Systems development life cycle (SDLC) The traditional methodology used to develop, maintain, and replace information systems. (2)

Tablespace A named set of disk storage elements in which physical files for database tables may be stored. (6)

Term A word or phrase that has a specific meaning for the business. (3)

Ternary relationship A simultaneous relationship among the instances of three entity types. (3)

Thin client A PC configured for handling user interfaces and some application processing, usually with no or limited local data storage. (9)

Third normal form (3NF) A relation that is in second normal form and has no transitive dependencies present. (5)

Three-tier architecture A client/server configuration that includes three layers: a client layer and two server layers. Although the nature of the server layers differs, a common configuration contains an application server. (9)

Time stamp A time value that is associated with a data value. (3)

Time-stamping In distributed databases, a concurrency control mechanism that assigns a globally unique time stamp to each transaction. Time-stamping is an alternative to the use of locks in distributed databases. (13)

Top-down planning A generic information systems planning methodology that attempts to gain a broad understanding of the information system needs of the entire organization. (2)

Total specialization rule Specifies that each entity instance of the supertype must be a member of some subtype in the relationship. (4)

Transaction A discrete unit of work that must be completely processed or not processed at all within a computer system. Entering a customer order is an example of a transaction. (12)

Transaction boundaries The logical beginning and end of transactions. (12)

Transaction log A record of the essential data for each transaction that is processed against the database. (12)

Transaction manager In a distributed database, a software module that maintains a log of all transactions and an appropriate concurrency control scheme. (13)

Transient data Data in which changes to existing records are written over previous records, thus destroying the previous data content. (11)

Transitive dependency A functional dependency between two (or more) nonkey attributes. (5)

Trigger A named set of SQL statements that are considered (triggered) when a data modification (INSERT, UPDATE, DELETE) occurs. If a condition stated within the trigger is met, then a prescribed action is taken. (8)

Two-phase commit An algorithm for coordinating updates in a distributed database. (13)

Two-phase locking protocol A procedure for acquiring the necessary locks for a transaction where all necessary locks are acquired before any locks are released, resulting in a growing phase, when locks are acquired, and a shrinking phase, when they are released. (12)

Unary relationship A relationship between the instances of a single entity type. (3)

Universal data model A generic or template data model that can be reused as a starting point for a data modeling project. (4)

Universal Description, Discovery, and Integration (UDDI) A technical specification for creating a distributed registry of Web services and businesses that are open to communicating through Web services. (10)

Update mode An approach in which only changes in the source data are written to the data warehouse. (11)

Update operation An operation that alters the state of an object. (14)

User-defined data type (UDT) SQL:1999 allows users to define their own data type by making it a subclass of a standard type or creating a type that behaves as an object. UDTs may also have defined functions and methods. (8)

User-defined procedures User exits (or interfaces) that allow system designers to define their own security procedures in addition to the authorization rules. (12)

User view A logical description of some portion of the database that is required by a user to perform some task. (1)

VBScript A scripting language based on Microsoft Visual Basic and similar to JavaScript. (10)

Vector aggregate Multiple values returned from an SQL query that includes an aggregate function. (7)

Versioning Each transaction is restricted to a view of the database as of the time that transaction started, and when a transaction modifies a record, the DBMS creates a new record version instead of overwriting the old record. Hence, no form of locking is required. (12)

Vertical partitioning Distributing the columns of a table into several separate physical records. (6)

Virtual table A table constructed automatically as needed by a DBMS. Virtual tables are not maintained as real data. (7)

Weak entity type An entity type whose existence depends on some other entity type. (3)

Web services Set of emerging standards that define protocols for automatic communication between software programs over the Web. Web services are XML-based and usually run in the background to establish transparent communication among computers. (10)

Web Services Description Language (WSDL) An XML-based grammar or language used to describe a Web service and specify a public interface for that service. (10)

Well-structured relation A relation that contains minimal redundancy and allows users to insert, modify, and delete the rows in a table without errors or inconsistencies. (5)

World Wide Web Consortium (W3C) An international consortium of companies working to develop open standards that foster the development of Web conventions so that Web documents can be consistently displayed across all platforms. (10)

XHTML A hybrid scripting language that extends HTML code to make it XML compliant. (10)

XML schema (XSD) Language used for defining XML databases that has been recommended by W3C. (10)

XSL A language used to develop style sheets. An XSL style sheet is similar to CSS but describes how an XML document will be displayed. (10)

XSLT Language used to transform complex XML documents and also used to create HTML pages from XML documents. (10)

Index

Note: **Boldface** terms are defined on the page that is boldface.